Invitations to Respond

As you read about these topics, I invite you to respond in a nu[mber of] ways. The most obvious is by **asking you questions** as I g[o,] prompting you to think about your own views on the major prob[lems of] teaching and learning. Sometimes I embed one of these questions in the text itself, and other times I highlight it in a special box called "In Your Own Voice." Where I place the question, though, is less important than whether you take up the invitation to respond. Unless you grapple with issues of teaching and learning, you cannot construct a useful framework for your later work as a teacher. Remember: inside my questions are issues, not simple facts. Reasonable people, including yourself and others like you, can expect to disagree about the issues.

To help you form considered opinions about teaching and learning, I frequently also invite you to **keep a written journal or portfolio** of your ideas and reflections, as well as stories about your experiences as a student or teacher. The exact content or format of your writing matters less, though, than your effort to reflect; a regular format simply makes the job more convenient.

A third way I invite you to participate is by **providing commentary from various teachers and researchers** about many topics in this book. Their comments are highlighted periodically in boxes called "Multiple Voices." These commentators vary widely in background. Some are widely published and known in the field of psychology or education, whereas others are well known primarily to the students in their own classrooms. Their variety confirms that useful, expert knowledge comes from many sources, only one of which is educational research. Useful teaching practices. In this important sense, we are all—yourself included—responsible for constructing the psychology of teaching and learning.

Other ways in which I invite your participation operate more indirectly. For example, each chapter opens with a **concept map,** called Chapter View, showing how key ideas or themes from the chapter fit together. But I intentionally leave the concept map sketchy or incomplete at the beginning of the chapter and invite you to fill in its gaps or even rearrange it fundamentally. At the end of each chapter the concept map appears again, but this time it's called Chapter Re-View and shows my version of how it might be made more complete. As you will see, there will often be more than one way to complete a concept map; mine will be only one of them, though hopefully it will be a thoughtful one.

Finally, I extend an indirect invitation through a stylistic feature of this book, its heavy **use of narrative or "stories"** about teaching. I have deliberately included more narrative than is typical for textbooks, especially texts about educational psychology, because I believe narrative is how most of us actually think about teaching and learning (Bruner, 1990; Phillips, 1994). The stories are based on real-life concerns about teaching and learning, but do not describe real people or incidents. To an extent, therefore, the line between fiction and fact will be blurred for these stories, just as it often is in memories of real life.

Like many stories, the ones in this book often have more than one interpretation. Most of the time, I have tried to indicate the interpretations that I intended. But since other meanings may lurk in the wings, I often invite you to explore alternative interpretations and how they relate to your own views on teaching and learning.

Excerpted from
Chapter 1

Constructing a Psychology of Teaching and Learning

Constructing a Psychology of Teaching and Learning

KELVIN L. SEIFERT

THE UNIVERSITY OF MANITOBA

HOUGHTON MIFFLIN COMPANY   BOSTON   NEW YORK

To everyone who has made this book possible—especially the teachers, who are also students, and the students, who are also teachers.

Senior sponsoring editor: Loretta Wolozin
Basic book editor: Karla Paschkis
Associate editor: Lisa Mafrici
Senior project editor: Rosemary Winfield
Senior production/design coordinator: Jill Haber
Senior manufacturing coordinator: Sally Culler
Marketing manager: Pamela Laskey

Cover design: Rebecca Fagan; Cover image: Daniel Root/Photonica

Reprinted by permission: Multiple Voices boxes by Virginia Richardson (p. 11), Adam Winsler (p. 58), Robin Stoeber (p. 89), Dean Page (p. 117), Janice Friesen (p. 140), Ned Noddings (p. 146), Deanna Melzian (p. 214), Mon Cochran (p. 232), Donna Olson (p. 237), Joe Kincheloe (p. 307), Steven Taylor (p. 325), Tom Barone (p. 378), Yvete Daniel (p. 441), Maria Matson (p. 463).

Excerpts from Margaret Wise Brown, *Goodnight, Moon* (pp. 151–152) copyright © 1947 by Harper and Row, Publishers, Incorporated. Text copyright renewed 1975 by Roberta Brown Rauch.

Printed in the U.S.A.

Library of Congress Catalog Card Number: 98-72084

ISBN: 0-395-70808-7

2 3 4 5 6 7 8 9-QF-02 01 00 99

BRIEF CONTENTS

CONTENTS

1

$\mathcal{S}$tarting with You

3

Thinking About Thinking

4

Developmental Change

PART TWO Relationships

5

What Teachers Do

6
*M*otivating and Managing Your Class   163

7

*A*mong Classmates and Parents

PART THREE The Social and Cultural Context   244

8
The Meaning of Classroom Talk   247

9

Gender and Culture as Influences on Learning

10

Teaching Students with Special Needs

12

Hearing Distant Voices: Interpreting Educational Research

13

Care and Justice in Teaching and Learning

PART FIVE Reflections

14

$\mathcal{L}$ooking Ahead

PREFACE TO INSTRUCTORS

I have written this textbook about teaching and learning because of experiences I had in teaching educational psychology—but especially because of frustrations I had. For nearly twenty-five years I have taught an introductory course in educational psychology to preservice teachers, searching all the while for a "best" way, or at least a good way, of doing so. How should problems of teaching and learning be organized, I wondered, so that inexperienced but motivated individuals could make sense of them and begin dealing with them? My quest for a best way to organize these topics led me eventually to write or coauthor three college textbooks (*Educational Psychology, Child and Adolescent Development,* and *Lifespan Development,* all published by Houghton Mifflin) that I could use in my preservice courses. I learned a lot from these projects, and that's one reason I was glad to have invested effort in them. The most important insight I gained was that in order to be effective, a book needs to engage students actively with its themes and ideas.

Approach of the Book: Students' Constructing Personal Understandings

Eventually I concluded that the "problem" of students' understanding rested not so much with the students as with my expectations about how teachers, and preservice teachers in particular, ought to think about educational issues and problems. I was not able to see or accept that educators, whether novice or expert, do *not* think about questions of teaching and learning in anything like the logical, scientific ways developed by academic psychology. Instead, they construct their views by simultaneously reflecting on previous personal experience, anticipating future experiences, and interpreting "official" canons of educational research and teachers' "lore" or wisdom. The result is a personal perspective about teaching and learning—one unique to each teacher, although often bearing a general resemblance to others' perspectives as well.

Given the inevitability and importance of this process, students need a book that attends to and encourages their active construction of knowledge and beliefs. That is the book that I have now tried to write. Judging by initial responses from reviewers and editors (and even from my own ed. psych. students!), I am extremely pleased with the result.

Where in some ways *Constructing a Psychology of Teaching and Learning* still resembles a textbook in educational psychology, with its chapters on topics commonly considered part of its domain, it is unique in its basis in constructivist views and philosophy, and especially those that are social constructivist. I have made every effort to present and interpret *all* major topics, themes, and research of educational psychology from this stance. Perhaps even more important, I have tried to model its tenets and spirit, devising multiple ways to invite students' active engagement with these topics, themes, and research, to help them actively build their own understandings about teaching and learning.

Struggling with a Compelling Question

Not all parts of teaching and learning, of course, assume philosophy(ies) of constructivism, and this fact presented me with the first challenge in writing the book: how to be fair to all prominent research and theories about teaching and learning? My goal has not been to debunk ideas or research that differ from constructivism but to present them as honestly as possible while still framing them in terms of teachers' and students' active sense-making. Take the case of behaviorism and applied behavior analysis. How should this perspective on learning be described in a book like this? That theory, and certain others in educational psychology as well, originated less in constructivism than in the empirical, positivist traditions of natural and social science. To be philosophically fair in cases like this, I have therefore framed the nonconstructivist assumptions of behaviorism as explicitly as possible, rather than leaving them implicit. And I have described them in terms that are informal, accessible, and capable of being related to key ideas of constructivism. To achieve the latter, for example, I addressed these questions: What does behaviorism say about how learners can control and influence their own learning behaviors? And what does it say about how learning principles operate between and among members of a group, such as a classroom? An example of this strategy of presentation occurs in Chapter 2, where I discuss different models (or "metaphors") of learning. Another happens in Chapter 12, where I discuss different types and purposes of educational research.

Content and Organization

As I wrote the book, I discovered that being true to its purposes required a different balance of topics, compared to conventional textbooks about educational psychology. I found that I needed more emphasis than usual on some topics and less on others, and I needed to sequence certain topics and ideas in unique ways. Yet in making these changes I did not want the book to seem unbalanced or to seem simply like constructivist "propaganda." To solve this problem, I have compromised between convention and innovation in text organization. Most chapters can be mapped onto classic topics or content of educational psychology, but they are often presented in new terms more consistent with constructivist ideas. And the sequencing of chapters resembles that of many ed. psych. texts—but not of all. But neither the content nor the sequencing is the only one possible. The *Instructor's Resource Manual* has suggestions about alternatives, and undoubtedly you as instructor and/or students will recombine these topics, now and in the future, to suit your own backgrounds, aims, and contexts.

With the constraints and responsibilities in mind, I divided the book into fourteen chapters, and grouped thirteen of the chapters into five major parts. Chapter 1, Starting with You, is not a member of a major part; rather it describes the overall purposes of the book and the philosophy underlying the selection and presentation of material used in later chapters. After this introduction comes *Part 1, Human Changes,* which consists of three chapters that discuss major forms of individual change and which challenges both students and instructors to think about the implications of an individual's learning and development for teaching and learning. Chapter 2, called Learning, in School and Out, describes three major perspectives about learning—behaviorism, cognitive science, and social constructivism—though, as the chapter points out, the distinctions among these are not clear-cut. Chapter 3, Thinking About Thinking, highlights the currently dominant learning perspective, cognitive science. The chapter explores several forms of cognitive psychology as well as their implications for teaching and learning. Chapter 4, Developmental Change, extends the exploration of cognitive psychology to include Piaget and Piagetian models of development and learning. As with Chapter 3, the emphasis is again somewhat cognitive, though in this case it is meant to reflect the typical focus of teaching on students' thinking.

The next two parts of the book also look at influences on students but from increasingly broad, societal perspectives. *Part 2, Relationships,* is about the face-to-face interactions that dominate classroom life. Chapter 5, called What Teachers Do, outlines three roles that all teachers play in various combinations: the teacher as instructional manager, as caring person, and as generous expert. It also invites students to reflect on how they expect to combine these roles, or others as well, into their own teaching. Chapter 6, Motivating and Managing Your Class, explores ways of thinking about classroom control that focus on students' positive learning and motivation, and not just on misbehaviors. A key theme of this chapter is the close link between motivating students, creating a positive learning environment, and managing students and their activities smoothly and wisely. Chapter 7, Among Classmates and Parents, describes the diversity possible both in students' families and in students' relationships with each other, and the implications of the diversity for managing a class and for fostering effective learning.

Part 3, The Social and Cultural Context, broadens the exploration of influences on learning still further. Chapter 8, The Meaning of Classroom Talk, looks at patterns of discourse and structures of participation in classrooms and how these can either help or hinder students' learning. This discussion is a natural extension of issues that emerged initially in Part 2 of the book, but which deserve a closer look by anyone wishing to teach well. The discussion also provides a bridge to Chapter 9, Gender and Culture as Influences on Learning, because many differences in students' (and teachers') classroom talk are related to differences in gender and culture. Chapter 9 goes beyond talk as such, however, to look at other aspects of gender and culture, such as the distinct meanings that "self-identity" has for boys and girls and for children from different cultural backgrounds. Chapter 10, Teaching Students with Special Needs, discusses the classroom diversity created by children with special needs, focusing especially on needs that classroom teachers are likely to encounter most frequently.

Part 4, Identifying Success and Value in Teaching, moves more directly to encourage reflection on teaching practice. For example, Chapter 11, Assessing Students' Learning, examines the issues of evaluation from the separate perspectives of students, of parents, and of teachers. It considers alternatives to conventional forms of evaluation, especially portfolios, and encourages the college student-readers of the chapter to reflect on both the opportunities and the problems of the newer methods. Chapter 12, Hearing Distant Voices, is about the nature and purposes of educational research and ways that classroom teachers can make use of the research even as beginning professionals. A major theme is the special value of teacher-conducted research; the chapter describes several examples of this kind of work and points out its unique strengths. Finally, Chapter 13, Care and Justice in Teaching and Learning, confronts the inherently value-oriented nature of both teaching and learning, and makes suggestions for how to understand students' (and teachers') implicit values, as well as how to foster mature, thoughtful moral thinking and moral actions on the part of students.

Part 5, Reflections, contains Chapter 14, Looking Ahead. The chapter invites students to take stock of what it will take to consider themselves truly accomplished as a teacher. It also invites students to reflect on what they have learned about teaching and learning so far and what they can expect to learn in the future. The chapter points to the key resources that students can expect to draw on—their personal experiences, their reading (including reading of this book), and knowledge and materials gained from colleagues. Since the chapter parallels the tone and purpose with which the book began, I was tempted to call it Ending with You (to match Starting with You in Chapter 1). But such a title might imply a finality to individuals' thinking about teaching and learning, which is definitely not a message consistent with the purposes of the book!

Fostering Active Understanding with Special Learning Features

In a number of ways, I have encouraged readers to develop their understandings about educational issues actively. Although some of the ways resemble standard pedagogical features of a college textbook, they are all integral to one of the major purposes of the book: to invite dialogue about teaching and learning.

- **In Your Own Voice** These are brief thought-provoking questions located throughout each chapter and set off in a visually distinctive type font. The questions can be used to generate discussion, to stimulate brief journal writing, or simply to encourage silent reflection about educational issues. They do not assume that readers have experience with classroom teaching, but they do assume that they care about teaching, learning, and students. In other respects the questions also honor the diversity among preservice (and among experienced) teachers. In general the questions call attention to difficult issues or dilemmas inherent in teaching, and they relate to issues and dilemmas discussed at the point in the text where the box is located. In responding to the questions, readers must deal with the open-ended quality of many educational debates—the fact that there may be more than one good solution to an educational problem.

- **Multiple Voices** These are brief comments by an educator to a topic discussed in one of the chapters. I invited both experienced teachers and college professors with specialties related to the topic of the chapter to comment on points raised in early drafts of the book manuscript. Not surprisingly, the two sorts of commentators call attention to different issues raised in the chapters, and they offer different solutions to educational problems. Their differences highlight the importance of dialogue in the formation of educational ideas, and illustrate vividly that there are multiple legitimate perspectives about many educational problems. Most chapters have at least one or two Multiple Voices excerpts.

- **Chapter View and Re-View** To help students to build their own models of teaching and learning, I have included graphic diagrams at the beginning and end of each chapter that depict the topics contained in that chapter. The one at the beginning, called Chapter View, illustrates only the main topics to be covered and invites readers to add to or construct the diagram with more detailed concepts and ideas as they develop their own thinking. The diagram at the end, called Chapter Re-View, illustrates one way of responding to this invitation; it builds on the initial diagram by showing more detailed subtopics and concepts in relation to the main ones illustrated earlier.

- **Terms for Further Thought** At the end of each chapter is a list of key terms called Terms for Further Thought. I selected these because of their centrality to the topics of the chapter, and not always because they were unusual, specialized, or technical. Some of the most familiar terms (such as *learning* or *teaching*, among others) are actually the most ambiguous—and as the name of this feature implies, they are deserving of further thought.

- **For Further Reading** At the end of each chapter is an annotated list of references called For Further Reading. I selected these to encourage reflection as well and also because they are relatively accessible conceptually. Calling the references "readings" may be a misnomer, though, since about half of the citations are to Internet web sites related to topics and issues discussed in this chapter. The web sites selected are all major ones in order to ensure their reliability and quality (they should not go out of existence by the time this book gets in print nor be excessively specialized).

Fabric of Presentation

But the most important ways in which the book fosters active understanding are woven into the manuscript itself. Throughout all chapters, I have made liberal use of *informal, first-person commentary* ("I think this . . ." or "My experience was . . ."), where appropriate, alongside more formal descriptions of research. I also freely interspersed *narrative sections and "stories"* of particular teachers' or students' experiences in the classroom. These elements of style do occur in other texts about educational psychology. But they are more prominent in this text, in order to make a crucial point about teaching and learning: that they are human endeavors and that they are actively constructed through human effort, rather than simply "received" from some distant authority. Dialogue and reflection account for much teaching and learning about education, or perhaps even all of it. The style of writing in this book is meant to embody that idea.

Instructor's Resource Manual

In addition to the book itself fostering active understanding of teaching and learning, the *Instructor's Resource Manual* also contains ideas and materials useful for reaching this ideal. In Part 1 of the *Manual*, for example, you will find discussions of general factors to consider in teaching educational psychology, such as the impact of time constraints on "coverage" of topics, alternate ways of sequencing chapters and topics, and implications of physical space on teaching educational psychology. Most important, Part 1 offers advice about ways to assess students' learning that are consistent with constructivist approaches, such as the use of group projects and portfolios and the use of conventional structured testing in innovative ways.

In Part 2 of the *Manual,* you will find suggestions for class discussions, in-class activities, brief out-of-class assignments, and resources for further exploration. These are organized around each of the chapters and take into account the book's overall nature and purposes. Part 2 also contains a selection of test items (both multiple-choice and short essay) for each chapter, which you can use either as is (that is, for conventional testing or grading) or in one of the alternative ways suggested in the *Manual* (for example, as discussion starters). Test items are also available in a computerized format.

Teacher Education Station Web Site

This web site (found at http://www.hmco.com/college, then click on "Education") provides additional pedagogic support and resources for beginning and experienced professionals in education, including the unique "Project-Based Learning Space." This special learning space links to five extended problem-based projects and background theory about project-based learning. The goal of this site is to help teachers learn by doing. The extended projects in this site support, and are supported by, the approach of *Constructing a Psychology of Teaching and Learning*. They integrate many forms of learning, encourage cooperation among students, create mentoring roles for both students and teachers, and draw on ideas and questions formulated by students themselves. In addition, the "Concept Carts" in the Teacher Education Station offer discussion and explanations about a number of key learning themes—cooperative learning, constructivism, inclusive classrooms, learning environments, and technology as a tool—which can significantly enhance the discussion of these same topics in this book.

Acknowledgments

This book lists only one author (myself), but it was really created by numerous people—in writing this Preface, I was often tempted to write *we* wherever the word *I* appears! There are so many participants, in fact, that thanking them all individually runs the risk of omitting someone by mistake. (If that has happened, in fact, let me apologize in advance to whomever has been left out.) But it is important to honor their participation because in various ways this book is as much "theirs" as it is "mine."

Special thanks go to the many reviewers who evaluated early versions of the book, in whole or in part, and who articulated both the problems and the potential of it in helpful ways. The reviewers, I should point out, included both supporters of constructivism and critics of it—but constructive (if not constructivist) criticisms were welcome from both:

Deborah Anders, *University of Arizona*
Suzanne D. Cormier, *Winthrop University*
Jerry L. Gray, *Washburn University*
Marlynn M. Griffin, *Georgia Southern University*
Walter Hapkiewicz, *Michigan State University*
Nancy Flanagan Knapp, *University of Georgia*
Molly Nicaise, *University of Missouri, Columbia*
Gwendolyn P. Quinn, *University of South Florida*
Geoffrey Scheurman, *University of Wisconsin, River Falls*
Mary R. Sudzina, *The University of Dayton*
Jonathan W. Vare, *Winthrop University*
Robert Otto, *Western Kentucky University*

Thanks also go to the contributors to the "Multiple Voices" boxes, who took time from their busy lives to offer thoughtful, alternative views of my own ideas about teaching and learning:

Thomas Barone, Arizona State University, comments on grades and alternative assessments.

Moncrief Cochran, Cornell University, comments on parents as mentors.

Yvette Daniel, a high school teacher in Toronto, Ontario, comments on teacher research.

Janice Friesen, technology coordinator in a Columbia, Missouri, high school, comments on the teacher's role as instructional manager.

Joseph Kincheloe, Pennsylvania State University, comments on cultural differences in the meaning of identity.

Maria Matson, a kindergarten teacher in Hawthorne, California, comments on fostering a morality of care.

Deanna Melzian, a first-grade teacher in Hawthorne, California, comments on young children's views of friendship.

Nel Noddings, Stanford University, comments on the teacher's role as a caring person.

Donna Olson, a guidance counselor in a Los Angeles high school, comments on effectively communicating with parents.

Dean Page, a Tampa, Florida, high school teacher, comments on teaching in light of developmental change.

Virginia Richardson, University of Michigan, comments on the role of dialogue in learning about teaching.

Rodelyn Stoeber, a high school teacher in Winnipeg, Manitoba, comments on problem solving in the classroom.

Steven Taylor, Syracuse University, comments on teaching children with special needs.

Adam Winsler, George Mason University, comments on learning as assisted performance.

And thanks must go to the editorial and production staff of Houghton Mifflin Company—especially Karla Paschkis, Loretta Wolozin, Lisa Mafrici, and (most recently) Ann Schroeder—for their insights and encouragement throughout the development of this book.

And finally, thanks must go to my wife and children, as well as to my own parents, even though the latter have long since passed away. Barbara, Michael, Elizabeth, Howard, and Mary do not know it, but they led me toward constructivist views of teaching and learning through their own intellectual curiosities and provisional searches for truth.

K. L. S.

Constructing a Psychology of Teaching and Learning

CHAPTER VIEW

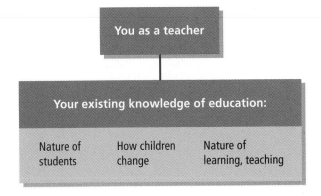

Chapter View: Starting with You This Chapter View is a concept map that indicates one among many ways of thinking about the chapter. It suggests a starting point, conceptually, for the chapter but is incomplete by itself. At the end of the chapter is a Chapter Re-View, which expands on the Chapter View, suggesting directions for taking your thinking further—though, of course, other directions are also possible.

1

Starting with You

This book revolves around two ideas, **teaching** and **learning**. It assumes you already know something about both and have experienced them in countless ways. You have witnessed teaching in classrooms, at home, and among your friends. You may have even done some teaching yourself. And you have experienced learning virtually every day, not only in the classroom but also during informal conversations with peers or when reading a book or watching a good television show. Your experiences with teaching and learning are unique to you; no one else has learned exactly what you have learned or seen what you have seen. In the course of these experiences, furthermore, you have already formed beliefs and views about the nature of the processes themselves: observations, impressions, and inferences about how teaching occurs or learning is experienced in general. Unless you have been a teacher, you may not have reflected much on your ideas; but it is impossible not to have them, given how experiences with teaching and learning pervade our society.

This book also assumes you are open to new ideas about what it means to teach and to learn, and willing to look at perspectives that have not been part of your experience until now. Over and over, as we journey together through the book, I will invite you to consider what you believe about teaching and learning in relation to ideas held by others—ideas expressed both in published writings and in informal conversations with peers. This task will be challenging for both of us. For me, it will be difficult because obviously I do not know you as an individual and therefore may not always ask a question or make a point that is the most relevant to your particular life. For you, reflecting on your beliefs about teaching and learning will be hard because it will mean questioning beliefs you may have held for a long time. Some of your ideas, even your most cherished ones, may turn out to be less reasonable than you first supposed.

In a sense you can consider this a textbook about **educational psychology,** the study of educational problems from the viewpoint of individual students and teachers. But I prefer not to call it that because of unintended meanings often associated with the notions of *textbook* and *psychology*. My reasons will become clearer as we go along, but just note two points for now. First, calling these pages a "textbook" may confer too much authority on its ideas and too little authority on yours (Apple & Christian-Smith, 1991). Second, saying the book is about "psychology" implies ways of understanding that may not prove useful to you as a teacher—in particular, that classroom learning and teaching can be understood through relatively general, scientific laws and everyday learning is fundamentally an individual rather than a social activity.

In the chapters ahead, I will often depart from both the general and individual perspectives. Instead, I will invite you to recognize your ideas alongside those offered here, even if (or perhaps especially if) they seem concrete or "local" in relevance. At the same time, I will urge you to recognize the value of systematic inquiry about teaching and learning. I will also call attention to the social quality of learning as you and other students and teachers actually experience it. In the classroom, for example, teacher and student talk to each other, write and make assignments for each other, and influence each other's actions in numerous ways, all in the interest of promoting learning. Among these social experiences are some that look solitary, such as when a student reads a book or writes an essay. But the "independence" of these actions is more apparent than real: always the book has been written and assigned by other people, always the essay ideas are based on dialogues with other human beings.

Instead of calling this book a "text," you might better think of it as a dialogue or conversation about teaching and learning, with you participating in that dialogue. It is guided by a specific but very broad philo-

How do you suppose first impressions will alter later experiences that these three people will form of each other? Will they reflect on their impressions in ways that will alter their opinions?
© Michael Newman/PhotoEdit

sophical perspective called **constructivism,** a belief that knowledge is created or "constructed" by active efforts to make meaning and by individuals' interactions with other people and with things in order to do so. You will see this term, and variants of it, frequently throughout the book, though most of the time you will simply see ideas that amount to, or point toward, constructivism. Various ideas and theories about teaching and learning will be described, as well as an assortment of experiences undergone by students and teachers. These will be invitations for you to think and to talk: to interpret the written descriptions with ideas and experiences of your own. The book will present not a single "truth" about education but a number of truths. Your own, personally evolving truth about teaching and learning can form alongside these others, and partially in response to them.

Experience: Pitfalls and Potentials

s you move closer to becoming a teacher, you may hear much about the value of personal experience. Experience is the best teacher, it is said: your encounters with students should show you how to teach effectively. We have all attended public school classrooms, for example, so this universal experience should help ready us to teach more than other, more deliberate experiences further removed from classrooms, such as reading books or attending discussions about teaching.

In Your Own Voice

Think about how your own experience may have misled you—for example, when your first impression of someone was mistaken.

What made you change your mind about the person later?

Of course, you may have had further experiences with the person, but think carefully: did the additional experiences also make you reflect or reinterpret your earlier impressions?

The trouble with this commonsense idea is that it assumes what you take or learn from experience will be obvious. Suppose I have indeed experienced many classrooms and teachers in my lifetime, but the classrooms varied widely in quality: some were good and some were very bad. If I am to benefit from this motley assortment of experiences, something must tell me how to sort the good from the bad—how to tell a good teacher from a bad one, or a helpful classroom practice from one that wastes time or even is harmful. At the extremes, intuition may indeed make this possible. We can all tell the difference (we hope) between a fabulous teacher and a horrible one. But many—perhaps most—experiences with education are not extreme, and sorting out their effects therefore takes thought. Was it good or bad that one of my former teachers assigned classroom tests; was it motivating or intimidating? Was it good or bad that another one worked a lot with individuals, or did this actually mean the majority often got neglected?

These questions have more than one response. If you do not agree with me that they do, try answering them yourself, trying deliberately to consider more than one point of view about them. Is there *always* a clear-cut answer about the effects of testing or about how much time to spend with individuals? If you still think these questions have unambiguous answers, try discussing them with two or three friends. Chances are that at some point in your lives, each of you has experienced classroom tests and teachers who sometimes worked with individuals. Do you all have the same viewpoint about the educational effects of these experiences?

As it is with notions of *teaching*, so it is with notions of *learning*: experience does not lead to uniform, predictable understandings of "what" learning is. Both you and your friend may have learned Spanish from elementary school onward, but you learned it entirely at school whereas your friend learned it partly from her family at home. Your ideas of what it means to "teach and learn Spanish" may therefore differ dramatically, even if you have achieved similar proficiency with the language. Experience has mattered, but mattered in different ways. If the two of you say—or anyone else says—that "we learned from experience," you will have to say what you mean by that idea.

Reflection: Partner of Experience

WHY is experience such an ambiguous teacher? One factor is probably the sheer diversity of human experience. But this is only part of the story. Another factor is the diversity of human **reflection** on experience, or how we consider, ponder, or tax our minds about topics and experiences. Everyone thinks about or interprets what happens in individual ways, and before you know it, we develop individual interpretations about events, interpretations that act as guides for further experiences and reflections (Russell & Munby, 1991; Schön, 1991). In school, the scenario might look like this: two of your friends take the same course from the same instructor, but their assessments of the course differ because they think about or reflect on the experience differently. As John thinks about the course, he sees different meanings in the experience (getting a good grade, finding a job) than Sara sees (learning new material, listening to an interesting professor). Their separate views grow out of separate reflections on experience. The stage is set for further differences to develop between John and Sara: for distinct interpretations of subsequent courses and for distinct choices of later courses. Eventually their thinking about learning may be more different than similar, and reaching common understandings about education may require still further reflections on both their parts.

The Results of Reflection: Celebrating Uniqueness

IT seems, then, that experience and reflection lead each of us to construct somewhat unique meanings for *teaching* and *learning*. The diversity of these ideas is pervasive. It exists in teacher education courses in college and even in textbooks such as this one (see Chapter 2 for some diverse definitions of *learning*, each based on a different root metaphor).

This diversity also occurs in teachers' lounges in schools and at professional conferences on education. The diversity can lead to disconcert-

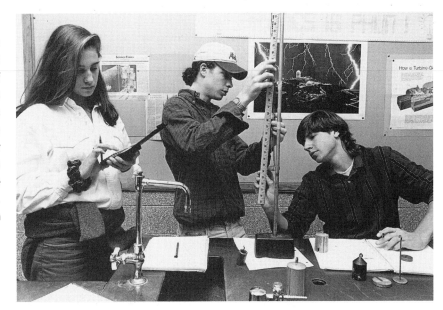

There are many ways to develop shared understandings, and not all of them require continuous conversation. These students may arrive at a common understanding of their experiment even though each is making a unique contribution to it.
© Gale Zucker/Stock Boston

ing misunderstandings. Consider the following two teachers, who work in a single school building. Jan and Frank differ in crucial ways. Yet both do something they call "teaching," and both encourage something they call "learning."

How different can two colleagues be? Jan Collins and Frank Burstow teach fifth grade in the same elementary school—in adjacent rooms, as a matter of fact. Jan uses a lot of self-chosen projects for her students, like the one three kids are doing now to "find out everything we can about space travel." She has her students keep journals about their projects and other activities, and reads to them without fail every week, or even more. She also keeps a journal for herself, in which she reflects on experiences and impressions about the students and daily activities.

When I visited Jan's room, she showed me her journal, now in its third binder even though it was only January. Her latest entries contained detailed personality sketches of each of the twenty-five children, collectively entitled "What I Know Now About My Students." She had gathered impressions from individual conversations she had had as well as from students' work and from informal conversations with parents and other staff. She could not talk with me during the lunch hour because of a teachers' meeting: "Several of us have lunch every few weeks to talk about the kids in each other's classes."

Next door, Frank prides himself in knowing his students. For him this means giving them frequent tests in all subjects and supporting the school district's program of standardized testing. He knows nearly all of his students' test scores by heart and keeps careful records of both their standardized and classroom-based scores, which he proudly showed me. The scores, he feels, are a prime indicator of what his students are learning, and help him to plan each week's instruction. The day I visited, Frank gave a vocabulary lesson: the kids read printed excerpts using difficult words, then took a practice test asking them to define each word. The test was multiple-choice. In fact, the test sheet looked a lot like a page from one of the standardized language tests; Frank had even printed his practice test using the same typeface used for the standardized test. Most students did well on it, though some had to take a retest on words they missed initially.

After school, I sat down with Jan and Frank to thank them for letting me to visit their rooms and express my appreciation for their work.

"One thing about this school," said Jan, "is that the teachers really know their students and *take students' learning into account.*" Frank nodded in agreement.

The gap that I had seen still fresh in my mind, I asked, "Tell me more about that. What do you mean by 'taking learning into account'?" I looked hopefully at both of them, ready for a long discussion.

As you can imagine, this question prompted very different responses from these two teachers, and I did not leave the school very soon.

If you were a mutual colleague of Jan and Frank, how would you have dealt with the differences between them? It will not do simply to ignore one person's views about *teaching* and *learning* and listen to another's; this strategy not only risks offending a colleague but also keeps you from learning from that colleague. Neither will it do simply to adopt one teacher's ideas about *teaching* and *learning* uncritically and completely. Chances are the ideas will be based on experiences somewhat different from yours, and therefore will neither fit your past nor support your future adequately. Your only option will be to develop your own personal perspective on *teaching* and *learning*, one tailored to your own particular experiences and goals. Ideas from others can help you do this, of course, but ultimately you will have to form your own opinions, claim ownership of your unique perspective, and be ready to explain yourself to teachers and parents who may disagree with you. Learning to do this in a way that maintains mutual respect between you and others can be a challenge, but it can be done. This book is meant to help you meet that challenge by stimulating your thinking and dialogue about the issues involved in *teaching* and *learning*.

Constructing *Teaching* and *Learning* Through Dialogue

 IALOGUE is indeed a key to dealing with differences in view-points about teaching and learning. Dialogue is valuable whether you are a student, a new teacher, or a veteran teacher.

Two students commenting about what makes a teacher good:

"She listens to me; doesn't just boss."

"When he talks to you, it sounds like he heard what you said, like it mattered. Like maybe I even changed his thinking a little."

Two first-year teachers commenting on why they like the school where they work:

"The old-timers take your comments seriously. It seems like they want to hear from me about my classes, even though they've seen it all before."

"The teacher in the room next door has taught for twenty years, and she gives me lots of good ideas for my kids. But she doesn't insist that I use them or insist that I agree with her."

Two veteran teachers commenting on why they have had a good year:

"The kids behaved OK this year, but they also had spunk. They really were willing to talk about things, like they were thinking for themselves."

"Those two new teachers at our building, they weren't afraid to talk about their classes. It makes conversation easier. I wasn't afraid of them being over-awed, of always agreeing with me just to be nice."

Not only teachers and students but also observers of education agree on the value of thoughtful conversation, dialogue, and other forms of give-and-take about educational issues. That is essentially what Virginia Richardson, professor of teacher education at the University of Michigan, is saying in the accompanying Multiple Voices box: be thoughtful, but be sure to share your thoughtfulness.

Dialogue in Person

These comments suggest that a good response to the differences among educators lies in **dialogue,** the active sharing of views intended to clarify differences and identify common ground. Dialogue takes many forms, from short exchanges to long conversations, and it can involve many people or just a few. It can even include people whom you never see, such as the author of a book or a media personality: sometimes you

In Your Own Voice

So one of my basic assumptions is that you cannot learn simply by absorbing information, as if you were a sponge.

You have to *engage with* learning, even if your engagement takes place silently, inside your head.

Can you and I agree on this basic premise?

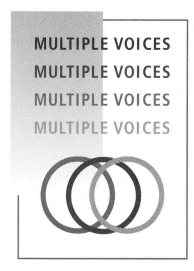

MULTIPLE VOICES
MULTIPLE VOICES
MULTIPLE VOICES
MULTIPLE VOICES

Dialogue! What a wonderful way to begin a book that deals with teaching and learning! After all, the work of the teacher is primarily oral dialogue. The teacher has educative conversations with students, other teachers and educational professionals, parents, friends and family members, himself/herself, and texts. So it really makes sense to think about dialogue as being important also in learning to teach.

What I like about the particular approach taken in this chapter is that Kelvin believes that both formal and informal dialogue are important in the learning process. Informal dialogue that goes on in an individual's head is intriguing to me, although I certainly acknowledge and have conducted research on the importance of formal dialogue in learning to teach. Informal/internal dialogue includes our conversations with texts, with ourselves in trying to figure out what just happened, and with others who are not present.

A very big piece of the current literature on teaching relates to reflection; and reflection may be considered as conversation with oneself. In fact, one of the most intriguing forms of reflection was called by Donald Schön [a professor at the Massachusetts Institute of Technology] *reflection-in-action*. This happens when the class is moving right along and something may jar the flow: a dilemma may crop up, or a quite unexpected student response may take place. At this point, the teacher may begin to have a dialogue with the classroom "action"—a reflection-in-action. What is going on? Why? What should I do now? These are important dialogues since they help us with next steps, and also provide learning experiences that allow us to avoid pitfalls next time.

Virginia Richardson, University of Michigan

"talk" with such a person in your mind as though she or he were sitting in the same room. Whatever its form, dialogue is marked by mutual respect among the participants, even when they do not agree on particular points. Its goal is common understanding, though not necessarily full agreement. For complex matters such as teaching and learning, dialogue often can continue for long periods, and may in fact never finish: you never really decide what teaching or learning is, once and for all. This does not mean you have to talk day and night for months to understand education. It means only that conversations about these things will never really end; they will just be interrupted periodically so that you and your conversational partners can eat, sleep, or teach the next day of school. Sooner or later, the dialogue begins again—and again.

Dialogue with Text

All this may seem plausible enough for conversations with your immediate community: your friends or your current teachers. But you may be less convinced that dialogue is possible with the unseen members of your educational community, such as the author of a textbook or a renowned authority on education. If a textbook author (myself, for example) asserts something in print with which you do not immediately agree, can you really do anything other than just accept the idea as authoritative? Even here, dialogue is possible and helpful. You can, of course, discuss an author's ideas with classmates or instructors. But you can also "talk" to the author in spirit, if not in fact. You can hold a sort of mental conversation between the author and yourself, as Jodi does in the following example. Jodi has never met the person who wrote the text she is reading, but she considers the author's ideas just as actively as she would if the author were in the same room with her. You may also sense a bit of skepticism in Jodi at times, a questioning that actually helps her come to terms with what she reads.

Jodi was reading her textbook in educational psychology, thinking and taking notes as she went along.

Conservation is the belief in or perception of constancy or invariance despite visible changes.

"Huh? Jargon again; I wish this author would speak more plainly." Jodi highlighted the word conservation with a bright pink felt-tip pen ("Sounds important," she thought).

Consider two glasses of water of the same size and shape. If a young preoperational child looks at these, he will have no trouble agreeing that they contain the same amount of water.

She highlighted the word *preoperational*. She remembered the prof using this term during discussion last week. "Little kids—preschoolers?" Jodi paused over the words *trouble agreeing* . . .

But if one of the glasses is poured into a wide, low jar, he may decide that it now has "less" water.

. . . and then over the word *decide*. "Sounds like a committee meeting—like the kid is discussing his thoughts with the water."

The lower height stands out perceptually and appears to distract him from noticing that it is compensated for by greater width. Older, concrete operational children are not distracted in this way. For them the amount of water in each glass stays the same regardless of how its shape changes.

Jodi wrote in her notes: "Conservation depends on paying attention." But then she crossed it out.

"No, that can't be what they mean by 'distraction.' Everyone gets distracted sometimes." She remembered a heated debate with a friend at a neighborhood hangout when the bartender brought "identical" drinks in different-shaped glasses. She was sure she received less for her money! Conservation might be something that even *she* lacked, not just little kids. Finally, she just wrote in her notes, "Ask Prof what they mean by 'getting distracted.'"

In theoretical terms, they "conserve" the amount of water in their minds in spite of visible changes that suggest an alteration.

Jodi heaved a sigh and closed her book, then looked again at her notes. "Who is 'they'?" she wondered. Was it really *all* older children or just a majority or just the ones who have been studied?

How Many Voices Create the Psychology of Teaching and Learning?

 OR various reasons, it can be tempting to accept an author's voice automatically in preference to your own; after all, whatever is in print should represent careful thought, if not "the" truth.

Published authors do have the advantage of time to reflect on what they write—in this case, to reflect on teaching and learning. Presumably they have also done a lot of talking about educational issues. In textbooks, in particular, authors try to summarize "the state of the field," meaning they try to speak on behalf of educators as a whole. In a sense, therefore, other educators are also talking whenever "the" author speaks, and when you read a text, you will actually "hear" many voices, not just one.

These are important reasons to take published perspectives on teaching and learning seriously, but they are still not good enough to justify accepting an author's perspective without question. No matter how many experts have discussed it, any particular theory of teaching or learning will not necessarily be appropriate or useful for your goals, values, or activities. Some theories may make assumptions that can seem wrong-headed. One may assume, for example, that learning is like the activities of a computer. Thinking of student learning in this way may be helpful in planning your classes—and then again, it may not. Even if you are skeptical of the computer metaphor, though, it is important to understand it as well as you can so that you can also understand *why* you object to it. Striking a balance between belief and skepticism can be difficult, but in the end it is productive: you will end up with a deeper understanding of both teaching and learning and of both your own thinking and that of the published authors.

Publications about teaching and learning thus merit your consideration; but so do your own ideas (Bereiter, 1994; Fenstermacher, 1994). To formulate your own perspective, then, you will have to "negotiate" your interpretations of *teaching* and *learning* with others' interpretations; that is, you will have to compare your ideas with the ones you read about as well as with those you hear about. The negotiation is in effect an internal, constructive dialogue, one that respects both your beliefs about teaching and learning and the theoretical perspectives described later in this book.

To summarize: dialogue can be either outward conversation or inward thoughtfulness. This book will invite you to do both. It will assume you already know something, or at least believe something, about teaching and learning. This assumption may not be as simple as it seems, since you may take a lot of your knowledge about education for granted or describe it in terms other than *teaching* and *learning*. Therefore, in the remainder of this chapter, I try to point to some of what you may already know and believe, the ideas that you can thus contribute to a dialogue on teaching and learning. In later chapters, the focus will shift toward

Even when we have the "same" experience, we may react to it differently. In the classroom, providing common experiences is no guarantee of common outcomes.
© Helen Nestor/Monkmeyer

what experienced educators and educational psychologists know and believe; but your own place in the dialogue, and its importance, will not be forgotten.

What Do You Already Know About Teaching and Learning?

In Your Own Voice

I'm trying to make reasonable assumptions here about areas where you have prior knowledge, but they are still just assumptions.

Is there a better set of headings than these three, one that more closely fits your way of thinking about education?

You probably already have significant knowledge about teaching and learning. You may not recognize it as such, though, because some parts consist of *assumptions* you hold about these activities, whereas other parts may be expressed in terms not typical of educational dialogues (Seifert, 1992; Seifert & Handziuk, 1993). To see what I mean, consider a number of topics about which you probably already have views:

- The nature of children and youth
- How people change as they grow older
- The nature of learning and of thinking

Chances are you already have views about these topics, each of which has a lot to do with teaching and learning. What do *you* think children and young people are like? How do they change over time? What do *you* mean when you say they "learn" or "think"? You may even have views about whether these are the most important questions to ask in the first place. When you stop and think, one question may seem more important than another; or you may feel that one topic or question should be phrased differently. Before you read further in this chapter, therefore, you might take a moment to reflect on how you would respond to each question. Or, if possible, talk to a friend or classmate about your views. Your ideas will be your particular starting point in constructing a psychology of teaching and learning. The ideas from classmates, from teachers, and from this book probably will not be your ending point, but they will assist you in deciding on directions in which to expand your beliefs.

The Nature of Children and Youth

Underlying any ideas about teaching and learning are assumptions about the nature of children and of young people: beliefs about human nature. One assumption is that children are capable of making decisions for themselves. In some situations, this is obviously true: ask an eight-year-old to choose a flavor for her ice cream cone, and she will almost surely be able to decide. But in other settings, a child's decision-making ability is more suspect. Is a kindergartner capable of deciding whether to attend school each day? Is a ninth-grader capable of deciding whether to engage in sexual intercourse? Between the extremes are decisions of ambiguous status. Can a third-grade student decide whether to spend more time reading a novel or learning science? Teachers, parents, and even students themselves disagree in answering this question. The reasons for the disagreement vary, but they all center on assumptions about a key issue: whether or not children can indeed make decisions for themselves.

Another assumption about the nature of children has to do with their inherent stability: do children have an "essence" that is basically fixed and stable or one that is changeable? Obviously some things about children do change—for example, they grow taller, their skills may shift sometimes even from day to day, and they may seem more competent (hopefully) from year to year. But are these changes merely superficial, or do they signify deeper, more profound alterations? To take an example that concerns teachers, think about this: if a student's reading skill improves dramatically during the course of schooling, does this mean the student is becoming *essentially* more intelligent with each passing year or merely more skilled? Perhaps "intelligence" does not grow simply because verbal skills grow; perhaps it remains constant in spite of changes in academic knowledge—or perhaps not. Teachers (and others who observe children) disagree about these possibilities. The disagreement may appear to be about the nature of intelligence, but it is really about something more: the fundamental stability of human beings. Are you the same yesterday, today, and tomorrow? You probably already have something to say about this matter.

How People Change as They Get Older

The problem of stability versus change suggests a related area in which you probably already have beliefs and assumptions—one that has to do not with *whether* people change as they get older but *how* or by what process. Obviously older individuals can do some things that younger ones cannot; with age, you learn to talk, catch a ball, read a book, and (perhaps) invite a friend to visit. But how do such changes come about? Is each change a response to specific events and relatively unrelated to other changes? Sometimes this must surely be true: it is hard (though perhaps not impossible) to imagine how learning to catch a ball will influence learning to read a book. The two changes seem rather unrelated, at least on the face of it. But what about learning to talk, learning to read, and learning to write? Those activities seem more related; therefore, maybe they have some underlying cause, and developing talent in one might improve talent in the other. But only up to a point. You may have met someone who talks better than he or she writes or who writes better than he or she talks. In fact, maybe you are one of those people yourself.

In any case, you probably make assumptions not only about *what* changes occur with age but also about *how* the changes come about (Overton, 1991). One common assumption, for example, is that change is like the growth of a seed or a plant: it occurs not in discrete bits but in complex, interlocking patterns, as when a seed sprouts or a flower blossoms forth. From this perspective, learning to talk and learning to read might be parts of a larger process of change, one that is part of a general pattern of language development and unfolds in a predictable way. A second common assumption is that human change is like the functioning of a finely tuned machine such as a clock or a computer. Separate changes (such as talking, reading, and writing) may only appear to be related; in reality, they may unfold together because of specific but separate influences. The chime on a grandfather clock, for example, often runs off of a different spring than the minute and hour hands on the clock; the hands may trigger the chime periodically, but in principle each could run without the other. In a similar way, a student may learn to talk, read, and write separately, even though one skill may trigger or make use of the others some of the time.

Even if you have not thought explicitly about how people change, you may already have used ideas such as these when you think or talk about *teaching* and *learning*. When you speak of a student being "ready" for a new learning experience, for example, you may be assuming that change consists of a process of patterned growth. To say that Joe is "ready" to begin kindergarten or that you are "ready" to begin college is to say that a number of changes have occurred simultaneously and somewhat predictably. When you speak of "improving your writing skills," on the other hand, you are more likely to be assuming that discrete, separate skills exist, could have been acquired separately, and can now be fine-tuned and performed separately as well. It is common, in fact, to speak of human change in one way on some occasions and in another way on others. Such "inconsistency" is not a problem in thinking about teaching and learning, as long as you are aware of its occurrence. The real challenge is to make yourself aware of your own diversity.

The Nature of Learning and of Thinking

In Your Own Voice

An interesting exercise is to collect a quick, informal survey of everyday definitions of the terms *learning* and *thinking*.

Try asking five people, and jot down their responses so you remember them.

But make sure the five people are diverse in terms of age, work or family arrangements, and so on.

Share your results with others, including the survey respondents themselves, if possible.

When you or I speak of *learning*, we are likely to have a metaphor in mind, a comparison of learning to a familiar object or activity (Bullough, Knowles & Crow, 1992). Sometimes learning is compared to a telephone network: you learn when you "make connections," as if multiple phone calls were criss-crossing your brain. Sometimes learning is compared to a bank: you "add to your storehouse of knowledge," making deposits and withdrawals as needed but otherwise letting your knowledge remain dormant and unused. Or learning may be likened to a job (you learn if there is a payoff, such as course credit or praise from your instructor), to eating (you "digest" ideas), or to combat (you are "challenged" to "master" the curriculum). These and other images serve different purposes in dialogues about learning; they are used with reference to different learning situations, curricula, and students. Maybe you can think of other metaphors or likenesses you have sometimes used. Some are probably shared with your friends and classmates, but others may be unique to you. *Learning*, it seems, does not mean the same thing to everyone.

Likewise, you probably already have views about **thinking**. Stop for a moment and consider this term. You may believe from experience, for example, that thinking is essentially equivalent to language: you often think silently in words or even openly talk to yourself when you are thinking hard. Or you may believe thinking is visual: sometimes you think in pictures, imagining an event, a place, or a person (e.g., "I'm trying to picture myself as a teacher"). Or thinking may seem equivalent to physical action, such as dodging quickly out of the way of a student charging down the hallway; "Quick thinking," you compliment yourself, as if thought were a matter of agility. *Thinking,* like learning, is like a chameleon, changing colors to fit its surroundings.

You may also regard thinking as a process that happens "inside" you. Most of us speak of "my" thoughts and "my" plans; yet it is hard not to notice how much your thoughts and plans are shaped by other individuals or events outside yourself. In the morning, you think about what to buy a friend for a birthday present, and decide to get something that day. But events at work—or, more precisely, the people there—distract you. You forget to go shopping after work. The next day you write yourself a note as a reminder to go shopping. This succeeds in reminding you, except that the store clerk shows you something better than what you had planned on buying—but also more expensive. You hesitate, and end up not getting anything that day. That night you are so tired from the extra shopping that you forget to write yourself another reminder note, and as a result you forget to act on the birthday present "problem," as it has now become, for two more days. Time is now running out, so you settle for something less desirable and less expensive than you had first planned. You end up annoyed with yourself: you seem forgetful and a poor planner! In taking responsibility for forgetting, though, you assume your plans have been "in" you all along rather than also "in" the daily world in which you participated. You therefore experience the distractions and delays as invasions instead of as transactions for which you are only partly responsible. You assume exclusive ownership of your plans, but in reality the plans have changed in focus and importance in response to events and other people as well as in response to you. In a very real sense, then, the thinking that went into your plans "belonged" to everyone, not just to you.

Taking Your Existing Beliefs
and Knowledge Seriously

I intend to take your existing beliefs and knowledge about teaching and learning seriously. I will do so in three ways. First, I will continually invite you to reflect on what you know and on the reasons for your beliefs. Second, I will attempt to express my own knowledge and beliefs as explicitly as possible. I will try, of course, to be fair to viewpoints other than my own, but I will also not try to pretend that I have no views of my own or that this book offers a "God's-eye view" of teaching and learning. Third, I will deliberately present a range of ideas, concepts, and theories about how learning occurs and how knowledge is constructed. These will vary in how much they either support or challenge your existing views about teaching and learning. Simply by showing you the variety, though, I hope to communicate a respect for differences of opinion, including your own. Whatever else you gain from reading this book, I hope you will discover that psychological and educational research is itself a human creation—a systematic one, perhaps, but one that is not eternally fixed.

What Lies Ahead

*I*N the rest of this book, I will explore the major themes or topics that bear on the ideas of *teaching* and *learning*. But my explorations will make sense only if you participate in them: this journey is one that we must make together. For this reason, I have designed this book to invite your thoughtful response. I hope you take up my invitation.

Explorations

The topics I will explore come from issues and problems as experienced in classrooms and other situations, but they also grow out of various published research and theories. Part 1 (Chapters 2 through 4) looks at how people change, in both their minds and their hearts and over both the short and long term. Part 2 (Chapters 5 through 7) explores the relationships surrounding children and young people, some of which go well beyond the classroom, and how they influence notions of teaching and learning. Part 3 (Chapters 8 through 10) broadens the focus on relationships to include students' ties with their culture of origin and with that special "adopted" culture called school. Part 4 (Chapters 11 through 13) looks at the deeply moral and evaluative character of classroom life and at how teachers' desire to encourage what is good and right influences every action of the day, including assessment of students as well as of teaching itself. Part 5 (Chapter 14) reroutes the focus back to you, inviting you to reconsider the nature of *teaching* and *learning*, but this time in light of your own increased awareness of teaching and your own future plans.

Invitations to Respond

As you read about these topics, I invite you to respond in a number of ways. The most obvious is by **asking you questions** as I go along: prompting you to think about your own views on the major problems of teaching and learning. Sometimes I embed one of these questions in the text itself, and other times I highlight it in a special box called "In Your Own Voice." Where I place the question, though, is less important than whether you take up the invitation to respond. Unless you grapple with issues of teaching and learning, you cannot construct a useful framework for your later work as a teacher. Remember: inside my questions are issues, not simple facts. Reasonable people, including yourself and others like you, can expect to disagree about the issues.

To help you form considered opinions about teaching and learning, I frequently also invite you to **keep a written journal or portfolio** of your ideas and reflections, as well as stories about your experiences as a student or teacher. The exact content or format of your writing matters less, though, than your effort to reflect; a regular format simply makes the job more convenient.

A third way I invite you to participate is by **providing commentary from various teachers and researchers** about many topics in this book. Their comments are highlighted periodically in boxes called "Multiple Voices." These commentators vary widely in background. Some are widely published and known in the field of psychology or education, whereas others are well known primarily to the students in their own classrooms. Their variety confirms that useful, expert knowledge comes from many sources, only one of which is educational research. Useful knowledge also comes from successful teaching and honest reflection on teaching practices. In this important sense, we are all—yourself included—responsible for constructing the psychology of teaching and learning.

Other ways in which I invite your participation operate more indirectly. For example, each chapter opens with a **concept map,** called Chapter View, showing how key ideas or themes from the chapter fit together. But I intentionally leave the concept map sketchy or incomplete at the beginning of the chapter and invite you to fill in its gaps or even rearrange it fundamentally. At the end of each chapter the concept map appears again, but this time it's called Chapter Re-View and shows my version of how it might be made more complete. As you will see, there will often be more than one way to complete a concept map; mine will be only one of them, though hopefully it will be a thoughtful one.

Finally, I extend an indirect invitation through a stylistic feature of this book, its heavy **use of narrative or "stories"** about teaching. I have deliberately included more narrative than is typical for textbooks, especially texts about educational psychology, because I believe narrative is how most of us actually think about teaching and learning (Bruner, 1990; Phillips, 1994). The stories are based on real-life concerns about teaching and learning, but do not describe real people or incidents. To an extent, therefore, the line between fiction and fact will be blurred for these stories, just as it often is in memories of real life.

Like many stories, the ones in this book often have more than one interpretation. Most of the time, I have tried to indicate the interpretations that I intended. But since other meanings may lurk in the wings, I often invite you to explore alternative interpretations and how they relate to your own views on teaching and learning. Indirectly, then, the stories ultimately invite participation; they ask for a dialogue among you, me, and the characters. I do hope you join in that dialogue whether you do so like Brent below, or Michele, or in some other way.

Michele and Brent have finished reading Chapter 1. Michele has read the chapter quickly, frowning as she went along. Brent has concentrated intently, smiling at certain points.

"Here we go again!" Michele bursts out. "Another education book with little to say! Don't ed profs know that we need answers, not questions? And need them soon, too; my school placement begins next month."

Brent looks perplexed. He enjoyed the chapter. "So what's the problem, Michele, really?"

"For one thing, I want to learn how to manage my class, especially misbehavior. Some students aren't exactly angels, and even the good kids are going to see that I'm new. I want to know *what* to teach. Exactly what. I wish Seifert would come right out and talk about that."

Brent can't contain himself. "Sounds like learning and teaching are, like, automatic skills. Like there's tricks that will always work. Right?" He glances cautiously at Michele. It looks safe, so he goes on. "It's not like writing a recipe for spaghetti sauce that you've made a thousand times. Every day is different."

"So how do I prepare myself ahead of time? No wonder this chapter sounds vague."

"But it's *not* vague. It—I mean Seifert—just says you have to think about what you believe about education and talk to others about it. Even 'textbook' knowledge can't give simple answers, or shouldn't. Dialogue. Give-and-take. Those are what help you find your way."

Evidently Brent agrees with me and Michele is skeptical. But I have sympathy for Michele's concerns; the first day of teaching is indeed coming soon, even if "soon" is actually still a year or two away. You really will have to decide exactly what to do on that day—and on all the days that follow. In the meantime, I hope you give Brent's opinion a chance to influence you. I hope you take the time, as he said, to think about what you believe and to talk to others about it.

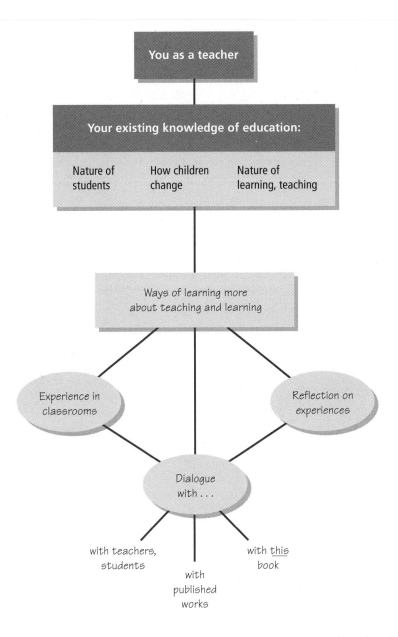

You as a teacher

Your existing knowledge of education:

Nature of students

How children change

Nature of learning, teaching

Ways of learning more about teaching and learning

Experience in classrooms

Reflection on experiences

Dialogue with . . .

with teachers, students

with published works

with this book

Chapter Re-View: Starting with You This Chapter Re-View suggests directions in which the chapter might have taken your thinking—though, of course, other directions are also possible. It expands the Chapter View, which suggests a starting point, conceptually, for the chapter. But this Re-View does not suggest an ending point. Like the Chapter View, it represents just one perspective among many.

Key Terms and Concepts

constructivism (5)   learning (3)   teaching (3)

dialogue (10)   reflection (7)   thinking (19)

educational psychology (4)

Annotated Readings

Dewey, John. (1933/1998). *How we think: A restatement of the relation of reflective thinking to the educative process.* Boston: Houghton Mifflin. A classic about the importance of reflection for becoming a highly skilled teacher. The language is sometimes a bit quaint (it was first published 65 years ago), but the ideas are still sound.

Hansen, David. (1995). *The call to teach.* New York: Teachers College Press. Accounts of three teachers who work under difficult conditions (e.g., because they have students who are at high risk for failure) and the sense they make of their work and of their own motives for teaching.

Schön, Donald. (1987). *Educating the reflective practitioner.* San Francisco: Jossey-Bass.

Schön, Donald. (1985). *The reflective practitioner.* New York: Basic Books. Donald Schön offers some of the best explanations of how practitioners think when they work in ever-changing, "messy" professions, including (but not limited to) education. He makes good suggestions for helping practitioners in these areas become more skilled at reflection.

Internet Resources

<www.classroom.net> Newsletters, videos, books, and interactive "chat" lines for discussing issues with teachers of all kinds.

<www.newmaine.com/progressive-educator> Materials about innovative approaches to teaching and learning, as well as an interactive "chat" line.

1
Human Change

As the title of Chapter 1 says, this book "starts with you." But teaching cannot stay with you: it is also about how you can create changes in students. Part 1 therefore looks at human change, or more particularly at change in students as individuals. Chapter 2 explores what psychologists, educators, and others mean by the term *learning*. It contains explanations of major theories of learning, noting the primary purposes and original metaphors intended for each theory. Chapter 3 discusses major forms of thinking, ranging from school-based forms to ones based in broader conceptions of problem solving and creativity. Chapter 4 discusses long-term or developmental change, comparing psychological conceptions of this idea with those held by teachers, parents, and students.

The discussion treats theories about learning, thinking, and development as useful constructions or as perspectives that can help teachers to support the learning engaged in by students. For purposes of teaching, therefore, each is "true" to some extent and for some educational purposes, but none is true to the exclusion of others. As a group, the theories share a strong focus on the student as an individual—as one person seeking to make sense of a curriculum and of personal experiences. This common strength will need to be supplemented, later in the book, by attention to students' relationships and to their place in the larger world. Let us begin, though, by considering students individually, by considering how "the" student might learn, think, and develop.

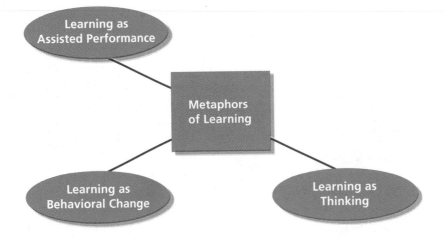

Chapter View: Learning, In School and Out This Chapter View is a concept map that indicates one among many ways of thinking about the chapter. It suggests a starting point, conceptually, for the chapter but is incomplete by itself. At the end of the chapter is a Chapter Re-View, which expands on the Chapter View, suggesting directions for taking your thinking further—though, of course, other directions are also possible.

2

Learning, In School and Out

What is learning, and what is responsible for it? Think about how you might answer these questions. Sometimes we hold an individual person responsible for learning, but just as often we think not of a person but of a person's circumstances as the source of learning. Consider Joe, one of my former students. Maybe you've known someone like him—or even been him:

Joe was new to the school, though not new to being a student. He and his mother had moved to the city three months ago, in time for Joe to start the school year in sixth grade. His new home was a hundred miles away, far from where he had lived before his parents' divorce, so Joe had a lot of things to get used to. There was a new teacher, for example, and new classmates. And there was a new problem of what to do with time after school: now his mother was working again, so she did not get home until 5:00 on most days.

Joe is rooted in circumstances that demand his attention and concern, and it is in the midst of these, rather than in the abstract, that we can ask what sorts of things will Joe learn—or, if you prefer, what sorts of things his new circumstances will encourage him to learn.

One possibility, given his situation, is that *learning* means becoming able to answer questions posed by the teacher, Mr. Gordon.

Fortunately, Joe thought, he was not doing too badly in school. Joe studied his teacher carefully: Mr. Gordon was calling the class's attention to a point about solids, liquids, and gases. "Water is one of the few liquids that actually get *larger* when they freeze. That's important; can anyone think of why?" Joe jotted down Mr. Gordon's point ("water—larger when freezes") and waited patiently for someone else to answer. He knew Mr. Gordon was driving at something in particular, but he was not sure what. Joe recalled the pipes freezing in their former house one winter; at that time, it had not occurred to him that they had burst because the ice got larger inside the confined pipes. He wrote down "pipes freezing" in his notes. Instead of raising his hand to make this point in class, though, he thought: let one of the science brains answer the question. As far as Joe was concerned, it didn't really matter exactly how much you "participated" in Mr. Gordon's class, as long as you paid attention, took notes at the right time, and avoided bothering anyone. Mr. Gordon always seemed to like you if you met these conditions. Joe had discovered that it was a "safe" class—predictable and not terribly demanding—just what he welcomed after moving to the city.

As his teacher intended, Joe has learned some academic content, that water expands when it freezes. But Joe has also learned other things accidentally, or even contrary to intentions. He learned about a setting called "Mr. Gordon's class"—that it is safe, for example, that it is not necessary to answer every question. And that Mr. Gordon likes students. Officially, Mr. Gordon may have been teaching only science, but unofficially Joe was learning about social relationships as well. In this sense, Joe and his teacher were experiencing different "curricula" without realizing it. But the changes that are occurring do indeed seem to be internal to or "inside" Joe; based on the (limited) information given, we don't see Mr. Gordon or other students changing as a result of Joe's rather passive response. Yet internal learning is not the only kind that occurs, especially if the circumstances of learning change as well:

After school, to fill time before his mother came home, Joe had joined an after-school program for kids his age. What a different world from Mr. Gordon's class! A dozen boys and girls came together every week, talking a mile a minute, doing projects, as they called their activities. Yesterday several of them had "done chemistry": one kid brought in substances (approved as safe by their adult leader) to experiment with: laundry soap, baking soda, vinegar, vegetable oil. Joe and three others had settled on a project to discover which substances would change colors when mixed together. They made notes on their observations, talked about why some combinations might change but others might not, and suggested other substances to bring from home (potatoes, window cleaner) to add to their observations. Everyone seemed to have ideas for new substances and about what would happen when they were tested. In fact, just *having* an idea seemed more important than whether the idea was a good one; even goofy suggestions were OK. So Joe talked eagerly and freely: "Bring some soda pop," he suggested, "and a can of chicken soup." Someone wrote his ideas on a master brainstorming list; Joe felt encouraged and more like he belonged. He paid close attention to the experiments.

Learning took place here, too; Joe was picking up ideas and information about how various substances combine. But learning in the program seemed different than learning in the science lesson. For one thing, official goals—the kids' conscious focus of attention—seemed less planned in the program. For another, it was obvious, and intended, that several goals were being pursued at once; not everyone was "doing chemistry," as Joe was. Unintended learning, like learning the rules of social participation, differed significantly between the two situations. In class, Mr. Gordon might hope for active participation, but he insisted only on your presence and quiet cooperation. Mr. Gordon seemed to assume that Joe would think actively about science even when not interacting with others. In the after-school program, active participation was virtually a condition of membership; thinking about chemistry experiments did not happen "in" Joe so much as between Joe and the others when they talked. In this sense, shyness and a need for privacy were tolerated less well in the program than in the class.

In Your Own Voice

I am arguing strongly that learning is diverse.

But does this make sense in your own life?

Think about something that you yourself learned *outside* school versus something you learned *inside* school.

Chances are they are different—but if that's so, then why are you calling them both "learning"?

Considering these differences complicates the question of what learning "is." Sometimes learning may result from deliberate teaching; that is the kind of learning educators usually think of when they talk of *learning*. At other times learning seems to occur on its own, or perhaps even *because* no deliberate teaching has been attempted (Cole, 1997). Still further complications arise when we consider the speed of learning, how slowly or quickly it comes about. For example, it took me literally years to learn to get along with my mother-in-law, but it took my five-year-old daughter only about one week to learn to tie her shoelaces. Do both these cases count as examples of "learning"?

These complexities pose a crucial question: does a common ground underlie situations of human change, a common thing, event, or process that we can call *learning*? Or is it more useful, accurate, and honest to regard human change as too diverse to call by any one name? Perhaps the term *learning* is just too ambiguous to do us much good. Or perhaps not. After all, teachers persist in using the term a lot, in spite of its multiple meanings. So it must have some value.

Metaphors of Learning

I HAVE no simple answers to the issues I have raised, but I can point toward some multiple, partial answers that, with a bit of effort, you can develop for yourself. The multiple, partial ideas about the nature of learning come from ideas of educational psychologists, offered in the form of (relatively) formal psychological theories of learning. Each theory gives a useful perspective, but none deals with all forms of learning equally well. For teachers and others responsible for children, the theories do not contradict one another directly as much as they speak past one another: they talk about different problems and events and view them in different ways (Derry, 1992; Lee, 1988). Theories of learning therefore can be regarded as **metaphors of learning**—images of learning modeled after particular and familiar objects, situations, and actions.

As you will see, each theory uses a metaphor as thoroughly as possible in an effort to understand human change as well as possible. Exactly how useful will the images be for you? This will depend on your personal and professional needs and goals, and on the learning situations you encounter in the future. For most teachers, though, all theories of learning prove useful in thinking about at least some of the learning that occurs in classrooms.

Learning as Behavior Change

> We become just by performing just actions, moderate by performing moderate actions, and brave by performing brave actions.
>
> Aristotle

Aristotle hints at an essential part of the **behaviorist** metaphor: that learning *is* change in actions. Admittedly he may mean more than this; he may be saying that actions are signs of deeper human qualities, and not only that they constitute the qualities as such. But in emphasizing the

A key notion of operant conditioning is that timely reinforcement makes a behavior more likely to occur. This girl is being reinforced for learning by notations on a chart of students' progress.
© Elizabeth Crews

importance of observable action, he points to a key problem of the human condition: we can know one another only by what we see one another do or hear one another say.

Teachers encounter this problem when they try to understand their students. Heather, a veteran elementary school teacher, had this to say:

Sometimes I get lulled by my students' quiet looks of attention. I think they're understanding me just because they're looking at me so steadily. But if I ask them to write something about the lesson, I'm usually in for a surprise! It's like half of them were not even in the room. It's better when they discuss the topic actively—I can be more sure that they are getting it. But even that can be misleading, because usually just a few students do most of talking. What are those silent ones actually *doing* when they sit there? Maybe they're listening, maybe not, but I just can't tell.

Like Heather, many teachers find overt action to be an especially attractive starting point to think about the nature of *learning*. Teachers often rely on overt actions from students to show that learning is "really" taking place: we need homework assignments actually turned in, hands raised at appropriate times, mouths shut for suitable intervals and open

In Your Own Voice

What would *you* consider an overt sign of learning?

Stop and think about this behavior: can you imagine circumstances where it might actually *not* signify learning?

at others. A major problem for teachers is to decide which behaviors constitute true learning.

Behaviorists have approached this problem in a particular way: by identifying several kinds of behavior change that they consider basic. I do not have space in this chapter to discuss all the forms, but I will describe two that are especially important to behaviorist theory: classical conditioning and operant conditioning. These two forms are the most "radical" in that they focus almost exclusively on outward changes in behavior and seek to reduce reliance on "thoughts" or other internal changes that might guide human behavior. (We will not ignore these latter forms of behaviorism entirely, however; versions of them will come up later in the book, when we look at cognitive and social influences on behavior.)

Both classical and operant conditioning are based on images of learning that portray a crucial kind of behavior change. Ironically—and perhaps significantly—both images involves a nonhuman animal, though each has been extended and elaborated to help us understand human learning in general and school learning in particular. Although starting with an image of animal learning may seem peculiar or even irrelevant to teaching, it may actually be helpful in understanding behavior change as such. Animals, after all, do not "think" in the same way humans do (except for my own dog, Ginger), but they certainly change their behavior on the basis of experience. So consider the images of animal learning in the following sections and what they suggest about how students learn.

The Dog and Its Food: Classical Conditioning

Imagine a golden retriever named Cory that is standing on a table—admittedly a strange place for a dog to be. Cory is a good-natured animal and has let himself be fitted with a harness that keeps him in one place so that he will not immediately dive for food that someone has put on the table in clear view but just beyond his reach. Cory is far from starving, but he has not eaten since yesterday. The mere sight of the food causes Cory to salivate slightly, but significantly; you know this because someone has installed a small tube at the corner of his mouth to drain the saliva into a small test tube that is tied to the harness.

Picture yourself as a behavioral psychologist in this odd but simple scenario. You show the food dish to Cory repeatedly. At first, you merely assure yourself that Cory indeed salivates when he sees the food and not at other times, such as when a bell rings or a light is turned on or off. Later, though, you make an important change: you try pairing a neutral sight or sound, such as the ringing of a small bell, to your presentation of the food. Cory, of course, still salivates to the paired event; after all, he still sees the food each time. But finally comes the crucial part. You present just the bell by itself, and behold: Cory salivates to the sound of the bell alone!

Cory's change in behavior illustrates **classical conditioning.** The dog has learned a response (salivating) to a previously neutral stimulus (a bell) because the stimulus has been paired repeatedly with another stimulus (the sight of food) that already has the power to elicit the response. Behavioral psychology has names for each part of the process. The originally automatic stimulus is called the *unconditioned stimulus* (sometimes abbreviated *UCS*), and the response the unconditioned stimulus originally causes is called the *unconditioned response* (or *UCR*). The stimulus that acquires new power is called the *conditioned stimulus* (or *CS*), and the response learned to it is called the *conditioned response* (or *CR*). The relationships among the terms for Cory the dog are diagrammed in Figure 2.1.

The image of Cory salivating may seem distant from your concerns as a teacher or a learner, but it has become a major vantage point for thinking about learning as behavior change. It is no coincidence that I described the image as I did; a situation much like it was actually studied and publicized at the beginning of the twentieth century by the Russian scientist Ivan Pavlov (1927). The change Pavlov demonstrated was called "conditioning" because the dog's learned response became conditional or dependent on being paired with a prior automatic response to a stimulus. As you will see shortly, behaviorists eventually studied other forms of conditioning. The form Cory experienced therefore is sometimes called *classical* or *Pavlovian* conditioning to honor Pavlov's historical priority in studying behavior change.

Jacqueline and Marcel both finished reading the passage above. "Weird," said Jacqueline, "I don't like tying down the dog like that. Or not feeding him since yesterday. Seems inhuman."

"You're not supposed to pay attention to that part of the story," said Marcel. "It's an image, a metaphor—remember? You're supposed to notice what happens when a bell and food get paired together, notice how the dog learns to salivate even when it's just the bell."

"But why would I limit a dog's actions like that? What does Cory think about being in a harness?" Jacqueline frowned. "Seems like showing him food repeatedly is just a kind of teasing. Naturally he's going to begin salivating just to the sound; it reminds him of the food. If you were handcuffed and teased, you'd act like that too!"

FIGURE 2.1

Classical Conditioning

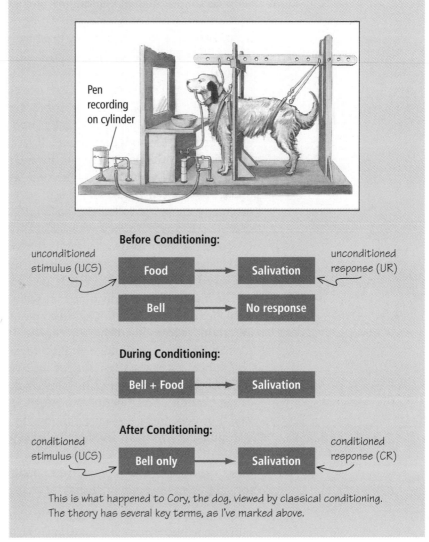

Pen recording on cylinder

Before Conditioning:

unconditioned stimulus (UCS)

| Food | → | Salivation |

unconditioned response (UR)

| Bell | → | No response |

During Conditioning:

| Bell + Food | → | Salivation |

After Conditioning:

conditioned stimulus (UCS)

| Bell only | → | Salivation |

conditioned response (CR)

This is what happened to Cory, the dog, viewed by classical conditioning. The theory has several key terms, as I've marked above.

Source: Douglas Bernstein et al., *Psychology*, Fourth Edition, copyright © 1997, p. 193. Reprinted by permission.

In Your Own Voice

Is Jacqueline missing the point about classical conditioning here or not?

How would you reply to her if you were in Marcel's place?

"But you're concerning yourself about what Cory *thinks* and *feels*," said Marcel. "He's just a dog, you know, not a person. I bet that whoever thought up this picture of learning picked a dog deliberately, precisely because it would make it easier to focus on Cory's *actions* instead of his thoughts."

Other Features of Classical Conditioning

Classical conditioning has a number of well-researched features, some of which are summarized in Table 2.1 (Gormezano, Prokasky & Thompson, 1987; Klein & Mowrer, 1989). The general trends shown in the table occur in human beings as well as in certain animals (such as Cory). **Extinction,** for example, refers to the *un*learning of a conditioned response: its gradual disappearance when the conditioned and unconditioned stimuli are no longer paired. Both children and other animals extinguish responses. Cory the dog will stop salivating to a bell if the bell is no longer presented with the sight of food; a student will gradually stop feeling natural curiosity about the curriculum if her teacher also stops presenting it with warmth and support. And so on.

Two other processes outlined in Table 2.1, spontaneous recovery and generalization, occur among children as well as other animals. **Spontaneous recovery** refers to the reappearance of an extinguished conditioned response after a period of disuse. Even if a student has extinguished curiosity about math, he may experience an initial return

TABLE 2.1   **Three Features of Classical Conditioning**

What It Is	Examples
Extinction The unlearning of a conditioned response, brought on when the unconditioned stimulus is no longer paired with the conditioned stimulus or when a new, competing stimulus is paired with the response.	1. After Cory the dog learns to salivate to the sound of a bell, the bell is rung by itself repeatedly. Gradually Cory stops salivating. 2. Katherine is anxious and cautious about riding her bicycle ever since she took a couple of spills from it last week. With further practice, though, she gradually feels less anxious and more confident again.
Spontaneous Recovery The reappearance of a conditioned response following its extinction—usually weaker than originally learned.	1. When Cory returned to the psychology lab 2 months later, he salivated to the sound of the bell even though he had previously extinguished that response. 2. After Katherine overcomes her worry about falling off her bicycle, she experiences the worry again the following spring, after putting her bicycle away for the winter.
Generalization The tendency for a stimulus *similar* to a conditioned stimulus to produce a conditioned response—usually weaker than the original learned response.	1. When Cory heard bells of other pitches and tone qualities, he also salivated, though not as much. 2. When Katherine first fell off her bicycle, she felt anxious not only at the sight of her own bicycle but at the sight of other bicycles and even pictures of bicycles.

of curiosity after a significant absence from it—perhaps in the fall, after a summer without math. As a result, forgetting does not necessarily increase steadily with time. **Generalization** refers to the tendency of a stimulus similar to an unconditioned stimulus to evoke a conditioned response. Once a student has become conditioned to respond indifferently to mathematics, she may also respond in a similar way to related subjects, such as science. Usually, however, generalized responses are not as strong as the originally conditioned response. The student therefore may disdain science, but disdain it less than mathematics.

Two qualifications about conditioning processes are especially important to teachers. One is that some responses are easier to condition than others. The easiest involve inborn reflexes, especially those that do not compete (or occur simultaneously) with other behaviors or previously learned responses. Cory the dog can be easily trained to salivate to a bell because salivating is one of his inborn reflexes. It would be harder for Cory to learn to peck in response to the bell, because pecking is not a typical behavior of dogs. It might also be harder for him to learn to salivate after a sudden loud noise, because another reflex, the startle response to sounds, normally *inhibits* salivation.

As with Cory, so with children: classical conditioning works primarily by modifying previous responses to stimuli. Suppose a child who is beginning school instinctively smiles and shows other signs of happiness and curiosity in response to a smiling adult. The child's response can potentially be paired or conditioned to other, more neutral stimuli, such as a curriculum activity, that the smiling adult presents. Suppose, on the other hand, that the curriculum activity is accompanied not by a smiling adult but by an adult who frequently scolds or criticizes. Then the activity becomes conditioned simultaneously to two responses, which we might call "happiness behavior" and "fearful anxiety," respectively. Since these responses compete (it is difficult to show happiness and fear at the same time), neither would be learned fully.

The second qualification regarding Table 2.1 has to do with the sources of its information. In general, extinction, spontaneous recovery, and generalization are patterns derived from experiments rather than from observations of naturally occurring situations. This means the concepts were initially devised to explain situations that deliberately limit or control the number and nature of distractions and irrelevant influences on a child or an animal. In the situation with Cory, for example, there are no unnecessary people in the room who might affect Cory's mood, no additional dogs barking and threatening to get the food instead of Cory, no unplanned noises or sounds other than the bell, and no extra food dishes competing for Cory's attention. A comparably controlled situation with a child or student would seem rather austere or barren compared to classroom-based learning situations. Would it therefore still be relevant to classroom learning? Would learning by students follow the same principles of conditioning as learning by Cory the dog?

Learning by Students Versus Learning by Dogs

A teacher's day is full of complexity, with many children and countless events that mutually influence one another. Social complexity and unpredictability are major departures from the controlled conditions assumed for classical conditioning and explored by Pavlov's research. Yet a form of conditioning takes place anyway.

Jacqueline and Marcel were taking educational psychology from the same instructor. For one assignment, they kept a log or journal with personal responses to the assigned readings. This week they wrote about classical conditioning:

Jacqueline's Log, April 12:

I remember hating mathematics, starting about 3d grade. Mr. Wilson used to call on each of us at random to answer word problems about division: "Just answer the question, please, and tell us how you got your solution." If you did it right, you got a brief word, "good." If you answered it wrong, there would be a long pause, then a question for the class, spoken with emphasis: "Can anyone help poor Jacqueline here?" I can still hear his voice asking this question; I would cringe all over and stare blankly at the textbook. In fact I still cringe when I see one of those "clever" word problems in a magazine.

Marcel's Log, April 12:

I fell in love with my kindergarten teacher: Mrs. June Kennedy. Was she ever nice to us! I remember her smile—seemed like she was never in a grumpy mood. She noticed you, said hello, how are you? It made such a difference. I hated going to school that first year, my kindergarten year. I remember crying at first—it seemed like every morning to me, though my dad tells me it wasn't that often. Too many new people, new kids. New everything. But Mrs. Kennedy kept smiling, kept saying hello, kept ignoring my gut-level worries. It made a real difference. These days when I'm someplace where I'm meeting a lot of new people, I still feel upset. But I also still remember kindergarten, and Mrs. Kennedy.

What did Cory the dog have in common with Jacqueline and Marcel? One thing is that all three experienced **stimulus substitution,** an essential process in classical conditioning. For Cory, a bell was substituted for food. For Jacqueline, the mere sight of mathematical word problems eventually substituted for the public shaming she experienced in third grade. For Marcel, a teacher's support came to substitute for the unpredictability of new social situations. For all three, both canine and human, the substitutions created new conditioned responses—unfortunately a negative one for Jacqueline.

Obviously, though, Jacqueline's and Marcel's experiences differed from Cory's in important ways, and understanding the differences is one of the challenges of using an image such as classical conditioning wisely. For one thing, both Jacqueline and Marcel were conditioned in the presence of other, competing influences: in the midst of other students, classrooms, and family experiences. The same can be said about Joe, the boy who introduced this chapter. His response both to school and to the after-school program probably are affected by a lot of previous experiences and people; we just don't know exactly how. We might begin to find out, however, if we could ask Jacqueline, Marcel, or Joe for more details of their school and personal lives. Meanwhile, we can only assume there is more influencing their changes in behavior than we currently know—an experience, incidentally, that teachers have with students rather frequently.

But a more important difference exists between Cory and the two students: both humans had some control over their behavior, whereas Cory was merely responding with an inborn reflex, salivation. It is true that both Jacqueline and Marcel were (presumably) compelled to attend school, like other children in modern society. They were also compelled to experience whatever joys or hassles their teacher happened to offer. But many details of their daily, moment-to-moment responses were also under their voluntary control to a significant extent. Jacqueline, for example, could (hopefully) minimize, though not eliminate, the embarrassment Mr. Wilson caused by studying her math assignments ahead of time; Marcel could solicit more of Mrs. Kennedy's warmth by approaching her frequently or initiating conversations with her. Cory, however, cannot walk away from the table to which he is harnessed.

Because students usually do control their behavior to some extent, the image of Cory salivating to a bell—the metaphor of classical conditioning—sometimes can be misleading when used to interpret classroom

In Your Own Voice

When my eighteen-year-old son read this section, he said, "Dad, you're too kind about students' experience of classroom life. Fact is, students just do as they're told basically all the time."

To convince me, he offered to arrange for me to talk with his friends.

Now I'm wondering whether he may be right.

How much control do you think students really have over classroom learning?

learning. The image works best for understanding times when students do lack major control over their lives. When a child has been violently abused at home, for example, classical conditioning offers an explanation for the child's fearfulness and shyness; the abuse has presented noxious stimuli that are truly beyond the child's control. More often, however, teachers need a different image of learning, a theory that emphasizes how the consequences of a deliberate response can lead to further learning. Another behaviorally oriented theory, operant conditioning, provides such an image, and that is where we turn next.

The Rat in the Box: Operant Conditioning

Imagine a gentle, white rat (not the kind associated with garbage cans, sewers, and disease) named Roseanne. Unlike a street rat, Roseanne is so mellow and trustworthy that she could be adopted as a house pet. As a matter of fact, she has lived her whole life in a psychology laboratory, and just now finds herself in a moderate-size wooden box on a table. It's an ordinary box, except that one wall has a small lever protruding from it and a food dispenser that looks like a small water or food dish.

You, the behavioral psychologist, watch and keep records on Roseanne's behavior. Roseanne is a good sport, and at first spends considerable time sniffing and pawing at random around the box. Eventually, though, she happens to press the lever, and immediately a pellet of rat food is dispensed into the food dish. Roseanne is a bit hungry, so she promptly eats the food. She resumes sniffing and exploring, and before long she presses the lever again: immediately another pellet of food appears! You note that the interval between level pressings is shorter the second time than the first time. As time goes on, in fact, the intervals continue getting shorter, until eventually Roseanne is spending most of her time pressing the lever and eating the food that appears on her dish.

Jacqueline scowled after reading this passage. "So I guess the point is that learning is in the relationship between the lever pressing and the reward? I like that better than the classical conditioning idea. Roseanne seems to have more choice than Cory had."

Marcel nodded, though with only mild enthusiasm. "Yeah, except I still suspect that we're not supposed to be thinking about the behavior as a conscious 'choice.' We might think about our own choices that way. Like in everyday activities: choice seems like a mental event—you know, something that supposedly happens 'inside' you. But I bet the point here is different. Here it's not what the rat thinks or feels that's important. It's the connection between overt actions and visible consequences that matters. I bet that's the point, not what Roseanne may be thinking about."

Jacqueline flipped back to page 34 in the text, where it described classical conditioning. "Seemed like before, with classical conditioning, Seifert was saying that learning depended on things that preceded a response—pairings of neutral and unconditioned stimuli. But now he's saying it depends on things that *follow* a response: pairings of consequences and responses. Agreed?"

"You got it, Jackie." And they smiled.

Like Cory the dog, Roseanne the rat changed her behavior and therefore "learned," but Roseanne's change illustrates an image of learning called **operant conditioning.** We all experience the crucial process of operant conditioning, which is simply that actions are influenced by the past and immediate consequences. Operant conditioning has specific terms for describing this principle: the action learned is called an *operant*, and the consequences are called a *reinforcement.*

"Strange names," thought Marcel. "Hope I can remember them." He looked up each in the dictionary:

> *Operant.* Any action that has an immediate consequence for a person or animal; so called because the action "operates" or acts on the environment.
> *Reinforcement.* Any consequence or outcome that causes an action to occur more often in the future; it may be valued consciously by the person as a "reward," but not necessarily.

Marcel put a bookmark at the page for each definition. Jackie might want to see this, he thought. But she had gone home for the day.

Operant conditioning has been studied more thoroughly than classical conditioning, perhaps for the reasons implied by Jacqueline and Marcel: that it focuses more on how behavior is affected by its consequences rather than by prior stimuli over which a person has little control (Klein & Mowrer, 1989; Skinner, 1974). Table 2.2 summarizes some key features of operant conditioning, along with brief examples that might occur in a classroom. Note that two of the terms associated with classical conditioning, *extinction* and *generalization*, are also used in operant conditioning.

These and other, related ideas about operant conditioning have proved useful in thinking about classroom learning and the behavior of

TABLE 2.2 Five Features of Operant Conditioning

What It Is	Examples
Extinction The unlearning of an operant behavior, brought on when the reinforcement is no longer paired with the operant behavior or when a new, competing operant behavior is reinforced.	When his teacher stoppped praising his comments during discussions, Frank stopped volunteering more contributions to discussions.
Generalization The tendency for behaviors similar to an operant behavior to occur in response to reinforcement—usually weaker in form.	When Colleen got positive comments and grades on her English assignments, her work in history improved somewhat as well.
Relativity of Reinforcers The tendency for some behaviors to be reinforcing only relative to other behaviors; sometimes also named the "Premack principle" after a psychologist who studied the tendency extensively.	Sherrie's teacher finds that Sherrie will do more mathematics problems if she is allowed to read a novel afterward, but she will read more of the novel only if she is allowed to spend free time in the library afterward. The novel is reinforcing relative to math but not relative to the library.
Partial Reinforcement Effect The tendency for an operant behavior to be learned more slowly if reinforcement does not occur on every occasion but also to extinguish more slowly after learning.	Karl clowns around in class a lot, but since the teacher and classmates acknowledge his behavior only some of the time, the clowning developed over a long period of time, and now it just won't go away when ignored.
Shaping Behavior Initial reinforcement of approximations or parts of a behavior, follow by gradual reinforcement of increasingly accurate or complete versions of the behavior.	Mike does nothing but whisper during class. You, the teacher, would like to priase him for being quiet for an entire class. But to do so, you must begin by praising him for being quiet for even just a few minutes; as this reinforcement begins to work, you can save your praise for longer periods of quiet behavior.

students (Davey & Cullen, 1988). They suggest, for example, why a student might persist with an inefficient method of taking notes: perhaps the method does work some of the time (partial reinforcement), and therefore it does not disappear quickly (extinction). Table 2.2 also suggests that identifying reinforcers may not be straightforward, since reinforcers can be individual and can vary over time.

Jacqueline's Log, May 3

Last week I was babysitting two kids, and I needed some way to limit their mischief, so I decided to try operant conditioning on them, like you talked about in class. They were being *terrible*—loud, rowdy, teasing each other, and teasing me, too! So I told them, "Each time one of you is quiet for 5 minutes I will give you one of these chocolate-covered candies"—I had brought some for a snack.

What happened next was strange. Joey did get quieter. Every time I gave him a chocolate, he ate it—until I realized that I was spoiling his lunch something awful! So I stopped, but then he was upset about my stopping and got more rowdy than ever.

Paul got quiet too, but started a "chocolates collection" on the kitchen counter with his reinforcements. About the time that Joey started getting stuffed, in fact, Paul asked me, "Do I have to eat these things?"

Professor's Response

Jackie's prof pondered this paragraph after he read it. What to write in the margins that would be helpful? Sounded like Jackie was on the right track, but five minutes was a long time to expect rowdy kids to be quiet! At least if they're not used to it. And did Jackie assume that everyone would welcome a chocolate candy, that it would be reinforcing for all? But best to focus, he thought, on one issue at a time. Let the question of diverse reinforcers go for the moment. He wrote in the margin,

5 minutes sounds long for some kids. Remember the "shaping" concept? Try approximations—e.g., shorter periods at first.

She is discovering, reflected her prof, the difficulty of finding and adjusting reinforcers. Sounds like Joey might have responded even with the candy given less frequently. In the margin he wrote,

Was Joey's "pay" too high? If you gave candy only every few times, maybe he would learn *and* extinguish more slowly—remember the "partial reinforcement effect"?

Ah! The individuality of reinforcers. What one child desires, another child may ignore. How, then, to influence every child's behavior? He wrote,

So Paul (and maybe others) don't really get reinforced by candy? Any idea how to discover alternative reinforcers for them? [Hint: observe them more . . .]

Then he wrote one more comment:

Good example, Jackie. Deserves more talk in class.

He set her log aside and went on to the next student's.

Jacqueline indeed identified a situation that can be understood and influenced by operant conditioning—getting Joey and Paul to be less rowdy—and she had partial success in handling it. Her professor's concerns, though, are worth noting. Not everyone responds to the same reinforcement, nor responds equally on every occasion. Partly as a result, a given reinforcement can seem like bribery to one student but a welcome reward to another. The resulting challenge is to individualize reinforcers: some students work for attention, others for academic credit, still others (hopefully) out of interest in a subject. Each student, furthermore, responds to different amounts of a reinforcement: a teacher's smile may seem like high praise to one student but seem trivial to another. And as if these complexities weren't enough, students actually control many important reinforcements themselves. They can reinforce one another, for example, by laughing at one another's comments in class or by talking to or looking at one another at odd moments. By the same token, they can withhold these reinforcers, thus extinguishing a classmate's behavior.

In a way, though, these complications miss the point about operant conditioning, because they are not a criticism of this theory of learning so much as a comment on typical conditions of classrooms. All teachers are challenged by the diversity among students, whether or not they think of learning in terms of stimuli, responses, and reinforcements. What these concepts offer is not a way to eliminate the complexities of classroom life but a manageable framework for understanding and dealing with the complexities. The framework has a particularly useful characteristic: it focuses attention on explicit behavior, on what teachers can actually see and hear of students' actions. In this respect it is distinct from other images and theories of learning, including the one discussed next, which focuses on thinking as a key to understanding learning.

Learning as Thinking

Cogito, ergo sum. (I think, therefore I am.)

René Descartes

Descartes, a well-known philosopher of the eighteenth century, is calling attention to what the behavioral theories of learning sometimes gloss over: that whatever else being human might mean, it also means being able to think. Perhaps, therefore, some theory of learning should be built around our ability to think. But what would it look like? One possibility is that it would show how we organize information. Perhaps it would also show how our ability to organize improves (hopefully) with age and with increasing education. And maybe it would suggest ways for us, as teachers, to assist children with the improvements. The result would be images of learning that looked like . . . what? Two candidate metaphors have captured the imaginations of psychologists: the modern computer and the growing but independent scientist.

The Computer: Information-Processing Theory

What better image than a computer, some have asked, to inspire ideas about how human beings think? A computer organizes and stores information; its structure and procedures are rather complex, but nonetheless they can be described in principle; and a computer will even allow us to test predictions about how information might be sorted, transformed, and stored in particular cases (Bara, 1996; Trefil, 1997). The newest computers, furthermore, can do surprisingly complex tasks—tasks that sometimes even seem human or "lifelike," such as responding to simple spoken commands or reminding you of appointments and errands when they arise. No wonder the computer has become a popular image of human thinking and of how learning may occur; perhaps the way computers acquire new information parallels the way people acquire knowledge. Perhaps it even parallels students' thinking in classrooms in particular. Perhaps.

The information processing approach points to the value of organizing information in order to remember it. How might these computers help these children to organize what they are learning?
© Paul Conklin/Monkmeyer

In Your Own Voice

Of course, you and I are human creatures, not machines.

So something must be missing from the information-processing image of learning, something that distinguishes you from a computer.

But what?

The computer on which I am writing this page, for example, has parts that correspond to important human mental functions. The keyboard receives information from its environment, much as my eyes and ears receive visual and auditory information. The electrical impulses from the keyboard are first stored temporarily in one part of the computer's memory, then sent to another, larger part of memory to be reorganized and compared to other information. These activities are called *information processing*. The initial storage corresponds, more or less, to the everyday human experience of momentary attention, for example, the sights or sounds that you happen to concentrate on from moment to moment as you drive down the street but forget immediately once you leave your car. The later reorganization of information corresponds somewhat to what we ordinarily call *conscious thinking*: the deliberate planning of an essay for a course, for example. In the computer, processing continues until one of two things happens: either the computer stores the information permanently on a disk drive or it "responds" by printing or displaying information on the video monitor. These outcomes, too, resemble human cognitive responses: the result of our attention and thinking is either to remember information or to respond somehow—in our case, with words or physical actions.

This sequence is commonly called an **information-processing model** of thinking and is diagrammed in Figure 2.2. The steps in the sequence are commonly called by names with a computerlike flavor, such as *short-term sensory store*, *working memory*, and *long-term memory* (Barber, 1988; Johnson-Laird, 1988). The model is helpful in explaining many organized thinking and reasoning behaviors. One obvious implication is that remembering something for a brief instant is not the same task as remembering something permanently. This seems to be what José believes:

JOSÉ, AGE TWELVE: Could you remember grandpa's phone number if I told it to you?

FIGURE 2.2

The Information-Processing Model

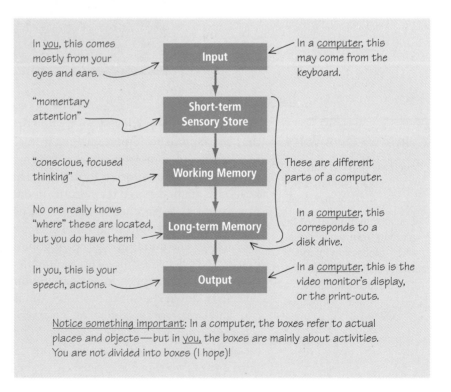

In you, this comes mostly from your eyes and ears.

Input

In a computer, this may come from the keyboard.

"momentary attention"

Short-term Sensory Store

"conscious, focused thinking"

Working Memory

These are different parts of a computer.

No one really knows "where" these are located, but you do have them!

Long-term Memory

In a computer, this corresponds to a disk drive.

In you, this is your speech, actions.

Output

In a computer, this is the video monitor's display, or the print-outs.

Notice something important: In a computer, the boxes refer to actual places and objects—but in you, the boxes are mainly about activities. You are not divided into boxes (I hope)!

YOUNGER SISTER MIRALDA, AGE FIVE: Sure. Just dial it.

JOSÉ: If I told it to you only once, could you still remember the number and dial without asking again?

MIRALDA: Sure.

JOSÉ: If I told you the number and then you had to get a drink of water, could you still remember the number and dial it even then?

MIRALDA: Yes.

JOSÉ: Won't you forget? They're just numbers, you know.

MIRALDA: I *won't* forget! Do you think I'm stupid? Let's try it.

José seems to suspect that Miralda *will* forget; he is like most adults in distinguishing between temporary memory of new information and long-term memories that are essentially permanent. His view is also consistent with the information-processing model in Figure 2.2. Miralda makes no distinction between short-term and long-term memory. Perhaps she assumes, unlike José, that a phone number will be personally meaningful and therefore easy to remember. Because of this assumption, Miralda may also believe her memory to be more powerful in this case than it really will be; after all, probably anyone learns phone numbers that belong to a friend or relative more easily than that of a complete stranger.

Strengths and Limitations of the Computer Image

This interpretation of José and Miralda is important in understanding both the strength and limitation of the computer metaphor as an image of learning. Its strength is that it has much to say about how thinking may be organized. Unlike with behaviorist metaphors, there is no need to know the detailed reinforcement history of an individual person. Its limitation is that unlike human beings, computers will process any information given to them, whether or not it is meaningful (Bruner, 1990; Shotter, 1993). "Garbage in, garbage out" is an old saying among computer experts, meaning a computer will process any numbers or words, however stupid or senseless. But the same cannot be said about people. Human beings learn information much better if it has meaning, that is, if it is significant and connected to prior knowledge and future goals. The computer image of learning has to account for this key difference between computer operations and human thinking. In effect, it has to suggest computerlike ways by which a human mind makes connections between new knowledge and old or in some other way discovers importance in new information.

The Importance of Meaning—Even to Computers

Discussing how information-processing theory might accomplish this task, or whether it even can, is beyond the scope of this chapter. But you can get a sense of why meaning matters by considering the following story and some elementary students' responses to it:

With hocked gems financing him, our hero bravely defied all scornful laughter that tried to prevent his scheme. "Your eyes deceive," he had said, "an egg, not a table, correctly typified this unexplored planet." Now three sturdy sisters sought proof forging along, sometimes through calm vastness yet more often over turbulent peaks and valleys. Days became weeks as many doubters spread fearful rumors about the edge. At last from nowhere welcome winged creatures appeared signifying momentous success.

"I can't make sense of this paragraph at all," Susan complained to her teacher, and several of her classmates nodded in agreement. The teacher had given the article to everyone to read for a discussion and possible quiz. Unfortunately, the teacher also had dropped it in the snow on the way to school, and the title had become unreadable on many copies, including Susan's.

"What's so hard about it anyway?" asked David. He looked around at his classmates, including Susan. "It's kind of poetic sounding, I suppose, but otherwise straightforward." He looked again at his copy; his was one of the few that had not been seriously damaged in the snow. He read the title silently: "Columbus Discovers America."

David, it seems, has found a framework for understanding the paragraph in an organized way, thanks to the title. Because Susan was deprived of this advantage, she finds the sentences rather obscure, not meaningful. Presumably, too, she will be able to remember little of it permanently. Her problem is to relate the paragraph to previous, meaningful knowledge—in this case to the story of Columbus, which both she and David presumably learned in the past but only David is able to put to use in this situation.

Expressed more directly in information-processing terms, Susan's and David's situation sounds like this: both students have previously acquired sets of concepts about an assortment of life experiences. Information-processing theorists sometimes call these **schemata** and consider them part of long-term memory (Howard, 1987). Chances are that both David and Susan have schemata for "Columbus Discovering America." In the case just described, though, only David was able to call on his schemata about Columbus, because he had the title to help him. He therefore was able to see a connection between the paragraph and his

In Your Own Voice

The notion of schemata raises interesting questions about where we find meaning in reading material.

What might be the schemata, for example, in reading a novel?

Is it different from the schemata for reading this book?

prior knowledge, an underlying similarity of structure between them. He experienced the similarity as "meaning" in the paragraph and therefore will be able to remember the paragraph as an example of his Columbus schemata. Susan, however, will have to remember the paragraph as a set of unrelated sentences—a much harder task, because she experiences it as not meaningful.

The Budding Independent Scientist: Piagetian Theory

Some cognitively oriented psychologists have noted a curious property of *schemata*, one that has led them away from the image of learning as a computer. Schemata, it seems, rarely match new knowledge or experiences perfectly. The paragraph David and Susan read is not a precise copy of their prior understanding of Columbus discovering America; almost surely it tells the story in a new way. The mismatch implies that schemata change when they encounter examples of themselves. David's understanding of Columbus will be altered, even if just a little, by his reading of the rather poetic account of Columbus. If so, David is experiencing two forms of learning at once: in one form he subsumes new experiences into a stable framework of knowledge (the "pigeonholes" examples), and in the other he alters the framework itself. From now on, we can guess, David will not think of the Columbus story as just history; from now on it may also be material for rich metaphors (as in the paragraph he deciphered), or at least material for clever word problems. His schemata will now be different than before.

Equilibration, Assimilation, and Accommodation

This two-way influence was of great interest to a highly influential cognitive psychologist named Jean Piaget (1977, 1985), who proposed an image of learning based on it. Piaget used the term **equilibration** for the interplay of experience and schemata (Piaget actually called them *schemas* instead of schemata), and he referred to their separate influences by the terms *assimilation* and *accommodation*. **Assimilation** refers to the interpretation of actions according to pre-existing structures of knowledge. **Accommodation** refers to the modification of knowledge structures as a result of actions. Piaget made numerous observations of children in developing these concepts, and interpretations of them have led to a particular image of learning: the child as independent scientist.

Four-year-old Tom is playing in a sandbox. Tom fills a tall, narrow bottle to the brim with sand, and then pours it into a wide pie plate. "This should make it be less," he says to himself. He looks carefully at the result and smiles with satisfaction. Then, using a funnel, Tom pours the contents of the pie plate back into the tall bottle: it fills exactly up to the brim again! Tom furrows his brow at this experience; "The same again?" he mutters, tentatively. Tom studies the tall glass briefly, then begins pouring the sand back and forth repeatedly. Just then you come up to the sandbox and sit with Tom.

"Is there more in the pie plate or more in the tall glass?" you ask, "Or the same?"

"More in the tall glass," says Tom, but he does not look completely convinced.

Like a scientist, Tom is making careful observations here, in this case of sand and its relationship to containers of differing shapes. Like a scientist, too, Tom has beliefs about the nature of the physical world, and the beliefs allow him to predict certain outcomes of his activity ("This should make it be less"). And like a scientist, Tom notes his observations even when they do not seem to fulfill his predictions ("The same again?"). In these ways, his learning is like "doing science." Certainly, at any rate, it is like doing an independent investigation.

What is not explicit in Tom's behavior is precisely *how* Tom's beliefs change as a result of experience—the process or mechanism by which Tom concludes, as he eventually must, that a volume of sand remains constant in spite of changes in its shape. This sort of learning is accommodation, and it unfolds much more slowly than assimilation (identification or pigeonholing of examples). Piaget observed that young children such as Tom need to experiment with volumes of sand and other materials for days, months, or even years before they become convinced, fully and permanently, that a volume of a substance remains constant in spite of any changes in the shape of its container (Piaget & Inhelder, 1974; Pinard, 1981). Most children finally acquire this belief early in the elementary school years, though the timing varies significantly among different tasks involving volume. Changes in the phrasing of questions such as those Tom was asked can make a task easier or harder, as can the specific materials chosen for the task. In general, familiar materials make a child seem more mature or "developed"; he or she may believe in constancy of volume a little sooner. Accounting for individual variations among students is an important problem for teachers, but not one in which the Piagetian image of independent scientist is fully helpful.

In Your Own Voice

Some say that the "budding scientist" is really based on the image of a growing organism.

The learner takes in mental nutrients (ideas, experiences, etc.) and organizes them into differentiated parts (leaves, branches, roots, etc.).

Taking in the nutrients is like assimilation, organizing the parts is like accommodation, and so on.

Do you think this is a valid image?

Strengths and Limitations of the Image of "Doing Science"

The image of learning as a form of "doing science" is compelling because it casts the child in an active, independent role as learner, a role that teachers certainly seek to encourage in students. It also has an attractively open-ended flavor: it is not the teacher's answers that the budding, independent scientist seeks but his or her own answers about the nature of things.

But this metaphor also has two hidden limitations. One is that in the image of the child as scientist, learning often seems to take more *time* than in other images and theories of learning. Although a child sometimes can acquire new knowledge quickly through assimilation to prior knowledge or schemata, she or he often needs long periods—days, months, even years—to accommodate or change schemata themselves. The slowness is consistent with the underlying metaphor of Piagetian theory: real scientific investigation itself often takes long periods, and human learning is thought to be a form of scientific investigation. But do teachers really have the time needed to foster long-term change? Sometimes they do, such as when they work with students literally for weeks to develop their reading skills. But sometimes the press of immediate goals interferes, such as when the school Christmas concert looms in December and preempts daily reading activities for several weeks, after which the long winter holiday prolongs the interruption.

The second problem with the image of the child as independent scientist is the isolation it implies. Tom, as child-scientist, seems to work alone, making observations and drawing conclusions primarily on the basis of solitary contacts with the physical world, and only gradually abandons his psychological independence for more social participation (Case, 1991). In some parts of the school curriculum, learning does happen this way; perhaps doing library research or taking measurements for a science lab experiment qualify as truly independent activities. Much, or even most, of the time, though, learning is very social indeed. Most assignments depend on instructions from other human beings (e.g., the teacher) and often on collaboration from others as well (e.g., classmates). These social elements may not always be explicit; supposedly solitary library research, for example, depends on the implicit participation of the teacher and the authors of library books. For our purposes as teachers, therefore, it is important to recognize the social influences on learning as well as a student's need to operate independently. Perhaps we even need to build a fundamental image of learning around the social, interactive events of classroom life.

Suppose, in fact, that we stand the image of independent scientist on its head and imagine that a child begins life not as an independent thinker but as a person immersed in social relationships and influences, a person who only gradually acquires independence of thought and action. This image is also consistent with everyday observations of children. The four-year-old at a family birthday party, for example, may be more confused than older relatives about the meaning of the celebration, but she is also likely to get more active guidance about how to act and what to say. Only when she is older will she move away from family traditions and devise more independent ways to celebrate birthdays. Looked at this way, *learning* is more like assisted performance, the heart of the next perspective.

Learning as Assisted Performance

If I have seen further, it is by standing upon the shoulders of giants.

Sir Isaac Newton

As Isaac Newton points out, we often know more when assisted by others. My voice sounds more musical in a choir than alone; your memory of this chapter's contents may improve if you try recalling it with a classmate; Elizabeth, my six-year-old daughter, sews better doll clothes if her mother helps her get started and encourages her to continue. And Elizabeth becomes a better basketball player if she practices with her team at school:

Two Ways of Learning to Shoot Baskets

On the driveway at home: Elizabeth looked at the basketball backstop, attempted a few shots, looked some more. For the moment no one was in sight up or down the block, just the retired man watering his garden two doors down. She looked up and down the street again; dribbled the ball, made one basket, stood still. Since coming outside, she had missed every shot but

In the gym at school: Elizabeth's teammates were already shooting baskets, dribbling actively around the court, calling to one another. Elizabeth was new to the team and not the best player; she looked carefully at Maureen, who was one of the best. Maureen successfully dunked a basket from almost twenty feet away. "Two hands," noted Elizabeth, "I should use two

The zone of proximal development is a psychological "space," if not a literal one, in which a less skilled person—like this boy who is learning to knit—can benefit from assistance by a more skilled person. © Mimi Forsyth/Monkmeyer

one. But, of course, she reminded herself that she wasn't really concentrating. She looked forward to the regular practice time, tomorrow afternoon, and took the ball back indoors.

hands like Maureen." The coach came over just then; "Ready to try some more free throws, Liz?" she asked. "Remember to stay loose in your knees this time, and take your time." Elizabeth tried several throws. She made every one, except the one when Maureen called to her, "Great shot, Liz!"

In this image, a learner is immersed in a network of social relationships: Elizabeth with her teammates and coach, me with my fellow choir members and director, you with your classmates and instructor. The relationships provide a framework for encouraging new skills beyond what we might be able to do alone. The network is sometimes called a *community of practice,* and the effects of the network on learning are sometimes said to comprise the *zone of proximal development.*

Communities of Practice

In Your Own Voice

Have you ever participated in a community of practice that did not function well?

What caused the problem?

A **community of practice** is a group of individuals who respond to one another and work together to accomplish some common goal (Britzman, 1991; Lave & Wenger, 1991). Communities of practice exist in diverse places in society and for diverse purposes. An athletic team constitutes a community of practice as members work together to win games and improve their skills. So is a group of teachers in a school or in a few neighboring schools as they share stories about teaching experiences and trade tips to use in their classrooms. But the most important example is the classroom itself, which can constitute a community of practice if it functions in a cooperative way and works toward goals that students and teacher truly hold in common (Tudge, 1990). If the curriculum is force-fed to students "for their own good," however, the classroom is not a community of practice in the sense meant here.

Frank had just finished reading *The Turkey Celebrates in His Own Way* with his second-grade class. In the story, Thelma the turkey has explained to Mr. Hobson that she has never cared for the Thanksgiving holiday; it makes her nervous. Mr. Hobson's response is ambiguous; he says he might therefore take Thelma to his house to celebrate Thanksgiving with his family. "We always like turkey," he adds. There is a double meaning here: is Mr. Hobson just trying to be friendly to Thelma, or is he saying that he will roast her for the Thanksgiving meal? None of Frank's students seem to be catching this double meaning.

FRANK: What did Mr. Hobson say he would do with the turkey?

JOSIE: He would invite . . .

SEAN: Ummm . . .

FRANK: Are turkeys *supposed* to like Thanksgiving?

ALL: Noooo. Hate it. Scared . . .

FRANK: Why do they hate it? [A few competing responses: turkeys are shy, they are bored, etc. But Frank attends mostly to Sean.]

SEAN: Get eaten. They get eaten then.

FRANK: So what about Thelma? What is *she* thinking about Mr. Hobson's invitation?

JOSIE: She's wondering if he's really a nice guy or really a hungry guy!

[Josie looks satisfied and smiles, but Sean looks at Josie, apparently puzzled about her last comment. Several students have not said a word during the whole time, but look on with interest.]

Frank's class constitutes a community of practice, at least during this particular discussion of this book. The students learn more because of assistance from Frank, though at other times they may also get assistance from one another. Note that as with all classes and other groups, some individuals seem more involved and central to the activity than others. To function well over the long term, the community has to allow for such differences in involvement and knowledge. The marginal students have a legitimate place as observers, where they can observe the entire activity of the community, gradually develop knowledge about the group's purposes, and develop skills at participating more actively (Lave & Wenger, 1991).

The Zone of Proximal Development

In Your Own Voice

The notion of a ZPD is attractive: can you think of an activity in your life that you perform better when you work with someone more expert than yourself?

But the notion can also be too seductive: maybe you can also think of an activity that you do better alone, *without* the assistance of experts.

Does your success at the second activity undermine the ZPD idea?

A community of practice influences learning by providing an assortment of people—the teacher and peers with various talents—who can assist an individual to perform more skillfully than he or she can perform alone. The gap between independent performance and performance with support from others is the **zone of proximal development** or **ZPD** (Vygotsky, 1985; Wertsch, 1991). In Frank's class, for example, many students discuss the book more clearly precisely *because* they do their thinking with others, some of whom already understand the book fairly well. Their improvement is an indicator that they are creating a ZPD for themselves. Much of the influence of a classroom community is indirect, through hearing classmates ask and respond to questions. The most talented member of the class usually is the teacher; but she or he is not the only person who assists students' performances. Nor is the teacher always the one with the most knowledge; on certain topics (e.g., dinosaur facts), a student may be the expert. All in all, class members function as coaches or mentors to one another, modeling learning, providing encouragement and support, and presenting challenges to individual students. Altogether their behaviors create a zone of proximal development

MULTIPLE VOICES

MULTIPLE VOICES

MULTIPLE VOICES

MULTIPLE VOICES

A common myth about learning as assisted performance is that the teacher (or the one doing the assisting) has to be a true expert in the domain being learned or in the activity being jointly performed with the student. In reality, one doesn't have to be an expert to provide good assisted performance experiences for children. In fact, often the true expert is so far ahead of novice learners in the domain that it is difficult for that person to "come down" to the learner's level and provide good scaffolding. A slightly more competent peer or an adult who knows a little more than the learner about an activity can often serve as a provider of assisted performance. Assisted performance, for me, means when the teacher and the learner are jointly engaged in a meaningful, goal-directed learning activity and the teacher is trying to allow the learner to do as much of the activity independently as possible by providing sensitive, leading questions and by carefully modulating the task demands and the assistance given in order to keep the learner in the zone of proximal development.

Adam Winsler, George Mason University

for the individual without which less learning would occur. Adam Winsler, a professor of psychology at George Mason University, describes something similar in his account of the ZPD. Note one of his points: in a community of practice, the teacher is not set apart from students but interacts with and learns from them in comparative equality.

But as you may suspect, there are also unsolved issues about communities of practice and the ZPD. The two concepts presuppose a sort of apprenticeship model of learning, with the less skilled learning at the elbows of the more skilled. But apprenticeships have two significant problems. First, experts may not always prove helpful to novices. The master tailor may never give the young tailor a chance to try complicated sewing projects; the classmate who knows a lot about computers may not actually assist less knowledgeable classmates to learn. Second, experts are by definition scarce, and therefore not always at hand. The best tailor may work across town, not in the novice's own tailoring shop; the best computer expert may be in another class or even in another school, not in the class where he or she is needed the most. Can communities of practice and ZPDs exist anyway? Cheryl and Jerod struggle with this question via e-mail:

TO: CHERYL@UMANITOBA.CA
FROM: JEROD@UARKANSAS.EDU
SUBJECT: SEIFERT'S COMMENTS ABOUT COMMUNITIES OF PRACTICE

Cheryl, my DEAR big sister <note my sarcasm>,

I still can't get used to using e-mail like this, but maybe the best thing is just to dive in and try!

This Seifert fellow sounds like he secretly believes in the last of his metaphors--that learning as assisted performance idea, zone of proximal development, and all that. I can sure support that "zone of prox dev" idea. Remember when you helped me figure out how to use the computer for e-mail? For the longest time it seemed like I could do SO much more only if you were standing over my shoulder. On my own, I could never get it to work.

What do you think?

<end of message>

TO: JEROD@UARKANSAS.EDU

FROM: CHERYL@UMANITOBA.CA

SUBJECT: LIMITS TO COMMUNITIES OF PRACTICE?

Jerod, DEAREST younger brother <note my sarcasm>,

I think you're right about Seifert's biases--he likes the "learning as assisted performance" idea. But I was troubled by the notion of COMMUNITY OF PRACTICE. It sounds like he's saying communities have to be face to face, like conventional classrooms, or maybe a church congregation.

But does a community have to be face to face? How about our family, for instance? Here we are writing e-mail notes to each other from distant cities, while our parents live in a third city, also far away. Yet in a lot of ways I feel like we form a small "community." Sure it helps to be together periodically--like at holidays--to re-new our connections. But do we have to be together all the time? Nope! <in my opinion, that is>

PS: Are you going home anytime soon? Mom and Dad complain (in their separate ways) about never hearing from you.

<end of message>

In Your Own Voice

Cheryl has a point, I think: a community does not have to be face to face.

But surely there has to be some common bond or common purpose holding the members together.

My question to Cheryl and Jerod (and to you): how strong does that bond have to be, and how minimal can the face-to-face contact among community members afford to get?

TO: CHERYL@UMANITOBA.CA

FROM: JEROD@UARKANSAS.EDU

SUBJECT: LIMITS TO COMMUNITY OF PRACTICE--EVEN IN SCHOOLS

Cheryl sis,

I hadn't thought about whether a community has to be face to face; just took it for granted that it SHOULD be. Makes me wonder just how much face-to-face contact is really necessary for people to help each other as a community of practice. Maybe none at all? Maybe just a little bit now and then?

Or does it depend on what the community--and the person--are trying to accomplish? Aren't there some things that have to have been learned in person, face to face? How about learning to drive a car? I suppose a computer could simulate driving on a TV screen, but sooner or later you have to try it on the real thing, don't you?

PS: I wrote to Mom and Dad--told them to get a computer and subscribe to an e-mail service. Then I'll write lots. Meanwhile, home by Xmas. University of Arkansas is nice. :)

<end of message>

TO: JEROD@UARKANSAS.EDU

FROM: CHERYL@UMANITOBA.CA

SUBJECT: ENOUGH OF THIS FOR NOW

Jerod,

I can think of other things, too, that have to be learned face to face--like learning to be a schoolteacher or learning to paint pictures or play the piano. Anything that can't be translated entirely into a string of words, like on these e-mail messages.

Still, Seifert's gotten me thinking that maybe a lot more of the usual school curriculum could, in principle, be learned through a range of communities of practice--some face to face, some using other ways of communicating, like these e-mail notes. Learning from a computer doesn't have to mean that you're sitting passively, waiting for a machine to dictate the material instead of waiting for a teacher to dictate it. You could be interacting actively-- like you and I are doing here.

Your comments?

<end of message>

In Your Own Voice

Cheryl and Jerod think I have a bias for learning as assisted performance.

Are they right?

If so, should I try to eliminate my preference, or at least hide it better?

Reconciling Metaphors of Learning

WHEN my children were preschoolers, the oldest one came to me one day and asked, "Daddy, which of us do you like the best: Michael, Elizabeth, or me?" Without even checking a parent-advice manuals, I knew instantly how to answer: "I like each of you in your own way. You're just simply different from each other, not better or worse." But the question made me realize something else, which is that I can make this claim to like each child in his or her own way only if I actually know each child well and really do appreciate each on his or her own terms.

Can They All Be True at Once?

It is much the same with metaphors, images, and theories of learning. Each is worthwhile in its own way, provided you can appreciate each on its own terms and know what each can accomplish (Seifert, 1992). For the purpose of being a good teacher, it is not necessary to determine the One Best Theory of Learning (note my intentional capitalization). It is true that each perspective on learning "contradicts" the others in the sense that it does not adopt the terms and focus of the others.

Classical conditioning, for example, at no time speaks of "communities of practice," and the information-processing theory rarely speaks directly of reinforcement in the sense intended by behaviorism. Rather than viewing the differences as conflicts, however, it may be more helpful to see them as differences in focus or attention. The behaviorist metaphor focuses most explicitly on the immediate consequences of action, for example, whereas the computer metaphor attends to the organization of knowledge. The notion of a community of practice recognizes that a lot of learning takes place in social situations, not solitary ones. As separate images of learning, no theory can portray every feature of learning or teaching equally well, just as no child can embody all possible qualities and no novel can tell every possible story that might be told.

Developing Your Own Metaphors of Learning

Ultimately only *you* can fashion a view of learning that makes the most sense to you. In my opinion, your best strategy for doing so is to regard

In Your Own Voice

Try it, you'll like it: let your mind play with metaphorical images of learning, and see if you can come up with one you like.

Don't worry if you shift to a different metaphor later; as I keep saying, no image of learning is perfect; none captures a final, complete truth about learning.

But each one reveals some of it.

the major theories of learning—the images I have described—as useful resources. Consider them thoughtfully, but then think also about how you can combine them with views and beliefs you already have. Your challenge is neither to accept professional theories of learning unthinkingly nor to dismiss them out of hand; your challenge is to synthesize them with your own beliefs and experience (Britzman, 1991). Be prepared, therefore, to accept some features of some theories, ignore other features that are irrelevant to your needs, and transform still others. And be prepared to do the same with your own prior beliefs. The result? You will be readier to teach than ever before.

Obviously, in a book read by many people, I cannot guess how you should focus your attention in developing a personal, coherent view of learning. But the metaphors and theories described earlier in this chapter hint at dimensions you may want to consider. One dimension is *time*. All psychologically based views of learning recognize that changes occur in both the short term and the long term, but often they emphasize one time span more than the other. Where do your particular beliefs about learning fit in? Another dimension is *relationship*. All psychologically based views of learning recognize that individuals often do a lot of learning when in groups. But some views give the impression that groups are crucial to learning, whereas others imply that social relationships are relatively unimportant or even irrelevant to the individual. What do *you* think: how central are other human beings in causing learning and influencing its direction? A third dimension is *evidence*. All psychologically based views agree that learning is shown both in action and in thought and that actions and thoughts somehow influence each other. But some seem to regard actions as more primary, more real, and a better source of evidence, whereas other views seem to give the same status to thoughts. You, like the people who developed academic theories of learning, will need to evolve your own positions on this question.

Using Metaphors in Practice

In resolving these issues, keep in mind that for you, understanding learning may serve a different purpose than it does for a research psychologist. As a teacher, you will solve particular learning problems experienced by particular students—by real, live individuals sitting across the desks just a few feet away. You must deal with their strengths and peculiarities, no matter what these may be and no matter how different one student may be from another. Research-based psychological concepts and theories, on the other hand, evolve out of a search for general knowledge, a search for universal truths (Shotter, 1991). Because of this purpose, they deliberately simplify certain features of human learners to create an account of learning that is coherent and universal. A theory based on the idea of classical conditioning, for example, downplays the highly organized, purposeful quality of much human behavior; one based on the idea of coaching and communities of practice may gloss over exactly which consequences (or reinforcements) influence a specific person's behavior in a given learning situation.

You, however, will not have the luxury of overlooking qualities of your students simply to achieve consistency in thinking about them. Students will not come to you as textbook cases of human learners. Instead they will be merely themselves: simply José, Miralda, Frank, Jacqueline, Marcel, Sean, Cheryl, and Jerod. Helping them to learn may therefore feel a bit like becoming multilingual, a speaker of many languages and a connoisseur of many cultures. In one of the many languages you must acquire, you will need to know your own general views about the nature of learning. But you will also need to "speak" several other psychological languages, one about how each individual student learns, day by day. Translating among these languages will often be necessary and always be challenging. With practice as well as reflection on your practice, though, you should succeed. Later chapters in this book can help move you closer to this success.

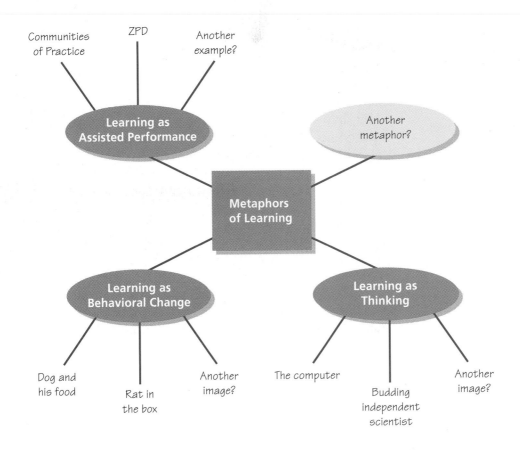

Chapter Re-View: Learning, In School and Out This Chapter Re-View suggests directions in which the chapter might have taken your thinking—though, of course, other directions are also possible. It expands the Chapter View, which suggests a starting point, conceptually, for the chapter. But this Re-View does not suggest an ending point. Like the Chapter View, it represents just one perspective among many.

Key Terms and Concepts

metaphors of learning (32)
learning as behavior change (32)
behaviorist (32)
classical conditioning (35)
extinction (37)
spontaneous recovery (37)
generalization (38)

stimulus substitution (40)
operant conditioning (42)
information-processing model (48)
schemata (50)
Piagetian theory (51)
equilibration (51)
assimilation (51)

accommodation (51)
learning as assisted performance (54)
community of practice (56)
zone of proximal development (ZPD) (57)

Annotated Readings

Martin, Gary, & Pear, Joseph. (1996). *Behavior modification: What it is and how to do it* (5th ed.). Upper Saddle River, NJ: Merrill. A down-to-earth explanation of the behaviorist point of view as it applies to professional settings, including both psychotherapy and education. The authors are not much concerned with comparing behaviorism to other metaphors of learning; they focus exclusively on using the conditioning ideas.

Sternberg, Robert, & Spear-Swerling, Louise. (1996). *Teaching for thinking*. Washington, DC: American Psychological Association. The authors discuss differences among types of thinking, as in this chapter, but their approach to the topic is based more on information-processing theory (or "cognitive science") and less on constructivism.

Weber, Sandra, & Mitchell, Claudia. (1995). *"That's funny, you don't look like a teacher": Interrogating images and identity in popular culture*. London: Falmer Press. This interesting book presents commonly held metaphors about the nature of teachers, teaching, and learning. The authors argue that the metaphors become the basis for popular stereotypes about teaching. Lots of attention to gender issues, but also to other, teaching-related issues.

Internet Resources

<www.wmich.edu/aba> This is the official web site of the Association for Applied Behavior Analysis, a major professional association committed to exploring the uses of behaviorism in many areas of human activity, including psychotherapy, management of child behavior problems, and education. The site includes information for contacting special-interest groups (for example, professionals concerned with helping children who are autistic or very withdrawn), as well as information about and samples from their publications.

<www.sunnyhill.bc.ca/Lalonde/JPS/index.html> This is the web site for the Jean Piaget Society, a professional association with a mix of individuals committed to understanding the implications of Piagetian theory. In spite of its name, the society does not consist exclusively of "true" Piagetians;

many study and understand learning more as assisted performance.

<www.massey.ac.nz/~ALock/virtual/project2.html>

This web site is totally dedicated to information about "learning as assisted performance," especially as originally espoused by an intellectual leader of the perspective, the Russian psychologist Lev Vygotsky.

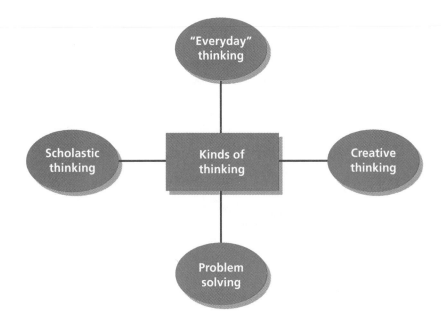

Chapter View: Thinking About Thinking This Chapter View is a concept map that indicates one among many ways of thinking about the chapter. It suggests a starting point, conceptually, for the chapter but is incomplete by itself. At the end of the chapter is a Chapter Re-View, which expands on the Chapter View, suggesting directions for taking your thinking further—though, of course, other directions are also possible.

3
Thinking About Thinking

Most people already have beliefs about what "thinking" consists of, especially when it has to do with classrooms and schools. For one thing, *thinking* is supposed to differ from feelings and emotions. We speak of "cold, hard" reasoning; if we say that someone's thinking is "soft," we are likely to be criticizing. *Thinking* is also supposed to be a general process, distinct from *what* you think about. Just as my computer can organize and process almost any possible string of words, so my mind should be able, in principle, to think about any possible topic or event: to say that an idea is "unthinkable" means only that we have strong negative feelings about it or conventions against public discussion of it, not that we cannot actually contemplate it. In structure, therefore, *thinking* is usually thought of as extremely general, even if in content it sometimes can be very specific. I can think about anything: my pet dog, my childhood, the meaning of my life. In thinking about *thinking,* therefore, we usually envision an activity that is detached from feelings and rather general. These qualities give the concept prestige; we usually believe it is good to be able to *think* well in the sense outlined here.

School-Based and Everyday Thinking Compared

*B*UT how realistic is this commonsense view of thinking, and how helpful is it to teachers? I invite you to consider the possibility that most of the time it is partially misleading, that thinking *is* not usually general or emotionally detached. I invite you to consider, furthermore, that one of the few situations where thinking most often does have these qualities is in school classrooms, in the interactions among teachers, students, and curricula. To an important degree, then, notions of *thinking* are like notions of *learning,* as discussed in Chapter 2, in that they refer to something different inside a classroom than outside. Bridging the gaps between the classroom and the rest of the world therefore becomes part of a teacher's job.

The Math Lesson in Class

Tom and Charleen are doing math in their second-grade class. Their teacher has been following the curriculum, which tells her to put the students in small groups to solve money problems. It also tells her to use small amounts of money; in its words, "children of this age learn best by manipulating tangible materials. They are unable to conceptualize large amounts of money, which are too abstract for them." The teacher has therefore given Tom and Charleen twelve "pennies" in the form of poker chips; their task at this particular moment is to divide the money in various ways to see how many combinations of candy they can buy from a price list the teacher has given them. The children are reasonably content as they work on the task, though they giggle a lot as they record their results.

"Can't buy much for 12 cents, can you?" says Tom to Charleen.

"Nope," she replies, "and anyway my mom and dad never let me buy candy ever, 'cept on my birthday." They continue working a few more minutes, experimenting with various combinations of poker chip "pennies." Then they record their results and wait.

Tom's Math Lesson at Home

Later, after school, Tom is home with his younger brother watching "junk" TV to pass the time before his mom gets home from work. Tom and his brother live with their mother; they barely know their father, who left home when Tom was about three years old. Today they have been watching cartoons, a practice their mom frowns on but tolerates for times when she is not at home. Today's cartoon show has been aggressively advertising a computer game called Space Blasters.

"Can I have Space Blasters for my birthday?" Tom asks his mom. He thinks this is a simple question, but he is wrong.

"Are you kidding?" says his mom. Her eyes widen and her voice becomes slow and measured. "One of those games costs almost $100! Do you have any idea how much money that is?" She stares hard at Tom, waiting for an answer.

"No, ma'am," Tom murmurs, trying suddenly to sound respectful. "I guess it's a lot . . . ?"

"Darn right it is!," says mom. "It's two weeks of groceries—that's what it is. Or all of your clothes to start school. Or our trip to see grandpa this Christmas!"

Tom withdraws to the living room again and shuts off the TV. "Mom's in one of her moods," he tells his younger brother. Privately, he can't decide whether he has actually done something wrong. Clearly amounts of money *do* matter and have consequences. Clearly, too, $100 is "a lot"—equivalent in consequences to several major activities he is familiar with.

Charleen's Math Lesson at Home

After school, Charleen is grocery shopping with her teenage sister. Charleen lives with her sister and both parents, but her parents work most evenings as caretakers for a building downtown. This particular evening, the two girls must buy food for the family for the coming week, and Charlene's special task is to choose breakfast cereal. She knows without being told that she should find the "best buy," meaning the most cereal at the lowest cost; her family is not poor, but she has been told, directly and indirectly, that money does need to be conserved carefully.

Charleen studies the cereal aisle closely. She has discovered that prices are posted on a small sticker under each type of cereal: an overall price in moderate-size print and a price per ounce in tiny print. The family's favorite type of cereal (bran flakes) happens to be on sale ($2) on one brand but not on another ($3). She starts to take the cheaper brand, but then peers closely at the prices and boxes. She notices that the box on sale is *smaller* than the other box. She hesitates.

Maybe the larger box is really a better buy? she wonders. She notes the quantity in each box: the on-sale box is 12 ounces, and the regular box is 14. That doesn't seem like much of a difference, she thinks.

In the end she takes two of the smaller boxes, though together they will cost more than a single box of the larger size. She takes them to her sister, feeling a bit nervous about her choice.

Charleen is relieved to find that her sister is happy with her choice. "You did right," says her sister. "These will be cheaper in the long run, and we'll get through both boxes eventually." Then she mutters, "Stupid grocery store. You almost have to have a calculator to figure out the *real* prices!"

Charleen feels a brief moment of pride at having succeeded in selecting this particular "best buy," but she's not sure whether she'll be able to do it again the next time she must choose from among prices, quantities, and sizes. Clearly, though, Charleen realizes that discerning prices is a serious business, that it must take skill if even her big sister has trouble doing it, and that she had better learn how to do it even if it *is* hard.

In Your Own Voice

As a student, presumably you've had extensive experience in thinking!

Some has been done in class (hopefully), but a lot has been done outside.

For you, how has thinking in class differed from thinking outside?

Do the differences coincide with my comments here or not?

As these examples suggest, there are differences between thinking as it occurs in classrooms and thinking as it occurs elsewhere. In classrooms, what counts officially as thinking is likely to be tied to specific problems set by a curriculum. Furthermore, the problems are likely to be sequenced in ways specified by the curriculum or by a teacher, either of which has usually based the sequencing on beliefs, metaphors, and theories of how children learn best, such as those described in Chapter 2. In learning about money, for example, Tom and Charleen were asked to deal with very small amounts, presumably on the grounds that small amounts would be easier for them to comprehend. Ironically, though, this curricular strategy may have made the money activity seem less important and motivating; as Tom said, "Can't buy much for 12 cents, can you?"

Outside classrooms, thinking often takes on a different character: there it is likely to be an emotional event as well as an intellectual one. Discussing the cost of Space Blasters, for example, involves serious financial issues for Tom's mother and therefore for Tom. So does Charleen's search for the best buy in breakfast cereals. Both children experience significant worries about money at the same time they learn important lessons about what money is for, how much it can buy, and consequences of various uses of money. These lessons are determined not by a curriculum or by theoretical images of learning but by the children's family circumstances. More well-to-do families might not show as much concern about costs, and different lessons in thinking might therefore be taught, at least lessons about money.

These contrasts do not mean that school-based thinking is always too tame and isolated from life; rather, it means that teachers inevitably face a problem of **transfer** of learning, or getting students to apply knowledge acquired in one situation to another, related situation. It is not good enough to be able to count money in class, as Tom and Charleen did; you should be able to count it at the store as well. It is not good enough to be able to read books and materials provided by your teacher; you should be able to read books and materials that you freely choose from the library or elsewhere. And so on. The challenge of transfer can be large, small, or anywhere in between. It may be relatively easy to induce students to use arithmetic skills learned in class to solve highly similar arithmetic problems on a unit test—unless a student lacks motivation to pass the test. It can be hard to motivate them to use their knowledge of high school chemistry in any situation other than the chemistry class itself—unless, of course, a student is planning a career as a chemist. Hard or easy, though, the problem of inducing transfer remains. Therefore, we return to it from various directions in later chapters. Sometimes it will reappear as a problem of motivating students, or of the similarity between life in the classroom and life in the community, or of observing the results of learning appropriately. In the meantime, it is important to clarify what you, I, or any other teacher means when we say we "understand students' thinking" and note how that phrase can mean different things in different situations.

A Thumbnail Sketch of Thinking

*L*ET'S look at three kinds of thinking in turn, then compare them with one another. First, we'll examine thinking that is generally considered "the" kind needed for school: thinking as scholastic aptitude. In our particular society, this form of thinking is often associated not only with high grades but also with high performance on standardized tests of scholastic aptitude and intelligence. Because of this historic association, we will also discuss the nature and purposes of such tests and how they have affected beliefs about what "good thinking" is, both in classrooms and out.

After considering the kind of thinking needed for success on tests of scholastic aptitude, we will consider two alternative forms: problem solving and creativity. *Problem solving* refers to the ways students (and teachers) deal with complex, ill-defined situations requiring solutions. *Creativity* refers to the ways people come up with innovative but still useful ideas and products. Together scholastic aptitude, problem solving, and creativity represent three major, distinct elements of what most of us think of as *thinking*. They also pose distinct challenges and opportunities for teachers, partly because of the conditions of teaching and of classroom life, which make some kinds of activities, conversations, and goals easier to arrange than others.

In Your Own Voice

As you think about *thinking* in reading this chapter, you might consider how much *you* value scholastic aptitude, problem solving, and creativity in your own life.

Don't limit yourself to your classroom life when you do this; think about *all* of your experiences: home, family, friends, job—everything.

Paper-and-pencil tests are so widespread, and have such a long history, that it is tempting to equate performance on them with what students actually learn. © Michael Newman/Photo Edit

Thinking as Scholastic Aptitude

ONE way to think of thinking is as scholastic aptitude: the skills needed to succeed in school, earn high grades, and the like. What might these skills be? One clue to this question comes from the many standardized tests designed to predict school success (Berlak, 1993; Frederikson, Mislevy & Bejar, 1993). Because of their purpose, they tend to call for the kind of thinking expected in school: verbal and numerical reasoning, as well as general "worldly knowledge" as shown, in particular, by having a large vocabulary. The following questions are typical in requiring these forms of thinking; they are similar to items (or questions) in the Stanford-Binet Test of Intelligence (Thorndike, Hagen & Sattler, 1986), one of the most widely used and respected tests for predicting scholastic aptitude:

- For a grade-school child: "Why is this foolish? 'A man had the flu twice. The first time it killed him, but the second time he got well quickly.'"

- For a high-school youth: "How are these alike: winter and summer; happy and sad; much and little?"

- For an adult: "Let's suppose that this box has two smaller boxes inside it, and each one of the smaller boxes contains a little tiny box. How many boxes are there altogether, counting the big one?"
- For an adult: "What does this proverb mean? 'Let sleeping dogs lie.'"

Do these questions seem vaguely familiar, as if you have seen something like them somewhere before? If so, the reason may be that you have been asked questions of this general "style" or type during your career as a student (though probably not these exact questions). The underlying style is widespread in public schooling and is characterized by the following qualities:

- The test item asks you to solve a problem or answer a question someone else has created rather than one you have set for yourself.

- It poses a problem that tends to have a specific answer or "correct" solution rather than one that has a number of alternative solutions.

- It requires you to read carefully (or sometimes listen carefully) to the exact wording of the problem or question.

- It rewards you for having knowledge of many terms and words, including several that are rarely used in everyday conversation.

- It expects you to solve the problem or answer the question by yourself, without consultation with peers or experts.

Altogether, the underlying qualities imply an image of *thinking*, one that depicts thinking as part of school learning and school success. As you might suspect, this view is not the only view of *thinking*; in fact, most thinking done outside of school does not have these qualities (Resnick, 1987; Resnick, Levine & Teasley, 1991). Nonetheless, the idea of *thinking* as scholastic aptitude is widely believed and respected in our society. How complete, useful, and fair this idea is will ultimately be up to you to decide; it will not necessarily be good for you simply because others believe it already. Because you should make up your mind intelligently, though, and because a school-based view of *thinking* is indeed so prominent, you should first consider it as accurately and fairly as possible. A good way to do so is to look a bit more closely at one of its historical origins and continuing supports: standardized tests of scholastic aptitude.

Tests of Scholastic Aptitude

Where They Came From

Even at their historical beginnings, tests of **scholastic aptitude** were designed to identify and predict how much students might benefit from conventional schooling. Early in the twentieth century, two French psychologists, Alfred Binet and Théodore Simon, were commissioned (that is, paid or hired) by French educational authorities for the specific purpose of identifying children who would *not* be likely to succeed in school—the ones who at that time were labeled "feebleminded" (Binet & Simon, 1908). For testing purposes, this goal led to less concern with what students actually learn in school than with finding *differences* in what students learn, and especially with identifying large differences. The result was a test in which most students had trouble answering some items correctly, few students ever answered them all correctly, and scores as a whole were distributed quite widely. To achieve a wide diversity in performance, of course, Binet and Simon had to adjust the questions to the ages of the children tested: younger children received somewhat different items than older children or adults, in recognition of obvious differences in knowledge and thinking skills due to age, maturity, and experience.

Later tests of scholastic aptitude and of intelligence have preserved and perfected the fundamental emphasis on identifying differences in academic thinking and school performance among individuals (Berlak, 1993; Linn, 1989). During this century, in fact, a minor industry has developed around designing and publishing standardized educational tests (Haney, 1993). These tests are now available in a wide variety of forms (for example, some to be taken in groups and others to be administered only to individuals) and for a wide range of groups (for example, tests in many languages and tests for members of specific occupations as well as students). It is safe to say that most students—literally millions in North America alone—encounter standardized tests of some sort and do so repeatedly during their school careers. The tests they take most often deal with either achievement in a specific subject or general scholastic aptitude.

What They Test

Given the history of scholastic aptitude tests, the most serviceable definition of "thinking as scholastic aptitude" is thinking necessary to succeed in school. Most tests of aptitude include school-like questions such as those already mentioned, questions about verbal reasoning, numerical skills, and vocabulary. It is not the content or style of the questions, however, that qualifies them as indicators of thinking as scholastic aptitude; it is the fact that they identify students who perform well in school. Since this amounts to defining scholastic aptitude strictly by its function, a long-lasting debate (now spanning more than a century) has developed about how to define it in terms of its content or "essence" (Horn, 1989).

A Single, Global Ability?

One school of thought proposes interpreting scholastic aptitude as a single, general quality or trait within individuals, one often called "general intelligence" and abbreviated for convenience with the single letter g. In this view, g (alias scholastic aptitude) is a quantity of which each of us has some amount. The amount is either inherited genetically, acquired and fixed early in life, or a mixture of both (Herrnstein & Murray, 1994). Put in crass terms, some people are smarter than others and always will be; school performance and scholastic aptitude tests merely reflect that fact. Teachers' job, therefore, is to adjust their expectations to fit the inevitable differences among students so that everyone can learn "to the best of his or her ability." Although most teachers feel this sentiment at one time or another, note something important about it: what's being talked about here is a *single, global* ability that governs performance in many areas, not a single, particular ability that influences only specific areas of performance.

One Talent Among Many?

A competing view of scholastic aptitude is that it is one among several important thinking abilities or "intelligences," each contributing to different forms of success in life. Scholastic aptitude is important because it contributes to school or academic success in particular, but as a term it is both too general and too specific. It may be too general because several more specific kinds of talent may create success in school; remembering facts, for example, may require a different kind of thinking than knowing how to plan your study time (Sternberg, 1990). It may be too specific, though, because some forms of thinking may be unrelated to scholastic aptitude and therefore rarely get honored fully in school: creative musical or artistic talents, for example, or sensitivity to the needs of others (Gardner, 1993). A successful student may have these attributes, but not necessarily. Teachers and classmates may appreciate these qualities in a student when they see them, but these abilities rarely get as much credit as talents in the more traditional curricular areas, such as language arts or mathematics.

The Experience of Being Tested

The latter interpretation—viewing thinking as a mixture of scholastic aptitudes—seems the more useful for understanding the full diversity of talents among students, but unfortunately it is full of ambiguity. The problem is that students' behaviors and achievements usually represent several skills or talents at once, and how are you to identify which ones they are displaying on any one occasion? On a particular test of scholastic aptitude, for example, a student may make dozens of responses; but do these show reading ability, reasoning ability, a cooperative attitude toward taking tests, or something else? Interpreting test responses can be a bit like watching a night sky full of stars: you can always "see" several patterns among the same overall set of stars, each of which may be right or convenient for certain purposes. Consider these four high school students as they encounter a particular item on a multiple-choice test of scholastic aptitude:

Question #25: Water lilies double in area every 24 hours. At the beginning of the summer, there is one water lily on a lake. The lake covers exactly 10,000 square feet. It takes 60 days for the lake to become covered with water lilies completely. On what day is the lake half covered?
   a) day 20
   b) day 30
   c) day 45
   d) day 59

Yolanda has taken advanced math courses in high school, and she recognizes the problem as one of exponential growth: it's something to do with logarithms and exponents, she says to herself. She sets about trying to determine the logarithmic formula for this problem, hoping she can calculate how many days from the beginning are needed to cover the lake halfway.

But finding this formula proves very difficult. Eventually Yolanda simply guesses at a formula, calculates an answer of "53 days," and picks option d (day 59) because it is the closest numerically and because she expects that the answer should not be a number divisible by 5. Yolanda has the distinct impression both that her guess is wrong and that she has spent too much time on the problem.

Paul has never seen a water lily in his life, so he spends valuable time trying to imagine what one looks like. He has the idea that if he can understand something about lilies, it might help him to solve the problem. Maybe, he thinks, the question is not really as mathematical as it appears; maybe lilies grow in a special way or at some special fixed rate, and if I could just figure these out, I could solve the problem quickly. Eventually he gives up and picks option b (day 30) because it is halfway between day 0 and day 60.

Morris is skeptical about tests. Surely, he says to himself, this question is a trick. He believes test makers would not really ask about exponents on a test of general ability, since not enough students know about them. What, then, is the trick? He agonizes over this question for a long time without success. Finally, at the last minute, he has an idea. If the lake is full on day 60, the terms of the problem imply that it must have been exactly half full on the day before, that is, on day 59. He considers option d (day 59), but decides against it because the last three questions on the test have been option d. So he picks option c at random and moves on.

Angela has always liked "clever" thought problems and feels familiar with this one even though she has never seen it before. It's like those "backwards reasoning" ones I saw in the library book last month, she thinks. Start at the end and work back: day 60 is full of lilies, so day 59 must be half full. She chooses option d (day 59) and moves on to the next problem.

These four students show some of the ambiguities of equating *thinking* with scholastic aptitude. Because this view is ultimately based on standardized testing, it contains the ambiguities of test-taking behaviors (Kamii, 1990; Perrone, 1991). Among the four students, Yolanda and Angela respond correctly, but for very different reasons; Paul and Morris respond incorrectly, but also for different reasons. Whether correct or not, responses on a standardized test are ambiguous, that is, have more than one possible meaning. Errors can occur because of

1. Thinking about or framing the problem inappropriately (as Yolanda did)
2. Lack of experience with a particular problem or type of problem (Paul)
3. Lack of motivation and daydreaming

In Your Own Voice

I notice that Yolanda, Paul, and Morris are spending a lot of time—perhaps too much—on this problem.

My instinct is to coach them on the test-taking strategy of "not taking too much time on any one problem."

But might this just encourage them to move too quickly through problems and to think superficially?

4. Unlucky guessing (e.g., Morris, who has been conditioned to expect tricks)

5. Combinations of these and other influences

Successes can result from

1. Familiarity or experience with a problem (Angela)

2. Lucky guessing (Yolanda)

3. Erroneous methods of solution that nonetheless lead to a correct answer

4. A combination of these and other influences

In Your Own Voice

When I reread this section, it seemed as though I was implying that skill at standardized tests is undesirable.

Indeed, I think that is true in some ways but not others.

To think about how "test-wiseness" can be good, read the novel *Stand and Deliver* by Nicholas Edwards (1989), or see the film by the same name.

The story describes the work of Jaime Escalante, a teacher in an inner-city neighborhood with students who were at risk for failure.

He coached the students to outstanding success on college entrance aptitude tests and in so doing made a remarkable difference in their lives.

Note, though, that these ambiguities do not invalidate the test of scholastic aptitude for its original purpose. If the test is intended to predict overall success in school in particular, and if it has been well constructed, the overall test results will indeed predict school success: high-scoring people will be more likely to do well in school, at least as schools traditionally have been organized and taught. This point applies to Yolanda, Paul, Morris, and Angela as much as to other individuals. Give them one hundred more problems that resemble school thinking tasks, such as the water lily problem, and their performances will suggest which of them is most successful academically. "What" they actually think in solving the one hundred problems, though, will still be uncertain.

To understand the nature of *thinking*, then, we will have to look in places other than standardized tests of scholastic aptitude, in spite of their historical importance in education. What if we looked at classroom events themselves? Would they show more than tests about what thinking "really" is? What if we saw activities in classrooms, for example, that required students to construct knowledge for themselves on their own initiative or to piece it together in collaboration with classmates and others?

Joe paused after reading the paragraph above, thinking about *thinking* in a classroom. Across town his friend Sara did the same: she took a break to think about *thinking*. Here is what each of them imagined:

Joe: A third-grade class—my third-grade class: Mrs. Kennedy, my favorite teacher of all time! We are doing two-digit subtraction

Sara: Senior high; tenth-grade English. Mr. Vittetoe has told us to write a short story—"not more than 5 pages long," he said. I am

problems: $43 - 26 = \ldots$? She lets us write down the problem and work on it before answering. We all scribble numbers madly. Then I've got it! I raise my hand and announce my answer: 23. "No, Joe, think again," says Mrs. Kennedy courteously. I look at my scribbles: I had reversed the digits in the "ones" column. She was asking us to "borrow," something we had just learned. I do more scribbles; "17," I say, without being called on.

writing just now; getting a sore wrist, in fact. But also it's not going anywhere, and I have just realized that. It had started out as an account of a girl running away to Canada. But it's stupid; no one ever "runs away to Canada." I sit there frustrated, not knowing whether to tear up my draft or shed a tear. What to do? Just then Mr. Vittetoe walks by; sees me. "Let's talk about it," he says. "Tell me your idea for the story." So we begin talking.

In homes on opposite sides of town, Joe and Sara daydream a moment longer about their separate examples. Separately, they both remark to themselves: funny how there's frustration in it, but also satisfaction, and social interaction. I wonder if my example is OK. And then they think: it's good that no one will see *my* example. It's probably not typical.

In response to my invitation to "imagine a time in class that showed a good example of thinking," Joe and Sara have both pictured examples of *problem solving*, a way of thinking about *thinking* quite different from the perspective based on testing scholastic aptitude. Even though both belittle their examples, they may be sensing something important—noticing another kind of thinking that deserves a closer look.

Thinking as Problem Solving

*S*UPPOSE that instead of defining *thinking* by what schooling requires, we defined it more broadly, by the requirements of various human occupations and everyday activities. What would *thinking* look like then? Considerable research has been done from this broader perspective, with *thinking* more often being called **problem solving,** the analysis and solution of situations that pose difficulties, inconsistencies, or obstacles of some kind. The research on problem solving both complicates and clarifies the scholastically based notion of thinking: some types of problem solving rarely occur in classrooms, either because they are impractical to arrange in classrooms or because they are not traditionally part of the school curriculum. On the other hand, as the examples devised by Joe and Sara show, much problem solving *does* occur in classrooms and may indeed be recognized as such by teachers. Looking at nonschool settings helps to put classroom thinking in perspective and to avoid the temptation to equate classroom activities with thinking itself—to believe that thinking is equivalent to completing worksheets or answering recitation-style questions. Looking at out-of-school examples also suggests qualities of problem solving that teachers need to import into classroom activities so that "good" thinking occurs there as well.

Kinds of Problem Solving

Since problem solving is embedded in everyday activities, it varies a lot from one situation to another. Knowing some of the variations makes it easier to understand how you might encourage problem solving in a classroom, even when the circumstances are quite different than outside of school (Hunt, 1991; Sternberg & Frensch, 1991). Look briefly at the following examples, which describe how a doctor, manager, lawyer, and

In classroom problem solving, as in this science experiment, students are likely to know what they are looking for and how to go about looking for it. Neither condition is as certain for problem solving outside of classroom settings.
© Gale Zucker/Stock Boston

psychologist solve problems. Then let's figure out what each of these problem solvers has in common with students' problem solving in classrooms.

Diagnosing X-rays

Imagine how a doctor might examine the chest X-rays of a patient. The patient may have a collapsed lung or lung cancer—or perhaps nothing wrong at all. The doctor cannot be sure, and the X-ray pictures give only fuzzy, ambiguous results. The problem is to decide whether the patient really does have something wrong with her lungs and what her medical problem may be.

What makes for good *problem solving* in this situation? Research studies have addressed this question by observing expert radiologists as they talk about X-rays while they diagnose them and comparing their comments with the ones made by inexperienced doctors (Groen & Patel, 1988; Lesgold et al., 1988). In essence the doctors "think out loud" while they work. When this happens, the experts show several important, interrelated differences from the novices:

- Expert radiologists comment on everything in the X-ray of the patient, not just on his or her lungs: *"This looks like a normal female chest, but what's that funny blob there?"*

- Experts begin suggesting general diagnoses more quickly than the novices, but also begin suggesting ways to test their suggestions: *"Left side looks like smoker's lung, or maybe a rib fracture in childhood. Can we ask her about that or at least get another picture from that side?"*

- Experts are more willing to drop initial diagnoses in the face of new, unexpected evidence: *"Oh I didn't know that she had been a star athlete until recently; no wonder her heart looks so big, like it's crowding the lungs."*

- Experts distinguish between relevant and irrelevant information more clearly: *"I might think her lungs were congested, but I can also tell that this picture is badly underexposed; that's probably what makes it so murky."*

These abilities do not necessarily improve steadily with experience. Other observations of medical diagnoses have suggested that certain kinds of cases, especially classic, "textbook" cases, are actually solved better by doctors who are either utterly inexperienced or highly experienced compared to those with moderate experience (Lesgold, 1988). Moderately

In Your Own Voice

Reading X-rays, of course, is only one kind of problem among many.

How do you think a challenge facing a radiologist differs from the one facing a teacher who must size up a student's learning needs?

experienced doctors perform worse with textbook cases, apparently because they are searching for unnecessary complications in these patients. Only the highly experienced doctors (more than ten years of practice) diagnose well in *all* situations—not only when a patient has an "obvious" problem but also when she or he presents an ambiguous one.

Solving Managerial Problems

A manager of a business faces rather different problems than a medical radiologist. He or she often must deal with many people simultaneously instead of with just one patient at a time, and deal more explicitly with human motives and preferences. Suppose you manage a large grocery store and your selection of coffee has not been selling well; you face the problem of improving the profits on your sales of coffee. How should you do this? You could lower prices (put on a "sale"), but that could also reduce your income; you could invest in more advertising, but that would also cost income; you could put a suggestion box by the coffee display asking customers for suggestions, but the people responding may not be representative of all customers. There is no time for market research on this problem, because each passing day means more money lost on the current selection of coffees. As manager, what should you do?

Studies of problem solving by experienced, skilled managers find they do not take time to analyze this sort of problem consciously and rationally. Instead they tend to act promptly, taking time to reflect only when the consequences of their initial actions begin to unfold (Wagner, 1991). Thinking about the business problem is closely interwoven with acting on the problem. Much of the expertise of management—perhaps even most—seems to consist of acting and responding to business circumstances in appropriate and timely ways; it is skill with procedures rather than skill in terms of conscious, verbal knowledge. You have procedural skills too: when you walk, you simply step forward "in an appropriate and timely way" rather than deliberating on which foot to lift or how far to place it! Only as the consequences of taking the step begin to occur do you reflect on the action: Is the step taking me where I want to go? Did I step in a hidden crack accidentally? These reflections lead to further actions—further steps, in this case.

Finding and Predicting Causes: Lawyers and Psychologists

Lawyers and psychologists show still other patterns of problem solving that differ from those of both managers and doctors, yet are similar in underlying purpose. Both lawyers and psychologists seek the *causes* of human behaviors—the links between earlier actions and later ones—but their orientations differ fundamentally. For lawyers, the major problem is to identify the causes of one specific event and to do so *after* it occurs. Suppose Jack drives his car into a tree and we now (obviously) know that this mishap has already occurred. As a lawyer, you seek the causes by looking back in time: did the collision happen *because* (1) Jack drank one glass of wine at dinner, or (2) the car manufacturer had installed defective brakes in his car, or (3) Jack's wife was giving birth and Jack needed to get to the hospital? Legal reasoning sorts out these possibilities and presents one chain of causes as more plausible than another (Amsel, Langer & Loutzenhiser, 1991).

For psychologists, in contrast, the major problem is not to account for specific past behaviors but to predict future ones, and to do so in general rather than for specific cases. Think about Jack's collision again. Psychologists would be less concerned than lawyers with why one particular person, Jack, had a traffic accident on one particular occasion. Instead they would focus on general causes and effects: Why do people, including but not limited to Jack, sometimes have traffic accidents? How much are accidents caused *in general* by drinking alcohol, or manufacturing defects, or family crises? Psychologists answer these questions in terms of probabilities: by how likely or unlikely an association is between an earlier event and a later one. Because the associations are phrased in general terms, they allow predictions of future events—or, more precisely, they allow for good guesses and bets about the future.

Commonalities in Problem Solving

The problems solved by doctors, managers, lawyers, and psychologists are diverse, but they have common features, features that suggest ways in which problem solving can and should occur in classrooms (Nye et al., 1988).

For one thing, all four examples require decisions or solutions based on information that is *incomplete* or *ambiguous*. X-rays are fuzzy, consumer purchases have many motivations, criminal actions usually have several possible "causes," and statistical trends never have clear-cut effects on any one person. Yet if one of these problems is to be solved, decisions and understandings must be found anyway.

For another thing, problem solving often takes **educated guesswork**— a form of trial-and-error behavior, but one based on experience and knowledge of the problem rather than on truly random responses. The manager tries a new pricing structure on the basis of thoughtful hunches, but does not know for sure whether the hunches were correct until after he sees the results of his new pricing structure. The doctor guesses at the medical history of the patient, and the psychologist's general predictions about traffic accidents translate into reasonable guesses when applied to individual drivers. Making reasonable guesses takes experience and familiarity with a field: a lawyer tends to solve legal problems more skillfully than a manager. But it also takes deliberate *reflection*, deliberate effort to consider alternatives and assumptions about the nature of a problem and its solutions.

The differences and similarities among problems to be solved raise issues for teachers about *how* to teach problem solving directly (Perkins, 1992). There are enough similarities to tempt us to try teaching problem-solving skills in general: to encourage students to practice "educated guesswork" with certain tasks or assignments, or to practice deciding when they have enough information about a problem to proceed even though the information is not complete. The trouble with this approach, though, is that using it effectively also requires knowledge and information that is very specific and detailed. Estimating the answer to an arithmetic problem, for example, calls for knowledge of certain specific arithmetic facts, not just for knowledge of guesswork strategies. So teachers end up having to foster general problem solving and specific knowledge acquisition simultaneously—which is why teaching can be so challenging!

Problem Solving in the Classroom

In spite of this dilemma about teaching problem solving directly, it is important to realize that genuine problem solving often does occur in classrooms, and at these moments the teacher does have an important contribution to make. Consider what happened in Jerry's classroom:

Jerry listened while his teacher gave the instructions: "Can you connect all of the dots below using only *four* straight lines?" She drew the following display in the middle of the chalkboard:

```
*   *   *
*   *   *
*   *   *
```

Jerry and his classmates stared at the display. Two kids volunteered to try solving it, but they were unsuccessful when they actually tried drawing lines on the board. Jerry stared awhile longer, puzzling over the problem.

When no one seemed to be getting anywhere, the teacher asked, "Think about how you've set the problem up in your mind: think about your *thinking*. Have you made any assumptions about how *long* the lines ought to be?" So Jerry thought—thought about his thinking. He thought especially about how long the lines "ought" to be.

"They need to be no longer than the distance across the square," Jerry said to himself. So he tried several solutions, reproducing the matrix on a piece of paper at his desk. His teacher had encouraged everyone to try as many solutions as possible.

But still he could find no solution, no way to draw only four lines that included all nine dots. He puzzled; he drew; he failed again at it. His teacher saw all of this happening; "Think about what you assume," she said again, "about how long the lines should be."

The teacher encourages actual efforts to solve the problem, even though initial attempts are unsuccessful and have not been fully thought through. She is calling for *educated guesswork*, for students to draw on their knowledge of other problems of this type.

The teacher encourages reflection on the problem. It is not satisfactory to apply solution methods automatically, without thought.

Now Jerry is trying more solutions, as encouraged by the teacher and as his classmates did earlier. More *educated guesswork* here. Possibly also a "zone of proximal development," arranged by the teacher, for working on this problem.

So Jerry thought again, and . . . "Aha! She did not actually *say* that the lines could be no longer than the matrix! Why not make them longer?" So he experimented with lines that went beyond the edges, and in just a moment discovered the following solution:

More encouragement to reflect, even to the point of questioning initial solutions.

Soon others in the class had found a solution, although not everyone solved the problem just as Jerry did. "Think about what's happened here," said Jerry's teacher. "Does this problem remind you of any other situations?"

Note that even this relatively simple problem has multiple solutions. It is *ambiguous* to some extent.

"The dots look like stars," said one of Jerry's classmates. "The lines are the constellations. It's as if there is more than one way to "draw" the constellations in the sky. They don't necessarily have to be drawn the way my science textbook shows them." The teacher nodded.

"You know what it makes me think of?" said Jerry. "Last year I never felt like I had time for homework because of baseball practice every evening after dinner. I finally figured out that I could still get both things done if I just did some of the homework *before* dinner. I wish I'd thought of it sooner."

The teacher encourages students to relate the problem to other situations of interest or concern: helping them to *transfer* their knowledge back and forth between this problem and others they consider relevant. The notion of *transfer* is important; see my comments that follow.

The teacher nodded again. "Interesting," she said, "but what's the connection to these dots?"

"Well, it's like I made assumptions about when I had to do homework. I assumed that it all had to fit *after* practice, all in the evening. But I could never make it fit afterward. I finally realized that I had set up the 'problem' wrong: no one had ever actually required me to work only in the evening. My assumption was wrong." The teacher nodded, then smiled.

As in this example, the teacher makes important contributions by asking well-placed questions and in that way guides students toward successful thinking. But the guidance can take a number of forms. The example here implies that the whole class was discussing the problem together. But as Rodelyn Stoeber, a high school science teacher, suggests in

MULTIPLE VOICES

MULTIPLE VOICES

MULTIPLE VOICES

MULTIPLE VOICES

As a math and science teacher, problem solving is very much a part of my curriculum. From my experience, it is indeed a skill that is difficult to teach. As is mentioned in the chapter, imagination, reflection, and educated guesswork need to be encouraged and developed in students in order for them to become competent in problem solving.

I found Jerry's situation as described in this chapter to be interesting. As a teacher, I think that I would have treated it somewhat differently. I would have had the students address the problem in partners or small groups first, thereby allowing them to discuss and try out their ideas with others. Using this strategy helps students better conceptualize the problem. As there might be several responses to the problem, a sharing of the different solutions as a class would also be a good option. After doing this, students could try to make up their own problems in partners and/or in small groups. However, the teacher needs to gauge students' background knowledge and also create an atmosphere of learning where the students are willing to take risks in sharing their own ideas.

Rodelyn Stoeber, High school science teacher, Winnipeg, Canada

the accompanying "Multiple Voices," the teacher can also organize students into small groups prior to a whole-class discussion to stimulate larger amounts of discussion or develop more solutions than a single, large group can accomplish alone.

Who Defines "the" Problem?

There are also differences between this classroom example and the ones described earlier that occurred outside the classroom. Note who defines the problem: to a greater extent than with the professionals described earlier, the students work on a task set not by themselves but by someone else, the teacher. "The" problem therefore means something different for students than for the professionals. To the students, it means finding answers or solutions to a problem to which someone else presumably knows the answer already and then showing this person their success (Denis, Griffin & Cole, 1990). To the professionals, the problem means the same thing, but more: it also means finding and defining the problem in the first place. For a lawyer, for example, "the" problem is not only to explain why a particular traffic accident occurred but also to decide whether it is actually important to create such an explanation.

Transfer

The difference in who finds and defines problems contributes to a problem peculiar to educators, namely how to ensure that students' solutions to tasks in class actually get used on tasks outside class. Educators sometimes call this the problem of *transfer* (Norris, 1992). One obvious way to encourage transfer is to make learning situations as similar as possible to situations where new knowledge or skills will be used. In learning to drive a car, for example, experience behind the wheel may be more helpful than an in-class discussion about driving. The trouble with this strategy, though, is that some forms of performance are difficult to simulate. Teachers can set up a "mock government" to demonstrate how laws are enacted, but making the arrangements takes considerable effort, takes time from other curriculum goals, and may lack some of the drama, tension, and genuine conflict of real government leadership.

Another strategy to encourage transfer was illustrated in the story about Jerry when the teacher makes an explicit effort to get students to relate the classroom task to other situations and problems important to them. As useful as this strategy presumably is, though, it still does not guarantee full use of learning to situations beyond the classroom—full transfer. Students, after all, could merely be learning to *talk* about how

In Your Own Voice

An interesting case in point was Tom and Charleen, the children counting pennies early in this chapter (see p. 70).

Suppose *you* were teaching them.

How could you get them to use their knowledge of counting money outside of class?

And how could you make sure they were not just learning to *talk* about using money outside of class?

a classroom task relates to nonschool tasks. This is a valuable skill, but not the same as learning to make these connections without prompting.

Clarity of Problems and Solutions

Another difference between classroom problem solving and much problem solving by professionals has to do with clarity. Outside the classroom, problems more often seem "ill defined": often it is not clear what the problem actually consists of or what a satisfactory solution may be (King & Kitchener, 1994). The store manager may not be selling enough coffee, but he also may not be convinced that coffee is the problem per se; perhaps other features of the store are annoying customers and discouraging purchases, or perhaps the store is not in a commercially strategic part of town, causing fewer people to shop in it. The manager may therefore puzzle over what "the" problem really is before he can know which particular business actions might lead to "solutions." Clarifying the problem requires imagination, not simply the logical application of business principles.

In the classroom problem of the nine dots, on the other hand, the goal is very clear: students are to locate a certain number of lines in a particular way. The orientation of the lines is a bit ambiguous—that is, in fact, "the" problem—but the range of imagination needed to create a solution is relatively restricted. Therefore, if students are to learn problem-solving skills as they are practiced outside of school, they will need tasks that are *more* ambiguous and complex than the nine-dots problem. I suggest some examples of such tasks in the next section.

Thinking as Creativity

*T*HESE comments hint at yet another way you can think about thinking, which is to focus on **creativity,** the making of ideas or things that are genuinely new but also useful or pleasing. Creativity requires a mixture of imagination, logical reasoning, and persistence (Feldman, 1988; Gardner, 1994; Tucke-Bressler, 1992). In the examples of problem solving described in the previous section, all of these qualities may have been present, but our discussion of them emphasized rational or logical activity. With the doctors and their X-rays, for example, we saw how expert doctors engaged in imaginative thinking, which I called "educated guesswork." My emphasis, though, was on the

Creativity is not just a matter of doing something unusual. It also involves using familiar materials and solving well-known problems in novel ways, as this girl has done in representing a house with straws.
©Myrleen Ferguson/PhotoEdit

doctors' reasoning skills, on their ability to justify a diagnosis logically. The example of the nine-dot problem showed an even stronger bias toward logical thinking: students were not so much coming up with a new idea as showing they could find a pre-existing one held by the teacher.

The bias toward thinking as purely logical reasoning is misleading; many human activities *do* create truly new ideas and products, even if they are small ones (Wallace & Gruber, 1992). Consider another classroom activity, one from a fifth-grade class. This one is rather different from the nine-dot task:

Jerry, Brendon, and Kalli looked at the job at hand: they were supposed to make a drawing that "uses five words at random from the dictionary." The instruction sheet told them to write down the first five words they encountered in the dictionary, each from a different page, along with the words' principal definitions. Then they were to let their minds range widely and flexibly to make up connections among the words, even outlandish, improbable connections. The instructions ended cryptically: "Draw something that shows the connections. But take your time; we won't share the drawings until two weeks from now."

For now, though, that last instruction was what the three students were staring at. Frowns and furrowed brows all around; occasional mumbles.

". . . must mean an object? Not a diagram?"

"Can't be done. . . ."

"Must be proving something. But what?"

Hmmm; all three nodded.

Dutifully the three students found five words at random: *dock, keystroke, partridge, ribbon, south.* Other groups did the same and, of course, came up with other lists. Jerry, Brendon, and Kalli brainstormed connections, and behold: they started enjoying it! After their first discussion, they even had a preliminary "picture" in mind: of a partridge with a ribbon around its neck, sitting on a boat dock facing south, typing on a computer.

But Jerry frowned at this first sketch. "It's dorky, too artificial," he said. And the others had to agree. It was a start, but they would need the whole two weeks to think about the drawing and overhaul it as needed. As it turned out, it was good that they had that time. But in the end, their final picture was completely different from their first sketch (see Figure 3.1).

These students faced a more ambiguous task than the ones who worked on the nine-dot problem. Instead of one possible solution, there were as many solutions as groups of students. Instead of relatively clear guidance about how to begin solving the problem ("Find four lines"), there was vague guidance ("Find any sort of connections"). But the teacher still defined "the" problem, even if she did it indirectly via the in-

FIGURE 3.1

Jerry, Brendon, and Kalli's Sketch

Preliminary Sketch

Final Sketch

struction sheet. In effect, she said to Jerry, Brendon, and Kalli, "You can choose any connections among words and make any drawing that you choose, but you *have* to choose something." The students were not really free to *not* do the task.

All things considered, then, does this drawing and free-association task call for creativity? Yes, in that it encourages students to see unique solutions to a problem. No, in that it still does not, any more than the nine-dot activity does, allow students to define or set the problem in the first place. But yes, in that some students may create interesting, pleasing relationships among word meanings. But no, in that other students may create solutions that are merely bizarre or strange. Giving Jerry, Brendan, and Kalli two weeks to create their drawing instead of one day may have encouraged persistence in deciding how to approach the project, and therefore made it more insightful and less bizarre. But there is still no guarantee of a truly creative outcome, one that is not only unusual but also pleasing.

Reconciling the need for something unusual with the need for something pleasing makes it harder to encourage truly creative activity in a classroom—but not impossible! Consider yet another student in another classroom:

Roberta had always *loved* plants. Her parents had encouraged her interest before she ever began grade 3, as her teacher had quickly found out in the first week of school. Roberta had brought Ms. Simon a potted plant as a gift—"something I put together myself, for you," Roberta had said. In free-reading times, and especially during trips to the school library, Roberta sought out books about growing things—houseplants, mostly, "but I also like ecology," she explained when she checked out a large picture book about the rain forest.

So Ms. Simon looked for ways to encourage this interest. "Would you like to enter the city science fair? It's extra work, but I'd give you time now and then. Some of it, though, would have to happen at home."

Roberta asked, "Can I do something on plants?"

"Yes. They want a 'project' or 'experiment.' I can show you the guidelines from the city; it's pretty broad."

Four weeks later, Roberta was immersed in her science fair project, which she was calling "The Effect of Centrifugal Force on Roots." She had gotten the idea from one of the library books on botany: you sprout bean seeds on a record player while it spins for several days and measure which direction the roots grow. Do they grow outward because of the centrifugal force of the turntable or downward because of the earth's gravitation? Day and night the turntable ran in the back of the class while Roberta perfected the technique

In Your Own Voice

One reviewer of this passage wrote that I sounded too critical of children's creativity, that children and young people *are* creative if only teachers and parents will let them be.

What do you think about this possibility?

If you support it, how would you then distinguish between the creative accomplishments of children and those of adults?

of sprouting seeds on it successfully. One time they fell off during the night because of the force of the turntable. Another time they dried out and died over the weekend. The third time it worked.

Eight weeks later, Roberta was showing a display of her project in the lobby of her school: a large poster with snapshots of roots growing and text printed in big, bold letters on the school's computer.

Twelve weeks later, Roberta was showing the same display at the science fair, in a big gymnasium with lots of other displays. A judge came by to talk with her. "What did you learn?" he asked.

"That the roots grow down, but sometimes out."

"Hmmm." He smiled.

". . . and that an experiment takes patience—seems like it's easier to describe than to do."

"Really!"

". . . that lima beans work better than mung beans."

A small chuckle from the judge.

". . . that I like growing things."

The judge gave her a good score.

Is Roberta's science project creative? Compared to the threesome who devised connections among random words, Roberta's activity fulfills the criterion of being "pleasing" and not simply unusual or bizarre. A pleasing result was more possible because Roberta chose to do the project— to solve a problem about root growth—herself; and presumably her self-motivation encouraged her persistence, a quality important for a creative outcome. Judged against her own developing knowledge, furthermore, it fulfills the criterion of being unique or unusual: she presumably learned things about roots and scientific experimentation that were entirely new to her.

On balance, then, this example comes closer than the others to representing true creativity. Notice, though, that it also veers back toward focused problem solving, the kind described earlier in this chapter in the work of doctors, managers, lawyers, and psychologists. Creativity and problem solving, it seems, may be similar in important ways, at least when they occur in children and youth. Solutions to problems can be both pleasing and unusual, and therefore creative in the sense I am talking about here. But sometimes solutions can also be expected and boring, the result of well-practiced skills known to all. In the latter case, problem solving may represent talent but not creativity (Feldman, 1986; Sosniak, 1990).

But even this distinction may be misleading. Careful observations of highly creative adults suggest, in particular, that their creative works develop out of a long, slow accumulation of knowledge, skills, and small achievements (Wallace & Gruber, 1992). The artist Picasso practiced painting techniques for years, and most of his practice yielded no masterpieces; Einstein toyed with interesting ideas about the physical universe for an equally long time, but without producing the theory of relativity. The common belief that creative works appear like a bolt of lightning out of nowhere appears to be just a myth. Or, to push the metaphor a bit further: inspirational lightning may sometimes strike, but the lightning itself is really the result of a long, complex build-up of electrical charges and storm formation.

If this interpretation of creativity is true, we should not expect full-blown creativity in the activities or behaviors of young people if what we are looking for are final products and masterpieces. We should instead look for activities that are precursors to full masterpieces, that make "showcase" accomplishments possible later in life. Viewed this way, which of the classroom examples described earlier in this chapter would be the most successful? Which would set the stage for fully creative achievement later, perhaps even months or years later? Would it be the nine-dot problem, the problem of five random words, or Roberta's science fair project? I have commented on their relative merits for promoting creativity in the short term, but what about the long term? A difficult question indeed, but therefore perhaps a good place to end this discussion.

A Conclusion: Thinking Is Various

No matter how much I think about thinking, it seems that I cannot pin it down, cannot identify "universals" that meaningfully explain students' cognitive activity. Instead, various kinds of thinking seem possible. There is scholastic aptitude, the kind of thinking that helps a child answer classroom test questions, but there is also everyday reasoning, the kind that helps her find the best buy in a grocery store. There is problem solving, both the kind that helps a professional find and define a problem in the first place and the kind that allows solutions to self-defined problems. There is creativity, the kind of thinking that creates truly new ideas and products.

Take a closer look at these forms of thinking when you think you see one of them happening. Ask yourself whether the thinking would be easy or difficult to encourage in a classroom, and why. Ask yourself whether the thinking might occur automatically because it fits naturally with the usual circumstances of classroom life or with the usual expectations of students, teachers, and parents. And ask yourself whether the thinking could survive a teacher's efforts to encourage it: would it be the "same" cognitive activity if students were told to do it rather than choosing to do it themselves? When you have begun asking these questions, you will be a step closer toward constructing a useful, unique vision of teaching and learning. You do not need to answer the questions to be a step closer; you just need to ask them.

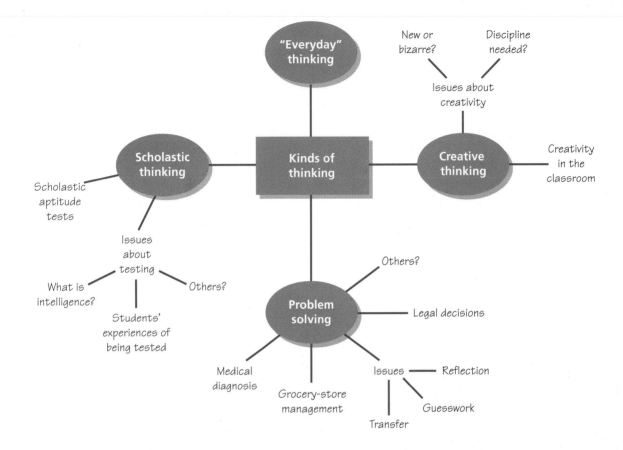

Chapter Re-View: Thinking About Thinking This Chapter Re-View suggests directions in which the chapter might have taken your thinking—though, of course, other directions are also possible. It expands the Chapter View, which suggests a starting point, conceptually, for the chapter. But this Re-View does not suggest an ending point. Like the Chapter View, it represents just one perspective among many.

Key Terms and Concepts

transfer   (72)
thinking as scholastic aptitude
   (74)

tests of scholastic aptitude
   (76)
thinking as problem solving
   (81)

educated guesswork   (85)
thinking as creativity   (91)

Annotated Readings

Gardner, Howard. (1994). *Creating minds: An anatomy of creativity seen through the lives of Freud, Einstein, Picasso, Stravinsky, Eliot, Graham, and Gandhi.* New York: Basic Books. Howard Gardner has written many readable but thought-provoking books about psychological issues. Here he explores the circumstances that supported creativity in the lives of several renowned creative individuals and, in doing so, reveals clues about the nature of creativity itself and how we might encourage it in ourselves and our students.

Hirsch, E. D. (1996). *The schools we need and why we don't have them.* New York: Doubleday. This is a book I disagree with strongly, but nonetheless it presents an important point of view about education. Hirsch's approach is best described as extremely traditional and "back to basics." At the heart of his viewpoint is an assumption that thinking and learning are at their best in academic settings, but only to the extent that the settings focus on transmitting crucial common content to students.

Perkins, David. (1992). *Smart schools: Better thinking and learning for every child.* New York: Free Press. The information-processing view at its best: a readable account of how to make the cognitive side of schooling as effective as possible. Many sensible suggestions and implications for teaching.

Internet Resources

<www.mensa.org> The web site for Mensa, the international organization for individuals who score in the top 2 percent of the population on standardized tests of intelligence. As you might suppose from this definition of their membership, the web site contains information about and support for a "scholastic" view of intelligence, but also for a more problem-solving view. It provides articles and materials, among other things, as well as a special section about the education of gifted children.

<www.fis.utoronto.ca/~easun/babette> This is a new web site for a group called the Special Interest Group for Arts-Based Methods of Research in Education. The group is a section of a large "umbrella" professional association called the American Educational Research Association. The Arts-Based group is dedicated to finding creative ways to use the arts (such as drama, music, poetry) to communicate the results and interpretations of educational research.

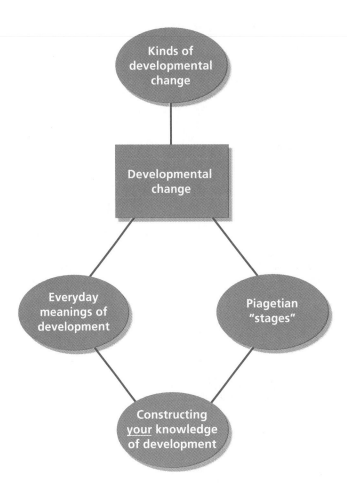

Chapter View: Developmental Change This Chapter View is a concept map that indicates one among many ways of thinking about the chapter. It suggests a starting point, conceptually, for the chapter but is incomplete by itself. At the end of the chapter is a Chapter Re-View, which expands on the Chapter View, suggesting directions for taking your thinking further—though, of course, other directions are also possible.

4
Developmental Change

Every year of my childhood I studied piano, and every year I participated in a recital. In the earliest years, around age six or so, I always played first on the program. Actually my father was the first: he would "begin" the recital by crawling under the piano to clamp extensions to the pedals so my young legs could reach them while I played. I was embarrassed by this help, but it was part and parcel of my musical childhood, of "me." So was daily practice, 365 days per year; practice was a staple of my childhood, along with a house deliberately kept quiet to facilitate practice. Music, especially the piano, defined a major part of "me," Kelvin Seifert.

Or did it? As a young adult, I avoided the piano for two decades on the grounds that I had never really enjoyed it and had been forced to practice as a child. I finally took up playing again near my fortieth birthday, and when I did, the piano filled a very different purpose in my life. In childhood, practicing had proven that I could focus attention, ignore distractions (such as after-school sports), and follow directions. Now, in adulthood, practicing proved I could *use* music to communicate and to offer enjoyment. Instead of performing in recitals for people who evaluated my musical progress, I now performed at churches and social gatherings for people who sought enjoyment. Instead of practicing dutifully every day, I now practiced only during the days or weeks leading up to performances. And instead of being given compositions to learn, I now selected pieces for myself, and with my audience in mind. I chose those that would fit a particular occasion, would make it more pleasing or meaningful.

Was the adult Kelvin who played the piano the same "Kelvin" who played decades before? Compared to the adult, the eight-year-old had followed directions more carefully: directions about exactly what to learn, how to practice, when and where to perform. In retrospect, enjoyment was secondary to child-Kelvin's musical experience. The forty-year-old Kelvin directed his musical activities much more autonomously; his guiding principle, in fact, was to enjoy the piano as much as possible, even at the expense of improving his technical skill. The emotional difference between the two experiences was dramatic: a stranger witnessing the two Kelvins might not recognize them as the "same" person. Yet both child and adult called themselves by the same name, Kelvin Seifert, and both played the same eighty-eight keys.

Even if you never studied a musical instrument, my experience hints at a psychological issue that is important for teaching and learning: the experience of long-term stability and change. In what sense do you or I change with age, and in what sense has each of us stayed the same? Are the changes more basic and prominent than constancies, or the other way around? These questions surround any human activity that persists over time. If you played softball at age six, did you experience it as the "same" game that you did at age twenty? Is being a friendly preschooler the "same" as being a friendly college student? Probably the experiences at the two ages differ significantly, yet they likely have similarities as well.

Put in psychological terms, these questions are about **developmental change**—relatively permanent, long-term alterations in skills, attitudes, or knowledge (Funder et al., 1993; Magnusson, 1994). Most of the time the changes are positive and desirable, or at least not negative. Some developmental changes can be quite broad, the result of countless minor experiences. The development of your sensitivity to others' feelings and moods may be like this. No single event taught you everything you know about how people show feelings; it was the accumulation of experience over decades that made the difference. But developmental change can also be focused and time limited: a child's knowledge of numbers and arithmetic may be more "developed" at age ten than at age six, thanks to four years of math lessons in particular. An even faster development is spoken language: a preschooler's speech is usually more developed at age three than at age one, thanks to two years of living among adults who already speak fluently.

The Varieties of Human Change

THESE examples suggest that the term *development* is similar to several other terms that describe change (Ford & Lerner, 1992). One related notion is *learning*, which usually refers to relatively focused, short-term change, especially change caused by deliberate study or teaching. When teachers speak of *learning*, they mean something that happens in a time frame short enough that you can identify specific experiences or actions (e.g., studying for math tests) that create the change. If learning experiences are outside of personal control, or unfold over an exceptionally long time, the term *development* is more common. But the distinction is a bit hazy; both *learning* and *development* refer to change in skills, feelings, or thinking. When I returned to the piano as an adult, you could say that I had "developed new attitudes" about it, but you might also say that I had "learned new attitudes." In any case, for convenience I will use the term *development* in this book to mean changes that take long periods of time, especially if the immediate causes of the changes are complex and not caused deliberately.

Several other common terms are related to *development*, though they are used less often in the work of teachers. One is *maturation*: among academic psychologists and biologists, this notion tends to refer only to physical changes, such as those associated with puberty among adolescents. In common conversation, however, the word and its variants often take on a larger meaning, referring to the acquisition of the social and personal qualities of older, established members of society, as in "Joe is showing a lot more maturity lately about handling conflicts with friends." Another similar term is *growth*. Strictly speaking, as used by biologists, *growth* refers only to increases in overall size or mass of a plant, a person, or some other animal. As with the term *maturation*, however, common usage has made *growth* a synonym for many kinds of long-term development, as in "Sara's vocabulary has grown by leaps and bounds." Because these broader, common meanings can cause confusion, I will adopt a policy in this book: I will always use the word *maturation* or *growth* in its strictest sense—and when I don't, I'll tell you.

Still other terms refer to important human changes, but changes that are negative. The term *illness*, for example, describes a change in a person's behavior, thoughts, and feelings, especially if the illness is serious. But the changes of illness are not usually considered desirable, even though psychological benefits (e.g., increased wisdom) may also result from the suffering. *Aging* is another term with both a narrow meaning and a broad one: used by biologists and medical professionals, it refers to human deteriorations near the end of life, both physical and psychological. In everyday speech, though, it can sometimes also be a synonym for *maturation*: "He is aging well" can mean "He is showing psychological maturity in his old age." *Illness* and *aging* are important for understanding human nature, but they usually are not our primary focus as public school teachers. More common for us are changes that are progressive, positive, and complex, the ones I am calling *developmental*.

Developmental changes matter to teaching because they affect assumptions teachers make about students' skills, knowledge, and beliefs, and assumptions about experiences that it's reasonable to expect students to have had. You cannot teach teenagers in the same way you might teach kindergarten children. This fact may seem obvious, but it is often taken for granted during the press of everyday teaching. Take Jill and Phil, both of whom are studying the "same" topic, medieval villages:

Jill, in grade 3, carefully placed the last "trees" in the village. She had made them from small sprigs of evergreen stuck in bits of clay. They stood nicely among the houses, though actually she had put most of them outside the village and beyond the castle that the village surrounded. She smiled slightly. "It still needs people," she announced.

Her partners were making the villagers, mostly from match sticks and bits of cloth. One was also working on the residents of the castle: a feudal lord and lady, two knights, and whatever others he would have time to make. Probably they would not be ready before tomorrow.

In the beginning, Jill's group had looked for pictures of medieval villages and castles; they had found especially good ones in an encyclopedia article the teacher found for them. They also read a bit—just a few pages—about how towns were laid out in the Middle Ages. After the display was complete, Jill was supposed to make labels for important parts of the town and its people, as well as write a short paragraph to put with the display, summarizing in big print what it showed. Next week they would enter the display in the school History Fair.

Phil, in grade 12, sat composing his essay on the computer: "Even in 1500, settlements had wealthy districts and not-so-wealthy districts. The local lord had the choicest spot for his residence, the castle: usually on the top of a hill or beside a river, to improve security. The common folk built their houses

In Your Own Voice

One test of whether Jill and Phil are learning the "same" material is whether they could assist each other with it.

What do you think: could one be of genuine help to the other with his or her work?

Would the helper necessarily be the older student, Phil?

around the castle, finding the best ground they could. They stayed close for protection—though of course they paid a price for it. Peasants were expected to give a big portion of what they grew to the lord and to serve in his army if commanded to do so. These were high 'taxes' even by today's standards, but they were better than . . ."

Phil paused and looked at what he had written. The essay was due in three days, and preparing it had taken more of his time this week than he had expected. His senior history teacher had given a couple of suggestions for references. The best one was an encyclopedia article that had good pictures of a medieval village and castles, but he had found he needed more written information to supplement the pictures. Two other books had helped, one from the school library and the other from the public library.

He sighed; it was good to be this far along but discouraging that he wasn't finished. On Friday he would turn in the essay. Next week he was supposed to give a brief oral report to the class about what he had learned.

Jill was in third grade, Phil in twelfth. Yet both were learning about medieval villages as part of a curriculum in history. Their teachers had arranged experiences to reflect the two students' developmental differences: long-term differences in reading skill, in writing, and in background knowledge. Since these developmental changes influenced how Jill and Phil learned, they influenced their teachers as well. The issue for teachers in general, in fact, is not *whether* developmental changes occur but precisely *what* the changes consist of and how they influence students (Pintrich, 1990). This issue is what we explore in the rest of this chapter. We look at the various kinds of developmental change that are relevant to teaching and how they affect teaching and learning.

Kinds of Developmental Change

How can you organize your knowledge of developmental change? Psychologists have explored a variety of ways to organize this knowledge (Tudge, Shanahan & Valsiner, 1997), but I suggest getting started by making three rather general distinctions: distinctions among age-graded changes, non-normative changes, and cohort effects (see Figure 4.1). First, let's look at what I mean by each kind. Later we'll come back to the first kind, age-graded change, and explore it more carefully.

1. Age-graded changes happen universally at predictable ages.	2. Non-normative changes happen to some people but not to others.	3. Cohort effects happen to everyone growing up at a particular time in history.

FIGURE 4.1   Kinds of Developmental Change

Age-Graded Developmental Changes

Age-graded developmental changes are events or processes that happen to nearly everyone at predictable chronological ages. Learning to talk, for example, is very age-graded: most children begin speaking in single words around their first birthday, link two words around their second birthday, and create simple grammatical sentences around their third. Among older children, puberty is age graded: in spite of wide individual variation, most boys' voices deepen around age fourteen and most girls first menstruate between ages twelve and thirteen.

Age-graded changes tend to obscure the influence of the environment, simply because the changes are so similar for each child (Dannefer, 1992). Language acquisition is a good example. Since almost every child learns to talk—rich or poor, black or white—it may seem as though experience has no influence on it. Yet obviously experience does matter: children learn the language of the people around them, not some foreign language, and children who are deaf do not acquire language normally (Feagans, Garvey & Golinkoff, 1984; Nelson, 1989; Volterra & Erting, 1990). Since nearly every child acquires language, furthermore, it is tempting to think that language ability is located entirely "in" children, unfolding through some natural, biological process. In some sense this idea is true;

infants do seem predisposed to acquire language (Chomsky, 1988, 1994). But it is also likely that language emerges from experiences normally taken for granted, simply because the experiences are so common.

To understand the significance of this misunderstanding more clearly, think about two school-related changes that are somewhat age graded: learning to read and learning to do basic arithmetic. Since children in our society are all about the same age when these abilities begin to emerge, a visitor from Mars might be tempted to think that learning to read and to compute occur universally "in" children, perhaps because of physical or biological maturation. The Martian might notice that the supposedly inherent changes unfold at different speeds for each child: some learn to read or compute sooner than others. But if the differences are relatively minor, the Martian might not attribute them to differences in the children's environments. In particular he (she? it?) might overlook the fact that society—or at least the "modern" ones—guarantees the acquisition of literacy and numeracy by arranging extended transactions between children and teachers to foster these skills (Gardner, 1991). Yet in reality, being universal does not mean a developmental change is either inevitable or biological in origin; it could simply be prompted by experiences that are so common as to go unnoticed.

Non-normative Developmental Changes

Non-normative means "not related to norms or standards." **Non-normative developmental changes** are those that happen to individuals or selected groups, but not to everyone. They can be either positive or negative, and they can be present at birth or acquired later (Mekos & Clubb, 1997). A child may be born with mild mental retardation or with the strength of an Olympic athlete. Either condition will make non-normative changes—changes that are unique—more likely for that child. She may also become physically disabled in a car accident later in childhood, or she may inherit a tidy sum of money from a great-grandparent when she is only ten. Either of these later events will also affect that child's life in ways not experienced by other children. Children with one skin color may experience social prejudice, but children with a different skin color may experience social prestige; individuals from each group will develop differently as a result.

Non-normative developmental changes account for much of the variety in students, and therefore make teaching interesting as well as challenging. One child receives encouragement from her parents to excel

In Your Own Voice

As a child, did you ever experience a situation where "everybody is doing it!"—wearing a certain kind of clothing, or holding the same opinion about music, or staying out to a certain hour, or . . . ?

What finally made you give up your belief in the inevitability of the opinion or behavior?

academically, but her sibling receives little of it; as the teacher of them both, you wonder why two children growing up in the same house seem so differently motivated as students. Or, more ominously, one student in your class has regularly witnessed a lot of violence in his home, but you as his teacher do not know this. You wonder why he seems to get in fist fights faster than other students. Or there is Judy:

When Judy was eight, one of her brothers died. Roger had been two-and-a-half years older—a friendly kid and, as siblings go, decent enough. Judy played with him more than with her sister and other brother, who were even older than Roger. He died suddenly one winter from complications of chicken pox. The doctors said he may have reacted to the aspirin he took for the fever; they said you weren't supposed to give aspirin to children, but Judy didn't know that, and apparently neither did her parents. Looking back, she found the suddenness worrisome. If the doctors couldn't save Roger from a common, almost universal disease such as chicken pox, what could they save you from? For a long time after Roger died, she was careful about her health, afraid that small problems might be about to become big ones. She missed more school days than most kids whenever she caught a cold, "making sure that I was really OK before I went back," she said.

For the rest of Judy's childhood, she lived in a three-child family, "with a hole in the middle where Roger had been," Judy said. It was not ideal for Judy, but it slowly became tolerable. She didn't have the playmate she remembered having, but of course she still had her family ("What was left of it!"). They did more things together, she noticed, than when her brother was still alive. That was fine with Judy; in fact, she encouraged family togetherness. Being together was reassuring. But it did mean she sought out friends less and got invited to friends' activities less. She developed a bit of a reputation as a loner—"spacey," one girl said, and "off in her own world" said another. On the other hand, by staying at home more, she always got her homework done and got better help with homework from her parents and remaining siblings. So her grades soared, though not until almost a year after Roger's death, when she had had time to settle down from it.

In Your Own Voice

What has been a unique, non-normative change in yourself?

It need not have been dramatic, like Judy's.

But it should be life altering: it has changed you, and only you, in permanent ways.

Judy's development was changed permanently by the loss of her brother Roger. She changed in ways that were both desirable and regrettable, but were in any case unique to her. On the regrettable side, she began worrying more than usual, and more than she needed to, about her health. We don't know whether this change stayed with her as an adult, but it apparently lasted for a substantial period, probably including the rest of her childhood. And she apparently withdrew from friendships more than usual for children of her age, keeping to the company of her family. Presumably, therefore, she gradually fell behind in learning the "social graces" of getting along in equality-oriented relationships with peers. But another change was desirable: one byproduct of her social withdrawal was stronger academic support from her family. Presumably her improved school performance will eventually provide her with more opportunities, even if she still would gladly give up her academic advantage to get her brother back. All things considered, losing Roger has shaped Judy's character and done much to make her the person she is.

Academic theories of developmental change often have ignored or minimized non-normative influences because they do not support the major goal of such theories, to generalize about and predict human behavior (Dixon, Lerner & Hultsch, 1992; Howe & Rabinowitz, 1992). Age-graded changes lend themselves to generalization much better: Piaget (described in Chapter 2), for example, outlines stages of cognitive abilities that supposedly happen to all individuals as they grow up. The sequences that he outlines can be helpful to teachers looking for general understandings of students' thinking, or for a basis for justifying particular classroom tasks.

Yet in planning for learning, the diversity among students is also important, and teachers have to recognize it at least as much as age-graded changes, if not more. Some diversity may, of course, represent age-graded differences in disguise; one student may simply be further along than another in reading, for example, or knowledge of numbers or social skills. But a lot of diversity probably reflects unique but permanent and life-changing experiences. As a teacher, it can be hard to discern the difference. A junior high student may deal comfortably with science experiments, for example, because her thinking has progressed farther along some universal, age-graded pathway of thinking, allowing her to think more abstractly and logically. Or the student may deal with the experiments comfortably because, alone among her classmates, she has a parent who works in a research laboratory and has frequently invited her there to visit. Furthermore, both types of change can operate at once: she may have had unique science experiences and developed thinking patterns typical of older students. As a teacher, you often have to keep such alternative possibilities in mind; to settle on just one of them too soon risks stereotyping a student unfairly.

Cohort Effects

Cohort effects are developmental changes that occur in individuals because of historical events and trends in society at large (Shanahan & Elder, 1997). They can happen to everyone in a society or only to a portion of a population. A simple example concerns the average height of human beings, which has increased during the past two hundred years due to slow improvements in sanitation and nutrition (Malina, 1991; Tanner, 1981). Particular cohorts of children—those born in particular historical years—grow to particular average sizes, with later cohorts growing taller than earlier cohorts. Partly for this reason, older adults currently are shorter, on average, than young adults. The difference is exaggerated because individuals also lose a bit of height as part of the natural aging process. But posture is not the only reason older people are currently shorter; they also grew up to be shorter people.

An example of a cohort effect with more educational and psychological impact is the effect of the atomic bombing of Hiroshima, Japan, in 1945. Nearly all survivors in that city were affected. Radiation interfered with children's physical growth; general destruction and poor health reduced attendance at schools and therefore the children's educational achievement; and massive numbers of premature deaths severed ties among relatives and increased antiwar sentiment in future years (Ishikawa & Swain, 1981; Lifton, 1982). But these effects were confined to people living in Hiroshima at the time of the bombing and during its immediate aftermath; those living there earlier (obviously) or much later were not affected.

The term **cohort effect** literally means "effect on companions or associates." The bombing of Hiroshima produced a cohort effect; only the residents living at that time were affected, not people living there before or after this event. Numerous examples of cohort effects are related to education, though often they are more gradual and less dramatic than the effects of an atomic bomb. Here are two examples:

- Average scores on standardized intelligence tests have risen slowly during the one hundred years in which these tests have existed. A likely cause is the expansion of public education and of contact with mass media, which tend to foster skills helpful for taking tests, such as a larger vocabulary and general worldly knowledge (Humphreys, 1989). The gradual improvement in intelligence test scores means that when older adults are compared to younger adults, the older adults tend to score *lower*. Without knowledge of the historical trend, we might interpret this difference to mean that people lose intellectual ability as they get older. In reality, a cohort effect may be operating: individuals born earlier in history tend to be less educated than those born later.

- Increasing numbers of women are working for paychecks than in years past, but the effect is more noticeable among younger women than among older, middle-aged women (U.S. Department of Labor,

1992). Does this mean women tend to give up their commitment to working as they get older? Do attitudes about jobs and gender change in age-graded fashion, with all women returning to traditional attitudes by midlife? Possibly, though a cohort effect may also be operating. Older women grew up at a time when working women represented a small minority of all workers and experienced more disapproval by society (Hudson & Lee, 1990; Spain, 1992). Younger women have also experienced gender prejudice in the workplace, but not to the same extent. On the other hand, younger women have had to cope with historically new problems, such as entering an economy in which fewer jobs offer security or a satisfactory, living wage. The new economic insecurities, combined with more equality-minded attitudes about gender roles, may encourage a disproportionate number of younger women to work, even though they may still end up—in spite of these gender and economic changes—doing the bulk of child care. History, that is, has changed attitudes about jobs and gender, not the simple fact of becoming middle-aged.

Both non-normative and historical changes highlight how social context may affect students' development, but they do so in different ways. Non-normative changes focus on individual events and experiences: what Joe experienced in his particular home or the motivation Susan developed from knowing one particular teacher. Historical changes highlight experiences that are universal but historically specific: for example, how students in general feel about getting an education even if the local economy is in recession or (on the other hand) now that a community college has opened up nearby. Between the non-normative and historical extremes are experiences that affect many people, but not all: those of nonwhite ethnic or racial groups, for example, or those of children whose parents get divorced. Whether to call such changes non-normative or historical, though, is not really important. What matters is recognizing that they can shape students' lives in important ways.

Ambiguities of Developmental Change: What Do We Mean by *Stage*?

OUR discussion so far may have implied that the different types of developmental change are clearly understood when people think or talk about long-term change in children. In fact, this is not always true: although the meaning of *developmental change* is sometimes acknowledged and understood, often it is just taken for granted or assumed unconsciously. This can cause confusion when two people—for example, a parent and a teacher, or a professor and a university student—use the same terms to talk about what amounts to different forms of developmental change. A good example of this problem is the way we use the term *stage*: parents, teachers, and psychologists often mean rather different things by it, depending on their purposes. Sometimes they refer to changes that are age graded, sometimes to changes that are non-normative, and sometimes to cohort effects. Yet everyone may believe they are talking about the "same" idea, *stage*. And that can create problems.

Everyday Meanings of *Stage*

In psychology, the term **stage** usually means something age graded: patterns of behavior that emerge together, in a predictable order and in all people as they grow older. Theories of language acquisition, for example, assert a predictable sequence: first, children use only single words ("hand!"); then they string two or three words in predictable but not necessarily grammatical ways ("two hand!"); and finally they begin constructing grammatical sentences ("You have two hands"). A few children (for example, those with a mental disability) may not experience this sequence, but these children are not typical.

This idea of *stage* seems clear enough, and we will come back to it shortly. But it is not what people usually mean by the term *stage* in everyday talk. It is also not what teachers usually mean by *stage* when they describe their students; we tend to use the term more freely or "loosely" than in formal theories of developmental change. Imagine, for the moment, what you would mean if you said that a student was "going through a stage." You might make either of these remarks:

- "Miguel is into this independence thing. Whenever I ask him to do something, he gives me this sarcastic look; then he says, 'I was *going* to do it in a minute; just give me time!' He didn't used to do that. It's new this term. Seems like he wants to feel in control of himself."

- "It just sort of evolved. Sharon used to be out of her seat—checking the goldfish, sharpening her pencil, using the bathroom. But I realized lately, you know, that sort of thing isn't happening anymore. She just works quietly until she's done. I hardly notice her now."

If you said these things, which student would you feel inclined to say is "going through a stage": Miguel, Sharon, neither, or both? Probably at least one of them is; after all, both have shown a change of behavior of some sort, and that may be enough to remark that either student is "going through a stage." Or maybe not. But in any case, you are not likely to think of Miguel's or Sharon's *stage* as necessarily universal (happening to everyone), patterned (involving not one but a set of related behaviors), or sequenced (having several levels).

Parents' Meanings of *Stage*

Research on the everyday meaning of *stage* has looked at these possibilities. One study interviewed parents, inviting them to describe their children at length, including how they changed with age. The parents used the idea of *stage* often, but not in the academic sense. Instead they used the term to refer to any change in a single behavior rather than to sequences or complex patterns of behavior. Parents used it particularly often to describe new behaviors that required active, inconvenient adjustments on their part (Harkness, Super & Keefer, 1994). Thus, they described a child's resistance to bedtime as a "stage" if the child had *not* resisted bedtime in the past. The resistance represented a change, and an inconvenient one at that. But the converse was much less likely: if the child used to resist bedtime but lately did not, the parents were not likely to describe the new compliance as a "stage." Unlike academic theorists, furthermore, the parents did not mean an entire pattern of related behaviors when they spoke of a *stage*. To qualify as "going through a stage," a child did not need to show resistance to bedtime all or even most of the time; just occasional resistance was enough, provided the occasions were inconvenient to the parents.

Teachers' Meanings of *Stage*

Do teachers who are not parents themselves think of *stage* in terms different from parents'? Though this question has not been studied directly, research suggests that teachers probably *do* think of developmental change differently than parents. For one thing, it seems to be true in general, as well as intuitively plausible, that adults' ideas about developmental change depend on their occupations, cultural backgrounds, and forms of involvement with children (Lightfoot & Valsiner, 1992). In one interview study, three university students, three parents, and three teachers of young children were invited to comment at length (several hours' worth!) on what they thought children and childhood were like—including, among other things, how children changed as they grew older

(Seifert, 1991, 1995). The students, parents, and teachers expressed radically different views about the nature of children, not only because of individual differences among them but also because of differences in their ongoing relationships with children.

The three teachers of young children, for example, described childhood as if it came in two stages: early childhood (roughly ages two to five), in which children are especially creative and free, and later childhood (age five and beyond), in which children become relatively conformist and dull compared to how they were in early childhood. Parents, on the other hand, described childhood more as if it were a never-ending soap opera: children (and their parents) had ups and downs, but never really reached resolutions of all problems at once so that stories of children's lives could finally be said to have ended. What about the university students? Perhaps because they had the least experience with real-life children, they tended to speak of childhood in age-graded terms, as a series of landmarks or stages marking particular ages. For them, and only for them, a *stage* was patterned, sequenced, and universal.

The studies mentioned so far imply that teachers are relatively homogeneous (or uniform) in what they mean by *stage*. In fact, however, this is not likely: both research and practical experience suggest that teachers *do* differ among themselves, and sometimes radically (Seifert, 1998*)*. Consider the implications of a common (but not universal) practice among teachers of kindergarten: retaining (or holding back) certain children for an extra year of kindergarten. Surveys have found dramatic variations in rates of retention even among teachers working in the same school; one teacher may retain far more children, year after year, than a neighboring teacher. Interviews with teachers suggest why (Smither & Shepard, 1989): some teachers see learning difficulties as a stage "in" the child, one that the child can grow out of simply given time. Others see learning difficulties as akin to failures of communication between adults and the child, located not "in" the child but "in" exchanges between teacher and student. The first group of teachers is more likely to recommend retention of students on the grounds that a learning difficulty is hard to modify quickly or deliberately. The latter group is more likely to pass a child on, where she or he will immediately encounter new, and hopefully more helpful, social relationships. The two types of teachers hold implicitly different views about the notion of *stage,* and the difference markedly affects their practices of retention and promotion.

Parents' and Teachers' *Stage* Compared

One reason differences such as these may occur is that the life circumstances of parents, teachers, and students present different challenges

In Your Own Voice

Am I being fair to university students here?

Do they really have less experience with children?

How about *your* way of thinking about change in children: is it primarily age graded, or is it something else—perhaps even resembling parents' or teachers' thinking?

related to their roles, and the challenges in turn create different understandings of developmental change. A major challenge for parents, for example, is to understand the long-term significance of puzzling actions of one particular child, their own: they wonder what it means that Joey does behavior X (resists bedtime, speaks sarcastically, refuses to eat his vegetables, etc.). Calling the puzzling behavior a "stage" implies that the behavior has a larger meaning in the child's life, while at the same time recognizing (or perhaps expressing the hope) that the behavior will not last forever (Harkness & Super, 1992). Calling it a "stage" also implies that the behavior really will lead to greater maturity eventually, and in this sense be a blessing in disguise.

Teachers too face the challenge of interpreting specific behaviors, but in a different context than parents. For one thing, teachers need to know how to influence the behavior of all children, no matter how diverse they may be. This makes teachers more interested than parents in predicting or estimating changes, as well as more supportive of children whose behavior can be predicted to some extent. For another thing, teachers are concerned with how their educational programs may affect children in general; hence they may be tempted to see childhood in terms of two stages: the ages at which children attend their classes and all the remaining years of childhood.

Piagetian *Stages*: Age-Graded Changes

An age-graded notion of *stage,* such as the one presented earlier, is basic to the widely known theory of cognitive development originated by the Swiss psychologist **Jean Piaget** earlier in this century and later elaborated on by other psychologists and educators. In essence, Piaget proposed that children's thinking develops through several patterned steps or stages (Piaget, 1983), that the stages occur in a fixed order for every child, and that each stage evolves logically from the preceding one and incorporates features of all previous stages. Piaget's claim is a bold one: he argued that every child, with few exceptions, experiences the same developmental changes in his or her thinking. Children differ only in how rapidly they progress through the sequence. From the point of view of teachers, who regularly deal with dramatically wide differences among children, Piaget's claim is either unbelievable or extremely helpful. That, for example, was the experience of Dean Page, a high school teacher of astronomy, as he explains in the accompanying "Multiple Voices" box. Before deciding what you yourself think about Piaget's belief in general stages, I invite you to look at what the stages actually

This girl's interests have shifted from infancy to age six, from playing peek-a-boo with her mother to counting and classification problems. Piaget would describe the change as a change in her stage of cognitive development—but are there additional ways of interpreting the change? © Elizabeth Crews

When I studied to be a teacher, concepts and research presented in textbooks—such as Piaget's developmental stages of learning—seemed to be remote and not very applicable. Practical experience in the classroom soon taught me that no two classes are alike or learn exactly in the same manner. Teachers have to pay conscious attention to the abilities of the students, which sometimes determine which concepts are learned easily and which are more difficult to grasp. The teacher therefore must learn the level of each class's ability to learn.

Sometimes something as simple as renaming a course and redirecting the focus of the curriculum can also improve learning. For example, I teach a course called "Astronomy," which grew out of the standard physical science high school curriculum. My fellow science teachers and I determined that many of the same concepts that were considered boring by students in a course titled "Physical Science" are received enthusiastically in a course titled "Astronomy"! The concepts of mass, weight, and density can be difficult for students to grasp. By applying these ideas to the study of stars and planets, though, and interjecting pictures of them from the Hubble telescope, students become more interested and achieve better understanding.

Dean Page, teacher of high school astronomy, Tampa, Florida

consist of. In doing so, keep in mind the potential power of an age-graded theory for teachers: if it proves even partially true, it can guide the selection of appropriate curriculum activities and teaching methods.

Sensorimotor Stage: Birth to Two Years

In Piaget's theory, the **sensorimotor stage** comes first; it is the time when infants learn mainly through their senses and motor activity. "Thinking" consists of handling objects, manipulating them, even tasting and biting them. It also consists of tracking objects with the eyes and listening to sounds attentively. In the sensorimotor stage, intelligence comes from learning by doing.

Through their actions, infants gradually construct concepts of their experiences and objects around them. To a one-month-old baby, a toy duck seems like an unpredictable, changing array of sights, tastes, and touch. As the months go by, though, these sensations crystallize into a stable notion of an object, *duck*. The concept takes on permanence: it

In Your Own Voice

. . . Or is a baby's search just a sign of growing memory and attentiveness?

Frequently I, even at my age, forget to search for lost objects, so in this sense I suppose I belong in Piaget's early sensorimotor stage, prior to object permanence.

What do you think?

begins to exist in the infant's mind whether or not she happens to be experiencing the duck at the moment. This is what Piaget meant by **object permanence.**

Not that the baby can yet call it by its name, *duck*; the concept remains intuitive rather than explicitly verbal at first. But, says Piaget, the concept exists in the child's mind nonetheless, even before her first birthday. How do we know? One sign is the infant's willingness to search for hidden objects (Piaget, 1952). Hiding the toy duck under a blanket reliably prompts a search by an older infant (eighteen to twenty-four months) but not by a younger infant (six months). In between these two age ranges, infants may sometimes search, but not completely or effectively.

The Preoperational Stage: Two to Seven Years

In the **preoperational stage,** children engage in intuitive, symbolic thinking, but the thinking does not yet exhibit full logic or coherence. These are new achievements in the preschool years, and children show them primarily through dramatic play and impressive improvements in language skill. Larry, a child care worker, notices the new achievements:

Larry looked around the room at the child care center. Children were playing freely in several areas. By a window was an area full of child-size furniture and implements. Two children were talking:

SOPHIE: I'm going to make a phone call (holding a ruler to ear and mouth). 'Cause I'm the doctor and that baby is sick (points to a stuffed teddy bear).

GEORGIA: What's the number? Here, I'll dial it for you. (Second child twirls finger in the air briefly, as if dialing.) Boy, this is sure a long phone number!

Larry looked in another direction and saw two other children, who had just arrived for the morning. They were talking happily, but more "at" each other than with each other.

MARTA: Look at my new shoes.

CARLOS: We're going to the store this afternoon.

MARTA: Brown ones.

CARLOS: Do you want to come too?

Larry glimpsed both the strengths and limitations of the preoperational stage as defined by Piaget. On the one hand, the preschoolers were remarkably fluent with language, could talk about objects and experiences that were not present (the doctor, the store), and could make objects stand for or represent other objects (a ruler for a telephone). On the other hand, the children sometimes talked past each other; Marta and Carlos were not really listening to each other.

Jeremy read the preceding paragraph and frowned. He thought, "But a lot of times me and my friends do the same as preschoolers. We don't really listen to each other when we talk. Sounds like a human quality, or maybe a human failing, not an 'age-graded stage.'"

Jeremy has a point: sometimes we act like young children and young children act like us. But he may also be missing Piaget's point: we differ from four-year-olds because we *can* attend to another person's thoughts by trying. Distinguishing between what a person *can* do—his or her capacity—and what the person *does* do—his or her performance—is crucial to age-graded theories of change such as Piaget's. Such theories deal with the capacity or potential possible at each age, not everyday, variable performance.

The Concrete Operational Stage: Seven to Eleven Years

By the time they are in grade school, most children are able to manipulate ideas and memories using logical rules. The rules seem very basic to adult minds, and they often operate unconsciously; for example, a newly emerging logical rule might be "If nothing is added or taken away, the amount of something stays the same." Piaget called this stage the **concrete operational stage** because children now "operate" on ideas and apply their new logical abilities most successfully to concrete or tangible objects and events. Later, as adolescents, they become able to think operationally about abstractions—but not yet.

Several features make thinking during the concrete operational period different from that during the previous, preoperational stage. The first is **reversibility,** or the ability to mentally go both backward and forward in working through problems. Both preoperational and concrete operational children can describe the steps in a simple science experiment, such as one to explore why some objects float and others sink. But only the concrete operational child can describe the steps in any order, including backward, forward, or a mixture. The ability comes from a second quality of concrete operational thinking: the ability to **decenter** attention, or focus on more than one feature of a problem at a time. Unlike the preoperational child, the concrete operational child can think about all the steps in an experiment as a group, as though they all existed at the same time; so he can name any step in any order without getting confused.

Of course, you and I might also have trouble judging whether two pieces of clay are the same if we had not actually seen them being deformed from identical balls.

I see a message for teachers in that fact: maybe students need to experience materials tangibly even after they can reason about them verbally.

Or am I reading too much into a simple experiment about clay pieces?

Probably the best-known examples of reversibility and decentration are Piaget's experiments with **conservation,** the belief in constancy or invariance despite visible changes in an object (Piaget, 1965; Grize, 1987). Consider two balls of clay of the same size and shape. If a young preoperational child looks at these, she will have no trouble agreeing that they contain the same amount of clay. But if one ball is squashed into a hot dog shape, she may decide that it now has a different amount—possibly more, possibly less, but definitely not the same. The new length of the clay mass stands out visually and apparently distracts her from noticing that the length is compensated for by thinness or narrowness. Older, concrete operational children are not distracted in this way. For them the amount of clay in each ball stays the same regardless of how its shape is deformed. In Piagetian terms, they "have conservation of quantity"; or, put differently, they conserve the amount of clay mentally in spite of its visible changes.

The Formal Operational Stage: Eleven and Beyond

In this stage, according to Piaget's theory, young people begin to reason about abstract relationships among ideas, and not only about their concrete or specific content; hence the name **formal operational stage.** Not all people reach this stage quickly or even reach it at all, but those who do have a marked advantage at **hypothetical reasoning,** the ability to think about imaginary or counterfactual relationships. Suppose a teacher asks, "What would have happened to history *if* the geography of North America had been reversed, with the west coast located in the east and settlers arriving first in this relocated 'west'?" To answer, the student must reason hypothetically. He or she must shift attention from what is to what might be. Hypothetical reasoning allows mental exploration or experimentation with situations and ideas, including those that vary in several ways at once. It is an important skill in scientific investigation, as Julie discovers:

Julie is watching and listening to her science teacher, who is explaining a problem for the class to solve. He is holding up a pendulum made from a string tied to a coffee cup. "What do you think determines how fast this pendulum swings?" he asks. "The length of the string, the weight of the cup, or the distance that I pull it out to the side?" He pauses, waiting while everyone thinks.

Julie squints at the pendulum while it swings. "Distance pulled out?" she wonders to herself. "Hmm; maybe not. Weight? Length! No . . . " She is stumped; it's the kind of problem her sister likes, but not one of her own favorites.

Julie is not the only student who is stumped. Sensing confusion, the teacher changes tactics. "Write me a brief paragraph," he says, "explaining a way to find the answer. Keep it brief, but make it clear!"

So Julie thinks . . . and thinks. "Make each thing—length, weight, angle—change independently of the others!" she thinks suddenly. So she begins writing her paragraph:

Procedure: (1) Get two lengths of string, two weights of cup, and decide on two angles for swinging. (2) Choose one of the lengths and one of the cups, and try both of the angles. (3) Go back to one of the angles and stick with it. (4) Try both of the weights of cup. (5) Go back to one of the weights of cup and stick with it. (6) Try both of the lengths of string.

The instructions seem awkwardly written, but she hopes the teacher will get the point: you have to control or keep irrelevant factors constant while you deliberately vary another factor.

Julie solved this problem using hypothetical reasoning. To make sure she has tested all possibilities systematically, Julie had to treat each factor as a mental (or hypothetical) object, imagining all possible combinations and keeping mental track of which ones remained to be tested. In essence, she designed an experiment; all that remains is to carry it out.

Piagetian Stages and Age-Graded Change

Piaget's age-graded theory of cognitive *stages* sparked a lot of interest among educators and research among psychologists interested in education and developmental change. They are important enough, therefore, that I have summarized them in a table (see Table 4.1). The reasons for the interest in Piaget are crucial to evaluating age-graded notions of change: rightly or wrongly, Piaget offered the possibility of *generalizing* about how children think as they grow older. To the extent that Piagetian stages (or some stages like them) are both true and truly age-graded, teachers and other educators can predict the intellectual skills possible in students even before meeting them.

Partly for this reason, numerous studies have been conducted to decide whether Piaget's ideas are indeed "right" or accurate (Case, 1992; Gelman & Baillargeon, 1983). In general, they have supported an age-graded account of change in children's thinking, provided you make the same assumptions Piaget made. You must ask children to respond to thought problems individually and without help; you must use problems

In Your Own Voice

An interesting challenge is whether Piaget's concept of formal operations also works for areas *outside* of science.

Do people think according to abstract, logical rules about politics, for example, or about family relationships?

What do you think?

TABLE 4.1 Piagetian Stages

Stage	Major features	Example
Sensorimotor (birth–2 years)	Coordination of sensory and motor activity; object permanence	Search for lost object
Preoperational (2–7 years)	Use of language; egocentrism	Make-believe play; children talking past each other
Concrete operational (7–11 years)	Rules or operations to solve concrete problems; decentered attention	Conservation (belief in constancy of amount)
Formal operational (11 years–adulthood)	Rules or operations to solve hypothetical problems; hypothetical reasoning	Systematic experimentation

that are not too emotionally charged; you must understand and speak the child's first language; and you must assume the children are trying their best to solve the problems you give them. As I will point out in later chapters, these assumptions often do not hold true in actual classrooms. When they do, though, there is usefulness in Piaget's stages and in the age-graded view of developmental change that underlies it.

Constructing Knowledge of Developmental Change

SUPPOSE you are not a research psychologist like Jean Piaget but a teacher. How do you know when to consider a change as a sign of development rather than of immediate learning? Part of the answer seems obvious: you can compare memories from different points in time or different periods of life. Sometimes the memories take the form of stories created by either yourself or others; other times they are simply recollections—"nonfiction stories." Often the distinction between *story* and *recollection* may be unclear; however, the blurring may not really matter in building an understanding of how a person has changed. Look, for instance, at these comments by teachers, all of which note developmental change in students:

Lee, grade 12 teacher: I remember that substitute well. It was grade 6, and we were doing math. I have always been good at math—got 100 percent, or close to it, on all the quizzes. The substitute was quizzing us orally that day, trying to challenge us by giving us really hard math computations to do in our heads. "How much is 18 times 19?" he asked. "342," I answered. "Wrong," he said, even though I was right and I knew it! I was sure annoyed, but I only got really angry when he followed up with "You can't get them all right. No one ever does." Well, then I was really steamed—but at least I didn't lose my temper like I did when I was in younger grades.

Ms. Smith, grade 5 teacher: I remember Jessie when she entered first grade. I had the first-grade class that year, and even then she liked to write. But you know, I didn't think about her liking to write so much then; what I mostly noticed was that she kept to herself—often didn't play with the others at recess, but would "hide" in a corner of the playground so that she could privately read or write in her journal. I didn't think about it again until this year, now that I have her again in fifth grade. She turned in a report on Monaco that was fifty pages long! Full of pictures and diagrams, as well as a good written text. When she turned it in, she said, "I couldn't find out everything, but I found out a lot." That's when I remembered her writing and reading at recess back then, instead of socializing.

Mr. Walker, school counselor: Today Jodi smiled at me when she entered school—so different now! Last year she acted like I was invisible when she walked in. Seems like I'm getting through to her finally. She's not quite so shy as she used to be.

Mme. Fillion, French teacher: I can tell Rick's catching on. He wrote *"Les deux chats mignons se chassent en jouer."* [The two cute cats chased each other playfully.] That's not quite how a genuine francophone would say it, but it's getting there.

Lee and Ms. Smith tell stories; Mr. Walker and Mme. Fillion report observations. All four note developmental change in a student, though in Lee's case the teacher reports on himself as a student. Lee and Ms. Smith point to changes over extended periods. Lee was always good at math but has grown more tactful, and Jessie was never outgoing but has become more confident in asserting her intellectual orientation. Mr. Walker and Mme. Fillion also report changes: Jodi is more sociable than last year, though still basically a shy person; Rick is "catching on" to French but is still (implicitly) a beginner, an amateur speaker of French.

The Strengths and Limits of Teachers' Knowledge About Development

There are real strengths to the narrative, personal knowledge of development shown by the four teachers above. It is based on experience and is easily accessible: recollections therefore have a vividness and authoritativeness that is harder to achieve with more formal theories, much like the vividness and authority conveyed by a work of fiction. In addition, the knowledge constructed directly by teachers is guaranteed to be relevant to teaching; otherwise, it would not be constructed in the first place. More formal theories of development (e.g., Piaget's) may also be relevant to teaching, but their relevance is less certain since they are often constructed to support or extend psychological theories rather than solve classroom problems.

In Your Own Voice

Can you think of a story about yourself that turned out to be misleading, though perhaps also a bit truthful?

Why was it mixed in that way?

But this form of knowledge has limitations as well, primarily because stories and recollections can mean something both *more* and *different* than they first appear. These qualities do not make them useless (far from it!), but it does mean they simply cannot be taken at face value. A story, for example, doesn't just report an event of the past, even if the storyteller claims it does: in addition, it expresses the current viewpoint of the storyteller. When Lee describes the incident with the substitute teacher, for example, he not only retells a past event but also implies his own assessment of his mathematics ability, both past and present; "I have always been good in math," he says, both explicitly and implicitly. Furthermore, depending on whom he is talking to, Lee may also be expressing an implied opinion about teacher-student relationships in general—that they can be humiliating, for example, or that relationships should be democratic and fair. Similar ambiguities occur when Ms. Smith tells about her successful student, Jessie. Whether or not her memories of Jessie are accurate, Ms. Smith may be expressing an immediate, current opinion about teaching: that teachers benefit from knowing students for long periods of time, for example, or that favoring academic work over social life may not be so bad in the long run.

Everyday observations are no less ambiguous than everyday stories. One problem is that events are usually remembered for a number of reasons, some of which may not be noted by the observer. The choice of what to remember from everyday events, furthermore, is far from automatic; noticing and remembering one event rather than another reveals something about the observer, not just about the event observed. When Mr. Walker noted Jodi smiling at him, for example, he implied *he* had something to do with her deciding to do this. But can we be sure of this? Maybe Jodi also smiled because lately her friends were treating her better, or because she had just received a high grade on a test, or even because she was amused by Mr. Walker's constantly looking to see *if* she was smiling. Likewise for Mme. Fillion: The fact that she chose to comment on Rick's writing says something about her priorities—perhaps that she is more concerned about students' written language than about their oral language. In a sense she is talking about two people at once: explicitly about Rick and implicitly about herself and her viewpoints.

Yet these ambiguities do not rule out the use of everyday stories and memories for understanding students' developmental change. Instead they do two things. First, they point to the importance of holding opinions about students tentatively, remaining open to new information as it continually comes to your attention. Second, ambiguities point to the value of holding explicit general views, interpretations, and theories of learning and human development—including, in particular, the views held by academic, age-graded theories of development such as Piaget's. The term *ambiguous* literally means "having many meanings"; it does not mean "having no meaning." Students' actions and thoughts are often ambiguous in this sense, that is, of being interpretable in more than one way. They are not—repeat, *not*—lacking in meaning altogether.

Resolving Disagreements About Developmental Change

In Your Own Voice

In the text, I sidestep the problem of how to respond to this particular difference between teachers, the one Joel is hearing.

Any suggestions?

Is it best to "lie low," as Joel seems to do?

Or is there a way for Joel to engage with the discussion himself?

Joel, who had just started teaching, remembered an unpleasant discussion in the teachers' lounge last week. He had overheard two veteran teachers disagree about whether young people really change much beyond age six. The first teacher argued that major changes are common throughout childhood and adolescence; his colleague argued that the key things about people do *not* change during the school years: "Just give students a test of intelligence; you'll see that they get similar scores each time they take it." Joel didn't know much about intelligence tests, so he didn't know how to take this comment; he made a mental note to find out more about IQ tests sometime soon.

But for now the conversation had become sharper than Joel preferred; the teachers' comments verged on mutual disrespect. It was almost like they were arguing about religion, about fundamental questions of existence! As a newcomer to teaching and to the school, Joel was uneasy seeing conflict so close at hand. What, he wondered, did disagreements between colleagues mean for educating the students in the teachers' respective classes? It was simplistic to take sides in the discussion-turned-argument; both teachers were respected and successful in the school. But seeing them debate so heatedly made Joel feel vulnerable: was tension such as this the price of professional dialogue? More to the point, he worried whether his own beliefs about development actually led him to actions that served his own students best. His viewpoint, it seemed, was only one among many. How could he, Joel, feel confident of his beliefs when other reasonable teachers obviously disagreed so much?

As Joel sensed, everyday beliefs about developmental change can be worrisome, even a bit fearsome, when they conflict with others' beliefs, and especially when students' educations are at stake. In essence, Joel is asking this: is there a way to judge the relative merits of a person's everyday beliefs, including my own? Is one person's opinion about teaching and learning just as good as another's? Is there any guarantee that my beliefs are somehow right for me and my students, even if my colleagues do not share them?

Developing Adequate Beliefs About Development

*I*N case you are expecting quick answers to these questions from me, I must disappoint you; you will need, sooner or later, to answer them for yourself. I can, however, point you toward my own positions, positions that I intend to echo throughout later chapters of this book. Yes, I argue here and elsewhere, there are ways to judge the relative merit of different opinions about teaching and learning. And no, one opinion is not necessarily just as good as another. And yes and no: you can never be absolutely sure that your views truly lead you to actions that are best for your students, but there are ways to make it more likely that they will. One way is to consider seriously the ideas generated by academic research on learning in general and developmental change in particular. Another is to reflect, at every chance you get, on your own views about human change in the light of developmental research (Fenstermacher, 1994; Greene, 1994). The remaining chapters in this book will continue to assist you with both of these strategies in various ways, beginning with Chapter 5, which explores the roles you might play as a teacher and how the relationships resulting from the roles often can affect students deeply.

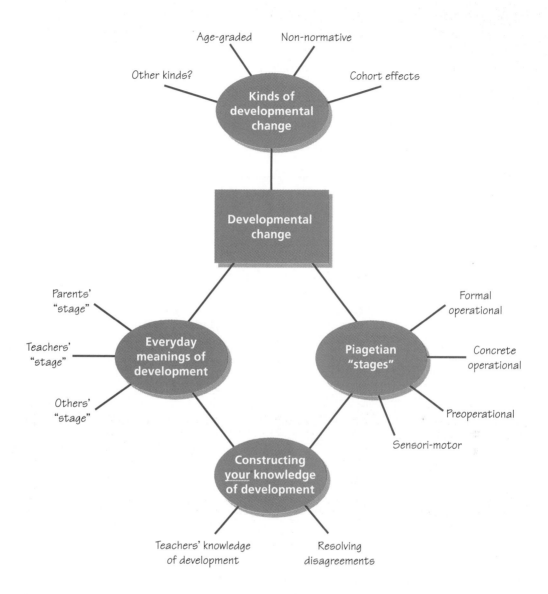

Chapter Re-View: Developmental Change This Chapter Re-View suggests directions in which the chapter might have taken your thinking—though, of course, other directions are also possible. It expands the Chapter View, which suggests a starting point, conceptually, for the chapter. But this Re-View does not suggest an ending point. Like the Chapter View, it represents just one perspective among many.

Key Terms and Concepts

developmental change (102)
age-graded developmental
    change (106)
non-normative developmental
    change (107)
cohort effects (109)

stage (112)
Jean Piaget (115)
sensorimotor stage (117)
object permanence (118)
preoperational stage (118)
concrete operational stage (119)

reversibility (119)
decenter (119)
conservation (120)
formal operational stage (120)
hypothetical reasoning (120)

Annotated Readings

Hwang, C. P., Lamb, M., & Sigel, I. (Eds.). (1996). *Images of childhood*. Hillsdale, NJ: Erlbaum. This is a collection of articles about how the notion of "childhood" has been conceived by different cultures, different historical periods, and different academic disciplines. It makes for interesting reading! See, for example, the chapter about the impact of common proverbs on views of child rearing and of children. Also read the chapter on how Navajo parents' belief in being respectful leads them to see children as inherently restrained and controlled rather than impulsive and distractible.

Matthews, Gareth. (1994). *The philosophy of childhood*. Cambridge, MA: Harvard University Press. The author is a philosopher by training and uses this perspective to explore how children themselves can "philosophize" about important matters (e.g., about death, ethics, democracy) more than we usually give them credit for. His account is reflective but also laced with examples from conversations with children of all ages.

Wadsworth, Barry. (1996). *Piaget's theory of cognitive and affective development* (5th ed.). White Plains, NY: Longman. A long-standing, readable account of Piaget's theory of development. In spite of its title, it is more about cognition (thinking) than about affect (feelings), reflecting the bias of Piaget himself. Wadsworth does not criticize Piaget; instead, he communicates the theory as clearly as possible.

Internet Resources

<www.sunnyhill.bc.ca/Lalonde/JPS/index.html> This is the official web site of the Jean Piaget Society, also mentioned at the end of Chapter 2. The society is dedicated to research inspired by the theory of Jean Piaget, but it has gone well beyond Piaget's ideas to explore all sorts of "constructivist" ideas. When you search the web site, look also for the links to other sites related to developmental change.

<www.journals.uchicago.edu/SRCD/srcdhome.html> This is the web site for the Society for Research on Child Development. A lot of it concerns matters that may not be of direct interest to teachers (such as how to become a member of this society), but the site also has links to its publications, including tables of contents of the latest issues of the society's major journal, *Child Development*.

II

Relationships

It is not appropriate to think of learning as a truly individual activity. Learning always happens with at least the indirect support of other people; even doing "independent reading" requires that other human beings (authors, editors, publishers) have written a book that can be read alone!

Part 2 therefore explores the most important of the relationships affecting students' individual learning. Chapter 5 begins with the teacher, describing major roles that this person must take on—and combine—in relationship to students. Chief among these are the roles of instructional manager, caring person, and generous expert. Chapter 6 discusses how teachers must simultaneously motivate students to learn, and manage their behavior when they do not learn—or more accurately, when they learn something other than the intended curriculum. Chapter 7 completes the discussions begun in the previous two chapters by exploring the remaining relationships that are important to students, those with their peers and families. It looks especially at how these relationships affect teachers and teaching, and how teachers can use them to support students' learning.

In discussing these topics, Part 2 shifts the focus from student to teacher but at the same time keeps students and their diversity in mind. As you will see in Parts 3 and 4, we will eventually have to return to the issues of diversity more directly. Before doing so, however, let us look at the complex demands placed on teachers and how the demands affect not only students' ability to learn the curriculum but also teachers' ability to learn about their students.

PART OUTLINE

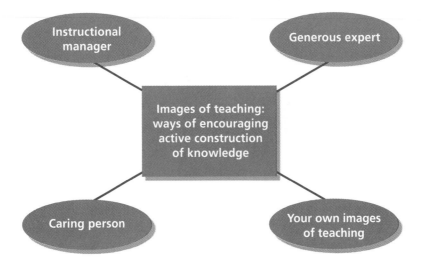

Chapter View: What Teachers Do This Chapter View is a concept map that indicates one among many ways of thinking about the chapter. It suggests a starting point, conceptually, for the chapter but is incomplete by itself. At the end of the chapter is a Chapter Re-View, which expands on the Chapter View, suggesting directions for taking your thinking further—though, of course, other directions are also possible.

5

What Teachers Do

How many ways can you teach? You likely have experienced some of them as a student: you have listened to a lecture or participated in a discussion, watched a classroom demonstration, or completed assigned homework. These are far from the only actions that constitute teaching. But they are among the ones most visible to students, and as such they have a strong influence on the relationships that develop between teachers and students. And the relationships, in turn, affect how students learn or, occasionally, even *whether* they learn. To see what I mean, consider these two teachers, Ms. Strathmillan and Mr. Shelmerdine, and how they teach. And consider how their students respond to each of them.

9:50 a.m.: Ms. Strathmillan looked around her class, tenth-grade general biology. Four students were talking quietly about a report they were preparing jointly. Six were working independently on different projects to be presented later in the term. Several were out of the room, visiting the library to find resources for their own joint project. Ms. Strathmillan worried about

9:50 a.m.: Across the hall, Mr. Shelmerdine finished a session on language and literature. Students were writing in journals they had begun early in the term. Each day they commented on current readings, relating them not only to literature read earlier but also to their personal lives and feelings. If they wished, they could also write brief fictional pieces or poems as a

sending them away as a group: would they "goof off" in the library, or even cause a disturbance? Three students were doing special work that Ms. Strathmillan had created because they didn't understand material on the last test; they were supposed to complete two worksheets and then discuss their work with the teacher individually. Ms. Strathmillan hoped to be done with these conferences before the other students finished their various activities. When the group returned from the library, she planned to lecture briefly on the current topic—migratory patterns in birds—before setting up everyone to work as groups and individuals again.

response, rather than expository comments, as long as the pieces were relevant. The most important requirement was to "speak from the heart": you had to mean what you wrote. Mr. Shelmerdine read everyone's journal as often as he could—usually once every week or two—and wrote comments in them. Sometimes he held conferences with individuals about what they had written, though time did not allow him to do this as often as he wanted.

Each of these teachers seems to have adopted a habitual pattern or style of teaching to use for specific educational purposes. Of course, it is hard to say with certainty how each teacher teaches in general. Yet this is a question that their students will ask themselves and that will influence the relationships they form with Ms. Strathmillan and Mr. Shelmerdine. Fair or not, for example, students will ask a question such as this: Is one teacher more concerned than the other with keeping organized? Perhaps Ms. Strathmillan is more concerned, because she has her students working in complicated groupings; or perhaps Mr. Shelmerdine is, because he has to keep track of many individual threads of dialogue in students' journals.

Or students will ask: Does one teacher care about students more than the other? Perhaps Mr. Shelmerdine does, because he has students "speak from the heart" in their journals. Or perhaps Ms. Strathmillan does, because she has troubled herself to arrange individual activities for her students. Or students will ask: Does one teacher share knowledge and expertise with students more than the other? Surely both do, even though Ms. Strathmillan may do it via group and individual activities and Mr. Shelmerdine may do it via student journals. Even if the meaning of teachers' actions is ambiguous, students will attribute significance to them, and their perceptions will affect the kinds of relationships possible between particular teachers and particular students. So the teachers' habitual ways of teaching will matter educationally. Take Murray and Shelley, students of Ms. Strathmillan and Mr. Shelmerdine, respectively:

10:00 a.m.: In Ms. Strathmillan's room, Murray looked at his teacher. Murray happened to be one of the students working independently. He liked Ms. Strathmillan's class; she always seemed so organized! What was good about it, he thought, was that you always knew what you were supposed to do. He noted that different students often worked on different activities. Murray rarely actually talked with Ms. Strathmillan directly, but this did not matter to him as long as he knew what he was supposed to be doing. He assumed his classmates felt the same way; certainly his own particular friends did.

10:00 a.m.: Back in Mr. Shelmerdine's room sat Shelley. She enjoyed writing in her journal; in fact, she wrote so much that Mr. Shelmerdine asked her repeatedly to limit the length of her comments! It was the personal aspect of writing that she liked: comparing her own life to those of characters in the current novel, for example, or her own feelings to the ones expressed in a poem or short story. In other humanities classes, Shelley's reactions had been mixed ("because usually you have to talk so abstractly," she said); here, though, it seemed as if Mr. Shelmerdine knew you as a person. That made it more worthwhile.

In Your Own Voice

I seem to be saying that among teachers, there is no such thing as "excellence" in general.

What do you think about that?

Can we reconcile the obvious differences among teachers with the possibility that some teachers are simply very good at all aspects of their work?

Here are two students who enjoy their teachers! Or, more precisely, each has construed the actions of his or her teacher in positive ways, ways that each personally values. On the assumption that each teacher has a number of other students who also respond positively to their classes, we can reasonably count each teacher as a "success," in spite of the differences in teaching methods portrayed earlier. Unfortunately, we *cannot* assume that all other students will appreciate either Ms. Strathmillan or Mr. Shelmerdine, or even that those who do like them will all do so for the same reasons. Relationships between teacher and students, in other words, will be diverse in nature. Murray and Shelley hint at the diversity that is possible:

10:09 a.m.: Just before the end of their respective classes, Murray and Shelley both sighed: soon they would have to go to their next classes. As it happened, they would switch places for next period, with Murray going to Mr. Shelmerdine and Shelley going to Ms. Strathmillan. Neither looked forward to the change.

Ms. Strathmillan doesn't even know me, thought Shelley.

Mr. Shelmerdine snoops into my life too much, thought Murray.

But then the bell rang, and Murray and Shelley got up from their desks, greeted each other briefly as they crossed the hallway, and sat down in their new rooms for the next period.

Murray's and Shelley's reactions suggest two important ideas about how teachers teach and how their ways of teaching affect relationships between teachers and students. First, teachers obviously teach in various ways, but no one way pleases all students or pleases any one student all of the time. The result is that relationships between teachers and students differ widely—among classrooms, within the same classroom, and from one occasion to the next. Second, even though teacher-student relationships are incredibly diverse and rather fluid, a lot of learning occurs anyway! Teacher-student relationships provide the medium or context for sharing knowledge and providing support for learning. Even classroom activities that seem solitary really involve social interactions: reading a book may look like independent work, but in fact it involves exchanges of ideas between author and reader, as well as prior understandings between student and teacher about when and what to read.

This chapter will explore the implications of these two ideas and invite you to do the same. We will look at three responsibilities typical for teachers: managing, caring for students, and sharing knowledge. Each responsibility calls for habitual sets of actions by teachers, which I will call **roles**—patterns of behavior that students witness repeatedly and therefore can be expected to influence relationships between teachers and students. Though I will describe each teaching role separately, I do *not* imply that the roles are mutually exclusive. Quite the contrary: teachers often enact elements of each role simultaneously. Whether students notice the complexity and multiplicity of a teacher's roles is another matter, one determined by what students want from a teacher as well as by what the teacher can provide.

Three Teaching Roles

To see how teaching roles influence relationships with students and their learning, imagine three different ways teachers can teach. One way is to be an **instructional manager**: to focus on orchestrating sets of activities for groups and individuals. Ms. Strathmillan seemed to be teaching this way, judging especially by Murray's comments. Another teaching role is to be a **caring person**: to focus deeply on students as unique individuals, noting and responding to students not only as learners but as individuals with lives beyond the classroom. Mr. Shelmerdine conveyed this impression to Shelley. Still another teaching role is to be a **generous expert**: to convey skill and familiarity with a subject, sharing competence freely and generously with students. Presumably both Ms. Strathmillan and Mr. Shelmerdine did this in their teaching as a whole, although generosity with expertise was not emphasized explicitly in the brief accounts given earlier. Each role or way of teaching encourages certain relationships with students, and therefore certain kinds of learning. It is important to remember two provisos about these roles, however. The first is that real-life teachers (not Ms. Strathmillan or Mr. Shelmerdine) usually enact *all* of the roles—and others besides—at various times, and sometimes simultaneously. The second is a result of the first: students often can interpret a teacher's behavior in more than one way. Even classmates sitting next to each other may construe or evaluate the "same" teacher differently.

In Your Own Voice

Do my comments here make teachers seem too changeable, as though they lack integrity or reliability?

Or simply flexible and sensitive to the needs of students?

The Teacher as Instructional Manager

What does it mean for a teacher to be an instructional manager, and what does it mean to students? Suppose I visit a "typical" but imaginary teacher oriented toward instructional management. In fact, suppose I visit her at different times of day and during several different activities. Of course, I will see her and her class do many things. One day I see small groups working on different projects; another time I see the teacher lecture or explain a topic to the whole class, though I notice a number of individuals working alone in the back of the room. One day is especially informative because it shows the teacher as instructional manager behind the scenes: I arrive after school and see the teacher reviewing goals and activities for the coming week. She crosses two off a list and shifts a third to another day. She writes the names of students be-

In Your Own Voice

According to both educational research and teacher lore, instructional management is a major struggle for *new* teachers (Bullough, Knowles & Crow, 1992).

Does this mean most beginning teachers eventually emphasize this role when they become experienced?

When playing the role of manager, a teacher is focused primarily on organizing students to learn. This may involve working with the whole class, but often it involves breaking the class into smaller working groups for various purposes. ©Nita Winter/The Image Works

side her notes for several planned activities. "Jerry has got to try this activity soon," she explains to us, "He's just not getting it." Looking over her shoulder, I notice a planning diary. It is barely legible, though also full of gaps; some days don't seem to have any plans, and most are rather sketchy. "The longer I teach," she says, "the more I just coordinate things in my mind." On the other hand, her record book is meticulous: all assignments, both large and small, are neatly recorded for every student.

After all of these visits I thank the teacher for showing us so much of her work; I leave the classroom and walk outside. What a well-organized teacher, I think. But then a curious thought occurs: in all of these visits, this teacher said little about *what* she was teaching or about actual individuals whom she taught! Instead, she focused on *how* she taught, on what she planned for when. For this teacher, or at least for what I could see of her work, methods commanded more attention than content, or students' personalities.

Organizing Others as a Priority: Pros and Cons

The focus on organizational problems is what I mean by the role of *instructional manager*. No teacher is concerned about management exclusively, but all are to some extent. As instructional manager, the teacher becomes especially concerned about coordinating learners and activities in numerous, complex ways. She does not participate in the learning directly so much as observe its progress and assess its results in students. In principle, the teacher could use the management skills with many grade levels and subject areas, because she distinguishes *how* she teaches from *what* she teaches. In practice, though, she would probably select and organize activities differently for other subjects or other grade levels; but she would keep a fundamental focus on the timing, sequencing, and coordinating of tasks, and only secondarily note the content of tasks themselves. She would also give high priority to keeping accurate and fair records of students' performance.

The teacher may be aware of and respectful of students' lives outside school, but she distinguishes these from classroom performance, which is her real concern. At times the distinction can make her seem insensitive to students' problems and goals, if these do not seem related directly to classroom learning. But as some educators have reflected, a deliberate lack of attention to the personal lives of students can have advantages (Berliner, 1990; Evertson, 1994). Dealing with students only as students helps to designate school as a place that clearly encourages learning and as a safe haven from distractions (or even dangers) that might interfere with learning. These are qualities that not all homes or neighborhoods are able to provide. As we will see later in the chapter, though, there are other ways to think about the role of teachers, including some that deliberately blur the distinction between students as learners and as people, and others that focus more on the content of teaching than on its methods.

Relationships Between a Teacher-Manager and Students

How are relationships with students affected when a teacher focuses on managing instruction? Some clues to these questions were given by Murray and Shelley at the beginning of this chapter. Their relationship with Ms. Strathmillan was businesslike: because Ms. Strathmillan focused on tasks and goals, Murray and Shelley focused on these as well. Yet, as Shelley's responses implied, not everyone likes this kind of relationship. What seems satisfyingly businesslike to one student can seem impersonal and uncaring to another. In spite of the relatively focused goals of management-minded teachers, then, the approach can easily produce reactions in students that the teacher does not intend. In this regard, the instructional manager is not really different from other sorts of teaching

So how does a brand-new teacher know what role to take? You don't! It takes time, experience, and reflection on what is happening in your classroom. In my first year of teaching, I put the emphasis on being an "instructional manager" and thought I was a failure as a teacher if I could not do that well. As a "caring person" who wanted to see kids grow and succeed, I was frustrated and overwhelmed by keeping up with everything. It was difficult to find time to reflect on these things, and there were few teachers who had time or the inclination to share their struggles with me. Now, twenty years later, as a technology coordinator, I can observe many teachers through all of the ups and downs of a school year. The most successful teachers are able to reflect on their role and to build on their strengths and weaknesses.

Technology can facilitate growth in all of these areas. A strong instructional manager will naturally lean toward using a classroom computer to keep records, to make plans, schedules, and class lists, and to print labels since these are organizational tasks. But the computer can also help the instructional manager in the other roles talked about in this chapter. Technology can aid in reaching individual students with diverse backgrounds and experiences. For example, sharing the rich resources of the World Wide Web and good searching techniques can enhance the "generous expert" role.

Janice Friesen, Technology coordinator, Columbia, Missouri

roles; not everyone likes teachers who act like caring persons or generous experts either. But the instructional manager may have a special challenge in dealing with the diversity of students' reactions simply because in playing this role, he or she can become more focused on "covering" or managing the curriculum than on anticipating the diversity that inevitably exists among students. In reality, of course, most teachers also care about their students, in addition to striving for a well-managed class, and they seek ways to combine both caring and management in their teaching. In the accompanying "Multiple Voices," Janice Friesen comments on how she used Internet technology in this way; she is a teacher responsible for helping other teachers use computers in education productively and in ways that provide for students' diversity.

A number of educational researchers have investigated some of the ways teachers' actions can have unintended effects on students. Derek

Edwards and Neil Mercer, for example, observed classroom conversations or dialogues between primary teachers and their students, and noted that the conversations often had different effects than the ones teachers intended (Edwards & Mercer, 1987). The teachers intended (commendably) to encourage students to think for themselves and to come up with answers to questions spontaneously rather than through detailed prompting by the teachers. They therefore used language strategies meant to accomplish this goal. For example, they often questioned students indirectly, asking questions such as "What are some things that make a pendulum swing faster or slower?" rather than "Does a shorter pendulum swing faster?" They also deliberately withheld answers to questions to get students to come with the answers themselves, asking "What do *you* think?" rather than "The answer is . . . ". Edwards and Mercer found these strategies often did work. But sometimes they also backfired: some students tended to interpret the teachers' strategies not as a call to think for themselves but as a challenge to guess what the indirect, "secretive" teachers were really thinking. They became adept at discerning hints and gestures, a skill that Edwards and Mercer called **ritual knowledge,** rather than at stating their own thoughts, which the researchers called **principled knowing.**

Another researcher and educator, Michael Siegal, reviewed and extended research about the extent to which younger children actually demonstrate and display their knowledge to teachers and other adults (Siegal, 1991). Siegal and his associates organized a series of interviews with the children that focused on their knowledge—on how much they knew about number, for example, or about the nature of friendship. The researchers deliberately varied the wording and sequencing of their questions, however, both within individual interviews and across interviews with different children. The variations allowed them to clarify the full extent of children's knowledge better than could conventional, school-like interviews.

What Siegal and his associates found was either disquieting or mildly amusing, depending on whether you have direct responsibility for helping such children to learn. Often, it seemed, children deliberately *held back* the full extent of their knowledge, apparently out of respect for the teacher or other adult who interviewed them. If a question was repeated, for example, a child was likely to fall silent the second time, even if he obviously knew the answer in other situations, simply because he believed (correctly) that the adult had already heard him the first time! The result was that the child seemed less certain or knowledgeable than he

In Your Own Voice

Both holding back knowledge and offering too much knowledge (offering "non-knowledge") sound like problems for teachers.

Do you have any suggestions for how to determine when a student may be doing either of these?

really was. On the other hand, if a topic of an interview interested a child (for example, "Why do the clouds move?"), she was likely to give obvious or "cute" responses—ones that she did not really believe—simply to keep the conversation going. Once again the inappropriateness of the responses created the impression that the child knew less than she really knew.

What is important about these unintended effects is that they are not experienced equally by every child, class, or teacher. Some students *do* display their knowledge accurately and appropriately when asked, and some *do* realize that teachers want them not to guess at hints but to express their thinking forthrightly. But only some; diversity in students' responses to the "same" teaching behaviors poses a constant challenge to teachers, one that the teacher as instructional manager must constantly face. The dimensions of the challenge vary with the format and content of an activity as well as with the students. Consider a class discussion and students' various responses to it. But imagine that you are not teaching it but have the luxury of sitting at the side of the class and observing the activity fully. What might you see?

Mr. Seifert, the teacher, is leading the class in a discussion intended to check students' understanding of a homework assignment. He is asking questions in rapid-fire sequence, each one a miniature test of knowledge: "How do you do problem number 3?"; "What's the first step in problem number 4?"; and so on. Mr. Seifert obviously knows the answers to all the questions he is posing; they are meant only to assess students' knowledge.

Student A and student B love this sort of oral testing. Over and over their hands shoot up, vying for the floor and for a chance to show their knowledge to classmates and to Mr. Seifert. But student C and student D seem quiet, almost indifferent to the proceedings. When Mr. Seifert calls on them, they answer dutifully but quietly, almost mumbling their replies. Are they ill prepared? you wonder.

Are they quiet because they failed to do the homework, or do they simply dislike showing off their knowledge so publicly?

The homework discussion ends, and Mr. Seifert shifts to a new activity, an exploration of a novel students have been reading. He invites opinions about the novel—how individuals felt about the characters and the theme of the book, among other things. Suddenly student C comes to life, freely offering personal opinions about the book. But students A and B fall relatively silent. Student D remains silent, and in fact draws intricate doodles on his desk while the discussion proceeds. You ponder the meaning of the changes and of student D's behavior and continued silence. Is student D alienated from the class, lacking oral language skill, or what?

In Your Own Voice

The fact is that I failed to notice these changes in participation because I felt so busy actually teaching.

I am still looking for a way to help me see more as I work with students.

Any suggestions?

I'm thinking about asking students themselves, even the first-graders with whom I work, to evaluate my teaching periodically.

And why have students A and B, so eager before, now fallen silent?

Finally, Mr. Seifert moves the class into individual seatwork dealing with the novel. And behold: participation levels change again. Student D comes to life, but in an unobtrusive way; you see him helping first one, then another student with their work. Then you see him go to the teacher with a (quiet) question. Students B and C work independently too, but not as helpfully or diligently as student D. Student A does not: now you see her drawing cartoons and staring around the room rather than writing as she is supposed to be doing.

Even if the manager-teacher achieves efficient management of learning, the students respond variously, in effect building a diversity of relationships with the teacher. Some become "public speakers," some become "individual helpers," and some combine these roles or create still others (Florio-Ruane, 1989). Hopefully, in spite of the diversity, all the students still learn something useful from the tasks and activities that the teacher works so hard to organize. It is legitimate to question, though, whether the students really learn the same content by the end of the school year, no matter how much a teacher tries to cover "the" curriculum or to provide similar tasks to all. Differences in students' responses are just too large—and too inevitable.

You can, of course, note differences among students in the short term, while students still belong to your class. As instructional manager, you can deal with these differences by reorganizing remaining assignments and activities so as to guide students back toward common curricular outcomes. If you discover partway through the year that John needs more work in multiplication but Sarah needs more work in division, you can provide for these needs while you still have time with these students. But as a manager, some differences will be harder to provide for. What if you discover that Sarah is losing interest in all things mathematical? Will there be time to rejuvenate her interest before the end of the year? And how would you do that? These questions are important, but they are better addressed through other teaching roles, those of caring person or generous expert. As the educator Nel Noddings has argued, a deep-seated attitude of caring for students as people can replace the "problem" of covering and organizing the curriculum with a different challenge, one of respecting and developing students as individuals (Noddings, 1994).

In the role of caring person, the teacher focuses on individual students' interests, goals, and differences. For the moment, at least, curriculum requirements may take second priority.
©Joseph Schuyler/Stock Boston

The Teacher as Caring Person

Suppose that instead of beginning with the organizational challenges of teaching, you focus on the diversity among students. Your class is nothing if not diverse: several students speak English as a second language, and two live in foster homes. Your class includes three students who are especially articulate at speaking and writing, but also several who you believe will need extra help to make it through the usual curriculum. Five students have witnessed the divorce of their parents sometime in the past, and one lost his father last year to cancer. Several enjoy music and play an instrument; two like art and draw rather well; and six enjoy sports and participate on schoolwide teams after school. But you happen not to teach physical education, art, or music, nor are you a school counselor. You happen to teach mathematics.

The Students as the Starting Point

How could you respond to such diversity? As instructional manager, the teacher faces this problem as well, but more as a challenge in planning the curriculum than as a fact to be celebrated in itself. For each unusual quality or experience that a student brings to class, the manager-teacher wonders how it will affect the student's mastery of the curriculum. The impact on learning differs, of course, depending on the quality or experience in question: a parent's divorce may hinder a student's achievement, but a long-standing interest in art might well help, even sometimes with school subjects not directly related to art. From the point of view of the teacher as manager, therefore, diversity complicates the job of teaching by forcing the teacher to plan multiple methods to move students toward common curriculum goals. Students' individuality becomes a necessary evil: something to be overcome when possible and at least minimized or controlled when not.

But what if we stand this approach on its head? What if a teacher simply celebrates students' diversity rather than seeking to overcome it? This is what happens when the teacher takes on the role of *caring person*. In this role, the teacher takes students' uniqueness as vital to their learning (Elicker & Fortner-Wood, 1995). Compared to the role of instructional manager, the teacher as caring person makes less of a distinction between who students are as people and who they are as students. Consider Ms. Althouse:

Ms. Althouse stares at her grade sheet, thinking about each student in turn. Their grades on the latest test run the gamut from poor to excellent. The trouble is not really their grades, she thinks, but that so many students have priorities in life other than learning math. Only Micky and Jocelyn really "think like mathematicians": they tackle problems out of sheer joy! Ms. Althouse easily understands their motivation; she loves math too. That's why she became a math teacher.

For the others, though, it is a different story. There are kids like Larry or Melanie, kids who are doing OK, but mostly because they know they need the math credit to get into college. Theirs is a rather functional approach: learn what's expected but not more than expected.

Then there are Wendy and Jerry—real puzzles. These two hang out a lot in the art room; in fact, as Ms. Althouse found out recently, they are doing quite well in art. Some of their sketches were selected this year for a citywide student art show. But neither Wendy nor Jerry did well on the recent math test. Ms. Althouse wonders why; she suspects there are important things about these particular students that she does not know. Jerry seems simply indifferent—casual, careless about homework, uncaring in class. Wendy does not seem indifferent so much as fearful, even hostile, toward all things mathematical. Ms. Althouse has gone over homework with Wendy a couple of times, and each time it simply ended in angry tears. When she did the same with Jerry, he cooperated nicely, but later continued with his careless ways anyway.

Two important issues arise here. First, Professor Seifert raises a question for Ms. Althouse: "Knowing that most students have no intention of becoming professional mathematicians, should she respect and support their nonmathematical priorities or work to create an intrinsic love of mathematics . . . ?" The two goals are not completely incompatible. I would choose to make the first primary and show my respect for the nonmathematical talents of my students. But I would also teach in such a way that these students might, at least occasionally, enjoy math and understand why some people love it as they love, say, art. Working together, we would "get through" as much math as minimally required by the school's standards; but, more important, we would come to respect one another's interests and talents.

The second issue reflects a widespread misunderstanding of what it means to care. Some students, like Murray, do indeed protest that they don't want to be "cared for." But these students, like many of my professional colleagues (who also make such a protest), *do* want people to detect and respond positively to their preferences with respect to styles of human interaction. So they actually do want care! To respond as carer means exactly this: to receive the other and respond as nearly as one can (consistent with your own moral commitments) to what has been received. Caring cannot be done by recipe. It requires sensitivity, flexibility, and a continuing commitment to increase our competence in human relations.

Nel Noddings, Professor, Stanford University

Although Ms. Althouse may behave less like a curriculum manager at other times, right now she is acting more like someone who cares about her students as people. But the caring role creates dilemmas for her. Knowing that most students have no intention of becoming professional mathematicians, should she respect and support their nonmathematical priorities or work to create an intrinsic love of mathematics, one more like her own? Knowing that several students have not really learned the most recent unit in the course, should she forge ahead anyway, or will doing so indicate disrespect for students' other, nonmathematical priorities? No doubt there is more than one way to resolve these questions; in the accompanying "Multiple Voices," Nel Noddings, professor of education at Stanford University, offers her own way of doing so, and especially of dealing with individuals who profess *not* to want signs of care from their teacher.

In any case, Ms. Althouse recognizes a responsibility to the curriculum—to "cover it," or at least teach parts of it—but she also recognizes responsibilities to the students. First and foremost, she says to herself, they should become useful, trustworthy members of the community, even if they do not love math or do not learn all parts of it. Sure she has to organize individual and group activities, but she does so in the service of fostering students' development as individuals. The larger goal of personal development is what guides her, and management becomes a means to that goal.

Armed with her concern for her students, Ms. Althouse decides two things. First, she must allow—in fact, encourage—retests for Wendy and Jerry. One or two remedial worksheets won't do, she feels, because their initial poor grades will stick in their minds, turn them off from math, discourage motivation, and even impair their self-esteem. They must have a *bona fide* success to counteract this recent bad experience. Second, she must learn more about Wendy's and Jerry's interests. It won't do to coax them too hard into loving math; overdoing the persuasion may even show disrespect for their non-mathematical priorities. She must discover what they do want most of all from life and see if there is any way to support these priorities even if they seem a bit distant from high school mathematics.

She thinks: I am not trying to turn everyone into a career mathematician here. I am trying to educate future members of the community—create persons who respect one another for who they are and who can trust one another to offer support when needed. And finally, she thinks: communities actually need the diversity of my students, so perhaps it *is* best that only some of them become devoted mathematicians.

If there is something to be learned from Ms. Althouse, then, it is this: caring for students as people does not free you from the challenge of orchestrating worthwhile activities in spite of the students' diversity. What it does do is focus your response to the challenge differently.

Dual Purposes or Cross-Purposes? Authenticity and Community

The caring teacher's concern for students as whole, unique individuals can hardly be faulted: who would not care about students in this way? Surely all teachers—you and I included—want students to develop themselves as individuals, whatever their particular talents and interests. And surely, like Ms. Althouse, we want students to feel valued by and committed to their communities, whether the community consists of classroom, neighborhood, or society as a whole. These beliefs are intrinsic facets of the teacher acting as caring person: in this role, the teacher rewards individual diversity and models commitment to the classroom community.

When taken in isolation from other teaching roles, though, the caring role encounters certain practical and ethical problems. Consider the practical constraints: in a modern school, how fully can a teacher actually relate to students as individuals? Classes may be large, time is probably scarce, and administrative expectations may emphasize curriculum coverage more than concern for students as individuals. The circumstances of teaching, in other words, direct a teacher toward the concerns of instructional management, the coordination of tasks and individuals. As a practical matter, therefore, being a caring teacher may take conscious effort, and perhaps more effort than being the instructional manager described earlier. Yet many teachers do make the effort! Kindergarten teacher Vivian Paley, for example, has published several books vividly describing her careful observations of students as individuals, along with her tolerance of and (especially) enjoyment in supporting their differences (e.g., Paley, 1997). Another educator, David Hansen, has documented similar commitments among teachers of high school students, in spite of the much larger numbers of students usually associated with secondary teaching (Hansen, 1995). Paley, Hansen, and other, unpublished teachers show that the role of caring person can be enacted; and they suggest, through their examples, that it is worth the effort to do so.

But the role of caring person poses ethical problems as well. Suppose a student does not really want to be cared for; what then? Like Murray, described at the beginning of this chapter, some individuals may not really expect or want a teacher to know much about them personally; they may actually seek a businesslike relationship or even relative anonymity. Creating a personal relationship with such a student, if not done carefully, may seem like an invasion of privacy. Suppose, for example, that a teacher asks all students to write personal reactions to an assignment. What if some students regard their reactions as unacceptable for social or personal reasons? Maybe a story read for English class makes a student truly angry, or arouses her romantically, or simply impresses her as a stupid choice by the teacher. Can this student feel safe sharing those feelings honestly? As the teacher, it would be nice to think that students are, of course, free to say anything they truly think of an assignment. But imagine the problem from the students' point of view: can you, the person being graded, be *sure* in advance that you can say "just anything" about an assignment? Or would some discretion be advisable? If you feel even some degree of caution about self-expression, the teacher faces a problem: your silence could mean you are *either* fear-

In Your Own Voice

How about you: did you ever prefer a class because it let you be *not* well known?

I had one like that—physical education.

I liked "blending into" it because I never felt very good at sports.

ful or diplomatic. In the first case, the caring teacher has a responsibility to draw you out, to make you less fearful. In the second case, he or she may have a responsibility only to respect your view. Somehow the caring teacher must learn to distinguish these possibilities.

At its root, teaching as a caring person values two goals that can conflict if either is carried to the extreme. On the one hand, the caring person values **authenticity** (or sincerity and integrity), self-expression, and the development of students' unique talents and interests. On the other hand, she or he values **community,** a civil and respectful concern for others. Most of the time these two values can co-exist, but a problem can arise if authentic self-expression leads to self-centeredness, to neglecting the needs of the student's community. A kindergarten child may refuse to share access to the classroom computer because he genuinely prefers using the computer by himself and learns more from it when he alone has full access. Or a high school student may resist sharing "her" girlfriend with the friend's new boyfriend; having the girlfriend solely for herself may feel, and in fact be, more fulfilling than sharing her. Or a junior high student may genuinely ("authentically") dislike most things mathematical, not necessarily unthinkingly but because he correctly senses that time given to mathematical activities means time taken away from other, truer interests. The intuition colors his attitude toward math classes, math teachers, and mathematically inclined students. How much should a caring teacher tolerate this sort of "uniqueness"? However authentic or well thought out the student's dislike of mathematics, a teacher may have to limit some expressions of personal development to protect the interests of the class as a community. Perhaps sarcastic remarks about math and math teachers will not be tolerated, for example, nor will skipping a math class even if other worthy activities take its place.

In Your Own Voice

One reviewer objected to this example, arguing that the teacher should simply *create* interest in math for students who lack it, that "respecting lack of interest" is equivalent to shirking responsibility as a teacher.

Do you agree?

When, if ever, should a teacher make peace with students' priorities rather than try to change them?

The Teacher as Generous Expert

It seems that teachers must not care for students' individuality so much that they neglect other major purposes of education, such as students' need for orderly activities or society's need for students with particular knowledge and skills. The role discussed earlier—the teacher as manager—helps to ensure that predictability and order. But still another role is needed to safeguard society's need for particular knowledge and skills. That role might be called the *generous expert:* the free sharing of key, valued knowledge with students to help them grow in expertise themselves. Compared to that of caring person, the role of generous expert

As a generous expert, the teacher shares his or her knowledge and enthusiasm freely. The focus is on the content, at least for the moment.
©Elizabeth Crews

more openly assumes an intellectual gap between teacher and student, with the teacher acknowledged as veteran and mentor on the one hand and the student seen as novice or protégé on the other. But the gap is not meant to be permanent. The generous expert works to overcome it. The next section looks at how this happens.

In spite of the importance of student diversity, it may be possible to be too concerned about it. Of course, students differ from one another, sometimes dramatically. But some differences may matter to teaching and learning more than others. If you teach science, for example, it may matter that one student has impaired hearing but another does not; this difference can affect how you teach as well as how the students learn. But is it important that one student has four siblings but another has only one? Perhaps this difference does affect how the students learn, but the reasons for the connection are neither obvious nor straightforward.

Expertise: Knowledge *and* Thinking

Rightly or wrongly, this line of thinking leads some educators to focus their efforts on the one dimension that is truly unique to educators: knowledge and comprehension of subject matter (Adler, 1984; Hirsch, 1996). When teachers adopt this stance, students become not so much diverse as unequal; some simply know or understand more than others. But they are unequal only along one specific dimension, one of knowledge or cognitive skill. In other respects, even to the generous expert, students may be quite equal: they may be equal in deserving common, friendly courtesy, for example. In still other respects, students may be unequal, but in ways quite different from their cognitive differences: individuals who are socially adept, for example, may not be the same ones who are academically adept (Haggerty, 1995). The teacher's job becomes one of sharing his or her knowledge and skill as helpfully as possible so that students can become more equal among themselves and more equal to the current resident expert, the teacher.

Even though this role means the teacher thinks and acts like an expert, it does not necessarily mean the teacher should rely on lecturing or other "full frontal" methods stereotypically associated with the sharing of expertise. That is because **expertise,** when properly understood, consists of knowing not only content but also *how* experts usually think about content. The expert science teacher not only knows scientific concepts and theories but knows how scientists develop these concepts and how they use them. The expert physical education teacher knows not only how various sports and activities can be played and used but also what the sports and activities were intended for when they were created and how they can be developed further in the future. And the expert primary-grade teacher, like Carolyn Eaton in the following example, not only can read well herself but knows how a child thinks when the child is learning to read fluently.

Joey is having a reading conference with his first-grade teacher, Carolyn Eaton. They are reading a book "together," except that Ms. Eaton wants Joey to read himself as much as possible. Joey's comments are in capitals, and Ms. Eaton's are in lowercase.

FIRST YOU READ—THEN ME. THIS IS WHAT YOU HAVE TO DO. I READ AFTER YOU; OK?

OK. [Ms. Eaton begins.] "In the great green room there was a telephone, a red balloon, and a picture of . . ." Are you going to read, or what?

YES.

"In the great green room there was . . ." Are you ready yet? Ready to read?

OK. "IN THE GREAT GREEN ROOM . . ."

"there was . . ."

"THERE WAS A . . ." [pauses, looking at Ms. Eaton rather than at the words]

"a telephone . . ."

YES, THAT'S IT, A TELEPHONE! "IN THE GREAT GREEN ROOM THERE WAS A TELEPHONE, A RED BALLOON, . . ."

"and a picture of . . ."

"AND A PICTURE OF [pauses, staring at the wall] . . . A COW JUMPING"?

"a cow jumping over the moon."

"OVER MOON." [Smiles from both Joey and Ms. Eaton]

Joey, what does this say? [Points to the word *telephone*]

"THERE WAS A TELEPHONE."

How about here? [Points to next page, which reads "And there were three little bears, sitting on chairs"]

"THERE WERE BEARS, THREE BEARS, AND THEY SAT ON THE CHAIRS."

Can you read this whole book?

SURE!

OK, then you start this time.

[Joey looks at first page, alternately at the picture and at the words]

"IN THE GREAT GREEN ROOM THERE WAS A TELEPHONE."

[Actual text: "In the great green room, there was a telephone,"]

"AND THERE WAS A RED BALLOON,"

[Actual text: ". . . and a red balloon,"]

"AND A PICTURE OF THE COW JUMPING OVER THE MOON."

[Actual text: ". . . and a picture of the cow jumping over the moon."]

"AND THERE WERE . . ." THREE BEARS? . . . "LITTLE BEARS SITTING ON CHAIRS."

[Actual text: "And there were three little bears, sitting on chairs, . . ."]

Could you read this book with your eyes closed?

SURE; WANT TO SEE ME DO IT?

Well, not right now; maybe another time. Could you read it without the pictures, just looking at the words? That's how I do best—when I see the words instead of the pictures.

[Joey pauses to consider this.] MAYBE, BUT NOT QUITE SO WELL.

Let's try it. [She proceeds to copy the words on a large sheet for Joey to "read" later.]

Compared to Joey, Carolyn Eaton is an expert reader. But her expertise includes knowing *how* reading occurs, and in particular how it develops in someone just beginning to read (Strauss, 1993). Judging by her questions, Ms. Eaton knows that "reading" takes many forms. It can involve making inferences from pictures, for example, as she implies by asking, "Could you read this story without the pictures?" And she knows that reading involves memory—remembering words or ideas that are likely to come next, as implied by asking, "Could you read this story with your eyes closed?"

Generosity as Access to Expertise

Furthermore, Ms. Eaton is generous with her expertise. For one thing, she shares her skills with Joey freely ("Maybe you don't need the pictures to read it") so that he, too, can become more aware of how he reads. For another, she suggests to Joey a concrete step ("Let's try reading it without pictures"), one that will move Joey a bit closer to becoming an expert reader like Ms. Eaton. Of course, she may discover that this move does not help; perhaps Joey is at a point where pictures stimulate his verbal decoding skills rather than distract from them. In that case, in an equally generous spirit, she will have to backtrack from her first suggestion and encourage Joey to use the pictures more rather than less. In any case, without acting and reacting in a generous way, her relationship with Joey would be cool rather than helpful and emotionally distant rather than educative.

To be effective, a generous expert also has to show his or her own ways of thinking and learning freely and clearly, even while they are occurring. Carolyn Eaton does this with Joey when she mentions how she prefers to read ("That's how I do best [looking at the words]"). But there are many other ways for teachers to demonstrate how they think and learn. In art class, students need not only to see good paintings but also to see how the teacher might create a painting himself, step by step. In science class, they should see not only the results of important scientific experiments but also the way the teacher might devise and conduct them. In literature, they need not only to read finished, publishable essays but also to see the early drafts of essays and hear the authors' thinking that leads to final copies (Seixas, 1993). In general, students should see you thinking, not just knowing; witness skillful reflection, not merely the results of reflection.

Obstacles to Expertise, Obstacles to Generosity

As you might suspect, a relationship based on expertise can also pose problems. For one thing, you may not really be an expert in every field in which you are supposed to teach. The problem is frustratingly familiar if you are a new high school teacher: you majored in, say, history in college, but on your first job you end up teaching only four of your six classes in this field, the other two being English and driver education. The same story goes if you are an experienced high school teacher, but

In Your Own Voice

I'm making it sound like it is necessary to "be an expert" in order to teach a subject.

But is it?

And if you do teach something you are unfamiliar with, can you still be a "generous expert," or do you take on some other kind of role?

with a variation: for years you have taught biology and chemistry, but this particular year you have to "cover" a math section for the regular math teacher, who is on temporary leave. If you happen to teach elementary school, these challenges may not be so formidable, but nonetheless you may have to cope with certain topics or subjects (math? music?) that feel alien to you. In all of these situations, you scramble to get organized and perhaps rely heavily on advice from other teachers as well as from textbooks and curriculum guides. Privately—and with some justification—you do not feel like an "expert." The role of generous expert does not fit as perfectly as it should.

For another thing, you may not always be recognized for the expertise you really do have. This problem is especially likely whenever a teacher does not fit students' preconceptions about the sort of person they "should" have as their teacher. The woman teaching algebra in a class dominated by somewhat "macho" boys, the African American teacher starting work in an all-white, racially prejudiced school, the male kindergarten teacher—each may know his or her field and seek to share it with students. But if colleagues, parents, and students do not help them do so, they may experience more frustration than they deserve.

Problems can occur with this role even for practical reasons, just as they do with the roles of instructional manager and caring person. Classes may be too large, too numerous, or too short to allow intelligent, thoughtful contacts with students. Normal pressures to follow an official curriculum may lead you to "cover" too much material, or focus too much on the convenience of teaching facts and answers and not enough on how to construct ideas (Wineburg, 1991). Like relationships based on managing and on nurturing students, therefore, relationships based on expert-novice differences cannot work for all possible situations or all purposes. This is unfortunate when it happens, but (ironically) it may not be all bad: research finds that teachers are often respected *more* if they play down their special expertise (Welker, 1991)! Being "just a regular person" can help, at least some of the time:

FRANK: I like my history teacher because she seems normal, natural—not like she's lording her knowledge over you.

KARLA: Well, he tells jokes. He's not "all math." He figures out what I'm doing wrong with the problem sets, but he's not all math.

LAURA: She listens to what you say. Knows me, even among all her students.

LAURA'S MOTHER: At the parent conference, I could tell that she liked her students. It wasn't all curriculum that she talked about. You could tell that she knew her stuff, had being teaching awhile. But she also knew her students as people.

Teachers' knowledge matters to these students and to the parent, but teachers' humanity seems to matter just as much or more. The implication? Be an expert, but be a person, too.

Common Ground: Active Learning

*W*HEN done well, the teacher-student relationships described in this chapter all serve a common purpose: fostering students' active efforts to learn. When a teacher takes on the role of caring person, for example, he or she deliberately recognizes and supports a range of choices by students, as well as a range of students' values, priorities, and activities. In this sense, the teacher as caring person is a constructivist, someone who believes that students create or "construct" their own learning rather than that they absorb ideas, facts, and skills passively.

But a focus on constructive learning also exists in other forms of teacher-student relationships, although teachers and students express the focus differently. As instructional manager, the teacher strives for a classroom in which students can learn without conflicts, confusion, or distractions, and in which students may take different pathways in learning a common curriculum. This approach focuses on challenges of organization and management because meeting these challenges enables students to learn in a crowded place, the classroom. Once again, as with the other teaching roles, it is students, not the teacher, who must ultimately make sense of assigned readings and practice needed skills. The teacher does not learn *for* the students. In this sense, the teacher supports constructivism, supports the belief that students create knowledge for themselves.

As a generous expert, the teacher is a constructivist in yet another sense. The generous expert's goal is not only to share knowledge with students but also to share knowledge of *how* expertise is created. When successful, this role makes students' active learning more possible by showing the way toward greater knowledge and competence: it models how others have already become competent. This sort of support is more focused, however, than the support of the teacher as caring person because it focuses on activities in which the teacher feels truly skillful—usually the official curriculum of a subject or of a grade level. The gen-

In Your Own Voice

To teach well, you will have to perform *all* of these roles—manager, caring person, expert—to some extent.

But even so, you may prefer one role over another.

Which would you prefer to emphasize?

And how would your preference affect your success with the other roles?

erous expert also expresses support differently than the teacher as instructional manager: unlike the manager, the generous expert involves himself or herself more actively in students' intellectual lives, noticing and commenting on their actual thinking and modeling reflective thinking as well. It is there, in students' intellectual lives, that the generous expert can offer help most effectively.

The common ground in constructivism offers a preliminary answer to a basic question posed in the first chapter of this book: "What is teaching?" The constructive quality of all teaching roles suggests two responses: first, the thing called *teaching* is any activity that encourages self-constructed learning; second, the thing called *teaching* can take a multitude of forms. No matter how diverse teachers and classrooms may seem to you, then, the successful ones are linked by engaging students' thinking and respecting their immense diversity. Typically, therefore, the successful teacher adopts and combines several roles—being something of a manager, a caring person, and an expert, either all at once or by turns. The precise combination, though, is largely a matter to be decided by individual teachers, including yourself.

Personal Metaphors for Teaching

WHAT kind of teacher-student relationship do you seek with your own students? As I have indicated, your relationship need not be one of the three described so far; you do not have to be *either* a manager *or* a caring person *or* a generous expert. These descriptions are really only metaphors, or implied comparisons between teachers and other types of people. As metaphors, they clarify some complexities about teaching while glossing over others. In your own relationships with students, therefore, you may find yourself combining these roles or creating new ones altogether. Perhaps you may find it better to construct your relationships flexibly, using any one role only for certain students or certain activities. Some educators have in effect argued for this sort of variety. The National Association for the Education of Young Children, for example, explicitly advocates a rather nurturing role for teachers of preschool, kindergarten, and primary classrooms (Bredekamp & Copple, 1997); their ideal teacher would emphasize what I have been calling the teacher as caring person, though not to the exclusion of the other roles. Educators concerned about college teaching and adult education, on the other hand, more often urge college instructors toward expert-novice relationships with students (see, for example,

In Your Own Voice

Many educators have also argued that which roles are appropriate depends on which subject you teach—that math teachers, for instance, should relate to students differently than English teachers (Shulman & Quinlan, 1996).

What do you think of this possibility?

Halpern, 1994). Still others have recommended that teachers vary their relationships depending on the subject or skill being taught and learned; maybe learning to read calls for an expert or a manager, for example, whereas developing oral language skill calls for a broadly caring person (Geary, 1995).

Whatever you think about these adjustments in teaching roles, you will eventually have to make choices about the relationships you personally consider appropriate between you and your students. One way to make effective choices is to depart deliberately and significantly from the metaphors—manager, caring person, expert—offered in this chapter. Try, at least for a start, to develop a metaphor that seems unique to you and to your aspirations as a teacher. That is what Connie Mandrich did. She saw herself as neither a manager, a caring person, nor an expert, but as a *translator* among languages or ways of thinking:

Professional Log for Connie Mandrich, Grade 6 Teacher

OCTOBER 19: Seems like I spent a lot of time this week explaining things in the science book. Like I'm a translator for the United Nations! The text speaks one language and the students speak another, or really several others. My job is to capture the spirit of the text and express it in other terms, terms that the kids actually use. Seems like I'm building bridges between content and kids. Except that real bridges just sit there, and I'm always active, always racing to keep up!

NOVEMBER 6: "Translator"—I still like that idea, but I realized today that I have to translate between more than content and students. There are times when I also translate among individuals. Seems like they talk past each other. They don't speak each other's language, even when we are all supposedly conversing in English. The cooperative work teams that I set up are the problem. Last week David said he would go to the library "soon" to get the reference books that his group needed, but his idea of "soon" apparently wasn't the same as his partners'. And his idea of "reference" books turned out to be wrong for Jill [in his group]. She wanted articles with less written detail and more pictures so that they could photocopy pictures to include in the report.

She got pretty cross because he "did it wrong." David was bewildered by her response. I had to mediate: explain that "soon" can mean different things, that "reference books" can mean different things, etc. There I was again, *translating* between students to avoid miscommunication.

JANUARY 20: Maybe me as "translator" isn't really right after all. Lately the problem is this: The more I work with the kids on math, the more it seems like I need to depart from the text, at least for some of them, just because they are missing key concepts from earlier in the curriculum. But that's not what translators do! I'm actually a composer—designing ideas and activities about math, at least for the kids who need extra help. Maybe I'm a translator for some but a composer for others. (Question for myself: I wonder who *else* I might be, and what I may become?)

Connie's metaphor of translator evolved over time, and in the end it worked only with some of her students. She is not unusual in developing a unique image of her relationships or in changing her metaphors over time. Educators Robert Bullough and David Stokes explored how first-year teachers thought of their work, and discovered a wide variety of images or metaphors (Bullough & Stokes, 1994). One teacher, upon reflection, described herself as a *nurturer,* another as a *problem fixer,* and still another as a *guide.* Several described themselves as surrogate *father* or *mother.* A relatively popular metaphor, especially for teachers at the secondary level, was one described in this chapter, the teacher as *expert.* But Bullough and Stokes also found that these metaphors did not remain fixed. As first-year teachers gained experience, new insights—and frustrations—about teaching led to revisions in their roles, usually in the direction of increasing complexity.

Whatever metaphorical description you adopt, the metaphor serves two purposes at once: it helps you to make sense of your work and your students, and it guides your actions in the classroom. You can sense these functions not only in Connie's comments above but also in the following comments from Tracey Wheeler, even though she chooses a different metaphor than Connie's. Tracey is a special-needs teacher in an elementary school:

KELVIN SEIFERT: So how do you like your new class, the one for children with attention deficit problems?

TRACEY WHEELER: Love it! But you know what? It's made me think about my teaching differently. Before, when I was doing a kindergarten class, I used to think that supporting students' choices was what mattered the most. Learning centers were a big deal! I would float from one center to another, one kid to another, offering help and coaxing individuals to make good choices, good use of time. I felt like a broker, offering options to "buy into" activities.

KELVIN: And now?

TRACEY: These overactive kids turned that idea upside down. These kids also like choices, and I still try to offer them. But I have to be awfully clear about exactly what they can choose. I'm framing choices a lot more explicitly: "You can do X or Y," not "You can do X or Y or Z or W or whatever." It helps, too, to keep the daily routine very predictable; we vary it a lot less in this

class than when I was teaching kindergarten. And I find myself making written "contracts" with individuals to get certain work done, just because they seem to like that! It's like I'm mainly a planner now, a master planner.

In a way, Tracey's newest metaphor for her teaching, master planner, was actually chosen by her latest students, and only by herself. They, not she, needed an instructional planner more than the classroom broker of her earlier kindergarten class. By seeing her role in this new way, Tracey and her students all benefited. Tracey felt more in touch with her students and could continue to think of herself as every bit as competent as she had been when teaching kindergarten. Her new students received the kind of teaching they needed. In the end, Tracey revised an important preconception that she had developed previously: choices matter, she now believed, but sometimes choices need to be framed clearly. Armed with this new belief, Tracey was able to teach her new class effectively, in spite of its unique needs.

More generally, Tracey's experience suggests again that teaching roles usually combine the activities of actual teachers. Whether she calls herself a broker or a master planner, Tracey always organizes and manages learning activities; she always cares about her students as individuals; and she always shares her knowledge with them freely. In other words, she is simultaneously an instructional manager, a caring person, and a generous expert, and probably plays other roles as well. Her skill comes from combining and varying the roles effectively, and her satisfaction comes from seeing students learn as a result.

Chapter Re-View: What Teachers Do This Chapter Re-View suggests directions in which the chapter might have taken your thinking—though, of course, other directions are also possible. It expands the Chapter View, which suggests a starting point, conceptually, for the chapter. But this Re-View does not suggest an ending point. Like the Chapter View, it represents just one perspective among many.

Key Terms and Concepts

role (136)
instructional manager (137)
caring person (137)

generous expert (137)
ritual knowledge (141)
principled knowing (141)

authenticity (149)
community (149)
expertise (151)

Annotated Readings

Bullough, R., Knowles, G., & Crow, N. (1992). *Emerging as a teacher.* London: Routledge. Robert Bullough and his colleagues have explored how teachers use personal metaphors to understand and guide their work. They have paid special attention to beginning teachers and teachers in training, and why those teachers sometimes shift from one metaphor to another as they gain experience.

Noddings, Nel. (1994). *The challenge to care in schools.* New York: Teachers College Press. One of the best explorations of the role of teacher as caring person. Noddings considers many implications of the role and discusses many objections to it. I find her conclusions quite persuasive, but not everyone does.

Sheull, Thomas. (1996). Teaching and learning in a classroom context. In D. Berliner & R. Calfee (Eds.), *Handbook of educational psychology* (pp. 726–764). New York: Macmillan. This is a chapter describing research on the various roles of teachers and students, including roles much like the ones discussed in this chapter. It is part of a larger volume summarizing research on many aspects of teaching and learning as seen from a psychological point of view. It is challenging reading at times, but clear and extremely thorough.

Internet Resources

<www.teachers.net> This sizable web site emphasizes discussion among teachers and provides lesson plans and other information tailored to different types of students and different approaches to teaching. You can join a "chatboard" (no charge) tailored to the level or kind of teaching you do; there's even one for substitute teachers.

<www.gsh.com> This web site, which calls itself the "Global Schoolhouse," supports teachers' needs for information and curriculum materials. It includes several discussion group "threads" on topics related to using technology (i.e., computers and the Internet) in the classroom. The site is sponsored by Microsoft Corporation (a prominent maker of computer software), so it leans strongly in favor of heavy use of technology.

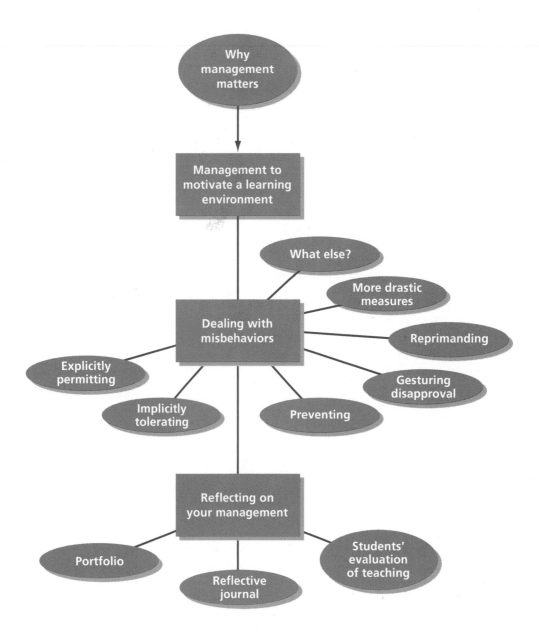

Chapter View: Motivating and Managing Your Class This Chapter View is a concept map that indicates one among many ways of thinking about the chapter. It suggests a starting point, conceptually, for the chapter but is incomplete by itself. At the end of the chapter is a Chapter Re-View, which expands on the Chapter View, suggesting directions for taking your thinking further—though, of course, other directions are also possible.

6

Motivating and Managing Your Class

The last chapter paid little attention to the immediate concerns of daily teaching. It is well and good to think in terms of metaphors and roles of teaching, as we did in Chapter 5, but what about questions that are more immediately pressing, such as these?

- Will students really follow my instructions?
- Can I possibly know enough about my subject area(s) to devise engaging activities?
- What if a student deliberately misbehaves?
- How strict should I be with *this* student *this* time?
- How do I deal with the differences in students' commitment—differences between Joe and Sara, or between Sara and Anne?

These questions raise issues about **motivation** and **classroom management.** The first term refers to rousing and guiding students' interests, and the second term refers to the techniques for maintaining a positive, productive learning environment. Both activities include planning, organizing, and coordinating activities, supporting students' initiatives where possible, and modifying and preventing negative behaviors where necessary. Management also includes the coordination or "orchestration" of techniques; a teacher's poorly timed action can be as ineffective as a poorly chosen one.

Motivation and management can be especially troubling to new and prospective teachers, though it remains an issue for veterans as well. It can be particularly worrisome because classroom life is not fully under a teacher's control. Events depend not only on your own actions but also on certain responses to your actions from students as well. How strict to be with a class, for example, depends in good measure on students' behavior, not just on yours. It may also depend on the standards of your school and community, as well as on the ages and personalities of your particular students. Yet in spite of these complicating factors, you are supposed to keep control, at the same time that you inspire students to learn. No wonder management matters to teachers, and no wonder it can be difficult to motivate—to energize—some students. In this chapter, I explore both challenges. I begin with the challenge of management, though as you will see, this topic soon leads to issues about motivation.

Why Management Matters

As various educators have pointed out, there are important reasons for teachers' concerns about management (Doyle, 1986; Zabel & Zabel, 1996). First, a lot happens in classrooms at once. In a mathematics class, for example, students may seem to be doing the "same" task, an assigned set of problems. In reality, though, they are doing many different tasks. Several are stuck on a particularly hard problem, but each for a different reason; several others completed only one problem before beginning to daydream or talk quietly with a classmate; a few may have finished and are wondering what to do next. At any one moment, therefore, each student needs something different—different information, different hints, different forms of encouragement—to use his or her time well. So much for students doing the "same" task! Obviously, too, if the teacher deliberately arranges multiple, overlapping tasks, students' diversity broadens still more.

Second, no matter how perceptive or experienced, a teacher can never predict everything that is going to happen. Lessons that take a lot of preparation may fall flat, but unplanned moments may sometimes lead to positive learning experiences. A student who you thought would enjoy a certain activity seems bored instead. Unexpected interruptions occur: a fire drill, a visiting administrator, a call on the intercom from the office are all in a day's work. Class discussions move off in unexpected directions in spite of planning the topics in advance. And so on. Days of-

In Your Own Voice

In spite of my comments here, some teachers do *not* seem preoccupied with classroom management!

Why do you think this is so?

The most important part of managing a class consists of creating a positive, motivating learning environment—like the kind experienced by these middle-school students in doing a science experiment.
©Paul S. Conklin

ten end differently from how they began, and differently from how you expected.

Third, classroom actions and reactions are public events, a feature that contributes to unpredictability. Students notice, for example, if a classmate makes a remark that is rude, sexist, or racist. And they watch how a teacher responds, or whether the teacher even notices the remark at all. They also notice whether a teacher treats all students equitably: is one student allowed to turn homework in late, but not another student? Does the teacher call on one student for discussion contributions more than on another? No matter how well intended a teacher's actions, they are often subject to multiple interpretations in classroom settings. What seems like welcome firmness to one student may strike another as harsh strictness.

Fourth, a teacher and students see each other so frequently that they develop a history in common, a collective memory of where they have come from and where they are headed in the time remaining. As the school year progresses, the emerging common history can both help and hurt the teacher's efforts. Part of the history can be agreed-on standards for how to behave in class: how to work cooperatively with classmates, for example, or when to ask for help. But part of it can be memories of undesirable events or difficult relationships: unforgiving memories of an explosive incident between two students or a grudge between two students that lasts for months.

In Your Own Voice

Think back to one of your own classes that went *very* well.

What accounted for its success?

What did the teacher do specifically to make it go smoothly?

Fifth, management becomes a problem because fundamentally classrooms are not voluntary settings. Many students enjoy coming to school, but not all. And some enjoy school only because teachers have worked hard to make school pleasant. But since the law and social customs ensure that all students come anyway, you cannot be sure of students' motivations in advance; you have to earn their commitment. Fortunately, it is possible to do so.

Management as a Way to Motivate Learning

*I*N spite of these features of classroom life, it is still possible to manage a class well—so well, in fact, that "management" becomes a way of motivating learning, rather than correcting misbehavior. You can do more than simply survive unexpected stresses, even when relatively new to teaching. The key is to begin not by focusing directly on students' misbehaviors but on building a learning environment that simultaneously encourages learning and diversity among students (Freiberg & Driscoll, 1996). As I will indicate later, this does not mean you will have no need to respond to misbehaviors and disruptions. It means only that your starting point in managing a class should be elsewhere—with what students can and do learn rather than with how their actions might interfere with learning. In making this change of focus, you come closer to motivating students, rather than simply controlling or correcting them.

For simplicity, think of management as a cycle of three basic activities. The first is *planning,* the creation beforehand of detailed methods or procedures for classroom tasks and activities. The second is *self-assessment* of teaching, an estimation of the significance or value of plans after a teacher has carried them out. The third is *revision,* the modification of plans as a result of self-assessment of teaching. In practice, these activities often overlap and lead teachers through extended periods in which the teaching and learning of large units or sections of a curriculum are gradually perfected. In the process of improving the teaching of a unit, students gradually learn more effectively or efficiently; but more to the point for this chapter, they also experience a more effectively managed class.

Figure 6.1 outlines this rather general model of management. To begin seeing what it means in practice and how it overlaps with motivating

FIGURE 6.1

The Cycle of Classroom Management

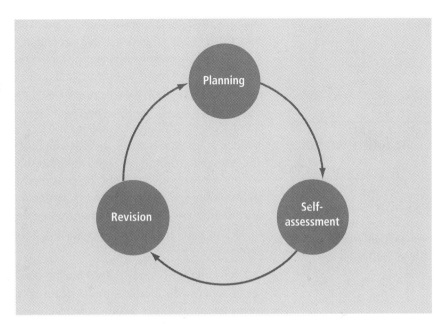

students, it helps to see how one particular teacher planned, assessed, and revised her own teaching and, in the process, experienced improvements in both students' learning and their classroom behavior. Barbara Fuller begins by planning a unit on community helpers.

Barbara Fuller, Classroom Manager

Scene 1: Good Intentions

It is late August.

Barbara Fuller, third-grade teacher, peers about her classroom, wondering how she will organize her program for the coming year. She has heard about cooperative learning—getting students to work together toward common goals—as a good way to create a productive environment. Ms. Fuller would like to try cooperative learning for a social studies unit this year, the one on community helpers that she is calling "How many people does it take to raise a child?" Students are supposed to explore how people outside the family contribute to the welfare of infants and children. Ms. Fuller hopes that by working in groups on this project, students can pool research, share ideas and interpretations, and make effective presentations as a group.

Ms. Fuller has read some very specific literature about how to get started with cooperative learning. One book (Johnson & Johnson, 1989) advises, for example, that she assign students to small work groups rather than let them select their own coworkers; this procedure is supposed to ensure that all students will belong to a group and none will be left out. Since assigning members would bring together relative strangers, however, groups will immediately need a task to make them begin feeling like a group. Perhaps they should begin by choosing a leader, and also a group name.

Ms. Fuller considers this advice carefully. She isn't sure whether assigning students to groups is wise; she has taught elementary school for five years, and something about assigned membership feels odd. She asks another teacher for his opinion about the practice; "It will probably work," he says. So Ms. Fuller sets aside her doubts: her colleague's opinion, plus the weight of authority of educational literature, suggests she should try it. She will assign groups, tell them to begin selecting a leader and a name, and see what happens.

Even though this scene does not involve immediate misbehaviors, it is really where Ms. Fuller should begin to deal with classroom management. She is thinking about how to ensure that students *can* learn: how to create a learning environment for the class as a whole. A time may come later (and in fact does come) when Ms. Fuller also has to deal with individual students' responses to the environment. Her actions at that time will also be part of her classroom management. But at this stage her challenge is an entirely positive one, a challenge to ensure learning—or motivate students—rather than eliminate disruptions to learning. Note that in planning she reflects on her purposes, and her reflections take deliberate effort that involves others. Ms. Fuller talks with a colleague before acting and also "consults" with educational research that she has read.

Of course, her planning might proceed differently if she had students of a different grade level, taught a different unit or course, or held different priorities for her teaching. If they were senior high students, for example, and relatively experienced with group work, she might concern herself less with how to constitute the groups and allow the students more leeway to choose and develop teams on their own. If she were teaching music, on the other hand, and if the students were supposed to perform together as a group, she might devote more attention to group membership to ensure that students within each group possessed roughly equal musical skills. If a group activity were a small part of her overall program, she might be less concerned about group membership; if the activity were a major part of the program, she might be more concerned. And so on. Barbara Fuller's particular approach to planning is not neces-

In Your Own Voice

Suppose you were in Ms. Fuller's place.

What other experiences, conversations, or reading would help prepare *you* for a cooperative learning project such as this?

sarily appropriate for other teachers' circumstances, though it is also not necessarily *in*appropriate for other teachers.

Once class begins, Ms. Fuller's focus will shift to the kaleidoscope of students' actions and responses. The pace will quicken and her decisions will become more fluid; her goal, however, will still be to provide an environment that supports learning. Because events in class will unfold rapidly, she will muster three skills as fully as possible: withitness, group focusing, and smoothness. These three terms were coined almost three decades ago by an educational psychologist, Arthur Kounin, and have been used widely by others since then (Kounin, 1970). **Withitness** is the ability to be aware of everything that is happening at once: to know that two students are talking on the far side of the room, for example, even while you are busy with a third student nearby. **Group focusing** is the ability to involve everyone in activities, leaving no one out: for example, to find a useful activity for students who finish their assigned work early. **Smoothness** is the ability to make clear and well-timed transitions between activities: to announce the end of an activity clearly so that everyone hears the announcement, for example, and proceed without delay to the new activity. (Table 6.1 summarizes these terms with examples.) In practice, being perfectly withit, group focused, and smooth about transitions are ideals, not skills that Barbara, or any other teacher, can perform flawlessly on every occasion. There is always more going on during class than any human being can keep up with! But Ms. Fuller will do her best and try not to fret unduly if her handling of the actual class session has some rough edges.

Scene 2: The Cooperative Groups Don't Necessarily Cooperate

Two weeks into the semester, Ms. Fuller announces the new unit on community helpers and the fact that it will depend on learning groups. She describes the purposes and advantages of working in groups: students can help one another, read more widely, and enjoy one another's company.

She tells them that to make membership fair, she herself will choose who is in each group. Both cheers and groans erupt as she reads the names.

"Ms. Fuller," says Tom, "I'm the only boy in my group."

"You'll be fine," she says. "If you look around, you'll see that everyone is with people they don't know terribly well." Tom scowls but remains silent. Chattering begins as she gets to the end of the list; the students are not listening well. But off they go to their groups, with instructions to choose a leader, a name, and, if possible, to begin work. Ms. Fuller is nervous about how things have started. "Should I be doing this?" she wonders. "Is it wise to

TABLE 6.1 Skills That Make Disruptions During Class Unlikely

Management Skill	Definition	Example
Withitness	Being aware of everything happening in the classroom	Talking with one reading group while attending simultaneously to ("keeping an eye on") other reading groups
Group focusing	Involving everyone in the class or everyone in a group	In leading a group discussion, deliberately calling on, and inviting contributions from, all members
Smoothness	Making transitions clear and well timed; in some cases, deliberately overlapping activities to achieve this goal	Warning students that an activity will end after a certain number of minutes; beginning the actual transition decisively; allowing one group to work a bit longer to assist another to finish promptly

Source: Based on Kounin (1970).

In Your Own Voice

Suppose Ms. Fuller had allowed self-choice of group members.

Could she have avoided these problems?

And even if she had, would other management problems have occurred instead?

put Tom entirely with girls?" But she lets events unfold, watching each group as she circulates around the room and straightens papers at her desk.

Before long, she notices that each group is developing its own character. In the first group (which Ms. Fuller dubbed "Group 1"), Jasmine takes over almost immediately; everyone seems to agree that she should be the leader. Unfortunately, Jasmine is not pleased to have this role: she reluctantly issues orders ("Kyla, you look up about nurses"), to which her group happily agrees. Jasmine's face looks a bit pained. In Group 2, Ken and Serge begin conferring about the project, ignoring the girls in the group. Ken and Serge apparently are already friends (in spite of Ms. Fuller's intention to split up friends) and seem content to proceed with all of the work themselves. The others draw doodles in their notebooks, chat quietly, or appear to daydream. In the third group, Ms. Fuller can hear voices periodically rising in anger. She can't hear all they are saying, but it seems to involve Jennifer and Sean, and possibly also Lavar. The other two group members are sitting quietly, simply observing the argument.

What to do? Ms. Fuller asks herself. Too many students are not involved. Several are focusing on power issues—who will be the leader—instead of beginning on the task. Should she step in, and when or with whom? Ms. Fuller is momentarily distracted by Jasmine, reluctant leader of Group 1, who comes up to ask a few questions about requirements for the assignment. But even while she answers Jasmine, Ms. Fuller keeps an eye on the other groups, especially the one where anger seems to be rising.

Ms. Fuller strives for withitness and succeeds to a large extent; she is aware of the variety of behaviors and reactions going on in the class, even when Jasmine distracts her with specific questions. She also shows a group focus in her concern that all students be fully, appropriately involved.

Possibly, though, Ms. Fuller has not been completely withit about the gender attitudes of her students; note that she glosses over Tom's concern about being the only boy in his group. As she assesses her experience with the groups so far, she wonders if she should have taken this opportunity to discuss his concern. There are arguments for doing so as well as arguments against. Tom's remark may conceal a gender bias against girls, and his bias may well be shared by other boys (and even by some of the girls). Bringing the bias into the open might give Ms. Fuller a chance to counteract it by encouraging more balanced attitudes about gender roles and the sexes. On the other hand, opening a discussion at this moment might take up valuable time that her students need to get organized for their groups. Perhaps she should simply note the possible gender implications of Tom's remark and plan on addressing the possibility of gender bias at a later time, using other activities. The right decision—to talk about gender or not—is not easy to predict. It will depend on Ms. Fuller's knowledge of her students—how biased they have seemed on other occasions, in particular. It will also depend on the priority Ms. Fuller gives to gender equity as an overall educational goal. We can assume she *does* support gender-fair attitudes in students, but we cannot assume this value takes precedence over other educational goals (such as learning to cooperate) in this particular situation.

In any case, Ms. Fuller has not yet had a chance to demonstrate smoothness in transitions to new activities, though that chance will come soon. Before that happens, a minor crisis forces a decision about where to devote her attention next. It again challenges her "withitness" and eventually leads her to revise her original plans for the cooperative learning groups.

Scene 3: When to Intervene?

After a few minutes, the angry group sends a delegation to Ms. Fuller.

"We can't choose a leader," says Jennifer, "because Sean and Lavar are being pig-headed. You've got to decide for us." Ms. Fuller scans the rest of the class, thinking about the other problems that might also need her attention right now, but decides to respond to Jennifer and to the angry group.

"What's the problem . . . " she begins, but before she can finish her sentence, there is a barrage of complaints. "Sean and Lavar are stupid and stubborn." "Jennifer just wants to be leader herself." "What about you—conceited or what?" Voices rise; a few heads turn from other groups to see what the commotion is about. Ms. Fuller is aware that the other groups are distracted, but only barely.

"All right! Enough!" commands Ms. Fuller. "Here is what you are supposed to do." She proceeds to explain their task in great detail: choosing a leader, choosing a name, deciding how to split up the research about community helpers. She writes the tasks down, and even writes precise suggestions for procedures ("ask for nominations, discuss the nominations, take a vote, . . . ") and for research tasks ("give each person one community helper to read about; choose from the following list"). Maybe detailed instructions will help, she thinks. But she is not pleased with her action; they were supposed to work together, not follow her orders. Privately, too, she wonders again about gender: the boys and girls do not seem to be getting along, judging by this group.

From Ms. Fuller's point of view, here's the problem: by intervening with the group, she fails to provide the sort of learning environment that she intended, one where students work cooperatively toward common academic goals. Instead of students selecting a leader, she has in effect become their leader herself. She is in danger, as educators Thomas Good and Jere Brophy have warned, of modeling direct, teacher-centered instruction even though she intends her students to adopt cooperation and self-regulation of learning (Good & Brophy, 1994; Brophy, 1996).

Yet Ms. Fuller should not be too hard on herself. Even if a cooperative environment has not worked for one of the groups so far, it may work at some later time if she can figure out ways to reorganize the group's task or coach its members on cooperative techniques. In arriving at this point, furthermore, Ms. Fuller has managed her own use of time and attention skillfully. Throughout the initial group session, she stayed aware of significant events and interactions in the class ("withitness"), and she showed concern about whether all students were indeed involved in their groups ("group focus"). Without these management skills, Ms. Fuller may not have noticed problems with the groups so soon. The fact that students' initial encounters had rough edges may not have mattered as much as the teacher's ability to respond to the students and their needs promptly and appropriately. How, then, does Ms. Fuller do so? How does she proceed without creating further confusion or chaos? There are several steps in the process. The first is to bring the initial session to a close smoothly—to use "smoothness." The next is to rethink her initial goals, taking into account her new knowledge of students' responses to group work. Her purpose in doing so, as before, will not be to control students' behavior directly, but to energize and guide their learning.

Scene 4: Moving On: Ending the First Session Smoothly

Ms. Fuller's detailed, emphatic instructions to Jennifer's group seem to have calmed that group down for the moment.

It is time, in fact, to call the class together and move on to the next activity. Ironically, though, it is hard to know exactly when to do so because each group shows a different degree of readiness to adjourn. Listening carefully to Group 1, Ms. Fuller hears them talking about irrelevancies: last night's television shows. Perhaps they can be interrupted immediately. Group 2, however, has settled into a heated but friendly discussion about the definition of "community helpers": do helpers include unpaid volunteers (such as people who assist at the food bank) or only people who get paid (police officers)? Since they are focused on the task, Ms. Fuller is reluctant to interrupt, especially because everyone is now participating, and not just Ken and Serge as at first. Group 3 members have gotten over their anger, but they are now confused about whether to move on to the assignment itself or take additional time to (finally) select a leader. Ms. Fuller wonders about this question herself, and wonders too about whether additional time will really help them to resolve it.

Well, we have to move on sooner or later, she thinks. But when and how? Her solution: give them a clearly stated, two-minute warning of the end, follow through on ending the session without fail, and be completely ready with instructions for the next activity.

Her result: five minutes later, the class is well launched into its next activity, and little confusion and few behavior problems arose during the transition.

It was indeed a smooth transition, something for Ms. Fuller to be pleased with and a reason to be hopeful about her educational plans and relationships with the students. The transition could have turned out differently; students could have become frustrated when interrupted, confused about what to do next, or bothersome to her or one another. As it turned out, though, Ms. Fuller could take satisfaction in how the first session ended, and in much of the session itself. But all did not go well. Students did not participate uniformly, and some were not very productive or happy during parts of the activity. There is still room for improvement, and this thought motivates Ms. Fuller's next actions, which

In Your Own Voice

Of course, instead of finding one best time to end the activity, Ms. Fuller could let different groups finish at different times, each when it is ready.

That strategy is sometimes called "overlapping."

Is it better than what she actually did?

Do you see any problems with overlapping?

In Your Own Voice

Suppose you were a student in Ms. Fuller's class.

Which of the groups would you be most pleased to be a part of, and why?

Is there something Ms. Fuller could do to make the less desirable groups meet your particular needs better?

we'll encounter soon. First, though, let us reflect further on what may have gone wrong initially.

Assumptions About Motivating Environments

In planning, assessing, and revising her program, Ms. Fuller has to make assumptions about the nature of learning and teaching in order to proceed. Whether she consciously reflects on these or not, she operates *as if* she believes certain things about what motivates students to learn, about how she therefore should teach them, and about the relationships she and her students should therefore have.

In Ms. Fuller's case, her initial assumptions are somewhat contradictory. She sometimes acts as if she is personally responsible for each individual student's learning; at other times, though, she acts as if only students, not the teacher, are responsible for learning. Viewed through the framework discussed in Chapter 5, her contradictions can be thought of as dilemmas about her teaching roles. How, for example, can she be a caring person? Is it more caring to arrange group activities on behalf of the students, thereby ensuring the groups' success? Or is it more caring to give students the experience of organizing activities for themselves, since someday they will have to take this responsibility anyway? Whatever the answer, her vacillation impairs the cooperative session somewhat by creating moments of confusion and misunderstanding between the students and Ms. Fuller, as well as among the students themselves.

Simply by forming the cooperative groups, for example, Ms. Fuller implied a belief that students can be responsible for their own learning. By definition—a definition announced to the students—the groups provided a forum for sharing ideas and offering support and encouragement. They also allowed students to develop their thinking and academic work in ways that they themselves consider appropriate. Ms. Fuller explains these purposes to the students when she introduces the unit (see the beginning of Scene 2). In effect, the group work invites the students to construct their own learning—to take responsibility for it.

As a result of students' uneven responses, however, Ms. Fuller doubts her own belief that students can take responsibility, and for one of the groups she eventually acts in a way that makes the opposite assumption. When Group 3 gets into conflict, she intervenes actively, orchestrates their procedures and tasks herself, and bypasses students' own efforts to take charge of their learning. Members of Group 3 therefore get a mixed (though implied) message. At first, along with the class, they hear, "I am

In Your Own Voice

Suppose Ms. Fuller were teaching tenth grade instead of third grade.

How would (or should) this fact have affected how she planned the unit, how students responded to it, and how she could (or should) have dealt with their problems in getting organized?

In Your Own Voice

Even if it sounds odd, I should ask this: are contradictory messages such as Ms. Fuller's really bad for students?

Maybe they *need* to hear two ideas—that they have freedom, but only if they can use it.

What do you think?

Maybe being totally consistent is not only impossible but educationally inappropriate?

giving you control"; but later they hear, "I am telling you how to act." The other groups hear the mixed message too, but less explicitly: they notice Ms. Fuller's actions with Group 3. In spite of her doubts and her actions, though, Ms. Fuller does not discard the cooperative group idea altogether. She leaves the door open for further cooperative learning activity. Her challenge now that she is busy with the groups themselves is to make herself aware of the unstated contradictions in her actions and use her increased awareness to make the next group sessions more successful. She can meet the challenge by talking to colleagues about relevant experiences, observing her students more carefully, and reading more research and published commentary about what works with cooperative groups. There is no fixed sequence for doing the tasks. As it happens, though, it is now lunch hour, and Ms. Fuller has a chance to do the first task: talking to colleagues.

Scene 5: Time to Seek Advice

It is lunch hour in the staff room. Ms. Fuller describes her first group session to two colleagues, Ms. Keating and Mr. Fernando.

"You can't let them get started with misbehavior," says Ms. Keating. "You've got to step in right away. But of course praise them, too, the minute you see individuals working well in the groups."

Ms. Fuller listens and nods, thinking that this sounds like the behavioral reinforcement idea she had read about somewhere, possibly in her educational psychology class. She is unsure about what to say.

"Actually, I disagree," says Mr. Fernando. "Stepping in like that—even to praise—just shows that you don't really think they take care of themselves. That you don't think students can work out differences, or know when they're being productive—that sort of thing."

"So what should I do?" asks Ms. Fuller.

Mr. Fernando hesitates; he is cautious about giving advice. But she asks, so he goes ahead. "Maybe you should teach group behaviors explicitly. Teach them things like taking turns listening and talking, asking the relevant questions, or keeping comments appropriate and on-topic. Maybe give the class practice with doing those things even before their first group sessions?" His voice rises at the end tentatively, as if he is merely proposing an idea for consideration.

Ms. Fuller still listens, still unsure about what to say.

"It's pretty crowded in a classroom!" says Ms. Keating. "That must have *something* to do with keeping order. Too many people talking, too many personal agendas. It may be a built-in problem. Isn't that why a teacher has to keep strong control?"

Ms. Fuller listens and ponders. The bell rings; her colleagues have to leave. What makes more sense to her are Mr. Fernando's comments: teach them how to handle themselves productively and courteously in groups. You can't just expect them to know how to do that, she thinks, if they've never tried it before. She gets up to leave, pondering how she can reorganize the next group sessions.

Educational research supports Ms. Fuller's decision: students do benefit from explicit guidance, practice, and support for working in groups. They also benefit from appropriate selection of tasks; not just anything works well in a group. The educator Elizabeth Cohen (1994), for example, pointed essentially to these same ideas after considerable research on classroom work groups. Here are three of her conclusions:

1. To work, a group task must be open-ended and amenable to multiple solutions. A project on "protecting the environment of the forests," for example, can be prepared several different ways. So can a project on "what parents should know about today's teenagers." Open-ended topics call for exchanges of ideas and perspectives, and therefore benefit from cooperative work.

2. Group members often need encouragement in adopting a group orientation rather than an individual one. The teacher can help by emphasizing the value of working in a group, both prior to and during a unit using groups. "You have a right to ask for help from group members," for example, is an important norm for group members. So is "You have a duty to assist someone who asks for help, though without doing the work for the other person."

In Your Own Voice

Can you think of another task (or two) that would be appropriate for group work?

How about one (or two) that would *not* be appropriate?

3. Some tasks are inappropriate for small-group work. Tasks and activities better suited to full-class or large-group formats include opening introductions to topics and projects, closing summaries of the achievements of individuals or small groups, and important classroom ceremonies or rituals (a prayer in a religious school, singing "Happy Birthday" to a classmate). Tasks and activities suited for individual work or for two-person tutorial review include practice at well-defined skills (such as going over "math facts"), reading, and writing.

Ms. Fuller has already implemented principles 1 and 3: she has selected an appropriate problem or assignment ("how many people does it take to raise a child?") that by nature can be dealt with in numerous ways. She still needs to pay more attention to principle 2: assistance for learning appropriate group membership skills. That is where she turns her attention when she makes the next revisions to her plans.

Scene 6: Two Days Later: Getting Ready for a Second Session

"Today we're going to work on our group projects again," says Ms. Fuller. "But first, let's talk more about how to do that. When I watched you last time, I think there was some confusion about how the groups were supposed to work. Did anyone else get that feeling?" There were nods of agreement and a few scowls.

"Ken and Serge hogged our time—acted like we didn't even belong," says Sheila.

"But not at the end!" says Ken. "Everyone just seemed tuned out, so we went ahead without you."

"That's what Jasmine did the whole time! She just went ahead by herself," complains Kyla, who was in Group 1, the group that appointed Jasmine as benevolent dictator.

"What?!" exclaims Jasmine, clearly offended. "You all *acted* like you wanted me to take over. Do you think I liked that?"

Many eyes turn to Ms. Fuller. "Well. How are we going to solve problems like these? Jasmine, Jennifer? Anyone? I need suggestions." She pauses a long time, determined to get the students to come up with at least some of the solutions.

"Ms. Fuller, for one thing, I don't see why we have to work with people we don't even know very well. Why not work with our friends?" This comes from Jasmine, and she stimulates murmurs of agreement.

"Good question, Jasmine," replies Ms. Fuller. "I'm not sure now that we really do need to work with 'strangers.' But what if there are some people no one wants to work with? Would it be fair to leave them out simply to work with your friends?" Several students show worried looks on their faces.

"How about a compromise?" suggests Sean. "We could choose one or two friends for our groups, and you could choose the others. Can we do that? That way everyone would be sure to be in a group."

Ms. Fuller realizes that the mechanics of this suggestion would need work, but it might have possibilities. "Let me think about it; it might work. I'll let you know tomorrow. Meanwhile, we have other things to talk about. I think we need principles or rules for how to behave in a group. Who can suggest one?"

To her relief, students do suggest rules for group conduct. They offer these:

1. Everyone should be involved.

2. You can have a leader, but only if you want one.

3. The leader does not have to do all the work, and should not.

4. Listen to others' ideas; offer your own.

5. Respect other groups, no matter how small a group is.

In Your Own Voice

What do you think of Ms. Fuller's compromise for constituting groups' membership?

Any problems?

The dilemma is how to include everyone in a group without forcing relationships artificially and without showing disrespect for students' own friendships.

In Your Own Voice

Why do you suppose the students included rule 5?

What connection did they see between it and the general problem of ensuring smoothly running groups?

The last rule was not strictly about conduct within a group, but several students wanted to include it anyway.

More remains, of course, to help students develop appropriate group skills. But Ms. Fuller and her students are off to a good start—and one that should motivate their efforts: they are collaborating to construct norms of group behavior rather than simply letting the teacher impose them. In this case, as a byproduct of collaboration, Ms. Fuller ends up modifying her earlier assumption about group management: that she must assign membership herself. Her revised practice—giving students some choice about membership—actually is more consistent with the experiences of many student-centered teachers (see Thorkildsen & Jordan, 1994). Even if it were not, however, it would be important to consider this approach, since students themselves have recommended it and Ms. Fuller's ultimate goal is to encourage students to manage their own learning.

Scene 7: Two Weeks Later

Students are working in their groups. Ms. Fuller looks around the room. None of the groups has the same membership as during the first group session.

Ken and Serge ended up together, of course, but also have reluctantly "adopted" Sheila. They seem to be including her, though often the adoption looks more like tolerance than full inclusion. They still talk only to each other sometimes.

Kyla did not want to work with Jasmine, and said so (confidentially) to Ms. Fuller. She ended up in a group of six girls, three of whom play together after school a lot. Ms. Fuller is concerned about whether that group is too large for effective involvement, but she is letting it go for now.

Jasmine and Lavar ended up together in a two-person group. Neither seems bothered by having crossed the gender gap, though Ms. Fuller notices that they never talk to each other outside of official work times. She is keeping an eye on them for signs of discomfort, especially if they become unproductive.

Sean worked with Ken and Serge for awhile, then one day drifted over to a brand-new group when he proved able to help them with a specific problem. Apparently there were no hard feelings about the change, so Ms. Fuller was not worried about it.

Two groups finally did select a formal leader. One leader (a boy) was called The King and the other (a girl) was called The Wizard. Neither leadership role seemed to amount to much, as it happened.

No group ever selected a name for itself. Ms. Fuller kept a list of who was working with whom to minimize confusion.

In one more week the groups, both large and small, will start presenting. Some have more work to do than others before they will be ready. Ms. Fuller knows she will need to get involved in the slower-developing groups. She wonders how to do that without meddling.

In the end, with appropriate modifications, the groups proved successful. This outcome did not, of course, solve all of Ms. Fuller's management problems—she is still wondering what to do next—but it has allowed her to move on to other issues and challenges. And it has kept annoying and unproductive behaviors from becoming more serious.

The whole story might have unfolded differently, of course, if Barbara Fuller had been teaching some other sort of class or other types of students. With senior high students, for example, the students' (and Ms. Fuller's) concerns about crossing gender boundaries might have led to different outcomes—perhaps with more of them tolerating coeducational work groups or even preferring them. With specialist classes—music, art, and gym, among others—the educational purposes may have reduced the importance of group work altogether, or at least given it very different meanings. Playing a team sport is a form of group work, though perhaps not one that involves the sort of verbal discussion that Ms. Fuller's groups needed to do. In spite of differences in circumstances, though, the general point remains: management of a class begins with organization and planning. These tasks must be done well for a class to run smoothly.

In Your Own Voice

I end up declaring Ms. Fuller's cooperative learning groups a success, even though not everything happened as she originally planned.

Is my assessment too optimistic?

Motivation: Is It Students or Circumstances?

As the story of Barbara Fuller shows, motivation has a lot to do with arranging circumstances that encourage learning. Ms. Fuller succeeded (eventually) with her students because she found ways to surround them, so to speak, with the support and encouragement to complete their projects. For each student, a lot of the support came from group partners—not surprisingly, given the nature of cooperative learning. But additional support also came from two other sources. One was Ms. Fuller herself, when she intervened at strategic times to ensure the effective functioning of the groups. Another was the task itself: it had a clear, attainable goal—learning about child rearing

In Your Own Voice

In your own experience, how would you know if a person is "motivated" or not?

What signs would you look for?

On the other hand, how would you know if *you* were motivated?

What signs would you look for in that case?

and the community—and was moderately valuable to students. Or more to the point, the project gradually became so, thanks both to Ms. Fuller's and the students' own efforts.

Among psychologists and teachers, however, the term *motivation* is often used not to refer to social circumstances, as I did with Barbara Fuller, but to a quality or state experienced *within* individuals. Used in this second, person-centered sense, motivation is like a mood or a feeling: it refers to the energy that arouses the person to action, and that gives direction or focus to action. Put in terms of classroom learning, motivation is the energy that arouses a student to learn, and that gives direction or focus to learning. Instead of being "in" the circumstances, as described for Barbara Fuller, motivation in this second sense is "in" students themselves. The task for teachers shifts from arranging circumstances for effective learning, to identifying when students feel motivated to learn, as well as when they do not. The task also becomes one of identifying which students habitually feel motivated, regardless of circumstances, and which feel motivated only rarely. The latter knowledge can help a teacher to focus her on energizing and guiding learning for particular students who need it the most.

There are several variations of the person-centered, "internal" notion of motivation, and to some extent they reflect the differences in models or metaphors about learning discussed in Chapter 2. To get a sense of them, look with me briefly at three that are especially common: motivation as reinforcement, motivation as beliefs about effort, and motivation as self-fulfillment. Each viewpoint is useful for certain teaching purposes, but each also has limitations.

Motivation as Reinforcement

From the point of view of behaviorism (one of the models of learning we encountered in Chapter 2), motivation refers to the impact of reinforcement on behavior. A reinforcement that works effectively is considered to be "motivating." If receiving gold stars for academic performance makes a student work harder, then gold stars are motivating; if praise is what works, then praise is motivating. Stated the other way around, motivation is what makes reinforcers work: it makes gold stars or praise (or whatever) effective in altering a student's behavior. The challenge for the teacher becomes one of figuring out which reinforcers really do work, for which students, and under what circumstances. The challenge has long been recognized by specialists in behavioral psychology (Premack,

JOYCE: It would surely be a lot easier if they all cared about the same thing. If they really all seemed to like being praised for good work, I could make sure to rely on praise. But some actually seem embarrassed rather than pleased by praise. Or if they all truly cared about grades, then I could rely on the grading system to motivate. But some just don't seem to care *what* they get. It might even be easier if they all cared about something irrelevant, as long as it was in common. For instance, what if students all liked listening to the *same* radio station? Crazy as it seems, then I could at least use that radio station as a motivator. Maybe find out if the station has been involved in our curriculum—in environmental causes. Or arrange to tour the station at year's end for students who did their work well.

But the fact is that not all students do respond to the same reinforcer, whether the reinforcer is a class activity, a teacher's priase or grade, or even a particular type of popular music. Nor do most students respond to the same reinforcer on every possible occasion. As a result, teachers have to observe students carefully, noting what interests them and what does not, and trying to offer the interesting as much as possible while avoiding the boring. This conclusion might not be a profound one, except for the fact that it can be so difficult to achieve: to provide truly interesting (that is, reinforcing) activities for as many students as possible, you often end up planning and managing more than one activity at once and searching hard for new, interesting approaches to old, familiar content.

Motivation as Attributions About Success and Failure

A more cognitive view of motivation focuses on the attributions that a person makes about the causes of success and failure. This viewpoint is sometimes called **attribution theory,** and it concerns the impact of a person's explanations for their actions. One well-known version of attribution theory, for example, calls attention to three kinds of attribution—locus of control, stability, and responsibility (Weiner, 1986; Graham & Weiner, 1996). *Locus of control* refers to whether success or failure is caused by factors internal to a person or external. Suppose you do well on a test. If you believe your success resulted from something "in" you, like high ability or effort, then you are attributing it to an internal factor (or in psychological terms, showing "an internal locus of control"). If, on the other hand, you believe success came from something "outside" of yourself, like the test's being too easy or sheer luck being on your side, then you are locating responsibility externally (showing "an external locus of control"). Attributions about *stability* refer to whether you attribute success and failure to factors that are temporary or lasting. If, after failing a test, you attribute the result to being sick or to neglecting to study (temporary factors), then you are making an unstable attribution; if you attribute the result to your lack of ability or to the teacher's permanent biases ("She/he always grades hard"), then you are making a stable attribution. *Controllability* refers to whether you interpret failure and failure as primarily influenced by yourself or by others. If you fail a test and attribute the failure to partying late the night before, you are attributing failure to a factor you can control or are responsible for (you could have avoided going to the party). If you explain the failure as the result of working at your job the night before, however, you are attributing failure to a factor beyond your control (you had to show up at your job or be fired).

Thinking of motivation in these terms challenges teachers to look carefully at how teaching practices might affect students' attributions of success and failure and to adjust their practices to encourage attributions that seem desirable. For example, giving random, unannounced quizzes may seem like a good way to assess students' typical study habits, but they may also send a message that studying (that is, effort) does not matter and that success is therefore beyond students' control. But adjusting teaching practices is often not straightforward. What complicates it is that students combine attributions in diverse ways and often combine them differently on different occasions. Putting students in cooperative work groups, for example, may make one student feel unable to influence success ("It will depend on who's in my group"), but make another one feel more in control ("I can influence my partners about how we divide the work"). Teachers need to be sensitive to complexities like these wherever possible.

In Your Own Voice

Think back to a teaching practice that you experienced as a student which reduced or spoiled your motivation, rather than increased or improved it as was (presumably) intended.

What was it about the experience that had a negative effect?

Motivation as Fulfillment of Needs

A **need** is a biological or psychological requirement for living, such as food or sex or love. When needs are not fulfilled completely (which is most of the time), we focus our actions so as to fulfill them better. So needs qualify as a form of motivation: they are the biological or psychological requirements that energize and give direction to our actions. This idea locates human motivation squarely "inside" the individual.

In both formal publications and informal dialogues, psychologists, teachers, and other educators have proposed many candidates for needs that are both motivating and relevant to classroom learning. One candidate, for example, is the *need for achievement,* which refers to a striving to compete with a standard of excellence, regardless of extrinsic reward (McClelland, 1985; Stipek, 1996). Another is a *need for self-determination* of our actions and wishes—or as one psychologist expresses it, a desire to be an "origin" of our actions rather than a "pawn" of other people's actions (DeCharms, 1984). Still another is a *need for self-actualization* or self-fulfillment; it refers to people's desire to reach their full potential (Maslow, 1970). For each of these needs, research suggests that some people (including some students) experience the need more frequently and strongly than do others, and that most people (and students) are more likely to experience it strongly and consciously only under certain circumstances. Most of us feel the need to achieve at times, for example, but not every moment of every day. The challenge for teachers is therefore twofold. First, the challenge is to identify which students are already guided by particular psychological needs, such as the ones mentioned above (though not necessarily limited to those). Second, teachers must arrange conditions that encourage the development and satisfaction of desirable needs.

But "meeting students' needs" can be surprisingly difficult, in spite of the intuitive meaningfulness of ideas like need for achievement, self-determination, and self-actualization. One problem is the generality or ambiguity of these concepts. How do I, during a busy day of teaching, recognize when one of my students is experiencing self-fulfillment? Is it happening any time the student simply seems happy, or is there some more subtle signs that I should look for? Another difficulty is that as teacher, my impressions of what students need do not always coincide with my students' own beliefs about what they need. If I give students freedom to choose their own project topics, am I meeting their need for self-determination? Or will some students feel that I am simply abandoning them—failing to give enough guidance in designing their projects? Ambiguities like these do not mean that teachers should give up trying to meet students' needs, but they do mean that they have to be cautious in naming and diagnosing them and to be continually ready to revise their diagnoses on the basis of new observations and information.

In Your Own Voice

Martin Woodhead, a sociologist, argues that teachers and others in the helping professions should not speak of children or young people's "needs" at all (Woodhead, 1997).

He argues that using the term either promotes stereotyping of students (they either "need" X, Y, or Z), or else using it leads to proposing and defining countless "needs" to honor diversity among students.

What do you think of this critique?

Is Woodhead right to caution us?

Using Concepts of Motivation to Guide Teaching

The person-centered theories that I just described all defined motivation as something primarily "in" individuals rather than as a set of circumstances "around" individuals. The teacher we visited at the beginning of the chapter (Barbara Fuller), however, dealt primarily with the circumstances of her students; she was concerned with arranging conditions in which they would feel like learning. But the difference in perspective is not necessarily as much of a gap as it may first seem. On the one hand, all theories of motivation recognize an important role for circumstances in influencing personal motivations. On the other hand, Barbara Fuller's teaching strategies were consistent with person-centered motivational theories. By setting up and perfecting cooperative work groups, she may have been helping students to reinforce each other for learning (a behaviorist explanation); or she may have been supporting students' beliefs that success depended on effort rather than luck (an attribution theory explanation); or she may have been meeting students' needs to achieve, to determine their own actions, and to fulfill themselves (a needs-based explanation). Any of these could have been happening—or all of them at once, for that matter—within her students. As the teacher, however, she could not affect these internal psychological processes directly; she could only arrange conditions where positive motivations were likely to develop.

The relationships between theories of motivation and teaching practices that motivate suggest a more subtle, complex meaning to the term *motivation* than I offered at the beginning of this discussion of the topic. I began there by defining motivation as "the energy that arouses the person to action, and that gives direction or focus to action" (pages 179–180). I implied that the "energy that arouses" was located within a person—sort of like hunger or desire. I also implied that the "direction or focus to action" came from within the person. A motivated student was therefore self-starting and self-guiding, a bit like an airplane running on automatic pilot toward a preset airport. But taken together, the theories of motivation and Barbara Fuller's teaching strategies suggest broader meanings to these terms. The "energy that rouses" really exists not only *in* students but *around* them as well. In a very real sense, teachers, peers, and students themselves generate each other's drive to learn. And the "direction or focus to action" comes from *both* the individual student and a student's social environment. Teachers, peers, and students jointly influence where an individual student directs attention and focuses effort—as they did in the cooperative groups of Barbara Fuller's class. If you are the teacher, then, some of the best advice for motivating students may be easy to name but challenging to implement: try to be full of energy when you teach; encourage fellow students to share their own energy and enthusiasms with each other; and create learning goals jointly with students wherever possible. To the extent that you can work toward these "simple" ideals, motivation will emerge, and learning will occur.

What to Do About Misbehavior?

As I have interpreted it, then, Barbara Fuller's experience suggests two crucial claims about motivation and classroom management. First, it implies that the ultimate source of inappropriate or annoying behaviors may sometimes be traced back to problems in the teacher's planning process and not necessarily to students themselves.

Ms. Fuller's students were not fully productive because they did not know for certain what Ms. Fuller expected of them. The students were

Students, in addition to teachers, can respond helpfully to many conflicts and inappropriate behaviors by fellow students. The boy in the center and the girl on the right, for example, are part of a student-led conflict management program at their school.
© Elizabeth Crews

uncertain because the teacher herself was uncertain. Second, Ms. Fuller's experience implies that once teachers' expectations are clarified, students will become more motivated and their behavior will improve. They will become more productive in their groups, in this case, and more truly cooperative about how they learn. That, at any rate, is what happened in Ms. Fuller's class. Both ideas are reasonable claims and are consistent with the views of a number of educators, including some who have studied the management of groups in particular (Cohen, 1994; Johnson & Johnson, 1989; Slavin, 1995).

Yet careful planning and clear expectations do not always ensure motivated students and therefore are not the whole key to successful classroom management. Students can also misbehave even when a teacher is quite clear about expectations and has made genuine efforts to communicate them well. At these times the challenge is not to rethink activities or tasks, as Ms. Fuller did, but to develop prior agreement among students about what constitutes appropriate classroom behavior and to deal consistently with behaviors that fall outside of agreed-on guidelines. But how does one do this?

One way to develop agreement about appropriate behavior is to hold *class meetings* for that purpose (Glasser, 1990). Students themselves can be in charge of the meetings, even in elementary school, and the meetings should focus on issues that affect the entire class, or at least a large part of it. "How much moving around the room is acceptable?" might be one topic, or "When is talking between students allowable, and when not?" With encouragement and guidance from the teacher, students of all ages, including kindergartners, can develop general guidelines for issues such as these. They can even suggest consequences for individuals who do not live up to guidelines, though you should make sure that the consequences are not excessive and that ensuring a good learning environment, rather than punishment, remains the major focus of attention. With democratic guidelines in hand (you can literally post them on the wall if you like), it becomes easier to deal with individuals who do not behave appropriately. Obviously, for best results, the class needs guidelines before misbehaviors occur—the sooner in the year, the better, though later in the year these guidelines can also help in revising earlier decisions by the class.

In spite of having classroom rules, though, and in spite of stating clear expectations to students, it is still possible for disruptions and misbehaviors to occur. It is important to respond to these promptly, because they can be "contagious," or spread to other students in the class, a process some have nicknamed the **ripple effect** (Kounin, 1970). Spreading disruption is precisely what confronted Mr. Collins, for example, a teacher of tenth-grade mathematics. An encounter between two students, Robert and Teresa, quickly became an interruption for several others.

Scene 8: Mr. Collins's Students

Robert comes in late to class, striding to his desk with a flourish. "Look what washed up on the shore," says Teresa sarcastically. Robert retorts, "Look at yourself, lizard-breath!" Teresa turns red and tells Robert to shut up. Several classmates stop working and become curious about what is going on.

Mr. Collins says, "OK, enough, you two. Robert, sit down and get started." But Robert takes this to mean that Mr. Collins sides with Teresa against him. He gets up as if to leave. Teresa mutters, "Good riddance, fat-face!" This is enough to drive Robert out the door and produces snickers from a few students. Mr. Collins follows Robert out the door, fearing the boy is likely to get in further trouble if left on his own during classes. Once the teacher is gone, Teresa smiles at others who are staring at her, and says with a mock-teacher tone of voice, "Time to work now, children!" There is more laughter; several conversations begin, including one between two students on opposite sides of the room. No one is working. Mr. Collins returns to class at this point, but without Robert.

The problem started with an action by just a single student—Robert arriving late—but it quickly escalated to involve a classmate (Teresa), then neighboring onlookers, and eventually the entire class. By this point, the disruptive ripples had become so complex that someone walking into the class at that time would have had trouble figuring out how it all began.

Could Mr. Collins have prevented the ripple effect once it had begun? Assume for the moment that he has already taken prior steps to prevent this sort of incident in the first place—that he has already discussed rules of appropriate classroom behavior with the class, for example. But Robert and Teresa still had a conflict, behaving inappropriately as described. What, then, could Mr. Collins do differently? Let's look at several options, modified from those suggested by another educator, Richard Wielkiewicz (1995). I will call these options *permitting, tolerating, preventing, nonverbally intervening, verbally reprimanding, response costing,* and *socially isolating*. Table 6.2 summarizes these options. They differ in how much they remedy immediate, short-term features of the disruption as compared to how much they focus on longer-term change in behavior. They also differ in how appropriate they are for Mr. Collins in this particular situation.

In Your Own Voice

My first response to this story was to blame the teacher; he should have prevented this disruption, I thought, before it even occurred.

But when I imagined myself in his place, I wasn't so sure of my judgment.

Could I have prevented the incident if I had been there?

Could you have?

TABLE 6.2   Options for Responding to Classroom Disruptions

Option	Description	Example
Explicitly permitting	Let it happen, and let students know when you permit it to happen.	Being late for class is OK if you have written permission from a parent or teacher
Implicitly tolerating	Ignore it and say nothing, or say as little as possible.	Using language that is coarse and colloquial but not vulgar or obscene
Preventing	Plan ways to make the behavior unlikely to occur.	Seating disruptive students far apart; negotiating classroom rules with students in advance
Nonverbally intervening	Show your disapproval or your expectations through gestures and actions, but not in words.	Smiling at a good comment from a student; catching the eye of a student about to disturb a classmate
Verbally reprimanding	State your disapproval or expectations verbally, either privately or publicly.	Taking aside and expressing your disapproval to a student who has been making rude remarks during a discussion
Response costing	Remove a privilege, a valued activity, or a valued resource because of a misbehavior.	Giving a demerit point for conduct to a student who got in a fight with a classmate
Temporarily isolating	Remove the student briefly from the classroom because of a misbehavior.	Asking student to sit in the hallway for one minute to "cool off" after a serious fight

Explicitly Permitting

In Your Own Voice

One reviewer found this passage controversial.

"It is never all right to let students tease in class!" she said.

The same reviewer believed in making a clear distinction between behavior allowed at home and behavior allowed at school.

I don't completely agree with this position, but what do you think?

At first glance, this may not seem like a realistic option for Mr. Collins; how could he explicitly permit students to arrive late or to insult each other? A closer look suggests, though, that what is not permissible is not the behaviors as such but the behaviors *in the context* in which they occurred.

There may be classes or situations when arriving late is permissible—for example, if a student has been sick or been delayed by another teacher. And there may even be times when insults can be at least tolerated if not encouraged, such as when students engage in ritualized teasing and banter that is good-natured but not vicious.

Since Robert and Teresa are not being good-natured, explicit permission may not be desirable in this particular situation. But Mr. Collins could possibly use it on at least some other occasions. His challenge, it would seem, consists of clarifying to students when questionable behaviors may occur ("It is OK to come late if you are quiet about it and have a good reason"), and not only when they *cannot* occur ("Tardiness will never be allowed here"). Put in terms of the operant conditioning theory explained in Chapter 2, explict permission not only allows students to reinforce one another for their behavior but adds reinforcement from the teacher: if coming late to class is (secretly) satisfying because it draws everyone's attention to you, the teacher merely adds to the satisfaction by permitting the behavior explicitly. So Mr. Collins will have to be sure that he can risk letting the behavior become so reinforcing that it gets out of control. Still, explicit permission may be worth this risk in some situations; it can help students to meet legitimate personal goals, especially when these goals may differ from or be poorly understood by the teacher. Tossing friendly insults back and forth, for example, may be an acceptable way to show personal interest (or even sexual attraction) in some settings, even if not in class. Forbidding all such remarks may therefore show disrespect for some students' out-of-class lives; permitting them explicitly—under limited conditions—may show respect.

Implicitly Tolerating

Even if Mr. Collins does not approve of the exchange between Robert and Teresa, could he simply ignore or tolerate it quietly? The answer depends in large part on whose problem the incident really is—who actually experiences the incident as a problem or, as some educators put it, who *owns* the problem (Gordon, 1991). **Problem ownership** refers to taking responsibility for a behavior as a problem. Some behaviors (e.g., nail biting, minor fidgeting) may annoy the teacher but not other students. In that case, the teacher owns the problem, but not the students. Other behaviors (e.g., a contemptuous look from a classmate) may annoy a student but not the teacher; then the student owns the problem. Still other behaviors may annoy several students at once, though for diverse reasons. Swearing out loud during class, for example, may intimidate one classmate, merely distract a second student from working, and exasperate the teacher, who has been trying to encourage better manners during class activities. In that case, ownership is shared, though in different ways and to different extents.

A problem is most likely to be tolerable to a teacher if it is owned only by an individual student rather than by several students or by the teacher herself or himself. Unfortunately, this condition does not hold for what happened between Robert and Teresa: both students own part of the problem, because neither can tolerate the other's behavior. Soon classmates own bits of the problem as well as they find themselves distracted from their work; and eventually Mr. Collins owns part of it when he has to leave class temporarily to find Robert. Under these conditions, the incident cannot be ignored, at least if Mr. Collins expects the class to continue working with as little disruption as possible.

As a management strategy, tolerating relies on what behavioral theory calls *extinction*, another process discussed in Chapter 2, in which naturally occurring behavior is simply ignored or not reinforced until it (hopefully) disappears. Since the process can take some time, it helps if the reinforcement, or lack thereof, is controlled mostly by the teacher. This state of affairs is most likely when the problem is confined to, or "owned" by, one student rather than many. This state of affairs might have occurred if Robert and Teresa had happened to stage their conflict at a less visible time and place, such as in the hallway after school, when classmates had not been witnesses. In that case, depending on its seriousness, Mr. Collins might still have wanted to intervene, but more simply to salvage the relationship between the two students rather than to maintain a smoothly running class.

Preventing

Could Mr. Collins have prevented the disruption from happening in the first place? Certainly prevention seems desirable, *if* it can be done. Put in terms of behavioral theory, prevention amounts to arranging classroom conditions so that a problem behavior (in this case, verbal conflict) cannot be reinforced in the first place; the power of operant reinforcement is rendered irrelevant. Successful prevention, however, means anticipating misbehaviors of students before they occur without also communicating lack of faith in the students' willingness to behave appropriately. If Robert and Teresa have already developed a history of bickering, for example, Mr. Collins might reasonably expect trouble on this particular occasion. Perhaps he therefore could have prevented it by seating the two students far apart in the classroom and by training himself to be alert to the early signs of conflict between them on this or other occasions. Perhaps—but not with certainty.

If other class members have had a history of verbal bickering and conflict as well, perhaps Mr. Collins should have prevented this behavior more systematically by encouraging the class to make rules limiting such behavior. At the least, perhaps he should have declared such a rule by unilateral, administrative decree. Then he would have had guidelines to fall back on if an incident such as the one between Robert and Teresa occurred. More to the point, the guidelines might have deterred Robert and Teresa from "making a scene" in the first place. So prevention seems like a promising strategy in this particular case.

Gesturing Disapproval Nonverbally

Once the incident between Robert and Teresa began, could Mr. Collins have at least shortened it by intervening nonverbally through appropriate or meaningful gestures? Mr. Collins can frown at a misbehaving student, stare at him or her, shake his head, or point his finger, among other things. These responses not only can indicate disapproval but have an advantage over verbal interventions, such as those described next, in that they can be made without seriously interrupting classroom dialogue or activity. But would they have helped in this case?

The answer depends on what Mr. Collins's gestures intend and how the students interpret them. Judging by the strength and speed of

Robert's and Teresa's responses, it seems unlikely that they might have noticed an unspoken gesture from the teacher; perhaps in this case their own verbal exchange was simply too reinforcing (as well as too vividly painful) to be influenced by nonverbal communications. On the other hand, classmates of Robert and Teresa might in fact have noticed gestures of disapproval, since they were less involved in the incident and may have been more interested in ending it promptly. If this speculation is true, gesturing nonverbally would have helped to at least contain the disruption to the original two students, even if Robert and Teresa themselves did not notice or respond to it.

Reprimanding

Why not just reprimand either Robert, Teresa, or both? Would this response not make future incidents less likely, even if it did not prevent or shorten the current one? Research on reprimands suggests that they often do have this effect, though only if used sparingly (Van Houten & Doleys, 1983). It also suggests that reprimanding is more effective if expressed privately or quietly to individuals and not delivered loudly for all to hear. When these conditions do not occur, a reprimand often makes little difference, possibly because the public shaming involved in a loud reprimand makes students feel they have little left to lose by further misbehavior.

In Your Own Voice

I mention here some risks involved if Mr. Collins delays his response to Robert and Teresa.

All things considered, do you think these risks outweigh the benefits of delaying?

How could you decide?

Whether a reprimand will solve Mr. Collins's classroom management problem, then, will depend on how it is done and on the circumstances surrounding this particular incident. A reprimand might be very effective if Robert's and Teresa's overall behavior has not yet driven Mr. Collins to use this strategy excessively—and indeed if other students' behavior has not led him in this direction as well. And it may be effective if Mr. Collins can find a way to state his disapproval quietly and privately to the students. Can he do that? Perhaps he can avoid responding until after the incident, speaking to each student privately after class. Unfortunately, this strategy does not stop the incident once it begins, so he will have to live with today's problem and hope simply to prevent future recurrences. By delaying, Mr. Collins will also fail to follow a common piece of advice from behavioral theory: provide consequences for behaviors as soon after the behavior as possible. Delaying either reinforcement or punishment is usually considered less effective than delivering them immediately; it is better, for example, to find out your grade on a test as soon as possible, whether the grade is high (reinforcing) or low (punishing). In the case of Robert and Teresa, a delay by Mr. Collins can not only reduce his effectiveness with the two students themselves but also risk having classmates fail to see that he responded at all. They might wrongly conclude that he is tolerating their behavior rather than (quietly) reprimanding it.

Response Costing

A **response cost** is like a fine: with each infraction of a rule, a student loses something desirable, such as a few minutes at recess or discretionary time at the end of the day. You can also think of response cost as a form of aversive behavioral conditioning, such as described in Chapter 2: an undesirable behavior is punished by removing a positive reinforcer or by imposing a (mildly) punishing stimulus. Will a response cost strategy help Mr. Collins? Presumably it will, so long as he can correctly identify reinforcers that Robert and Teresa actually value and therefore will find unpleasant to lose. Does Robert, for example, care about being granted free time at the end of a class session? Perhaps the students will indeed care about the costs of inappropriate behavior. The only way to be sure, though, will be for Mr. Collins to actually try the strategy and later revise or abandon it if it does not work.

Temporarily Isolating

A relatively drastic form of response cost is to impose brief social isolation (sometimes also called "timeout"). A student who disrupts the class can be sent or placed where he or she has no people and few interesting sights and sounds with which to interact. The isolation need not, and indeed should not, last more than a few minutes, but it should be long enough to interrupt reinforcements that may be encouraging disruption. In the case of Robert and Teresa, Mr. Collins could separate the two students far enough that they could not interact at all, even nonverbally with scowls or gestures. Complete separation might mean sending one student to the hall, to another classroom, or to the school office.

But note that risks are involved. On the one hand, either or both of the students might find the isolation very humiliating, in fact so humiliating that Mr. Collins might damage his relationship with the student permanently. On the other hand, either student might actually find isolation just as interesting, or even more so, than being in the presence of classmates (note that Robert actually did leave the classroom voluntarily, implying that departure was no punishment for him). In that case, a student may experience isolation as reinforcing, and even seek to arrange for more of it by misbehaving again.

Choosing the Right Response to Misbehaviors

These considerations suggest both good news and bad. The bad news is that no response to a disruption is foolproof; there are always circumstances where any particular management strategy will fail. The good news is that many strategies work at least some of the time; there are almost always circumstances where a certain response by the teacher is reasonably likely to *succeed*. Mr. Collins's challenge—and yours, too, when you teach—is to identify those circumstances, the times and places where a particular management strategy will in fact be likely to work. There are no simple formulas or maxims for learning which strategies will work when, though it does seem that some are likely to work more of the time than others. Response costing and isolation in particular are relatively drastic and unpleasant actions to take and therefore should be used only sparingly, if ever. Permitting, tolerating, and silently intervening have a gentler impact and thus should be used more often, provided you can time them appropriately. Reprimanding falls in between in severity: it can be quite effective as long as you use the strategy quietly and as sparingly as possible.

Further discussion about exactly when, where, and how to manage your class is beyond the scope of this book, though a number of other books on this topic are helpful (see, for example, Alberto and Troutman [1994] or Canter [1989]). Full specification of "what to do when" about serious misbehavior may even be impossible, since no one can anticipate your particular students, teaching circumstances, or the experiences that lie ahead. Inevitably, therefore, and in spite of guidelines such as those given earlier, you will need to develop and exercise judgment in responding to classroom misbehaviors. Let's finish the chapter, therefore, by looking at ways to undertake this larger task, the search for sound judgment about classroom management. As it happens, the advice is also helpful in learning how to motivate students effectively.

Reflecting on Management and Motivational Strategies

*G*IVEN that universal prescriptions for motivating students and managing disruptions are scarce, how can you improve your skills in these areas?

In the long term, the best way is to become a skilled, reflective observer of your students, of your classroom program, and of yourself. What matters most is not mastering specific management or motivational techniques but assessing the impact of your techniques and modifying them appropriately for later occasions. Acquiring such judgment depends partly on reading about the experiences, research, and advice on management published by other educators. But it also depends partly on sharing your experiences and reflections directly with other professional teachers. As it happens, both Ms. Fuller and Mr. Collins follow this latter strategy, though each in different ways. Ms. Fuller finds support for reflection in talking with a friend.

It is important to realize that you are not alone in dealing with classroom management problems. Discussions with fellow teachers can help you to develop new approaches and strategies for handling difficult situations—and for keeping your emphasis on positive motivation.
© Elizabeth Crews

Scene 9: Ms. Fuller and a Friend

It is the weekend. Ms. Fuller is visiting a friend, talking about the cooperative groups in her class.

"I can't complain too much," she says. "Most students are participating, more or less. But I can't help worrying about the pace of the groups; some are *much* farther ahead than others. It doesn't seem fair to individuals in the slow groups!"

Her friend pauses before answering. "Are you saying it's better to be fast or to be slow? Do you mean that faster groups learn more, enjoy working more—that sort of thing? Or that the slow ones are being more thorough?"

Now it is Ms. Fuller who pauses, even longer than her friend. "You're onto something there. . . . "

"Have you looked at what's happening in the slower groups?" her friend continues. "Is their activity 'bad' in some way?"

Ms. Fuller stares out the window. "No, not 'bad'; just slower, more relaxed. It's like they have a different idea about how to pace their conversations, how to let work flow from one stage to the next. More easygoing."

"And that's bad?"

"Well, it's certainly slower. Maybe bad eventually, when time runs out. I'm not sure."

Mr. Collins, on the other hand, finds support in corresponding with other teachers on the Internet.

Scene 10: Mr. Collins's E-mail Group

It is the weekend. Using his computer at home, Mr. Collins checks his e-mail and discovers a posting from an Internet discussion group of teachers called SURVIVAL-LIST. Today's posting is part of an exchange that has been unfolding for a couple of weeks. The posting reads like this:

```
TO: SURVIVAL-LIST

FROM: teacherwizz@ualaska.edu

RE: No-win times

>>>>>I'm having an awful time with two students who insult each
other whenever they get a chance. What to do? Last week one of them
actually left class in anger over a remark made by the other. I let
her leave, and apparently she didn't get in further trouble--this
time. Also tried ignoring the incident, but it left everyone gloomy
for the rest of the hour. What to do?
```

The comments rang a bell! It's not identical to what I experienced, thinks Mr. Collins, but it has some resemblance. He posts a reply:

TO: SURVIVAL-LIST

FROM: CollinsSearcher@educserver.edu

RE: No-win times

>>>>>>Right on, Teacherwizz! Reminds me of what happened to me this week, too. It was like this: [Mr. Collins goes on to describe the encounter between Robert and Teresa.] Can't decide yet when and whether it's better to ignore behavior like that or to respond actively. But I'm thinking about it. I'm thinking that you have to judge intrusiveness--low intrusion means you can ignore a disruption. But how do I respond when intrusion is "low"? Comments most welcome.

These two teachers found professional support and stimulation in a friend and in the Internet, respectively. But these are not the only ways to reflect on issues of management and of teaching generally. The choices abound: you can keep a professional portfolio, for example, or write a reflective journal, use student evaluations in your programs, or attend professional development activities. The strategies for professional development are important enough that I will mention them again in other chapters of this book. For now, though, look briefly at how each might help you to think about how to manage a classroom.

Professional Portfolios

A **portfolio** is literally a flat, ample folder or case used to carry documents, drawings, or other portable materials. As used in education, a "portfolio" usually means a collection or assortment of materials related to the work of a student or a teacher (students' portfolios are discussed in detail in Chapter 11). Ms. Fuller can use a portfolio, for example, to compile plans and materials for teaching, including teaching the cooperative learning unit in particular. For this unit, she can keep copies of all assignments, as well as special materials such as overheads, handouts, or advice sheets and instruction sheets to students and to herself. If students give permission, she could also keep samples of their work.

How can a portfolio help you with managing and motivating students? If done thoroughly, it brings together materials to help with planning and orchestration of your teaching; and, as we saw in the case of Barbara Fuller, these activities are a foundation for a well-managed program. A portfolio can also assist in reviewing and revising units of teaching, both as they occur and later when a teacher plans for subsequent semesters or years (Anson, 1994). The contents are like archaeological remains: tools and objects full of meaning and left behind by a previous civilization. Of course, a portfolio also has the limitations of archaeological remains. One limitation is that only certain materials may seem worthy of being saved. Ms. Fuller might save her final, successful plans for the cooperative groups, for example, but throw away her earlier, less successful attempts, even though the earlier plans might contain information or clues that would prove helpful to review at a later time.

A second limitation of portfolios is that not all elements of classroom "culture" are capable of being saved, in spite of their importance or success. Just as a culture's pottery can be saved but not its music, so a classroom's written documents can be saved but not its oral dialogues. This limitation poses a challenge in using a portfolio to improve your teaching strategies, because these often occur "on the fly" and leave little physical evidence behind. Students may produce disappointing written work, for example, because a teacher has managed an activity inappropriately. Then again, their written work may look quite satisfactory in spite of *mis*management. In either case, samples of the writing may end up in the portfolio, but there will be few clues about the interactions, behaviors, and teacher's responses that led to the writing. A bias toward physical evidence can be a problem for a reflective teacher, but it can easily be remedied by supplementing a portfolio with a reflective journal, such as that described next.

Reflective Journal

A more direct way to reflect on motivational and management issues is to simply write about them. What happened in your class today, and why did it happen? How could you respond next time? Mr. Collins uses a variation of this approach, called a **reflective journal,** in writing about the incident with Robert and Teresa for the Internet discussion group. To get full benefit from this sort of exchange, however, he may need to enter into more dialogue with the discussion group about the significance of the incident and about the issues it raises for him. Doing this may take time (one week? three weeks?), but if Mr. Collins has the time, it might be worth the effort.

Whether on the Internet or in an old-fashioned notebook, the key to reflective writing is elaboration on and interpretation of classroom experiences as fully as possible. Many teachers and educators therefore find the task easier if they share their writing with peers (Black et al., 1994). The sharing stimulates dialogue about issues and thus develops individual teachers' thinking more fully. In fact, when a journal becomes quite developed and a teacher keeps it for an extended period, it can become a form of **classroom research,** or **teacher research,** such as discussed in Chapter 12: a sustained, systematic inquiry into issues and problems defined by the teacher rather than by educational theories. Over time, as classroom research, the journal can provide answers to the issues or problems in terms especially relevant to the teacher's particular classroom and students.

Note, though, that there are limits to what reflective journals provide. For one thing, writing and reflection take time and effort and, by nature, have to take place before or after school hours. As people busy with students and other personal responsibilities, even the most dedicated teachers may not have time to write fully about every important issue or problem, much less share and discuss it with others. For another thing, teachers may have certain classroom experiences they are not willing to commit to paper, especially those that include mistakes or problems in dealing with particular students. A teacher—perhaps even Mr. Collins— may occasionally respond in personally unacceptable ways (such as shouting or even cursing in class) or have personally unacceptable feelings (for example, an unusual attraction to or dislike of a certain student) that she or he feels self-conscious about and prefers not to retell to others. Dealing with such feelings and experiences calls for an especially safe setting and an exceptionally trusted listener. If a teacher is fortunate, he or she may find such a setting and person in a close friend or relative. But even when this is not possible, a teacher can usually find needed, safe privacy with a counselor or therapist.

Student Evaluations of Teaching

By "student evaluations," I do not mean evaluations *of* students but evaluations *by* students of you, the teacher. In many ways, students, whatever their ages, are especially well suited to assess your actions as a teacher (Theall & Franklin, 1990). They see you every day for most of the time you are in class, though not when you are talking to colleagues, making lesson plans, or privately reflecting on your program. They also know whether they are enjoying whatever is going on and whether they believe they are learning. They may not be able to say precisely *why* they get these feelings, of course, but their comments give clues about your teaching nonetheless.

In one sense, teachers use students' evaluations all the time when they notice individuals' reactions to the flow of activity. Mr. Collins noted how classmates reacted to Robert and Teresa, for example, and Ms.

Fuller noted how different combinations of students reacted to working in groups together. In addition to such informal observations, though, it is possible—and useful—to invite more deliberate assessments from students. Periodically you can inquire, either from individuals or from the group, about reactions to classroom activities and procedures. The best questions are somewhat open-ended: Do you feel as if you are learning from this class? Are the expectations reasonable? Questions can also focus on classroom procedures, in which case they are more likely to resemble the *class meetings* discussed earlier in this chapter (Glasser, 1990). Is the classroom policy about "no talking" working well enough, you can ask, and if not, what should we do about it? Students' responses to all such questions—whether the questions are procedural or substantive, and whether individually or in a group—suggest what motivates them as well as ways to revise classroom policies, procedures, and goals related to motivation and management.

With older students, the same invitation to assess the class can be extended in writing, a technique that can encourage students to state their opinions more freely because it protects their anonymity. (But not entirely: you might still recognize their handwriting, and students may realize this.) Mr. Collins tried this technique, in fact, with his tenth-grade class, though not on the same day that Robert and Teresa had their argument.

Scene 11: Hopes and Fears

2:40—near the end of class. It is the second week of the semester. Mr. Collins distributes a 3-by-5-inch card to each student in the class.

"On one side," he says, "I want you to write the word *HOPES*. On the other side, I want you to write the word *FEARS*. Then take the rest of the class today to indicate briefly what each of these are for this class. Write your hopes on the HOPES side of the card and your fears on the FEARS side. Never mind about perfect English—just use terms, or an outline, or whatever. You can even draw me a diagram or picture, as long as it shows your hopes or your fears."

Teresa raises her hand. "Do we put our names on the card?" she asks.

"No," says Mr. Collins firmly. "I'm interested in your hopes and fears this time, not in who is saying them." A few students glance at one another when they hear this; then they start writing. Five minutes later the class is over, and Mr. Collins has a stack of brief student assessments. He tucks them away to read that night, feeling just a bit nervous about them. Anonymous feedback, he suspects, can contain more criticism than face-to-face conversations with students. But he feels he needs their opinions and responses.

That night he reads the cards, and here is some of what he sees:

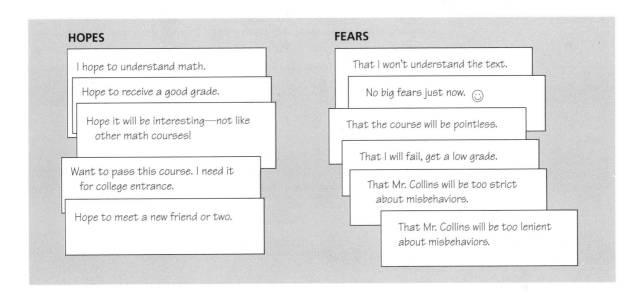

HOPES

I hope to understand math.

Hope to receive a good grade.

Hope it will be interesting—not like other math courses!

Want to pass this course. I need it for college entrance.

Hope to meet a new friend or two.

FEARS

That I won't understand the text.

No big fears just now. ☺

That the course will be pointless.

That I will fail, get a low grade.

That Mr. Collins will be too strict about misbehaviors.

That Mr. Collins will be too lenient about misbehaviors.

After finishing the stack of cards, Mr. Collins breathes a sigh of relief: they contain nothing devastating, and the students *do* have some hopes!

It is late; Mr. Collins wants to forget about school for today. Before he does, though, he gets out a transparency and a felt-tip pen and begins listing some of the hopes and fears on it. Tomorrow he will show it to the class and invite them to comment on the lists orally.

Classroom Management to a Reflective Teacher

A personal teaching portfolio, a reflective journal, and student assessments of teaching all have two important effects on a teacher's approach to motivation and management. First, they encourage solving the challenges of teaching through a mixture of personal thoughtfulness and respectful consultation with others. Second, they encourage blending or combining questions about immediate behavior problems with longer-term questions about curriculum planning, teaching, and students' learning needs. To the extent that you can take your reflections and consultations about management seriously, classroom management turns into something not primarily about fixing undesirable behaviors but about motivating appropriate behaviors time after time, behaviors that not only do not disturb others but lead to focused, enthusiastic learning.

To make reflection and consultation work, you need to think of your classroom—and indeed of the entire educational enterprise—as a community of learners: as individuals with interests and skills that are incredibly diverse but nonetheless legitimate. The community comes in different versions based on size: the smallest may be your own classroom, somewhat larger may be your school, and largest of all may be the educational world in general. You yourself are a member of each community simultaneously, and you are challenged to learn from its members in spite of its diversity and to assist your students to do the same. Meeting this challenge means understanding the various kinds of relationships that can develop in them and it is to this topic, therefore, that we turn in the next chapter.

CHAPTER RE-VIEW

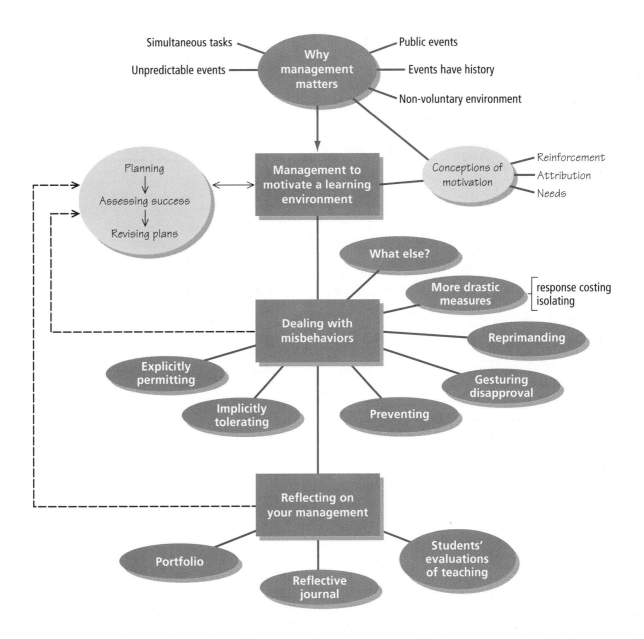

Simultaneous tasks

Unpredictable events

Why management matters

Public events

Events have history

Non-voluntary environment

Planning
↓
Assessing success
↓
Revising plans

Management to motivate a learning environment

Conceptions of motivation

Reinforcement

Attribution

Needs

What else?

More drastic measures — response costing, isolating

Dealing with misbehaviors

Reprimanding

Explicitly permitting

Implicitly tolerating

Preventing

Gesturing disapproval

Reflecting on your management

Portfolio

Reflective journal

Students' evaluations of teaching

Chapter Re-View: Motivating and Managing Your Class This Chapter Re-View suggests directions in which the chapter might have taken your thinking—though, of course, other directions are also possible. It expands the Chapter View, which suggests a starting point, conceptually, for the chapter. But this Re-View does not suggest an ending point. Like the Chapter View, it represents just one perspective among many.

Key Terms and Concepts

motivation (163)
classroom management (163)
withitness (169)
group focusing (169)
smoothness (169)

attribution theory (181)
need (182)
ripple effect (186)
problem ownership (190)
response cost (193)

portfolio (197)
reflective journal (198)
teacher research (199)
classroom research (199)

Annotated Readings

Kohn, Alfie. (1996). *Beyond discipline: From compliance to community.* Alexandria, VA: Association for Supervision and Curriculum Development. This book offers a stimulating challenge to most books about classroom management. Essentially the author argues that teachers should concern themselves less with maintaining control of students and more with building a sense of community with the classroom and school. Most classroom management strategies, he says, are based on rather negative beliefs about the nature of children and youth. You may or may not agree, but this book is worth a look! So, too, is Kohn's *Punished by Rewards: The Trouble with Gold Stars, Incentive Plans, A's, Praise, and Other Bribes* (Boston: Houghton Mifflin, 1996), which argues that external rewards, rather than motivating people, end up making them lose interest in what they are doing. Kohn offers alternatives to reward-based motivation.

Wielkiewicz, Robert. (1995). *Behavior management in schools* (2nd ed.). Boston: Allyn and Bacon.

Zabel, Robert, & Zabel, Mary. (1996). *Classroom management in context: Orchestrating positive learning environments.* Boston: Houghton Mifflin. These two books are relatively "mainstream" in their approach to classroom management. Each has chapters on individual features of the topic, such as preventing individual behavior problems before they occur, dealing with them once they do, and developing classroomwide programs to create smoothly functioning activities.

Internet Resources

<www.pacificnet.net/~mandel/ClassroomManagment.html> This is a teachers' forum, a site where teachers can exchange information, ideas, and problems on the World Wide Web. The section named above is all about classroom management in the sense discussed in the second half of this chapter. The site also has sections devoted to other forms of curriculum planning and classroom planning that are more related to classroom management as discussed in the first half of this chapter.

<www.state.ky.us/agencies/behavior/homepage.html> This site is sponsored by the State of Kentucky Department of Education. Intended for classroom teachers, it is devoted entirely to information and advice about how to handle difficult behaviors in the classroom. Among other things, it has descriptions of difficult situations, along with alternative strategies for dealing with them.

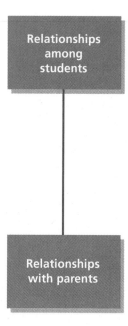

Chapter View: Among Classmates and Parents This Chapter View is a concept map that indicates one among many ways of thinking about the chapter. It suggests a starting point, conceptually, for the chapter but is incomplete by itself. At the end of the chapter is a Chapter Re-View, which expands on the Chapter View, suggesting directions for taking your thinking further—though, of course, other directions are also possible.

7

Among Classmates and Parents

Look around the schoolyard: you'll find bullies and leaders, victims and loners, talkers and listeners, friends and enemies. Relationships underlie everything that happens; they are both implied by actions (who hangs out with whom) and stated by words ("I won't be your friend"). Skills at the relationships have partly been learned elsewhere—usually at home—but also at school itself. The result is a kaleidoscope of social patterns, though a kaleidoscope with regularities if you look carefully. Joe often bosses Jeff rather than the other way around; Rosa usually keeps her eye either on Susanna, a popular girl, or on Serge, a handsome boy.

Judging by the energy students put into them, social relationships are high-priority concerns. But unlike their experiences at home, where relationships first originate, young people face major obstacles in maintaining relationships in school: time to socialize is scarce, and time guided by teachers is plentiful. In high school, breaks between classes are only five or ten minutes; in elementary school, recesses last only fifteen or twenty minutes; at both levels, lunch "hours" are often much less than an hour. Most discretionary time is commandeered, so to speak, by teachers and other school authorities.

CHAPTER SEVEN

These circumstances have distinct effects on teachers, students, and parents, some of which we will explore in this chapter. We'll initially focus on this question: how does a student establish connections to peers when there is so little time to do so? Later in the chapter, we'll examine parents' influence on students' relationships, as these affect students' academic performance and general well-being.

As my comments will suggest, students cope with the social conditions of school in ways that seem diverse and universal at the same time. To appreciate the diversity, look at how Kirsten, grade 1, copes:

Looking at the clock, Kirsten realizes it is ten minutes before recess. She had better be ready. She turns to her current best friend, who is the girl across the aisle from her, Gillian: "Let's run to the swings today before anyone else gets them." Gillian nods in agreement. They have used class time to make recess plans like this before; in fact, they have to in order to ensure someone to play with and equipment to play on. As they whisper together, they notice Penny, a girl across the room, watching and listening to them talk; but then Penny looks down and continues working. Penny has no classroom neighbor with whom to make similar plans. You are not supposed to roam around the room before recess for this purpose. She will have to fit in as best she can after she gets out on the playground.

And here is how Arturo, grade 6, copes:

For the third time, Arturo is visiting the principal as punishment for talking to friends during the library period. "Can you listen to the story next time without getting into trouble?" asks the principal. "It depends on the story," says Arturo. "Yes," says the principal, "I suppose it does." Aside, to me, he smiles just slightly and says, "He's definitely not stupid!"

And here is how B.J., grade 11, copes:

It is lunch hour at the high school. "Let's go to the grocery store," says B.J., searching for entertainment until afternoon classes start. There are five of them—three girls and two boys— all from the same English class. They often do things together. The trouble is that today there are *seven* people: two extras from another English class. They are nice enough, but don't usually "belong" to the five. Should I invite them along? wonders B.J. No, she decides; the regulars have so little time together anyway. "On second thought," she says to the group, "it's pretty crowded and there's not much time left before class. Let's go another day."

In spite of the differences in their situations, these students have three qualities in common, two of which are visible from the examples. First, whatever their age, they all show significant concern about their social lives. No one wants to be alone. Second, their efforts to connect with others are influenced heavily by the priorities and routines of attending school. Social activities are determined by the convenience of seat assignments (as with Kirsten), by the channeling of schedules (as with B.J.), or by the competition of social with academic needs (as with Arturo). Third, although not immediately visible from the examples, the students' parents and other immediate family have also influenced their attitudes about social relationships, as well as their strategies for developing them with both classmates and teachers.

In this chapter, we will further explore how students deal with such complex influences and manage to be sociable in an environment that is only partially designed for that purpose. Our explorations will rest on a few assumptions throughout. First, I assume that students generally *do* wish to be sociable at least minimally and that few actually prefer having no friends or acquaintances at all. The existence of occasional loners or bullies does not change this picture. I also assume that different students express sociability differently: some seek more contacts than others do, and some have relationships thrust on them more than others. Finally, I assume that teachers can help students and their parents meet students' needs for satisfactory peer relationships while at the same time encouraging them to take their academic work seriously, and I'll suggest ways to do this. I hope to persuade you that with students, the challenge is to avoid pitting academic motivations against social motivations, and that with parents, the challenge is to be realistic about how they can and should participate in their children's education.

In Your Own Voice

As you read through these descriptions of different types of relationships among students, think about how they fit your own past experience as a student.

What differences did your social relationships make in your overall feelings about school?

(It is one thing to have had a lot of peers, for example, but another to have had just a few special friends.)

Relationships Among Students

WHAT sorts of ties and connections are we talking about in discussing students' relationships? It is risky to answer this question with generalizations, since each relationship has a "personality" and unique qualities, just as the individuals involved in them do. Even so, let me suggest several general types to facilitate reflection on why relationships among students matter to teaching and learning.

True friendships make academic challenges and worries much more bearable —as long as they do not preempt time that should go to studies.
© Harry Cutting/Monkmeyer

Peer Relationships

Although some people define "peers" to mean special or even intimate friendships, I will use the term **peers** to refer to a person who is your social equal and with whom you have relatively casual or passing contact. As a child, peers include the majority of classmates that you ever have; as an adult, they include most (though not all) coworkers and neighbors. You may either like or dislike peers, or feel a bit of both, but your reaction in any case is relatively mild. Peer relationships often have high turnover: that is, new peers come into your life and former peers leave, such as when you move into a new class at school each year or when you join (or quit) an extracurricular activity. You may remember individual peers after your relationships end, but since the relationships are relatively casual, you typically make little effort to sustain them once circumstances change.

From the point of view of teachers (but not necessarily of students), casual peer relationships are the social backbone of classroom and school life. Peer relationships dominate classroom activities, even if special, self-chosen friendships dominate the social lives of some students out of class. On a small-group project, for example, many—or even all—group members may be casual peers, or at least begin the year as such. Successful cooperation on academic tasks may depend, in fact, on the social ties among students being casual and open to all participants. Intense feelings between specific individuals, whether positive or negative, can actually interfere with group functioning, whatever their benefits or harm to individuals (Lane, 1995). As it is with teacher-student relations, so it is with relations among group members: "playing favorites" in a group activity or avoiding an individual like the plague causes overall learning to suffer.

Since it is therefore in a teacher's best interests to encourage casual but positive peer relationships, he or she can be tempted to believe that students who excel at casual relationships are the happiest with their social lives or even the most talented academically. Research, in fact, confirms that teachers tend to hold this belief, but it also suggests that students themselves often do not agree with it (Gandara, 1995; Ramsey, 1991). Students with relatively few friends or acquaintances sometimes rate themselves as just as satisfied socially as the most popular students, and often they prove themselves no less successful academically because of having fewer social relationships (Rubin & Asendorpf, 1993). At the extremes, however, an exception exists: students who are extremely withdrawn socially or are actively rejected by their peers tend to perform less well academically and to think poorly of themselves socially (Asher & Coie, 1990). These young people require separate comment at the end of this chapter.

To see how a bias favoring casual relationships might develop for the more middle-of-the-road majority, consider Ms. Gillis, the grade 1 teacher of Kirsten, described at the beginning of the chapter:

Ms. Gillis is looking at the results of her survey of friendship patterns that she recently completed for her class. A **sociogram,** they called it at the workshop she'd just attended. Each student was asked to list a classmate whom he or she liked the best. Since some students were picked by more than one classmate, and some picked each other, Ms. Gillis could diagram the results (hence the name: *socio-* for social relationships and *-gram* for diagram) as shown in Figure 7.1. Interesting patterns, she thinks; they give a rough idea of who is friends with whom. The boys choose one another; that makes sense, she notes, based on what she has seen at recess. The girls outnumber the boys, but she also notes that they have concentrated their votes more fully on just a few individuals. What does that mean?

In fact, what does the whole sociogram mean? How is she to interpret it? Ms. Gillis begins asking this question as she ponders the diagram. Some in-

FIGURE 7.1

Sociogram (Partial) of Ms. Gillis's Class [Students responded to the question, "Who do you like the best?"]

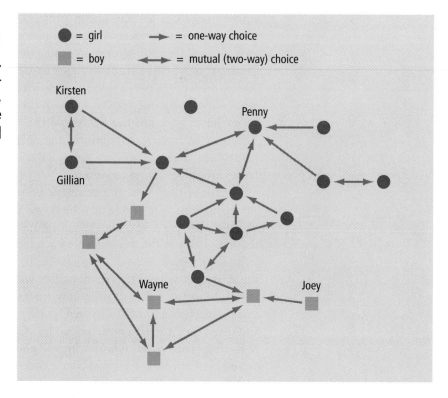

dividual choices and group patterns don't make sense. Kirsten and Gillian choose each other (no surprise there), but they actually turn out to be *less* popular overall than Penny, who never has any one person to play with at recess. And the result for Joey was unexpected: he wasn't picked by anyone, even though Ms. Gillis knows he participates well in group activities and seems well liked by others at recess. Apparently he just didn't make the top nomination of any one person in spite of his obvious popularity. Wayne, on the other hand, got chosen three times even though he is well known for getting into conflicts and insisting on having his own way. The sociogram is not picking up these particulars of student relationships. The inconsistencies concern Ms. Gillis. Maybe she should have asked for several nominees rather than just one; or maybe she should have phrased the sociogram's questions differently, asking not whom a student liked but whom a student liked to work with or liked to play with at recess. The leaders at the workshop had in fact suggested these options, but only now did they seem important.

Still, thought Ms. Gillis, the diagram has its uses even as is. It does give clues about students' opinions of one another, even if the resulting information doesn't speak for itself. The bottom line, she thinks, is whether a sociogram helps her to know if students are willing to work with one another, if some are getting left out a lot. Besides the sociogram, how else can I find this out? she asks herself. And what I can do about it if I discover problems with their relationships?

Ms. Gillis has already implicitly answered the first question by her actions: in addition to using the sociogram, she can find out about students' relationships by observing their reactions to one another in the course of each day's teaching and by reflecting on her observations thoughtfully. And what of her second question: how to encourage positive relationships? We will consider this problem later in the chapter. First, though, we'll look at a form of connection that sometimes competes with peer relationships, those between special friends.

Special Friendships

The term *friendship* is often used loosely to mean any sort of positive relationship, even if rather casual (Erwin, 1993). As used here, though, the term means something more precise: a **friendship** is a strong, lasting bond between particular individuals. As such, a friendship tends to survive changes in circumstances at least to some extent; friends who cannot see each other on one occasion, or in the context of one particular activity, are often willing to delay contact and change activities to sustain the relationship. Though friendships certainly can involve more than two people at a time, there is an inherent limit to how many can participate in a true friendship, simply because the time committed to any one friend reduces the time available to other potential friends.

Friendship as Experienced

Viewed this way, friendships between classmates often look different to participants on the inside than they do to observers on the outside, such as psychologists, parents, or teachers. To a participant, a friend provides secure companionship and affirmation of personal worth. These benefits can be especially valuable in school, where peers often hold diverse values and interests, only some of which are compatible with your own, and where individual performance is constantly being evaluated by teachers and others in authority (Rizzo, 1989). A few good friends—or even just one—can make dealing with these uncertainties easier. Because of these benefits, teachers can add a lot to students' self-confidence by supporting friendships among students. Deanna Melzian, a first-grade

Friendship to a first-grader . . . it certainly has a different meaning to a child than it does to us reading this book. To a six-year-old, a best friend can be someone whom he or she met at the park for the first time yesterday and played with for fifteen minutes. Friends can be easily bought, sold, and bargained for: "If you let me use your ball, I'll be your best friend." Friends can be very possessive: "If you play with anyone else, I won't be your friend anymore." Yet sometimes six-year-olds can be quite inclusive, welcoming new children and becoming "best friends" in a day. Cliquishness has not started yet. But even in first grade, children start gravitating to those who are outgoing, cute, or athletic.

Are all first-grade friendships fleeting and superficial? By no means. Many pairs of friends choose to sit together, run errands together, and play together the whole year. They quietly support and care for each other, or chatter away and entertain each other. The rest of the class is well aware of these undying loyalties, and often complain that "Yvette always chooses Amanda."

Friendship is frequently a curriculum theme in first grade. There is much opportunity to teach the value of friends and the methods for making and keeping them—a real mystery to some children. Books like the *Frog and Toad* series by Arnold Loebel are great springboards for discussion. As a teacher, I feel it is worth my time to help students relate to each other in a warm and friendly manner. But I also know that a child's view of relationships is not like mine, and that only time and practice will teach children to develop the deep, intimate friendships that we as adults cherish.

Deanna Melzian, First-grade teacher, Los Angeles, California

teacher from Los Angeles, California, shares this conclusion in the accompanying Multiple Voices box.

Friendship: A Psychologist's-eye View

But friendship as experienced in school often is not what special friendship means to outside observers. To a psychologist, what is often important about friendship is not that it makes school easier to bear but that it indicates developing social and cognitive maturity. Phases or stages of friendship unfold in a predictable sequence, with each stage representing a more sophisticated understanding of interpersonal relationships and resolving the limitations of the stage preceding it. One widely cited theory of this sort is the one originated by Robert Selman and his associates (Selman, 1980; Selman & Schultz, 1990), which describes individuals' ideas of friendship at different ages. According to Selman's account, preschool and early-school-age children think of a "friend" merely as someone to play with for the current moment. Whether or not their actions coincide with this idea, their notion of friendship includes little sense of loyalty, give-and-take, or reciprocity, which older people often assume in their definitions of friendship. As preschool children move into the elementary school years, they redefine friendship to include one-way assistance: a friend is now someone who helps you, though not necessarily someone whom you must help in return! By later elementary school, a friend becomes someone with whom you share activities and resources (games, snacks, and such), though the reciprocity implied by these activities is still tied very much to the current moment. Only in adolescence do young people begin defining friendship in terms of long-term continuity, mutual affection, and (eventually) concern for the friend's underlying psychological needs.

These are useful landmarks for thinking about students' relationships with special friends, but they also have two important limitations from the viewpoint of teachers. First, note that Selman is talking about *knowledge of* friendships, not about the actual enactment of a friendly relationship. It is quite possible, therefore, that a child or youth may develop a mature, general understanding of friendship without being able to implement or express the understanding in everyday relationships. Psychological stage theories, including Selman's, do not speak to this gap between experience and knowledge; yet it occurs frequently among students in classrooms.

The second limitation of Selman's stages is that the stages primarily concern the development of individuals and deal little with the impact of individual friendships on the groups or communities in which they occur. As with other stage theories (for example, Piaget's, described in Chapter 2), "higher" stages are assumed to be better than lower stages. In Selman's theory, a more sophisticated understanding of the concept of friendship is better than a less sophisticated concept. Although such an assumption is hard to argue with when viewed in isolation, its value is less clear when embedded in the complexities of everyday life in communities, including classroom communities. In the context of a classroom, is it always important that students develop the highest levels of interpersonal understanding? What if achieving the highest forms of understanding takes class time away from other valuable pursuits, such as developing better reading or math skills? Or what if fostering sophisticated interpersonal understandings in a class leads to more special friendships forming, causing "nonfriend" classmates to feel socially excluded or even rejected? Although these negative outcomes are not

In Your Own Voice

If the idea of a gap between knowledge of friendship and the experience of friendship seems odd to you, consider the relationships in your own life: are there some that have had unsatisfying, "immature" conflicts even though you can in principle imagine a better way to relate to the person?

(Think of a difficult parent or a difficult coworker.)

inevitable, they *do* result because of excessive attention to the needs of individuals at the expense of needs of the group.

Friendships: A Teacher's-eye View

To a teacher concerned with encouraging classroom learning, therefore, students' friendships present a complex picture. Though friendships often can assist students' learning, their effects are not always so benign. Consider the advantages: best friends may enjoy working together on cooperative projects, answer each other's questions about homework assignments, and offer support and consolation if one friend performs poorly on a test or an assignment. But consider the problems, too: best friends may form an exclusive clique when working within a larger group, literally do each other's homework, or fail to confront each other with hard truths (such as when one friend is not trying hard enough at schoolwork) in order to protect friendly feelings.

Lucille Logan remembered her best friend during high school: Megan Hill-Carroll. She recalled tenth grade, when they used to go to the library together after school, supposedly to study. In reality they spent a lot of time talking about cute boys. "I also remember perfecting the art of dividing homework so that we each did half and copied the other half from each other. I added in slight changes so that it looked like it was totally my own work. We saved a lot of time that way!" I asked, "Did your friendship help Lucille with learning?" "Oh, for sure! Megan helped me in a lot of ways—like when she always understood science classes better than me."

Rick Thain remembered a special friend from high school: "Jim and I used to send each other e-mail messages using the computers in the school lab, until the teachers told us that we had to stop." "Do you remember helpful things about knowing Jim?" I asked. "Well, when we had to give an oral report, we used to challenge each other to include some irrelevant word somewhere in the report—like *broccoli* or *snails*. Then we would sit and listen for the irrelevant word and try not to laugh when it came up. It actually made both of us pay more attention, but I doubt if the teachers would have approved!"

In Your Own Voice

One teacher who read this section told me that students' social relationships are more of a concern for elementary teachers than for secondary teachers.

Do you agree?

If so, why might that be true?

How, then, should a teacher respond to special friendships among students? (Surely you are not supposed to discourage friendships!) Mull over your own answer to this problem while you also consider mine: that the challenge for teachers is neither to encourage nor to discourage special friendships but to *use* them educationally (Wunsch, 1995). Can the empathy and commitment of friends somehow be enlisted to support students' learning? That is the question to ask—and to answer. One possible answer is to explore the usefulness of another type of special relationship, the one between mentors and protégés.

Mentoring Relationships

A **mentor** is someone who devotes himself or herself to developing the skills of another person, who is often called a **protégé**. Mentoring resembles a tutoring relationship, but also includes broader concerns such as sharing personal feelings and offering emotional support (Otto, 1995). It usually extends over time: for weeks, months, or even years, though rarely for a lifetime. All in all, a mentor behaves like or resembles other important, helpful people in a person's life while duplicating none of their roles exactly: the mentor is simultaneously like a parent, a teacher, and a special friend.

People of all ages participate in a variety of mentoring relationships, such as when a veteran teacher helps a new teacher to get established, or when an experienced coworker "adopts" a new staff member helpfully (Glover & Mardle, 1995). Mentoring relationships can also develop in classrooms in spite of the relative uniformity of students' ages. Mentoring is possible because of two facts of classroom life: even in a single classroom, students differ widely in background skills and talents, and

Mentoring relationships are based on clear differences in skill or experience between two individuals. A student who is older—or at least more knowledgeable—can be helpful to another student in ways that are partly like a teacher, and partly like an acquaintance or friend.
© Jean-Claude Lejeune/Stock Boston

the nature of school life encourages students to focus relationships on academic matters (Rizzo, 1989). These circumstances create the potential for some students to assist others in ways that are both caring (like a friend) and informed (like a teacher or parent): some students, in other words, can become mentors to other students.

As a teacher, how can you transform potential mentorships into actual ones? One way is to create work groups that deliberately include individuals with different levels of experience. This strategy does not guarantee helpfulness among students, but it does set the stage for it. For example, Mr. Lee tried creating diverse work groups in his end-of-year activity for his grade 8 class:

Annual Spring Life Days, Alexander Vincent Middle School

This year, we will be going camping! But you have a job to do to get ready. First, you must choose partners—at least one, and not more than three. There is an important rule about partners: your partners must include at least one person who has gone camping several times before and at least one person who has not! So ask around the class before you settle on partners. If you have trouble finding two people (including yourself) who meet the requirements, then see me and I will help you to look.

When you know your group members, you must plan your trip, using the guide provided on the other side of this sheet. As you will see, you will have to (1) find a parent sponsor (to help with planning and camping equipment as needed), (2) decide on a food menu, (3) plan an evening social activity for the whole class, and (4) select an environmental learning project for your group for the days that we will be away. You can choose from the suggestions on this sheet, but you may want to consider other ideas that you devise yourself. I will need all of this information no later than two weeks from today. Good luck!

In Your Own Voice

Perhaps Mr. Lee's problem is not that mentorship won't work but that a camping trip may not be the best activity on which to try it.

What do you think of this possibility?

If you agree, can you suggest an activity better suited for mentoring relationships?

Mr. Lee hoped that requiring veterans and novices to mix would promote helpful, mentorlike relationships. He pictured experienced students sharing their knowledge of meal planning, campsite social activities, and the like. Before the groups could even finish forming, however, Mr. Lee discovered a problem: there were not enough experienced campers—not enough potential "mentors"—to go around. Two of the veterans, furthermore, had not had the kind of experience helpful for planning a school-sponsored camping trip. They had always slept in a recreational vehicle rather than in tents on the ground, for example, or they had always left trip planning to their parents. One veteran camper did not enjoy her role as "expert" about camping to classmates: she had always felt dragged along on family camping trips, and now wanted as little to do with it as possible. That left three students qualified and willing to be experts to about twenty novice students. These three found their way in camping groups and began planning promptly. They were not happy, however, about having to expand their groups to include students who still lacked access to an experienced camper.

All in all, it seemed, expertise was not as widely available as Mr. Lee had originally assumed, nor as generally appropriate for students' needs.

Discovering these problems was frustrating, but Mr. Lee realized that lack of expertise among classmates did not have to rule out a camping trip altogether, nor rule out the sharing of knowledge in some form. He reflected on what to do. Invite an adult with camping experience to class to help the students plan? Regroup students according to motivation to learn about camping rather than according to their experience with it? The bottom line, he reminded himself, was not to insist on mentorship experiences as such but to stress the positive features underlying mentorships: mutual helpfulness in spite of diversity among students. Mr. Lee thought about this idea as he got ready to revise his preparations for the camping trip.

If Mr. Lee had had access to students from more than one classroom, he could have also tried another way to encourage mentorships: deliberately mixing students of different ages together for an activity or even for the entire school year. Students from grades 4, 5, and 6, for example, might be placed in a single classroom group in roughly equal proportions, creating a wider spread of ages and maturities than a typical single-age or single-grade class. Research to evaluate mixed-age programs has found the practice helpful to both older and younger students (Katz, Evangelou & Hartman, 1990). Older students are more likely to teach or tutor material to younger students, both formally (at the teacher's request) and informally (without the teacher knowing it). Learning results not only for the younger students but for their older peer-teachers as well (Foster-Harrison, 1997). And there are social benefits: because of the range of maturities, older, experienced students are more likely to help younger, inexperienced students learn the routines and expectations of the teacher. Veterans also offer support to newcomers, introducing them to other children and to play activities. The "protégés," for their part, also give something to the relationship in the form of respect for the experience of their mentors: they learn the ways of the classroom community and appreciate the help they receive. That is what happened to Kyla (grade 1) and Elizabeth (grade 3) in their multi-age class:

In Your Own Voice

This is all well and good for elementary-age students, but will it work for adolescents in high school?

Could you imagine yourself in a peer-mentoring relationship as a high school student?

If not, think about how else teachers might encourage helpfulness among students.

It was lunchtime. Most students were putting away their work and getting their coats. Kyla stood in a daze, looking just a bit worried. It was her first week in the multi-age class—her first week, in fact, in the school itself.

"Here," said Elizabeth, "you're supposed to put your papers there [points to boxes by the side of the room]. Then go get your coat." Kyla did as Elizabeth told her, but kept one eye on Elizabeth all the while. "You can come with me at lunch; I'll show you where we eat. Though I warn you, it's going to be mostly big kids!"

In this situation, Kyla gets help and Elizabeth gets appreciation. A potential mentor-protégé relationship is born. Note, though, that what the students "get" is not equivalent: Kyla may eventually receive enough help before Elizabeth receives enough appreciation, or vice versa. This assymmetry suggests that sooner or later, the basis for the mentoring relationship will need to change. Teachers can help this process so that a mentorship that begins as a satisfying social tie does not end as an annoyance to the mentor.

How can you help develop mentoring relationships and help keep them positive once they have begun? One way is to recognize the inherent limits on this sort of relationship so that you do not expect more from it than it can provide. In some situations, for example, mentors may be scarce: many students may need extended help and support with math, but relatively few have expert knowledge or a sustained desire to be helpful. Worse yet, some potential protégés may be hard to match with a mentor, no matter what their needs. A student with a dark skin color or with a particular disability, for example, may be less likely to find a helpful friend than equally deserving classmates. As the teacher, you can (and should) counteract biases such as these by deliberately arranging for students with differences to work together on tasks and projects. The resulting relationships may not develop into true mentorships, but often they will at least become truly cooperative ones (Slavin, 1995).

Once a mentoring relationship has begun, you can help it to flourish by recognizing the frequent need to gradually transform mentor and protégé from unequal partners into equal ones. As Elizabeth and Kyla's situation implies, these two girls may not always want to be leader and follower forever; a day may come when Kyla does not need or even want Elizabeth's advice any longer, or when Elizabeth grows tired of giving it. An early sign of change is often budding competition between mentor and protégé: the mentor may seem to dismiss a protégé's ideas and actions unfairly, or the protégé may challenge a mentor more openly and frequently (Devlin, 1995). If and when these changes occur, you as the teacher can help by (gently) encouraging the partners toward defining their relationship in new ways, ways built on more equal, nonmentor foundations. Even so, either or both partners may feel some loss, since a valued relationship will be transforming or even dissolving. Loss and disappointment, however, are preferable to the alternatives, which can include never having friends at all.

Few Relationships

Unfortunately, some students withdraw from most relationships, not because they have been rejected by others but because they experience more than usual amounts of shyness in the presence of others. **Shyness** is a predisposition to be extremely concerned about the evaluations of others, and especially about the possibility of rejection by others. Most of us feel it at some time, no matter how outgoing we usually are. Shyness provides protection—a sensible response to unfamiliar situations and people, and especially to those who have power to hurt us or put us to shame. When carried too far, though, it creates too much caution. A shy student may never speak in class, for example, for fear of looking foolish (Zimbardo, 1990). He or she may never ask a peer for minor help on an assignment for fear that the request will be rejected, and as a result make it less likely that the favor will be returned or that a friendship will develop.

The Nature of Shyness

In certain ways, shyness feels different than it looks. From the inside, it is dominated by low self-esteem; from the outside, it seems dominated by a mixture of submissiveness and unfriendliness. Listen to what Edwin, a fourth-grader, told his school counselor, and then listen to his teacher, Ms. Overton:

Edwin: I don't know . . . it's hard for me to look at the teacher—I forget what I'm going to say when I do that. I keep wondering what she will think of what I say, whether it'll be wrong. Then she can't wait for me, and skips to others. [Long pause] The kids get impatient with me, too, 'cause I stumble over my words—take a long time, correct myself. [Pause] But I *do* listen

Ms. Overton: Edwin sure is quiet! I probably only heard him speak maybe once in the last week. But he gives up so easily, too: if he can't think of what he wants to say, he clams up, puts his head down, looks away—that kind of thing. So the others stop asking him for advice, like they do with each other in group work; when one girl did ask him for the answer to a

pretty well. [Pause] Umm, and it's easier when I can talk to someone one at a time, alone. I hate groups, especially the group oral reports that we had to do last month. Nobody really wanted me in their group. I can see why.

math problem this week, he just said, "I don't know," even though I knew he did have the answer. It frustrates me! He's perfectly bright, but he defeats himself by turning into this "bland" sort of creature. What am I supposed to do?

Both Edwin and Ms. Overton agree that Edwin doesn't talk very much, because his silence is plainly observable. But Edwin also describes attributes to which Ms. Overton has little access: self-blame ("No one wanted me . . . I can see why") and fear about what others may think when he speaks. Ms. Overton, on the other hand, describes attributes that Edwin apparently does not see in himself. He seems to give up too easily, she thinks, and he gives an impression of being defensive when he pretends not to know an arithmetic answer that he really did know.

Students become shy for a variety of reasons, and the reasons make some difference in how teachers can respond to shyness most helpfully. One possibility is genetic: research suggests that human temperament (or personality "styles") is to some extent inborn. Even from birth, some infants seem more inhibited than others in their responses to adult smiles, for example, or more fearful of strangers (Kagan, 1994). Such tendencies are not the same as social shyness per se, but they could predispose some individuals to shyness. Most psychologists agree, however, that certain childhood experiences and kinds of relationships are necessary for shyness to develop significantly (Wolff, 1995). It does not help, for example, for parents to hold excessively high standards of achievement, since overly high standards can convince the child that he or she is really valued only for achievements and not for himself or herself. On the other hand, parents are not necessarily the cause of shyness: the problem can also be triggered or exaggerated because a child has qualities that society stigmatizes, such as particular racial features or a physical disability.

Helping Shy Students

As a teacher, you can do certain things to make shy students more comfortable in class and therefore more likely to interact more freely (Ramsey, 1991). The strategies vary from specific to broad:

- *Minimize activities in which some children may get left out.* A classic example is the exchange of valentines in elementary school. If this activity is not handled tactfully, some students may end up with fewer valentines or even none at all, and the shy student is one of the more likely ones to be shortchanged. Another example is invitations to birthday parties: since such parties are by definition "private" activities, students are entitled to invite whom they please—and also to leave out whom they please. But as the teacher, you can either spotlight the informal exchange of invitations with offhand comments of your own ("Ah, so you got an invitation too?" spoken so others can hear) or gloss over the exchange. For the shy student's sake, glossing over is more desirable.

- *Be reasonable about requiring activities that make many students self-conscious.* Giving an oral presentation, for example, is a nerve-wracking experience for many students, even though it may also be a good experience for building confidence and clarifying students' thinking. But if a student is so anxiety ridden that she or he simply cannot think coherently, the activity may simply function to shame the student. In such a case, you can find a less threatening way to work toward the same educational benefits, such as making a presentation to a small group instead of the whole class or making sure the topic is one in which the shy student has special expertise.

- *Have realistic expectations for your students, including the shy student in particular.* This advice may seem obvious, but it is easy to forget in the case of a student who is very withdrawn. For one thing, the student may seem "incompetent" because he or she rarely speaks or asks questions. Your expectations may therefore go down—ironically, sending a message that you lack confidence in the student. For another, you may also be tempted to continually urge the student toward greater effort, since it may seem as if he or she is simply "lazy" or not trying hard enough. In this case, you may appear to be blaming the student's problems on himself or herself when the "laziness" really results from not understanding the current material.

- *Devise activities that give respected roles to the shy student.* These activities can be woven into normal routines, such as when you simply acknowledge the student when she or he arrives in class, or when you manage whole-class discussions to ensure calling on the shy student occasionally as well as on other students. Or the activities can be more deliberately chosen, such as when you assign stories or literature that portray the problem of shyness sympathetically or arrange group projects in a way that guarantees a meaningful, comfortable role for the shy student in the group.

- *Avoid labeling a student as "shy."* If you must describe the student for any reason, focus on the student's behavior using neutral terms: "He/she takes longer to get to know people" or "He/she is selective about his/her friends" is more diplomatic and less stigmatizing than "He/she is shy." The label can take on a life of its own, especially when used by an authority such as the teacher. The shy student is inclined to take your diagnosis at face value rather than challenge it; and, to some extent, nonshy classmates may do the same.

Enemies, Temporary and Otherwise

More noticeable than shy students because they can be more disruptive are students who dislike each other. As in any other group that lives or works together for extended time, most classes contain some unpleasant relationships. From the teacher's point of view, students' personal dislikes are not necessarily something for which you are responsible, any more than you are ordinarily responsible for students' choices of friends. You may have to involve yourself, however, if personality conflicts interfere with learning and teaching. It becomes a problem—*your* problem—if hostility between individuals prevents cooperation on assignments, keeps other classmates from interacting normally, or spreads so widely that others must "choose up sides." When dislikes have these effects, someone must seek to contain or resolve them so that classroom life can proceed. That someone usually includes the teacher.

Sources of Conflict

How do negative relationships develop in the first place? One possible source is students' normal human discomfort with behaviors, attitudes, and qualities that seem alien or that students lack in themselves:

After school, grade 5: Michael is taking his "secret" detour home today, because the other boys started following him again, teasing him as he walked. "Hey, geek!" they called to him, and "if you're so smart, why can't you throw a ball straight?" The first time this happened, Michael tried answering them, but later he decided it was easier simply to avoid them. So he started taking a long, indirect way home. It hurt to think about why he was doing so, but he was starting not to care, starting simply to dislike the "gang."

Noon hour, grade 9: Today Jorgé has made it through the first week at a new school, and he is discovering a new challenge at lunch hour. He sees that most students eat bag lunches outside the school and seem to belong to unofficial "eating areas." A group of African American students have sat by the main door each day. Some "nerds" have adopted an area on the side of the building. Under the windows of the main office, mainly girls congregate (it's less rowdy there), but the Hispanic girls sit separately from the white girls. Around back seems to be a lot of jocks. Where, wonders Jorgé, should I eat?

At the heart of both of these situations is the pain of exclusion: the shame that you can be (or already have been) excluded by peers, or even rejected actively, and the fear that friendships may therefore become impossible. Shame and fear can loom as potential threats, as with Jorgé, or come closer to realization, as with Michael. Or they can strike vividly at the heart, as with Valerie and Sheila:

Five minutes before class, grade 11, Monday morning: Valerie has taken her usual seat. She is waiting for the bell to ring. Others drift in, talking cheerfully. Her best friend, Sheila, arrives and takes her seat, one just across from Valerie. She greets Valerie cheerfully: "Hi! How was your weekend?" Valerie mumbles something, looks down, fidgets. Sheila watches, puzzled. Then she does it: Valerie gets up and takes a different seat, one far from Sheila. Why? thinks Sheila. She will not find out right away, even though Valerie could easily tell her the reason if she chose: on Saturday Valerie saw Sheila at the movie theater, sitting with a boy Valerie had been dating.

There is no denying that students involved in events such as these find them disturbing and that teachers should respond to the students in ways that are sympathetic and supportive. But should you, as a teacher, do more than this? Should you intervene actively? Think about what "active intervention" might mean, for example, in the three cases just described. If you found out about Michael's situation, should you reprimand the boys who are teasing him and forbid them to hassle Michael? In Jorgé's situation, should you talk to the students about the importance of inviting newcomers into existing social circles, of being flexible and open about whom you eat with? If you suspected that Sheila was hurting Valerie's feelings, should you try to find out why, or even try doing something to repair the damage between them?

Dealing with Conflict

How much to intervene in a conflict depends partly on your own personal values—how much you believe, for example, that individuals should solve personal and social problems by themselves. But it also depends on the impact of the conflict on your major purpose as a teacher, which is to encourage learning to the fullest extent possible. If conflict seems to prevent respect among students, mutual support for learning, or the sharing of ideas, it may in fact be time to intervene. You must recreate, in other words, a community of learners, even if the learners are not necessarily personal friends.

How can you accomplish this task? There are no simple formulas, since every conflict relationship is different. But there are also numerous strategies to consider, strategies used with some success by teachers, educational leaders, and university researchers. (In fact, you might want to consult some of the references cited in the next several paragraphs, because they give more detailed suggestions than I can do here.) Here are just five of them. They may help, but do approach them cautiously! You will have to decide how well they fit your particular circumstances.

Classroom Rules of Civility It often helps to insist on basic civility—courtesy and good manners—for all classroom activities and for schoolwide activities if you can enlist support from other teachers or from the principal (Zuelke & Willerman, 1992). A good time to establish an expectation of basic courtesy is at the beginning of the year, before students have had time to develop personal friendships and dislikes that might make some students selective in the people to whom they are courteous. But rules and guidelines can also be discussed periodically throughout the school year, particularly when and if conflicts arise that create rude behaviors or exclusionary attitudes in certain students.

Community Building Some activities can build general commitment to classmates as a community and in this way help to prevent conflicts from arising or becoming difficult (Johnson & Johnson, 1991). With elementary students, for example, you can challenge them to solve a set of coded messages cooperatively and then piece the messages together into a coherent paragraph. High school students can try the same activity with more difficult codes, or they can create coded messages themselves and use them to challenge classmates.

Role Playing Significant Conflicts Often it helps to have students act out conflicts that affect the class as a whole and then discuss their reactions to the dramatization (Macbeth & Fine, 1995). To protect individuals' privacy, however, it may be wise to modify the details of a role-played conflict, making it relevant to as broad a range of students as possible. Instead of acting out Valerie and Sheila's conflict exactly, for example, you might propose role playing a slightly different story of personal betrayal and its aftermath. Discussion after the dramatization can take the form of a class meeting, such as those recommended in Chapter 6 (see page 191) for establishing guidelines for appropriate classroom behavior (Glasser, 1990).

Involve Others When Conflicts Escalate Besides teachers, there are other professionals to assist with conflicts among students, both inside and outside school—school counselors, the principal, social workers, even the police (Besag, 1989; Hill & Hill, 1994). Whom to call on depends on the nature of the conflict: is it chronic or occasional, violent or verbal, widespread or confined to a few? It also depends on the services actually available in your school or community. As a rule of thumb, large urban school districts tend to have access to larger numbers of professionals in supporting roles, though many exceptions to this trend exist.

Involve Parents in Particular Research on parent-teacher relationships has concluded repeatedly that students are helped by almost any form of parent involvement in the school and by many types of communication between parents and teachers (see, for example, McCaleb [1994]).

In classrooms and communities that are multicultural, communication among parents, teachers, and students can sometimes be challenging. But it can happen —particularly if teachers make an effort for it to happen.
© Robin L. Sachs/Photo Edit

When conflicts between students become difficult or chronic, therefore, it can sometimes help to seek advice and support from parents about how to handle them. In some schools, parent advisory committees assist in developing policies about appropriate school behavior, and recommend or even organize new programs that defuse difficult relationships among students, such as racism or gang-related violence. In the long term, however, parental involvement is most effective if it begins *before* difficulties among students arise so that communication with parents is already established when you or the students need it the most.

Relationships with Parents

s the previous paragraph suggests, the roles of parent and teacher sometimes overlap: both can act as either mentors or caregivers, though each emphasizes different life problems and does so for different assortments of children and for different periods of time. For the sake of students, therefore, it is important for teachers to work as closely as possible with parents—though, as we'll see soon, "working closely" does not always mean a parent must literally visit the classroom on a regular basis. Also for the sake of the students, it is important for teachers to notice when family relationships do not seem to be working well and to respond appropriately. The rest of this chapter will address each of these key points.

At first blush, parents and teachers seem to have different relationships to young people, the one acting as primary caregiver for children and the other as primary mentor, or developer of talent. In reality, though, their roles overlap considerably, or at least they do when they are carried out effectively (Epstein, 1990; Martin, 1992). Like teachers, parents often relate to their children as mentors: they set up conditions for their children's learning, provide periodic academic guidance, discuss ideas, encourage the use of language for self-expression, and set standards for both school-related and other learning. Parents create small "communities of learning," like those described for teachers and classrooms in Chapter 2 (see page 56): they assist children's (or students') thinking and skills until children themselves can perform independently (Vygotsky, 1978). Teachers, for their part, often concern themselves

In Your Own Voice

Can you think of something that a parent or relative consciously *taught* you?

How about some way in which a teacher showed care or concern for you as a person?

If you cannot, is the reason because of you, because of your teachers, or because my ideas are overstated?

with the welfare of their students as human beings without regard for academic performance: they seek to bolster students' confidence and self-esteem, they make allowances for personal stresses (such as when a student's parents divorce), and they intervene if they suspect a student is being abused, either at home or elsewhere. Viewed in these ways, parents and teachers are not as different as they first appear.

To understand how parents' and teachers' activities potentially overlap, let's think about their respective activities more closely. First, we'll look at exactly how parents can assist learning in the manner of teachers; later we'll look at how teachers can show the kind of personal concern usually associated with parents. Keep in mind that the two kinds of overlap are only potentials: at some time, every parent does not—or cannot—support a child's learning, and no teacher can be concerned with students' personal lives exclusively (Procidano, 1993). These distinctions are also important, so I will comment on them where appropriate.

Parents as Mentors

In what ways, exactly, do parents sometimes resemble teachers? Put briefly, parents act like teachers whenever they ensure regular work habits in children, provide academic guidance and support, or encourage discussion of ideas and the use of school-like language (Kellaghan et al., 1993). To see how this can happen, consider a relatively clear example: a family with two parents, one child, one breadwinner (the father) with a satisfactory income, and one homemaker (the mother) who enjoys her role. Suppose further that this family is currently experiencing no major stresses. (Never mind for now that a family of this sort may actually be statistically unusual or even privileged economically in current social realities; later we will consider the impact of other configurations, incomes, and stress levels on how parents can act as teachers.) We'll call this two-parent, middle-class family the Stauffers, their third-grade child Vicki, and the child's teacher Ms. Tennyson. The Stauffers and Ms. Tennyson have each posted a chart in their respective territories, the kitchen and the classroom. The charts in Tables 7.1 and 7.2 summarize individuals' regular responsibilities.

Judging by the two charts, both Ms. Tennyson and the Stauffers encourage regularity in completing tasks. Each chart, furthermore, includes both academic tasks (homework, language arts) and activities that are personal or social (tidying bedroom, preparing for recess). Each

TABLE 7.1 Chart on the Stauffers' Refrigerator

Family Chore Chart		Mon	Tues	Wed	Thurs	Fri
7:00	Feed cat	V	M	D	V	M
7:15	Make breakfast	D	M	D	M	D
7:30	Wash dishes	M	V	V	D	V
4:00	Homework (as needed)	V	V	V	V	V
5:00	Cook dinner	M	D	V+M	M	D
5:30	Set table	D	V	M	D	V
6:30	Wash dishes	V	M	D	V	M
7:00	Homework (as needed)	V	V	V	V	V
8:00	TV or reading	V/M/D	V/M/D	V/M/D	V/M/D	V/M/D
9:00	Bedtime	V	V	V	V	V

V = Vicki, M = Mom (Ms. Stauffer), D = Dad (Mr. Stauffer)

TABLE 7.2 Chart on Ms. Tennyson's Classroom Bulletin Board

Classroom Daily Routine	
8:30	Attendence and announcement
8:45	Language arts
9:45	Free reading
10:10	Recess
10:30	Mathematics
11:15	Science
12:00	Lunch
12:45	Social studies
1:30	Physical education
2:15	Recess
2:35	Art/music (alternate days)
3:15	Dismissal

Note: Schedule will change for assemblies and holidays.

chart implies academic guidance and support for Vicki: time is made available for homework (at home) or learning tasks (at school). Apparently both Ms. Tennyson and the Stauffers know at least something of what Vicki should currently be learning, as well as something about her recreational needs. In these important ways, parents and teacher are reinforcing each other's efforts.

Less visible in the charts, but no less important, are other similarities in the ways the Stauffers parent and the ways Ms. Tennyson teaches. When Vicki was young, for example, the Stauffers read stories to her almost every day; this activity helped Vicki to learn about the nature of print and learn "literate" ways of speaking. Ms. Tennyson built on this knowledge of print and of literacy, asking Vicki to read further and talk in class about stories that she assigned or that Vicki selected. For years, too, the Stauffers often used school-like ways of talking with Vicki, a style that linguists call *Standard English*. At the dinner table and elsewhere, their sentences were complete and grammatically correct, and their vocabularies relatively large. Ms. Tennyson spoke in this same style in class and expected it from students, including Vicki. In later grades, Ms. Stauffer often helped Vicki with homework problems, essentially acting as an unpaid teaching assistant, though in this case an assistant located at Vicki's home. Thanks to all of these similarities between the Stauffers and Ms. Tennyson, it should not be surprising that Vicki prospered both in school and at home. Guidance, support, and involvement all came together for Vicki's benefit, thanks to her good fortune in having parents with the time, economic security, and motivation to support the teacher's work.

In Your Own Voice

The reality, of course, often is not as I portray it here for the Stauffer family; for various reasons, parents are not always fully available.

When this happens, how should a teacher (or the teacher's school) respond to compensate effectively for the support a student is missing?

The Varieties of Families: How Many Mentors, How Often?

As I already implied, the problem with the example of the Stauffers and Ms. Tennyson is that relatively few families actually resemble the Stauffers in composition, economic advantage, or motivation. Time pressures and the stresses of breadwinning mean that realistically, most parents cannot truly act as complete educational mentors for their own children, as Mon Cochran, professor of family studies at Cornell University, points out in the accompanying

MULTIPLE VOICES

MULTIPLE VOICES

MULTIPLE VOICES

MULTIPLE VOICES

In reflecting on the idea of parents as mentors, I find myself making a distinction: parents *mentor* their children part of the time, but they are not *mentors* in the sense that teachers are. The distinction has to do with the healthy irrationality of parent-child relationships. Parents are (and should be) crazy about their children, whereas teachers bring a more reasoned, thoughtful orientation to relationships with students in their classes.

Put their emotionally based relationship together with the time pressures that parents face, and the result is mentoring that may be only occasional and is often unconnected with academic learning. Hence the need for structured ways to create consistency between what is expected of children at home and what is expected from them at school. Teachers can facilitate development of common expectations by providing students and their parents with parent-child activities that make use of the knowledge and skills taught in the classroom. Parents will appreciate the opportunity to interact with their children around games, puzzles, and other activities linked to classroom learning, especially if the teacher and principal make it clear that such home-based interaction is legitimate "parent involvement," with as much value to the school as volunteering in the classroom or serving on a parent-teacher council.

Mon Cochran, Professor of family studies, Cornell University

Multiple Voices box. As Professor Cochran also points out, though, the problem is lack of time, knowledge, and resources, not lack of interest.

However, some families also face additional stresses. About 70 percent of all mothers in the 1990s work outside the home, including somewhere between 30 and 50 percent of mothers of early-school-age students (United States Department of Labor, 1994). About one-third of all children witness their own parents' divorce, and most of these children live for significant periods in single-parent households or in "blended" stepfamilies (Procidano & Fisher, 1992). Furthermore, in some communities and families, children are now raised by various relatives, such as an aunt or a grandparent, in addition to their biological parents (Chavkin, 1993; Francasso & Busch-Rossnagel, 1992). Do these circumstances affect whether parents can act as mentors for their children? The general answer is "it depends." Family configuration *may* influence parents' ability to assist children's learning, but it does not determine it in any simple way.

Single-Parent Families

Depending on the community in which you work, anywhere from 15 to 50 percent of all families will be headed by a single parent, usually the mother (Carlson, 1992). How might this circumstance affect a child in school? In and of itself, having only one parent may make little difference; the majority of such families, in fact, function quite well (Alexander, 1994). The "problem" of single parenthood stems more from conditions often—but not always—associated with this type of family:

- Some single parents are single because they have separated from a spouse recently; as a result, they may still be feeling the stress and conflicts associated with this change. Others may have been single parents for years, have received substantial support from relatives and neighbors, and currently be experiencing little stress with the responsibilities involved (Miller, 1992).

- Because of separation or divorce, some single parents do not live with their children full time; a former spouse often has custody part of the time, a circumstance that makes consistency in child-rearing practices difficult or impossible (Maccoby & Mnookin, 1992).

- Some single parents are very young (even adolescents) and therefore may lack the psychological and material resources needed to care for a child skillfully.

- Most single parents are women and hence are relatively likely to experience society's economic biases against work stereotypically associated with women: they earn relatively low wages.

- Low income is especially likely for the youngest single mothers, but most older mothers also experience a substantial decline in standard of living if and when their marriages dissolve (Everett, 1994).

- Since single parents must function as both breadwinner and homemaker, they experience relatively heavy demands on their time.

If several of these conditions converge on one family, they can interfere with the sort of support that the Stauffers were able to provide for Vicki. Time becomes scarce, so visits to a child's teacher become difficult to arrange; even scheduling a phone call to the school can take effort. Income can also become scarce, or at least decrease, so issues of economic survival may loom larger in a parent's mind than a child's progress in school. Consistency in household routines becomes hard to arrange and enforce: if the child visits the ex-spouse, she or he may encounter household routines and standards different from those of the first parent (Maccoby & Mnookin, 1992).

Stepfamilies

About 80 percent of all people remarry after a first divorce (Cherlin, 1992). When the remarriages involve children, they create "blended" families or *stepfamilies,* families in which some members are related legally but not biologically. From a child's point of view, a parent's remarriage can be either good or bad, depending, as always, on the circumstances. If a child used to live with his or her mother, remarriage may mean a rise in standard of living, so worries about money may subside. But the child may also face new challenges in getting along with a stepparent or stepsiblings; the two formerly distinct families may have developed different habits, styles of interacting, and standards of tidiness, and—most important for teachers—different levels of motivation for academic work. A child may have to adjust to these differences at the same time she or he must adjust to the loss of daily access to one parent due to an earlier divorce. It may take effort, therefore, to develop consistent expectations for all children in the family such as the consistency the Stauffers were able to provide in our earlier example. It should come as no surprise, therefore, that some children's academic performance may decline in the aftermath of divorce and remarriage, or that behavior problems may occur or increase.

Dual-Earner Families

In families with two parents, and unlike the Stauffer family, about 70 percent of mothers now work outside the home (United States Department of Labor, 1994). The trend has developed relatively quickly by historical standards, beginning in the 1940s and continuing up to the present. Does the presence of two breadwinners affect a child's welfare, and in particular affect a child's educational progress? Obviously parents who each hold a job should have less time for family matters than parents who hold only one job between them. On the face of it, dual-earner families therefore should experience time-related stress, and at least some of that stress might affect their children. In general, though, research has consistently found only time-budgeting problems, not ill effects on children (Lerner, 1994). As with the other family variations discussed here, the impact on children depends heavily on the surrounding conditions:

- *Psychological support for working:* Gender roles still encourage more guilt in mothers about working outside the home than in fathers. This particular gender gap is alleviated considerably, however, if family members (spouse *and* children) support the idea of the mother working as wholeheartedly as possible (Lerner, 1994).

- *Material support for working:* Gender and family roles also induce fathers and children, on average, *not* to increase their contributions to household work even when the mother works (Apter, 1994). But this tendency is only an average; fathers and children who do "pick up the slack" on housework can significantly reduce the stress of both parents working.

- *The real demands of the parents' two jobs:* Some jobs create more stress than others, and some jobs require more time away from spouse or children. If both parents hold high-demand, high-stress jobs, time and attention to parenting may indeed suffer. More commonly, however, at least one parent holds a job that is lower-demand or even part time; so the negative impact on parenting may be reduced or eliminated.

Judging from the research, having dual-earner parents will not harm children if family members support the mother's working, if family members take up a larger share of housework, and if neither parent's job involves excessive demands or stress. These conditions probably do hold for many dual-earner families, though not for all.

Bilingual and Bicultural Families

Approximately 10 to 15 percent of all families in North America are bilingual (that is, speak more than one language), and the proportion is much higher in other parts of the world (Arias & Casanova, 1993). This circumstance obviously can affect relationships with teachers: you cannot speak directly and fluently with a parent if you do not speak the parent's language. Even when both parent and teacher do speak the same language, though, culturally based beliefs and expectations about children can create misunderstandings and impair communication.

In one recent research study, observations of parent-teacher confer-

In Your Own Voice

Note that the research emphasizes that the parent who needs support for working is the mother, not the father.

This implies a question about whether the mother should work, but not a similar question about the father.

What do you think: is this a subtle form of gender bias in the research or merely a reflection of reality?

ences suggested that Hispanic parents tended to express different values and priorities about children in the conference than did Anglo teachers (Greenfield, 1995). The parents assumed a more communal view of human nature and the teacher a more individualistic view. Awkwardness was the result, as in this meeting between Ms. Hamilton and Ms. Davila:

Ms. Hamilton Meets Ms. Davila

It is parent conference day at Ms. Hamilton's school. Ms. Davila walks in with her daughter, Maria, looking a bit uncertain. Since it is still early in the school year, Ms. Davila is not sure what to expect from the conference.

Ms. Hamilton begins by showing Ms. Davila a folder full of Maria's written work. "She has made wonderful strides in writing, Ms. Davila! Look at this story about cats—she wrote it just last week. Her sentences are a lot longer now, and show her new vocabulary. . . . She's been working hard. . . ."

Ms. Davila looks at the folder, but says nothing for the first moment. "She's a good girl, Maria," she says, patting her daughter on the back gently. "Helpful to everyone; listens well. 'People smart,' she seems to me!" She continues to read the story about cats, though she isn't really concentrating on it.

Ms. Hamilton shifts to arithmetic, pulls out recent number problem sheets, and shows a one-page description of the semester's arithmetic curriculum goals. "She's having some trouble with borrowing in subtraction problems, but overall I'm pretty satisfied. What do you think?" She spreads out a sample of Maria's work for Ms. Davila to look at.

Ms. Davila looks at Maria, not at the problem sheets. "She knows where to get help when she needs it. Her brother can do arithmetic really well; he can be really helpful." She pauses; Ms. Hamilton is also pausing. Both are wondering what to say next. Each is thinking the same thought: something is not quite right about this conversation. It's like we're talking past each other, thinks Ms. Hamilton.

The two women smile at each other cautiously. Ms. Hamilton shows Ms. Davila other material by Maria, but she says less about it now. There are more pauses. The conference ends early, with neither parent nor teacher really satisfied.

What went wrong in this meeting? Perhaps it was that Ms. Hamilton and Ms. Davila wanted to talk about different topics. Ms. Hamilton focused on Maria's individuality and academic achievements, but Ms. Davila focused on Maria's ability to cooperate and take advantage of others' strengths, including academic strengths. For Ms. Davila, these are important life skills, and Maria's "individuality" lay (perhaps paradoxically) in her ability to fit in with the community. Both women are

MULTIPLE VOICES
MULTIPLE VOICES
MULTIPLE VOICES
MULTIPLE VOICES

Everyone, whether teacher or parents, needs to feel recognized and validated. As a counselor in a multi-ethnic primary school, I feel the responsibility and challenge for creating positive communication with parents lies mostly with the classroom teacher or other school staff. Occasionally, though, personal worries or issues can make communicating a challenge even for a professional teacher!

Here's an example. Ms. Jones taught a third-grade class with many Spanish-speaking bilingual children. She was determined that José Garcia be kept in third grade for another year. She had several reasons: José was physically small, his behavior was impulsive and immature, and academically he was at first-grade reading level. Ms. Jones was also aware that José was part of a large family, that Spanish was spoken in his home, and that both parents worked. These facts had nothing to do with wanting José to repeat third grade, but they had made it tricky this year, and at times frustrating, to communicate with the Garcia family.

School staff arranged a meeting to decide about José's future, and Ms. Garcia was able to get time off work to attend. Through a bilingual interpreter at the meeting, she discovered, among other things, that the family was facing severe financial difficulties, that José was the only (and highly valued) son, and that both parents were in marital counseling (father was a recovering alcoholic). This last fact had been shared reluctantly, with tears and embarrassment. Ms. Garcia delayed signing the agreement to keep José in third grade, saying it would "hurt his feelings about himself" and that José's father would be "very upset." Everyone, including Ms. Jones, agreed to wait for a final decision until Mr. Garcia could be present.

Speaking in English, and in Ms. Garcia's presence, Ms. Jones mentioned that she found it easier to talk with José's father because he spoke more English, and that she was certain that she could "get him to agree" to the grade retention. Ms. Garcia left the meeting with further tears—although, because of the language barrier, it was not clear how much she had understood. Because of the language barrier, furthermore, and because of Ms. Garcia's obvious respect for authority figures (like teachers and her husband), Ms. Garcia was too anxious and discouraged to explore other ways the school might help with José's lack of academic progress.

So connection did not occur. Ms. Jones felt like she had failed and, in a kind of ripple effect, so did Ms. Garcia. What went wrong? It seems to me that as professionals, teachers need to recognize that students and parents need support and respect at all times. Unpleasant or difficult news can be more palatable if coupled with positive recognition of a student's qualities and accomplishments. All parents, regardless of background, appreciate such recognition! Teachers have a responsibility for promoting this part of communication with parents. That's their job, after all: to be heard, understood, and accepted.

Donna Olson, Elementary school counselor, Hawthorne, California

challenged to communicate effectively; in particular, they need not only to listen to each other's words but also to understand the unstated priorities guiding those words. As the teacher, though, Ms. Hamilton faces not only the challenge to communicate but also a professional responsibility to meet the challenge. Unlike Ms. Davila, she is being paid to understand diverse students' needs; achieving such understanding involves hearing parents' true concerns about their children, as those concerns are meant to be heard. A parent should be able to get through to the teacher because of, rather than in spite of, the teacher's efforts to understand. This is also the conclusion reached in the accompanying Multiple Voices box featuring Donna Olson, an elementary school counselor in Hawthorne, California; as she points out, in fact, the encounter sometimes can be even more frustrating than the one between Ms. Hamilton and Ms. Davila if the teacher cannot meet a parent more than halfway in communicating or fails to include positive comments about the child when doing so.

Responding Appropriately to Parents

RECOGNIZING uniqueness is the key to understanding relationships, whether among students, within families, or between parents and teachers. Like individual people, individual relationships are one of a kind, full of unique chemistries that create peers, friends, and (even) enemies. This principle is equally true for the relationships that define families, relationships teachers sometimes catch glimpses of in parent-teacher conferences or other community contacts. Therefore, there are few generalizations or predictable patterns for understanding the ties that bind your classroom of students among themselves or to their local community. The families and children that you meet are not necessarily similar to you or your own family in particular, nor similar to other families you know well—nor should they be. This can be a hard lesson to learn even for seasoned professional teachers, but it is an important one on which to reflect.

In spite of this disclaimer, however, there are two principles about parents as mentors that are universal and that you can safely assume in working with them. One is that in general, *parents do care* about their children's education; it is a rare mother or father who is truly indifferent (Epstein, 1990). The other is that *time can be scarce* to visit school, as it can be for other important activities of parenting or teaching. A family's configuration can aggravate this problem, but to some extent all parents share it: everyone who raises children has to juggle time among a paying job, homemaking responsibilities, and—last but hopefully not least—contacts with teachers and the school.

The most helpful way to relate to parents, therefore, is by respecting their good intentions and the stiff competition for time that they face. Can you find ways to communicate with them that do not require their physical presence at school? How about frequent newsletters sent home? Occasional phone calls focused on positive achievements? On the other hand, can you also encourage parents who are able to do so to visit school? Can you do some "creative" scheduling of meeting times or think of unconventional places to get together? (Does it *have* to be in a classroom?) Finding solutions to these challenges will take effort, but the results may be worth it, since parents are important mentors of your students as well as their caregivers—just as you are.

Ms. Hamilton wrinkled her forehead. What had gone wrong? she wondered. She closed her eyes and recalled the particular comments she and Ms. Davila had made. The mother's had all been about cooperation, she noted; the mother seemed unconcerned about Maria's achievements.

Or was she? Maybe Ms. Hamilton had just jumped in too quickly with news of Maria's schoolwork? Maybe more respect for Maria's personality would have been in order? Trouble was, it was too late now; Ms. Davila had already gone home.

Perhaps a follow-up note would help, she thought. Except I can't talk only about Maria's achievement; that would seem as if I were ignoring her personal qualities again. But I also can't totally ignore her achievements, since she *is* a good student and school *does* have something to do with scholastic achievement!

A follow-up note, she thought again, but the right kind. Ms. Hamilton looked at her watch: 3:20, still early. I do have time before my next parent comes.

She got out a sheet of school stationery and began writing:

Dear Ms. Davila,

Just a note to follow up on our meeting today, because I think I got carried away talking about the curriculum! Maria has been a joy to have in class. I have repeatedly seen her help other students with their work. But that has made others more willing to give her help in return when she needs it. So everyone is coming out ahead.

In addition, Maria's work has generally been very good, especially in language arts. Here's a copy of her story about cats—the one I told you about earlier. And, of course, her grades have generally been good. But I don't need to go over that again—I already talked about that when you visited.

Thanks again for finding time to talk with me about Maria. Do call or send a note if you have any questions or concerns.

Yours truly,
Ms. Hamilton

Before she sealed the note in an envelope, she found Maria's story about cats and began walking it down the hall to the photocopier. She wanted to save a copy for herself before enclosing it with her note. On the way down, she passed the teacher from the room next door.

"You're looking cheerful!" she said. "What are you doing?"

"Finishing up a parent conference," said Ms. Hamilton.

As Ms. Hamilton discovered, there is more than one way to communicate with parents, and what matters is not the format of communication—ten-minute oral conference, note home, phone call, or whatever—but its effectiveness. Effective communication, in turn, results from developing positive networks of relationships between and among all the people relevant to students' learning: among students themselves, of course, but also between the teacher and the most important people in students' lives, their families. The challenges in communicating with such a variety of people are great. They are so great, in fact, that we should take a closer look at what classroom communication is like, how it can go wrong, and what a teacher can do to make it go well as much as possible. That is where we turn in the next chapter.

Chapter Re-View: Among Classmates and Parents This Chapter Re-View suggests directions in which the chapter might have taken your thinking—though, of course, other directions are also possible. It expands the Chapter View, which suggests a starting point, conceptually, for the chapter. But this Re-View does not suggest an ending point. Like the Chapter View, it represents just one perspective among many.

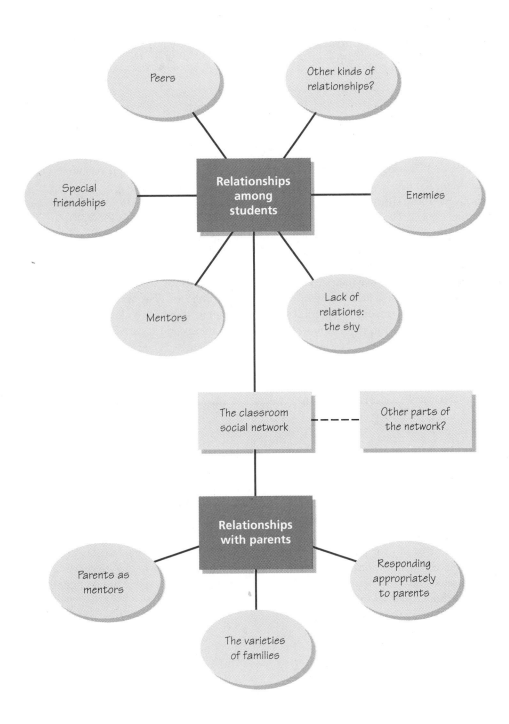

Key Terms and Concepts

peers (210)   mentor (217)   stepfamily (234)
sociogram (211)   protégé (217)
friendship (213)   shyness (221)

Annotated Readings

Wallerstein, Judith, & Blakeslee, Sandra. (1989). *Second chances: Men, women, and children a decade after divorce*. New York: Ticknor & Fields.

Wallerstein, Judith. (1995). *The good marriage: How and why love lasts*. Boston: Houghton Mifflin. In these two books, Judith Wallerstein provides accounts of two parts of a major, longitudinal research program focusing on marriages. The first book looks at the impact of marital breakup, and the second focuses on the reasons for marital survival. As these books point out, there is more than one kind of divorce, and also more than one kind of successful marriage.

Johnstone, Marilyn. (1996). *Dealing with bullying*. New York: PowerKids Press.

Zarzour, Kim. (1994). *Battling the schoolyard bully*. Toronto: HarperPerennial Books. Bullies, and what to do about them, have increasingly become a concern for many teachers. These two books speak to that concern. The first is intended for school-age children themselves (late elementary and beyond), and the second speaks to their parents and teachers.

Internet Resources

<www.pta.org> This is the national web site for the Parent-Teacher Association, the major volunteer organization of parents who work in support of teachers and schools. PTAs exist in numerous American schools and in numerous Canadian schools under the name PTO (Parent-Teacher Organization). The site includes information about the PTA's educational programs for parents, as well as links to other, related organizations.

<www.schoolcounselor.org> This is the web site for the American School Counselors' Association, a major professional organization for guidance counselors in public schools. The site has links to related sites, some of which discuss relationship issues (e.g., aggression, shyness) as they affect teachers and students.

<www.yahoo.com/Health/Mental_Health/Diseases_and_Conditions/Shyness> This site is really a category of Yahoo!, a major search engine of the Internet. In this case, the category lists other sites that discuss and offer help with shyness. Not all of them focus on school-age children, but all are relevant, at least indirectly.

III

The Social and Cultural Context

As a teacher, you are involved with more than personal relationships with students as individuals. You also serve the broader community and culture in which you and your students live and work. The beliefs, customs, and behaviors of the community and culture frame much of life in school—and much of students' daily behavior and thought in particular. They form the *social context* of teaching and learning. Part 3 explores the social context of teaching in detail.

Each chapter in this part highlights a different aspect or meaning of the term *context*. Chapter 8 explores how patterns of communication in the classroom affect learning: what kinds of participation result from different forms of activity. Chapter 9 discusses society's beliefs about gender roles—about which sex is (supposedly) good at doing what or which sex (supposedly) *prefers* to do what. That chapter also discusses the importance of language and ethnic background, especially as these guide how we talk with others, solve problems, and express our feelings. Finally, Chapter 10 discusses society's beliefs about special education for people who are disabled, whether physically, emotionally, or cognitively. The chapter is guided by the viewpoint that these people can and should be included in classroom life as deliberately and fully as possible.

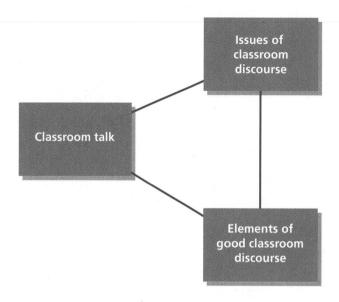

Chapter View: The Meaning of Classroom Talk This Chapter View is a concept map that indicates one among many ways of thinking about the chapter. It suggests a starting point, conceptually, for the chapter but is incomplete by itself. At the end of the chapter is a Chapter Re-View, which expands on the Chapter View, suggesting directions for taking your thinking further—though, of course, other directions are also possible.

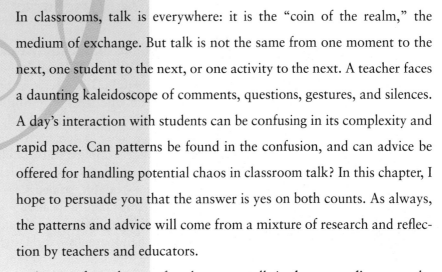

8

The Meaning of Classroom Talk

In classrooms, talk is everywhere: it is the "coin of the realm," the medium of exchange. But talk is not the same from one moment to the next, one student to the next, or one activity to the next. A teacher faces a daunting kaleidoscope of comments, questions, gestures, and silences. A day's interaction with students can be confusing in its complexity and rapid pace. Can patterns be found in the confusion, and can advice be offered for handling potential chaos in classroom talk? In this chapter, I hope to persuade you that the answer is yes on both counts. As always, the patterns and advice will come from a mixture of research and reflection by teachers and educators.

A more formal name for classroom talk is **classroom discourse,** the verbal interactions among members of a class, including that especially important member, the teacher. To explore how discourse gets organized and affects learning, we will begin by reflecting on some very common classroom activities, ones that you probably have experienced yourself in your years as a student. We'll examine each activity first from the teacher's point of view, focusing on how a teacher might think about the activity as he or she initially plans it and watches it unfold. Then our viewpoint will shift to how students respond to the activity and the extent to which they actually participate in the discourse the activity makes possible. It is here, among students' responses, that complications can arise. The teacher may plan for a particular pattern of discourse to occur, but in practice individual students vary widely in the patterns they perceive or to which they have access. Two students therefore may not experience activity as the "same," and the outcomes the teacher intends may differ from those constructed by the students. Differences in students' responses are not necessarily a problem, but teachers do need to understand that the differences occur so that they can ensure that classroom discourse is indeed as educational as possible.

Structures That Influence Classroom Discourse

SOME activities occur frequently enough that we can describe their recurring pattern. Educational researchers call the pattern itself a **participation structure,** a set of rights and responsibilities expected from students and teacher during an activity. Sometimes the rights and responsibilities are stated explicitly by the teacher ("Students, one of our class rules is 'Don't interrupt when someone else is talking'"), but often they are merely implied through class members' actions, and individual students must catch on to them for themselves. During a lecture and recitation, for example, students are usually responsible for listening, raising their hands before speaking, being brief if called on, and sticking to the topic or theme of the lecture when they speak. The teacher, on the other hand, usually has the right to speak as long as he or she wishes, to change topics at will, to grant the floor to any particular student, and to evaluate publicly the quality of a student's question or comment. Altogether, the students' and teacher's rights and responsibilities constitute much of the participation structure of the activity that we all know as a "lecture."

Teachers use a lot of different participation structures, depending on whom, what, and where they are teaching at the moment, but only a few structures account for the majority of activities in schools (Cazden, 1986). Here is a partial list of the most common structures, listed not by how frequently they either are or should be used but by roughly how much the teacher controls or determines the talking the participation structure involves. The list may sound familiar because you have probably experienced many of these forms of participation in your own career as a student:

In Your Own Voice

Think back over the courses you have had.

Which ones used forms of participation that you enjoyed and learned from the most?

Did the forms of participation influence your preferences for certain subjects or teachers?

- *Lecture:* The teacher talks; the students listen. Maybe the students take notes, or maybe not; hopefully the students think about what is said, but there is no way to be sure without arranging for one of the other participation structures to occur.

- *Recitation:* The teacher leads a question-and-answer session; the students raise their hands to be recognized and give answers that are (hopefully) brief and relevant; classmates learn (hopefully) by listening to others' responses as well as answering for themselves.

- *Discussion:* The teacher sets a topic, an issue, or a problem and invites comments or solutions to it; students are supposed to know something about the topic or problem already, and to say or ask something that is relevant to it and responds to other students' comments.

- *Collaborative group work:* The teacher sets a general task, and group members work out details of implementation among themselves. Group members are supposed to make sure that everyone on the team is included and respected. Occasionally the teacher monitors (or visits) the group as it proceeds, but most of the time the group proceeds on its own initiative.

- *Individual dialogue:* The teacher converses or works with just one student, ignoring the rest of the class, which is otherwise occupied or perhaps not even in the classroom at the time.

- *Recess breaks and lunch time:* Students interact freely among themselves, usually outdoors; the teacher takes a break or gets activities ready for the next part of the day, but usually does not interact with students.

Each of these participation structures makes certain kinds of discourse relatively easy and other kinds more difficult. Put differently, each has its own rules about questions such as these: When is speaking expected? When is it optional? When should you be quiet? To whom should you talk? What kinds of comments are considered appropriate? Students learn and practice these rules but, for various reasons, do not do so equally. The results are differences in how much students learn and in the nature of what they learn.

Each participation structure is also facilitated by certain physical arrangements of a classroom, such as those illustrated in Figure 8.1 (Imel, 1996). Desks facing forward or arranged in a single large circle lend themselves to activities that are teacher led, such as lectures or recitations. When interaction does occur under these conditions, it is not evenly distributed. In a lecture hall arrangement, the most actively in-

In Your Own Voice

Participation rules are sometimes written down and stated openly to students, but not always.

How did you learn them, especially any rules that had to be "caught" and were not taught?

How would your experience of school have differed—or perhaps did differ—if you were unfamiliar with the participation rules?

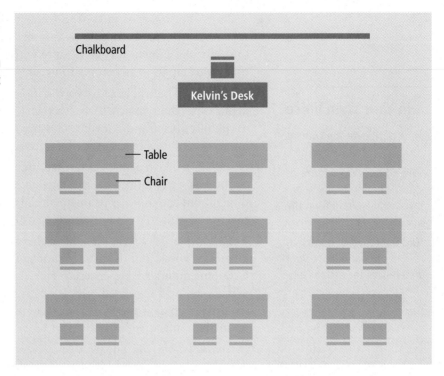

FIGURE 8.1

Lecture-Style Room Arrangement

volved students tend to be those seated near the front and center of the room. When they have a choice, in fact, school-wise students sometimes choose seats in this "active zone" if they wish or expect to interact, and avoid it if they do not. In a large, single-circle arrangement, students sitting across from the teacher tend to speak the most and those sitting adjacent to each other speak to each other very little, unless it is for purposes not related to the ongoing discussion. More widespread participation, as well as conversation among students, can be encouraged by arranging desks in small groups, though this arrangement also makes it harder for the teacher to monitor the quality and progress of individual conversations.

The Impact of Participation Structures on Learning

F course, every classroom activity has explicit content that students (one hopes) learn. But every activity simultaneously has a form or structure that also conveys an implicit message or lesson about how,

Using a variety of participation structures can help a wide variety of students to take an active role in the class. This second-grade teacher, for example, is mixing whole-group with small-group formats.
© Elizabeth Crews

when, and whether to participate. To see what this idea means, take a look at some typical classroom activities, what each assumes about students' participation, and the consequences of its assumptions for students' learning. I will use my own college teaching as a source of examples, and in particular my teaching of one topic—children's play—in an introductory course for teachers of young children. I have chosen my teaching of this topic, however, not because I have been particularly gifted at teaching it (you will see that I have not) but because changes in how I have taught it over the years show the differences among participation structures especially well. In all cases, my intentions remained constant: to stimulate students' thinking about the nature and purposes of play, to see the relevance of play to teaching and learning, and to choose to explore the topic further through term projects and other, related activities. As it turned out, though, my first teaching methods created forms of participation that did not support my educational goals.

Lecture

The first time I taught about children's play, I lectured about it. This was not because I had reflected on alternative methods of teaching and decided that lecturing would help my students the most. Rather, I chose to lecture because it was convenient and apparently also a widespread practice. Here is a section of my notes from an actual class session where I did so:

Year One: Mr. Seifert's Lecture Notes:

Characteristics of Children's Play (for "Introduction to Early Education")

1. Introduction to topic: What do we mean by play?
    a. Excess energy
    b. Seeking stimulation—relieve boredom
    c. Escape from work

2. Six qualities that define play
    a. intrinsic motivation—no one makes children play
    b. attention to means, not ends—it's the process, not the outcome
    c. nonliteral behavior—"make believe" is important
    d. no external rules—children make up their own rules
    e. self-governed, not object-governed—use objects any way you want
    f. active engagement—visible involvement

3. Implications for teaching
    a. Find classroom activities with playlike qualities (give 2–3 examples)

b. Watch children playing—what can a teacher find out about their learning?

In Your Own Voice

What do you think of my assumption that students were attending and remembering what I was saying?

To me it now seems naive, but I still wonder how I could have moved beyond it sooner.

Any suggestions?

As a lecture, this bit of teaching went reasonably well: I covered the material efficiently (in around twenty minutes), related the topic to other previous ones in the course, defined and explained all key terms clearly, and at the end related my ideas to what I believed were students' interests. In all of these ways, I implemented what I later found out were the recommendations of educational research for "good" lecturing (Christensen, 1995; Flowerdew, 1994). I also discovered that students were quiet during the lecture (at least mostly), even though some were as old as I and others had more experience with children and teaching. About a third of the students even took notes; the rest, I had to assume, committed the important ideas to memory while they listened. As someone new to college teaching, I was relieved that I made it through the class session without embarrassment or obvious resistance from the students.

But there were also certain negative signs and outcomes. In spite of their courtesy, few students lingered after class to talk with me about the topic of play or about their own experiences with it. Worse yet, few students chose children's play as a focus for term projects, even though I was convinced it would be a highly enjoyable topic. On the final exam (which was several short essays), many were able to repeat back the six criteria for defining children's play, but few seemed able to relate these to their experiences, either personal or classroom based. Some, however, were not even able to recall the criteria I had described for defining play.

In Your Own Voice

As a participation structure, lecture often gets a "bad press": teachers and students often criticize it.

Are there times, however, when you have found a lecture valuable and helpful?

What were the conditions or circumstances that made this possible?

Even though my lecture overtly focused on a topic (play) that praised action, intrinsic motivation, and self-choice, it also implied a different message: that learning can be done passively and should follow a preset intellectual path. Even the physical layout of my classroom sent the message: desks faced forward, as if reminding students to look to the leader for information (see Figure 8.1). I, the designated leader, stood at the front of the room behind a podium, along with notes and other materials to help me provide knowledge for all of us. Later I discovered educational researchers and writers who criticized these participation features of lecturing (McKeachie et al., 1990; Scott, 1995). For some students, I now suspect, my lecture format may have even implied that "learning" is equivalent to daydreaming, since both activities call for the same behavior: you sit quietly and show little expression. The obvious solution, of course, would have been to extend invitations during my lecture for students to think about and tell about their own knowledge, experiences, and beliefs about children's play. But in my first year of college teaching, I offered few of these.

It occurred to me that previously, as a grade-school teacher, I had invited students' active participation more frequently and deliberately. Yet even there, when I had taught kindergarten, I realized I had expected students to sit quietly and restrain themselves from talking more often than I cared to admit. Like when I read a book to the class: no matter how captivating the story might have been, reading it meant that individual students—in this case, just five years old—had to attend quietly to words and actions that I had designated for attention. Just as during my college lectures, the students were not supposed to take charge of deploying their attention, not supposed to choose where, when, and whom to think about.

During my first year of university teaching, in any case, my lecture medium contradicted my lecture message, or at least it took for granted that students would think constructively on their own. When many of them seemed not to do so, I began to wonder what I could do to remedy the problem. Was there a way to ensure active engagement with the topic?

Recitation

Because of these ongoing concerns, I modified my approach to the topic and turned my lectures on children's play into recitations. In other words, I still did a lot of organized telling, but now I frequently interspersed questions among my comments, prompting students to state prior beliefs, for example, or to describe experiences they had had related to children's play. One immediate tangible result was that my "lecture" notes changed in appearance, because I began prompting myself explicitly to ask questions:

Year Three: Mr. Seifert's Class Session Plans

Characteristics of Children's Play (for "Introduction to Early Education")

1. Introduction to topic: What do we mean by *play?* [*First ask 1–2 students to answer this question.*]
   a. Excess energy [*Ask: What evidence is there for this?*]
   b. Seeking stimulation—relieve boredom [. . . *or for this?*]
   c. Escape from work

2. Six qualities of children's play [*Invite students' definitions—but keep them brief*]

   a. intrinsic motivation—no one makes children play

   b. attention to means, not ends—it's the process, not the outcome

   c. nonliteral behavior—"make-believe" is important

   d. no external rules—children make up their own rules

   e. self-governed, not object-governed—use objects any way you want

   f. active engagement—visible involvement

   [*Can you think of examples and/or counterexamples of each quality?*]

3. Implications for teaching

   a. Find classroom activities with playlike qualities [*What playlike activities have you seen in classrooms as a student? As a teacher?*]

   b. Watch children playing—what can a teacher find out about their learning? [*How could you do this? Invite suggestions from students.*]

Asking questions and inviting brief comments reassured me, because now I was continually finding out whether students were listening and understanding my remarks; the questions served both to motivate students to listen and to assess their knowledge of the material.

In this regard, I was not unique among teachers who use recitation: research on this method has found it generally useful for giving teachers an informal indication of students' comprehension as a class session is actually occurring (Willen & White, 1991). To be sure, involving students took more class time; lecturing on children's play took twenty minutes, but a structured, recitation-style discussion now took more than forty minutes. But we always covered the topic eventually, because I still was keeping tight control over the direction of the classroom discourse and because I always limited how much any student could speak. I felt the extra time was worth it.

And in some ways class participation did improve, though not as much as I had hoped. On the written essay test in particular, more students seemed able to accurately recall the qualities that define *play*. But I was still disappointed at how infrequently students applied ideas about play to their own future plans as teachers or to their current and past histories as individuals. There were still too few who chose "play" as a focus for term projects or who wrote well about how to integrate play into their philosophy and plans for teaching. Why, I now wondered, didn't they take advantage of these opportunities, since it seemed clearer than before that they were thinking about the topic?

Again, clues appeared during the recitations, though I did not understand their significance at first. For example, how carefully students listened sometimes depended on who was talking; even though students were supposed to benefit from hearing classmates' comments and answers to questions, many students listened more closely to me than to others. I had a vague feeling that students were violating their responsibilities (such as those mentioned at the beginning of this chapter); they should be listening to each other more, I thought, and listening to me less exclusively:

Clue No. 1: Who Is Worth Listening To?

ME (KELVIN): Can someone define *play* for the class? Joanne?

JOANNE: [Pause; all classmates except two stare into space.] Kind of "excess energy"? Like when kids need to burn off steam?

ME: That's right. [Suddenly six to eight classmates pick up their pencils and get ready to take notes.] One theory of play is that it allows children to use up excess calories, excess energy. What else is a theory about play? Bill? [Another pause; most classmates put their pencils down again and stare into space.]

For another thing, students sometimes hinted at differences in priorities that I ignored. Certain comments and questions implied that although they shared an interest in children's play in general, they did not necessarily want to emphasize the content I had chosen for class time. They had their own priorities:

Clue No. 2: Invitations to Follow Tangents

ME (KELVIN): . . . and so you see that there is not one but several bases on which children's play is usually defined. Questions so far?

HEATHER: Professor Seifert, I'm curious about why some children engage in so much dramatic play or make-believe. Can we talk about that for a minute? [Two other students nod in agreement.]

ME: An interesting topic! [I look at my watch.] I wish we had time for it. Can we save your question for another time? ["Another time" never occurred that semester.]

These and other experiences made me wonder whether I was still keeping too much control over the "floor time" of the class. It was as if by relying on recitation, I was trying to control the thought processes of the students, and in particular trying to make sure they thought about children's play in one particular sequence: *my* sequence.

Furthermore, I wondered whether recitation would work if I were teaching other subjects or students of younger ages. What if I were teaching art, or music, or creative writing in high school? There is a place for dialogue in these subjects, but often it is to explore ideas rather than to guide students' thinking in particular ways. I realized I wanted my own students to explore ideas freely, too; maybe then they would begin using knowledge of children's play outside of class discussion times. Somehow I had to give students more influence over classroom discourse. That meant, among other things, that I had to stop worrying quite so much about whether I was covering all of the "official" content about play.

Classroom Discussion

After more than five years of giving lectures and leading recitations about play, I took the plunge: I quit lectures and recitations on children's play and held full-class discussions instead. The decision significantly changed my planning; instead of outlining detailed content, I now made planning notes that focused on issues about which students might have opinions:

Year Eight: Mr. Seifert's Discussion Notes

Characteristics of Children's Play (for "Introduction to Early Education")

Talk about possible explanations for play—what do students think is its purpose? (10 minutes?)

Can we define *play*? Brainstorm defining qualities and illustrative examples.

Question for all: Are there exceptions—examples of play that do not show some of the qualities? (30–40 minutes)

What is important about play? (20 minutes?)

For teaching? Can play be used in teaching?

For the general welfare of children?

Etc. (whatever the students bring up)

When I began using discussion instead of a question-and-answer format, I also changed the furniture in my classroom, from rows of tables and chairs facing forward to a single, large circle of chairs (see Figure 8.2).

In Your Own Voice

I notice that my planning notes became more sketchy when I shifted from lecture/recitation to discussion.

It makes me wonder if discussion would have worked, even if I had tried it, when I was new at my job, still "green" and relatively unfamiliar with the content.

But I also can't really believe that new, "green" teachers should avoid class discussion!

Can you resolve this dilemma for me?

FIGURE 8.2
**Circular Room
Arrangement**

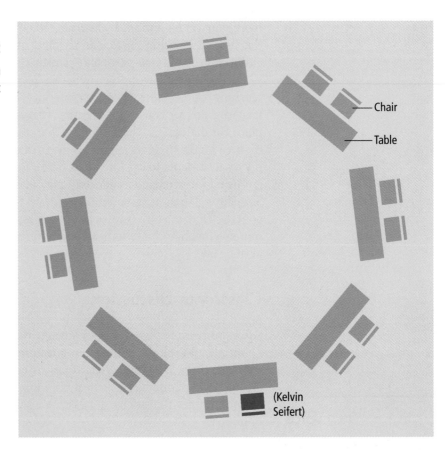

Chair

Table

(Kelvin
Seifert)

In Your Own Voice

In this paragraph, I am identifying a dilemma that teachers at all grade levels face: how much are you responsible to the curriculum you are supposed to teach, and how much to the students who actually populate your classroom?

Given your own experience, what would your answer be, at least at this point in time?

Shifting from recitation to discussion made several positive things happen from my perspective. More than ever I could now see whether students cared about the topic; they now showed their interest explicitly through their comments. A lot more students seemed motivated than in earlier years; exchanges were frequently lively, even heated, and lasted past official ending times for class sessions. At long last, a number of students indicated interest in doing term projects about children's play, especially projects in which they observed children playing or drew on their personal experiences facilitating and participating in children's play. All of this was good.

But then again, it was not *all* good. Sometimes it seemed as if certain students spoke too freely. Had they done any reading? Did they really listen to one another's comments during discussions, or only wait until they could hear themselves speak? On some occasions, the discussion about play seemed more like empty-headed verbiage than thoughtful consideration of knowledge and perspectives. Even when a discussion went well, I worried continuously about whether it had really covered the crucial core ideas about children's play. For one class, the discussion would focus on whether "play was really motivated intrinsically"; for another, it would emphasize whether "play can be used in teaching." By shifting to discussion, I had gained more support and loyalty from the students, but had I become disloyal to the subject itself and neglectful of my students academically? I hoped the motivation of participation through discussion was worth the risks and that what students were learning was still authentic intellectually. In these respects, too, I later learned I was not alone in my concerns, nor was I being unreasonably anxious. Educational researchers have also pointed out the danger that too much emphasis on getting students to learn actively can sometimes compromise the quality of their learning (Newmann, Marks & Gamoran, 1996). Students were busy talking, but not busy enough thinking, exploring beliefs, and formulating worthy goals of their own.

Quality of discussion had also been a concern when I taught school-age students. With a bit of persistence and luck, I almost always could get a good discussion going, even in the youngest grades. I remembered one day, for example, talking with a class about "How to make school safe and friendly." I loved the discussion: heated, friendly, and enthusiastic. But had students really listened to one another's ideas or developed their own thinking on the basis of hearing other students' thinking? I wasn't sure. Some students, I suspect, did not regard the discussion topic—achieving safe and friendly schools—as being important to their lives; so for them the discussion was an artificial rather than an authentic issue. The same problem probably was occurring, I realized, with my college students: some regarded children's play as a vital concern, perhaps for personal or career reasons of their own, but others did not. Was there a way, I wondered, to find discussion topics and activities that everyone would regard as authentic and vital?

Collaborative Group Work

I still was not satisfied with my approach to teaching about children's play, partly because some students still never spoke in class and partly because I was starting to seek better evidence that students were actually acquiring a deep understanding of children's play and not merely sounding as if they had by talking a lot during discussions. My solution was to

Although I make it sound as though group work was the solution to my long-standing dissatisfactions with my teaching, it actually was not.

Some students find this form of participation artificial.

Have you ever had this reaction to working collaboratively?

If you were in my place—teaching about play—how would you deal with students' assertions that group work is artificial?

assign **collaborative group work**: small teams of students designed a project on an aspect of children's play that interested them, made observations of children at play, reported the results briefly in class, and wrote a common, group report about their work. Collaborative work, I hoped, would avoid the danger of shallowness that I had sometimes sensed in class discussions by immersing students for extended periods in issues they developed for themselves. Discussion within work groups would not be for show, so to speak, but for the more authentic purpose of solving the problems students set for themselves.

Since team members tended not to be friends prior to the project, and since they usually had limited time to meet outside class, I started by changing the furniture again, from the large circle I had preferred for discussion to several small circles or groupings in which group members could focus on one another more easily (see Figure 8.3). I also provided students with guidelines not only about the content of the project but also about how to collaborate. Here is an excerpt of the guidelines:

FIGURE 8.3

Small-Group Room Arrangement

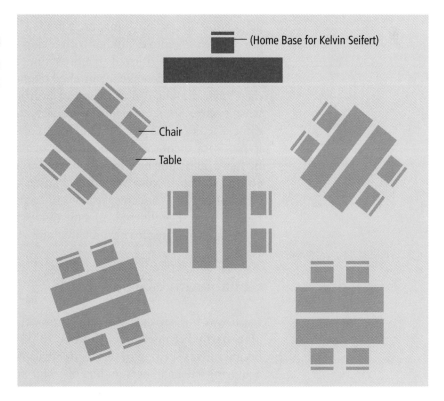

— (Home Base for Kelvin Seifert)

— Chair

— Table

Year Sixteen: Mr. Seifert's Guidelines for Collaboration

Characteristics of Children's Play (from "Introduction to Children's Play")

Suggestions for Working Together

1. Make sure that you listen to everyone, and not just to the people you agree with most. Part of the challenge of this project is to *include* all team members.
2. Keep in mind that you don't have to be best friends with someone in order to be partners with him or her for this project. The key thing is to get the work done.
3. It takes many abilities and insights to succeed at the project: (1) understanding research literature about children's play, (2) observing children well when they play, (3) having confidence in describing your observations and knowledge to a group (our class), (4) having skill at writing and reporting your experiences, and (5) being tactful in listening to and using partners' ideas. Find out who has each of these abilities in your group, and use what they have to offer!

What happened when students collaborated? With encouragement and reminders about how to work together, many groups did approximate the preceding guidelines. They listened, showed mutual respect, and diversified their activities. As a result, a number of formerly quiet students became active—even talkative—when working with their team members. Participation apparently was at an all-time high for my unit on children's play, particularly when I combined collaborative work with discussions and recitations, which certain students still seemed to prefer. I marveled over my new success, especially because I had heard stories from other teachers (such as Barbara Fuller, described in Chapter 6) about cooperative learning not working well. One difference between my experience and some of the less successful ones, I speculated, had to do with students' maturity: my college students were fairly experienced—and generally successful—as students, so they may have acquired more diplomatic and cooperative skills than, say, children in the primary grades. But maturity was not the whole reason; some of my colleagues at the college had also had stressful teaching experiences using cooperative learning. "Too many prima donnas," one had said. I looked up *prima donna* in the dictionary and found that it means a temperamental, vain, or self-centered person, qualities that did not seem to describe my particular students. In the end, I suspected that age or grade level as such did not affect whether students cooperated well, but maybe individuals' personalities and prior experiences working in groups did influence success. Without knowing it in advance, I discovered that my students enjoyed working together in groups, and did well at it.

Yet even now, problems developed. Some students complained that the classroom became too noisy when teams were meeting together; their collective voices made quite a din. Other groups never worked well together, in spite of guidelines and encouragement, and neither they nor I ever really understood why. And since I deliberately did not intervene in group planning, projects became even more diverse than class discussions had been, and occasionally the final results verged on being strange or even bizarre. I worried all over again about whether I was covering the material about children's play as I should and whether I had failed my students by letting them take possession of the learning process to such an extent. One night I wrote about it:

Year Twenty-Three: Mr. Seifert's Professional Journal (confidential)

October (4th week): I still worry about my coverage of children's play as a topic, but I am not willing to rely primarily on teacher-led lecturing or recitations again. I will compromise with the need for specific content by including recitations, specific readings, and occasional brief lectures to supplement readings. I'm thinking these should happen alongside student-initiated activities like the group projects. "I've got to have many ways to participate" is my present thinking. But of course I keep evolving and changing, so who knows what I'll think about this next year, or the year after?!

I do need to continue finding ways to learn what students think about this topic when they are working freely and not constrained by specific tasks or my "official" thinking as instructor. Today I found it helpful to hang around during the lunch hour immediately following class, listening to students' comments to one another about assignments and class sessions. I suppose that they concealed their worst complaints because I was nearby, but even so they spoke rather more freely at lunch hour than during class time!

The solution to gaining participation, in other words, was for me to worry less about *which* participation structure worked best and think more about how to combine a *variety* of structures strategically to benefit students. I realized, furthermore, that the participation structure I preferred the most (discussion) cannot accomplish everything I value in education and that the format I least preferred (lecture) does nonetheless accomplish important educational goals and deserves more credit than I used to give it. The success of any participation structure depends on when it is used and for what educational purposes. Therefore, in teaching about children's play (I still do, even as this book goes to print), I think about my purposes more deeply than ever. What do I want my students to be able to say, think, and do as a result of the unit—and why? These are such fundamental issues in education and psychology that I return to them at length later in the book (see especially Chapters 11 and 12): about ways to decide what is worthwhile to teach and ways to assess what students learn. First, though, let's look separately at the detailed nature of classroom discourse and at teachers' and students' contributions to it.

How Teachers Talk

*W*HEN actively teaching, teachers have an identifiable way of talking that linguists call a *register*. A **register** is a pattern of vocabulary, grammar, manners, and types of comments that people associate with a social role. An example would be the "baby-talk" used when speaking to a toddler or an infant. Its features (e.g., repeated nonsense words and exaggerated pitch changes) mark the speaker as an adult or a mature caregiver and mark the listener as an immature infant or a young child.

Teacher-talk register works in a similar way; it conveys a message that "I am a teacher and you, my listeners, are students." Teachers use the register to varying degrees, of course, and use it more in some situations than in others. But the register is widely noted by educational researchers (e.g., see Bloome [1994]), and it is common enough that most people who have attended school (which includes all teachers) can recognize its teacherlike quality. You should have little trouble deciding who is the teacher and who are the students in the following exchange, even though I identify each person simply with a letter of the alphabet:

PERSON A: All right now, I want all eyes up here. All eyes on me. Person B, are you ready? Person C? Listen carefully. We are going to try a new kind of math problem today. It's called *long division*. Does anyone know what long division is? [Three hands go up.] Person D, what do you think it is?

PERSON D: Division with bigger numbers? [Pauses hesitantly; five more hands go up; Person A scans the group.]

In Your Own Voice

Psychologists call a parent's baby-talk by the name "motherese," so by analogy teacher-talk could be called "teacherese."

But this makes mothers seem like teachers, or teachers seem like mothers, or both.

There may be some truth to the analogy, but it may also be misleading.

What do you think?

PERSON E: Division by two-digit . . .

PERSON A: I only call on people who wait to be recognized [scans group further]. Person F, can you help Person D with her answer?

PERSON F: Division with remainders. [Two hands shoot up a second time.]

PERSON A: Close. Actually, you're both partly right. Long division can involve larger numbers, and often it does involve remainders. But not always; there's more to it than that. Listen now while I explain it. [Person A goes on to explain the nature of long division.]

In this scene Person A must surely be the teacher, if only because she or he makes so many comments designed to control or influence the others' comments and behavior. Person A uses a lot of control talk, and it is this feature that marks the teacher-talk register most clearly. Numerous observational studies of classroom discourse confirm the prevalence of controlling comments in teachers' classroom discourse (Cazden, 1986; Lemke, 1990). As the preceding example suggests, though, it is also not hard to imagine or recall examples from personal experience as a student.

Control talk takes a number of forms, depending on the immediate purposes of a teacher and the needs of the class. In a lengthy study of science teachers' discourse, Jay Lemke identified more than a dozen strategies and tactics of control (Lemke, 1990). He noted teachers using talk in each of the following ways, and the ways also apply to all teachers, not just those in science:

- *Nominating speakers:* By calling on one student rather than another, teachers influenced the direction and pace of dialogue in ways they considered productive. ("Joe, what do you think about the question that I have posed?")

- *Terminating and interrupting speakers:* Just as teacher-talk can grant the right to speak, so it can also take that right away, sometimes even before a speaker is ready to end his or her turn. ("Thanks for that, Jasneth; let's give someone else a turn.")

- *Asserting irrelevance:* Sometimes during a speaker's turn, teachers channeled the direction of discourse by asserting that a comment was not relevant. ("We're talking about Shakespeare's plays here, not the movie version that you saw.")

- *Marking importance:* On the other hand, teachers also influenced the discourse by pointing out when an idea was important. ("That's a good question, Jill; I'm glad you brought it up.")

- *Signaling boundaries between activities:* Teachers declared when one activity or discussion was over and a new one was beginning. ("Look-

In Your Own Voice

Imagine how classroom dialogue would seem if a *student* adopted some of these features of teacher-talk.

What impression would the student create if he or she terminated or interrupted a speaker, for example, or signaled the boundary between activities, or asked another student (or even the teacher) a "test" question?

ing at the clock, I see that we have to move on to journal writing. Put away your books and find your journals.") Exercising this form of control, of course, powerfully altered the current discourse.

- *Using "test" questions:* Frequently teachers asked questions to which they already knew the answers, and followed these with evaluations of students' answers. ("How much is 11 times 12? [132] Right, good.") Test-and-evaluation sequences can be helpful educationally, but they also mark the teacher as an expert and therefore more deserving of controlling the general direction of discourse.

Woven into the directly controlling features of teacher-talk are certain other features that are less unique to teachers but may signal to students that they are listening to someone who is doing something called "teaching" and that this person expects them to be doing something called "learning" (Cazden, 1986):

- *Exaggerated changes in pitch:* With all students, but especially with young ones (e.g., kindergartners), teachers vary the pitch of their voices, from high to low, more than usual. The changes might be diagrammed in print like this:

Teacher: Gilbert, I want you to find a book, and take it to your desk.

Exaggerated pitch also occurs in the baby-talk register, incidentally, but in even more extreme form than in teacher-talk.

- *Careful enunciation:* In teacher-talk, a teacher speaks more slowly than when talking with another adult. He or she also is more careful than usual to pronounce words correctly. The combination creates an impression of formality, especially when combined with characteristic vocabulary and grammar, mentioned next.

- *Formal vocabulary and grammar:* Teacher-talk includes fewer than usual words and expressions that are slang or casual and uses more that sound formal, as if being read from a book. Instead of saying, "Get out your stuff," for example, the teacher is more likely to say, "Get out your materials." Instead of saying, "It ain't right," the teacher is more likely to say, "That's incorrect."

In and of themselves, the indicators of control and formality are not necessarily bad, nor are they equivalent to being dictatorial or bossy. Control often can help others, and the control that marks teacher-talk often can help students. Two educational researchers, Mary Catherine O'Connor and Sarah Michaels, came to this conclusion when they observed elementary school teachers' strategies for "marking importance,"

In Your Own Voice

Is it really necessary for a teacher to adopt these indicators of teacher-talk?

Imagine a teacher who used ordinary changes in pitch, ordinary enunciation of words, and informal vocabulary.

Would it work?

If so, under what conditions?

one of the control strategies listed above (O'Connor & Michaels, 1996). O'Connor and Michaels called the strategy *revoicing*, because they noted that teachers often used it to strengthen the contributions of students who lacked social status with their peers. By paraphrasing the comments these students made, the teachers were able simultaneously to advance the class discussion and to create opportunities for quieter students to participate on a more equal footing with talkative students.

Mr. Lee was leading a science demonstration and discussion about balance beams. He had a beam set up with an assortment of weights available for trying to balance it. "So what do you think will happen," he asks the class, "if I move these weights this way?"

Two hands go up: ever-eager Kathleen and normally quiet Jocelyn. Mr. Lee knows that Kathleen probably knows the answer and that she will express herself well if he calls on her. It is easy for other students to listen to her. But she has already spoken several times today and twice during the current discussion. Jocelyn—well, Mr. Lee is not sure. She rarely speaks, but when she does, she sometimes sounds hesitant. It can take patience to listen to her. But she needs the experience; she deserves to be listened to. In the split second Mr. Lee has, he wonders which student to call on: Kathleen or Jocelyn.

He calls on Jocelyn. The girl hesitates, then says tentatively, "Um . . . I think that it . . . might tip to the right?"

"OK," says Mr. Lee to everyone, "you're saying that moving these like so [demonstrates] will make the scale tip. Interesting idea; why do you think so?"

As it happened, O'Connor and Michaels concentrated their observations on positive instances of revoicing, which were essentially instances of teachers' control talk used for constructive, educational purposes. At the same time, though, they noted that revoicing can also have negative effects. In marking the importance of one student's idea, for example, they may unintentionally slight another student's contribution. Or a teacher may imply criticism when apparently praising a student's comment ("Good idea, Sam—nice to hear from you for a change"). The possibilities for harm mean that teachers have a responsibility as well as a right: their privileges in controlling the flow of classroom talk carry with them a responsibility to support students' own contributions to the talk as fully as possible. A successful class or lesson, in other words, is not necessarily one in which you, the teacher, have had a lot to say but one in which students have had a lot to say.

The possibility of discouraging or even silencing students is especially high if a student comes from a family or community in which the conventions of teacher-talk are not normally used by parents or other adults in authority. In research observing language patterns in three rural communities, Shirley Brice Heath and her colleagues found differences among the communities in how closely speech at home resembled speech at school (Heath, 1983; Heath et al., 1991). In one community, for example, parents spoke to children comparatively little, and when they did, they did not mark or alter their speech in ways comparable to teacher-talk register. Parents also were unlikely to ask "test" questions, concentrating instead on real questions (i.e., the ones whose answers they really did not know themselves). When the children first entered school, therefore, they were unfamiliar with the conventions of teacher-talk—to their detriment. If presented with a "test" question, for example, a child might not respond at all, since such a question appeared either foolish ("Does the teacher really not know what is 2 plus 2?") or humiliating ("Why would the teacher want *me* to state something so obvious?"). Heath found that as the children moved up through the grade levels, they performed less well than their counterparts in other communities.

But a gap in style of communication need not work against students. In another research project, Roland Tharp and Ronald Gallimore assisted teachers of ethnically Hawaiian children to tolerate and adopt another nonstandard style of communication typical of Hawaiian culture, the "talk-story" (Tharp & Gallimore, 1991). In the talk-story, individuals interrupt one another freely during conversation in order to build a topic or story jointly. In a conventional classroom, this behavior might be considered rude, since it preempts the teacher's right to interrupt a speaker and to determine the direction of conversation. Tharp and Gallimore found, however, that when teachers learned to expect this sort of participation, and even more when they supported and encouraged it, students' motivation and learning improved significantly. The key, in this case, was a sensitivity to differences among families and cultures, combined with flexibility about how dialogue and participation occurred in the classroom.

In Your Own Voice

Tharp and Gallimore's approach has been criticized because all children need to learn school-like ways of talking sooner or later.

Supporting culturally inherited forms of dialogue, it is argued, just delays that learning, even if the support also has other benefits.

How would you respond to this point?

Is there a way to reconcile support for school-talk register with support for home-talk register?

How Students Talk

TUDENTS also have a characteristic *student-talk register*, used in class and especially in the presence of teachers. Like teacher-talk, the student-talk includes a lot of control talk, though often the control is less direct or explicit than the teacher's. Various forms of student control talk have been observed in more than one type of classroom, including junior high science (Lemke, 1990), senior high and adult second-language classes (Johnson, 1995), and elementary classrooms (Cazden, 1988). Teachers may sense the influence of student-talk when an exchange is moving in an unexpected direction. But because of its indirectness, and because events sometimes move too quickly to analyze precisely, it can be difficult to know how to respond on the spot. That is what happened to Jane Gladstone, a first-year teacher with a sixth-grade class, who puzzled over this exchange:

Who's In Charge Here?

Ms. Gladstone announced the first activity, language arts. "OK, everyone, we'll start with language arts. Turn to where we left off yesterday, page 46."

"But Ms. Gladstone," said Paul, "we actually left off at page 32. You promised we would pick up from where we left off."

"No, dummy!" whispered Katherine, quiet but annoyed. She sat next to Paul. "You were absent yesterday, and the day before was a holiday. Remember?" Suddenly three or four others were talking quietly to one another about which page number was correct.

"Page 46!" Ms. Gladstone said firmly—actually a little more firmly than she intended. And so the lesson began. The reading turned out to be a short story about an athlete who trained hard for local competitions. Students took turns reading selections and formulating questions about it to pose to the rest of the class. In this way, they got halfway into the story. But then something happened.

"Ms. Gladstone," asked Joe, "do you think it is a crime for athletes to take steroids—those drugs that make them really strong?"

Ms. Gladstone was taken off guard; she had not expected this question! All she could think of was "Well, I don't know; that's a hard question."

"My dad says it *is,* and that no one should have doubts about that. You mean you don't really care, Ms. Gladstone?"

Where was this discussion going? Ms. Gladstone thought to herself. And how could she get it back on track? Or should she even try to get it back?

Jane Gladstone is asking herself valid questions, but unfortunately she cannot stop the clock to ponder them properly. As readers, however, *we* have that ability (at least in our imaginations!): we can interrupt Jane's activity and look at precisely how her students influence the flow of classroom discourse. Then we can look at additional methods of influence used by other students in classrooms.

In Your Own Voice

Before you read the following paragraphs, take a minute to think about Jane's question yourself.

Think, too, about how her students are influencing the direction of the discussion and how, for the moment, Jane has become a follower, rather than a leader, of the students.

Is the reversal of roles a problem for you or not?

Look at Jane's class more closely. Her students used student-talk to influence events in three ways:

- *Agenda enforcement:* A student interrupts the discourse to insist on what he or she understands to be the agreed-on agenda. In Ms. Gladstone's class, Paul made this move by proposing to start the activity on a different page (page 32), which he understood to be where the class should be starting.

- *Digression:* A student asks a question or brings up a topic that is only tangentially related to the teacher's intended plan. In Ms. Gladstone's class, Joe did so by asking the teacher's opinion about athletes' use of steroids.

- *Side talk:* A student talks to another student, often to be sociable ("Hi, how are ya?") or to get information needed to participate in the official activity ("Which problem did she say to do?"). In Ms. Gladstone's class, Katherine used side talk with Paul, but primarily to silence his objection by giving him information that he was missing or had forgotten. Several others (unnamed in the narrative) did the same.

None of the strategies directly usurps the role of the teacher. No student tries explicitly to set the class agenda directly, for example; Paul comes the closest, but even he attempts not to create an agenda but just to enforce the existing, teacher-made agenda. Students rarely directly grant or deny one another the right to speak in class, as a teacher commonly does; to do so would seem brash. Because students do not (or are not supposed to) manage the class, their efforts to influence classroom discourse are relatively indirect, and sometimes may not even be perceived as "control" at the time they occur.

Agenda enforcement, digression, and side talk are not the only ways for students to influence classroom discourse. There are other tactics that are more indirect:

- *Calling out:* A student speaks out of turn or without being officially given the floor by the teacher. A variation on this strategy might be called "aggressive hand raising," in which a student raises his or her hand before hearing what the teacher is actually asking simply to gain priority in being called on to speak. In observing this behavior in first- and second-grade classrooms, one researcher named these students "turn sharks," ever preying on others' hesitations about taking their turn in the discourse (Erikson, 1996).

- *Answering with a question:* Instead of answering a "test" question from the teacher directly, a student responds with a question of his or

Eye contact also differs by gender: research reports that girls and women look directly at a speaker more of the time than do boys and men.

How do you suppose this difference might affect girls' and boys' relationships with teachers?

(And would the effect be different for male and female teachers?)

her own, either for clarification ("Is X what you are asking about?") or about the content itself (Teacher: "How can we measure air pressure?" Student: "Can we find a barometer?"). The effect in either case is to shift the discussion to ground that is safer or more familiar to the student.

- *Silence:* A student says nothing, perhaps even when asked directly to respond. Although at first glance this strategy may seem like nonparticipation, it can also serve to move the ongoing discourse in new directions. When met with silence, a teacher (or even a talkative student) is less likely to continue the current topic or exchange and more likely to seek a new one.

- *Eye contact:* A student either does or does not look directly at the teacher while the teacher talks, and perhaps especially when the teacher is speaking to the student in particular. According to conventions of classroom discourse, students show motivation to learn, respect for the teacher, and implicit acceptance of the topic or activity by looking directly at the teacher. Looking elsewhere implies the opposite.

Since in most classes students are quite diverse, the student-talk register is likely to be more familiar to some students than to others, with consequences for a student who is not familiar with it. Take eye contact. In Navajo Indian communities, for example, eye contact has a meaning almost directly opposite to its conventional school meaning (Chisholm, 1996). Averting gaze, that is, conveys respect for the speaker, and direct eye contact signifies challenge or disrespect. Ironically, a child who uses this form of eye contact could create an impression quite unlike what she or he intends. The teacher may take this student to be lazy or disrespectful when actually the student feels the opposite. Or the teacher may take the student to be interested and respectful when in fact he or she is angry and frustrated. As with differences in expectations about teacher-talk, the way to avoid misunderstandings about student-talk is to listen and watch students as closely and with as much openness as possible. It also involves learning whatever you can about cultural and family differences in communication, not just in general but also as they apply to your particular students.

Rules about discourse and participation are constantly being broken—as may be happening with these two girls whispering to each other. But sometimes these infractions serve a useful educational purpose.
© Gale Zucker/Stock Boston

Issues of Classroom Discourse

A number of issues have been raised or objections made to what I have said so far about classroom discourse and to the research that backs it up. As it turns out, none of the issues really disproves the usefulness of regarding teacher-talk and student-talk as distinct registers or styles of speech or of understanding students' learning in terms of these registers. The issues do suggest, however, that classroom learning should be understood *solely* in terms of classroom discourse and the impact of discourse on class participation.

Is Classroom Discourse for Control or for Motivating Learning?

The answer is that it can be for either, but most often it is for both at once. When a teacher asks "test" questions, for example, or selects who gets to speak, she or he does control or influence students' behavior. But the teacher also creates content that can be learned: the questions are al-

Classrooms are not the only places where discourse serves multiple purposes.

Think about family conversations at the dinner table: if a parent inquires what homework a child has to complete, is the parent (1) curious about the homework, (2) feeling concerned about the child's general welfare, or (3) indirectly pressuring the child to get started on the homework promptly?

Or some combination of the three?

ways about *something,* and the selection of speakers is always done partially to give "floor time" to important ideas. The opportunity to learn is woven into the requirements for discourse and for participation in classroom life.

Likewise, students' discourse tactics often—or, perhaps, usually—serve both to control and to learn. It is true that students sometimes deflect or redirect classroom exchanges that may hurt them: if you do not know the answer to a teacher's question, for example, you can avoid revealing this fact by falling silent, by digressing, or by suggesting that the question is not part of the agreed-on agenda of activity. Sometimes these amount to tactics of survival because they may reflect students' lack of authority in the classroom. But often classroom survival is not an immediate worry, and in those cases the contributions of students are more accurately thought of simply as "influential." Because of students' comments, questions, digressions, and silences, the teacher may rephrase an important question, retract a request, propose a new topic, or the like.

Yet whether students are actually controlling discourse or merely surviving it, the same tactics can also indicate that students are actively learning! A student may be silent for either of two reasons: simply to resist being called on or to think hard about a question the teacher has posed. A student may offer a digression to avoid answering the teacher's real question or to make a connection with a related idea that simply failed to make it into the mainstream of the class discussion (such as the students mentioned on page 256, where I was describing my own recitation-style teaching). A student may talk on the side to a neighbor out of boredom with or disapproval for the current activity, or because he or she needs to express enthusiasm and interest in it. Or perhaps a student feels both at once: a bit of resistance to being called on, for example, together with sincere thought about a teacher's question. Somehow the teacher must see these verbal moves for what they are: actions that serve more than one purpose. Other researchers have come to similar conclusions. Gordon Wells (1993) and Claude Goldenberg (1996), for example, note that instructional conversations are often inherently ambiguous—having multiple meanings—in that they not only contain or exchange content but also influence individuals' behavior at the same time.

Are Rules and Regularities of Classroom Discourse Constantly Being Broken?

In Your Own Voice

Can you think of a teacher who often broke the conventions of teacher-talk—who didn't sound like a teacher?

What was the effect of this behavior on students?

Yes, indeed they are, though some are broken more often than others. In effect, there are always moments when a teacher or student does not talk as if he or she is "in school." Think about your own classroom experiences to confirm this fact. Do you remember a teacher occasionally changing character—talking slang for a moment, for example, even though she or he usually spoke rather formally? Do you remember a teacher who sometimes tolerated speaking out of turn, even though the official rules of discourse forbade doing so?

However, the occurrence of "infractions" may not suggest that classroom talk does not exist so much as that students and teachers sometimes have conflicting interests. When Jay Lemke observed discourse in science classes (described on pages 264–265), for example, he noted that the most frequently broken "rule" of discourse was the rule against side talking and that this rule dealt with an area where teachers and students have legitimate goals and needs that differ or even conflict (Lemke, 1990). For teachers, limiting extraneous, unofficial conversation allowed classroom activities and dialogue to proceed more nearly as planned; hence the teachers Lemke observed all supported the rule against side talk. For students, and contrary to the teachers' fears, side talk rarely seemed a threat to learning; it rarely became very loud anyway. On the contrary, students needed occasional side talk to understand bits of classroom dialogue they had missed hearing. They also needed it indirectly to ensure good relations with neighboring classmates (a point I made in Chapter 7 about social relationships in the classroom), because they could expect to need help from classmates at later times. Students' and teachers' interests conflicted, and were resolved in this particular case by making a rule against side talk but at the same time allowing it to be broken frequently.

Do Some Students and Teachers Use Classroom-Talk More Than Others?

Yes, they do; as with any other human behavior, some people do more of it than others. Have you known a teacher who constantly asked "test" questions and another who did so only rarely? Have you known a classmate who specialized, consciously or accidentally, in digressing during a class discussion but also known a classmate whose comments usually seemed relevant? The differences come from a variety of sources, including cultural and societal expectations, which we will focus on in the next chapter. But they also reflect individuals' beliefs about the nature of teaching and learning.

The impact of teachers' beliefs on styles of classroom discourse was well illustrated in a research project by Lynn McAlpine, Alice Eriks-Brophy, and Martha Crago (1996). The three researchers investigated beliefs about teaching held by elementary school teachers serving a Mohawk Indian reserve in Quebec, Canada. The entire school had developed a curriculum focused on Mohawk heritage, culture, and language. All teachers supported the curriculum and implemented it in various ways in their classrooms. But individual differences in teachers' beliefs about teaching, learning, and language led to very different experiences in different classrooms, judging by interviews and classroom observations made by McAlpine and her associates. A teacher named Beth, for example, described Mohawk culture and Mohawk language as essentially equivalent; she was a native speaker of Mohawk herself and used the language throughout the day with her students. To assist students in acquiring Mohawk, she emphasized informal interactions and informal, homelike participation structures. She saw little need to control the flow of discourse to achieve her purposes as long as the discourse was conducted in Mohawk, and thus she needed rather little "control talk" of the kind I have been describing in this chapter.

In the same school was another native Mohawk teacher, Anne, whose beliefs led to a different discourse style. Anne did not speak Mohawk (she had been sent to boarding schools like many children in her community, and had been encouraged to speak only English), but she still identified strongly with the Mohawk community and culture. Because of this experience, Anne distinguished language and culture in her mind, and identified the latter more squarely with the purposes of the school, the school's curriculum, and her classroom. Teaching about Mohawk culture in English posed problems, however, because existing English-

In Your Own Voice

These observations suggest that a visitor to these classrooms could be misled by first impressions in visiting each room.

Anne might seem more directive than she really is, and Beth might seem more permissive or even overly permissive.

If you were one of these teachers, how would you deal with these possibilities?

language materials often were culturally inappropriate in style or content. She found herself constantly revising and altering the English materials to fit her purposes, and therefore constantly explaining to the students how the storybooks, textbooks, and worksheets needed to be used. Unlike Beth, therefore, she used considerable amounts of control talk in her class to guide discussions and activities appropriately. (She did not, however, use more control talk than a non-Mohawk teacher, Carole, who also taught at the school.)

For these two teachers and their classes, classroom discourse was highly individual and reflected the influence of values held by each teacher. Judging by their experiences, there is more than one way to talk with students, and to some reasonable extent one perspective may be as legitimate as another. Beth's class went more smoothly than Anne's in the sense that Beth rarely needed to state instructions or guide the flow of discourse explicitly. On the other hand, Anne's class accomplished more when judged against the Mohawk-focused curriculum that the teachers had collectively developed; and this was true even though most discourse occurred in English.

To say this much, however, is not to imply a "theory of relativity" about teaching, in which *any* style of classroom discourse is just as acceptable as any other. Are there not some universally desirable qualities of classroom talk toward which all teachers should strive? This is the problem that we discuss next, and with which we conclude this chapter.

Using Discourse to Motivate Learning

*E*VENTUALLY you will have to make up your own mind about this question, but in the meantime I will offer you my own advice about it: the goals of classroom discourse are, or should be, to encourage the broadest possible participation by students, combined with genuine educational challenges for the greatest possible number. In essence, discourse should motivate learning. These are goals shared by most educators, especially those concerned with providing for social, cultural, and academic diversity among students (Heath et al., 1991). Participation as well as challenge can be provided by following three general guidelines in combination: using a variety of participation structures, adjusting participation structures to the subject or topic at hand, and adjusting participation structures to students' expectations. Let me explain.

Using a Variety of Participation Structures

All other things equal (which, of course, they often are not), discourse is more successful if you provide a variety of participation structures rather than just one or a few. Any one instructional format can be overdone: just as there can be too many lectures, there can also be too many collaborative projects or group discussions (Johnson & Johnson, 1991; Slavin, 1995). Varying discourse formats not only relieves boredom but also provides for diversity among students, who are likely to differ in how they prefer to interact with one another or with the teacher. At the same time, a variety of participation structures can challenge students to learn new ways of interacting: a student who is relatively uncomfortable with working as part of a team, for example, may gain new social and academic skills by participating in a collaborative group project.

Adjusting Participation Structures to the Subject or Topic

Some subject matter, topics, and educational goals lend themselves to certain forms of participation better than to others; or, put in more everyday terms, they need to be talked about and acted on in particular ways. This is essentially the lesson I learned, and described earlier in this chapter, about my teaching theories and issues about children's play. A complex or controversial social issue, such as "eliminating poverty," seems naturally suited for discussion, though it may still be possible to lecture about it if the teacher makes sure to offer balanced viewpoints. Some topics are learned better if approached by a group rather than by individuals; "current community views about sex education," for example, might benefit by having each team member survey the attitudes of a different segment of the community. Still other topics seem to require relatively large amounts of demonstration and practice, and relatively little discussion or recitation. In music, for example, it is possible to discuss a performance by the school band, but doing so may be less important than rehearsing a selection further. Selecting the appropriate discourse patterns for a subject or topic should help students to understand the material more deeply. They will learn, for example, the nature of a controversy firsthand by seeing that it necessarily creates discussion and disagreement.

Just because an activity works best with a particular form of partici-

In Your Own Voice

I almost make it sound here as if you must choose only one participation structure at a time.

But is this really necessary?

What, if anything, would keep you from having some students work in small groups, for example, while others work independently?

In Your Own Voice

Here's a problem for you: suppose an imaginary school could use only *one* participation structure to teach *all* of its subjects.

What should that structure be?

Is there one "special" way of participating that might not be ideal for all subjects but nevertheless might work satisfactorily across the board?

pation, though, does not guarantee that every student will initially enjoy or feel comfortable with that particular form. A student who is uncomfortable speaking in front of classmates may be uncomfortable in a social issues class, even if the class is organized the "right" way, by emphasizing discussion. Another student who finds repeated practice boring may tire of his concert band classes, even if repeated practice is essential to the band's success. Eventually these students may change their opinions of these forms of participation, provided they stay with them long enough to see their benefits. But their initial discomfort is a reminder that choosing structures of participation depends not only on the nature of the subject or of your educational goals but, to an extent, also on the expectations and preferences of the students. The "best" form of participation may represent a compromise between what a subject demands and what a student expects.

Adjusting to Students' Expected Styles of Participation

How do your particular students prefer to participate? To the extent that you can find out, discourse in your classroom will succeed more fully; more students will be involved, and interaction can be tailored to challenge students appropriately. Who among your students often prefers to "call out" responses and comments, and who will speak only when spoken to? Who seems to think that interrupting others' comments is a sign of enthusiasm rather than a sign of rudeness? Who will say more if given a few extra seconds to think before speaking? Who will talk in a small group but not in front of the whole class? Try to answer these questions even partially, and try to keep them in mind when designing activities and interacting with students. If you accomplish these tasks, you should be able to increase class participation significantly and ensure that it is appropriately stimulating at the same time.

Admittedly it is challenging to diagnose students' discourse styles accurately, since diagnosis must take place in the middle of numerous conversations all through the day. You can't always ask students outright; they may not have thought about it, or their conscious preferences may not always coincide with preferences implied by their actions. Yet students' styles of participation can be sized up at least tentatively. One way to get started is to focus deliberately on just one student per day or per class session, noting only the most important ways in which he or she influences (or fails to influence) classroom activity and discourse. You can note your observations in a professional journal such as described in Chapter 12.

Patterns in the Confusion of Talk

*I*N spite of the diversity and unpredictability of classroom life, it does exhibit patterns. Conversation tends to occur in certain formats, called *participation structures,* and the participation structures influence the kind of learning that takes place. Teachers themselves tend to talk in a predictable style, or register, that identifies them to students as the teacher. Both students and teachers talk in ways that influence the course of discussions—or whether discussion occurs at all. Not surprisingly, though, the way teachers talk normally influences classroom talk more than the way students talk. Amid all the typical, recurring patterns is room for you, as a teacher, to alter your own discourse and interactions to help students learn as well as possible.

The challenge is to decide exactly *what* alterations in your discourse to make. I have offered a few suggestions in this chapter, such as recording observations of individual students' participation in a journal. But there is more to answering this challenge than observation. An additional, less direct strategy for understanding students' styles of talking is to learn as much as possible about students' social and cultural backgrounds. Then ask yourself how the backgrounds influence the ways individual students interact in class. For example, do their cultures of origin support the use of direct eye contact when speaking, or do they not? Does a student's gender also influence a behavior such as eye contact? And, for that matter, how much do gender and culture affect your particular students? These questions are the focus of the next chapter.

CHAPTER RE-VIEW

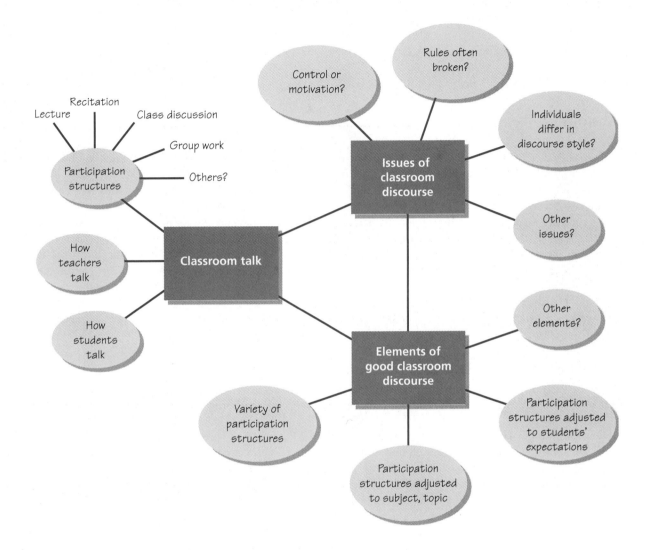

Chapter Re-View: The Meaning of Classroom Talk This Chapter Re-View suggests directions in which the chapter might have taken your thinking—though, of course, other directions are also possible. It expands the Chapter View, which suggests a starting point, conceptually, for the chapter. But this Re-View does not suggest an ending point. Like the Chapter View, it represents just one perspective among many.

Key Terms and Concepts

classroom discourse (247)   classroom discussion (257)   control talk (264)
participation structure (248)   collaborative group work
lecture (252)   (259)
recitation (254)   register (263)

Annotated Readings

Cohen, Elizabeth. (1994). *Designing group work: Strategies for the heterogeneous classroom* (2nd ed.). New York: Teachers College Press. Based on an assortment of research and wisdom, the author offers suggestions for making group work successful. Some of the suggestions involve the teacher structuring activities before students get started on them, as well as maintaining leadership of the class during group activities to ensure their success.

Johnson, David, & Johnson, Robert. (1994). *Learning together and alone: Cooperative, competitive, and individualistic learning* (4th ed.). Englewood Cliffs, NJ: Prentice Hall.

Slavin, Robert. (1995). *Cooperative learning: Theory, research, and practice* (2nd ed.). Boston: Allyn and Bacon. These are two of the most widely used texts on the opportunities and challenges of using cooperative learning in the classroom. Both include advice to teachers about how to implement cooperative activities. Johnson and Johnson are broader than Slavin in that they explicitly discuss participation structures other than cooperative learning.

Internet Resources

<www.review.org> This web site contains an online journal with information for colleges and universities that wish to make their educational programs more accessible to students with diverse educational and cultural backgrounds, as well as to any students who "have difficulty meeting their educational goals." Some of the topics are not related directly to classroom life (e.g., the high cost of postsecondary education), but many are; see their archives of past issues, and especially Volume 3, Number 4, which concerns linguistic (or language) practices that influence a student's classroom success.

<www.inform.umd.edu/EdRes/Topic/Education/> This is part of a web site sponsored by the University of Maryland that presents the results of educational research in accessible form. Information is organized by topics. One topic is cooperative learning, but other interesting topics are featured as well.

<www.ed.gov> Here is the official—and huge—web site of the United States Department of Education. Among other things, it contains online versions of many of the department's publications. When you get to the home page listed above, click first on the "search" category; then ask for any topic of interest. When I asked for government publications about cooperative learning, for example, it returned a list of more than two hundred articles, all of them online.

Chapter View: Gender and Culture as Influences on Learning This Chapter View is a concept map that indicates one among many ways of thinking about the chapter. It suggests a starting point, conceptually, for the chapter but is incomplete by itself. At the end of the chapter is a Chapter Re-View, which expands on the Chapter View, suggesting directions for taking your thinking further—though, of course, other directions are also possible.

9

Gender and Culture as Influences on Learning

In this chapter, I invite you to consider how learning and teaching might be affected by two important experiences: gender and culture. **Gender** refers not to biological sex differences as such but to patterns of social behaviors and attitudes associated with biological sex. **Culture** refers to the organized context of behaviors, attitudes, and customs that constitute a distinctive society or way of life. To discuss these topics effectively, though, I need your help. Specifically I need you to be aware, or to make yourself aware, of your own attitudes about gender and culture. As you may notice in the chapter, gender and culture can be difficult topics, not because there is no useful research about them (actually there is quite a lot) but because individuals, including teachers, often do not agree about their moral and educational significance. In the course of the chapter, I will point out these issues. First, let's consider the research itself and what it implies about life in classrooms and about students' learning. We'll start with gender.

How Important Is Gender in Your Own Life?

A good place to begin thinking about gender is with your own beliefs. Before reading further, take a moment to consider each of these questions, and remember your answers to them as you read on through the chapter:

- Do you think that in general, teachers respond differently to boys than to girls? And how about you personally: have any of *your* teachers responded differently to you because of your sex?
- How important are gender-role expectations in the lives of most children? How important have gender-role expectations been in *your* life?
- Who or what is most responsible for creating gender-role expectations: teachers, parents, the media, or children themselves? And who or what has been the most responsible in *your* life?

There are several ways to answer these questions, and each affects how you evaluate information and issues about gender such as those presented in this chapter. You may, for example, believe that gender influences human lives—but mostly other people's, not your own. Conversely, you may believe that gender expectations have affected your own life a lot, that you have missed certain opportunities because of your gender even though others seemed to have escaped these influences. If you respond in either of these ways, the chapter's contents may seem useful, but not universally or fully. On the other hand (or perhaps "on the third hand"), gender roles may not seem important for either yourself or others. In that case, I expect you to be rather skeptical about the significance of this chapter, and I have an especially difficult job ahead as writer!

My own answer to the first two of my opening questions is this: gender *does* matter in human relationships, including relationships in classrooms. Whether or not you agree with this position, I ask you to consider it as you read this part of the chapter. If you and I do disagree, part of the gap between us may be narrowed by considering research about my third opening question: sources of gender influence. Often the responsibility for gender expectations, it seems, is not where it first appears to be. But more on that later. We will begin, as usual, with teachers and their classrooms.

One way that some teachers respond to gender roles is by talking at closer range to girls than to boys. But this gender difference is not created simply by the teacher; many girls (and boys) are more comfortable with it as well.
© Fredrik D. Bodin/Stock Boston

What Teachers Do Differently with Boys and with Girls

CLASSROOM research has documented several ways in which teachers, on average, respond differently to boys than to girls. The differences can also be seen through casual observation as well, but only if you look closely. Many arise so quickly that they may be obscured by later events the moment after they occur.

Responding to Students' Knowledge

Systematic observations of classrooms find that teachers tend not to praise boys and girls for the same behaviors, nor do they criticize them for the same behaviors. Look at this classroom:

Ms. Paschkis is leading her second-grade class in a lesson about environmental studies. Lisa is there; so is Mitchell; and, of course, so are others. As usual, Ms. Paschkis keeps things moving at a fast pace—"to hold their interest," she says.

"Lisa," she asks, "can you remember the kinds of animals we read about last time?"

Lisa pauses. "Birds, fish, insects, . . . ?"

"That's right, but there's one more. What is it?" Ms. Paschkis pauses. Another pause. "I'm not sure."

Ms. Paschkis frowns slightly. "You should know this—maybe you have to read the pages again. Mitchell, can you help?"

"Mammals," says Mitchell.

"Good. Good thinking," says Ms. Paschkis.

In Your Own Voice

Would teachers be less likely to show these gender biases if they taught same-sex classes (all girls, that is, or all boys)?

How about if they arranged and worked with same-sex groups within a mixed-sex class?

What would be gained, and what lost?

What is going on here? Lisa was criticized for not knowing an answer, but Mitchell was praised for knowing. Was this coincidence or gender bias? There is never a way to be sure if we observe only a single brief incident such as this. Research observing interaction over extended periods, however, has found that such "coincidences" occur more than we would expect. Teachers, it seems, tend to praise boys more than girls for giving right answers and to criticize girls more than boys for *not* knowing right answers (Delamont, 1996; Measor & Sykes, 1992). In other words, when it comes to giving right answers, a boy is more likely to be praised and a girl is more likely to be overlooked; and when it comes to giving wrong answers, a boy is more likely to be overlooked and a girl is more likely to be criticized. Yet the incidents that create these trends are so brief and ambiguous in themselves that neither children nor teachers may sense a pattern in them.

Responding to Behavior

One difference, then, is in how teachers respond to students' knowledge. What happens when teachers respond to students' behavior? There is a trend here as well. Can you pinpoint it in this next exchange?

Mr. Hoffer is also teaching a unit about environmental studies. Karla is there, and Jason; Joel is there as well, sitting near Karla. It so happens that Mr. Hoffer is having a discussion with his class on the same topic as Ms. Paschkis's class.

"We talked about several kinds of animals last time," says Mr. Hoffer. "Did everyone read the pages that I assigned?" Several hands go up.

Mr. Hoffer continues, "And did you make an outline of the key points, like I told you to do?" This time only two hands go up, Karla's and Jason's.

"Good, Karla." Jason makes a face at her, which she returns in kind. Instantly Jason is spotted by Mr. Hoffer, even though Mr. Hoffer is now busy writing something on the board.

"I saw that, Jason," he says. "And I don't want to see any more of it." Karla smirks quietly to herself.

The psychologist Carol Gilligan and her associates interviewed students in a private girls' school (Gilligan, Lyons & Hanmer, 1990).

The girls, she discovered, did feel compelled to show "good" behavior (compelled, that is, to be careful, respectful, and well behaved).

But they attributed the pressure both to teachers' expectations and to classmates' expectations.

How does the experience of these girls compare to your own, and why do you think it is similar or different?

Not much time has gone by in this example—probably less than one minute. So does it show anything significant about teachers' gender expectations? In this case, the teacher has praised a girl and criticized a boy, but for behavior rather than knowledge, as in Ms. Paschkis's class. At the same time, he ignored a girl's misbehavior (Karla's) and even a boy's compliance (Joel had done the work but sat quietly). Like the first example, though, the incident is ambiguous taken by itself; it suggests gender bias only if a pattern of similar incidents occurs over time. As it happens, a pattern is in fact what classroom research has found (Golombok & Fivush, 1994). When it comes to "good" classroom behavior, in other words, boys are more likely to be overlooked and girls are more likely to be praised; whereas when it comes to classroom misbehavior, boys are more likely to be criticized and girls are more likely to be overlooked. Table 9.1 summarizes these trends. Just as with teachers' responses to students' knowledge, though, the incidents creating these trends are individually ambiguous and difficult to discern through casual observation.

Public Talk Versus Private Talk

On average, teachers are more likely to talk to boys from a greater distance than they use with girls (Wilkinson & Marrett, 1985). This tendency parallels a general gender difference in society as a whole:

TABLE 9.1 Gender Differences in the Basis for Praise and Criticism Although there is variation among any one teacher's responses to students, teachers as a group tend to respond differently to male and female students. One way to think about the trends is that if you are a girl, it is a bit easier to be praised for good behavior than for knowing correct answers, whereas for boys the reverse tends to be true.

Type of Response from Teacher	Boys	Girls
Praise	Correct knowledge	"Good" behavior
Overlooked/ignored	"Good" behavior, wrong knowledge	Misbehavior, correct knowledge
Criticized	Misbehavior	Wrong knowledge

Source: Golombok & Fivush (1994).

figuratively and sometimes literally, males often talk from across the room, whereas women talk at each other's elbows. In classrooms, however, it does not matter whether the teacher is male or female; teachers of both sexes incline toward the gender-stereotypic distance in conversing with male and female students, as in this classroom:

The eighth-grade class is working at their seats on a set of math problems. Ms. Mafrichi is circulating among students, helping individuals who are having difficulties. From a few desks away, she notices that Loretta has made a multiplication error: she has written "8 x 16 = 118."

Ms. Mafrichi approaches Loretta's desk and quietly says, "Take another look at 8 x 16. See if you think it's right."

Meanwhile, from two rows away, Rob is raising his hand for help. "Ms. Mafrichi, is this right?" he asks while she is still with Loretta and without being called on. He holds up his paper for her to see. He has made an error with a decimal point.

"You're doing pretty well, but check the decimal point," says Ms. Mafrichi, without moving.

Here the teacher's conversation with Loretta is relatively **private** because only Loretta, the person being spoken to, can hear and respond. But the one with Rob is relatively **public** because it has an audience other than the person spoken to directly. Does this matter? On any one occasion, probably not. As a steady pattern, though, it may teach a hidden lesson: that boys' efforts are more worthy of public comment than girls'. Whether or not boys' efforts are successful is not part of this lesson; their mistakes are just as worthy of notice as their successes. Why else would they be discussed in view of others?

Attention Paid

Overall, teachers interact with boys more often than with girls (Leder, 1990; Meason & Sykes, 1992)—10 to 30 percent more frequently, depending on the class and grade level. Why do teachers do this? Do they actually believe boys deserve this much more attention than girls? The answer probably is not simple. Part of the reason may relate to boys' and teachers' willingness to converse at a distance; they have conversations not only up close, as girls do, but also at longer distances. Another reason may be boys' assertiveness about conversing. When participating in the same class discussion, boys tend to contribute out of proportion to their numbers or their level of preparation for class (Koehler, 1990). As in the preceding example, it can be a boy, not a teacher, who initiates an

In Your Own Voice

Of course, Ms. Mafrichi's quiet approach could also *favor* Loretta in another way: by building a more personal relationship with her than with Rob.

What do you think of this possibility?

In Your Own Voice

Of course, you could ask whether it really *matters* that teachers interact more often with boys than with girls.

Are the students to whom teachers talk the most necessarily the most important students in teachers' eyes?

What do you think?

additional interchange. Still another possibility may have to do with teachers' perception that boys more often misbehave, a perception that gives teachers more to talk about with (some) boys: they must discuss behavior as well as academics.

Is a Gender-Biased Classroom Inevitable?

*E*VEN though it is common for everyone in a class—boys, girls, and teachers—to interact on the basis of gender-role expectations, it is by no means inevitable. Becoming aware of gender expectations helps to reduce them, because it makes it possible to counteract them deliberately. You build awareness by simple self-reminders, of course, but other strategies that are less direct are also helpful. The indirect strategies work by making the classroom more equitable (or fair) in general (Leaper, 1994). Here is a sampling:

- *Support spontaneous work-related contacts between the sexes.* A number of years ago, Lisa Serbin and her colleagues demonstrated that early childhood teachers could easily learn to reinforce children for interacting with the opposite sex (Serbin, Tonick & Sternglanz, 1997). Serbin also found that when teachers did so, children reduced how much they spontaneously segregated themselves by sex and interacted more than before with members of both sexes. It is testimony to the power of children's own gender biases, however, that the children reverted to highly segregated playmates soon after the teachers stopped supporting cross-sex interactions!

- *Arrange for cooperative, cross-sex work groups.* In the early grades (e.g., kindergarten), boys and girls provided with similar materials tend to use them in similar ways (Pellegrini & Perlmutter, 1989). At these grade levels, therefore, one simple way to encourage a gender-fair classroom is to create play and work groups that include members of both sexes. With older children, adolescents, and young adults (middle school, high school), this strategy can also work, but with less certainty. Whereas some boys and girls may develop more equitable relationships as a result of working together, others may simply reproduce the gender stereotypes of the larger society: boys may seek too much leadership, for example, and girls may be too willing to comply (Hourigan, 1994).

  Some educators have argued, in fact, that cross-sex "discomfort" pervades so many students and learning tasks that the sexes should be educated separately, as they sometimes have been in the past (Riordan, 1990; Ruhlman, 1996). A small but significant assortment of schools have been founded in recent years based on this idea (Lewin, 1997; United States Department of Education, 1993). Proponents, including many of the students themselves, argue that separating the sexes allows students to focus better on learning. Less time is given to managing the impressions made on the opposite sex. Girls speak more freely in class and worry less about their physical appearance; boys are less tempted to think that school success is the domain of girls or behave so that girls become focused on their social and physical attractiveness. In these ways, the self-esteem of girls in particular may benefit from single-sex settings.

But these arguments post problems. One is that there is little evidence that boys and girls discard gender roles very much simply because the opposite sex is not present. Research on life in single-sex schools suggests that conventional gender roles still guide the behavior of students even in the absence of the opposite sex (Brown & Gilligan, 1992; Ruhman, 1996). Another problem is that educating the sexes separately does little to bridge the gender gap directly; girls acquire little experience in dealing with boys as equals in learning, and vice versa. A third problem is that historically, policies of "separate but equal" education often have not worked: in the case of separate education for African Americans and white Americans, for example, the policy led to separate but *un*equal provisions for African Americans (Kluger, 1976). A similar effect has tended to occur with gender and sports, where separate programs and facilities for males and females have led to inferior programs and facilities for women (Mitchell, 1995). In both cases, the group with lower status maintains its lower status under policies of "separate but equal" provisions. Some educators argue that similar problems might occur if single-sex education became widespread (National Organization for Women, 1996) and that it therefore should be prohibited by law, just as direct forms of gender discrimination are currently prohibited.

In any case, whatever the merits of single-sex schooling, you may sometimes find it prudent to be moderate in your expectations of cross-sex cooperation. Often cooperation works just fine. But sometimes there may be students who do not work well with members of the opposite sex. There may also be tasks in which members of one gender do not feel comfortable displaying their knowledge and interest in the presence of members of the other. Boys may conceal interest in and knowledge about young children, for example, and girls may minimize interest in and knowledge about mathematics. If this hap-

In Your Own Voice

What do you think of my analogies between gender segregation and racial segregation?

What about the analogies between gender segregation in academic classes and in sports?

Are the analogies appropriate or misleading?

pens, you may find it more productive to tolerate temporary segregation on some activities, or even promote it for the moment, and look for ways to promote cross-sex interaction later.

- *Arrange for informal training that counters gender stereotypes.* In one research project, Phyllis Katz and Vincent Walsh (1991) trained and videotaped students in tasks that were not typical of their own sex. Girls demonstrated the use of carpentry tools, for example, and boys demonstrated ways of playing with a new doll. To close the videotape, the modeling students were deliberately complimented, sometimes by another child and sometimes by an adult. What happened after classmates viewed videotapes of the demonstrations? Katz and Walsh found they were then more likely than before to show flexibility in gender roles; for example, they indicated more interest in leisure activities *not* traditional for their own sex, and were more flexible about which occupations they considered appropriate for each sex. However, this flexibility was evident only if the classmates actually saw the model child being praised for his or her work; without this sign of support, the nontraditional demonstrations had little impact.

- *Avoid using gender to organize the classroom.* In a two-year study of classrooms, Barbara Lloyd and Gerard Duveen (1992) found that teachers often used gender not to discriminate but simply to organize activities and behaviors. When leaving the classroom, for example, many teachers asked students to form lines separately for "boys" and "girls." Others used gender-related terms to control behavior ("Boys, please be quiet" rather than "Michael and Donald, please be quiet"). Though these practices did not discriminate as such, they did heighten the importance of gender in the minds of students, increasing the chances that students' own gender biases might operate more strongly in other interactions with classmates (Eder, Evans & Parker, 1995; Thorne, 1993).

Even though gender roles are virtually universal, then, there are ways for you, as a teacher, to influence them to create a more equitable atmosphere in the classroom. Most of the strategies take conscious effort on your part; you cannot count on students to remind you of them! In working toward gender equity, in fact, it is important to keep in mind that students themselves create much of their own gender-role differences, based on their experiences elsewhere. Therefore, even though you can reduce gender biases in your classroom, it may be difficult or even impossible to eliminate it altogether. This fact does not mean you should give up influencing students, only that you need to know how students create their own gender differences.

How Children Create Their Own Gender Differences

Y comments so far may have given the impression that teachers bear major responsibility for gender-related bias and discrimination in the classroom. This conclusion, however, is not fair to teachers. It is true that teachers can contribute to the problem, and can minimize gender differences if they try. But teachers are not the only source of the gender-role stereotypes and behaviors exhibited by students, including even those that are expressed only in the classroom. Every member and institution of society makes a contribution: parents, the media, and children themselves. Properly understanding gender issues would therefore require discussing the beliefs and actions of all of these groups. Since space is limited, however, we will restrict ourselves to discussing only children. They are the group most influenced by teachers, and, as it happens, in a sense children actually *are* more responsible for their own gender biases than any group of adults (Maccoby, 1990).

Essentially children seem to create their own gender-role beliefs and behaviors in three ways: (1) through their own cognitive maturation, (2) through mutually reinforcing one another's gender-appropriate activities, and (3) through preferring compatible friends or playmates. Observational research supports the importance of each process, though their comparative importance remains unclear. As with the biases in teachers' interactions described earlier, students' construction of their own gender roles can be seen if you look. But you have to look carefully and for sustained periods.

Cognitive Maturation

In Your Own Voice

If children gradually become less stereotyped about gender roles, perhaps they ought to gradually become more willing to play together during the school years.

Yet they do not; segregation remains high well into high school.

What do you suppose accounts for this fact?

As children grow, they acquire increasingly sophisticated knowledge about society, including knowledge about gender and its significance. The basics of gender-role knowledge are in place soon after a child begins school: seven-year-olds know (or at least believe), for example, that "boys hit" and "girls cry" (Maccoby, 1994). They also have considerable knowledge of gender stereotypes about toys and activities: that boys (supposedly) play with vehicles but girls play with dolls.

Two changes unfold as children refine and elaborate on this knowledge during their school years (Martin, 1994). One is that they slowly realize there are many exceptions to the stereotypes. In fact, they discover, some boys do cry and some girls do hit. In this sense, children become more flexible about gender roles as they get older. Unfortunately, a second change occurs that acts at cross-purposes to the first: children also slowly learn about other children's reactions to gender-role behaviors. Approval comes for behaving in gender-appropriate ways, and rejection comes from not doing so. The result is that for many years through childhood and adolescence, young people increasingly shape their behavior to fit their personal images or knowledge of how each sex is *supposed* to behave, even though they increasingly know that gender roles can be and often are flexible. The resulting effort to be gender appropriate can be painful. Take this junior high boy:

David banged his head against the wall several times, crying. He had rushed out of the class just moments before to escape teasing. For the umpteenth time, it seemed to him, the same three boys had made fun of him.

"Your glasses are too thick," said one.

"David actually *does* his math homework!" said another sarcastically.

"A true nerd," said the third. "Hey, smarty, when are you *really* going to get smart?" (meaning quit taking schoolwork so seriously).

After being teased so many times, David couldn't hold back tears this time; so he left. The message, it seemed to him, was "learn not to trust anyone, especially boys." He cried a bit more, feeling quieter now but more depressed. The bell rang; the class ended and students came out to go to their next classes. But two girls, Bev and Carol Lynn, stopped to check on David.

"You OK?" asked Bev. "It got pretty rough on you in there."

David stifled further tears and looked at them. "Yeah, I'm OK, thanks," he said.

"The creeps should lay off," said Carol Lynn, scowling. "Get a life of their own."

It seemed to David like he should say something else, something that showed appreciation to Carol Lynn and Bev. But all he said was "Yeah. Thanks; I'm OK now," and walked to his next class.

What happened here? David failed to uphold a gender expectation: that boys do not cry. On the other hand, he did uphold another gender expectation: to say little about his feelings. Somehow he has already acquired knowledge about gender stereotypes along with knowledge about their limits. By his age, he knows something about what boys *should* do and feel (stand up to teasing) as well as what they *actually* do and feel (cry sometimes).

David was not a passive recipient of society's beliefs about gender any more than any of the rest of us are. He wrestled with them of his own accord, to the extent that his growing cognitive maturity allowed. A large part of what he wrestled with, it seemed, was his knowledge of the reactions of his peers, the second way in which young people construct gender roles for themselves.

Mutual Reinforcement for Gender-Appropriate Behavior

When a child's behavior is consistent with conventional gender expectations, he or she is more likely to be supported and praised by peers than otherwise. Observations of children and students suggest that the trend is already under way when children begin kindergarten and continues all the way through the end of schooling (Eder et al., 1995; Serbin, Powlishta & Gulko, 1993; Serbin, 1994):

Learning to Dance in Kindergarten

Ms. King was teaching the "Mexican Hat Dance" to her kindergarten class. The dance called for jumping in rhythm and for a number of related arm movements. A few girls volunteered, and soon were having a good time. Several children, both boys and girls, were watching. "Come on," said Julie, "it's fun!" The others just giggled and looked at one another with embarrassment, but then two, Marni and Joseph, came forward. Neither was as skilled as the first volunteers, but they did their best to keep up. "That's it, Marni!" said Julie. "Wait. Let me show you." And she stopped to demonstrate a step for Marni. Meanwhile Joseph continued dancing as best he could. The boys on the sidelines looked at one another and snickered some more; then they left.

Calculus Versus Shopping: Twelfth Grade

"What'ya been up to this week?" asked Marylee.

"Cramming for the city math competition—every night this week," replied Ginny. "Mostly calculus, but there's a bit of geometry. Oh, and I went shopping Wednesday afternoon—bought a new outfit."

"Am I impressed!" said Marylee. "Is it the one you're wearing?"

Marni and Ginny were both supported and noticed for a gender-conventional behavior: Marni for dancing and Ginny for clothes shopping. Joseph was honored for nothing, and in fact was scorned by other boys. Although the behaviors and responses could have been coincidences having little to do with gender roles, systematic observations suggest otherwise. Lisa Serbin and her colleagues noted significantly more praise

In Your Own Voice

Try to imagine these two examples if the boys were girls and the girls were boys. Would they still be plausible?

If you were the teacher in the first example, would you have an explicit obligation to support Joseph's dancing?

and support from peers in preschool classrooms when a child engaged in gender-appropriate activities, such as when a girl painted or a boy played with vehicles (Serbin et al., 1994). And in high schools, Donna Eder and her colleagues observed both praise and pressure from peers for individual boys and girls to enact appropriate gender roles (Eder et al., 1995); girls who did not show enough concern about their attractiveness, for example, tended to be ignored by other girls or even teased.

Peer reinforcement helps to explain how peers maintain and strengthen gender biases once those biases have formed. But it does not really explain why reinforcement begins in the first place, even at young ages when children have not yet formed sophisticated stereotypes. Why should nontraditional gender behaviors in early childhood seem unworthy of notice by peers or even threatening enough to merit teasing? And why at this age should traditional gender behaviors seem satisfying enough to merit praise? These initial biases must come from someone other than peers, presumably from parents or media images of adults. Once the bias is initiated, however, it may be possible for peers to sustain it themselves, at least in situations where they are not otherwise being guided by adults, such as the school playground or during classroom "chatting" out of earshot of the teacher.

Choosing Compatible Playmates and Friends

Children and young people may not initially be concerned about conforming to gender roles, but simply be seeking playmates (if they are young) or friends (if they are older) with whom they feel compatible. Perhaps members of a child's own sex tend to be more compatible, and over time the sexes therefore choose to segregate themselves: boys gradually prefer to interact with other boys and girls with other girls. The process need not happen consciously, and in fact research on children's choices of playmates and friends suggests that it rarely does (Martin, 1994). In early childhood, choices are made much too rapidly for reflection, as in this example:

Greetings from Joe

Recess has just begun; children are on the playground. Joe, enrolled in first grade, runs vigorously toward two classmates, Jill and Charlie. "Let's go; I'll beat you to the swings before they get taken!" he shouts to them while he is still at least fifteen feet away. He is smiling, and approaching fast.

Students vary widely in how much they prefer conventional gender role activities. The two girls in the top photo enjoy talking about their clothes, but the martial arts students in the bottom photo include both boys and girls.
© Elena Rooraid/PhotoEdit

Jill eyes Joe warily and says nothing. Her heart beats a little faster because she is unsure what to do, not because she is getting excited.

Charlie returns the smile and takes off for the swings. "Me first!" he yells over his shoulder, racing across the yard, and taking no time to notice Jill's reactions.

Over time, as individuals increasingly choose members of their own gender, the two sexes drift apart socially. Eventually, so the argument goes, the self-imposed segregation creates two different gender worlds or ways of life (Maccoby, 1995). In one, members concern themselves more with personal relationships and in the other with activity and mutual competition. When interacting freely (which often occurs only *outside* class), teenage girls will share intimacies by telling secrets, exchanging clothing, commenting on one another's appearance, and grooming one another's hair. Meanwhile, boys learn to avoid intimacies or other expressions of vulnerability, engage in mock fighting, and turn numerous activities into contests (e.g., "Who can drink their soda the fastest?").

Unlike the process of peer reinforcement, self-selection of compatible friends helps to explain how gender differentiation might begin: children simply sort themselves out, and one basis for the sorting is (supposedly) gender. As an explanation, mutual compatibility has an intuitive appeal: you may be able to remember times when you felt more comfortable interacting with a member of your own sex. But there are three problems with the mutual compatibility explanation.

First, observations of preschoolers do not actually support the idea well. Three- and four-year-olds, who are just forming their first friendships, do not actually choose playmates of their own sex more often than those of the opposite sex (Maccoby, 1994). If children sort themselves by compatibility, then, they initially must do so rather slowly or tentatively, taking well into the elementary school years to complete the process. Teachers' observations on the playground, however, suggest that gender segregation is already well established by the time children begin kindergarten. Second, compatibility may explain why the sexes drift apart, but not why gender roles take on their conventional forms as children grow up. Given that the sexes do drift apart in childhood, why do they move in traditionally "male" and "female" directions, directions that occur widely or even universally in all societies? Third, why do some children and teens seem more gender-typed than others? Not every young person acts stereotypically masculine or feminine; in fact, observations of youngsters on school playgrounds suggest that many have numerous daily contacts with the opposite sex and, in this sense, do not live in separate gender worlds. This happens in part because some boys

In Your Own Voice

I raise an important issue here that other psychologists and teachers have also noted: whether gender differences are "in" children (and in us adults) as individuals or are triggered by the situations in which we find ourselves.

Is it that I am a manly man (in my case), or are there times when I am *expected* to act like a man?

What do you think?

and girls do not frequent activities (such as the school dance) where gender-typed behavior is prominent, and instead build their social lives around activities (such as a club with teacher supervision) where gender typing matters much less. If self-segregation occurs, then, it does so more for some people than others, and more in some situations than others.

In spite of these qualifications about the influence of peers, the research evidence is strong that children and youth do contribute to the development of their own gender roles (Maccoby, 1994; Leaper, 1994). Because this conclusion is especially true for school-age children compared to preschoolers, it is important for teachers to recognize. At the same time, of course, students are not totally responsible for creating gender biases any more than teachers are; each is simply one source of them among many. This fact complicates teachers' most important responsibility with respect to gender roles: to decide how to respond to them.

What Should You Do About Gender Roles?

ALL things considered, the implications of gender roles for teaching are not straightforward. No teacher wants to treat individual students unfairly on account of gender or see anyone's opportunities limited by discriminatory practices related to gender. As the previous sections suggest, teachers therefore can examine their interactions with students and often can make them more gender-fair. But unfortunately it is not that simple: the issues of gender discrimination are beyond teachers' power to control fully. Especially disconcerting is the possibility that for some purposes, students themselves may prefer a degree of gender segregation and, in this sense, bear some responsibility for their own gender roles, including responsibility for status differences between boys and girls that they create as a result. If you are a teacher who believes in gender equity, you may therefore find yourself working at times against students' preferred styles of interaction: there may be girls who resist encouragement to assert themselves, for example, and boys who resist encouragement to listen and hold back their assertiveness. At times you may also agree with some experts on gender development (for example, Maccoby, 1995) that self-imposed gender segregation in childhood serves purposes that are valuable, or at least acceptable. All-boy peer groups, for example, may channel and control excessive male aggressiveness; the boys learn to compete with one another and to avoid doing so in other situations. All-girl groups may develop commitments to mutual emotional support and cooperation, and in this way foster girls' self-esteem. The trouble is that simultaneously with these benefits, same-sex groups also foster gender stereotypes and deny their benefits to members of the opposite sex. Girls do not learn to assert themselves, and boys do not learn to give and take mutual emotional support.

What, then, is a teacher to do? When should you discourage gender-role differences, and when should you tolerate them? Should you ever actively support them? Ultimately you will have to formulate answers to these questions yourself as you gain experience with students. For now, though, I offer two principles to help guide your search.

First, *the more likely that a traditional gender-role behavior will cause harm, the more you should challenge it or even oppose it.* Conventional gender roles often may seem innocent enough, but sometimes they can hurt either self or others. At the extreme are behaviors whose harm is obvious. Violence by or among males is an example; they are actions performed to feel powerful. Another example is attempted suicide by a female because of self-blame or a belief in powerlessness. In either case, the action hurts both the person and his or her friends and relatives, and therefore should be opposed.

But most gender-role behaviors have more ambiguous consequences than these. Consider these examples:

- Sharon, grade 12, decides to quit school before completing the year in order to get married. She assures her best girlfriend that it is not because she is pregnant.

- Jerry, grade 11, decides to continue playing on the high school football team even though he has seriously injured his knees twice in doing so. His reason: his friends admire the football team, and he wants to be a part of it.

- Deb, grade 8, decides not to enroll in the college prep sections of math and science for high school next year. Her reason: her girlfriends are not taking these sections, and "What do I want with math and science anyway? They're for boys."

Can we be sure that harm will befall each of these students? Sharon seems the most likely victim, since modern urban society usually regards early marriage as limiting a person's future. But saying this is different from saying that Sharon in particular will suffer bad consequences. Can we be certain that she would be hurting herself—certain that she is not psychologically ready, or that her husband is not, or that she will be trapping herself into a low-income job as a result of early marriage? At

---

In Your Own Voice

One reviewer who read these examples argued that the first two are not really about gender roles, although they certainly involve decision making.

But I still think all three are expressions of gender-role expectations. What do you think?

Can you see a case both for them being about gender-role differences and not being about these differences?

What Should You Do About Gender Roles?   **299**

best we can consider these outcomes to be disconcertingly possible. Ethically, therefore, it is more honest to question or challenge Sharon's decision rather than to oppose it outright.

Similar considerations apply to Jerry. Physically, he puts himself at risk by returning to football after two previous injuries. But that is all we know for sure; we do not know for sure that he will in fact have another injury. In talking to Jerry about his decision, then, we must admit our ignorance of its consequences; but we also can, and should, question his decision. In the end he must decide about football for himself, just as Sharon must ultimately decide about her marriage for herself.

And what about Deb: is she making a mistake by following the lead of her girlfriends and declining the college preparatory sections of math and science? It may be harmful if Deb is considering careers that require math and science, such as nursing or medicine; but it may not be harmful if she is headed in some other direction, such as teaching the humanities in high school, that does not depend on advanced knowledge of these subjects. As her teacher, you can and should point out these possibilities before she makes her final choice. But when all is said and done, Deb will have to make the choice herself, and you will have to respect it. Yet even then, your responsibility to Deb may be unclear: what if you suspect she will change her mind later and eventually regret having dropped math and science? Maybe you should say so to her. But once again you have to admit to her that you are dealing in uncertainties: you do not know the future well enough to predict whether she really will change her mind at a later date.

When students' behaviors, attitudes, and choices are full of ambiguities such as these, making it impossible to predict the long-term consequences of students' actions, there are no simple guidelines about gender roles for teachers to follow. Another, more positive approach is needed, one that recognizes students' right to shape their own lives, yet also recognizes the power of gender as an organizer of society and of the individuals within it. That approach is summarized in the second guideline.

Second, create options related to gender roles for students wherever possible. Options can be large or small, immediate or long term. Here is a sampling of a few, though many more exist:

■ *In a class discussion:* Be thoughtful about whom you call on to speak. Are girls getting enough chances, even when they do not raise their hands as quickly as some of the boys? Are boys seeing that you respect all students' contributions, and not just "turn sharks" who seek the floor most actively?

In Your Own Voice

One idea for ensuring fair chances to speak is to have individuals pass around a "speaking object" (maybe a ball or an orange) and insist that a person can talk only when she or he is holding the speaking object.

How well do you think this would work?

- *When students are working independently:* Be mindful about *why* you praise or criticize a student. Is he or she getting noticed for performance as well as for compliance with procedures? Are you "broadcasting" your opinions of some students by speaking to them from a distance but concealing your opinions of others by speaking to them only close by?

- *When students talk to you about academic and career choices:* Encourage the nontraditional, both in courses and in career options! By definition, students are likely to need more information and encouragement about unconventional choices than conventional ones. A boy interested in teaching elementary school is less likely to have support for this idea than a girl interested in doing so; a girl who would like to be an engineer is less likely to have support than a boy with the same interest. Encouraging nontraditional plans does not mean, however, that gender-traditional choices should be criticized. The boy who loves engineering and the girl who loves elementary school teaching also need information and support for their choices. Remember: the guideline is to provide options for students, not to channel individuals in preconceived directions.

- *When planning a specific lesson:* Consider methods that all students, boys and girls, can connect with actively. In teaching mathematical problem solving, for example, it may be important to encourage students to share their thinking with trusted partners rather than to hear only from the teacher or only from those who currently feel entitled to speak (Becker, 1995). Engaging students in collaboration may be especially helpful to some girls, those who have already taught themselves to "collaborate" in social relationships with other girls. But it can also help all students, whether or not they have shaped their social lives around peer collaboration.

- *When planning a whole course:* Provide as many ways to gain recognition as possible! Ideally, your course should offer an assortment of avenues to success: it should be possible to be a good contributor to a discussion, or a writer of good essays, or a skillful collaborator with classmates, or—who knows what else? The more avenues to success you can create, the less likely it is that students will feel they are being forced to compete with one another and the more everyone can respect one another's individuality. When you have established respect for individuality, you have begun to deal with the other challenging aspect of context that affects teaching and learning: students' cultural diversity.

With these guidelines in mind, you can broaden the ways in which students think about their roles and relationships with others, without denying them the right to create their own versions of what it means to be masculine or feminine. When all is said and done, the most noticeable feature of students' beliefs about gender is likely to be their diversity, a reflection of another area where diversity will be prominent: students' cultural backgrounds.

Culture as Context for Teaching and Learning

*E*VEN broader in influence than gender is culture, the patterns of attitudes, behaviors, language, and roles that constitute a distinctive way of life of a society. When the pattern belongs to a group within a society rather than to an entire society, it is sometimes termed *ethnic culture* or simply *ethnicity*; it is really ethnic cultures that concern teachers, and how such cultures relate to one another and affect teaching and learning. Culture includes elements that are relatively obvious, such as special holidays, a unique language, or distinctive clothing. But it also includes elements that are more important but less easily discernible by an outsider, such as deeply held values about what consti-

Without knowing much about the society or culture where it was taken, it is hard to interpret this picture. What are these people doing? What is the relationship between them? Are they enjoying their work or not?
© Elizabeth Crews

tutes "true" intelligence, beliefs about the nature of worldly success, or preferences about how children should act with respect to their elders. When students come from many different ethnic cultures, therefore, they may bring with them a variety of assumptions about very important matters such as these. It helps, of course, for a teacher to know something about students' cultural assumptions. But as I point out at the end of this chapter, if prior knowledge of students' cultures is impossible, it also helps for a teacher to stand ready to learn about students' cultures as they get acquainted and gain more experience with each other (Hoffman, 1996; Ogbu, 1994).

What Is Culture?

Since important features of any ethnic culture are often subtle or invisible, it is not surprising that students can have trouble understanding the general term *culture* when they first encounter it. There are two reasons for the difficulty. The first is that, as already mentioned, the concept is so broad (Grossberg, 1994). Take a look at this initial attempt by a middle-school class:

Ms. Emond wrote the word *culture* on the board and posed her question: "When I say 'Mexican culture,' what do you think of?"
"Tacos—tamales."
"OK, so 'culture' includes food. How about if I say 'Japanese culture'?"
"Kimonos. Buildings with pointed roofs."
"So 'culture' includes clothing. And architecture, styles of buildings. How about if I say 'British'?"
"Queen Elizabeth. And Parliament."
"So 'culture' includes ways that a people govern themselves."

As a starting point, there is nothing wrong with this discussion; students have to begin somewhere in thinking about the term *culture*. But notice that distinctive societies and peoples could easily be stereotyped if the discussion is not extended or elaborated. Left as is, the exchange could leave students with the stereotypical impression that all Mexicans like tacos, all Japanese women wear kimonos, or all British people support the monarchy. It might leave the impression that *culture* refers only to something "nonwhite" or foreign; why, for instance, didn't Ms. Emond ask about American culture? It could also leave the impression that culture has little to do with underlying beliefs or attitudes about life, but is only a list of specific, observable traits: food, clothing, architec-

In Your Own Voice

A teacher who read this section said I should make the point more strongly that "White Americans" also constitute a cultural group.

I saw her point, but wasn't sure how to describe "White culture"—perhaps because I myself am white.

Can you help?

How would *you* describe White American culture?

ture, parades or ceremonies involving royalty, and the like. Yet the observable traits may matter less than the meanings underlying them. Typical foods may matter less in defining a society, for example, than a society's beliefs about who should cook food and why. Typical clothing styles may matter less than the social occasions and rituals where the clothing is worn.

The second reason culture can be difficult for students to understand is that individuals from the "same" cultural tradition often adopt different attitudes to it. One African American will emphasize the "African" part of her identity, but another will emphasize the "American" part. Still another may have relatives from more than one cultural heritage, and therefore will feel torn about which part to value or will embrace first one, then the other, depending on the situation (Morrison & Rodgers, 1996). The dilemmas create diversity among individuals, a diversity that is nearly universal in a multicultural society such as the United States. Asha, a teenager whose family came from India, experienced such a dilemma. Her family happened to be Hindu:

8:00 A.M. Asha looked at her hair, black and falling to her shoulders. How should she wear it today? Her mom still preferred her to wear one or two thick braids, with her hair parted in the middle. But that looked stupid! She had been refusing to wear it that way for almost two years now, since tenth grade. The other way that her mom liked, and even her dad, was to tie it tight in a bun on top of her head. But that, as her friends had already told her, made her look like a grandmother.

What she wanted was to let it hang down loose, the way half the girls in her class were already doing. But her parents did not approve of loosely hanging hair, and said so: "You *know* what it makes you look like, don't you?" And she did know what they were hinting at; it was something not appropriate in polite company. But she didn't agree with her parents' opinion, in spite of their ominous tone.

So how to wear it this morning? Asha took a good look in the mirror and decided. She formed a bun but tied it loosely: that would do it. Kind of "with it" and attractive, she thought, but not tight like an old lady—an old Hindu lady. When she walked out to the kitchen, her parents looked at her and paused, but then just said, "Good morning." "Good morning to you," said Asha brightly, hoping to have a pleasant breakfast conversation.

Like a lot of adolescents, Asha experienced conflict between her parents and her peers about dress and personal appearance. But Asha's particular experience had culturally based overtones that might not be obvious to her peers. In Hindu culture, a girl or a young, unmarried woman typically wears her hair either in one or two long braids and a

In Your Own Voice

Have you ever had divided cultural loyalties, or do you know someone who has?

How did you (or he or she) resolve them?

In Your Own Voice

Technically, Hinduism is a religion, not a cultural group as such.

But even if it is, Hinduism is influencing Asha's daily behavior here.

Can you think of ways *your* religion (or lack of one) has influenced your daily behaviors?

married woman wears it tied up in a tight bun (Miller, 1995). To wear hair down loose is to suggest that a woman is menstruating; that is the impression her mother fears Asha will create.

So cultural beliefs and practices, it seems, are not valued unquestioningly or uniformly. For any one person they often must be coordinated with the beliefs and practices of several others, including parents, teachers, and friends, some of whom may identify with cultural frameworks that differ from the individual's. Any one classroom therefore may contain not only many different cultures but multiple versions of what is supposedly the "same" culture. Each deserves appreciation and support by teachers and classmates.

9:00 A.M. The teacher, Mr. Leclerq, sees Asha sit down in his twelfth-grade English class. He scans the twenty-two students, noting among other things that four other Hindu students are also present this morning. Vidya Bhakar is sitting near the back, quiet as always and neatly dressed. Mr. Leclerq finds him polite when called on or spoken to, but not inclined to initiate comments. Bal Johnson is sitting near the front, not far from Asha. Both of these students contribute freely to class discussions and seem rather extroverted to Mr. Leclerq. He thinks they could be friends if they wanted to be, though he suspects that in fact the two rarely speak to each other outside class. And then there is Indira, the girl who says she also speaks Punjabi and always wears a spot, a *bindi*, in the middle of her forehead. Occasionally she has even worn a *sari* to school, a sort of long, decorated cloth draped all around her. It seems to Mr. Leclerq, though, that she usually does not seem comfortable with the way classmates look at her on those days.

In Your Own Voice

What has been your own experience in encountering people from a cultural or ethnic group other than your own?

Positive, negative, or mixed?

Or nonexistent?

What factors account for the quality of your encounters?

As far as Mr. Leclerq and the other eighteen students are concerned, do Asha, Vidya, Bal, and Indira truly share the same culture of Hinduism? Or are their experiences with it more different than similar? Each seems to have constructed a different version of Hinduism to guide his or her life, at least judging by dress and classroom manner. Or have they? Clothing and deportment seem to be rather superficial reasons for concluding that the four students differ in their Hinduism. Is there some better basis for deciding the extent and similarity of students' Hinduism? An obvious starting point would be to ask the four students themselves to describe their various relationships to Hinduism and experiences with being Indian American. In fact, Mr. Leclerq could extend this strategy to the entire class: he could give an assignment, for example, in which all students must describe something about their own cultural background and their opinions of it.

In responding to the ambiguities of ethnic culture in this way, Mr. Leclerq would be doing what many experts in multicultural education

Am I being too optimistic in concluding that "culture is not in the eye of the beholder but in the affiliations experienced by members of the culture"?

How can this idea be reconciled with the facts of racial prejudice, which definitely originate not with members of a race but with all the "beholders" of a race?

recommend: to define *culture* not in terms of objective behaviors and associated underlying values but in terms of conscious *identification* with behaviors and values (Marrett, Mizuno & Collins, 1992). By this definition an "ethnic group" consists of all the people who consciously share knowledge of common historical or religious experiences, value particular cultural symbols in common (e.g., clothing, rituals, and language), and value personal or social values in common. These are not necessarily the same people who happen to *have* these qualities. There may be (and probably are) Italian Americans who do not value their Italian heritage, for example, and may not even know much about it; these individuals are not, by this definition, part of the ethnic group of Italian Americans. Among all people with Italian background, in fact, there may be—and probably are—many kinds and degrees of conscious affiliations with Italian American ethnic culture, just as Mr. Leclerq's four students probably represent a range of affiliations with Hinduism. Culture, in other words, is not in the eye of the beholder but in the affiliations and attachments experiencd by members of a culture. That is the lesson Mr. Leclerq must keep in mind and help his students to learn. Although classmates may think they know whether Asha is "really" Hindu, at a deeper level Asha must eventually decide this for herself.

It is June. Asha and a number of friends are looking for summer employment—not an easy task! Several of them are at the employment office of a company that hires a lot of high school students. They are filling out an information form. The questions are routine and short: your age, your work experience, your preferred forms of work, and so on. Near the end, though, is one question that makes Asha pause. Here it is, including the parenthetical disclaimer at the beginning:

(Optional—for confidential records only) What is your ethnic culture of origin? Please choose one:

_____White	_____Asian
_____Native American	_____African American
_____Hispanic	
_____Other (specify):_____	

Asha stares at the question, wondering whether to answer it and how. She does not think of herself as Asian but as someone with Asian parents. Even her parents, though, are more Hindu than Asian. And Hinduism, she knows, is a religion rather than an ethnic culture; there are Asians who are not Hindu and non-Asians who are. She suspects, though, that most of her classmates and potential employers would not understand these distinctions or share her own opinion of her ethnicity. So maybe she should leave the question blank—or would leaving it blank make it seem as if she has something to hide? Asha hesitates.

"How are you going to answer that last one about ethnic origin?" asks Juanita, who has been filling out the same form.

Cultural Differences in the Meaning of *Identity*

In spite of their ambiguity in some situations, ethnic cultures are distinctive when viewed in general. One way they differ is in how they define personal **identity** or *self*. In middle-class, white American culture, the self is a unique, independent individual, and an entity that is consistent or predictable across many situations. This definition is also well ingrained in schools and in the minds of many teachers, whatever their personal ethnic backgrounds: a teacher is likely to agree with the idea that "every student is special and unique," even if she or he cannot always follow up on this belief by individualizing instruction completely. The majority of nonwhite cultures, however, do not emphasize the self as unique but the self as interdependent with and socially responsive to others. In Native American, African American, Mexican American, Asian American, and a number of other cultures, it is your relationships, not your autonomy, that characterize you as a person (Greenfield, 1994;

MULTIPLE VOICES
MULTIPLE VOICES
MULTIPLE VOICES
MULTIPLE VOICES

Not only do teachers educated in mainstream professional education programs ground their pedagogy on a view of the self abstracted from the social context, but so do many educational psychologists. Most of the psychological tests administered to students simply do not take into account their socioeconomic and cultural backgrounds. In this context, the usual language of psychology claims to measure the ability/aptitude/efficiency of a "central processing mechanism" [such as discussed in Chapter 2]. In fact, such measurement is shaped less by some innate ability than by the individual's familiarity with "modernist consciousness": knowledge of and comfort with the conventions of white mainstream culture, Standard English, the conventions of schooling, and middle-class concerns with success. Due to no fault of their own, those who operate outside of this cultural framework are punished by the discipline of psychology.

Joe Kincheloe, Professor of educational foundations, Pennsylvania State University

Morris, 1994). In these cultures, the psychologically healthy person is not someone who stands apart from the crowd; that person would be regarded as isolated, lonely, or alienated. Rather, it is the person who gets along well with family and familiar others, and who fulfills ongoing responsibilities to them. Remember Ms. Davila in Chapter 7, the mother who had the awkward parent-teacher conference with Ms. Hamilton? The conversation between Ms. Davila and the teacher was awkward in part because Ms. Davila assumed an interdependent view of her daughter Maria's identity. She gave priority to talking about her child's success at relating to others rather than to talking about Maria's individual academic achievements. Ms. Hamilton, however, focused more on Maria's academic abilities, abilities that she apparently assumed existed independently of Maria's social relationships. Her belief is widespread among educators and may contribute to other educational misunderstandings as well. As Joe Kincheloe, professor of educational foundations at Pennsylvania State University, points out in the accompanying Multiple Voices box, an individualistic view of the self also lies at the heart of a lot of educational testing, and therefore may contribute to cultural misunderstanding and injustice.

Classroom Impact of Valuing the Interdependent Self

Awkwardness can result when students assume interdependent or relationship-oriented notions of self but their teachers assume independent or individualistic notions. To these students, the teachers and the school in general may seem egotistical and appear to expect self-centered behaviors from students. To the teachers, the relationship-oriented students may seem to lack confidence, ability, or motivation. Both perceptions are culturally biased, though in different ways.

Ms. Damon looked at her class: they had just begun working in groups, and what a difference it made in students' interest! She had just finished a whole-class discussion for health class about "how to spread the word about the dangers of drug abuse." But no one, it seemed, wanted to speak. They're eighth-graders, she thought, and they still don't know how to participate well in class discussions! She would ask a question, pause; rephrase the question; pause some more. Students would look at one another, not at her, until finally someone volunteered an answer. A brief and mumbled answer.

But that was a few moments ago. Now things were different: students had moved to groups to create a "publicity campaign" about the dangers of drug abuse. They attacked the task with gusto, talking among themselves, interrupting one another with further ideas. Most groups transformed the task into designing an antidrug poster, and some were already sketching it out. It was great to see them finally working! But what had made it happen?

This was not the first time Ms. Damon had seen such a transformation. She had taken the job at the Indian Reserve School four months ago, and since then she had noticed a pattern: passive silence when she tried to lead whole-group discussion, but animation when students worked together with peers. So far, though, she could not bring herself to get rid of further teacher-led discussions. I can't just teach the whole program using groups, she said to herself. They won't be prepared for high school. She knew the styles of some of the high school teachers; they were based heavily on recitation and public discussion. And besides, she thought, the students need to try asserting themselves more.

Experiences such as Ms. Damon's have been documented by cross-cultural educational research, both with Native American populations (Philips, 1983; Tharp, 1994) and with other nonwhite ethnic groups (see Greenfield & Cocking [1994]). When it happens, students' aversion to teacher-led activities stems not from a general lack of confidence or ability but from a commitment to peers: they see themselves functioning as equals, responsible for helping peers to learn and eligible for help from peers. In general, the students define their identities by their peer relationships, not by their independence, uniqueness, or difference from the group. This attitude makes them most comfortable with participation structures (see Chapter 8) that are cooperative and group oriented. This sort of participation supports this form of self-definition better than whole-class discussions or whole-class "public" recitations led by the teacher. It also leads to responding cautiously to teachers' invitations to talk in class; holding back shows respect for elders, who are important guardians of social ties and interdependence in the community as a whole. A lively class discussion therefore might show disrespect for an important cultural value, even though it might also show acceptance of a major educational value, that of fostering thinking and problem solving.

Ms. Damon faces a genuine problem in deciding how to structure her class activities. In the short term, it does seem as if the students will learn most effectively if she emphasizes group work and minimizes or eliminates teacher-led discussions and other teacher-led activities. But in the long term, will this approach prevent the students from becoming comfortable in traditionally oriented classrooms that may lie ahead? Will too much peer-oriented activity also prevent them from learning to be self-assertive in public, a skill that might help them in dealing with the non-native world? Strategies for resolving these questions have been

In Your Own Voice

How would you resolve the dilemma of honoring students' preferred modes of participating while also preparing them for other, more traditional forms of classroom participation?

Can you suggest one or two ideas?

proposed by multicultural educators (see Osborne, 1985, for examples). In general, the best strategies involve supporting students' preferred forms of participation but at the same time introducing alternative, individualistic forms of participation deliberately but not coercively. In Ms. Damon's case, students would indeed be encouraged to work heavily in peer groups; but "learning how to contribute to a teacher-led discussion" would also be identified to the students as a curriculum goal and practiced periodically.

Self-esteem: Motivator or Source of Embarrassment?

Valuing the interdependent self also can create awkwardness when teachers try to bolster students' feelings of self-worth or **self-esteem**. This idea may seem counterintuitive from the perspective of the individualistic, unique self, but a bit of reflection on students' reactions shows why it is valid:

When Ms. Elliott began teaching first grade, she made a point of greeting every student personally at least once each day, either before, during, or at the end of the school day. "It sort of tells the children that I think highly of each of them," she explained, "and that I know each of them as an individual. They need to have confidence in themselves, and maybe this will help." She pointed out that two-thirds of her class were Asian Americans, primarily Japanese Americans, Korean Americans, and Filipinos.

But the effects of the greetings were not what she expected. Although students generally were very polite in class, they seemed embarrassed by this particular practice. Some would mumble a response, and others acted as though they had not heard it. Instead of gradually becoming more cordial in responding, as she expected, students' haphazard responses persisted well into the year. Finally, she gave up her goal and simply greeted individuals sporadically, when she thought of it. What was the matter? she wondered.

The problem here is not politeness as such, because the students generally were very well mannered. Rather, the problem is that Ms. Elliott's explicit bolstering of self-esteem has an unstated purpose, which is to encourage each student to think of himself or herself as a unique individual; only by adopting this belief could her greetings make sense. Yet uniqueness may not have been a quality the students' families were encouraging in them. Instead, parents and relatives may have been nudging the children toward fulfilling responsibilities to others, including responsibilities to teachers for completing schoolwork. Ms. Elliott might have had better success, therefore, if she had *not* praised each student in a general way but encouraged him or her to think about how to improve performance on schoolwork, or how to develop better habits of self-discipline. Expressed in terms of operant conditioning, which we discussed in Chapter 2, the reinforcer turned out not to be reinforcing after all, and the teacher needed to look for a more effective alternative.

In any case, for students committed to an interdependent view of self, general self-esteem depends heavily on circumstances largely outside the control of teachers, namely on the strength of social ties, both in and outside of school. One research study of African American children found that the children felt happiest about themselves to the extent that they lived in an extended network of relatives and family friends (Walker et al., 1995). When it comes to schoolwork, an area where teachers can expect to have considerable influence, feedback focused on performance, and not merely supportive of the student as a person, often is more welcome and more effective in promoting learning. Interestingly, educational research has come to much the same conclusion for all students, regardless of cultural background (Bandura, 1993).

Strategies for Multicultural Teaching

GIVEN the cultural subtleties of terms such as *culture, identity,* and *self-esteem,* how can you teach a multicultural class successfully? I already mentioned some ways in previous sections of this chapter, but there are others as well. The strategies range from general principles to methods specific to particular ages or ethnic cultures (Osborne, 1985).

- *Use content that draws on students' cultural origins.* In a multicultural kindergarten class, for example, you can create "prop boxes" filled with materials from several cultures (Boutte, Scoy & Hendley, 1996). One can have shoes such as Indian moccasins, Chinese slippers, and boots or sandals from various cultures; another can have items related to food and eating, such as an empty container of tortillas, or child-oriented cookbooks from lots of different cultures. In elementary classrooms, you can incorporate celebrations from holidays meaningful to the children's families—complete with culturally relevant items of food or costumes, if possible. At all grade levels (even high school), you can invite members of students' families or leaders of students' cultural communities to visit or to assist with classroom activities. Best of all are invitations to take leadership in your class: to demonstrate a recipe, for example, or describe important celebrations or historical events from the students' perspective.

Activities such as these not only show respect for students' cultural origins but also challenge students to learn and understand cultures different from their own. An additional, interesting way to accomplish these purposes is to ask them to interpret pictures or slides of people or scenes from a culture unfamiliar to some students but known to others. If chosen carefully, these pictures can elicit dramatically different interpretations from children who are familiar with the culture compared to children who are not. The anthropologist George Spindler (1987) calls this method "transcultural sensitization"; he has used it successfully to help students understand rural life in France, though the method can easily be adapted to ways of life in North America. For example, Spindler showed one picture to students that depicted an older woman bending low over a row of vines on a steep hillside, apparently picking something off the plants. Students unfamiliar with the rural way of life in France missed several important points about the picture. They failed to note, for example, that because the vines grew on a hillside, farms had to be split into many small plots of land, harvesting could not be mechanized, and vines had to be harvested by hand. Harvesting by hand, in turn, made hand labor valuable and encouraged the development of extended families so that many family members (such as the old woman in the photograph) could help with the harvest. This outcome, in turn, encouraged somewhat interdependent self-identities of the kind discussed earlier. Many students projected their own cultural experiences onto the picture and assumed the woman was tired, bored, or anxious to get out of working. In the actual context of the picture, however, family members such as the old woman are proud of their valuable ability to contribute to family income.

In Your Own Voice

Showing pictures of an unfamiliar setting also makes an interesting activity in school classrooms. Try it sometime, either with pictures of places from your own life or, better yet, from your students' lives. Can classmates really understand what they are seeing without it being explained?

- *Include and respect all of the students' languages in the curriculum.* In classrooms with students who speak languages other than English, it may be tempting to impose an "English-only" rule about speaking and writing in the hope of accelerating students' learning of English. But this policy has two problems. One is that when implemented fully, it can convey disrespect for students' cultures of origin by treating their languages as if they have nothing to contribute to students' education. The other is that allowing bilingual students to use only a single, unfamiliar language of communication may actually retard literacy development more than if multiple languages are tolerated. A better approach is to encourage children to switch freely between their first language and English. This is easier for teachers to implement, of course, if they understand and speak a child's first language! Even if they do not, however, teachers sometimes can find conversational partners from elsewhere—from classmates or other school staff members, for example, or from occasional volunteers from the community.

The advantages of including a student's first language were illustrated by the educational researchers Luis Moll and Joel Dworin (1996), who observed the writing development of Hispanic elementary children whose teachers encouraged free switching between Spanish and English when the children wrote. The result was markedly greater fluency, better grammar, and more coherent organization as the children matured—and in *both* languages, not just in English! A student named Delia, for example, produced increasingly longer writing samples during first grade, and the samples contained fewer errors and more self-corrections by the end of the year (see Figure 9.1). Such progress is common, of course, for monolingual children; what is remarkable is that Delia was making the progress in two languages at once.

■ *Emphasize private and indirect interactions; be cautious about spotlighting individuals excessively.* Giving whole-class, "public" instructions and leading whole-class question-and-answer periods may seem like sensible teaching strategies, but they may bypass the network of ties that students (and their families) have established for each other, and in this way they can imply disrespect for students' interdependence (Greenfield, 1994). Where possible, therefore, teachers should deal with students' needs individually or in small, relatively private groups or settings. Cooperative group work often facilitates this approach, as Ms. Damon found out in the earlier example of her class at the American Indian Reservation. Even when it seems important for students to learn to speak publicly, though, teachers can still find ways to support their commitment to interdependence. Instead of expecting individuals to give oral reports, for example, a teacher can allow students to tape record their presentations, make the presentation with a partner, or speak from a script.

Note, though, that the advice to be indirect needs several qualifications. One is that less time spent in public, whole-class interactions means that more interactions will be private and unmonitored among students. But will students actually respond helpfully and fairly to one another? This concern was discussed earlier (see Chapter 8) with regard to classroom structures of participation. There I cautioned that when students work in groups independently, there is a danger that they will reproduce society's biases about gender and ethnicity: girls and nonwhites may receive less respect and be given fewer chances to

In Your Own Voice

How could a teacher assess whether small groups are actually promoting equity in class or interfering with it?

Can you suggest a strategy or two for doing this?

FIGURE 9.1 Delia's Writing in English and Spanish Delia, a Hispanic student, had teachers throughout elementary school who encouraged her to use *both* Spanish and English and to switch between them freely. Even during first grade, she became more skilled at writing in both languages: her writing samples became longer, had fewer errors, and contained more self-corrections.

A mí me han dicho que los gatos son los animales más limpios que hay. Yo tengo un gatito y le he enseñado muchas cosas diferentes. Yo le he enseñado a cazar, subirse a los árboles, comer lo que le doy y le enseñé a jugar.

En este mundo hay gatos de toda la clase.

En selvas, bosques, zoo y en tu propia casa o barrios hay gatos. En las selvas y en los bosques hay toda clase de animales salvajes que comen o atacan a la gente y a los animales.

En la casa o barrios algunos gatos son domesticos porque la gente los cría y los cuidan. Los gatos que no son domésticos o no están domesticados por la gente so salvajes y si los tratas de agarrar te rasguñan la cara o manos.

They have told me that cats are the cleanest animals there is.

There are many kinds of cats, there tigers, lions, mountain lions, cheetas, panters and cats that you take care of at home.

The cats that you take care at home are domestics, and tigers, lions, mountain lion, cheetas and panters are wild. Their wild because they kill people, eat other animals and they are not domesticated by people.

If you play around with a kitten the kitten mite bite you, run away or keep on playing.

Wild cats like to hunt other wild animals.

Domestic cats are little and wild cats are big and strong.

Translation:
They have told me that cats are the cleanest animals there are. I have a little cat and have taught him many different things. I taught him how to hunt, climb trees, eat what I give him, and I taught him how to play.

In this world there are all kinds of cats.

In jungles, forests, zoo and in your own house or neighborhoods there are cats. In the jungles and in the forests there are all kinds of wild animals that eat or attack people and the animals.

In the house or neighborhood some cats are domestics because people raise them and take care of them. The cats that are not domestics or domesticated by people are wild and if you try to grab them they will scratch your face or hands.

Source: From L. Moll and J. Dworkin (1996), Biliteracy development in classrooms: Social dynamics and cultural possibilities, in D. Hichs, ed., *Discourse, Learning, and Schooling*, pp. 221–246 (New York: Cambridge University Press). Reprinted with the permission of Cambridge University Press.

In Your Own Voice

How could you accommodate students who like speaking in front of a group as well as students who don't?

Are there ways to make both groups of students feel valued and to induce *them* to respect one another without feeling *de*valued themselves?

contribute. Whether such biases will actually occur, however, will depend on the personalities and cultural composition of a particular class and on how teachers prepare students for such work. When you teach, therefore, you will have to assess the risk of biases in your particular students.

The other qualification for the advice to be private and indirect is cultural: cultures vary in the value they place on children performing publicly and in the support they give children for learning to do so. A good example of valuing public performance is in some parts of contemporary African American culture. Educational researchers Catherine Dorsey-Gaines and Cynthia Garnett (1996) argue that African American churches in the United States often encourage public verbal performances: the preacher is highly respected for providing a verbal sermon rich with subtleties and Biblical allusions, and children growing up in the church are valued for reciting Bible passages well and retelling Bible stories with feeling. To *deny* certain black children the chance to verbally perform in class, therefore, may be as unjust as *requiring* children from other cultural backgrounds to do so. As the teacher, you need to balance these competing concerns. (Perhaps you can begin by asking students themselves about their preferences and by observing their actual behavior when you use different forms of participation.)

■ *Reflect on how students respond to activities, and act on your reflections.* Reflecting on your practice is the most important piece of advice of all; only by doing so will you truly allow for cultural diversity in the classroom. For it is not just that cultures differ from white, mainstream culture but that cultures also differ among themselves, that individuals differ within any one culture and may even belong to more than one culture at a time. As obvious as these ideas may seem in principle, in practice it can be just as easy to overlook differences among individuals as it is to overlook differences among cultures. Either way, a teacher risks stereotyping something—either a culture or a student. One way to guard against these twin dangers is to reflect continually on your efforts to know your students, as well as your efforts to know their backgrounds. That is what Mr. Jackson tried to do and what led him to use a questionnaire flexibly to evaluate his approach:

Mr. Jackson passed out the questionnaire to his homeroom class. An inner-city school, ninth-grade class, lots of bilingual and ESL students, mostly low income and a few migrants—a real cultural salad bowl! Six weeks had passed, and it was time to find out how he was doing as a teacher in their eyes. So he circulated a simple questionnaire to evaluate his teaching. It looked like this:

1. How are we doing? Is this class what you expected? Am I what you expected?

2. How about class sessions: Too much discussion? Too little? Too often? Too . . . what?

3. Should we have: More lectures? More discussions? More group projects? Or . . . ?

4. How about assignments: Did you like having partners on the first assignment? Dislike it? Tell me why, if possible:

5. Anything else that you want to say, now that you think about it?

"You can do the questionnaire in more than one way," he said. "One is just to write your answers on the questionnaire. Another is to fill it out with a partner, or even with two partners—just turn it in jointly. Another is to come to me after class, or at noon, or after school, and tell me your answers orally, and privately if you prefer. You choose. But do respond! I need your comments."

In soliciting such evaluations from students, it is important to actually *use* the information they provide. You must actually consider their suggestions and act on some of them—though you do not need to act on all of them. Otherwise students are likely to consider your request mere window dressing, just the appearance of concern about their opinions, rather than real concern. To make your concern genuine, of course, you must ask genuine questions: if you ask about the amount or difficulty of homework, for example, you must actually be wondering whether the amount or difficulty is appropriate.

Beyond Tolerance for Diversity

*I*F one idea pervades this chapter, it is that students and teachers live in a society much bigger than themselves, and that the society creates a context for teaching and learning that cannot be ignored. Gender roles were invented, so to speak, long before students, classrooms, or schools, and they influence virtually every society in the world. And culture and cultural differences are fundamental to the human condition; it is not realistic to think they will play no part in modern schooling or in your students' learning.

Yet gender and culture are not just facts of life to which students and teachers must adjust. They are also sources of meaning and motivation. We actively create relationships to gender roles (either using them, changing them, or actively ignoring them); and we actively adopt (or reject or ignore) our cultural backgrounds. Teachers in constructivist classrooms owe it to their students to assist them in developing perspectives about gender and culture that they can live with. The job of assisting students, in fact, is actually part and parcel of a larger mission of teaching: to support the full diversity of students as they seek education. The next chapter carries this idea further by discussing another source of diversity, teaching and learning among students with special educational needs.

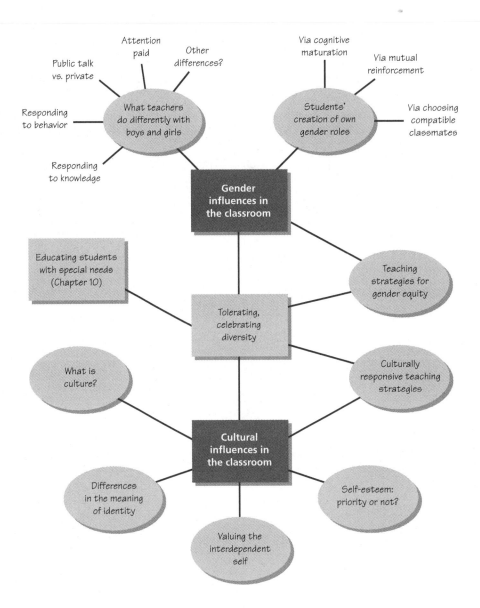

Attention paid

Public talk vs. private

Other differences?

Via cognitive maturation

Via mutual reinforcement

Responding to behavior

What teachers do differently with boys and girls

Students' creation of own gender roles

Via choosing compatible classmates

Responding to knowledge

Gender influences in the classroom

Educating students with special needs (Chapter 10)

Teaching strategies for gender equity

Tolerating, celebrating diversity

What is culture?

Culturally responsive teaching strategies

Cultural influences in the classroom

Differences in the meaning of identity

Self-esteem: priority or not?

Valuing the interdependent self

Chapter Re-View: Gender and Culture as Influences on Learning This Chapter Re-View suggests directions in which the chapter might have taken your thinking—though, of course, other directions are also possible. It expands the Chapter View, which suggests a starting point, conceptually, for the chapter. But this Re-View does not suggest an ending point. Like the Chapter View, it represents just one perspective among many.

Key Terms and Concepts

gender (283)
culture (283)
public talk (287)

private talk (287)
identity (307)
interdependent self (308)

self-esteem (310)
multicultural teaching (311)

Annotated Readings

Cushner, K., & Brislin, R. (1996). *Intercultural interaction: A practical guide* (2nd ed.). Thousand Oaks, CA: Sage. This book offers information and advice about interacting successfully with individuals from nonwhite, non–North American cultures. It is intended for people living abroad, but is also helpful for people (e.g., teachers) who interact with families and individuals from a variety of cultural backgrounds. One chapter specifically focuses on schools, teachers, and teaching.

Taylor, J., Gilligan, C., & Sullivan, A. (1995). *Between voice and silence: Women, girls, race, and relationships.* Cambridge, MA: Harvard University Press. One of several good books by Carol Gilligan and her associates, this one describes interviews with teenage girls of color who come from families that are relatively poor economically, though not necessarily poor in spirit. If you don't think gender affects students much, this book will change your mind.

Thorne, Barrie. (1993). *Gender play: Girls and boys together.* New Brunswick, NJ: Rutgers University Press. The author describes in vivid and poignant detail the contacts between the sexes during elementary and secondary schools, and the frequent pain and anxiety they cause. She has a knack for making the commonplace exchanges between the genders seem extraordinary and full of meaning for children's development.

Internet Resources

<www.yahoo.com/education> Most Internet search engines have a category about education, and this is the one for the search engine called Yahoo! Within this category are others relevant to the topics of this chapter. These include, among others, links to women's education, gender equity issues, bilingual education, and Native American education.

<www.ncbe.gwu.edu> This is the web site of the National Council for Bilingual Education, a nonprofit professional association dedicated to supporting bilingual students, their teachers, and their educational programs. This web site, based at George Washington University, has many components.

<www.ed.gov/offices/OBEMLA> This web site serves the Office of Bilingual Education and Multilingual Affairs, a branch of the United States Department of Education. It is a bit more focused on organizational and funding issues than the NCBE site, but it still has much to offer classroom teachers concerned about equity and cultural inclusiveness in teaching.

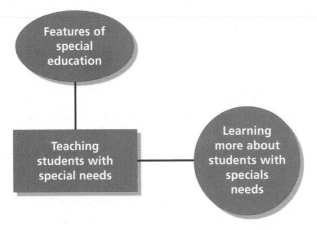

Chapter View: Teaching Students with Special Needs This Chapter View is a concept map that indicates one among many ways of thinking about the chapter. It suggests a starting point, conceptually, for the chapter but is incomplete by itself. At the end of the chapter is a Chapter Re-View, which expands on the Chapter View, suggesting directions for taking your thinking further—though, of course, other directions are also possible.

10
Teaching Students with Special Needs

"Frankly he made me uncomfortable at first, though I'm a little ashamed to admit it. Cerebral palsy, that's what he had. Mild CP. The way he moved was odd—kind of jerky—and he didn't really look at you straight, I guess because of his motor problem. The first day he was in the class, I worried about whether he would knock something over. I kept wondering how much help, plain physical assistance, to give him. Should I help him find the page in the text? Should I help him put on his coat?"

Joyce was talking about Peter, a student in her seventh-grade English class. She took another sip of coffee and went on.

"In fact, he was behind the others academically. I thought: How am I supposed to do the curriculum with him? Was I supposed to plan a modified program—not expect him to meet the usual goals for seventh-graders—or what? Peter could speak easily, but he couldn't write very well. The jerkiness was the problem. So he used a computer to type all written work. They gave me a computer just for Peter! I had to find space for it where it didn't distract the others and remind them that Peter got priority with it."

Joyce looked at me, then out the window, then heaved a long sigh.

"I kept thinking: Will anyone help me do this—help me with Peter? That's what I kept wondering. It was a real stress at first."

I looked at her furrowed brow, and asked what I thought was the basic question: "Do you wish that they had never given you Peter?"

"No, not at all!" she exclaimed. "Don't get me wrong. In principle he was no problem, no problem at all. It was the practice that was hard. Peter was a bright kid, but a kid with special needs. I felt a real respect for him. . . ." Joyce trailed off for a moment. She took a last sip of coffee. "But I *did* wonder how much he would be respected by other students. If I made too many changes in what I expected from Peter, would that call attention to his differences and make the others lose respect for him? Or would it simply help classmates to respond to Peter more helpfully? I didn't know. Actually, I expected that most students would probably not reject him socially, but probably would ignore him. They're good kids, that class, but not *that* good!"

I smirked at this. "And so . . ." I began slowly, "what happened?"

"You mean academically or socially?"

"Both. Each." I looked at Joyce expectantly.

"Well, that is another story," she said. "Or really *two* other stories. I'll have to tell them later, when I can have another cup of coffee." The recess bell had rung, and Joyce left to meet her class, Peter included, for the final part of the morning.

If you were in Joyce's place, how would you feel? Consider her reactions. At first she felt general uncertainty about and discomfort with Peter's disability, as well as concern about how to accomplish the usual curriculum given his needs. These are serious issues because they complicate an unwritten commitment of teachers, which is to accept *all* children and youth who come to school, no matter what their skills or backgrounds, and provide them with the best possible education. Students with special needs test that commitment; they challenge a teacher to find alternative and often unconventional ways of educating. Can it be done? Could *you* do it if you were the teacher?

In this chapter, I will answer the first of these two questions in the affirmative. We will see that education for students with special needs can indeed happen in regular classrooms and therefore *should* happen there. The basic challenge is **inclusion,** or educating students with special needs in regular classrooms. We'll explore some of the adjustments teachers and other school staff must make for such inclusion to take place. Whether you personally will want and be able to make the adjustments, however, is a question that I cannot answer. I suspect that most of you will indeed strive to include students with **special needs** as much as pos-

In Your Own Voice

There are several questions to consider here.

One of the most important is this: How much is education a privilege, and how much is it a right?

Think about how you answer that question now; then come back to it from time to time as you learn more about **inclusive education** and its implications.

sible. Doing so, however, may require not only adopting a few special classroom techniques but also modifying important educational beliefs. You may need to rethink your mission as a teacher and consider your beliefs about the nature of teaching and learning. In particular, you will have to broaden your educational priorities for students to include social skills alongside academic skills (Siegel, 1996). Only you can make such important changes; I can only point to the issues involved.

We begin with a sketch of **special education** in society as a whole, with an emphasis on how official, societywide policies affect individual classroom teachers. As we'll see, the general policies have made particular assumptions about the nature of special needs and about how students with such needs should be taught. You will need to consider these assumptions, decide how they affect your own teaching, and therefore decide how you can work with the policies to create true inclusion in your classroom. Toward the end of the chapter, I offer my own advice about how to achieve inclusion given policies and procedures that you are likely to encounter currently. Most of the advice will *not* focus, though, on students with particular disabilities—on how to teach students with hearing impairment, for example, or students with mental retardation. I leave that important, complex task to courses and books dedicated to that purpose. We'll focus instead on strategies of general value, ones that serve all students with special needs, no matter what those needs happen to be.

Key Features of Special Education

*I*N all English-speaking societies, national policies and laws heavily influence the education of students with special needs. In the United States, the key legislation is federal **Public Law 94-142,** currently referred to as the **Individuals with Disabilities Education Act,** or **IDEA.** The act affects local schools, and therefore individual teachers, in three important ways: by supporting the *least restrictive environment* for all students, by requiring *individual educational plans* for students who need them, and by *funding a variety of services* for students with special needs. Such involvement of federal authorities is unusual in education, which is normally considered a responsibility of state, provincial, and local governments. Steven Taylor, professor of special education at Syracuse University, comments on this fact in the accompanying Multiple Voices box. As he notes, there are good reasons for government involvement, though also some reasons for caution as a result.

A key feature of special education is inclusion of students with special needs in classroom activities as much as possible. While inclusion may require modification of the usual classroom procedures and expectations, the modifications are not necessarily difficult to arrange.

The Least Restrictive Environment

The IDEA legislation shifts priorities for students with disabilities away from segregated, special classes, which were in common use in past decades. Instead the act requires placement in the **least restrictive environment** (or **LRE**), defined as a combination of settings that involve students in regular classrooms and programs to the greatest extent possible. Support for the LRE reflects the results of research in the 1960s and 1970s suggesting that students with disabilities performed no worse, and sometimes better, when educated in regular classrooms for some or even all of the school day (Gartner & Lipsky, 1987; Lipsky & Gartner, 1996). LREs are also more democratic than segregation into special classes. Just as segregation based on race did not in fact create equal educations for all children, neither does segregation based on ability create equal educations.

A policy favoring the least restrictive environment means you can expect to have students with special needs in your classroom or classes rather often, perhaps even every year. The precise number and frequency

In Your Own Voice

Later I'll talk more about the impact that a policy of least restrictive environment has on teaching.

Before you read further, though, think for a minute about the impact: how might it affect *your* teaching, and what help would *you* need to make the policy work?

MULTIPLE VOICES
MULTIPLE VOICES
MULTIPLE VOICES
MULTIPLE VOICES

Reading this chapter, I wondered about what new students in education must think: "What have I gotten myself into?!" Not only must students learn how to teach students with disabilities; they must learn a whole new language, complete with baffling abbreviations. As you explain, IDEA requires that students with disabilities have an IEP (individualized educational plan) and be educated in the LRE (least restrictive environment). Of course, the centerpiece of IDEA is the right to a FAPE ("free, appropriate public education"). If students continue in these fields, they can look forward to learning more of these abbreviations!

The chapter correctly points out that the education of students with disabilities has been heavily influenced by national laws and policies. The current language of the field reflects this. Education is increasingly driven by legal requirements and procedures. Why, an astute student might ask, is the national government so centrally involved in these matters when education is primarily *not* its responsibility? Put another way, what does a politician in Washington, DC (or Ottawa, Canada), know about educating Johnny or Mary? Good questions.

When the first legislation was passed in 1975, the plain truth was that state and local governments were not doing their jobs in educating students with disabilities: as many as two million of them were excluded. The "least restrictive environment" was included in the law because students with disabilities often received education in segregated classrooms and special schools. The "individualized educational program" was added because these students' individual needs were often overlooked. Even today, observers note that local school districts often violate the spirit, if not the letter, of the law.

So we still need legal protections to protect students with disabilities from discrimination. Yet I hope that future teachers will look beyond the law and focus attention on doing what is right for students with disabilities. Unless they are committed to providing children with the best possible education, legal requirements like the IEP or LRE can be little more than empty bureaucratic exercises. The spirit underlying the legalities is this: do not exclude or segregate students based on disabilities; treat parents with respect, and involve them in educational decision making; plan for students as individuals; if one approach doesn't work, then try another. Are not these what any good teacher should do?

Steven Taylor, Professor of Special Education, Syracuse University

will depend not only on the nature and needs of the community you serve but also on the range of support staff your particular school is able to provide for students. In general, more support staff tends to mean students are present in regular classes more rather than less often because the support staff participates in a general program of inclusion of students with disabilities.

Of course, the precise nature of students' special needs also varies from year to year and from class to class, simply because they vary from student to student. Among the most common special needs are *learning disabilities (LDs)*, difficulties or impairments in specific aspects of learning—often reading—experienced by students who are otherwise capable and cooperative. Another common type of need is *speech and language disorders*, difficulties with grammar, pronunciation, or other aspects of oral language and verbal communication. Together these two forms of needs occur in nearly 10 percent of all children under age eighteen, most of whom are students enrolled in public schools (United States Department of Education, 1997). They are numerous enough that most teachers can expect to have several students with learning disabilities or speech and language disorders in their classes. Because of their frequency, I describe these conditions more fully later in the chapter, as well as other special needs that classroom teachers encounter less frequently.

Individual Educational Plan

The IDEA legislation also guarantees individual attention to students with special needs. It does so by requiring teachers and support staff to develop an annual **individual educational plan** (or **IEP**) for each student. The IEP is created by a team of individuals who know the student, usually including at least the classroom teacher, a resource teacher or other special educator, and the child's parents. The IEP can take many specific forms, but it always describes a student's current level of achievement, specifies educational goals or objectives for the coming year, lists special services to be provided for the student, and describes how the student's progress will be evaluated following implementation of the plan. Figure 10.1 on page 327 shows a simple IEP used by one school for a boy named Billie, a third-grader whom we will meet shortly.

Requiring IEPs for all students with special needs means two things to classroom teachers. First, they should expect to make definite, distinct plans for each student with a disability. Second, they should not expect to do so alone, as teachers often do in planning regular classroom pro-

FIGURE 10.1
Individual Education Plan

INDIVIDUAL EDUCATION PLAN

Student: Billie Lakoff	Birth Date: 26 May 1992	Period Covered by IEP: 9/19xx–6/19xy
Address:		Phone:
School: Grant Park Middle School	Grade Level: 3	Teacher(s): G. Eidse

Support Team

List specialties (educational, medical, or other) involved in assisting student:

Resource Teacher, Instructional Aide (part-time)

_____

_____

Special Curriculum Needs to be Addressed

List general needs here; use separate sheets(s) for specific, short-term objectives as appropriate:

Billie can read short, familiar words singly, but cannot read connected text even when familiar. Needs help especially with decoding and other "word attack" skills. Some trouble focusing on reading tasks. Billie speaks clearly and often listens well when the topic interests him.

_____

Special Materials or Equipment Needed

Modified tests and reading material as required.

_____

Signatures:

Parent or Guardian: K. Lakoff   Principal: L. Stauffer

Teacher(s): G. Eidse

Date of IEP Meeting: 26 October 19xx

Some educators have argued that IEPs should be developed for as many students as possible, or even for every student, regardless of whether they have special needs.

What do you think of this proposal?

Is it a good idea?

grams, but to plan collaboratively with others (Roach, 1995). A team approach to individual educational planning helps to ensure a voice for everyone concerned about a student: not only can the teacher be heard, but so can the principal, the resource teacher, the local school psychologist, and the student's parents. But collaboration also complicates the planning process, both philosophically and procedurally. Working as a team, not one but several people must make sure to formulate their thoughts about a student, accommodate one another's educational philosophies and experiences, and literally journey to the same room at the same time to express themselves and make decisions. For busy parents and teachers, these can be real challenges. Consider what happened when a group of people met for an IEP conference about Billie, a third-grade boy who was having serious difficulty learning to read. Billie has recently been classified by school authorities as "learning disabled," a move that has entitled Billie to part-time assistance from a teacher aide (TA). But final decisions have not yet been made about exactly when or how to use the TA or about exactly what Billie's educational program should look like. That is what today's meeting is for:

Ms. Eidse looked around the table. The psychologist was late for the meeting, she noted, even though he was the one who had asked for the mid-morning time slot. Hmph. Ms. Eidse had not wanted to meet then; "Who's going to cover my class?" she had asked. She thought this was a question without an answer, but the principal had in fact answered it for her. "Get the teacher assistant, Ms. del Boca," he said. "She can take the class for you." Obviously the principal did not know Ms. del Boca very well or Ms. Eidse's class either, for that matter.

What did the principal "not know" here? It is possible, of course, that Ms. Eidse was simply being defensive or overly possessive about letting someone take charge of her class. But it is also possible that Ms. del Boca did not share Ms. Eidse's approach to teaching. Perhaps she was more lenient, for example, or more strict, and when Ms. Eidse returned after the meeting, there was a real risk that she would find significant disorder in the classroom. Perhaps, too, the principal did not know the class had certain students who were difficult to manage in the best of times—though never difficult enough to come to the attention of the principal or of the resource teacher. Ms. Eidse may have been worrying about how these students might behave in her absence, when Ms. del Boca was in charge.

But mid-morning it was, because that was the "only" time the psychologist could attend. No one had consulted with Billie's mother, Ms. Eidse also noted, about when she could come; she had certainly been invited cordially enough, as the law required, but in effect was simply informed of the time. Now the principal was chatting with Billie's mother, Ms. Lakoff, making pleasantries to break the ice. She looked uneasy—as well she might, thought Ms. Eidse. The two women exchanged smiles in the midst of the principal's conversation; they had gotten rather well acquainted this fall in the course of talking about Billie's difficulties. Ms. Lakoff looked across the table as well and acknowledged Ms. Ashmore, the resource teacher. The two of them got along well enough, but with a touch of awkwardness; Ms. Ashmore had turned the initial informal conversations about Billie into a formal referral, with the classroom visits by her and the psychologist, conferences with Ms. Lakoff, and formal testing.

Why the awkwardness between Ms. Lakoff and Ms. Ashmore? Again, it is tempting to dismiss their relationship as a mild "personality clash," but doing so does not explain the causes of the clash or suggest how Ms. Eidse, the classroom teacher, might respond to it constructively. A more helpful way to think about the parent and the resource teacher is to look at the meaning of what has happened between them: once the resource teacher made a formal referral, Billie moved much closer to being officially and publicly acknowledged as a "student with special needs"—in his case, as a "student with a learning disability." As a caring professional, of course, Ms. Ashmore may be very careful not to use this label in speaking of Billie; but the risk has increased that the label will be used by someone, somewhere, whether in school or out. From Ms. Lakoff's perspective, Ms. Ashmore may seem responsible for having created this risk.

As soon as the psychologist arrived, the meeting began. "Sorry I'm late," he said. "But you know how it is. . . ." Ms. Eidse wasn't sure she *did* know "how it is," but no matter. She did not have much time, because she had promised her TA that she would return by 10:30.

Ms. Ashmore looked around the table. "I'm sure we are all busy today. Maybe we can save time if I share with you a plan that I drafted informally yesterday. Take a look at them and see what you think." She passed around copies of a tentative IEP (see Figure 10.1).

Everyone began reading her proposal silently. The psychologist nodded as he read, murmuring things like "Yes," "Umhm," and "That's like what we talked about on the phone last week, isn't it?" Ms. Eidse wondered what "that" was that they had talked about, just the two of them; but she kept silent. Ms. Lakoff said nothing, and showed little reaction one way or the other.

There is a hint here that the psychologist and the resource teacher are shutting the other people out of the discussion because they already talked about Billie on the phone last week. It is an uneasy, "dark" feeling: perhaps the future of a child is being "railroaded" through without proper consultation. Not even the mother has much to say; is she being silenced unjustly, we wonder? The meeting time, we remember, has been set without consulting with the mother, and the time chosen is inconvenient for the teacher. What is going on here? Is a democratic process not being followed? If so, the actions of the psychologist and resource teacher are definitely unacceptable! Billie's mother should speak up; she should demand that she be more involved in planning Billie's IEP. So should Ms. Eidse: why should she, the teacher who sees Billie the most and therefore might have a lot to say about Billie's capacities, experience such strong time pressure by simply attending the meeting?

All these possibilities may be true, but there is another, rather different interpretation of what just happened in the meeting. It depends on understanding a key feature of a good IEP planning process: the formal IEP meeting usually follows considerable informal consultation among the people with knowledge about the child and expertise about programming options. In this case Ms. Eidse, Ms. Ashmore, and Ms. Lakoff are likely to have talked already, and perhaps repeatedly, about what Billie needs educationally. The people not involved with Billie on a daily basis—the principal and the psychologist—are less likely to have participated in these conversations, although even they may have been asked their opinions and offered the opinions of the others on one or more occasions prior to the meeting. In the best cases, the prior discussions lead toward partial agreement about what a future educational program for a student should look like—what, in other words, should be written onto the IEP. In these cases, the meeting itself simply completes the process of achieving consensus, and to an extent simply affirms or ratifies the earlier discussions about the child.

If these earlier discussions have in fact occurred, then, it may matter less than it first appears whether Billie's mother has little or a lot to say on her son's behalf at the meeting. And it may be unfortunate (but not disastrous) that Ms. Eidse is under pressure to leave the meeting early; in other IEP conferences, other staff members may sometimes be the ones under time pressure. But the existence of the earlier, informal communication is crucial to this more forgiving interpretation of the events described here. Informal communication *should* have occurred; we will hope that it has.

But the principal had some questions and began putting them to Ms. Ashmore and the psychologist. Ms. Eidse did her best to follow along with the discussion, but noted that her watch now said 10:26. She would have to leave soon, even though the meeting had barely begun. She felt she knew Billie and his needs especially well; after all, she had taught him every day for three months! She didn't want to be rude, nor did she want to be silent. But she was also remembering her class and wondering how things were going with the TA, Ms. del Boca.

Smiling, and in a cordial tone, she said, "I'm so sorry, but I'm going to have to leave. I promised the TA I would be back by the end of recess, which is in just a few minutes. I suspect Ms. Ashmore's plan will work fine, though I can also live with any changes you decide on."

There could be something odd about Ms. Eidse's comment here. As Billie's classroom teacher, she is likely to have partial responsibility for implementing Billie's individual educational plan. Shouldn't she know, then, about any changes in the plan before agreeing to them? Why would she be relatively accepting of changes made sight unseen? There are, of course, the ominous possibilities mentioned earlier: perhaps an IEP program is being pushed through without real consultation and Ms. Eidse has given up trying to influence it. But there are other, more hopeful possibilities: as we noted before, informal conversations may have occurred previously so that Ms. Eidse already has a pretty good idea of what lies in store for Billie and what she can expect to do as his teacher. Perhaps, too, she knows the crucial remaining decisions do not involve Billie's classroom activities but concern arrangements that others at the table have to make, such as which TA should tutor Billie periodically and when the tutoring should be worked into the TA's timetable. It would still be better, of course, for Ms. Eidse to stay until the end of the meeting; but we have to remember that she also has obligations to the rest of her class and that she made a promise to the TA to return by 10:30. What is happening to them now, she thinks? But saying all of these things would distract the meeting from its purpose, so here is what she says instead:

"I suspect Ms. Ashmore's plan will work fine, though I can also live with any changes you decide on. But I do have to go. Goodbye for now. Goodbye, Ms. Lakoff." She added the last greeting to Billie's mother on purpose; she deserved it, she said to herself.

Never enough time, she thought as she walked back to her classroom. And if only the psychologist had come on time, or could have met after

In Your Own Voice

Am I being too tolerant and accepting of what happened in this IEP meeting?

Think about the teacher in particular: is there something Ms. Eidse should have done differently for the meeting to serve Billie better?

school, when I'm not so rushed. But then she remembered: Billie's mother couldn't have come at that hour anyway, even if she had been asked to come then (which she hadn't been). She worked after school. So there had been two reasons for meeting in the mid-morning.

It is tempting to think there are heroes and villains in this collaboration, but this judgment may be too hasty. By being late, for example, the psychologist did limit Ms. Eidse's participation in the meeting; but on the other hand, the psychologist probably served a large number of students, had to travel among a number of schools, and faced challenging problems regarding balancing time commitments among them all. It is possible that if the principal had known the TA and Ms. Eidse's class better, he might have suggested better ways to cover Ms. Eidse's class, and Ms. Eidse therefore might have felt freer to stay longer at the meeting. But it is also possible that no other choice was available; and in any case, the principal cannot be expected to know each teacher's students as well as the teacher herself or himself knows them. Finally, it is possible that both Ms. Lakoff and Ms. Eidse should have been invited more explicitly to speak at the meeting. But it is also likely, as indicated in the anecdote, that numerous conversations about Billie involving both Ms. Lakoff and Ms. Eidse, as well as the psychologist and Billie's parents, had already occurred. In a sense, therefore, the IEP meeting itself may serve a partially ceremonial function: it may simply ratify earlier thoughts and discussions that have already evolved over time (Mehan, 1986).

If there is a real "culprit" in the story, it may be the inherent scarcity of time: the fact that the educators and Billie's parents are all busy people, and therefore it can be challenging to get them together to make final decisions about services for a student with special needs. Yet, as these comments suggest, time pressures in scheduling meetings do not in and of themselves force compromises in the final quality of an IEP. Relevant people can still consult one another prior to larger, more formal meetings, and in doing so facilitate everyone's common goal: to devise the best possible program for the student (Garner, 1995).

Support for a Range of Services

The third way the IDEA legislation affects teachers is by providing money to local schools to organize a range of services for students with disabilities. The services tend to emphasize inclusion to a significant extent, especially for students with relatively mild disabilities, who form

In Your Own Voice

Relevant people *can* still consult with one another, but we cannot assume they always do.

What if consultation were difficult to conduct informally—for example, what if a parent spoke little English, or the school had only limited, part-time resource teaching help?

Can you make any suggestions for how to make the IEP process caring and fair in cases such as these?

the majority of all students with disabilities. An example might be a resource teacher, such as Ms. Ashmore, in a local school, who is usually a teacher with a background in special education who helps colleagues to work effectively with students who have learning difficulties. But other services help the smaller number of students with moderate or severe disabilities. These tend to involve settings that are more segregated, though often not completely so. An example might be a special, self-contained classroom in the school building for students with moderate physical or mental handicaps. Even though the students in such a class spend a majority of their days apart from other students, they may join in social or schoolwide events on a regular basis. Although these arrangements may seem to contradict the principle of least restrictive environment discussed earlier, in fact they do not, because they still strive to provide these more seriously disabled students with as much involvement and as many educational options as possible.

The provision of a range of services means that you, as a classroom teacher, can expect to work together with others not only in creating IEPs but also in implementing them. The pressures of time and large classes can make true collaboration difficult; it is tempting, as with the IEP conference described earlier, for a teacher to shorten and simplify his or her relationships with other educators who see a student during part of the student's day. To ensure coordination and mutual support for the student, however, it is best to strive for continual communication among involved staff. That is what Pat and Sharon tried. Sharon taught seventh grade, and Pat was a resource teacher—a teacher whose official job is to assist classroom teachers in working with students with special needs. Sharon's seventh-grade class contained several students with reading difficulties:

As a resource teacher, Pat was enthusiastic when she heard she would be working with Sharon. She knew Sharon shared her commitment to inclusion, and she liked how Sharon had worked in past years with the students with reading difficulties. So she wasted no time proposing a meeting: "Let's talk about our roles, about how we might coordinate my work with yours."

The discussion was productive indeed. First, they agreed that a lot of integration in the past had not gone far enough. Not only should they devise a way to keep students with reading difficulties in Sharon's class, but they should also keep *each other* in Sharon's class as far as possible!

"Why not have me attend one of your classes every day?" proposed Pat. Since Sharon had several students from Pat's caseload anyway, it seemed like a good idea. So it was agreed: Pat would come every morning for about an hour during Sharon's seventh-grade language arts sessions. They would share the teaching, including the planning responsibilities. Communication, they agreed, would be the key to real success.

What Pat and Sharon are planning is commendable but somewhat unusual. Both teachers are busy people with distinct job responsibilities: Pat's to work with and support individuals needing help and Sharon's to orchestrate an entire classroom's progress through a language arts curriculum. Neither has a shortage of potential work to do! The only reason for working together is to improve their understanding of each other's work and of the challenges each of them faces. Improved understanding, they hope, will make each more effective at what she does. Pat will know the language arts curriculum better and gain a sense of the full range of students' achievement, not just the achievement of students having difficulty. Sharon will learn more about how to help individuals who, in a classroom context, seem especially difficult or even "impossible" to help. But learning from each other will take more of the teachers' time—time to talk together and, for Pat, time to work in Sharon's class.

At first the decision seemed to work well, with each teacher making significant contributions to the program. Sharon designed the overall language arts program, but she availed herself of Pat's knowledge of the special-needs students and responded to her suggestions about activities. When Sharon described the books her students would read in the first month, Pat realized some of the special-needs students would find some of the books difficult, and she suggested a few alternative selections. Pat also suggested that Sharon allow certain students—the ones who had a lot of trouble writing—to prepare oral or tape-recorded versions of their written assignments. Sharon seemed amenable to these changes.

But it wasn't long before differences began to emerge between Pat and Sharon. Pat did lead activities with the whole class sometimes, but more often she ended up helping individuals whenever they had unusual problems with an assignment or when some other sort of crisis arose. Since handling these problems often meant leaving the room, Sharon sometimes ended up teaching on her own. Before long, the students themselves began reacting to these differences as well; they took questions about assignments, and even questions about misbehavior, to Sharon, not Pat. Apparently they saw Sharon as the "real" teacher and Pat as her helper.

We can't be sure what caused the teachers' roles to diverge, but we can guess at some reasons. One is that the teachers' prior experiences and expertise "nudged" them gently, but unceasingly, in separate directions. After all, Pat did have more experience working with individuals

In Your Own Voice

Given the benefits of collaboration, why do you suppose so little time has been made available to Pat and Sharon to help make it happen?

Why do they have to go "above and beyond the call of duty" to attempt a collaboration?

In Your Own Voice

In this example, I have implied that Pat and Sharon may have been overzealous in trying to collaborate.

Do you think that in fact they were?

Can you think of a way to save their plan, to help them work together after all?

Or should they plan to learn about each other's work in some less ambitious way?

having unusual learning difficulties. Sharon, on the other hand, had more experience planning whole-class curriculum activities; perhaps she could do it more easily or quickly than her newcomer partner. In spite of the teachers' desire to share their work, then, it might be in students' best interest for Pat to look after special learning problems and Sharon to plan and lead whole-class activities. Perhaps this division of labor, rather than the reverse, felt more comfortable to the teachers as well. And eventually students might notice, even if unconsciously, where and when each teacher worked most effectively and comfortably. The divergence would unfold over time and would not be troubling at first.

Since she had plenty of work to do helping students, Pat didn't really mind the changes in her role at first. Pat did start to worry, though, when she and Sharon began cutting corners on mutual planning times. The fast pace of activities meant Pat and Sharon sometimes postponed agreed-on appointments, whether to talk about the special reading students or about the classroom program generally. Now, thought Pat, I am truly becoming the assistant and not even a partner behind the scenes. What to do? Sharon suggested that they meet less frequently but not sacrifice regular times altogether. By the winter holidays, therefore, they were meeting only twice per month instead of weekly as they had begun. And Pat settled into being the "invisible teacher," as she began to jokingly refer to herself. Privately she wondered how she really felt about these changes.

How would *you* have felt about the changes if you were in Pat's place, or in Sharon's for that matter? You may be able to think of other ways for Pat and Sharon to have collaborated and handled the changes in their working relationship. But whatever strategies you can imagine, one option was not available: neither Pat nor Sharon could work with the students with special needs in isolation from each other. Consultation and coordination with other responsible educators have to be part of their plan, no matter what form the consultation and coordination take or how often they occur. Students with special needs pose unique challenges to classroom teachers, since the students' learning can require additional planning and assistance to implement. Official school district policies and even state and federal laws reflect this circumstance by requiring consultation and coordination at certain key times (such as at the IEP meeting we read about earlier). But the need to consult and coordinate is far more than legal: it is intrinsic to educating students with special needs.

In Your Own Voice

When I wrote the next several sections, I did my best to make them accurate.

But I constantly came up against figures that do not "add up" as they should, presumably because of the ambiguities about classification categories discussed here.

Given the imprecision of categories, do you think it is still helpful to use them? What purpose, if any, would they serve *you* in your work as a teacher?

A student with a learning disability functions well in most areas of classroom life but needs help with a specific area of study—often reading or arithmetic.

Major Types of Special Needs

So far I have talked mostly about what it is like to *teach* students with special needs. The stories of Joyce and Peter, of Ms. Eidse and Billie, and of Pat and Sharon all concentrate on teachers and other adults, not students. But who are these students—the Peters and Billies and others—and how do they actually learn?

It is overly simple to say, even if true, that students with disabilities are incredibly diverse as individuals, just as other students are. Teachers need to know more about what that variety consists of and why it is described with terms such as *disability* or *special needs*. In this section, therefore, we explore the four types of disabilities that classroom teachers are most likely to encounter: learning disabilities, attention deficit disorder, speech and language disorders, and mild mental retardation. Together these conditions account for 4 to 5 percent of all students in school and 85 to 90 percent of students with special needs (United States Department of Education, 1997; Wenger, Kaye & LaPlante, 1996). The uncertainty about the figures stems from several factors. One is the ambiguities of categories of special needs, described in more detail shortly. Another is that the behaviors underlying the categories overlap, and a child therefore may be classified, either informally or formally, as belonging to more than one category of need. A third is that surveys of frequency of special needs sometimes focus on populations that truly differ in frequency. Speech problems occur in all segments of society, for example, but occasionally they may be confused (wrongly) with the normal problems of learning English as a second language; in these communities, as a result, speech problems may sometimes be "overidentified."

In any case, since this book cannot devote itself entirely to special education, I will not describe relatively infrequent kinds of disabilities, such as blindness, deafness, or serious chronic health problems (childhood cancer or childhood AIDS, for instance). Nor will I discuss behavioral or emotional problems unrelated to learning disabilities, attention deficit, speech and language problems, or mild retardation. These difficulties are certainly important for the students who have them, as well as for their families and teachers. But (as Figure 10.2 shows) they are not needs that most classroom teachers are likely to encounter very often.

FIGURE 10.2

Percentages of Students with Special Needs in the United States, 1995

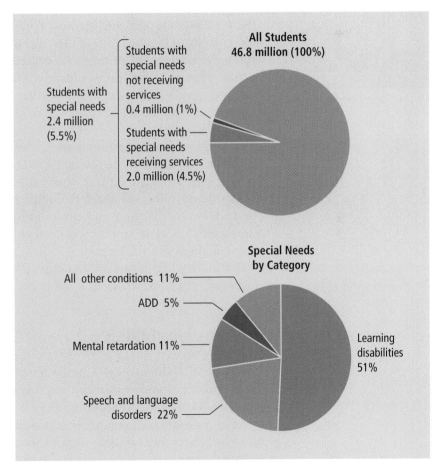

I must admit that I feel uneasy framing descriptions around "types" of disabilities. Doing so implies that disabilities are relatively fixed, stable, and distinct, much as different kinds of fruit or vegetables are. As you will see, the reality is somewhat different. The behavior of a particular student with a particular disability can be hard to categorize: he or she often (but not always) experiences the same difficulties in learning other students do, as well as difficulties similar to those experienced by students with other types of disabilities. Any particular learning difficulty, furthermore, usually poses a problem only in some situations but not others. A student who reads poorly may be "disabled" in language arts class but not in physical education or other activities that rely on skills other than reading. Official descriptions of types of disabilities tend to overlook these complexities, and therefore risk stigmatizing the real, live human beings to whom they are applied (Finlan, 1994; Kliewer & Biklen, 1996).

Still, categories of disabilities do serve useful purposes. For one thing, they give teachers, parents, and psychologists a frame of reference for talking about the social and learning-related difficulties faced by particular children and youth. For another, categories are necessary in order to arrange for services for students, as well as to procure funding for them. A student has to "have" an identifiable, namable special need if teachers and other professionals are to provide help. For these reasons, authorities in special education have continued to use categories or labels for types of disabilities in spite of continuing disagreement and concern about whether doing so may hurt students' self-esteem (Hallahan & Kauffman, 1995; Lipsky & Gartner, 1991). Perhaps the best strategy for teachers is to avoid using them wherever possible, understand their limitations when others use them for legitimate purposes (such as official classification for funding purposes), and stand ready to explain their limitations to parents and other members of the public who may use them inappropriately (Adelman, 1996).

That said, what in fact are the types of disabilities most common in education? Let's take them in order, from highest frequency to lowest.

Learning Disabilities

A **learning disability** (or **LD**) is a specific impairment of learning related to language that makes a student unable to achieve in some aspect of schoolwork at a level appropriate for his or her age. LDs show themselves as a major discrepancy between a student's ability and some feature of achievement: a student shows a serious deficit or delay in reading, writing, listening, speaking, or doing mathematical calculations, but not

In Your Own Voice

Some of you may have been labeled, either officially or informally, as a "special-needs student."

Or you may know someone who was.

How did that feel, and what effect did it have on your attitude about school and your academic performance?

in all of these at once. LDs do not include students whose learning problems stem from physical, sensory, or motor handicaps, from mental retardation, or from cultural or economic disadvantage. Genuine LDs are all the learning problems left over after these other, more obvious causes are accounted for or excluded. Typically an LD has not been helped by teachers' usual efforts to assist students who fall behind academically. Typically, too, an LD is focused on a relatively specific area of academic learning. A child may be able to read and compute well enough, for example, but be unable to write.

LDs are by far the most common form of special needs, accounting for half of students with special needs in the United States in 1996 and for anywhere from 5 to 20 percent of all students in public schools (United States Department of Education, 1997). Students with LDs are so common, in fact, that most classroom teachers regularly encounter at least one, and often more than one, per class in any given school year.

Defining Learning Disabilities Clearly

With so many students defined as having learning disabilities, it is not surprising that the specific features of disabilities vary considerably. Any of the following students, for example, might qualify as having a learning disability, assuming they have no other disease, condition, or circumstance to account for their behavior:

- Albert, an eighth-grader, has trouble solving word problems when he reads them ("If Frank has 2 cents more than Joe and 3 cents less than Sarah, how much more money does Sarah have than Joe?"). But he can solve them easily if he hears them orally.

- Bill, another eighth-grader, has the reverse problem: he can solve word problems only when he reads them but not when he hears them.

- Carole, a fifth-grader, constantly makes errors when she reads textual material aloud, either leaving out words, adding words, or substituting her own words for the printed text.

- Doug, a third-grader, forgets things easily and frequently, his homework materials in particular. His desk is a mess.

- Emily, a seventh-grader, has terrible handwriting; her letters vary in size and wobble well above and below the line.

- Denny reads very slowly, even though he is in fourth grade. As a result, he sometimes forgets the beginning of a sentence by the time he reaches the end, so his comprehension is not good.

- Garnet's spelling is inventive, no matter how much he practices official, conventional spellings. Garnet is in sixth grade.

- Harmin, a ninth-grader, has particular trouble decoding individual words, especially if they are unfamiliar; he reads *conceal* and *alternate* as "concol" and "alfoonite," respectively.

- Irma, a tenth-grader, adds multiple-digit numbers as if they were single-digit numbers: for her, *42 + 59* equals *911* rather than *101*. On the other hand, *23 + 54* equals *77*, as it does for other students.

- Jake, a fourth-grader, gets distracted easily; thus, he loses track of where he is in a written assignment and seems not to notice whether he is understanding material he reads.

- Kelly privately knows she has not been performing well academically for several years; she is now in seventh grade. She clowns around about schoolwork, claiming it does not matter to her very much.

With so many expressions of LDs, it is not surprising that educators often disagree about their nature, about the kind of help students consequently need, and even about whether the term *learning disabilities* describes something meaningful about human behaviors and qualities at all (Finlan, 1994; Ingersoll, 1993). The controversy is inherent to LDs: by definition, we are unsure of their causes or origins. Often a student's learning difficulties can be explained in terms of more than one major learning theory, and each explanation implies different remedies for the student.

Accounting for the Difficult-to-Explain: Reasons for LDs

Take Irma, the girl mentioned earlier who adds two-digit numbers as if they were one-digit numbers. Put more formally, Irma adds two-digit numbers without carrying digits forward from the ones column to the tens column or from the tens column to the hundreds column. Figure 10.3 shows what her faulty strategy looks like on a sample of her homework. What is going on here? Each of the psychological learning theories described in Chapter 2, for example, would explain Irma's problem plausibly but differently.

Behaviorism: Reinforcement for Inappropriate Behaviors

Perhaps Irma persists with a single-digit orientation because it has been rewarding or reinforcing in the past. Assuming she did learn to add single digits correctly (*3 + 5, 7 + 8*, etc.), she must have received good evaluations of her computations from her teachers during her earlier grade levels. Even with two-digit addition, she may also have performed better than expected initially: note that many two-digit problems can be solved correctly without carrying digits. Two-digit addition without carrying

In Your Own Voice

Which of these learning difficulties would pose more of a problem to a *teacher*, and which would pose more of a problem to the *student*?

If a problem were relatively difficult for a teacher, how might this fact affect the tendency of teachers to label the problem a "learning disability"?

And in the long term, how might it affect the overall frequency of particular kinds of LDs among students?

In Your Own Voice

The "bottom line" about these theoretical explanations is whether they lead to different ways of teaching a student with a learning disability.

We saw one example of this with Irma's homework paper.

Can you think of another example, either from your own experience or from the list of students with LDs described earlier?

FIGURE 10.3

Irma's Math Homework: Double-Digit Addition

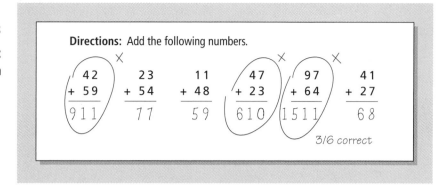

Directions: Add the following numbers.

may have been especially plentiful in the introductory stages of learning two-digit addition, and therefore may have encouraged Irma to persist with a procedure that had been appropriate for single-digit problems. Even though the procedure now causes numerous errors, Irma may persist with it because it still rewards her intermittently; on every few problems, she still solves a two-digit problem correctly.

From a behaviorist perspective, the cycle of persistent, partial reinforcement somehow has to be broken. But how? Perhaps the teacher needs to reinforce behaviors that compete with Irma's inappropriate adding behavior and actually make it impossible for her to continue with them. For example, the teacher could grade less on coming up with correct answers and more on "showing work," including the work of carrying digits from one column to the next. To do so, the teacher might rearrange the homework assignment to look something like that shown in Figure 10.4, though this is not the only way to do so.

Information-Processing Theory: Faulty Processing Strategies

Perhaps Irma has selected an inappropriate procedure for dealing with two-digit addition, one meant for one-digit problems in particular. Her solutions are not random or unthinking but systematic and intended; it is just that they are neither conventional nor "correct" by adult standards. Of course, Irma may have used the one-digit procedure so much that her choice is now automatic and once again has become unconscious.

From an information-processing perspective, if this is the case, she needs first to become aware of what she is doing and of its impact on her solutions; only then can she adopt a procedure effectively. So perhaps the teacher needs to encourage Irma to reflect orally and explicitly on

FIGURE 10.4

Irma's Math Homework: Encouraging Competing Responses

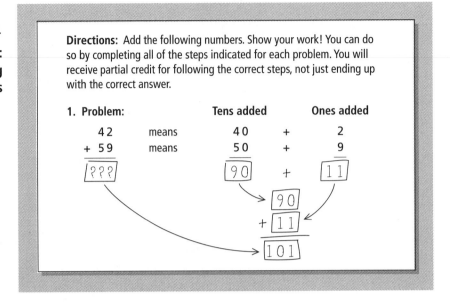

how she solves addition problems—perhaps by thinking out loud, for example, as she solves problems. This would foster a form of what information-processing theory calls "metacognitive awareness," or thinking about *how* thinking itself occurs. Once she learns to reflect in this way, Irma may become ready to try new, more appropriate ways to solve two-digit problems in writing. Her homework assignment might then look more like that shown in Figure 10.5.

FIGURE 10.5

Irma's Homework: Encouraging Reflection

Directions: Add the following numbers. Show how you solve the problem—write out all of your steps, and use brief written notes, where necessary, to explain what you are doing.

$$\begin{array}{r} 1 \\ 4\,2 \\ +\ 5\,9 \\ \hline \end{array}$$

~oops!
(forgot to carry)

1 0 1

1) I added the "1's" —— 2 + 9 = 11

2) I added the "10's" —— 4 + 5 = 9

3) I moved the extra "1" to the "10's" column.
                    —— 1 + 9 = 10

4) I wrote the remaining digit from the "1's" column at the right, and the final sum of the "10's" column to the left: 101.

Constructivism: Lack of Mentoring Support

Perhaps Irma has not received enough attention and support as she has learned to add. To a large extent, therefore, she has had to devise methods of addition on her own, through a combination of borrowing ideas from classmates and figuring out what she could from the textbook. The one-digit procedure has been the result, and was the best Irma could do under the circumstances. Her mistaken outcome was neither the teacher's nor Irma's fault: classes were simply too large and school life too busy to allow her teachers to notice her work in enough detail or to help her with it when difficulties first began.

As constructivist theory might say, no "zone of proximal development" ever occurred; in fact, none could have been arranged easily given the commotion and pressures of Irma's particular classrooms. Yet at this point Irma still does need coaching, does need assistance in finding her way toward appropriate methods for solving two-digit addition. Perhaps her current teacher could therefore arrange for an experienced classmate to work with Irma individually. Or perhaps a parent volunteer could work with her. Or the teacher herself could now take time with Irma in spite of her own busy schedule. Now that she knows clearly what Irma's learning problem is, assisting Irma might not take excessive time away from other students; at least she would no longer waste time diagnosing reasons for Irma's errors, and Irma could focus sooner on learning a more successful strategy for two-digit addition. A constructivist response to Irma's difficulty, then, might not depend on precisely what was written as directions for the homework paper, although the teacher might consider adding a note to the homework such as that in Figure 10.6.

Frank puzzled over the examples of homework in Figure 10.5. "Actually, looking at these examples, I don't see why you shouldn't just try all of the strategies at once. Is there any reason not to?" He looked over at Jenn for an answer.

"Can't think of any," she said. "Except maybe practical things. Maybe one way of setting up the homework takes more of a teacher's time than another. How many students can you do individual tutoring with if you're teaching a full load of classes in high school?"

"But there's also another problem, it seems to me," said Frank. "The 'show-your-work' strategy looks like it limits the number of problems that you can present in an assignment. So does the 'reflection' strategy. Each problem takes up a lot of space and a lot of students' attention."

Jenn glanced back at Figures 10.4 and 10.5. "True enough," she said. "But

FIGURE 10.6

Irma's Homework:
An Invitation for
Dialogue

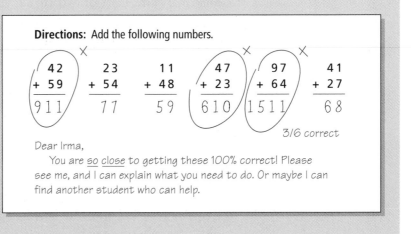

Directions: Add the following numbers.

×   ×   ×

42   23   11   47   97   41
+ 59   + 54   + 48   + 23   + 64   + 27
911   77   59   610   1511   68

3/6 correct

Dear Irma,
    You are *so* *close* to getting these 100% correct! Please
see me, and I can explain what you need to do. Or maybe I can
find another student who can help.

the point is that you're getting a better guarantee that students are really *thinking* correctly about the problems. Isn't that the point? If you have that guarantee, maybe you don't need as many individual problems per homework assignment."

"You're probably right—except if I could only pick a few problems, I would still worry about whether I had picked the best ones for the students. I hope there are ways to get help doing that!"

"Maybe from the curriculum manuals?" offered Jenn.

"And maybe from other teachers," added Frank. "Maybe even from my own good sense in choosing math problems!"

Jenn smiled at this, pondering all of the comments. Then she said, "But you're right about that first point. No reason not to borrow from *all* theories. If Irma were my student, and if I had ample resources and time, I'd combine strategies: give her work that *prevents* her from using an incorrect way to add. But I'd also ask her to reflect on her work in writing. But first I'd find time to talk with her face to face."

Attention Deficit Disorder

Attention deficit disorder (ADD) is a problem with sustaining attention and controlling impulses. Often, but not always, it also includes *hyperactivity* (or excessive activity), in which case the condition may be called **attention deficit hyperactivity disorder (ADHD)**. In a classroom, the ADD or ADHD child fidgets and squirms a lot, has trouble remaining seated, continually gets distracted, has trouble waiting for a turn, and tends to blurt out answers and comments. The child may also shift continually from one activity to another; she or he seems unable to play quietly, may talk excessively and without listening to others, often misplaces things, and is more likely than other children to try risky activities. The child with ADD or ADHD won't do *all* of these things, of course; but over a period of time (such as a year), he or she is likely to do several of them, and do them not only at school but at home as well (American Psychiatric Association, 1994).

When Is It Really ADD?

It is important to read the description in the previous paragraph carefully, and especially the last sentence, because a casual reading may suggest that a *lot* of students—perhaps even a majority—show symptoms of ADD. Who of us, as children, did not sometimes fidget or have trouble sitting still or waiting for a turn? Who of us has not sometimes talked to others without listening well or been frustrated by misplacing things? School and home in particular are places that put heavy demands on *not* exhibiting ADD-like behaviors. At home children are supposed to play reasonably quietly, listen to adults when spoken to, keep out of danger, and the like. At school they must not only do these things but also sit still for extended periods during lessons, avoid interrupting others, and keep their materials (and their minds) organized, among other tasks. Given these challenges of home and school, it should not be surprising that many children show occasional signs of attention deficit or impulsiveness. It also should not be surprising that ADD and ADHD are the most common reasons parents and teachers refer children to psychiatrists (Weiss & Hechtman, 1993). Parents in particular show a lot of concern about this condition. In one survey, fully half of all parents of preschool and school-age boys considered their children to be so active as to be a cause for concern or even deserving of referral to specialists (Smith, Wood & Grimes, 1987).

When psychiatrists, psychologists, and special educators speak of ADD and ADHD, however, they are not speaking of occasional lapses of attention, such as those most children commit. They are referring to inattention and impulsiveness that occur on numerous occasions and in more than one setting. A relatively select group of children—about 5 percent of students with special needs, or much fewer than 1 percent of all students—display these problems to this extent. The large majority of children with ADD (75 to 80 percent) are boys, although the reasons for the sex difference are not clear. These true ADD children are frustrating to themselves as well as to others. Scott, a fourth-grader, is a good example:

10:45, the end of recess. Scott comes back to the classroom, supercharged and happy as a lark. Off comes his coat; he leaves it on the floor because he is busy giving quick smiles to everyone who happens to glance his way. He tousles the hair of a boy who happens to be standing near him. The boy can't decide whether he likes this or not; but just to be sure, he walks away from Scott.

10:50. The teacher gives students instructions to begin a math lesson. "Get your workbook and a pencil, and come sit with me on the carpet," she says. THUD! Scott's chair falls on the floor, along with half the contents of his desk. Scott begins picking the things up. He looks a bit embarrassed, but mostly he just seems to be in a hurry.

Partway through cleaning up, he notices that one of his pencils needs sharpening. Leaving the rest of the mess, he goes to the sharpener. On the way he stops to look at the fish tank and calls everyone's attention to one of the fish.

"Wow! Look at that one!" he blurts out, apparently to anyone who will listen. But no one in fact is listening, because most students have already gathered on the carpet as the teacher requested.

Forgetting why he is out of his seat, Scott scans the room. He notices a book on a side shelf and leafs through it briefly.

Then Scott "discovers" the unsharpened pencil still in his hand. He finally remembers wanting to sharpen it, but now another student is already starting to use the sharpener. Butting ahead of the student, Scott inserts his own pencil, breaks the lead turning the crank too hard, curses to himself, and teases the classmate.

10:55. All other students except Scott are now settled on the carpet. Scott has left the sharpener again and is fixated on the fish tank. The teacher is definitely getting annoyed.

"Time for math, Scott," she says sharply. "Just bring your pencil and book so we can get started."

"What about my stuff?" he asks, referring to the mess on the floor by his desk. But Scott comes to the carpet without waiting for an answer. He has his pencil, but not his book.

"Where's your book, Scott?" asks the teacher. "I told you to get it."

Scott looks as if he hasn't heard the teacher's question. He notices two pigtails on a girl sitting in front of him. He gives them a yank and gets up again. The girl looks annoyed and acts as if she might cry. But Scott doesn't notice; he is back at his desk. The teacher begins the lesson without him.

"I can't find my book," Scott announces loudly from across the room, interrupting the teacher.

Only a few minutes have passed here, but it already seems as if Scott craves excitement, stimulation, and change. It is as though there were little difference between thinking and action: in Scott's world, one seems nearly equivalent to the other and leads all too soon to the other. He may be too "busy" mentally to be aware of the impressions he is making on others. He is at risk for making fewer friends and for performing poorly. The risks will continue into adolescence and beyond (Weiss & Hechtman, 1993).

Causes of ADD

Most psychologists and medical specialists agree that true ADD (not "mere" intermittent distractibility or high activity) reflects a problem in the nervous system, but they are not sure of the exact nature or causes of the problem (Rutter, 1995). Research has found slight but systematic differences in the functioning of a key part of the brain, the *cerebral cortex,* which is normally involved in controlling voluntary actions. But *why* the differences occur is largely a matter of speculation. Is it from mild brain damage before or during birth? Or is it from the child's exposure to toxins (such as from a serious infection) early in life? Or is it even a result of a lifetime of eating the wrong sorts of food? All these possibilities have been suggested, but none has been supported by research conclusively or consistently.

Research has also shown that ADD tends to run in families, with children of ADD parents somewhat more likely than usual to have the condition themselves. Such an association does not necessarily mean, however, that ADD is "inborn" or genetic. Observations of parents of children with ADD do show that the parents impose strict rules of behavior on their children. But observations of ADD children who later become less active (for example, because of medication) show that their parents subsequently become less strict in behavioral expectations of the child (Barkley, 1985). The change can be interpreted either as strict parenting causing ADD or as ADD causing strict parenting: strictness may contribute to a child's restlessness (an ADD-like behavior), or it may represent a *parent's* response to the challenges of a restless child. There is no way to be certain about the direction of causation, about what is causing what.

In Your Own Voice

The trouble with speculating about the causes of ADD is that, from a teacher's point of view, it does not lead to helpful instructional strategies.

Some would argue, in fact, that it tempts us to *give up* on a child with ADD, since the causes may be not be subject to educational influence.

Do you agree?

Is it helpful, or even relevant, to know about the possibilities in these two paragraphs?

Helping Students with ADD

Since there is no clear, single cause for ADD, there is no single way to help a student with this condition. The most common strategy is a combination of medication for immediate symptoms and support for the student's efforts to organize and monitor his or her own behavior. *Ritalin,* a drug known more formally as *methylphenidate,* is the most common medication used for children with ADD. It works, surprisingly, by stimulating or "waking up" the nervous system; increased alertness apparently helps the child pay better attention to the choices he or she is making and to the impact of actions on others. In spite of concerns by some parents and teachers, Ritalin has not been found to have serious negative side effects, such as making the child lethargic, depressed, or drowsy (Johnston, 1991). But sometimes it does have practical disadvantages. It costs money, for one thing, which is a problem if parents do not have much income to begin with or lack medical insurance that pays for medications. For another, Ritalin must be taken regularly in order to work, including on weekends. The drug will not work well if parents' schedules (for instance, from working night shifts) prevent them from making sure the child takes regular doses.

From the point of view of a teacher who wants to help a child with ADD, medication actually may not be as important as helping the child to organize choices and actions. Clear rules and procedures, for example, can reduce the "noise" or chaotic quality in the child's classroom life significantly. The rules and procedures can be generated jointly with the child; they do not have to be imposed arbitrarily, as if the student were incapable of thinking for himself or herself. A peer can also be enlisted to model slower, more reflective styles of working; a child with ADD can watch a favorite classmate complete a set of math problems, for example, and the classmate can be encouraged to say what he or she thinks about while doing the work. Sometimes it can help to make lists of tasks or of steps in long tasks. Also, it might help to divide focused work into small, short sessions rather than present it in single, longer sessions. Whatever the strategies used, they should be consistent, predictable, and generated by the student to whatever extent is possible. If they have these qualities, they will strengthen the student's attention-directing capacities and minimize the confusing distractions of classroom life while at the same time treating the student with the respect she or he deserves as a member of the classroom community.

In Your Own Voice

Are the suggestions in this paragraph out of keeping with the constructivist spirit of this book?

If you were the teacher who implemented them, could you and the child with ADD remain members of a cooperative, learning-oriented community?

How could you avoid becoming a "dictator," imposing additional rules arbitrarily on one particular student?

Speech and Language Disorders

Speech and language disorders are problems with understanding and expressing information, ideas, or meanings (McCormick & Loeb, 1997). A common example involving speech is stuttering, in which a child repeats or prolongs sounds. If *language* is involved, a child may pronounce words clearly enough but use excessively short, simple sentences compared to other children of the same age; he or she may fail to indicate relationships among sentences using conjunctions. As you might suspect, speech and language problems are often associated with other difficulties, such as partial loss of hearing or general cognitive limitations (mild retardation). But the association is not perfect: some children with speech or language disorders do not have other obvious limiting conditions. While it is possible, therefore, that speech and language disorders have a biological or physiological basis (as do hearing impairments, for example), it is not at all clear that they do. Their cause (or causes) often remains ambiguous.

Students with speech and language disorders are common, but only about half as common in the schools as students with learning disabilities. Estimates of the frequency of speech and language disorders vary, but they average between 1 and 3 percent of the school population as a whole, depending on whether the estimate includes students with other conditions, such as deafness or mental retardation, that usually also affect language and speech (United States Department of Education, 1997). Note, though, that estimates of speech and language disorders do *not* include students who speak English as a second language, even though this "condition" can sometimes impair oral communication for some individuals.

Like students with learning disabilities, those with speech and language disorders are a diverse group. In addition to a student who stutters, for example, any of the following students might qualify as having a speech and language disorder:

- Larry, a seventh-grader, speaks in a squeaky, nasal tone, as if he constantly had a nose cold and were about to sneeze. Some of his classmates joke about his voice behind his back, although a lot of the others just seem to ignore it.

- Even though she is in third grade, Mary continually omits certain sounds from her speech: she says *ar* instead of *car,* for example, and *ike* instead of *like*. Everyone can understand her, but the omissions are noticeable and sometimes annoying.

- Ned is a boy of few words. Though his first-grade classmates typically speak in five- and ten-word sentences, Ned tends to be quiet and never uses more than two words at a time.

- Peter used to speak like Ned—just one or two words at a time—but now that he is in middle school, his sentences are more complex. The trouble is that his grammar is terrible, even when he tries to speak correctly, and teachers often find his speech garbled and distorted, as if he had a "personal accent" that they cannot understand.

- Quinn, an eighth-grader, has had a moderate hearing impairment from birth. She prefers to communicate by signing (with American Sign Language, in particular), but she can vocalize to some extent. When she does vocalize, though, she speaks slowly and with a thick accent.

- Randy has mild mental retardation. Now that she is in sixth grade, she can carry on simple conversations, especially on everyday topics; but her vocabulary and sentence structures remain limited.

Given the ambiguous origins of problems such as these, how can a teacher begin helping the students who show them? Frank and Jenn wondered about this question themselves:

"I'm sure part of it has to be genetic," said Jenn after looking over the list. "It even says so with Quinn: 'Quinn has had a moderate hearing impairment from birth.' Proof positive."

Frank looked up. "I beg to differ, Jenn! It depends on how you take Seifert's question. He asked, 'What might *create* communication problems?' Maybe he means how are they created and *re*created all through life, not just at birth. Including for Quinn. Having a hearing impairment is only a problem if you are surrounded by people who communicate with oral language. If Quinn were among people who signed all the time, she would not have a problem."

Jenn considered this. "So if I could surround myself with people who dislike and avoid learning Spanish as much as I do, then I wouldn't have a 'problem with French'?"

"Um, not exactly. The Spanish language would still exist in the wider world. With all the Spanish and Spanish-speaking people who live in our part of the world, you'd have to have something to do with it sooner or later."

"So if Quinn surrounds herself with people who sign, isn't she just hiding

In Your Own Voice

I have cited these students as examples of speech and language difficulties.

But suppose you encountered them in your students: how could you know for certain that they did not simply have unusual expectations about how to participate in classroom discourse?

What could you do to rule out this possibility?

her head in the sand like me, just denying that she lives in a world of oral communication? An ostrich is an ostrich, I'd say."

"I didn't say anything about ostriches!" said Frank. "What I was driving at is that whatever leads to a communication difficulty, a good part of it is bound to be *learned*. A lot of the difficulty gets 'created' and modified by experiences. Or else it gets remedied or even 'defined as irrelevant,' also depending on a child's experiences."

Jenn was silent, thinking about this idea.

"It's like when a person is nearsighted," Frank continued. "Then you 'have a problem'—right?—and the problem may be one that you were born with. But it's a 'problem' only if you have to look at a lot of things that are far away, right? And whether you do *that* depends on your experiences, right? And whether nearsightedness remains a problem depends on whether you have the experience of getting glasses, right? Then, once you've seen an optometrist, once you get glasses, nearsightedness is no longer a problem. Right?"

"Hmm . . ." Jenn pondered these ideas while she took off her own glasses to clean them. "So if you're right, teachers do not need to concern themselves first and foremost with underlying causes, genetic or otherwise. They should focus on arranging successful *experiences* of communication for students."

"You got it," Frank said. "And it seems to me, Jenn, that teachers do that best anyway."

In Your Own Voice

Are you satisfied with Jenn's conclusion that teachers do not need to be concerned with origins of communication difficulties?

Or is she too extreme in her views?

Can you think of a time when it *would* help a teacher to know why or where a learning-related difficulty came from?

As Frank implies, speech and language are inherently *social* activities; it takes two to converse—and two to fail at conversing as well. Difficulties with communication arise, or at least can be accentuated by, social experiences. They can be seen as mismatches in how individuals expect messages to be conveyed and interpreted, such as the ones discussed in Chapter 8 that are related to cultural differences in communication. The difference, however, is that children with speech or language disorders are not trying (even if unsuccessfully) to honor the discourse patterns of a non-English culture or language; instead they are failing to uphold the rules of any culture or language (Bunce, 1997). The student therefore may speak too slowly, ungrammatically, or haltingly to suit any language community at all. In the process, of course, she or he would violate classmates' and teachers' expectations about how conversation and dialogue should flow. As with cultural mismatches, these more general mismatches of expectations about how to communicate gradually leads to simplifying interactions, to making them less frequent, or, eventually, to ignoring the child altogether (Rice, 1993). The deterioration of communication is a serious educational problem over the long term.

But just as speech and language disorders may gradually be created by social interactions, so can remedies for them. If you are a teacher and have a student with a speech or language disorder, you can minimize the child's speech or language problem, and sometimes reverse it, by emphasizing certain positive strategies of communication (Kaiser & Gray, 1993). You can try all of the following strategies in particular, both by modeling them yourself and by supporting classmates who use them:

- *In responding to the child's language, be patient and accepting.* This strategy sounds obvious enough, but sometimes it can be hard to implement during the busier moments of classroom life! "Being patient and accepting" means taking enough time to listen to the child, even if he or she speaks more slowly than usual. It also means refraining from pointing out specific language or speech errors in public, because doing so can make the child self-conscious and bog down communication even further. And it means responding to the child's comments at a rate that is relaxed and somewhat slow, but also natural: too rapid a rate can be hard to comprehend, and too slow a rate can be insulting to the child.

- *Model good language and speech yourself, and encourage it in classmates.* In addition to meaning that you should use correct grammar and pronounce words clearly, this strategy means adjusting your vocabulary and sentences to levels your particular students can understand—good advice, incidentally, for communicating with all students, whatever their needs. "Modeling good language and speech" also means paraphrasing a comment from the child if you think you understand it but classmates do not. Saying "Joe asked for the eraser" is insulting if the classmate who has the eraser already understands Joe's request, but it is helpful if he does not. The usual style of teacher-talk—the "teacher-talk register" discussed in Chapter 8—generally can support these strategies. Teacher-talk normally includes careful pronunciation and correct grammar. It also allows teachers to rephrase students' comments for emphasis ("Joe is right; Washington *was* the first president of the United States") and for the benefit of others' learning.

Modeling good language and speech also means encouraging situations where the child who needs help can hear and participate in conversations with peers; seating him or her in the middle of several classmates, for example, can encourage achieving this goal better than

In Your Own Voice

On doing what the research in this paragraph recommends: imagine coaching *your* students to include in discussion a student who has a speech or language difficulty.

What might be your first step in doing this?

locating the child off to one side or near the front of the class. Research has found, furthermore, that classmates can be coached successfully to include or "draw in" students with speech and language disorders, deliberately involving them in peer-dominated conversations more than would be possible otherwise (Ostrofsky, Kaiser & Odom, 1993).

- *Provide for practice at communicating.* A child with a speech or language disorder should be encouraged to participate in oral activities to the greatest extent possible, rather than being "saved the embarrassment of participating," and therefore being prevented from practicing his or her language skills. "The greatest extent possible," of course, will depend on the level and type of language of which a child is capable; but the principle of striving for inclusion remains, no matter what the child's qualities or abilities. "Providing for practice" also means praising the child for efforts and successes at using emerging communication skills. The praise need not, and probably should not, be public, but it should occur from time to time. "Providing for practice" also means ensuring that *all* students have chances to contribute to oral activities. In class discussions, not just one or two students should dominate; all students should be invited to participate, including the child with a speech or language disorder. In role-playing activities, not just a few verbally oriented volunteers should get turns; everyone should be allowed—and expected—to take part in some way.

- *Work with the speech-language pathologist, and try to implement his or her suggestions.* Because students with speech and language disorders have highly individual difficulties in communicating, their needs are usually assessed or diagnosed individually and in detail by a specialist called a *speech-language pathologist.* The specialist talks with the child's teachers and parents, observes the child, and administers a number of tests of language, speech, and hearing ability. On the basis of this information, the speech-language pathologist will propose a program of activities tailored to the child's particular strengths and needs (Lowe, 1994; Norris & Hoffman, 1993). Since some programs may involve individual speaking and hearing, they may require pulling the child out of class periodically to work in a separate, quiet room. But others, particularly those involving language in groups, lend themselves to classroom practice, and therefore often become the responsibility of the classroom teacher. Because the speech-language pathologist's recommendations focus on the child's unique communication needs, they are worth taking seriously and implementing to the best of your ability. On the other hand, your own observations of the child—the ones required for creating an IEP, in any case—are also worth thinking about and discussing with the pathologist because they often provide further clues about how to help the child.

Mental Retardation

Mental retardation refers to significant limitations in a person's intellectual functioning and daily adaptive behaviors (Jacobson & Mulick, 1996). Like someone with a speech or language disorder, a child with mental retardation may have limited language or impaired speech; and like a student with a learning disability, he or she may not perform well academically. But there are important differences from these other conditions. Children with mental retardation have broader, more significant impairments in their intellectual functioning than children with learning disabilities. They score poorly on standardized tests of intelligence (such as those discussed in Chapter 11) and have limited performances on most academic tasks. Their adaptations to daily life are limited in more than one area that most people take for granted. Caring for themselves physically (for example, getting dressed) may be more work than usual; health and safety might be a concern (knowing whether it is safe to cross the street); or (for older individuals) finding and keeping a job might require help from supportive others.

Mental disabilities sometimes appear to have physical causes, such as genetic abnormalities or difficulties during childbirth. One of the most common genetic causes is **Down syndrome;** it is a genetic disorder (a child is born with it) in which a child has either an extra chromosome (chromosomes are the genetic "building blocks" that direct normal growth) or a particular chromosome that is defective. Down syndrome affects about one out of every eight hundred births and is somewhat more likely to occur when the parents (including the father) are relatively old.

But as with many other children with special needs, there is often no obvious physical cause. In the vast majority of cases, mental retardation is relatively mild and therefore may be overlooked until a child begins elementary school. Then even mild retardation may become obvious, since it is in school where a child must begin simple routines of self-care, such as going to the toilet unsupervised, and it is in school where he or she begins using language and cognitive skills.

For a disability that has physical and genetic influences, however, mental retardation shows important signs of being "created" by social circumstances. To see what I mean, consider some of the facts about prevalence, along with Frank's and Jenn's reactions to the facts:

- Experts estimate that about 1 to 3 percent of people of all ages—preschoolers, school-age children, and adults—have at least mild mental retardation, a percentage that has remained fairly constant for several decades. But the frequency of mental retardation also is significantly higher among school-age children in particular; some reliable estimates put the figure at more than 10 percent for children between ages six and eighteen (United States Department of Education, 1996). Why would the percentage increase for individuals in school and decrease for those beyond school age?

"Weird," said Frank. He looked over at Jenn and put on his mock "news announcer" voice. "Scientists prove that going to school 'causes' mental disability, at least in some kids. Once finished with school, students show remarkable improvement in intellectual functioning! Story at 11:00!"

"Don't be ridiculous, Frank. Think about it!" said Jenn. "School is where people get screened the most systematically: *everybody* is right there, in classrooms, available to be observed and tested. And school is where you need thinking skills just to survive—and where you need simple social skills too, like knowing how to play at recess compared to how to play in the gym. When kids leave school, they don't have to struggle with courses anymore, so there's one less way to be mentally retarded than before."

- Since 1976, the number of school-age children and youth diagnosed as mentally retarded has declined by almost 40 percent, from about 880,000 in 1976 to about 530,000 in the 1990s (United States Department of Education, 1996). Why the decrease?

"You know what I think?" said Frank. "I think the notion of mental retardation must be pretty ambiguous. Maybe it even goes through 'fashions.' Why else would the numbers go down like that?"

"Yeah, that is a puzzle," said Jenn. "Remember what Seifert said earlier about learning disabilities *increasing* a lot in frequency during the seventies? That's the same time diagnosis of retardation fell. I wonder if more and more parents and teachers tend to classify children as 'learning disabled' than as 'mentally disabled.'"

- In general, milder cases of mental retardation are *more* frequent among families living at low income levels and in poverty and much less frequent among well-off families (Drew, Hardman & Logan, 1996). But moderate and severe cases of mental retardation are about equally frequent no matter what the economic level. The mild cases

In Your Own Voice

By the same token, it is not reasonable to assume mental retardation actually "disappears" when students finally leave school.

More likely, society begins to ignore their special needs.

Some educators argue, in fact, that schools should do more to help students plan the transition away from school to the world.

What do you think of this idea?

Any suggestions about how to begin doing it?

make up the large majority of all children with mental retardation; they also include the children who can learn most easily, either individually or in group settings such as classrooms.

Frank whistled softly under his breath. "If I understand what Seifert's getting at, it's that privileged social circumstances—the kind that higher socioeconomic status can buy—helps give children what they need. That part makes sense. It's not fair to families with less income, but I guess it's not surprising."

"What surprises me," said Jenn, "is that higher economic status can sometimes 'buy' enough help that a child might not seem retarded at all."

"Yeah," murmured Frank, looking troubled. "Although maybe it's another example of official categories of disabilities being ambiguous. Maybe being 'mildly retarded' really means '*might* be a little retarded.' Maybe some of those kids are not retarded at all but are experiencing some other sort of disability, like a specific learning disability or even chronic poor health."

Jenn raised her eyebrows; she just thought of something. "And for the ones who are in the 'might be retarded' group, coming from a family or a neighborhood with more money would make it more likely that your true difficulties might be discovered."

". . . or that the other problems—the ones confused with mental retardation—would not even occur in the first place," added Frank.

Jenn pondered this for a moment. "You know what I'm thinking?" she finally said. "I'm thinking that the 'problem' of mental retardation is not just one that kids have. It's also a problem of inequality—a problem that the community and society also has."

Teaching Children with Mental Retardation

Three general strategies can help you become an effective teacher of children with mental retardation. Stated in very general terms, (1) give more time and practice than usual, (2) teach in the context of daily life activities wherever possible, and (3) include the child in school social events and activities as much as possible. Let's look briefly at what each of these strategies entails.

- *Give more time and practice than usual.* If a child has only a mild mental disability, he or she probably can learn important fundamentals of the academic curriculum—basic arithmetic, for example, and basic reading. Because of the disability, though, the child may need more practice than most students in your class. He or she may know that two plus two is four, for example, but need help in applying this idea to real objects. You (or someone) will have to show the student

In Your Own Voice

Since teachers are usually very busy people, schools often provide a teacher with assistance in individualizing the curriculum in the ways described here.

The help might come in the form of a teacher assistant, a "resource" or consulting teacher, or some other professional consultant.

If *you* were working with one of these people, what would be the first thing(s) you would ask?

that two *pencils* plus two *pencils* make four *pencils;* and, having helped him or her to make this application, you may have to help with further generalizations, such as the addition of books or shoes or chairs.

Giving all this help takes time and therefore can try the child's patience. To compensate for this problem, you may need to reward the child frequently for effort and successes, either with well-timed praise or with tangible signs of praise such as gold stars. You may also need to set reasonable goals: work on academic skills the child actually can learn without becoming excessively discouraged, however different or simplified the skills may be compared to those of classmates. At the same time, it will be important not to insult the child with curriculum materials designed for children several years younger, even though they provide a convenient solution to the problem of simplifying the curriculum. In many curriculum areas, fortunately, there already exist materials that are both simplified and appropriate for older students (Hickson, Blackman & Reis, 1995).

- *Include adaptive and functional skills in the curriculum.* A child with mental retardation presents a dilemma especially clearly that all teachers face: since there is not time enough to teach everything, how is a teacher to select what to teach? One answer is to relate learning goals to everyday activities as much as possible, just as you would normally do with all students. These goals lead to skills that help a child to *adapt* to the needs of everyday living and serve a clear *function.* Instead of teaching about addition and subtraction only in the abstract, for example, you can teach about buying common objects (e.g., food) and making change for the purchases. Learning about equivalences among coins in this way gets at important principles of addition and subtraction, but at the same time confers a practical and (hopefully) motivating daily skill. Similar considerations can guide reading instruction: instead of learning just any group of words, tailor the words to those especially useful to the child (*go, stop, school, fire,* etc.).

An adaptive, functional approach can help in nonacademic areas as well. For children who need help in learning everyday tasks, the tasks can be analyzed in specific parts. Instead of beginning by teaching how to tell clock time in general, you can start with learning times on the clock that are important to the student (such as when he or she gets up in the morning or when school starts). Add knowledge of other times that are personally meaningful, gradually working toward full knowledge of how to tell clock time as circumstances permit. With this strategy, the student is sure to have learned the most important knowledge first, whether or not he or she actually achieves full, accurate ability to read the minute-hand and hour-hand on a clock face.

- *Include the child in both social events and group learning activities.* The key word here is *inclusion:* a child with a mental disability should participate in and contribute to the life of the class as much as possible. If the class attends a special event or goes on a field trip, for example, the child should go if at all possible. If the class plays a group game, the child should be one of the players. If you assign class members to cooperative group projects, the child should be assigned as a member of one of the groups. All of these actions foster the potential for a type of mentoring relationship, such as that discussed in Chapter 7. On the one hand, inclusive cooperative groups foster acceptance and helpfulness toward the child with the disability; on the other, they stimulate the child to learn as much as he or she can from class members and class activities. Inclusion also helps the child with a mental disability to observe and practice socially appropriate behaviors, such as how to greet a classmate without overwhelming or offending the classmate, or when and how it is appropriate to ask the teacher a question. These skills are especially important if the child is to be fully accepted as a classmate.

[It is morning recess in Ms. Hodgson's second-grade classroom.]

KELVIN SEIFERT: So how has it gone for Sherrie in your class? [Sherrie has a mild mental disability.]

MS. HODGSON: Well, she's made a *big* change in her attitude toward reading. In the fall, she just hated it! I struggled just to get her to look at a book, even one with no words and just pictures. But now she's much better about it.

SEIFERT: Better?

MS. HODGSON: Several of the kids decided that they like "reading" to her. They really just look at the pictures with her and talk about the pictures. Sherrie's thrilled with the attention, and talks some too. At the beginning of the year, the others were just ignoring her completely. But not now. Now I'd like to organize the peer reading sessions a little more—get some of them to actually tutor her in sight vocabulary.

SEIFERT: Any idea what made them start reading to her? Whose idea was it at first?

MS. HODGSON: That depends whom you ask. Personally I think I planted the idea in their heads, but I don't think Joe would at all agree with me. He likes to take credit for deciding to read to her.

[Later the same day]

KELVIN SEIFERT: So Joe, what do *you* think about having Sherrie in your class?

In Your Own Voice

For the teacher, a key challenge is to identify students who are as potentially helpful as Joe.

Have you ever known any (or feel you are one yourself)?

What qualities should such a student have?

JOE: Well, at first she used to yell when she had to work—like go "yaaaaaaah." Everybody would look around and wonder what was going on. I remember one time she even punched Ms. Hodgson.

SEIFERT: And then?

JOE: I don't know. Most of us stopped paying attention to her. Then she just stopped yelling. Maybe Ms. Hodgson did something while I wasn't looking. How am I supposed to know?

SEIFERT: It must have been better after she stopped yelling.

JOE: Last week, me and Charlotte each read a book to her a couple of times. She liked that!

SEIFERT: Can Sherrie read?

JOE: No, she likes to look at the pictures and talk about them.

SEIFERT: Do you like reading to her?

JOE: Yeah, it's OK. You can relax when you read to her.

Chances are that Joe and Ms. Hodgson both contributed to calming Sherrie down. Their experience suggests the importance—and potential satisfactions—of involving classmates in the challenges of teaching and including students with special needs. But it also suggests that inclusion can lead to redefinition of what it means to "teach." With a student with special needs, "teaching" no longer can mean a solitary activity done by an individual (if indeed it ever really meant that). Instead, "teaching" now refers to a collaboration among several people or even among many. Of course, this new, collaborative role presents new challenges; in Ms. Hodgson's case, for example, it meant taking seriously the potential contributions of a fellow student, Joe, in teaching Sherrie, and possibly even modifying her usual ways of teaching reading to support Joe's contributions. But as Joe, Sherrie, and Ms. Hodgson show, such challenges often can be met.

Learning More About Students with Special Needs

*T*HE comments about Joe and Sherrie suggest that this chapter has only scratched the surface about teaching students with special needs. There is much more to learn about them: about their tremendous diversity and about strategies for including such students in classroom life as fully as possible, whatever their particular educational difficulties. A large body of literature exists to help teachers with these tasks; for example, entire books have been written exclusively about teaching students with learning disabilities (Lerner, 1993), those with speech and language disorders (Bobrick, 1995), and students with mental retardation (Drew, Hardman & Logan, 1996). In fact, specialized books have been written about disabilities that are much less frequent than these, such as teaching individuals with blindness (Kennedy, 1993), deafness (Welsh, 1993), or chronic health problems (Wishnietsky, 1996), among others. In the space of a single chapter I have been able only to hint at the complexities, challenges, and satisfactions of working with each of these kinds of students.

In spite of its limitations, though, the chapter expressed several key themes. One is that inclusion is definitely desirable and possible, but collaboration among staff, which inclusion calls for, can also be a challenge. Another is that as a classroom teacher, you will encounter some kinds of disabilities much more frequently than others; in particular, the large majority of "your" children with special needs are likely to have learning disabilities, speech and language disorders, or mild mental retardation. Third, the major categories of disabilities are not clear-cut but are ambiguous to a significant extent. Some children can reasonably be viewed as belonging to more than one category and others as belonging to only one, and then only marginally. The ambiguities exist because, to a certain extent, special needs are socially constructed: difficulties with learning or behavior tend to be problems in some social settings but not others and with some people but not others.

KELVIN SEIFERT: David, do you remember the first time you met Howie? [a sixth-grade classmate who stutters]

DAVID: Yeah, no one would talk to him, 'cause he took too long.

SEIFERT: So what did Howie do?

DAVID: He kept to himself mostly. One day he bopped me one on the head, though! He had gotten really mad that time. I guess it was because I had ignored him a lot.

SEIFERT: Do you have any advice for other sixth-graders who might have someone in their class who stutters?

DAVID: Yeah, just take your time. Just listen before you talk. Just take your time listening. Then it'll work out.

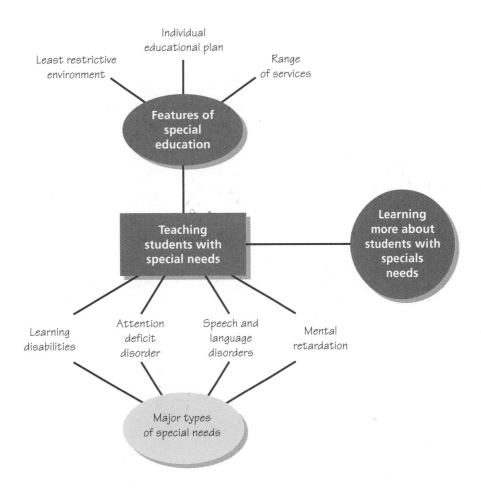

Chapter Re-View: Teaching Students with Special Needs This Chapter Re-View suggests directions in which the chapter might have taken your thinking—though, of course, other directions are also possible. It expands the Chapter View, which suggests a starting point, conceptually, of the chapter. But this Re-View does not suggest an ending point. Like the Chapter View, it represents just one perspective among many.

Key Terms and Concepts

special needs (322)
special education (323)
inclusion (322)
inclusive education (322)
PL 94-142 (323)
Individuals with Disabilities
  Education Act (IDEA) (323)

least restrictive environment
  (LRE) (324)
individual educational plan
  (IEP) (326)
learning disabilities (LD) (338)
attention deficit disorder
  (ADD) (344)

attention deficit hyperactivity
  disorder (ADHD) (344)
speech and language disorders
  (349)
mental retardation (354)
Down syndrome (354)

Annotated Readings

Howe, K. R. (1992). *The ethics of special education.* New York: Teachers College Press. The author focuses on ethical issues in special education: how teachers and others in authority should protect the legitimate interests of students with special needs and their families, even though they may be more helpless than other children and families. It is a major feature of this field and one we only touched on in passing in this chapter.

Paul, J. (Ed.). (1997). *Foundations of special education.* Pacific Grove, CA: Brooks/Cole. Although the title sounds like this is a conventional textbook, each chapter actually is written by an acknowledged expert in the field. The topics cover the spectrum from relationships to parents, to individualized educational planning, to ethics, and more.

Turnbull, A. (1995). *Exceptional lives: Special education in today's schools.* Englewood Cliffs, NJ: Merrill. This book is noteworthy because of its emphasis on examples of the lives of children with special needs and their families. As such, it does an unusually good job of communicating the feeling and flavor of existence for such children.

Internet Resources

<www.ldanatl.org>, <www.aamr.org>, <www.asha. org>, <www.add.org> Information about particular kinds of special needs is plentiful on the Internet. Each of these four web sites belongs to a national association concerned with some form of special need: www.ldanatl.org is about learning disabilities; www.aamr.org deals with mental retardation; www.asha.org focuses on speech, language, and hearing disorders; and www.add.org concerns attention deficit disorder. Each web site offers a mixture of information about the nature of the problem itself and about the organization's activities on behalf of individuals with the particular form of disability.

IV

Identifying Success and Value in Teaching

As discussions in the previous chapter have indicated, teaching and learning are tied closely to questions of value and success. Behind your actions and those of your students are choices and judgments about what is good and desirable: Is this activity, this reading, this assignment more desirable than those others? Does a student's completion of these tasks represent more success than the student's previous performance? Answers to questions of success and value are fundamental to education.

Part 4 explores these problems. Chapter 11 begins by discussing the problems of assessing students' learning. It views the issues from several perspectives—students', parents', and teachers'—and offers suggestions for making assessment as reliable and valid as possible. Chapter 12 broadens the discussion to explore how you can use educational research to develop your teaching in new, more effective directions. It pays special attention to ways that you can organize research of your own, even as a classroom teacher. Chapter 13 concludes by looking directly at how students develop ethical judgments—beliefs about the good—and how teachers can assist that development.

CHAPTER VIEW

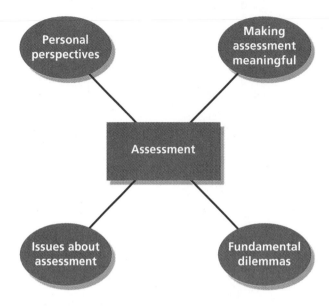

Chapter View: Assessing Students' Learning This Chapter View is a concept map that indicates one among many ways of thinking about the chapter. It suggests a starting point, conceptually, for the chapter but is incomplete by itself. At the end of the chapter is a Chapter Re-View, which expands on the Chapter View, suggesting directions for taking your thinking further—though, of course, other directions are also possible.

11

Assessing Students' Learning

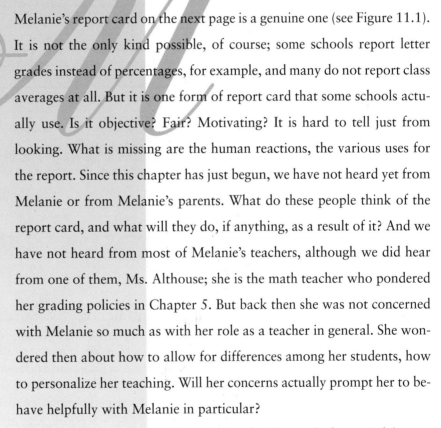

Melanie's report card on the next page is a genuine one (see Figure 11.1). It is not the only kind possible, of course; some schools report letter grades instead of percentages, for example, and many do not report class averages at all. But it is one form of report card that some schools actually use. Is it objective? Fair? Motivating? It is hard to tell just from looking. What is missing are the human reactions, the various uses for the report. Since this chapter has just begun, we have not heard yet from Melanie or from Melanie's parents. What do these people think of the report card, and what will they do, if anything, as a result of it? And we have not heard from most of Melanie's teachers, although we did hear from one of them, Ms. Althouse; she is the math teacher who pondered her grading policies in Chapter 5. But back then she was not concerned with Melanie so much as with her role as a teacher in general. She wondered then about how to allow for differences among her students, how to personalize her teaching. Will her concerns actually prompt her to behave helpfully with Melanie in particular?

All of these people participate in the familiar and often painful experience of "grading" students' performance. Lingering behind report cards and grading policies is a set of activities called **assessment,** ways in

CHAPTER ELEVEN

367

FIGURE 11.1

Melanie's Grades

Fort Richmond High School
Student Grade Report: Term 1

Student: Melanie Sikorsky   Grade: 11

Course	Teacher	Term Grade	Class Average
Mathematics	Althouse	74/100	66/100

Comment: A good effort!

Course	Teacher	Term Grade	Class Average
English	Courtney	78/100	69/100

Comment: A cooperative student. Keep up the good work.

Course	Teacher	Term Grade	Class Average
Art	Zubrick	94/100	88/100

Comment: A good artist.

Course	Teacher	Term Grade	Class Average
Phys Education	Glaveen	79/100	81/100

Comment: Showing improvement. A good effort!

Course	Teacher	Term Grade	Class Average
Chemistry	Wilson	82/100	75/100

Comment: Off to a good start. Keep up the good work.

[Explanation of grades: 91-100 = A; 81-90 = B; 71-80 = C; 61-70 = D; less than 61 = Fail.]

Principal: Brendon MacDougal
Date: 6 February 1997

In Your Own Voice

Students often tend to equate assessment and evaluation—they imagine that the only information a teacher pays attention to are activities to which the teacher assigns grades.

Did you ever think this when you were in elementary or high school?

How do you think it affected your attitude about school?

which teachers identify or diagnose strengths, weaknesses, and unique qualities of students. Assessment permeates all education, and it creates important ethical issues for teachers and students alike, because it inherently leads to **evaluation,** a judgment about whether students' learning is worthy, useful, and desirable. What are the signs or indicators of assessment? Educators have created various solutions for making detailed, informative assessments. As we will see in this chapter, though, the solutions do not bypass the need for evaluations based on assessments; they simply allow teachers to be consistent and explicit in their judgments of students, as well as in their observations.

To understand these generalizations, it helps to go back to Melanie's grade report and look more closely at how Melanie, her mother, and Ms. Althouse each responded to it. Their personal "takes" on the report will allow us to consider the major issues of assessment in general terms and to look even further back to the activities on which Melanie was assessed, both deliberately or incidentally. The activities will point to decisions that you will need to make about how to organize your own teaching and how to facilitate the kinds of learning that you value.

Evaluation and Assessment: A Student's Perspective

 UT I am getting ahead of myself. Let's start by listening to Melanie as she thinks about her grade report soon after receiving it:

Melanie was halfway home on her regular thirty-minute ride by city bus. She stared at the figures in between the bouncing of the bus: 74/100, 78/100. Those were the only two that mattered, math and English. Her mom had threatened to ground her if those two ended up below 70. So she was safe, at least theoretically.

Why math and English? she wondered again. The other grades were actu-

Assessment has different meanings to teachers, parents, and students, as a result of their separate roles and relationships to each other. It also poses different issues and problems.

ally higher, and might have compensated overall. But the others didn't seem to attract her mom's attention; they were just decorations framing math and English. "Because of college," her mother had said, and Melanie had smiled dutifully. Math and English for college. Oh well, at least now her mom would get off her case; Melanie closed her eyes, listened to her portable tape player, and took deep, relaxing breaths.

When she opened her eyes, she happened to notice her art grade: 94/100! No wonder; art class was a whole different world. Melanie relished her art classes: she moved happily from one project to the next, from drawing her pet cat to sculpting a dinner setting with "artistic meaning," to weaving a small kerchief for—who else?—her mom. You can't be penalized in art class, she thought, as long as you really explore the materials and try to be honest with yourself. 94/100.

Still, though, it was "only" in art where she got that grade, not in math or English. Not something you could brag about. Best to wait, she thought; best to wait out school. Someday she would not have to keep chugging away at the Important Subjects. There would come a time and place where art would be the Important Subject. Where? she wondered. But she had no answer. Melanie closed her eyes again and daydreamed.

Math and English, she thought. The grades should be OK with mom. And, she reasoned, I can always point out that I was above the average for the class; I just won't mention that I'm below average in math among my own friends. And only ordinary in English. Only one more year, she thought, and then . . . She lost her train of thought in the music of her tape player. In fact, she started humming softly to the music, then singing to it as the bus bounced along. The bus driver looked at her strangely, but said nothing; he had gotten used to Melanie singing on the bus. She had a nice voice.

In Your Own Voice

How do you think Melanie might think about her report card if she habitually received very low grades?

Or very high grades?

Do you think her report card serves high-achieving students better than low-achieving students, or both equally well (or equally poorly)?

Embedded in Melanie's thoughts are two issues that touch on both assessment and evaluation at the same time. One issue has to do with purposes (Eisner, 1994; Scriven, 1991): is evaluation supposed to motivate students, or to guide teachers' program planning, or to inform parents and other educators about the success of students and the worthiness of educational programs to society? Melanie has certainly learned about her standing from the report card, but will the information motivate and guide her future learning? It seems unlikely that it will, since each grade summarizes numerous experiences and activities. If Melanie is going to be motivated by any information about her performance, it will need to be information that diagnoses her activities in much greater detail. Perhaps her teachers provided her with such detail about herself during the preceding term, but we cannot tell from the grade report itself, nor from Melanie's comments. If the final report motivates her at all, therefore, it would seem most likely to affect her self-identity in general. "You are artistically inclined," the report may seem to say, "so take more art and fewer academic subjects if you can." Whether Melanie *should* assume her grades accurately reflect this sort of information is another question, and depends on the quality of the assessments underlying them. Let us assume, for the moment, that these assessments were fair, valid, and accurate; later in the chapter you will be able to decide better for yourself, after you have found out more details about them from one of Melanie's teachers.

Another issue is the comparative importance of different skills and forms of knowledge (Gordon & Bonilla-Bowman, 1996): are some more important than others, and if so, who is to decide about what is important? Melanie experiences these issues not as questions but as the privileging or elevating of certain subjects, especially math and English, compared to others. Note that the higher status of academic subjects is not necessarily something Melanie believes in herself; rather, it is merely a fact about school that she has learned to live with. Math and English have become valuable not for themselves but because her mother nags her about them and because universities expect good grades in them. In art, on the other hand, where she does sense intrinsic, personal value, she has performed much better.

Evaluation and Assessment: A Parent's Perspective

*M*ELANIE'S responses do not represent the only perspective on grading in particular or on evaluation and assessment in general. Her mother offers a view that highlights different issues, ones related to her position as a parent:

Ms. Sikorsky stared through the kitchen window, sipping her coffee; Melanie had just left for the evening, after handing her the final report card. Not great, she sighed with relief, but definitely good enough. I won't have to ground Melanie; I was afraid I might actually have to! Her grades are good enough.

Ms. Sikorsky took a deep, relaxing breath, and let it out slowly. It's hard enough being Mel's only parent, she thought, without also getting into battles about grades. I just hope colleges will think that 70s in the academics are "good enough." I suppose they will—or at least the colleges that we can afford will. Those won't be as picky as the fancy ones.

Ms. Sikorsky looked at the grade sheet again, brushing off a few bread crumbs. What actually went into the marks? she wondered. The teacher's comments look so stereotyped; they could almost have come from a computer. What has been going on in those classes of hers? It's so hard to find out. When I get home from work, it's already too late to call the school. And what exactly would I ask? "Hi, I'm Melanie's mother, and I'm wondering what you've been doing in math class so that I can help her more"? Awkward at best, brash at worst.

Ms. Sikorsky did go to parent information nights when Melanie was in tenth grade, but this year Mel discouraged her from attending—"It's dorky, none of the older kids' parents do it." Well, she has been too tired in the evening to fight that advice; she stayed home. So Melanie's classes have become something of a mystery that Melanie's descriptions of them haven't really solved: "Oh, you know, we don't do much. The teacher just leads discussions and lectures. Teaches stuff. You know, . . . " You should have probed her more anyway, Ms. Sikorsky told herself. Maybe then you'd know more about her day, and her grades would have been better.

Ms. Sikorksy blamed herself for the science fair fiasco last winter: Melanie had had such a great idea: the effects of day length on the health and blooming of poinsettias! In the end, though, it hadn't turned out well. To do the experiment, they had to buy plant lights and at least two poinsettia plants ("Four would have been better," Melanie said later). But plant lights and poinsettia plants cost money, which was something they did not have a lot of. Then Melanie needed to find some place to control the length of each plant's exposure to light. The basement worked for one plant, except that they kept forgetting to turn its plant light on and off at the right times. The second plant needed a different proportion of day and night, so they settled on a neighbor's basement, and installed the plant and its light with an automatic timer to make sure the light came on and off at the right times. That arrangement worked fine, except that Melanie kept forgetting to go to the neighbor's to water the plant, and eventually it died before the end of the experiment. So the great science fair idea never blossomed, so to speak, and Ms. Sikorsky blamed herself for the failure.

But she did not blame Melanie. Melanie has lots of good ideas, she thought, and keen curiosity even about a "boy's" subject like science.

Her coffee was almost gone. That pesky report card, she thought. It may recognize her talent in art (she sees that "94/100" on it), but it leaves out so much about my daughter! Leaves out that she *does* enjoy science, if she can just get the help with it that she deserves. Or that she reads avidly and writes her own poetry. Or that she sings beautifully—even on the bus. Or that she can be responsible for herself better than a lot of kids her age; living with just one parent has taught her that. She's so friendly, thought her mother, a kid with a winning personality. Where is all of that on the grade report? she wondered, holding back a tear.

In Your Own Voice

Have you ever received a final grade that you felt did not reflect some quality or achievement that deserved recognition?

If you could go back and talk to the teacher about this problem, what suggestions would you make for a better way to evaluate and grade students?

Just as Melanie is, Ms. Sikorsky is coping with the interplay of assessment and evaluation, except that the issues for her are not the same as for Melanie. One issue for Ms. Sikorsky is who is entitled to evaluate students, and entitled to evaluate Melanie in particular. As a parent, Ms. Sikorsky has not been invited to evaluate her daughter's academic capacities, presumably because she is not an expert on the school curriculum. Yet as a parent she does have expertise of another kind: she knows quite a lot about Melanie's talents and qualities, including talents that are academically relevant and that the grade report appears to have ignored. From Ms. Sikorsky's point of view, the final grade report implies that neither Melanie's special qualities nor Ms. Sikorsky's special knowledge of them matter. Presumably curriculum standards have guided the grading decisions instead, standards that (hopefully) are thoughtful, balanced, and widely accepted in public education. Even if the standards have these good qualities, though, the grades tell much less about Melanie than could be told, and much less than is relevant. Ms. Sikorsky senses what many educators have stated: that parents have valuable knowledge of students that could improve both their learning and their assessment (Goldberg, 1997; McCaleb, 1994).

Another issue for Ms. Sikorsky is the sorting function of evaluation, including final grades in particular. She knows that grades often channel individuals into educational programs and activities that differ in the opportunities they provide (Brantlinger, Majd-Jabbari & Guskin, 1996). So Melanie's mother is concerned about college entrance, and insists that Melanie achieve minimum percentages in key subjects. Her role as mother, however, makes coping with the sorting function of grades especially difficult: as a mother she is an advocate for her child, and therefore cannot allow herself as much detachment from her daughter's grades as Melanie's teacher may feel. As a busy single parent, furthermore, she has little time to influence school grading practices directly. All she can do is accept the system (mostly) as it is, and urge her daughter to make the best of it.

Her position as consumer rather than producer of evaluations makes Ms. Sikorsky vulnerable to a parental equivalent of students' "grade grubbing": caring more about Melanie's grades than about her actual learning. To her credit, this attitude has not taken over her relationship to Melanie or to Melanie's teachers unduly. The mother still appreciates her daughter, and not just her grades. And she is still willing, at least in principle, to learn from Melanie's teachers about how to help Melanie to learn.

"At least in principle": that phrase is a clue to a third issue embedded in Ms. Sikorsky's comments: how to design evaluations so that they actually communicate to people (such as herself) who have a stake in them but know little about the daily activities of classrooms. As far as Ms. Sikorsky is concerned, Melanie's grade report fails to accomplish this task. Information about Melanie's educational life is much scarcer than Ms. Sikorsky would like. The scarcity might not matter if the mother had no desire to assist her daughter's education. But in fact, the opposite is true: she believes she could and should help her daughter academically, if only she could find out how.

Many teachers would applaud Ms. Sikorsky's attitude (Goldberg, 1997). But how, they might wonder, to succeed at sharing detailed knowledge of the educational program with busy parents? They might answer their own question by saying that more than the usual means of communicating are needed: more than occasional, brief parent orientation nights or stark numerical scores sent home at periodic intervals. The strategies for communicating might pose some of the challenges we explored in Chapter 8, where we focused on the obstacles (and some solutions) to effective discourse in the classroom, and in Chapter 7, where we looked at potential difficulties in relationships between teachers and parents. But even if these challenges and difficulties can be resolved, where does the resolution leave us? Exactly what other assessment practices would communicate more successfully? Later in this chapter, I will suggest some alternatives. For now, just note that Ms. Sikorsky and other parents like her obviously *do* care about their children's education and intend to help with it if they know how.

Evaluation and Assessment: A Teacher's Perspective

*M*ELANIE's teachers have still other views on assessment, views that are colored by their roles as makers and interpreters of grades. Having this role may mean feeling less vulnerable than Melanie or her mother, but it can also create new worries about the fair use of power in guiding students' futures. Teachers must be careful about "playing God" in assessing students, because doing so leads so easily to making evaluative judgments. Sometimes it may seem as though teachers' responsibility to observe and evaluate students is too much to expect even of adults who are thoughtful, caring, and experienced. Ms. Althouse, the math teacher whom we met in Chapter 5, felt the weight of responsibility in these terms as she reflected on her current set of grades:

Darn! Ms. Althouse thought, these report cards are going to be the death of me. She scrolled through several computer screens of her students' grades, which the office had conveniently put on the schoolwide computer network. How is anyone supposed to know, she wondered, what my students actually *learned* this term or how they grew?

Ms. Althouse called up the grades for the eleventh-grade math class and flipped through them. "There's Melanie," she said out loud, even though no one was in the staff room. "She got 74/100. That's OK, but not great."

Melanie's a good example, she thought. How is anyone supposed to know that Melanie started the term by nearly failing it? Something good happened to her, but what? I should have watched her closer, should have asked her why *she* thought she was doing better, asked her what was going on. Whatever it was, it helped. Melanie climbed from 50/100 on the first quiz to 88/100 on the last one, which averaged to 74/100. At that rate, if the course had been longer, the girl might even have gotten a final percentage that was higher.

Too many students, she sighed to herself, too many to keep up with. But you would think that the district would at least come up with a grade sheet that showed the kind of change that happened to Melanie. I'll have to bring that up at the staff meeting again. Last month the others sounded like they were almost ready to look at alternatives. To try a reporting system that actually tells you details about the student or that inspires students to feel actual ownership of their achievements.

Ms. Althouse shut off her computer. The eleventh-grade class, she reflected. Even those major tests don't tell enough about students. What do they really show about Melanie? With a student load of 100 faces per day, I had to write tests that wouldn't take forever to mark; so I borrowed questions from last year, mostly short-answer and multiple-choice. But I happen to know that Melanie isn't at her best with questions like that. Her homework—the problem sets—is *wonderful* compared to her tests: she figures out all of the problems, shows all her work clearly. She can think, I can see that. And didn't I see her help others with some homework last week? She had a knack for explaining things that time; didn't make them feel like dummies. But her homework counts for only a little in her final grade, and her helpfulness with others doesn't count at all. She was "just" 74/100.

74/100 probably won't get Melanie into the field trip to the state capitol, thought Ms. Althouse. The state legislators choose the kids, and they go strictly by grades. What a shame! Mel would do well on a trip like that, get

In Your Own Voice

If Ms. Althouse is justified in feeling disappointed in current reporting systems, why haven't more schools dropped them in favor of newer, more informative alternatives?

Can you think of any reasons?

so much out of it. And she probably won't get there on her own; her mom is so busy since her divorce. And some of the kids who *do* go have probably already been there. Really "fair," eh? All because of those stupid grades, she muttered in frustration. There has got to be a better way.

It is important to note that Ms. Althouse is not criticizing assessment per se so much as the way assessment-related information is used (or ignored) to make evaluative judgments. One problem she points to is the lack of attention in the grade report to students' change or development. Melanie has "grown" during the term, but we would not know it from her final report, which focuses on everything *but* how she has changed. The report gives a simple snapshot; it gives performance at a particular moment in time, term's end. It also compares Melanie not with her own past achievements but with a curriculum standard and with other students. Melanie got 74 in math against an implied standard of 100; and she got 74 against a class average of 66. In highlighting these comparisons, the report card assumes a commonly held view of human intelligence or ability: that it is fixed rather than changeable. Apparently Ms. Althouse does not make this assumption in her own thinking about students. She would prefer assessments that showed more detail about students' long-term development—about how students learn and change over extended periods of time (Wolf & Reardon, 1996).

In Your Own Voice

Are structured test questions really a "regrettable necessity," as Ms. Althouse seems to think?

Are there times when they are exactly what students need, regardless of whether they are convenient for teachers?

Another issue worrying Ms. Althouse is the information on which grade evaluations are based. In the case of the report card, the sources are not unusual in nature: a combination of tests, quizzes, and homework assignments. But Ms. Althouse is dissatisfied with them because they are weighted toward structured questions and problems. In her opinion, these do not reveal the ability of some students (including Melanie) to think mathematically, which presumably is a major goal of her math course. Ms. Althouse implies, in fact, that she is a critic of structured test questions in general: they are a regrettable necessity for coping with large numbers of students. With fewer students, Ms. Althouse could observe and interact with individuals more and arrive at richer, more complex understandings of their achievements. Presumably the richer understandings would provide the basis for more effective assessments and evaluations, ones that would simultaneously inform parents, motivate students such as Melanie, and guide future teachers' instructional plans (Darling-Hammond, 1994; Shepard & Bliem, 1995).

Like Ms. Sikorsky, Ms. Althouse knows there are worthy talents that final report cards don't recognize. Melanie, for example, has talents that would both give much and gain much from the trip to the state capitol, except that her talents did not translate into numerical grades on the report. But Ms. Althouse frames this injustice differently than does Melanie's mother. She is thinking not just about one specific student, Melanie, but about all of the students who might, or might not, be recognized fully for their talents. As a teacher, her issue is general equity rather than personal advocacy—ensuring fairness to all rather than getting the best opportunity for a single student. Some students, she notes, may be fortunate enough to have their talents fully recognized because those talents happen to coincide with the existing grading system. But others will not. Some students, in fact, may need the support of positive school evaluations just to have a fair chance at life. Melanie may be among these students. For her, good grades would make possible a first and only visit to the state capitol, and not merely an additional visit that duplicates a family outing that might take place anyway.

All in all, Ms. Althouse is not as critical as she first appears. Not only does she wish openly for richer forms of assessment, but she also hints implicitly that she supports the principle of evaluating—of judging—students' performance. It is the practice of assessment—this particular grade report, used at this time—that frustrates her. She does not question, for example, whether Melanie's grades are an accurate "snapshot" of her progress at one moment in time; rather, the issue is the lack of developmental information they provide. She has not questioned the quality of the multiple-choice and short-answer tests that she wrote and gave; she is concerned only that these tests draw on too few thinking skills. And she has not really questioned whether students *other than* Melanie should visit the state capitol; she regrets only Melanie's inability to be selected and questions the value placed on final grades for this purpose. The problem is only this time, this particular occasion. "There has got to be a better way," she said, not "there is no way."

Taking Stock of Issues About Assessment

*L*ET'S reorganize the issues that Melanie, her mother, and her teacher talked about into a more formal list. I will list them according to three related themes: purposes and assumptions, power and privilege, and influence on teaching and learning. As you will see, the themes overlap, but the format will be serviceable even so. With the list at hand, you (and I) will be able, in the last part of this chapter, to consider assessments and evaluations that go beyond final report cards and that hopefully prove to be clearer and more motivating to everyone concerned.

It is easy to understand the distress of Melanie and her mother over grading practices that masquerade as real assessment. Their interests are clearly not being advanced by the practice. But why is this kind of letter/numerical grading still so prevalent? I can think of at least two reasons. First, given the realities of teacher workloads, the practice is functional in a narrow sense. Grades are, after all, relatively quick and easy to provide. But more significantly, special interests within the larger culture are served by maintaining the practice. Individual course grades and GPAs are often used by employers for discriminating among competing candidates for available jobs. Selecting the "best" person for each job promotes economic efficiency, and grades are useful for comparing, sorting, and ranking students according to narrow (often language- and math-related) characteristics that represent but a sliver from the broad spectrum of human talents, abilities, and forms of intelligence.

So business and economic interests override those of Melanie and her mother. And not even the university is the ultimate recipient of benefits of the "grading game"; it merely extends the practice on behalf of these larger, societal interests. Finally, the truly professional teacher, whose broader definition of *education* demands attention to a much wider array of human attributes than grades can measure, also loses. What to do? The teacher must consider the possibilities of alternative forms of assessment and evaluation: portfolios, performances, journals, exhibits, anecdotal records, and so on. These strategies are usually more labor intensive in comparison with traditional grading. And they may appear strange and inappropriate to some administrators, parents, and even students, who are accustomed to the familiar and comfortable. But Melanie and her mother have offered us a valuable lesson about the costs of maintaining a practice that fails at promoting the real education of our students. Good teachers will learn from it.

Tom Barone, Professor of Education, Arizona State University

Issues About Purposes

1. Why assess or evaluate at all? To inform, to motivate, to make decisions? To accomplish these purposes with students, with parents, with other teachers? Is it enough to say that assessment and evaluation should serve all three purposes and all three groups, or would doing so mean evading more specific educational responsibilities? Tom Barone, professor of education at Arizona State University, gives one answer to these questions in the accompanying Multiple Voices box. You may not agree with his opinions about whose interests conven-

tional assessments really serve, but his point of view deserves serious consideration: it suggests an urgent need for more equitable and sensitive forms of evaluating students.

2. What purposes of assessment and evaluation are assumed or unstated? Do they implicitly reaffirm a view of human intelligence, for example, as being essentially the same "thing" in all people, except that some of us have more of "it" than others have? Do assessment and evaluation sort students into various educational programs or activities, either implicitly or explicitly?

Issues About Power and Privilege

3. Do assessments and evaluations emphasize the importance of certain content, subjects, and skills at the expense of others? Are the resulting differences in status justifiable?

4. Who is entitled to assess and evaluate students? Only teachers? Only experts in educational evaluation? What kinds of observations and judgments are appropriate from students themselves, or from their parents?

Issues About Influence on Teaching and Learning

5. When and why do assessments and evaluations sometimes distract students from learning rather than focus them on it?

6. Can (and should) assessments and evaluations be designed that summarize students' individual development rather than compare students with one another?

As we have seen, the report card at the beginning of this chapter stimulated a student, her mother, and one of her teachers to answer these questions in particular ways, ways that none of them found completely satisfactory. Are there evaluation alternatives that give richer, more satisfying answers? That is the problem we will explore in the rest of this chapter. In our search for alternatives, we will follow the thinking and actions of the person who is in the best position to find and act on them: Melanie's teacher, Ms. Althouse. As you will see in the next section, Ms. Althouse based her final grade for Melanie on much more information than was obvious to Melanie's mother or even to Melanie herself. The challenge, as she saw it, was not *whether* to collect a variety of information but *how* to collect it so as to produce the clearest picture possible of Melanie's learning, one that can be communicated as easily as possible to Melanie's mother while having the fewest negative consequences for Melanie's motivation. Ms. Althouse thinks of assessment, and especially of evaluation, in terms of a prescription drug: it may be good for you, but it also has side effects that you need to know about and that will need watching.

Assessments That Motivate and Inform

*A*s you may suspect, there are alternatives to the conventional assessments, such as that Melanie received, that deal with the problems we have discussed. The alternatives differ in name and details. **Authentic assessment** refers to assessment procedures based on tasks with real, ongoing value to students. For example, instead of learning about fractions simply through paper-and-pencil exercises, students might learn about them by devising and executing recipes for a bake sale (cooking the right amounts requires converting many fractions). Assessment of this task would involve observing students' success at baking appropriate amounts for the sale (and at producing tasty products in the end!). Students could use the same task to learn about money more authentically than with conventional textbook-based problems: they would need to price the products appropriately to cover their costs and keep track of both expenses and income. Again, an authentic assessment of this (authentic) task would focus on students' financial success. Furthermore, since students might well be able to observe their own successes on these tasks, it would make sense to involve them in their own evaluations, at least to some extent (Darling-Hammond, Ancess & Falk, 1995; Valencia, Hiebert & Afflerbach, 1994).

In Your Own Voice

Have you ever experienced one of these alternative forms of assessment as a student?

How well did it work for you?

Were there problems with it?

An increasingly common form of authentic assessment is **portfolio assessment,** assessments of collections of students' work, which are called "portfolios" (Calfee & Perfumo, 1996). The collections might be pieces of writing or progress reports on a science project. With some forms of portfolio assessment, students select the materials and evaluate the results; in others, the teacher may do this work or share it with students. Depending on students' and teachers' purposes, a portfolio may deliberately include all work over a period of time—even rough drafts—or it may include only polished, final products. We will explore portfolios further in a moment, because, as it happens, Ms. Althouse began using them.

Performance assessment is similar to authentic assessment in that both terms refer to assessments of tasks meaningful to students. Compared to other forms of authentic assessment, however, performance assessment is less often associated with assessments generated by teachers (such as portfolios) and more often with those by external authorities, such as school districts or state education departments (Smith & Levin, 1996). As such, they are intended somewhat more to compare students' success relative to one another and against a predetermined criterion, such as the officially mandated curriculum of a district or state. In a performance assessment of high school English, for example, all students might first be given material to read in common (e.g., a play by Shakespeare), then participate in a common amount of discussion of the readings with classmates, and end with writing an essay on the readings that has a common topic. The assessment is more authentic in that it resembles the teaching and learning activities typical of a high school English class but is conducted in a way that facilitates comparisons between students' actual skills and those expected in the English curriculum, as well as comparisons between one student's skills and another's.

Mastery learning is a way of organizing learning so that all students learn material to an identical, high level, even if some students require more time to do so than others (Guskey, 1994; Shuell, 1996). In a typical mastery learning program, the teacher introduces new concepts or topics in relatively small units. After initially teaching a unit, he or she gives an ungraded assignment or test to assess which students have learned the material and which ones need more help with it. The students who have already learned the unit to a high level are given enrichment activities; those needing more help are provided with tutoring from classmates or peers, for example, or with additional, self-guiding materials until they have learned the materials fully. When the system is working well, all students can in principle end up with the highest grades or scores, although some students will have taken longer than others to do so. "Working well," of course, depends on a teacher's having ample materials for both remediation and enrichment and on having a curriculum to teach that can feasibly be broken up into small units.

Most of these alternative methods share a commitment to assessment and evaluation that is meaningful to students, teachers, and parents while also taking into account the concerns of these people and of curricular authorities. The methods also share a common problem, which is how to "translate" the results of assessments into terms conventionally understood by parents or by other teachers who do not know about or do not wish to begin using these forms of assessment. We will return to this second problem later in the chapter. First, we should look in more detail at why some teachers do use alternative assessments and at how parents and colleagues react when they do. Let's start with Ms. Althouse, one year following the last time we saw her.

After School, One Year Later: A Visit to Ms. Althouse's Classroom

KELVIN SEIFERT: So . . .

MS. ALTHOUSE: . . . so about the time of that grade report [one year ago], I had already started having students do a portfolio. It was more than just collecting work in a folder. They were also supposed to select and interpret mathematical materials, and supposed to create them too. The "creation" part was two projects: one using everyday math and one using "pure" math. I tried to encourage people to choose their own topics as much as possible. Like for everyday math, someone studied how the weather bureau combines weather measurements mathematically to make forecasts. For pure math, someone read about and explained permutations and combinations, which is a topic we don't usually cover. Then she made a few predictions about their properties and tested them mathematically. I made sure to talk with each student about the projects now and then, or at least briefly every couple of weeks.

KS: And the "selecting and interpreting"?

MS. A: For selecting and interpreting, they had to find an example each week of other people using math and write a commentary on it. The weekly entries could be on the same topic as the creative projects, but they didn't have to be. Somebody included news clippings about the election polls, for example, and commented on the statistical reliability. Somebody else included her parents' tax returns and wrote about whether a computerized tax return was really workable in principle. I responded in writing, adding to the ideas or correcting misconceptions.

Ms. Althouse is not finished talking, but already she is hinting at how she will handle assessment. By opting for portfolios, she is inviting diversity and self-choice, and she is implying that motivating students is a priority—issue number 1, which I listed in the last section. Presumably her assessments will reflect this priority. But instead of assuming this, of course, I should actually ask her:

KS: Wasn't the diversity in the folders a problem? What about covering the curriculum?

MS. A: [Raises her eyebrows and sighs] Good point. But when I really thought about it, I realized that what I cared about the most was motivating the students. Making them enthusiastic about math. Making them see its real value, its personal value. Covering the curriculum is important, I suppose, but it won't matter if a student ends up hating math.

KS: But how can you evaluate portfolios when each is so unique?

MS. A: Simple. I judge students against themselves, not against one another. I look at how they grow. Like Melanie—that's whom you're really interested in, isn't it? She's a perfect example. Her first portfolio items were pretty straightforward; I think she just put in her mom's weekly grocery list and talked a bit about budgeting. But you should see her now! Last week she found an article about digital art on computers. She loves art and is really good at it, did you know that? She evaluated its pros and cons for school art and wrote a piece about it *for* elementary-age students, deliberately using simple language for their sake. Now she wants to use it to do a demonstration of digital art when the first-graders come here to Ft. Richmond next week.

So I was right, at least about one thing: Ms. Althouse is indeed giving priority to motivating students. And since motivating students means allowing diversity, she is also led to focus on students' individual development and away from comparing students with one another (issue number 6 from the last section). Or perhaps she is guided by assumptions or beliefs about intelligence: that it is not a single "thing" of which each student has either more or less, but many qualities that may be difficult to compare. Maybe this belief guides her, or at least allows her, to search for changes within individual students, and diversity in portfolios is one way to find it. Should I ask if there is something to this alternative interpretation?

KS: Does it make sense to say that some kids are always smarter than other kids? Can you see it in their portfolios?

MS. A: [Looks puzzled] I suppose you could say that, but I haven't really thought about it that way. At least not anymore. Before I started using portfolios, I used to try hard to justify final, summary grades. It was for my sake as much as the students'; I continually worried about the information that was left out of final grades, and whether that meant summary grades were fair. I worried a lot less about that after I started using portfolios.

KS: So portfolios solved your dilemmas about grading?

MS. A: Hardly! It's more like I traded one problem for another. I used to worry about fairness—about whether final grades reflected what students had actually done. Now I worry about explaining what portfolio achievements actually mean to parents and other teachers—explaining portfolios in terms of conventional grading and assessment practices. That's a tough one for me these days. But I have some ideas that I like about how to "translate" portfolio results into conventional language. Let's talk again so I can tell you about them. Right now I have to go to class.

The bell rang for the next period of the day. I wrote in my notebook, "communicating/translating portfolios—how?" and made a mental note to follow up on her invitation to talk further.

Although Ms. Althouse seems not to have thought about the nature of achievement consciously, she does hold beliefs about it: she believes, for example, that a fundamental truth about students is the noncomparability of their abilities. Therefore, she does not base her evaluation on individual growth merely because portfolios make it convenient to do so (Elbow, 1994). She sees individual development as philosophically and educationally more desirable than comparisons and rankings. Whether others—teachers, administrators, and perhaps yourself—agree with her is, of course, another matter, as we will see shortly.

Later That Day: In the Staff Room, Talking with the Department Head

KS: Ms. Althouse was telling me about her portfolios—she's really "sold" on them now! But I can't decide what to think. You're the department head, right? Responsible for the math teachers and the overall math program here?

MR. NELSON: Yep. [Scowls and stares off at the wall; then changes abruptly to cheerful friendliness.] Now don't get me wrong: I have a *lot* of respect for Ms. Althouse's teaching. She's experienced, and it's not my place to criticize her choices. She gets very good results from her students with those portfolios—some very motivated students. They love it! [Pauses]

KS: But . . . ? Is the other shoe going to fall?

MR. N: Umm, but I don't think she appreciates the problems that she creates for the rest of us. I teach sections of the same course, and I find that students sometimes try to figure out whether Althouse's class is easier than the others—or harder—because of the portfolios. Some think the portfolios make it easier; others think they make it harder. Either way it's awkward; they come to me as the department head, complaining and wanting to change teachers.

KS: Is that so bad?

MR. N: No, but it's a hassle. I really don't *know* how to compare the work in Althouse's class with the other math classes. Officially we all use the same curriculum, but the portfolios make it seem like every one of Althouse's kids is doing something different. Even the principal and superintendent's office grumble about it occasionally. If her students weren't so motivated, I might have to step in, get her to change [smiles wryly]. Not that she would ever take advice from me!

In Your Own Voice

Do you sympathize here with Ms. Althouse's belief about the noncomparability of students' achievements?

Can you think of a situation where you might *not* agree?

In Your Own Voice

Suppose you were teaching in a high school where you suspected students were "shopping" for particular teachers.

How would you respond to a student who you thought was doing this?

How would you respond to a colleague who was concerned about students' doing this?

In Your Own Voice

What can you suggest for responding to Mr. Nelson's concern about the ambiguities of portfolios?

Or should he just learn to live with the ambiguities of the grades that result?

Mr. Nelson is talking about the purposes of assessment (issue number 1). Unlike Ms. Althouse, however, he is not concerned about how assessments inform and motivate "insiders," such as learners and (perhaps) their parents. He is talking about how it affects "outsiders"—students or other teachers who are not familiar with the details of Ms. Althouse's program. How are outsiders to know, he wonders, precisely what a given grade or evaluation from Ms. Althouse represents? Because of the portfolios, her system appears to represent different accomplishments for each student. The ambiguity seems to be the price paid for her students' high motivation. When tests and assignments are the same for all students, it seems more plausible to assert that all students are mastering the same material. But even then, as Ms. Althouse might argue, the material they master may only *seem* the same. Two students may solve a problem using very different sorts of thinking: one by reasoning it out, for example, and the other by remembering a solution strategy from another, similar problem.

Mr. Nelson is using everyday terms to describe a key problem in making assessments of students: the problem of *validity*. Current evaluation experts recognize two forms of validity. The first is *construct validity*, how well an assessment really reflects or represents what it is supposed to represent; the second is *consequential validity*, how beneficial and predictable the assessment process itself is for the lives of students (Linn & Baker, 1996; Shepard, 1993). (Forms of validity are discussed in more detail later in this chapter.) In picturing Ms. Althouse's portfolios, Mr. Nelson sees mixed validity. What the portfolios represent is too diverse to specify (low construct validity). How they influence or affect Ms. Althouse's own students is mostly positive, though how they affect other teachers' students is either neutral or negative (consequential validity that, overall, is positive but not perfect). Whether Mr. Nelson is being fair in making these judgments is, of course, another question. Before making up our own minds about these issues, however, we should listen further to his comments:

KS: But what you complain about—the students shifting sections—wouldn't that be fixed if *every* teacher used portfolios? Then no one could feel that the "grass was always greener on the other side of the fence," that the assessments in an unfamiliar section of the course were necessarily better?

MR. N: I suppose it might. But not completely; it could also just make the course *more* ambiguous. With portfolios everywhere, some kids and their parents might be mystified about the entire math program, not just about Althouse's version of it!

The real question, it seems to me, is this: is there a desirable curriculum, a definable subject, called "mathematics," or is there not? You're writing a book about this, right? Put that in your book. I say that there is a "core" to math—things about it that every student must learn. How can diverse portfolios, self-chosen portfolios, ensure learning the core? Actually Althouse agrees with me, but I find it hard to see evidence of her belief in a common core of math, hard to see it in all the diversity of the portfolios.

In Your Own Voice

Suppose we created a curriculum committee that consisted of equal numbers of math teachers, university math professors, and political leaders.

Would such a committee provide the best view of the "core" of mathematics?

Why do you think it would or would not?

"Is there a 'core' to math—things that every student should learn?" In posing this question, Mr. Nelson is referring to issue number 3: whether assessment and evaluation should emphasize certain content at the expense of other content. Chances are that he and Ms. Althouse generally agree on the answer—that there is indeed a common core—but so far only Mr. Nelson has stated this position explicitly. Perhaps Ms. Althouse will too, if invited to do so. Their views about the issue are important because they influence their opinions on issue number 4: who is entitled to evaluate students? If mathematics does have a common core, classroom assessments should be constructed by the people with greatest knowledge of the core. But who these people are is debatable. Are they the teachers of the subject? The subject-area teachers would have knowledge of math as well as of how students typically learn math. Or are the true experts university professors of mathematics? They probably know "pure" mathematics the best, although they may not have as much sense of how children and adolescents learn it. Or are those with the best knowledge of the core really political and business leaders, since they may have the best sense of where mathematics is actually needed and used in modern society?

However, even if Mr. Nelson and Ms. Althouse agree that a "core" to mathematics exists, it is unclear whether the two teachers differ about the nature and importance of the core essentials of high school mathematics. One teacher may believe the essentials consist of different topics than those chosen by the other, or one may conceive of the core as being smaller or less important overall than conceived by the other. Such differences are common among teachers and would influence their beliefs about another feature of issue number 4: the appropriateness of students' self-evaluations (Agran, 1997; Azwell & Schmar, 1995). To clarify these subtleties and their impact on Mr. Nelson's and Ms. Althouse's students, we will eventually have to go back and talk with each teacher further. First, though, we should hear from Melanie's mother; she too has thoughtful opinions about portfolios and authentic assessments.

Six Months Later: Assessments That Communicate

KS: The last time we talked, you didn't sound very pleased with the reporting system used by Ms. Althouse. Still true?

MS. SIKORSKY: Well, actually I'm more satisfied now than I was last time. After that last report card Ms. Althouse changed her system, started using "portfolio assessments" of students' work. Started sending more work home, and the work had more written comments on it and fewer grades or scores. I started getting a better idea of Melanie's actual daily work. Melanie was supposed to go over the portfolio materials with me each time they came home. And we did, mostly.

KS: How did all of this affect you in particular?

MS. S: I liked it! Though not completely. I could see that Melanie was putting out effort for the course. When she made mistakes on problem sheets, or when she found limited resources for her "pure math" paper, it was not from laziness but from struggling to do her best. That was reassuring. And I could see where I could help with some of Mel's work—and where it was beyond me. So I trusted Melanie's motives more and felt able to help her more effectively, or at least to give encouragement.

KS: But . . . ?

MS. S: I also worried about how the new system might be affecting Melanie's future. Since I knew that everyone in the math class was doing a different project, I couldn't help wondering how Melanie's compared to the others: was it "A"-quality material or "B"-quality, and so on? Althouse gave it no summary grade or score until the end of the term, when the project was complete! Was Althouse really expecting the same from Mel as from other students? There was no way to tell; I just had to trust her to be fair.

In Your Own Voice

If other parents, like Ms. Sikorsky, are uneasy with portfolios because they do not compare students, what do you suppose the effect of their uneasiness might be on students?

How do you think it might affect students' opinions about the purposes of grading and evaluation, and about the best ways to be graded or evaluated?

Ms. Sikorsky has mixed feelings, both worries and satisfactions. The satisfaction is real: with the new emphasis on meaningful work and descriptively oriented assessment, she can understand Melanie's activities better than before and support her education more effectively. As a parent, this advantage counts for a lot—but not for everything. Like Mr. Nelson, Ms. Sikorsky is concerned that the diversity of students' work prevents comparisons of work. Although she may not realize it, her concerns are common among parents whose children's teachers use alternative methods of assessment (Adams & Young, 1995). The very emphasis on narrative in assessments—on describing a student's performance in words—makes it more difficult or ambiguous to compare students to one another (Elbow, 1994). The ambiguity is exacerbated by the diversity of students' projects (Adams & Young, 1995); they are like apples and oranges, as Ms. Althouse said (Egawa & Azwell, 1995).

This parent is fundamentally satisfied, then, though beneath her satisfaction lies one more worry:

MS. S: One more thing that made me nervous: I noticed that Mel evaluated *herself* on several pieces of work, including even the final math projects. She wrote brief appraisals of the quality of her work. Did those self-evaluations really count? Melanie said that they did, but I can't quite believe her. What if she praised herself too much? Would Althouse still honor the assessment? Of course, maybe it wouldn't matter exactly what Mel said about herself, since there are so few letter grades or scores on any of the work. And to be honest, I noticed that Melanie often did *not* praise herself highly for some of her work. I actually wondered if she was sometimes too hard on herself!

Self-assessment? This is something Ms. Althouse did not tell us about. Whatever Ms. Althouse's reasons for having students evaluate themselves, the practice has caused Ms. Sikorsky to confront issue number 4, concerning who is entitled to assess student learning. Conventional wisdom limits this activity to teachers. Since Ms. Althouse breaks this convention, however, Melanie's mother has had to reflect consciously on the assumptions behind this belief. Can students judge themselves fairly? Can teachers be relied on to respect students' self-assessments and to use them in ways that truly contribute to learning? Or should self-assessments be regarded as an educational exercise, one that guides students' learning but does not count toward a final evaluation? Ms. Sikorsky does not have answers to these questions—or, more precisely, she does not know how Ms. Althouse might answer them. Space does not allow us to reason these questions out fully, but note that a significant number of educators have offered answers that indeed give a role for self-assessments by students (see, for example, Garcia [1994] or Schmar [1995]).

As these researchers point out, a major advantage of self-assessments is their power to motivate students by enticing them to take responsibility for their learning. How does that power feel to students? To get a firsthand look at it, let's talk again with Melanie:

Six Months Later: Living with Self-assessments

KS: What about self-grading in your math class? How did that go?

MELANIE: Well, for one thing, it wasn't really self-*grading*; it was self-*assessment*. The point was that we were supposed to reflect on the quality of our work. Comment on it in writing so that Althouse could also comment more helpfully. That was how it was supposed to work.

KS: And did it really work out that way?

M: Yes, most of the time it actually did. I would write something about the quality of my work before I turned it in—just a sentence or two. And she would respond underneath my comments. But commenting made more sense on the bigger assignments compared to the daily work.

KS: Meaning what?

M: With daily work—mostly responses to reading assignments and answers to problem sets—there wasn't that much to say, except "I had trouble with problem number 3," or whatever, or "I found these pages easy to understand." It was hard to pinpoint my own reactions when the assignment was already so specific.

With the big projects, it was different. Like on the "applied math" assignment. We had to report on our work in stages, and I could comment on how well I thought I was doing—whether I was finding enough library material, or understanding the material, or still thought my project idea was a good one. That sort of thing.

KS: So did you give yourself actual "grades" or scores on your work, or just written comments?

M: On daily work we gave ourselves a grade, but it was only pass-fail—whether I thought a homework paper was basically acceptable. Althouse circled the grade and recorded it. On the big projects, we wrote more and gave ourselves letter grades. But I'm still not sure whether she will consider them real grades. She says she will, but I don't quite trust her!

From Melanie we learn two important points. The first is that Ms. Althouse used self-assessment primarily to encourage reflection about and responsibility for classroom work. Most of the grades, as Melanie says, are "only pass-fail." The second point is that we still cannot tell clearly whether Melanie actually likes self-assessment; she has not showered it with criticism, but neither has she praised it explicitly. It is time to ask:

KS: Do you like doing self-assessments?

M: They *can* be good, but it gets to be a burden when you have to do them a lot. It feels like everything is being graded all the time—and I mean *everything.* Like there's nothing that does *not* count!

KS: But you said that the actual grading was mostly pass-fail. Wouldn't that make it easier? Or did you fail some of the daily assignments?

M: No, no. But I had to scramble to make sure that I got everything in, every blessed homework paper, so that I did not have to give myself any "fails."

KS: But that's no different than what happens with any teacher who requires a lot of daily assignments. How did *self*-assessment affect it: how did it make your job harder?

M: [Pauses] I suppose there were two reasons. One is that I felt more responsible. I worried about giving myself a "fail"; she's not the one doing it. Another reason is that I never really understood whether my self-imposed "passes" and grades counted the way Ms. Althouse's do. She claims that they did, but I still can't quite believe it. I would have to give myself a ridiculous grade just to find out her reaction. But I never had the nerve, even on just a small homework assignment. "Pass" myself for a lousy piece of work or "fail" myself for something really good.

In Your Own Voice

Have you ever been skeptical of a teacher's invitation to assess your own work or the work of another student?

What kept you from trusting the invitation?

What did you think really motivated the teacher's invitation?

In a sense, Melanie is saying that self-assessment is working almost *too* well because so many pieces of work have become her personal responsibility. Her taking on responsibility might be entirely good for her, except that Melanie remains privately unconvinced that she in fact does have the authority to assess her own work. Lingering in the background is a continual worry that the teacher might eventually contradict Melanie's grading decisions; after all, society still gives Ms. Althouse the power to do so. In effect, therefore, Melanie lives with conflicting messages. One comes from Ms. Althouse, granting students autonomy to assess their own work. The other comes simultaneously from society, keeping this autonomy from "mere" students. As a result, and as critics of portfolios sometimes point out, Melanie risks being distracted by the evaluation process itself (issue number 5 described earlier). She also verges on feeling overevaluated: there are few times when she feels truly safe to fail, if necessary (Elbow, 1994). She is inhibited from laziness, therefore, but perhaps also from taking risks in her learning.

But What About Testing?

$\mathcal{I}$N searching for assessments with greater authenticity, Ms. Althouse has succeeded, albeit not perfectly. But where has her new practices left the most important traditional method of evaluation, the classroom test? She and Melanie have mentioned her using tests, but only in passing. Should she (and we also) be concerned about how to use them well and about how to ensure their quality? The short

Paper-and-pencil testing has many advantages but also poses certain problems — including achieving satisfactory levels of both reliability and validity.

answer is a definite *yes,* as long as we (and she too) understand how tests affect students' construction of knowledge and understand the assumptions conventional tests make about the essential nature of human knowledge.

In particular, most classroom tests usually have the following characteristics, whatever their style, form, or subject:

- *Charactistic 1: Sampling.* Tests sample knowledge of skill from some larger domain. On a test of arithmetic, it is never possible to include every conceivable addition problem; only a selection can be included. On an essay test, it is usually not possible to ask every important essay question; only a few can in fact be asked.

- *Characteristic 2: A designated time and place.* A test takes place at a special time and place, which is usually the classroom on a date announced (typically) in advance. The testing occasion is regarded as distinct from other occasions, which are usually regarded as occasions for learning knowledge, not displaying it. The distinction is widely held, even though many teachers and students often also note that a test may "make you think," meaning it also serves as a time for new learning.

- *Characteristic 3: An assumption that learning is individually stored.* Tests focus on knowledge as a "thing," an object that individuals accumulate in some measurable amount. During a test, the knowledge held by friends, family, or teachers is deliberately ignored, even if a student could normally access that shared knowledge easily and normally would do so.

These qualities of classroom tests are responsible for two major issues or challenges in constructing tests: reliability and validity. It is important to understand what underlies these two issues and how they are affected when a teacher—such as Ms. Althouse—modifies her assessment methods to make them more authentic. As you will see, there is no way to ensure perfect reliability or validity. But shifting to more authentic assessments redefines the issues in ways that may provide partial solutions.

Reliability

The first issue, **reliability,** refers to the consistency of test results—to how similar a student's score, grade, or performance would be from one testing occasion to the next. If you get 80 percent on a test the first time, you should get close to 80 percent if you take it again later. Achieving high

As an alternative form of assessment, some teachers help students to construct portfolios of their work. This student, for example, is writing a journal entry that will be part of a series of writing samples that she will later edit and assess for herself.

reliability is both challenging and important because of the testing characteristics just mentioned. For various reasons, scores may vary from one testing occasion to the next. Questions may be ambiguous or open to multiple interpretations, either in answering them or in grading them. Or questions may be too hard and therefore cause students to answer essentially at random. When these things happen, tests become unreliable to some extent.

There are various strategies for assessing how reliable a test actually is, although none are perfect for use in classrooms. One strategy is to assess **test-retest reliability,** by simply comparing the results of the same test given twice. If the test is reliable, students should tend to produce similar scores each time. However, giving a test twice takes up valuable class time, and it provides no insurance that students do not simply remember answers from the first testing and thereby perform similarly on the second testing. Another strategy is to assess **equivalent forms reliability.** This involves finding or devising two parallel or equivalent forms of a test, each given to different groups of students. In testing students' knowledge of addition, for example, you might write two tests, each with a different specific addition problem. This approach works if the test is fairly easy to write (such as the addition test in my example) or when you can procure equivalent forms from another teacher or from a commercial publisher. Otherwise it can be burdensome to write two versions of a test that you feel sure are truly equivalent. A third strategy, one that bypasses this extra work, is **split-half reliability,** which assesses reliability by using only one version of a test but dividing it into equivalent halves and seeing whether students' scores are similar on each half. If they are, the test may be reliable; this conclusion is justified, though, only if each half of the test, considered separately, contains a reasonably large sample of items or problems. It also assumes that each half truly measures or reflects equivalent knowledge rather than different knowledge. For example, if one half of the test contains addition computation problems but the other contains multiplication word problems, performance on the two parts may differ as a result, and the test may therefore seem "unreliable" when part scores are compared.

Validity

The second issue, **validity,** refers to how well a test measures, reflects, or demonstrates what it claims to measure, reflect, or demonstrate. If you get 90 percent on a ten-problem addition test, the result should imply

In Your Own Voice

As a teacher, you usually won't take the trouble to make the checks on reliability described here.

Yet surely that does not mean we should not trust the results of teacher-made tests.

Or does it?

What do you think?

Some have criticized the terms *face validity* and *content validity* because they imply that the content of a test is "in" the test rather than in the way a test is used.

For example, two spelling tests might look essentially identical on the surface.

But one could be used to assess students' ability to sound out unfamiliar words and the other to assess their ability to remember previously learned words correctly.

Do you think teachers should be concerned with this sort of ambiguity in face validity?

that you can perform addition problems in general, not just that you are good at guessing answers or can solve the ten problems that happen to be on the test. To be valid, a test must first of all be reliable in the sense described earlier. Unless the scores "sit still," there is no way to judge their relationship to what the test claims to measure—no way, that is, to judge validity. But a test also needs more than reliability.

One additional quality is **face validity** or **content validity,** meaning the test looks, on logical grounds, as if it covers what it purports to cover. A test of arithmetic should look as though it is testing arithmetic skills— for example, by containing problems about this subject and not some other subject. Stipulating this sort of logical connection may seem obvious, but if you stop and think, many of us can remember classroom tests in which face validity was questionable at best. I recall a biology test that seemed to assess my ability to remember and spell difficult terms rather than to understand and use the terms meaningfully. I also remember more than one history test that seemed to assess not my understanding of history but what my classmates variously called "poetry-writing ability," "the gift of gab," and worse.

Another needed quality is **criterion-related validity,** which refers to how well a test predicts a particular type of knowledge or skill (the "criterion") regardless of the precise content of the test. A language test in Spanish, for example, might predict students' performance in French or German (or even English!), even though the grammar and vocabulary of Spanish is only indirectly reflected in the other languages. By definition, criterion-related validity cannot be assessed simply by inspecting the test itself; it has to be observed by comparing performances on the test with performances on the criterion.

Although testing experts used to distinguish sharply between face validity and criterion-related validity, current opinion more often integrates the two into a single, more comprehensive notion of **construct validity,** or how well a test is logically related to its content as well as how well it in fact succeeds at assessing what it is supposed to assess (Messick, 1989, 1994). The more general notion of construct validity corresponds more closely to teachers' actual concerns about classroom tests, such as Mr. Nelson's. In creating and using a classroom test, a teacher is likely to wonder simultaneously whether the questions are appropriate (content validity) and whether they actually reflect students' knowledge of a subject as a whole (criterion-related validity). The teacher may also be concerned with the consequences of the test itself on students' motivation and learning, an issue sometimes called **consequential validity** (Shepard, 1993). Consequential validity becomes an issue, for example, whenever the teacher asks: will the test itself focus students' attention on the subject being studied, or will it simply create stress or focus attention on grading?

Why Reliability and Validity Can Be a Problem

Even though some of the problems we have mentioned may have happened to you and your classmates repeatedly, the basic issues of reliability and validity are not actually inevitable. They are the result of how tests, and therefore assessments, are conventionally organized and conducted in schools. The fact that tests are usually samples rather than whole domains inevitably creates ambiguity about how accurately, and even whether, tests represent the larger educational goals held by teachers: essentially the questions of reliability and validity. Likewise, the fact that testing times are normally distinct from "learning" times creates ambiguity about how closely knowledge displayed during testing reflects knowledge used in more important situations, such as class discussions or everyday tasks. This ambiguity is the problem of **transfer** of learning, which we discussed in Chapter 3, but it is essentially also a question of validity. The ambiguities created by the nature of testing make the connections between conventional classroom testing and learning imperfect: it is often possible to perform well for the wrong reasons and to perform poorly for commendable reasons. Consider what happened to these four high school students who were taking a midterm test in physical science when each encountered the following short-essay question:

Question #4. Explain how you would estimate the height of a skyscraper—or any very tall building—using a barometer. Write no more than one brief paragraph.

The first student, Joe, pondered the question. I assume, he thought, that the teacher is referring to our unit on air pressure. We learned that pressure decreases with higher altitudes. It's just a matter of using the formula that we learned for calculating that relationship, for calculating altitude from air pressure. So he wrote the following:

I would measure the air pressure on the ground floor of the building, and again measure it on the roof of the building. Then find the difference in pressure. Then use the difference to calculate an estimated height, using the formula that you taught us: Height = millibars × 30 feet/millibar.

The second student, Mary, restrained her annoyance with the question. The teacher has forgotten to include all the information again, she grumbled to herself. I suppose you could estimate the height from the difference in air pressure between the ground floor and the top of the building. But that would be a pretty rough estimate—pretty inaccurate! She pondered how to answer the problem in spite of its seeming to be incomplete. Finally, she wrote this:

Get a large ball of kite string, and take with the barometer to the roof of the building. Tie the string to the barometer and lower the barometer over the edge until it touches the ground. Then measure the length of the string; that will be the height of the building.

The third student, Olivia, also thought the problem was ambiguous ("unclear," as she termed it). She didn't really care whether she figured out the answer. In fact, she enjoyed the ambiguity of the problem. There's got to be a way to have a little fun with this question, she thought. She had an inspiration:

Take the barometer to the top of the building, along with a stopwatch. Drop the barometer off the edge and time how long it takes to hit the ground. Don't hit anyone when you do it! Then plug the time that it falls into the formula we learned for the acceleration of gravity: distance = $1/2(9.8$ meters/second^2) $\times$ time^2. That should give the distance from the roof to the ground, more or less.

The fourth student, Dennis, disliked science courses intensely, and especially science tests. These problems are always so artificial, he thought. When will anything like this ever happen in *real* life? He stewed about this briefly, and in the process discovered that he couldn't think of an answer that he thought might be acceptable to his teacher. Since he had to move on to the next question, he finally wrote this:

I would take the barometer into the building, asking to see the building's caretaker. I would show him the barometer and say, "Sir, I'll give you this barometer if you tell me how tall this building is."

But of course Dennis knew his answer would not get credit. So he erased it and dredged his memory further. He really did not understand how barometers work or exactly what they have to do with altitude, but he remembered reading something about it in the text. Still not really knowing what he was talking about, he eventually settled for repeating what he had read:

Compare the barometric pressures at the top and bottom of the building. Use the formula that relates air pressure to altitude.

In reading these examples, your first instinct may be to evaluate the students, to wonder who deserves credit for their answer and who does not. You may also wonder who deserves credit for their thinking and who does not. Note that if you were the students' actual teacher instead

In Your Own Voice

Suppose you actually were the teacher of these students.

To whom among the four would you give credit for their answers?

To whom would you not give credit?

Should you give credit for "creative" answers that you don't expect, or might doing so lead to other problems with the class as a whole?

of a reader of this book, you would have access only to the students' written answers and not to their private thoughts as well. In that case, both Joe and Dennis might get credit, even though Dennis's thinking suggests that he does not understand either the question or his answer. Both Mary and Olivia might fail to get credit for their written replies even though Mary's thinking suggests that she may actually know the right answer and even though both girls make creative use of the science they do know.

Taking all four responses into account allows us to shift perspective from evaluating the individuals to evaluating the validity of the test question itself. The question does seem to have some validity, but the validity is far from perfect. It does look as though it belongs on a science test, and at least one of the students who actually understands the question seems likely to get credit for his answer. But another student (Dennis) may get credit even though he does not understand what he is talking about. Two others (Mary and Olivia) may not get credit, not necessarily because they fail to understand but because they have displayed valid knowledge that happens not to relate to the question. Olivia even sounds as if she might display still other valid knowledge if it were posed to her again just to see if she could think of another innovative solution. In this sense, her response may lack not only validity but reliability as well.

The looseness of fit between test questions and knowledge may not be equally prominent, of course, for all possible questions; I have created these examples to make a point about validity. Furthermore, validity might increase if we consider an entire classroom test as a whole instead of just one item. The ambiguities of the individual items might cancel one another out if they are written well, creating a more reliable and valid classroom test. This is in fact the position of most testing experts (Thorndike, 1997) and the working assumption of most teachers when they do use conventional classroom tests. In a very real sense, however, the problem remains even for tests as a whole: even if reliability and validity improve, they never become perfect. What, therefore, is a teacher to do?

Reliability and Validity with Alternative Assessments

ONE answer, of course, may be to simply live with the problem. Perhaps we accept that classroom tests always have imperfect reliability and validity in order to get on with the business of teaching. But another answer is to modify the three fundamental assumptions of classroom tests—assumptions about sampling, about designating a special testing time and place, and about where learning resides. When this is done, the resulting modifications point to very different forms of classroom assessment, modifications that call into question whether the term *testing* is still appropriate (Moss, 1994):

In Your Own Voice

How do you suppose sampling more of students' work makes assessment more reliable?

Or more valid?

One way to answer these questions is to ask yourself this: If you were a student being assessed, which would seem fairer to you—a larger amount of your work or a smaller amount?

(And why?)

- *Modified Characteristic 1: Make the sample much closer to the size of the domain.* Instead of relying on a relatively small sample of a domain, make the sample much larger—as close as possible, in fact, to being identical to the domain it is supposed to represent. The closer the sample itself is to the domain, the more fully reliable and valid the test is likely to be. As a practical matter, of course, there are only so many questions or tasks that can be put into a typical classroom test; how much, after all, can you really ask during a one-hour midterm or even a two-hour final exam? The first modified characteristic therefore leads to modified characteristic 2: it requires "testing" students over a period of days or weeks, and not just over minutes or hours. In language arts, for example, instead of an essay examination, samples of students' expository writing can be accumulated over a period of weeks. Or instead of being based on a single, final revision, the grade can be based on a series of drafts, each of which is evaluated. When strategies such as these are used, the result is closer to what educators usually call *assessment* rather than *testing* (Eisner, 1994). It is also closer to what Ms. Althouse did in using portfolios to evaluate her students.

In Your Own Voice

Again, suppose you were a student being assessed.

Do you see any problems with broadening the types of knowledge of skill that you display for assessment?

Do you think it could hurt the evaluations of certain students, and if so, would that be fair or not?

- *Modified Characteristic 2: Broaden the types of knowledge displayed.* In addition to "testing" (or, perhaps more accurately, assessing) frequently, validity can be increased by drawing on a broader range of tasks and skills than is possible in a conventional classroom test. If a student's knowledge can be displayed only during an hour-long window of testing time, much of it cannot be displayed at all. He or she will not be able to write a research essay or conduct a full-length experiment in the relatively short duration of a classroom test. But a student can still be tested on larger tasks such as these if what we mean by "being tested" is akin to what educators have been calling *assessment*.

- *Modified Characteristic 3: Consider the social context of learning.* Instead of regarding learning as residing solely within individuals, we can assume that all displays of knowledge reflect group contributions of some kind and that these contributions are often positive and desirable. A teacher's challenge is to identify precisely what classmates, parents, and others have contributed and to decide whether he or she

In Your Own Voice

The suggestion given here is for evaluating a group project.

Can you think of a learning activity in which this approach might *not* work—in which individual evaluations seem necessary by the very nature of the activity?

approves of them. Sometimes the contributions of others may seem obvious, such as when students deliberately produce a group presentation with clearly delineated roles for individuals. But at other times their contributions may be obscure: how much did a student produce an excellent entry to the science fair because of her own efforts, and how much because of strong support from parents? From this perspective, a conventional test is a display not of knowledge but of an individual's contribution to knowledge shared by peers, parents, and teachers. To "test" the individual's contribution therefore requires evaluating the group's contributions as well as the individual's. One way to do so is to create projects or assignments with both common and individual elements (Slavin, 1995). In doing a project about the "ecology of Africa," for example, a group of students might contribute individual pieces (such as short essays) on specific aspects of the ecology. These might be evaluated individually. But they might also create a common essay that ties the individual contributions together, and the essay might be evaluated in common, with each member receiving the same grade for it. In taking this approach, the teacher moves away toward assessment: he or she observes or diagnoses individuals' learning, but also takes into account the context of their learning.

Taken together, these proposals for alleviating the inherent problems of reliability and validity have transformed the meaning of the term *classroom testing,* the activity that created the issues in the first place. Following the modifications listed, testing no longer resembles specific, paper-and-pencil activities on particular class days but something broader and more inclusive, such as the portfolio procedures used by Ms. Althouse. Under the new assumptions, "testing" now encompasses a broad range of tasks over extended periods of time. And it considers the impact of context on learning—the inputs from peers and family.

The modifications reflect the process by which students construct knowledge more fully than do the traditional assumptions of testing given earlier. The construction of knowledge is complex, takes time, and involves more than the student himself or herself. Note, though, that this constructivist perspective on testing and assessment is not free of problems, no matter how much more authentic it may be. Melanie pointed out one problem: blending occasions of testing and learning can make students feel they are eternally being tested and create an unwillingness to take risks. Melanie could end up like the first-grader who supposedly asked his teacher, "Today, teacher, do we *have* to do what we *want* to do?"

Other problems lurk in the wings with constructivist assessment. Peers and parents are now regarded, for example, as co-learners with each student; but as we saw in Ms. Fuller's class in Chapter 6, their new collaborative status creates the danger that they may fail to be good partners in learning. For example, what if a classmate on a cooperative project insists on having his or her own way or, on the other hand, fails to show interest in collaborating at all? Furthermore, a constructivist approach to assessment entitles students to evaluate their own work more than before, just as Melanie did. But what if, as Mr. Nelson and Ms. Sikorsky pointed out, this practice raises questions of bias or expertise?

For classroom teachers, however, perhaps the most immediate problem with alternative assessments is how to use them in a world that so often expects conventional summary grades. For example, how can you "translate" the diverse results of students' portfolios into percentages or traditional letters that are supposed to represent an entire semester or year of work? I have already hinted at strategies for solving this problem; now it is time to look at them more directly.

Getting Along with Grading Systems

THE fact is that even if a teacher does use alternative methods of assessment with students, eventually most have to report on students' performance in terms of conventional summary grades. Adopting the three modified characteristics discussed earlier (larger sampling, broadened types of knowledge and skill, and allowing for context) does not prevent this from happening; school districts almost universally expect grades of some sort, as do parents, other teachers, and many members of society at large.

Because grades are by nature general and ambiguous, however, assigning them can make teachers (and, of course, students) uneasy. When they function well, grades serve a sorting purpose: they tell students, parents, and the community something about students' progress in a subject area, and thus help everyone adjust their expectations and plans accordingly. School counselors and principals sometimes use grades to promote or guide individuals into programs or courses where they seem most likely to succeed. Employers sometimes use grades in evaluating job applicants, though often only if the jobs involved resemble jobs experienced at school.

To accomplish these purposes, grades require making comparisons either of one student with another or of each student with predetermined standards of achievement. The first of these requirements, comparisons among students, is precisely what some alternative forms of assessment try *not* to emphasize, on the grounds that comparisons distract students away from learning and toward competition with one another. Portfolios in particular are often intended to highlight details of individual progress rather than comparisons among students. (Of course, students or others compare one another's work anyway, or even compete to see who produces the "best" portfolio. But that is another matter, a choice that they make rather than one encouraged by the nature of portfolio assessments.)

Using Rubrics to Summarize Alternative Assessments

The second requirement of grading, comparisons with standards, can be handled by the use of **rubrics,** guidelines that serve as scoring criteria. Where appropriate, rubrics sometimes contain potential or hypothetical responses that illustrate different levels of performance along several dimensions of learning. Help in devising reasonable rubrics is widely available from some school districts, most state departments of education, and many government agencies and national professional associations. Rubrics exist in areas as diverse as mathematics (National Council of Teachers of Mathematics, 1996), science (National Research Council, 1996), elementary language arts (Swearingen & Allen, 1995), and teaching students with special needs (Kentucky Systems Change Project, undated).

Table 11.1 shows a scoring rubric for two dimensions of a writing portfolio, and Table 11.2 shows one for scoring problem-solving sets in mathematics. In either case, a teacher evaluates a student's responses by comparing them to the guidelines provided in the rubric. Hopefully, this technique lends at least moderate reliability and validity to the teacher's judgments, though how much it lends will depend on the care the teacher takes in judging students' work and on the depth of the teacher's understanding of the skills or knowledge being evaluated (Airasian, 1996). Adding together the resulting scores gives a final summary score for the portfolio that reflects the quality of the student's work relative to the standards used.

Note that the final score may form part of a student's final grade for a course or only part of it, depending on the importance or weighting attached to it. In using rubrics to evaluate portfolios, it is perfectly possi-

In Your Own Voice

Since, as I explain next, rubrics do not ultimately spare you from dealing with issues about the fairness of grades, do you think rubrics are worth using anyway?

Would you be worse or better off without them?

Why?

TABLE 11.1   Scoring Rubric for a Writing Portfolio

Dimension 1: Diversity in Types of Writing		
Score	Name of Level	Description of Performance
4	Outstanding diversity	Good-quality example of all of the following: critical essays, poems, short stories, news articles
3	Good diversity	Good-quality examples of 3 of the 4 types of writing, *or* all 4 types present but only 3 of good quality
2	Satisfactory diversity	Good-quality examples of 2 of the 4 types of writing, *or* all 4 types present but only 2 of good quality
1	Insufficient diversity	Good-quality examples of 1 of the 4 types of writing, *or* all 4 types present but only 1 of good quality
0	Lacking diversity	No good-quality examples of any type of writing, *or* certain types not attempted

Dimension 2: Quality of Writing		
Score	Name of Level	Description of Performance
4	Outstanding quality	Written piece has all of the following: strong voice; sophisticated ideas; stays on topic; is well organized; paragraphs with specific details; few errors of spelling, punctuation, or usage
3	Good quality	Written piece has 5 of the 6 qualities listed above
2	Satisfactory quality	Written piece has 4 of the 6 qualities listed above
1	Fair quality	Written piece has 3 of the 6 qualities listed above
0	Poor quality	Written piece has 2 of the 6 qualities listed above

ble to combine the results with other, more conventional forms of assessment, such as tests or term papers, as long as the results of all activities are converted to a common scale of ratings. Table 11.3 illustrates how this might be done for a science course. Any letter grades on papers (or, in this case, lab reports) are converted to equivalent numerical values using a formula like the one shown beneath the table. When all

TABLE 11.2   Scoring Rubric for Problem-Solving Sets in Mathematics

Score	Description of Performance
5	Answers on problem set mostly (90%) accurate, labeled if appropriate, and work is shown
4	Answer is close but incorrect because of minor computational error or miscopying
3	Answer is incorrect, but the solution is generally on track; specific aspect of problem was misunderstood
2	Answer is incorrect, but written solution shows some understanding of problem
1	Answer is incorrect, but written solution shows evidence of thinking beyond simply copying the given information
0	No evidence of understanding beyond simply copying the given information

grades are shown in numerical form, the results are then multiplied by a fraction or percentage that represents their comparative importance in the course as a whole. The converted scores can then be combined because they now reflect performance on a single scale of value.

TABLE 11.3   Combining Rubrics with Other Final Scores: An Example from a Course in General Science

Assignment	Actual Numerical Score	% Weighting	Weighted Score
Problem set 1	80	10%	8
Problem set 2	90	10%	9
Midterm test	75	20%	15
Portfolio (Lab research project)	80	60%	48

Total score for course: 80 (out of 100 possible weighted points)

Note: If letter grades are used for individual assignments, they must first be converted to numerical form by a formula such as this: A = 4.0, B+ = 3.5, B = 3.0, C+ = 2.5, C = 2.0, D = 1.0, F = 0

The Meaning and Ethics of Grades

Using rubrics and weightings to calculate final scores lends some order to evaluating students, but it does not determine what grade to finally give a student. Still unanswered are questions such as these:

In Your Own Voice

Was your grade from a teacher or course ever higher because of "improvement" such as described here?

Did you ever suspect your grade was held back because of a *lack* of improvement?

How did you feel about each of these events?

- *Should you take improvement into account in determining a final grade?* If one student's performance improves over a semester or school year, should the student receive a higher grade than another student whose performance remains constant during the same period, or if it even decreases? Is it fair to grade on effort, to distinguish between these two students? Should you have told the students about this possibility before you began teaching them?

- *Should you take effort into account in determining the final grade?* Regardless of whether their scores have changed over the semester or school year, some students may seem to have tried harder than others. Should two students with the same final score get the same final grade if one seemed to try harder than the other? How can you be sure that a student really has "tried hard" rather than merely tried to please or flatter the teacher? If you do distinguish between the two students, should you have told all students that you would be grading partly on effort as judged by yourself?

- *Should the mix of activities affect the final grade?* Suppose one student's final score is high because she produced numerous book reports that are good, but short and oral, whereas another student's final score is equally high because he produced one or two good written term papers. Should they receive the same grade, or should one receive a higher grade than the other? Is it fair to distinguish between the two students for this reason? Theoretically, the weightings you assigned to the two activities (as in Tables 11.1 and 11.2) should reflect their comparative importance. Since final scores are by definition summaries of numerous learning activities, though, the scores may leave out distinctions among activities that are subtle but significant, and about which the students may have been unaware.

- *In years to come, will people understand the basis of the final grade?* It is well and good—and perhaps even preferable—to base a final grade on an unusual mix of innovative activities. You can explain the basis of the grading to the students themselves, and perhaps also to the students' parents and to current administrators and other teachers. But what explanation will remain in a few years' time when you, the student, and your original colleagues may have moved to other schools and may not be easily available anymore? Will the final grade still have the same meaning for these later "generations" of educators and students? Perhaps they will wrongly assume, for example, that the grade was based on "classic" forms of testing and other assignments, and that no portfolio work occurred. Would it be fair to the students if later generations interpret the final grade differently than you intended? On the other hand, would it be fair to your current students to give up a desirable teaching practice (such as portfolios) because of this danger?

Dilemmas at the Heart of Assessment

*A*T the heart of every approach to assessment and the grading practices that come out of them lie questions about how students learn. Does each student construct a different understanding of the curriculum? Indeed, *should* every student construct a different understanding, using active help from teachers? These crucial questions lead to others that plague assessments closer to the surface. If every student acquires something different from the curriculum, how can a teacher make comparisons among students? But then again, *should* a teacher be concerned with making comparisons, even if parents or others demand them?

In this chapter, I have attempted to answer these questions in a particular way, both explicitly and implicitly. I have proceeded on the belief not only that students routinely do construct different understandings but also that as both an ethical and a practical matter, they should be encouraged to do so. This perspective has solved one perennial problem of assessments but created another. It has solved the problem of the shallow and arbitrary quality of some comparative evaluations of students. It has also highlighted diversity among students—so much so, in fact, that direct comparisons of students become more difficult. However, this perspective has created the problem of how to communicate the true nature and extent of each student's learning to parents, educators, and students themselves. We have looked at some ways to resolve the trade-off: ways to preserve the intrinsic validity or meaningfulness of alternative assessments (such as portfolios) while also communicating their meaningfulness successfully.

As it happens, we will see a related dilemma or trade-off in the next chapter, where we come to terms with understanding, interpreting, and using published research about education and teaching. There the problem has to do with comparability of research studies and findings: it is certainly valuable to be able to compare one research study with another, but perhaps not if comparisons mean that research findings are neither meaningful nor useful to teachers. That chapter will also offer compromises to resolve apparent dilemmas between meaningfulness and comparability. You will have to be judge—as (hopefully) you have been in this chapter—about whether the particular compromises are good ones. But you will not be able to avoid making compromises of some sort.

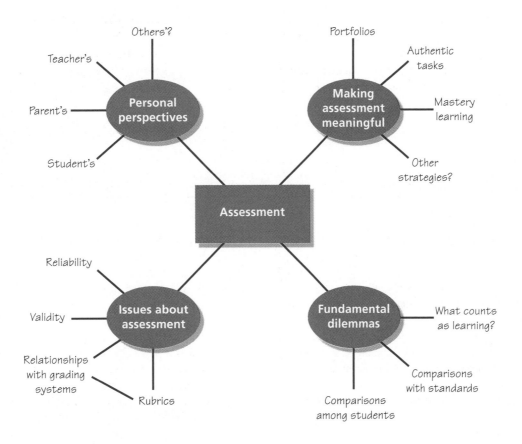

Chapter Re-View: Assessing Students' Learning This Chapter Re-View suggests directions in which the chapter might have taken your thinking—though, of course, other directions are also possible. It expands the Chapter View, which suggests a starting point, conceptually, for the chapter. But this Re-View does not suggest an ending point. Like the Chapter View, it represents just one perspective among many.

Key Terms and Concepts

assessment (367)
evaluation (368)
authentic assessment (380)
portfolio assessment (380)
performance assessment (380)
mastery learning (381)
validity (393)

construct validity (394)
consequential validity (394)
face validity (394)
content validity (394)
criterion-related validity (394)
reliability (392)
test-retest reliability (393)

equivalent forms reliability (393)
split-half reliability (393)
transfer (395)
rubric (401)

Annotated Readings

Thorndike, Robert. (1997). *Measurement and evaluation in psychology and education* (6th ed.). Columbus, OH: Merrill. This is one of many texts explaining issues about measurement, evaluation, and assessment from a relatively "classical" viewpoint. If you are wondering about the nature and issues of reliability and validity, for example, this book gives a good account of them, and indirectly helps in understanding the alternative views in the books listed below.

Baron, J., & Wolf, D. (Eds.). (1996). *Performance-based student assessment: Challenges and possibilities: 95th yearbook of the National Society for the Study of Education.* Chicago: University of Chicago Press. This volume provides authoritative reviews of alternative assessment methods, written from a number of points of view. Each chapter is written by a different expert in assessment; some are rather critical of alternative assessments, although most tend to be at least cautiously supportive. The book offers a good balance and range of views.

Darling-Hammond, L., Ancess, J., & Falk, B. (1995). *Authentic assessment in action: Studies of schools and students at work.* New York: Teachers College Press. These authors describe, and advocate for, the use of authentic assessment in schools. Most of the book is a series of case studies of how this style of assessment was implemented in several specific schools, along with commentary about why authentic assessments worked in each case. If these kinds of assessments appeal to you, this book makes for good reading.

Internet Resources

<www.nagb.org> This is the web site for the National Assessment of Educational Progress (NAEP), a nonprofit agency sponsored by a consortium of government agencies and private foundations. The NAEP is dedicated to developing effective standards and methods for assessing students' learning in a variety of areas of school learning. The web site contains its recommendations for several academic subjects

(e.g., math, science, reading). The recommendations include a lot of paper-and-pencil testing, but also some innovations on these classic procedures. <www.ericae.net> This web site is sponsored by the Clearinghouse for Assessment and Evaluation, one of the ERIC Clearinghouses. It contains numerous articles about testing, evaluation, and assessment from a wide range of perspectives, including "authentic" assessments and portfolios. Information is organized by subject area and grade level of students; included are several short articles about assessment in early childhood education, adult education, and the teaching of English as a second language.

CHAPTER VIEW

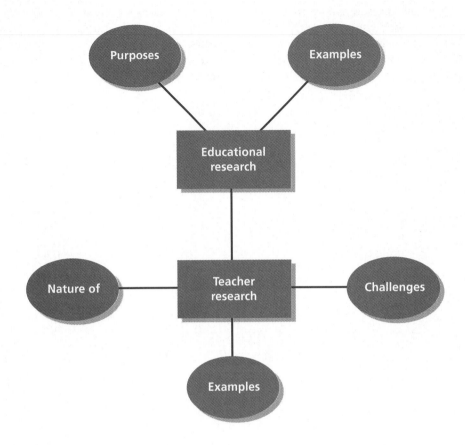

Chapter View: Hearing Distant Voices This Chapter View is a concept map that indicates one among many ways of thinking about the chapter. It suggests a starting point, conceptually, for the chapter but is incomplete by itself. At the end of the chapter is a Chapter Re-View, which expands on the Chapter View, suggesting directions for taking your thinking further—though, of course, other directions are also possible.

12

Hearing Distant Voices: Interpreting Educational Research

Imagine you are having a dinner party, the purpose of which is to offer you advice and support for your teaching and to answer questions specific to teaching and learning that may be nagging you. You can invite anyone you like, from anywhere on earth and from any time in human history, without regard for practical difficulties and without worrying about whether other people would consider your guests "appropriate." Whom would you invite?

Once you start thinking about it, the possibilities are endless. Of course, you could invite an experienced teacher whom you admired as a child or whom you currently admire; this person would likely have important wisdom to share. But you may have other, less obvious choices as well. Maybe there is a trusted relative whose opinion you would value about an activity as important as teaching (for me it was my grandmother, unfortunately long since deceased). Or maybe there is an author or two who you suspect would understand your world and the challenges you face. Or perhaps a renowned leader of a political or social movement or a religious leader you have known or would like to have known. Never mind whether all your guests speak the same language; we will assume they have all learned English just to attend your dinner

In Your Own Voice

If *you* designed your dinner, of course, you might prefer a different mix of people than the one suggested here.

Who would be in your particular group, and why?

party! We will assume, furthermore, that this evening they are all happy to attend to your wish: to discuss general issues and specific problems related to your teaching.

Once your dinner party is assembled, three things could happen. First, and most generally, the guests might comment helpfully on why teaching is a good choice of profession for you given *your* particular circumstances. Initially they might make only general comments about the value of teaching in society and on the nature of teaching and learning as they see it. But you could guide your guests to focus their comments on you: you could tell them of real, personal experiences that shaped your views of teaching and learning, or that motivated you to enter this field. The resulting interplay of ideas would help you develop a way of thinking about teaching. It would "frame" your own ideas about education, give you a perspective for interpreting your ideas and for understanding your place in the educational world.

Second, your guests might offer specific advice about appropriate teaching practices. Maybe you would talk about how you might handle a certain classroom disruption that you recall from your own schooling or that one of your guests recalls from his or her experience. Or you might talk about a challenging curriculum task, such as how to "get through" to certain students about the meaning of a difficult concept in science. The advice might come up in the course of more general advice and reflection, such as that just mentioned, but it would have a more practical flavor: here is how I would do this; how would you do it?

Third, you might sometimes find your guests persuading you of the importance of certain actions related to teaching. "You have got to know your students personally," one might say; or "You have got to get your parents comfortable with talking with you and visiting their children's classroom"; or "It is important for you to include *all* students in your class, even the ones with special needs." The immediate focus in these comments would not be on *how* to do these things (that too might happen, but at other points in the dinner party). The focus would be on the *rightness* or *desirability* of the actions and on getting you or others to agree about their rightness. As with your guests' specific advice, their persuasive comments would likely be interspersed with their general advice and perspective taking. If your dinner is a long, leisurely one, there will be time for it all: time for framing, offering practical advice, and persuading.

Three Purposes of Educational Research

*W*HOEVER your particular dinner guests would be, the resulting conversation would share purposes intended by **educational research,** or the systematic study of educational problems. First, both the dinner and educational research *provide a framework for thinking about teaching and learning* (Hittleman & Simon, 1997; Hubbard & Power, 1993). A "framework" in this context means a perspective or general viewpoint for understanding specific events and actions—including, in this case, the events and actions related to teaching and learning. Second, both the dinner and educational research *offer advice to be applied to appropriate teaching practices:* How might I initiate reading instruction to first-graders? What could I do on the first day? What if I were initiating reading instead with a fourth-grader who's been having learning difficulties? Or what if I were teaching a course in literacy to adult learners? Educational research exists that has tried to answer these questions and others with a similarly practical slant. Third, both the dinner and educational research *advocate ideas and persuade others* to take actions benefiting students and society. Is it a good or a bad idea to retain (or hold back) a student in grade level for another year if the student fails the curriculum the first time? Some educational research makes recommendations about this sort of a question, in this case retention in grade. But since the recommendations may not coincide with all teachers' initial beliefs, the authors of the research may make an effort not just to present their findings but to persuade their readers or audience of the merits of their recommendations. Note that opening yourself to people whom you respect does not mean giving up thinking for yourself about education. At our imaginary dinner party, you are seeking others' opinions precisely to develop and clarify your own views and distinguish them from others'.

At its best and when properly understood, educational research creates an analogous relationship between others' ideas and your own. It provides general perspectives about teaching and learning, recommends appropriate teaching practices, and persuades educators and members of the public that certain educational practices are desirable. Yet doing so does *not* mean you cannot or should not think about these matters for yourself. On the contrary—and like your dinner party—educational research is meant to stimulate your own knowledge and beliefs: it should create rather than undermine your individuality as a teacher. Authors of research articles are like the guests at the dinner party: each has poten-

In Your Own Voice

If you could immediately, today, get access to any educational research at all, what topic or problem would you want it to tackle?

Would it be about classroom management, as suggested here, or about some other topic?

tial contributions to make, but none has final answers. Not all of the guests' contributions will be equally helpful; some comments may be true and useful, but not for you at this time. If you are just now starting as a teacher, for example, you may be especially interested in anything said about classroom management but less interested in the problems of administering schools or of the political issues that always accompany the educational enterprise. Your dinner guests may talk about both sorts of issues anyway, and your job will be to sort out their more useful comments from their less immediately useful ones.

To experience educational research in this way, however, you must read the authors of research literature as if they were collaborators as well as authorities. You must think of their printed comments as part of a dialogue about teaching and learning that may include you if you choose to participate in it. There are several strategies for adopting this attitude—more, in fact, than we have space to discuss. To keep the discussion short enough for one chapter, we will focus on just two strategies for hearing the voices of educational research. One strategy is to understand the **purposes** of any particular piece of research that you encounter in order to assess its current usefulness to your daily work and your long-term professional goals. The other strategy is to begin thinking about whether—and how—you, as a teacher, can contribute to the purposes of educational research by creating your own *teacher research*.

Why Was This Research Published?

*M*ost published studies on teaching do not address every purpose of educational research equally. Instead they emphasize only one of the major purposes: either providing a framework, specifying teaching practices, or advocating educational ideas (Floden & Buchmann, 1990). The emphasis of a particular publication affects its style, content, and significance in ways that are both obvious and subtle. The effects in turn influence how a reader, including yourself, should interpret or understand the research. Let's look briefly at the differences in style, content, and significance, and then at their impact on you as a developing, reflective teacher interested in gathering information and ideas about teaching. In the next section, we'll consider several examples of educational research, each chosen because it emphasizes a different mix of purposes and therefore calls for different interpretations and responses from readers.

First, the major purpose of a research article affects how completely the research tries to create *universal truths as opposed to truths that are local or dependent on circumstances.* If the purpose is to give you a perspective on how students learn *in general,* for example, the research may gloss over or tend to ignore obvious differences in how students learn in the interest of being relevant to as many learning situations as possible. In reading this sort of research, your job is to make allowances (mentally) for this fact given what you already know from experience, reflection, and other reading about students' learning. You must ask yourself whether the circumstances of your students and classroom dilute the relevance of a general "perspective" piece of research. This will be challenging if you lack experience and are too new at teaching to have done much reading of research—though you should always be able to reflect on the conclusions contained in a research piece. In fact, because of the challenges of evaluating the adequacy of general claims about teaching and learning, you may initially prefer to read research that focuses more directly on classroom teaching practices. This choice may be fine, but it may also limit how quickly or completely you can develop a perspective of your own; the "framing" perspectives contained in some research studies can help you to do so.

In any case, the second difference that the purpose of the research makes is by influencing the **response that an author expects** from you, the reader: does he or she expect you to actually do something new or simply to consider doing something new? Or even just to be aware of a new idea? Advocacy research, for example, may deliberately sound as though it expects action. If it is about the benefits and problems of including students with special needs in regular classes, for example, you may take a moral position: you should include these students, it may seem to say. A teaching practice article, on the other hand, may merely ask you to consider alternatives to your normal ways of teaching: certain strategies worked here (in the research you just read about), it says, so think about whether they might work for you as well.

Less obviously, any piece of published research will make unstated **assumptions about prior experiences and attitudes** of its readers. A framework piece may assume, for example, that you are already familiar with theories of learning, although if it truly is educational research, it may primarily assume familiarity with everyday classroom applications of the theories. Therefore, an education-oriented study to assess the behaviorist concept of reinforcement may be relatively accessible to you even if you never made a career of studying the theoretical details of behaviorist theory. (Behaviorism was one of the theories discussed in Chapter

In Your Own Voice

As you read this book, what experiences and beliefs does it seem that I, Kelvin Seifert, am expecting from you, the reader?

(And are they reasonable?)

2.) It might seem more accessible than you expect because, for example, it uses teachers' praise of students' learning, a notion with which you do have some experience, as the chief reinforcement observed in the research.

Similarly, research that focuses on specific teaching practices or on moral advocacy makes assumptions about your experiences and attitudes. A teaching practices piece may assume that you have taught a class in the past, or at least that you are familiar enough with classroom life to understand discussions of teaching practices. The idea of "withitness" (discussed in Chapter 6), for example, originated from observations of teachers managing large-group classroom activities; but even if you have not yet begun your teaching career, it is possible to understand the idea and its potential value when you eventually do teach. An advocacy piece of research, on the other hand, may assume you do in fact enjoy persuading others of your point of view, even when others initially disagree or react indifferently. The assumptions may show up as much in what the writing omits as in what it explains: if the term *cooperative learning activity* is used without explanation, for example, the researcher may be assuming you are the sort of person—perhaps a teacher—who already knows what that term means and therefore believe in the value of cooperative learning.

Having made these distinctions, I must qualify them by saying that an individual research study or publication rarely serves *only* one purpose at a time; it merely emphasizes one purpose more than others. A study that offers a theoretical framework may also use its framework to suggest specific teaching practices or to advocate new ways to organize education to benefit students. And vice versa: a study that describes new, effective teaching practices may as a result suggest, or at least imply, a new way to understand students' learning in general or new actions that educators in general should take. In these ways, research studies are like the guests at the dinner party discussed at the beginning of the chapter: although each person may contribute primarily to one area of your thinking, each is likely to have useful things to say about other areas as well.

Let me illustrate these ideas about the purposes and effects of research by describing and commenting on several examples of actual research studies relevant to education—studies that I found meaningful in some way. The studies are not a full cross-section of educational research, but they do convey a sense of the variety possible (and necessary) among research studies. Each serves a mixture of purposes, but with an emphasis on one of the particular purposes (perspective taking, teaching recommendations, or advocacy) described earlier. The differences in purpose reflect the assumptions the authors of the studies make about their readers and about the mental work the authors hope readers do and the motivations they hope readers will acquire.

Example: How Do Children Acquire Moral Commitments?

In 1997, Herbert Saltzstein and several colleagues published an article about how children acquire moral beliefs (Saltzstein et al., 1997). The researchers were all graduate students and professors of psychology, mostly at the City University of New York. Their affiliation in psychology affected my expectations: I suspected they would talk about moral beliefs in general and take relatively little responsibility for relating their observations to moral issues (e.g., cheating) that often arise in classrooms. Still, the article interested me because as a teacher, I had felt a long-standing concern with fostering characteristics such as integrity, honesty, cooperation, and loyalty in my students. It also interested me as an educational researcher because moral development was a topic that potentially could "test" the adequacy of major theories of learning. I reasoned that if I could find out about the mechanism or process by which children acquire mature moral beliefs, maybe I could modify my teaching to take advantage of that knowledge.

So I began reading the article. I discovered some parts were challenging and required careful reflection, whereas others were easier to read. One of the most challenging passages came almost immediately, in the second and third paragraphs; in fact, they required prior knowledge (though not a lot of it) about research on moral development. I was glad I concentrated on these paragraphs, though, because they clarified the rest of the study. Here are (on the left) what I read and (on the right) my thoughts as I read it:

In Your Own Voice

Suppose you were reading the Saltzstein article on your own, without my accompanying remarks.

Where else could you get help in understanding its purpose and perspective?

Initial Problem

We began by re-examining the phenomenon of heteronomy, Piaget's assertion (1932/1965) following Kant (1785/1959) that young children equate moral obligation with deference to authority when justifying their moral judgments. The concept is important because it is central to the organismic account of moral development as a series of differentiations and integrations. . . . [p. 37]

This was one of the difficult paragraphs, perhaps especially because I have never read the specific book by Piaget referred to, nor the one by the philosopher Kant. But I did recall reading, at various times over the years, about Piaget's views on moral development. He believed that at first, children define morality in terms of what adults think: an action is "good" if and only if adults (e.g., parents) consider it good, and "bad" if and only if adults consider it bad. This is the idea of "heteronomy" to which Saltzstein refers (and, incidentally, it is also an idea borrowed and studied by other psychologists, such as Lawrence Kohlberg, described in Chapter 13). In this view, children take an extended time to develop or "grow into" truly autonomous moral beliefs; these beliefs form slowly out of earlier beliefs in the same way a living plant or other organism grows. This is the "organismic account of moral development" to which Saltzstein refers.

. . . This account has been challenged by Turiel's domain theory (Turiel, 1983). According to Turiel and his colleagues, even young children intuitively distinguish moral from conventional rules. [p. 37]

Here was an idea that intrigued me! Saltzstein and his colleagues were pointing to research (by the person cited, named Turiel) suggesting that even preschoolers know the difference between truly moral rules and merely conventional rules. Apparently they believe, for example, that it would be wrong to steal toys or to hit someone, even if adults gave you permission to do so. But they also know it would be all right for traffic lights to use different colors—for red to mean "go," for example, and green to mean "stop," provided everyone knew about and agreed on changing the rule. That is what the researcher named Turiel concluded from the studies that Saltzstein cites here.

The introduction continued in this fashion for about two pages, requiring me to read slowly and carefully in order to understand its points. I was not discouraged from continuing, though, because I wanted to find out more about how, in general, children acquire moral beliefs. Do moral beliefs take time to develop—do they "grow" on children slowly after initially being borrowed from parents or other adults? If so, then maybe I owed it to my students to adopt and express desirable moral attitudes myself so as to provide them with a good model for their developing beliefs. Or were students' crucial moral beliefs already in place when they entered school, almost as if "hard-wired" in their minds or as if learned quickly during infancy and the preschool years? In that case, it might still be desirable for me to adopt positive moral attitudes, but not primarily to model them for my students to learn. Since students already would understand essential moral beliefs, they might need something else from me, such as firm enforcement of desirable moral behaviors. Take cheating: the students might already understand the nature and undesirable implications of this behavior. As a result, they might not need demonstrations of honesty and integrity from me so much as affirmations from me of the importance of honesty and integrity, along with consistent enforcement of appropriate sanctions against cheating when it did occur.

For me, therefore, the outcomes of research on moral development—including Saltzstein's, which I was currently reading—posed issues of classroom management, and the issues were related both to my university classrooms and to the public school classrooms in which I assisted teachers. So I read on. Saltzstein proposed resolving the issues about the origins of moral development by distinguishing between *moral conflicts* and *moral dilemmas*:

In Your Own Voice

If you already believe one of these alternative ideas about handling students' cheating, it may be tempting to read Saltzstein to confirm your belief.

But what if the article *doesn't* confirm it?

Should you simply change your mind, or dismiss the article, or what?

Moral conflicts are conflicts between moral duty or right and a nonmoral desire. An example might be the conflict between whether to return a wallet to its rightful owner or keep the coveted wallet with its extra cash. In contrast, moral dilemmas are conflicts involving two moral rights or duties. For example, [a person might feel a dilemma between] whether to steal a drug to save a spouse's life. [p. 38]

The distinction looked promising to me. Moral conflicts looked fairly simple in cognitive terms, even if they were sometimes difficult emotionally. The "right" action was obvious. Moral dilemmas were more complex cognitively as well as emotionally, because two "goods" were being weighed against each other. The moral alternatives might both be right and wrong at the same time, and their relative "rightness" might not be immediately obvious.

Saltzstein and his colleagues proposed that when young children show awareness of moral rules, they may be doing so in the simpler context of moral conflicts. A young child might believe that you should return a dollar to its owner even if the child has trouble in practice overcoming a selfish impulse to keep the dollar. The same child might have trouble deciding, however, whether it is "right" to inform his teacher if a best friend has cheated on a test. In that case, two moral principles compete for attention: honesty and loyalty to a friend. To sort out the implications of choosing between these principles, a young child might need to rely on older, wiser minds, such as parents or other adults. And the minute he or she does so, the child is showing the moral heteronomy to which Saltzstein referred early in the article.

Understanding these ideas took effort on my part, but once I had begun figuring them out, the rest of the article became much easier to follow. In reading the pages that followed, I noted in passing that the researchers used several techniques common in psychological and educational research. For example, they **interviewed** participants, a common way of gathering systematic information about individuals' thinking. They also imposed **controls** on their procedures and on the selection of participants. Procedures were controlled, for example, by posing the same three moral dilemmas to all participants so that individuals' responses could be compared meaningfully. The selection of participants was controlled by selecting two age groups for deliberate comparison with each other, one composed of seven-year-olds and the other of eleven-year-olds. Since the researchers wanted to generalize about moral development as much as possible, but obviously could not interview

In Your Own Voice

I describe Saltzstein's choices of research methods as if they are "persuasion devices."

Is that fair?

Do you think there is more to them than that?

every child in the world, they also **sampled** participants: they selected a manageable number (sixty-five, to be exact) from the larger student population of one particular school. In the second part of the investigation, they also selected a comparable number of children of the same two ages (seven and eleven) from the city of Recife, located in Brazil. The Brazilian group's responses were compared deliberately with the American group's to allow for the impact of cultural beliefs on moral development in general. I recognized this research strategy as an example of using **control groups.** In research terms, the Brazilian group "controlled for" the impact of American culture on children's moral beliefs. And vice versa: the American group "controlled for" the impact of Brazilian culture on children's moral beliefs. Altogether, these techniques helped to ensure that the interviews about children's moral beliefs really illustrated what they were supposed to illustrate—that they were *reliable* and *valid* in the senses discussed in Chapter 11. As I noticed Saltzstein's attention to good research techniques, I gained confidence in his observations and in the interpretations he and his colleagues made from them.

What did Saltzstein and his colleagues find out—or, perhaps more to the point, what did I, Kelvin Seifert, infer from what Saltzstein and his colleagues wrote about? Here are three ideas that I gained. One was that in everyday life, children probably deal with moral beliefs of all levels of cognitive complexity, and not just "simple" moral conflicts and "complex" moral dilemmas. Saltzstein found that children's solutions to moral dilemmas depended a lot on the content of the dilemma. Children advocated strongly for truthfulness in some situations (for example, in deciding whether to tell the teacher about a friend's cheating) but not in other situations (such as in deciding whether to back up a friend who is being teased and has lied in an effort to stop the teasing). But rarely did all children support any one moral principle completely; they usually supported a mix.

Another idea that I gained from Saltzstein's research was about *how* children expressed moral heteronomy versus moral autonomy. Age, it seemed, did not affect the beliefs children stated; younger and older children, that is, took similar positions on all dilemmas initially. But age *did* affect how steadfastly children held to initial beliefs. Younger children were more easily influenced to switch opinions when an adult "cross-examined" them by asking probing questions; older children were more likely to keep to their initial positions. Moral heteronomy was revealed not by a child's views as such but by the kind of dialogue the child had with adults.

In Your Own Voice

Do you find it reasonable or not reasonable that eleven-year-olds might think adults have beliefs similar to those of seven-year-olds?

Before you read the following passages, can you think of a reason why they might do so?

A third idea that I gained concerned children's perceptions of *adults'* moral beliefs. Saltzstein found that even though older children (the eleven-year-olds) showed more moral autonomy (were more steadfast) than younger children, they tended to believe that adults thought about moral issues in the same way younger children did. In the "teasing" dilemma mentioned earlier, for example, the eleven-year-olds opted much more often than the seven-year-olds for remaining loyal to a friend, even though doing so meant further untruthfulness with peers. Yet the eleven-year-olds also more often stated a belief that adults would resolve the same dilemma in a way characteristic of seven-year-olds— that is, by telling the truth to peers and thus betraying loyalty to a friend. This finding puzzled me. Why should older, and presumably more insightful, children think adults are more like younger children than like themselves? Saltzstein suggested an interpretation, however, that helped me make sense of the apparent inconsistency:

. . . Consistent with our past research, children attributed the kinds of moral choices made by younger children to adults. In our view, this finding tends to support a constructivist rather than than a [social modeling] view of morality, which would predict that the child's judgments mirror (or develop toward) their representation of adult judgments. [p. 41]

In other words, if children learned moral beliefs by imitating (or modeling themselves after) parents or other adults, they ought to see themselves as resembling adults more and more as they get older. Instead, they see themselves as resembling adults *less*, at least for the middle part of childhood. This would happen only if they were preoccupied with "constructing" their own beliefs on the basis of their experiences and therefore failed to notice that they are gradually arriving at beliefs increasingly similar to adults'.

In Your Own Voice

What do you think would happen if Saltzstein and his colleagues assumed *no* prior knowledge about psychological theory?

Do you think they would "pay a price" for this approach as well, although perhaps a different price?

Relevance: A Truly Universal Framework?

The research by Saltzstein offers a way to understand how children develop moral beliefs, and especially to understand the change from moral heteronomy to moral autonomy. By imposing controls on the procedures (uniform interviews) and on the selection of participants (particular ages, particular societies or cultures), the researchers eliminated certain sources of ambiguity or variability in children's responses. Furthermore, by framing their project in terms of previous general research and theory about moral development, they made it easier to interpret their new results in the general terms of these theories as well. In these ways, the investigation aspires to provide universal truths about children's moral development, and it is to this extent a good example of "framework" research in the sense described earlier in this chapter.

But note that the authors pay a price for orienting the research in this way. By framing their work around existing general theory and research, they must assume readers already have some knowledge of that theory and research. This is not an unreasonable assumption if the audience is expected to be fellow researchers; after all, many of them are paid to "know the literature" of psychology. It is quite possible, in fact, that Saltzstein and his colleagues may have had such an audience in mind when they published their article. But knowledge of theory can also be an obstacle if the authors' purpose is to communicate with nonpsychologists: in that case, either the authors must make more of an effort to explain the relevant background research or readers must educate themselves about the research. The latter activity is not necessarily difficult (the background knowledge for Saltzstein's work, for example, took me only a few paragraphs to explain in writing), but it must be done to make full sense of research that tries to provide a universal framework of psychological knowledge.

Note, too, that Saltzstein and his colleagues did not really claim their conclusions were truly *universal*, only that they were *general*. One sign of the difference is the fact that they interviewed children from two distinct societies, Brazil and the United States. By doing so they implied that one society could not, in principle, provide truly universal information about moral development; there would always be something about the beliefs of "merely" American (or Brazilian) children that was unique only to the children's home society. Providing information from two societies, however, also failed to establish knowledge about moral development that is truly universal. Studying both Brazilian and American children gives us a more general idea about children's moral thinking, but there is still the possibility (in fact, a likelihood) that other, even more exotic societies might produce results different from these first two. At best, then, Saltzstein's work offers general ideas about how children develop moral beliefs. It cannot claim to offer fully universal truths about it.

The Reader's Role: Interested Observer of Children

In conducting and reporting their research, Saltzstein and his colleagues were not acting as schoolteachers, nor were they expecting readers necessarily to respond as teachers. As they put it in the first paragraph of their article, their purpose was to offer "a more contextualized perspective for understanding the development of moral judgments" [p. 37]. They seem *not* to be intent, as teachers often might be, on recommending how children's moral judgments ought to be fostered. Observation of children is their purpose, not intervention. The meaning of the term "contextualized perspective" isn't obvious when they first use it, but soon becomes more clear: they are talking about the importance of taking cultural influences into account in explaining how children acquire moral beliefs. They do note information relevant to teaching; for example, they point out that for cultural reasons, teachers in Brazil do not command high respect and therefore, compared to American children, Brazilian children may feel less compelled to tell the truth to their teachers. But this educational fact is not the primary focus of their research, nor do they discuss what (if anything) ought to be done about it.

Yet the nonteaching perspective of the article did not keep me, a former schoolteacher and current university teacher, from responding to the article in terms of educational concerns. As I mentioned already, I was attracted to the research because of my own concerns about character development in my students: how do they acquire moral beliefs and commitments, and how should I help them in doing so? I did not expect to find an answer to the second question given the "observation" orientation of the authors. I did expect to find an answer to the first, although even here I also expected I would have make allowances for the fact that the research interviews were not identical to classroom situations. Children might respond differently when interviewed individually by a researcher than when responding to a teacher in class—or perhaps not. So I had to be careful to note the context and purposes of Saltzstein's study, and to remind myself that once I went beyond simply observing children to intervening with them, I might have to draw my own conclusions. But in spite of these cautions, or maybe because of them, I found much of value to my teaching in the article.

Example: The Impact of Bilingualism on Reading

In 1995, three education professors—Robert Jiménez, Georgia García, and David Pearson—published a study that explored the impact of bilin-

gualism on children's ability to read English. The three specialized in curriculum studies, literacy acquisition, and bilingual language development, and therefore were motivated by a concern for the academic success of bilingual children—or, more precisely, by a concern for identifying why some bilingual children have difficulty learning to read English. Too much research on bilingualism, they argued, was based on what they called a "deficit" framework: it identified qualities that bilingual children lacked and that prevented them from learning. They sought an alternative framework, one focused on bilingual students' competence, and especially on their competence to read a second language.

To search for this alternative framework, the researchers mounted a large research program that consisted of several related research studies. The article published in 1995 was just one of the studies. It caught my interest not only because of its topic but because of its approach. Instead of interviewing or observing several dozen students, as Saltzstein had done to study moral development, these investigators relied on a few selected case studies. Each **case study** consisted of detailed and somewhat lengthy observations and interviews with just *one* student! Unlike Saltzstein, these authors were not seeking to study a representative sample of students; instead they were seeking to identify the complexities of students' thinking processes. So in their study, it was not important

---

Why Was This Research Published?

whether the students were "typical" of all students in their thinking. It mattered only whether their thinking was complex in *some* way, a way that would suggest how thinking could be organized in other students' minds.

For their case studies the authors chose just three students, each selected for a particular research purpose. One was a highly proficient reader who was also bilingual (Spanish and English); a second was a marginally proficient reader who was bilingual (Spanish and English); and a third was a highly proficient reader who was monolingual in English. To "qualify" for the study, furthermore, all of the students had to be comfortable reflecting on and talking about their own reading processes so that the authors could interview them at length on this topic. The researchers asked each student to read six one-page passages in English and (where relevant) in Spanish. They invited all three to think aloud about their reading as they went along, commenting on how they figured out particular vocabulary or the meanings of passages. The oral readings and think-aloud commentaries were taped and transcribed, and became the basis for the research study the authors published. When I read about these procedures, I recognized them as research methods common in **qualitative research,** an approach that relies on rich verbal description of behavior or, in this case, of students' thinking.

Using these procedures, Jiménez, García, and Pearson discovered important differences among the readers. The proficient bilingual, Pamela, used her growing knowledge of *each* language to aid her in learning vocabulary from the other language. When she encountered the English word *species,* for example, she guessed correctly that it meant the same thing as the similar Spanish word *especies;* and when she encountered the Spanish word *liquído,* she guessed correctly that it meant the English word *liquid.* Her focus on learning vocabulary was stronger than for the proficient monolingual, Michelle, who commented less on specific words than on how the overall reading passages related to her prior general knowledge. The difference presumably stemmed from Michelle's greater familiarity with English vocabulary—so much greater, in fact, that Michelle did not need to think about individual words consciously. Both Michelle and Pamela differed, however, from the less proficient bilingual reader, Christine. Like Pamela, Christine focused on vocabulary, but she did not think of her native Spanish as a resource to help in this task. When reading a Spanish word, she sometimes was reminded of English equivalents (or "cognates," as language teachers call them), but she did not use her much greater knowledge of Spanish to assist with her

In Your Own Voice

When you think of the researchers' goal—to learn about the effect of bilingualism on literacy—do you find it misleading that they focused on so few students?

Or do you find it illuminating?

more limited English. In this sense, bilingualism became a barrier to reading comprehension rather than an advantage.

Relevance: A Framework, But Also Recommendations for Practices

In this study, the authors do offer a way of thinking about how bilingualism, when considered in general, affects children's reading comprehension. But the ideas they offer point more directly than those in Saltzstein's research toward particular teaching practices. Jiménez and his colleagues emphasize the importance of regarding a child's native language as a strength in the process, not a liability, and they point out the importance of facilitating vocabulary development. But they do not make this claim to be universal, one true for all forms of bilingualism in all circumstances. Instead the authors focus on a particular form of bilingualism in a particular situation: bilingualism that involves languages that are relatively similar by world standards (Spanish and English) and bilingualism that occurs in a society where one language (Spanish) has experienced more disrespect than the other (English). This is certainly a common form of bilingualism, but it is not the only form either in the United States or in other countries of the world.

If these two conditions did not exist, their conclusions might not hold true. For some students (e.g., Chinese Americans), the native language and the second language are much more different in vocabulary, pronunciation, and grammar than Spanish is compared to English, and therefore may provide less of a resource to a child learning to read. Furthermore, in some settings, relationships between languages are more equal than in the United States. In certain parts of Canada, for example, both the numbers and the overall social status of English speakers and French speakers are more equal than in the United States. In both of these situations, if a child fails to learn to read the second language, it may be not for the reasons suggested by Robert Jiménez but for other reasons, ranging from difficulties with reading as such to cultural differences in what a child expects to be taught (Edwards & Redfern, 1992; Hoffman, 1996).

The Reader's Role: Both Teacher and Researcher

In the published version of their research, Jiménez, García, and Pearson assume readers have some familiarity with bilingual students and with issues related to learning to read and learning a second language. They begin their article by describing more than a dozen previous research studies in these areas. Later they describe numerous responses of the three bilingual students to the passages the students were asked to read.

In Your Own Voice

The limits on Jiménez's conclusions imply a question for teachers: how should you help students who are bilingual in ways *other* than those studied by Jiménez?

For example, how can you be most helpful to students whose first language is Chinese rather than Spanish?

At the end of the article, they make suggestions not only for teaching ("focus more on vocabulary development") but also for continuing the research (we need to further study "children who are learning to read English as a second language"). When I read these various comments, I found my prior knowledge of and reflections about teaching helped me to make sense of them. But I also found I did not need to be fully expert to understand the authors' messages; I have never, after all, taught English as a second language, nor have I conducted research on reading or bilingual language development.

Example: Reviewing Inclusive Education

In 1996 two special educators, Dorothy Lipsky and Alan Gartner, published a review of recent political and societal developments related to special education in general and in particular to *inclusive education,* the practice of placing children with special needs in regular classrooms while simultaneously modifying their programs individually to accommodate their needs (Lipsky & Gartner, 1996). Their purpose was partly to assess the extent to which schools have in fact implemented inclusive education, but partly also to argue for the desirability of this approach on both ethical and educational grounds. I was attracted to their article

The trend toward more fully inclusive education has led many educators to wonder how well inclusion has actually been practiced in public schools. This question, in turn, has led Lipsky and Gartner to review inclusion practices systematically.
© R. Hutchings/Photo Edit

In Your Own Voice

Lipsky and Gartner never observed actual special education programs for this research but instead reviewed reports and other research about programs.

Do you think they are at risk for misunderstanding the current state of special education as a result?

In what sense is their document orientation useful in the first place?

because its purposes coincided with some of mine. Here were two educators, I expected, who could bring me up to date on current practices about this important area of teaching and learning.

I noted, however, that to accomplish their purposes, the authors did not actually interview anyone or administer any tests or surveys. Instead they provided a **review of the literature,** meaning they looked at government statistics and legal documents as sources of information. Since inclusive education has been studied heavily, this approach worked well; the researchers had voluminous material to draw on, and they were able to discern important trends in inclusive education on the basis of the work already done. First, in reviewing government statistics, they noted that the schools were currently serving far more children with special needs than in the 1970s, but the growth had occurred primarily for one particular kind of child: the child labeled "learning disabled" (see Chapter 10 for more discussion of this term). Next, the authors analyzed the provisions of important legislation related to inclusion (such as PL 94-142, also discussed in Chapter 10). From these reviews, they concluded that many children with special needs still received educations that at the time of publication were not really integrated but were separate from that of other children; even those who spent parts of the day in a regular classroom, they pointed out, experienced little sense of being included. Finally, the authors reviewed publicly accessible court cases related to the inclusion of children. From the cases, the authors noted that parents as well as court judges have been moving steadily toward stronger beliefs in full inclusion of children with special needs.

Having set the stage in these ways, the authors concluded that inclusion had not gone far enough even by 1996, the year they published their article. They also concluded that teachers and other school leaders should work harder to achieve full inclusion. They cited several educational practices that promote inclusion effectively, noting research studies that tested the practices and found them successful. One practice, for example, is to vigorously encourage collaboration among school staff, including teachers, who have responsibility for students with special needs. Another is to develop strong programs of participation for parents of these students. A third is to encourage a range of instructional techniques found effective for special-needs students, such as cooperative learning activities and computer-supported learning.

Relevance: A Framework That Is Timely

By offering a broad overview of special education, Lipsky and Gartner do provide a framework for understanding this field. In reading their review, however, I realized that their overview is deliberately limited to the current state of the field and that this quality is simultaneously its strength and its ultimate limitation. By being tied to a particular time or year, it can better help educators who are currently involved with improving services to students with special needs. Yet as the authors themselves might admit, focusing their findings on a current point in time ensures that they will eventually become "old news" and that a new review may have to be written. In this sense, their research differs from the research of both Herbert Saltzstein and Robert Jiménez described earlier. Both of the latter authors might agree that their ideas may someday prove inappropriate or dated, but neither designed their studies to be deliberately tied to the calendar, to be an update as of the particular year, 1996. Saltzstein's notion of *moral heteronomy* and Jiménez's recommendations for teaching bilingual children are meant to last as long as possible, until better ones are found. The trends in inclusive education in 1996 presented by Lipsky and Gartner, however, are not offered in this spirit; by the year 2006, their review will be less current than it was in 1996, and therefore less useful for its original purpose. It will begin gaining value later, however, for documenting the long-term history of inclusive education.

The Reader's Role: Educational Activist

In Your Own Voice

Think about how the role of educational activist assumed by Lipsky and Gartner fits you and your goals.

Do you respond to the news that "inclusion is not progressing well" by feeling more committed to inclusion?

If not, why not?

After finishing the review by Lipsky and Gartner, I felt moved to act: more motivated to work for fuller inclusion of students with special needs and more frustrated with school policies that delay or limit inclusion. I pondered my reaction: why, I wondered, did I feel more "activated" by their research than by either Saltzstein's or Jiménez's? Part of the reason was in me; I have a personal history of interest in special education, though I have never fully immersed myself in this field. But part of the reason was also in how Lipsky and Gartner framed their article. By organizing their topic in a time-focused way, the authors imparted more urgency to their findings. "This is how inclusion is now," they seemed to be saying, "this particular year." And by tracing the recent history of inclusive education, they highlighted the *lack* of change in this area. "Education could have been more inclusive by now," they also seemed to be saying, "but in fact it is not." In sending me these implicit messages, the authors coaxed me into focusing my attention more on intervention than on insights. In other words, at the moment when I finished their review, I was more interested in changing school practices regarding inclusion than in understanding *why* change in practices had recently been slow.

Many teachers would like to be able to focus their attention on the school life of particular children as individuals. The demands on teachers' time makes this difficult, though not necessarily impossible—as the research by Vivian Paley suggests.
© Ilene Perlman/Stock Boston

The Voices of Teacher Research

*E*VEN though I enjoyed the challenges in reading the three studies—by Saltzstein, Jimenéz, and Lipsky/Gartner—I sensed something missing in all of them, something that was also missing in other research studies I had read. Stated briefly, the problem was this: although teachers are often the objects of educational research—indeed, crucial to it—their role in influencing the design and interpretation of most research remains unclear. In the world of educational research, people other than teachers, typically professors or other professional researchers, speak for teachers more often than not. All three research studies described earlier had this shortcoming. Teachers were talked about, and perhaps included as readers of the research, but they definitely did not decide on the research topics or specify whether to use interviews, case studies, or reviews to answer educational questions.

The information that emerges from this arrangement certainly has to do with teaching and learning, and often contains useful insights. But by definition, it is framed by people whose experiences and fundamental commitments are not with classroom teaching. As a result, the studies

In Your Own Voice

How would *you* conduct the studies about moral beliefs or about inclusive education?

As a teacher, would you have different priorities for these topics than Saltzstein or Lipsky and Gartner?

are somewhat more likely to start from problems posed by academic disciplines or by educational administrators. Two of the three studies described earlier showed this quality. Although Jiménez, Garcia, and Pearson did deal with a problem of classroom teaching (bilingual reading instruction), neither Saltzstein nor Lipsky and Gartner did so directly. Saltzstein began with a problem in psychology (moral development), and Lipsky and Gartner began with a problem of general school reform (inclusive education). Classroom teachers are concerned, of course, about both of these latter problems. But if they were designing the research projects on their own initiative, they might reframe both Saltzstein's and Lipsky and Gartner's topics to focus more explicitly on the challenges of classroom teaching. In studying moral beliefs, for example, they might focus more fully on whether and how moral beliefs can be fostered in particular students. In studying inclusive education, they might focus more fully on the practical difficulties teachers face in implementing full inclusion.

The Nature of Teacher Research

In Your Own Voice

Teacher research is sometimes also called *classroom research* and sometimes also *action research*.

Can you think of advantages (or drawbacks) to each of these alternative names?

In view of the issues about the nature of educational research, a particularly important kind of investigation for teachers is called **teacher research,** systematic and intentional inquiry by teachers (Stenhouse, 1985). Teacher research is not to be confused with "research about teaching," which consists of investigations by professional researchers of the topic of teachers or teaching. Teacher research has several defining characteristics. First, it originates in the problems and dilemmas of classroom practice, such as a gap between what a teacher is doing and what she or he would like to be doing, or a chronic problem with certain students, materials, or activities. Second, its outcomes offer information about particular teachers and classrooms rather than about teachers in general or students in general. Skeptics argue that this feature makes teacher research less useful than conventional educational research, but its supporters point out that focusing on particular people and settings makes teacher research more valid simply because it is more attuned to differences among classrooms, teachers, and students. Third, although the audience for teacher research can certainly include professors and educational administrators, it tends to be other teachers (Fenstermacher, 1994). Teacher research is therefore in a stronger position than other research to provide an "insider's" perspective on the problems of teaching (Cochran-Smith & Lytle, 1993).

"It's like that joke," thought Howie after finishing the page above. Julia winced slightly, knowing she couldn't stop him from telling it:

This person is looking for his car keys under a street light at night. So a second person walks up, see? And the second one says, "Did you lose something?"

"Yeah, my car keys."

"Under this street light?'"

"No, way over there," said the first man, pointing out into the darkness.

"So why are you looking over here?"

"Because this is where the light is!"

Educational research is sometimes criticized for being like the person in Howie's joke: looking where there is already the "light" of information and theories rather than where the most important educational problems are. But the criticism is not entirely fair. It is true that research studies tend to build on one other and, in this sense, gravitate to where the "light" of previous research and previous thinking already exists. The studies by Saltzstein, Jiménez, and Lipsky/Gartner all cited previous research studies, previous theories, or both as justifications for the problems they addressed. But it is also true that the previous research those three studies cited was based on lasting, important problems of human development and of education. Moral development, bilingual literacy, and inclusive education are all important concerns of teachers and educators, whether or not research has been done about them. The reason later studies gravitate around certain topics, in other words, may have as much to do with the importance of the topic as with the fact that others have already studied it.

From a teacher's point of view, it might be more accurate to say that the problem with a lot of educational research is lack of access to the most appropriate examples of it at the most helpful times. If I am teaching first-grade mathematics for the first time, for example, I need the benefit of research on *this* topic, not on some other educational topic, and I need it *now*, not at some later time in my career. How am I to locate that research? And even if I do find it, how can I be sure I am understanding the special language and research procedures often embodied in many educational research studies? These problems are not impossible to solve, but they do require becoming familiar with the research literature in general, much as you can begin finding books in the public library more easily after you start visiting the library regularly and get to know how it is organized. Interpreting research studies, furthermore, is a skill in itself, one that takes time to acquire and often benefits from guidance by others who already have some of it. It is a professional challenge to acquire skill at finding and interpreting educational research, but far from an impossible one.

Teacher research offers one way to begin meeting that challenge, because it begins with problems of classroom practice and therefore stimulates you (as a teacher) both to observe your own students and to search for published educational research about particular problems of high concern to you. In a sense, it transforms Howie's joke about the man looking for car keys under the light rather than where the keys actually are. With teacher research, the joke should now be told like this:

"That's *so* ancient, Howie," Julia said disdainfully. "I've heard it before, and I bet some of the other readers have too."

"So? So tell a better one." Howie was annoyed, but was willing to listen.

A teacher is sitting outside in the dark with a flashlight in her lap.

Another teacher comes up and asks, "Why are you sitting in the dark like this?"

"I'm looking for something," says the teacher.

"But you're just sitting there, not even using your flashlight!"

"I know," she says. "First, I have to decide what to look for."

Perhaps, suggest some educators, educational research should be more like this teacher's search: before you can begin, you have to figure out what you are looking for. In that case, when you do begin to search, maybe you will need only a small light—a flashlight—as long as the light is portable and can shine where you really need it.

In Your Own Voice

I use a flashlight analogy here, but this too may be misleading because it implies that you do your teacher research alone and that you focus your attention into a narrow "beam."

Do you think these assumptions are accurate?

If not, can you think of a better analogy for explaining the nature of teacher research?

Teacher Research in Practice

Teacher research has a number of features in addition to the defining ones already mentioned (Richardson, 1994). To varying degrees, most such studies support some combination of these ideas:

1. Teaching is really a form of research.
2. Teacher research, like teaching itself, requires substantial reflection.
3. Collaboration among teachers is crucial for making teacher research meaningful and for the improvement of teaching.
4. Teachers' knowledge of teaching has to be shared publicly, especially when gained systematically through teacher research.

To see how these features look in practice, let's look at several examples of teacher research studies.

Example: Focusing on Motivating Students

In 1993, Patricia Clifford and Sharon Friesen published an account of their effort to develop a classroom program based on students' outside interests and experiences. Clifford and Friesen were co-teachers in a double-size classroom that deliberately included children from first, second, and third grades.

Because of prior experiences, the teachers were led to their research by three major questions, which they phrased like this:

- *How can a curriculum remain open to children's unique experiences and connect with the world they know outside the school?* The teachers believed that all too often the official school curriculum lacked meaning for children because it seemed cut off from the rest of the world. The result was unmotivated students and poor learning.

- *Why is imaginative experience the best starting point for planning?* The teachers believed that imaginative experiences—make-believe play, stories, poems—provided access to children's lives outside school. Perhaps somehow these could be connected to the goals of the official curriculum.

- *What happens when teachers break down the barriers between school knowledge and real knowledge?* In drawing on children's outside experiences, would children actually become more or less motivated? Would children take over the program and fail to learn the official curriculum goals?

To answer these questions, the teachers kept extensive diaries or journals for one entire school year. In the journals, they described and reflected on their daily teaching experiences. The teachers also talked with each other extensively about classroom events and their significance, and the results of the conversations often made their way into the journals. For example, the teachers recorded in their journals an experience with students about ways of telling time. In preliminary discussions, the students became interested in how a sundial works. So the teachers and students went outside and created a human sundial using the students themselves. The teachers' journal chronicled these events, and noted the comments and questions students developed as a result:

- If you stood in the same place for a whole day you would see your shadow change places because the earth changes position.

- Why is my shadow longer than I am in the evening, but shorter at noon?

- Clouds can block the sun's rays, so sundials won't work on rainy days.
- How did people start to tell time?

As the year evolved and observations accumulated and were recorded, the teachers gradually began to answer their own three questions. They found, for example, that connecting the curriculum with children's interests and motives was most effective when they could establish a personal bond with a child. They also found that imaginative expression helped certain children to feel safe to explore ideas. And they found that blending school knowledge and "real" knowledge caused children to learn much *more* than before, although much of the additional knowledge was not part of the official curriculum. With these conclusions in mind, and with numerous examples to support them, Clifford and Friesen published their study so that others could share what they had learned about teaching, learning, and students.

The study by Clifford and Friesen is interesting in its own right, of course, but for our purposes, try stepping aside from its content for a moment and look at the research as an example of teacher research. First, the research incorporated teaching: Clifford and Friesen were teaching while they studied their program, and studied their program while they were teaching. Second, the research required considerable reflection over a long period of time: their journals and conversations contained not only descriptions of events but also their interpretations of the events. Third, the study involved collaboration: not one but two teachers were studying the major questions. Finally, the teachers developed their results and conclusions not only for themselves but also for others. These four qualities make the study by Clifford and Friesen a clear example of teacher research. Note, though, that other studies conducted by teachers may be less clear-cut; they may show some of these four features, but not all, as in the next two examples.

Example: Focusing on Development

In 1986, Vivian Paley published a short book called *Mollie Is Three,* one of a series based on her observations of children as a prekindergarten teacher. Paley was interested in how young children develop or change over the long term, and in particular how the development looks from the point of view of a classroom teacher. She observed one child in particular, Mollie, from the time she entered nursery school just after her third birthday until after she turned four years old. Paley's interest focused not so much on curriculum, as Clifford and Friesen's had, as on Mollie as a whole person; "the subject which I most wished to learn," wrote Paley, "is children" (p. xiv). She therefore wrote extended narra-

In Your Own Voice

If you were a teacher reading the study by Clifford and Friesen, how would you make allowances for the differences in circumstances between your own students and your own teaching compared to the students and teaching goals described in their article?

How might you avoid overgeneralizing from their work to yours while still drawing useful ideas from theirs?

In Your Own Voice

Suppose Vivian Paley had written about children's learning and development not in the form of a story but in the form of an essay.

Would an essay format seem more general and therefore more convincing?

Or would it seem less vivid and therefore less convincing?

tive (or storylike) observations about the whole range of activities of this one child, and included periodic brief reflections on the observations. Because the observations took a narrative form, the resulting book reads much like a novel: some themes are simply implied by the story line rather than stated explicitly. Using this approach, Paley demonstrated (and occasionally also stated) several important developmental changes. At age three, for example, Mollie's language was often disconnected from her actions: she would talk about one thing but do another. By four, she was much more likely to tie language to her current activities, and in this sense she more often "said what she meant." A result of the change was that Mollie also began understanding and following classroom rules as the year went on, because the language of rules became more connected (in her mind) to the actions to which they referred.

Vivian Paley's book had some of the characteristics of teacher research, but had differences as well. Like the research by Clifford and Friesen, Paley's work was based on her teaching and her teaching was based on the research; and once again the research involved periodic reflection on teaching and the public sharing of the reflections. Unlike Clifford and Friesen, though, Paley worked independently, without collaboration. And compared to Clifford and Friesen, she deliberately integrated observation and interpretation as one might do in a piece of fiction to make the "story" imply or show its message without having to tell it in so many words. In this regard, her work resembles what some educators have called **arts-based research,** studies that take advantage of an artistic medium (in this case, narrative writing) to heighten readers' understanding and response to research findings (Barone & Eisner, in press). If you are studying the use of space in the classroom, for example, photographs, drawings, or scale models of the room may be especially helpful in strengthening your conclusions. If you are studying children's musical knowledge, on the other hand, recordings of performances by the children may be more appropriate. Of course, you can also write about classroom space or children's music, but both forms of understanding may lose something in "translation" to a written format.

Example: Focusing on Collaboration

In 1996, an example of teacher research was published that was intended for classroom teachers and university researchers at the same time and focused on the challenges of collaboration among educators. Wendy Schoener (a teacher) and Polly Ulichny (a university researcher) jointly published a study in which they explored how, or even whether, teachers and university researchers could participate as equals in the study of teaching (Ulichny & Schoener, 1996). Wendy (the two used their first names throughout their published study) was a teacher of adults learning English as a second language (ESL); Polly was a specialist in multicultural education and wanted to observe a teacher who was especially successful at reaching the ethnically diverse students who normally study ESL. Polly therefore asked Wendy for permission to study her teaching for an extended period of time: to visit her class, videotape it, interview her about it, and the like.

What followed is best described as an extended "negotiation" between teacher and professor for access to Wendy's class on the one hand and for mutual respect for each other's work on the other. In the published article, the negotiations are described separately by each participant to honor the differences in their concerns and perspectives. Before, during, and after the observations, Polly and Wendy each had to adjust her expectations of what the other could do and was willing to do. As the authors put it, some things were "easy to hear" from the other and some things were "hard to hear." Wendy, as a teacher, found it easier to hear criticisms of her teaching if they came from herself rather than from the higher-status university professor, Polly. Polly, for her part, found it easier to hear Wendy's self-criticisms if she matched Wendy's self-evaluations and disclosures with some of her own; Polly began telling about dilemmas and problems she experienced in her own (university) teaching. Because of tendencies such as these, the two educators eventually focused less on Polly's original purpose—studying multicultural teaching—and more on the problem of how teachers and university researchers might collaborate effectively.

Overall, this study qualifies as a piece of teacher research, but it can also be considered an example of research *about* teaching. Consider the criterion described earlier: the study meets them, but always ambiguously. First, the research did involve collaborative reflection by the participants, but the reflection was only partly about classroom teaching; the rest was about how the relationship between Wendy and Polly developed. Second, the research observations did focus on classroom teaching—Wendy's teaching; however, they originated not with Wendy's concerns about her own classroom but with Polly's need to study multicultural teaching. Third, the researchers did share what they learned by publishing their observations and ideas, but their article speaks not only to teachers but also to university researchers and educators of future teachers. Their dual audience is understandable given their focus on the relations between these two communities. But it makes the study less clearly a piece of *teacher* research as such.

In pointing out these differences, I am *not* implying praise for pure, "politically correct" examples of teacher research or criticism for mixed

In Your Own Voice

Suppose Wendy and Polly had been two teachers instead of a teacher and a university researcher.

What would be gained by this difference, and what would be lost?

Or suppose both had been university researchers.

Could the study have been done at all in that case?

or "impure" examples. Quite the contrary: the point is to notice how diverse studies by teachers can be and to appreciate the diversity. Whatever their specific features, classroom studies by teachers hold in common a commitment to giving a voice to teachers as they reflect on their work, and reflect especially on problems and challenges intrinsic to classroom life. This goal can be accomplished through more than one method: through journals and other recordkeeping methods, through oral discussions with colleagues, and through written reflections created either for themselves or for others concerned about teaching and learning. The diversity of topics and methods should not surprise us, in fact, since students, teachers, and classrooms are themselves so diverse.

The Challenges of Teacher Research

*W*ELL and good, you may say. Teacher research offers teachers a way to hear one another, to learn from their own and others' experience. But this benefit comes at a cost, both in time and effort, as it did for Wendy (and Polly) described in the previous section. By definition, no one can do teacher research *for* teachers; they must do it for themselves. In fact, given the stresses often experienced when you begin teaching, you may need to satisfy yourself at first with appreciating other teachers' classroom-based research, whether you see it in writing or hear about and discuss it orally. Sooner or later, though, you will need to confront the fact that other teachers inevitably study problems and dilemmas that occur in other classrooms, and that these may not coincide with the ones you experience with your own students. Ultimately, the only solution to this problem is to initiate teacher research of your own, focusing on classroom challenges unique to yourself. Your projects need not be as long term or comprehensive as the ones described in this chapter, but they will need to be systematic and reflective.

Doing your own teacher research raises several important questions. First, how do you know what, from all of your experiences, deserves special study and reflection? Second, is teacher research practical for the circumstances, or will it detract from your teaching and from students' learning? Third, will others, especially principals and teachers, support your engagement with teacher research, and perhaps even try to help create conditions that support doing such research? These questions do not have simple or definitive answers, but let's consider briefly how you might begin answering them for yourself.

What Is Worthy of Study?

In Your Own Voice

What topic or problem might be worthy of study for *you* if you were a teacher researcher?

Would it be the same topic or problem that you identified on page 413 in connection with "conventional" educational research?

Since this question has moral overtones, it is indeed complex. But a brief, preliminary answer is easy to give: teachers should study either what intrigues them the most about their work or what troubles them the most. The chapters of this book describe potentially intriguing and troubling features of teaching and learning for teachers as a group. But only you can decide which features or issues deserve priority in your particular case, and therefore might merit some form of classroom research. How can you decide what your priorities actually are? Try reflecting on your work frequently, and try discussing it with other educators or other individuals whom you trust. In a way, this is the major advice underlying this book.

Is Teacher Research Practical?

From one perspective, the answer has to be "Of course not!" Teacher research is not practical because it takes time and effort that presumably could be used in some other way. Viewed very generally, however, teaching itself is not "practical" in one sense: it takes time and effort to implement any sort of classroom program, and the resulting work often is labor intensive. Teaching students always takes a lot of work. Since systematic reflection on teaching (i.e., classroom-based research) is also work, the question should be whether time invested in reflection improves your effectiveness as a teacher and students' effectiveness as learners. If it does, teacher research is "practical."

In Your Own Voice

It seems that not all educational problems are equally easy to study.

Is there one that you might have information about but might be especially difficult to study, either as conventional research or as teacher research?

Looked at in this way, teacher research is indeed practical, though perhaps not in every way on every occasion. If you choose to learn about the quality of conversational exchanges between yourself and students, for example, you will need some way to record these dialogues, or at least to keep accurate, detailed notes on them. Doing so may or may not be practical, depending on your circumstances. On the other hand, if you choose to study how and why certain students remain on the margins of your class socially, this problem too may or may not be practical as a topic for teacher research, depending on whether you can find a way to observe and reflect on students' social interactions or lack thereof. It all depends on your circumstances: on the attention you can afford to divert to your problem and the demands placed on you as a teacher in relation to the benefits that solutions to the problems will give you.

In essence, Kelvin asks here whether teaching interferes with research. Some might argue that it does, that there is a great divide between teaching and research. This happens, I think, because we tend to think of research in terms of surveys and statistics, and not as something engaging and self-renewing. The verbs used to represent teaching are *act, choose,* and *decide* as opposed to *understand* and *observe* for research. In my opinion, though, the "chasm" is irrelevant and artificial. Empirical inquiry should not be viewed as a separate entity with goals different from teaching. As a teacher, my choices and decisions are based for the most part on my understanding and observations of my students—which are essentially research activities. Observing the subtleties and nuances of students' behavior is the key, and this can often be done best by a teacher who knows the students on a daily basis.

Yvette Daniel, High School English Teacher, Toronto, Ontario, Canada

Nonetheless, educators continually debate the potential of teacher research. Some argue that the nature of teaching is inherently incompatible with the nature of research (Wong, 1995); hence the two cannot be combined. Teaching calls for action, choice, and decision: classes need materials, students need ideas, and programs need choices in order to function. Research calls for understanding and observation: from this perspective classes need to be observed, students and teachers need to be interviewed, and programs need to be analyzed. The two sets of activities, it is argued, are incompatible. One set is done at the expense of the other.

Other educators argue that the dilemma is illusory. This is the view expressed by Yvette Daniel, a high school English teacher, in the accompanying Multiple Voices box. As Ms. Daniel implies, teaching and research conflict only if you define both activities narrowly; with broader definitions, they become compatible. For example, teaching involves more than the interactions with students that take place during class sessions; it also includes preparations and planning times before and after class sessions. If these are included, teacher research is always possible; that is, teachers can always reflect on the events of the day (Wilson, 1995). Research, for its part, is more than passive observation of students and classrooms; it also includes educational interventions, efforts to stimulate students to new thinking and new responses. Even under these broader definitions, of course, some classroom studies are ruled out as impractical or even unethical. You cannot prolong dialogues excessively, for example, or deliberately teach incorrect information to students "just to see if they notice." But some investigations are impossible for *any* form of research. In medical research, for example, you cannot investigate a medical treatment that is extremely painful or deliberately withhold a drug of proven value "just to see what happens."

Will Others Support Your Teacher Research?

Since teacher research is tied closely to teaching itself, both critics and supporters agree that success with teacher research means challenging traditional beliefs and practices about the conduct of teaching (Eisner, 1991). The reflectiveness called for by teacher research in particular means less time working alone than is customary and more time working with colleagues who support your work and who might even be potential collaborators. To sustain a commitment to classroom inquiry, in other words, you will need people with whom to share teaching experiences, problems, and ideas. The number of such individuals need not be large; in the studies described earlier in this chapter, each teacher had only one collaborator. But they must be supportive so that you can trust them with information about your difficulties as well as your joys and be willing to listen carefully to theirs. They need not, however, agree with everything you do or believe; in fact, both you and your supporters may learn more if you *disagree* sometimes about the significance of particular educational goals or classroom experiences. And a supportive colleague need not actually be another classroom teacher. The study by Polly and Wendy involved a collaboration between a teacher and a university researcher. You may find helpful others where you do not first expect them, such as among the administrators of your school or among teachers at other schools.

Benefiting from All Kinds of Research

I do not advocate teacher research at the expense of other forms of educational research. Rather, I encourage you to consider a broad range of approaches to studying teaching and learning. The studies described in the first part of this chapter—the ones about moral development, bilingualism and reading, and inclusive education—are all fine examples of educational research. They are "conventional" in the sense that they were designed, conducted, and published by individuals other than classroom teachers; but this fact does not, in and of itself, make them either more or less relevant to classroom teaching. When well done and focused on issues of concern to teachers, educational research by nonteachers has distinct advantages. For one thing, it can be more objective (though not always): in comparing different methods of teaching, for example, someone who is not using any of them may find it easier to be unbiased. As a practical matter, furthermore, researchers who are not teachers may have more time for and experience with conducting research. The review of inclusion practices described earlier (Lipsky & Gartner, 1996), for example, would require time spent in libraries reviewing documents to which most classroom teachers probably lack access.

At the same time, the studies described in the latter part of the chapter—the ones about curriculum development, a preschool child's growth, and university-school collaboration—are also good examples of research. But as examples of teacher research, they are less conventional in authorship and are able to accomplish certain unique goals as a result. As teachers in particular, the researchers had an excellent sense of what *they* needed and wanted to learn about their classrooms, their teaching, and their students. As teachers, furthermore, the researchers had unusually good access to and knowledge of the classroom lives of students whom they studied. Vivian Paley (1986), for example, was able to describe Mollie's thinking in numerous activities over an entire school year. These benefits can also occur from research by nonteachers, but they are more difficult to arrange.

The challenge for you, as a classroom teacher, is to see the value in *all* forms of research, without being tempted to think that only a few, or even only one, can provide useful guidance for teaching (Eisner, 1996; Phillips, 1992). If you can do this, your ways of learning about teaching will be enriched. You will have more ways to understand life in classrooms empathically, but also have some of the benefit of objective distance. You will have more ways to grasp the individuality of particular students, but also to see what they have in common. And you will have more ways to interpret your own experiences as a teacher, but also be able to learn from the experiences of others. Realizing these benefits fully is a challenge, because the very diversity of teaching and learning makes educational problems and solutions diverse as well. But you will also have plentiful company in searching for better understanding, and your company will include both professional researchers and classroom teachers.

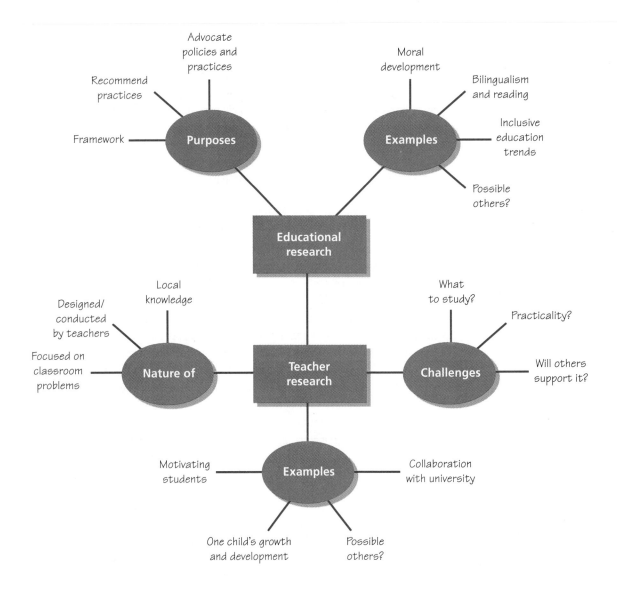

Chapter Re-View: Hearing Distant Voices This Chapter Re-View suggests directions in which the chapter might have taken your thinking—though, of course, other directions are also possible. It expands the Chapter View, which suggests a starting point, conceptually, for the chapter. But this Re-View does not suggest an ending point. Like the Chapter View, it represents just one perspective among many.

Key Terms and Concepts

educational research (413)

purposes of educational
   research (414)

responses expected in reading
   research (415)

assumptions about readers'
   experience (415)

interviews (420)

controls (420)

sampling (421)

control groups (421)

case study (425)

qualitative research (426)

review of the literature (429)

teacher research (432)

arts-based research (437)

Annotated Readings

Anderson, G., Herr, K., & Nihlen, A. (1994). *Studying your own school: An educator's guide to qualitative practitioner research*. Thousand Oaks, CA: Corwin Press.

Hubbard, R., & Power, B. (1993). *The art of classroom inquiry: A handbook for teacher-researchers*. Portsmouth, NH: Heinemann.

McKernan, James. (1996). *Curriculum action research: A handbook of methods and resources for the reflective practitioner* (2nd ed.). London: Kogan Page. As their titles imply, these books offer guid-ance for conducting classroom-based research. They make good resources for getting started.

Jaeger, R. (Ed.). (1997). *Complementary methods for research in education* (2nd ed.). Washington, DC: American Educational Research Association. This book offers a chapter on each of the major forms of educational research. Each chapter is written by a different authority on educational research, and is both authoritative and accessible in its language. Overall, the book offers a good way to gain perspective on the place of teacher research in the larger landscape of educational research.

Internet Resources

<www.aera.net> This is the official web site of the American Educational Research Association, one of the major "umbrella" professional associations sponsoring educational research in the United States and, indeed, in the entire English-speaking world. The opening page has links to an assortment of divisions and special-interest groups, each specializing in some form of educational research. One special-interest group is called "teacher as re-searcher"; another is called "arts-based research in education."

<www.ed.gov/offices/OERI> This is the web site of the United States Office of Educational Research and Improvement. It summarizes current research initiatives and programs sponsored by the U.S. federal government, and includes links for finding more information about individual initiatives and programs.

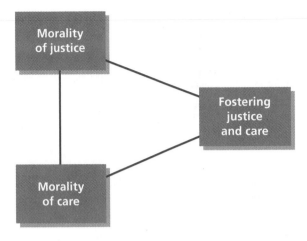

Chapter View: Care and Justice in Teaching and Learning This Chapter View is a concept map that indicates one among many ways of thinking about the chapter. It suggests a starting point, conceptually, for the chapter but is incomplete by itself. At the end of the chapter is a Chapter Re-View, which expands on the Chapter View, suggesting directions for taking your thinking further—though, of course, other directions are also possible.

13

Care and Justice in Teaching and Learning

Some say that teaching is all about ethics or morality—about constantly choosing between actions that are right and actions that are wrong, and constantly fostering "right" actions among students. Ethical choices arise so frequently during every school day and in such ordinary situations that you may not notice them. For example:

■ You are teaching first grade, and it is getting close to recess. You have been working with a reading group while other students work quietly at their seats. You ask yourself, "Should I give this group a final few minutes? Or should I take the final minutes to help one or two students at their seats, individuals who I know need a bit more help?" More time with the group means less time with the individuals, and vice versa.

■ You are teaching eleventh grade. A student comes to you the day before a test and asks to take the test a few days later than the rest of the class. Her reason? "My parents were away last week, and I had to take care of my younger brother and sister." Should you let her take the test later or not? You wonder whether her family responsibilities were reason enough, and even whether they are real. And you wonder whether postponing the test for her would be fair to other students, some of whom may themselves have struggled to be ready on time.

- It is late one day after school; you are planning the next day's lesson. You consider whether to plan another day on the current topic because you know that doing so might help certain students to grasp key parts of it. Or should you move on to the next topic so as not to bore students who already understand the material perfectly? It seems that being more helpful to some means being less helpful to others.

- It is lunch hour. You are finally relaxing; it has been a hectic morning and indeed a hectic week. A student comes to you for individual help about the current unit; he is not understanding certain key material. Should you give up your lunch hour to help? Of course! you think; but then you remember how tired *you* are, how much you need a break before your afternoon classes. How can you be fair both to your need for a rest and to the student's need for help?

- You are grading students' essays. On one essay, you encounter a passage that is awkwardly expressed; you know it needs rewriting. But how to help the student to do so? You begin by inserting alternative phrasings on the manuscript; but then you hesitate to finish. You look at the clock; you have thirty more essays that need a response. You wonder if you should you devote more time to this student's work, even if that means less time for other students' essays.

The Ethical Nature of Teaching

THESE examples are ordinary incidents of teaching, the kind that every teacher encounters. But they all have an ethical or moral dimension: in every case, the teacher must choose how to be simultaneously considerate of students, self, and the class as a whole. Being helpful to one person may mean being less helpful to another, such as when a teacher has time to help some individuals but not all. Or sometimes being fair to a class comes at the expense of an individual, such as when grading standards cause one student to just miss an "A" even though he or she tried much harder than another student who earned an "A" through luck or coasting. And the opposite may occur as well: one person's needs may be important enough to override customary rules of fairness for the group. A teacher's policy when leading discussions may be to call on every student equally, but in fact the teacher

Dilemmas about how to use time are really part of a more fundamental problem of human choice: we often face alternatives, each of which has both good and bad consequences.

Choosing to study education, for example, has both benefits and drawbacks, as did the alternatives you gave up as a result.

What were the benefits and drawbacks in your case?

may call on certain students a bit more often than others because they need to develop confidence, to "come out of their shell" (Streitmatter, 1996).

In the short run, of course, there is a way around each dilemma, but it always involves some cost. You can take more time with the reading group *and* with individual students, for example, but that extra time will have to come from somewhere. But where? Perhaps you can give up your lunch hour to a student who needs help, as the teacher did in the third example above. No matter how dedicated you are to your work, though, you will need to relax sooner or later. Perhaps, then, you can deliberately save relaxation for evenings or weekends—although in that case, you will have to make sure you do not have too many other work-related responsibilities at those times, such as grading, or lesson planning, or caring for your own family. Yet even if you have no children, spouse, or others for whom you are responsible daily, and even if you work around the clock, seven days a week, there will still be teaching-related tasks that you could do to help your students. In other words, you cannot "off-load" your free, discretionary time onto other periods of the week indefinitely. Eventually you will have to leave some tasks, both personal and teaching related, undone. The problem is built into the nature of teaching. There are always more ways to help students than an ordinary mortal has time to accomplish: more curriculum materials to develop, more thorough feedback on student projects, and the like. This principle in itself might not pose a problem, except that it has a twin: because teaching is so complex, it is continually difficult to decide when you have helped "enough" or when you are being truly fair to all of your students as a group. Yet you must decide.

Underlying the decisions are two broad issues. One has to do with *justice,* the broad principles of fairness that apply to as many people as possible. The other has to do with *care,* sensitivity and commitment to individuals' unique needs and circumstances. Because teachers deal with groups as well as individuals, they encounter these two issues both singly and in combination. They also see their students struggle with issues of justice and care, with treating one another fairly as well as with consideration. If you teach, then, justice and care will be central concerns—so central that we will take a close look at them in this chapter. As we will see, the ethics of justice and of care have different roots and take different forms. Therefore, one may sometimes seem more important than the other, depending on the situation at hand and on the priorities of students and teachers. I hope to persuade you, however, that a completely ethical teacher (or student) is necessarily concerned about both kinds of morality: about both justice and care, both fairness and consideration (Bubeck, 1995).

Morality of Justice

ORALITY is a system of beliefs for understanding and choosing between good and bad or between right and wrong. A **morality of justice** is a collection of beliefs and choices based on principles of fairness or impartiality, and that is therefore meant to apply as universally as possible. The key values of a justice-oriented morality are equality and the fair use of power (Gilligan & Wiggins, 1988). A person must not be hurt because he or she is weak or disadvantaged compared to other people; might, that is, does not make right. A student who stutters, for example, should not be shut out of class discussions even though his classmates can speak faster and more fluently. He has a moral right to be heard. A student who gets very sick on the day of a test should have another, fair chance to take the test, one equivalent to other students' chances.

What complicates life for teachers is that principles of fairness sometimes can conflict with one another. In fact, the potential for conflict

Kohlberg's stages of moral reasoning are based on the form or structure of thinking, not on specific positions taken or beliefs held. These teenagers, for example, may be picketing because of principles formulated individually (postconventional reasoning), or they may be picketing because their friends are also doing so (conventional reasoning).
© Michael A. Swyer/Stock Boston

abounds. Take the student who stutters. Even if a teacher and class agree that the student should receive respect and get ample time to speak, a second moral principle says that all students, including those *without* communication difficulties, should still get some chance to participate in discussion. The problem is that the student who stutters may need much more "floor time" than others to communicate effectively; how much more time is he entitled to? Is there a point at which his time should be limited so that others can also have turns?

And dilemmas of justice are easy to imagine for the student who missed a test because of illness. Granted, she has a right to take the test on another day; but a competing moral principle says that all students should be guaranteed equal chances to perform well on any test. One student's taking the test on a later day reduces that guarantee, whatever the reasons for the lateness, since the late student has more time than others to study for the test or even to learn answers from classmates.

Because of complications such as these, two people can sometimes reach opposite moral conclusions, even though both are principled and base their actions on considerations of justice. What matters in understanding justice-oriented morality, therefore, is not just a person's specific beliefs and actions but also whether the beliefs and actions are guided by an underlying concern for equality and fairness. How, then, can we detect whether such a concern is operating? If you are a teacher, how do you know how well you think or one of your students thinks about justice? Kohlberg's account of moral development provides some help with this problem.

Kohlberg's Six Stages of Beliefs About Justice

A well-known way of thinking about how the morality of justice relates to education is organized around work originated by the psychologist Lawrence Kohlberg. Beginning in the 1970s and continuing into the present, Kohlberg and his colleagues developed an account of how justice-oriented beliefs develop across the lifespan (Kohlberg, Levine & Hewer, 1983; Guidon, 1992; Schrader, 1990). Kohlberg proposed six stages through which children, youth, and adults go as they struggle to construct general principles of justice. The stages were based on how a person responds to hypothetical or imaginary ethical dilemmas, which Kohlberg took as indicators of moral thinking in everyday, "real" situations as well. Here is one of the dilemmas Kohlberg used in his original research as I posed it to an elementary student named Jocelyn:

In Your Own Voice

Have you ever been caught on either side of this form of dilemma—either wanting a special favor from a teacher or resenting it when another student seems to have received one?

What should a teacher do to resolve or minimize this sort of problem?

KELVIN: I'm going to tell you a story and ask you to think about it. It's about a man named George.

JOCELYN: Good. I like stories.

KELVIN: Once there was this man named George. Something sad happened: his wife got very sick with cancer. She needed a special medicine or else she might die. George didn't have much money, even after he worked very hard to get all that he could. He went to the only pharmacy that sold the medicine, but it was still much too expensive. He only had half the money that he needed. So you know what he did?

JOCELYN: What?

KELVIN: He went during the night and broke into the drugstore and stole the medicine so he could give it to his wife.

As Kohlberg designed it, the story deliberately poses a conflict between two principles of justice. One concerns theft and the idea that everyone should be protected from burglary, whatever their circumstances, personal values, or individual vulnerabilities. The second principle concerns the preservation of life and the idea that everyone should be protected from pain, suffering, and death, whatever their circumstances.

How did Jocelyn reconcile them?

JOCELYN: That wasn't a good way to get it.

KELVIN: Was George right or wrong to steal the medicine?

JOCELYN: Some ways right, some ways wrong. He was right to really care about his wife. But he was wrong because what if he got arrested? What would his wife do without him?

In one way Jocelyn seems indecisive, "wishy-washy": George is both right and wrong to steal the drug, and Jocelyn therefore has no clear position on the issue. In another way, though, she answers consistently: she shows concern for the personal relationships in the story, and for George's relationship with his wife in particular. He is right to care, but at the same time he is wrong for a closely related reason: getting arrested would interfere with his caring for his wife. Caring and commitment in relationships is what Jocelyn's response is about.

It is another question, however, whether Jocelyn's response represents good—that is, highly developed—moral thinking or just some ideas unique to her. Kohlberg's six-stage model offers a way of making this interpretation, a model we will get to in a moment. Before doing so, keep three limitations in mind if you want to understand the model fairly (Emberley, 1995). First, Kohlberg was interested in moral *belief*, not moral action—how people *think about* right and wrong, not how they actually act when confronted with real ethical dilemmas. Second, as mentioned earlier, he was interested in a particular kind of moral development, that having to do with principles of justice. The model therefore can shed light on young people's ideas about general issues of fairness and equality more than it can clarify their ideas about caring and responsibility to others. Third, the model is about how morality changes or transforms as the majority of children and youth grow older, among individuals at any one point in time. In framing moral development in this way, therefore, Kohlberg's model resembled Piaget's more general theory of cognitive development, which also searched for age-related changes during childhood and adolescence.

With all these caveats in mind, then, what stages did Kohlberg in fact propose, and where would Jocelyn fit into them? Table 13.1 summarizes the six stages (Colby & Kohlberg, 1984; Puka, 1994). Kohlberg orga-

TABLE 13.1   Stages of Moral Judgment According to Kohlberg

Stage	Nature of Stage
Preconventional Level (*emphasis on avoiding punishments and getting awards*) *Stage 1* Heteronomous morality; ethics of punishment and obedience *Stage 2* Instrumental purpose; ethics of market exchange	Good is what follows externally imposed rules and rewards and is whatever avoids punishment Good is whatever is agreeable to the individual and to anyone who gives or receives favors; no long-term loyalty
Conventional Level (*emphasis on social rules*) *Stage 3* Interpersonal conformity; ethics of peer opinion *Stage 4* Social system orientation: conformity to social system; ethics of law and order	Good is whatever brings approval from friends as a peer group Good is whatever conforms to existing laws, customs, and authorities
Postconventional Level (*emphasis on moral principles*) *Stage 5* Social contract orientation; ethics of social contract and individual rights *Stage 6* Ethics of self-chosen universal principles	Good is whatever conforms to existing procedures for settling disagreements in society; the actual outcome is neither good nor bad Good is whatever is consistent with personal, general moral principles

Source: From Kelvin Seifert and Robert Hoffnung, *Child and Adolescent Development,* Third Edition, Houghton Mifflin, copyright © 1994, p. 491. Reprinted by permission.

nized them around children's developing knowledge of social conventions. Put briefly, the youngest child (age four or so) judges fairness and rightness in a way that is oblivious to conventions, society's usual moral agreements, beliefs, and practices. Some time in the elementary school years, however, he or she becomes focused on conventions—what others approve of—as determinants of fairness and rightness. So it is somewhere here, in this middle level, that Jocelyn's responses belong; in her answer to the dilemma above, she focuses primarily on people's concern for one another. Eventually (young adulthood), a person goes beyond conventions and assesses fairness and rightness relatively independently. Not surprisingly, Kohlberg named the earliest stages **preconventional,** the middle ones **conventional,** and the final ones **postconventional.** You can sense the implications of this framework by looking at each of the six stages in more detail, which we do in the next section.

Stacy, the Skeptic

"Hmph. Some theory!" Stacy stewed about the passage above, which she had just read. "Obviously Jocelyn *is* principled about her ethics. And maybe not just 'middling' in her development of it. Her particular ethics are to care for the people around her. Shouldn't she get more credit for that? Seifert's going to a lot of trouble to make her valuable attitude look lame-brained." Stacy makes a mental note to write off Kohlberg's model of moral development unless Seifert can redeem it by the end of the chapter. Or at least redeem his own ethical attitudes: doesn't he believe that caring about others is important? Meanwhile Stacy reads on, with skepticism.

Preconventional Justice

In early childhood, according to Kohlberg, beliefs about justice are preconventional in that they have little to do with commonly held beliefs about right and wrong but much to do with events the child experiences personally, events that may be irrelevant to the experiences or needs of others. The first stage of preconventional moral belief is called *heteronomous morality,* or *ethics of punishment and obedience.* In this stage, the child defines right and wrong actions not by their impact on others or by the child's intentions but by consequences imposed externally on the child. "Good" actions are followed by rewards, and "bad" actions are followed by punishments or other negative consequences. The rewards and punishments, furthermore, are not ones the child creates for himself or herself, because the child has not yet figured out how to do this. Instead they result from what seem to be the arbitrary responses of powerful people such as parents or teachers. If helping yourself to a cookie brings affectionate smiles from the authorities, that action is believed to be "good"; if it brings frowns or a slap on the wrist, it is believed to be "bad." In a way, morality at this point is like the weather: you cannot do much about it, but you certainly prefer "good" weather over "bad" weather. The trouble is that you have to live with the weather you get, and you are only beginning to know how to influence it.

Early in the elementary school years, though, the child begins achieving significant control over the moral weather. The change marks the second of Kohlberg's stages, which he calls the *ethics of instrumental purpose* or *ethics of market exchange*. Instead of being at the mercy of powerful authorities' responses, the child learns how to *produce* positive responses deliberately. In essence he or she now exchanges actions for approval (hence the name "market exchange"), and the exchanges may involve not only parents but also teachers and peers. However, the actions always apply to only one other individual at a time. "Good" now becomes any action that produces a satisfying response from someone else, and "bad" becomes any action that produces a painful or unpleasant response. If deliberately speaking courteously in class produces a positive response from the teacher, that action is now seen as ethically "good"—at least with that person in that situation. If deliberately cursing and swearing produces approval from a friend, that action also becomes "good"—with that particular friend. At this point, the child sees no inconsistency in regarding the same action as good for one person or situation and bad for another; what matters is whether the action produces a satisfactory exchange: performing an action and getting approval from another person in return.

Stacy, Still Preconventional

"Something is wrong with Seifert's picture," thought Stacy, "though maybe not what I first thought." She was still simmering with annoyance. "Preconventional thinking is supposed to be immature. So I'm supposed to get over it by my age." Stacy was 25. She furrowed her brow and pondered whether she really felt as though she had moved beyond believing that authorities, not she, define what is right. Had she actually grown to this point? Well, maybe, but . . .

". . . But don't I still usually tell my professors what they want to hear? Just write the essays, do the assignments, answer questions, whatever—exactly as they ask?" Stacy thought about this. "I conform to one professor in one class and to another in another class. And I assume it's ethical to make the switch. It doesn't really matter whether I think their expectations are good for students; I just do as I'm told." A discouraging thought. "A market exchange: I do what they ask, and they give me approval or grades. So I'm no better than a preconventional child. No better than one of those preschoolers."

But then Stacy listened to a new voice: "Are you really so unusual, Stacy? Don't most students deal with teachers by cooperating with their expectations?"

She liked that voice better. "I bet, she said to herself, that we all carry elements of preconventional thinking around with us. And anyway, is being childlike really so bad?"

Conventional Justice

In the late elementary school years, says Kohlberg, children begin trying to reconcile the differing moral expectations of the various individuals in their lives. The effort creates a new interest in conventional justice, or social expectations about fairness and equality. At first, the concern with conventions leads to an *ethics of interpersonal conformity* or *ethics of peer opinion*, Kohlberg's third stage of moral development. In this stage, the child assesses actions by how they are evaluated by his or her primary community—by immediate peers, for example, or by close family relations. Deciding right and wrong becomes like taking an informal vote: an action is "good" if all (or at least most) of the child's peers favor it and "bad" if they disapprove. Unlike in the previous stage of market exchange, though, which took account only of the approval of self and a single other, group consensus now matters. Do all my friends approve of doing daily homework whenever assigned? If so, doing homework is good. If they all disapprove, on the other hand, it is bad. And if my friends disagree among themselves, then . . . what? In that case, perhaps doing homework is simply a matter of personal preference, such as whether you prefer vanilla ice cream or chocolate.

As you might suspect from the example, a problem with this sort of ethics is that community opinion may not always be a reliable moral guide. For one thing, a child usually belongs to more than one community, and the communities may differ in how they appraise specific actions. The family may think one thing (doing your homework is good), but peers may think another (take it easy; homework is for nerds). For another, as the preceding example suggests, disagreement can exist even within a single community. Some peers (or family members) may think it is good to stand up and fight when insulted; others may think it is

In Your Own Voice

Some psychologists (including Carol Gilligan, discussed later in this chapter) might argue that Stacy is coming to the wrong conclusion in deciding her "cooperative voice" is indeed immature.

They would argue instead that something is wrong with Kohlberg's theory if it creates this impression.

What do you think?

If you agree, what exactly might be missing or mistaken in Kohlberg's theory?

In Your Own Voice

Perhaps you have been caught in the middle of an ethical conflict (such as whether to report on a friend who has cheated in school or has shoplifted at a store).

In that case, you may have experienced some of the dilemma of the ethics of interpersonal conformity.

How did you resolve the dilemma?

good to practice tact and avoid violence at all costs. At this stage, a child still needs some way to reconcile such disagreements so as not to be pulled to and fro by others' conflicting opinions.

This ethical danger subsides in Kohlberg's fourth stage, called the *social systems orientation* or *ethics of law and order,* which emerges during adolescence. At this stage, the teenager tries to reconcile the differences among the various relationships and communities in his or her life. The moral challenge is to find common ground among them—to find the beliefs held in common by both friends and family, or by different circles of friends at school or at home. Maybe they all have positive things to say about education, for example, but what do they all really say about education in common? Whatever that common ground is, it is likely to be more general or abstract than in the previous stage. Everyone may believe in "getting an education," for example, without necessarily believing in "doing your homework" every night. When fully developed, this form of ethics becomes based on expectations held by society as expressed in its laws and other official documents. "Good" becomes what is legally approved or at least universally tolerated. "Bad" becomes what is illegal or universally disapproved of.

The good news about the ethics of law and order is that a young person can now distance himself or herself from the tyrannies of immediate peer pressure. It is no longer necessary, for example, to support an idea such as "Be nice to everyone except Rachel" just because your friends happen to agree on it. For many unsatisfactory ethical ideas, chances are that at least one of your communities (perhaps your parents in the preceding example) would not approve of the idea, and a broad ethics of law and order therefore will spare you from the excesses of any one group of peers.

The bad news is that it is still possible that society as a whole will create laws and agree on beliefs that may be ethically bad. Discriminatory laws and attitudes—about women, racial groups, or whatever—are perfectly legal, and may sometimes be held universally. So are laws permitting the pollution of the atmosphere or laws permitting the accumulation of fabulous wealth at the expense of citizens living in poverty. If these laws and the attitudes underlying them are morally wrong, they are wrong for reasons other than legality. A person guided by an ethics of law and order may have trouble understanding this idea and difficulty grasping the idea that existing laws and beliefs may not be the best or only ones possible.

Stacy, Still Conventional

Stacy reread the section on conventional justice, still remembering her annoyance with the example of Jocelyn on page 452. Seifert had said that Jocelyn was at a middling, conventional level of moral development because she showed primary concern for others' feelings. Stacy thought about Seifert's interpretation again, and begrudgingly agreed with it. What bothered her, she now realized, was the implication that human care and responsibility for others might not be as ethical as acting on abstract principles of fairness.

She thought too about her own relationships and her efforts to develop and maintain them. Over the years it had been a mixed bag: trying to be liked by others and trying to stay connected often guided her actions and judgments. In high school she had dressed like her friends, gone to the same movies they had, listened to the same music, eyed the same boys. . . .

Stacy wondered about these efforts. Some had succeeded, had truly connected her with others. Like her friendship with Jody, a relationship still alive and well after all these years. But some had also been destructive failures, like the times she had skipped classes because her "friends" invited her to do it. It really had seemed like the right thing to do at the time, but not now, eight years later. She had genuinely cared for her girlfriends back then, but now she wondered if she had sometimes cared too much. Which brought her back to Seifert's example of Jocelyn: obviously Jocelyn cared about human relationships, but was this necessarily "good"? Was it possible for Jocelyn to care too much?

Postconventional Justice

When individuals discover the limitations of conventional justice—usually during young adulthood—they begin developing new, more comprehensive beliefs that Kohlberg calls *postconventional*. The first sign of a postconventional orientation is Kohlberg's fifth stage of moral development, called the *ethics of social contract and individual rights*. Actions in this stage are evaluated not by whether they conform to public opinion or even by whether they happen to be legal. Instead, actions are judged according to whether they have been created through fair, democratic processes, respect the rights of all individuals, and take into account differences in individual beliefs and perspectives. For instance, is legally requiring attendance at school morally "good"? At this fifth stage of ethical thinking, the answer will no longer depend simply on whether your friends, family, and teachers believe education to be good, or on whether society currently has laws about mandatory attendance. Now the moral status of compulsory education depends on how society has collectively arrived at a decision to require attendance. Have all affected parties been consulted? Is compulsory attendance actually demeaning or useless to certain cultural, ethnic, or religious groups that might prefer to provide their own forms of education? Might some students flourish better if they left school relatively early to work instead of completing high school, and have they and their families been consulted?

If questions such as these have indeed been considered and the relevant people consulted, a nationwide decision to compel attendance at school might be ethically "good." But only for the moment! Because of the complexity of the democratic process, any consensus about compulsory attendance is likely to be provisional. Given enough time, important changes in the curriculum—in what students are being compelled to do by attending school—surely will occur. Various changes will take place regarding compulsory attendance: the starting and leaving ages, the mandatory lengths of school days and school years, and the like. Procedures for opting out of compulsory attendance also will change: over time, a family may need permission from more or fewer authorities, or may need to make more elaborate or simpler justifications. As a result, what society means by "mandatory attendance" will gradually change, and the ethical worthiness of the policy will have to be reassessed in response to the changes.

But even the ethics of social contract has limitations. One is that it puts excessive faith in rational, democratic discussion: actions are judged to be "good" regardless of their content, as long as they have resulted from such discussion. But this may not always be true: it is possible, for example, to decide democratically to institute a dictatorial, fascist government; such decisions in fact occurred in Europe earlier in this century, and were a factor that led to World War II. A second problem is related to the first: the ethics of social contract tends not to speak to the ethical issues of personal life; by nature, it focuses instead on broad community or societal issues. It has something to say, for example, about the general merits of compulsory schooling. But it has less to say about how, or even whether, to motivate a student who is dropping out of school in spite of being legally compelled to attend, or about when to intervene in the life of a child who is becoming dangerously thin because she refuses ever to eat. Yet issues that are personal and irrational arise frequently among both teachers and students: the high school dropout and the anorexic girl may both have heartfelt reasons for their actions, and no amount of rational, democratic consultation may change their minds.

To some extent, this limitation is resolved in the final, sixth stage of moral development, which Kohlberg calls the *ethics of self-chosen, uni-*

versal principles. At this point the "good" becomes more than democratic consultation (stage 5 ethics); it begins to also include personally held principles that are relevant to everyday life as well as to the larger events within the community or society. A person at this stage may believe in the inherent dignity of all human beings, for example, and will let this principle guide his or her personal relationships, using it to sort out his or her position on larger, communitywide issues. Is it "good" to include all students in regular classrooms, as we discussed in Chapter 10, regardless of physical or mental disabilities? The answer now depends not only on how democratically the policy is instituted in the community or society at large but also on how well it might promote human dignity individually. The stage 6 thinker asks two questions: first, "Will individuals with disabilities have better lives as a result of inclusion?" and second, "Will the individuals, their teachers, and their classmates all be consulted and respected if this policy is implemented universally?" The second question was essentially the only one asked at the previous ethical stage of social contract. By adding the first question, a person at the final stage achieves a more complete, comprehensive form of thinking about justice. But the demands for clear thinking are relatively high at stage 6, which is perhaps why Kohlberg and his associates believe relatively few people reach it (Kohlberg, Levine & Hewer, 1983).

Stacy, Postconventional

Stacy was feeling better about this whole chapter, though she was not yet completely at ease. She realized that the section she just read on postconventional thinking held the clue. She remembered a day in high school when she had finally refused to skip a class with her friends. At the time, she had primarily felt challenged to avoid hurting their feelings. It was, she had thought, an exercise in caring for others. But now, years later, she sensed another dimension that she had missed at the time.

"Why?" they had asked. "Why not come shopping with us?" They certainly looked hurt, as though Stacy had just taken a knife and cut a cord that bonded her to them. Now they were at one end and she was at the other—alone.

"Because I've got to think of myself, too," she had said. She had put it as nicely as she knew how. "If you want to skip, it's your business. But my business, at least today, is to go to class." Stacy had looked pained, as did they. "Have fun, though," she had said, and smiled weakly.

Stacy remembered that incident as if it were yesterday. Had it been only about caring for others' feelings? At the time she had thought so. Now she thought it was about caring for herself as well. She realized, in fact, that

In Your Own Voice

Notice again that it is not a person's moral *conclusion* that determines his or her stage of moral judgment but the *reasoning* behind the conclusion.

A student can sound postconventional simply by borrowing the "morally correct" conclusions of someone else.

Is there a way for a teacher to discern whether a student is sounding "good" merely for public consumption, so to speak?

there was a principle guiding her decision that day, a principle of caring about everyone's choices and needs, even when one of the parties was herself. "If that's not principled thinking," thought Stacy, "then what is?" She picked up her book again and continued reading.

All things considered, what sense can we make of Stacy's and Kohlberg's ideas taken jointly? One conclusion is that even though stages of moral judgment may characterize children of different ages, evidence of the stages may live on in all of us no matter how old and (presumably) wise we get. Another is that the ethics of justice and the ethics of care may not really be distinct (Bubeck, 1995). As Stacy's reflections suggest, it is quite possible to develop a sense of care or responsibility for others based on principles of justice or fairness. In fact, combining the orientations may be especially important for teachers, since teachers must be concerned about students as individuals while at the same time juggling the needs of many such individuals. Neither justice nor care can accomplish this goal alone; whatever morality teachers develop, then, and whatever beliefs and practices they encourage in students, it must allow for both kinds of ethics. To see why this is so, let's look at the next section, where we explore the morality of care and how it both supports and determines an ethic of justice.

In Your Own Voice

Can you think of a choice you made that now seems preconventional by Kohlberg's standards?

Or one that seems conventional, or postconventional?

Morality of Care

A **morality of care** refers to beliefs and actions that are based on responsiveness to others and therefore are tailored to circumstances and individual relationships as much as possible (Noddings, 1992; Steitmatter, 1996). Its key focus is not equality and fairness, as in the case of a justice-oriented morality, but responsibility for and connections with others. Individuals should not be ignored or neglected simply because they exist on the fringes of social life of a group or community; a morality of care requires that you draw those people into the mainstream as much as possible. When confronted with a student who stutters, therefore, a care orientation makes the same recommendation a justice orientation does: the student should have a chance to participate in class discussions, even though his or her classmates can speak faster and more fluently. But the care orientation is less concerned about the student's right to participate than about the teacher's and classmates' *responsibility* to ensure inclusion and social participation. The starting assumption is connection and relationship, not autonomy

A morality based on care rather than justice, such as Gilligan's, focuses on your concern for others—but also on how well the concern is reconciled with your own needs as an individual. © Ilene Perlman/Stock Boston

and freedom. In following a care orientation, the teacher should do more than simply provide opportunities for the student to speak. He or she should also encourage participation actively, though without at the same time making the student self-conscious about doing so.

Shifting the focus from rights to responsibilities changes the character of moral thinking, making it focused less on general beliefs and more on strategies for developing and maintaining human relationships. A care orientation therefore is appropriate for anyone, such as a teacher, whose stock-in-trade is social interaction with diverse individuals. But a care orientation also poses issues of its own, issues that can be just as challenging as those posed by a justice orientation. Consider again the student who stutters. Suppose the teacher and most classmates agree on a fundamental caring value: that everyone should be included in the life of the class. But suppose also that involving the student with the language disorder requires active effort on the part of the teacher. Perhaps the teacher not only must call on him a reasonable number of times during discussions but also deliberately make friendly conversation with him after class and take time to persuade classmates to include him in their social and learning activities. Perhaps she must also use many seatwork times to support the student's academic work, which is suffering because of his lack of confidence; and perhaps other students see the teacher less during these times as a result.

Eventually one student privately but vociferously complains that the time given to the student who stutters is excessive. Since the teacher is

Creating a caring atmosphere—one of acceptance and encouragement of growth—is a challenge for any educator. It is especially a challenge when a student looks or learns differently than others. Since teachers set the tone and model caring behavior for students, I believe they must first know their own style, limitations, and experiences. All children can learn, but their rates, techniques, and styles of learning are unique. So the role of the teacher is to make sure that inclusion and participation are available for all. Caring for individuality, furthermore, will vary daily, along with the ease and frustrations in implementing your goals.

Maria Matson, Kindergarten Teacher, Hawthorne Public Schools, Hawthorne, CA

committed to considering *everyone,* including the student who complains, she listens respectfully to the objections. However, when the complaints are repeated by a parent and later by another student, the teacher eventually begins to ignore them. Eventually she senses that a few students seem more distanced from her and respond less and less enthusiastically to invitations to participate in activities. In this case—a rather plausible one—has the teacher fulfilled the expectations of a caring morality? Taking responsibility to include one student, it seems, has competed with responsibility to include other students; a benefit for one has, to some extent, become a cost to another.

So a morality of care does not necessarily provide easy answers to moral dilemmas any more than a morality of justice does. However, it can foster attention to and concern for individual needs and circumstances, a point also made by Maria Matson, an experienced kindergarten teacher, in the accompanying Multiple Voices. Since individual needs and circumstances are important to teachers, a morality of care deserves our closer attention. How does it develop during childhood and adolescence, and what are its benefits and problems? The ideas about a morality of care developed by Carol Gilligan speak to these questions.

Gilligan's Morality of Care

In one key respect, Carol Gilligan approached the problem of moral development differently than Kohlberg: instead of inviting individuals to

In Your Own Voice

Why would gender roles encourage an ethics of care in girls and an ethics of justice in boys?

When you reflect on common gender stereotypes, what features of them might support such a difference?

On the other hand, what features of boys' and girls' lives might ensure that both sexes support both moralities to some extent?

comment on moral dilemmas they imagined, she asked them to talk about moral dilemmas they had really experienced. In her original research, for example, she and her colleagues interviewed women who had either had an abortion or were considering getting one (Gilligan, 1982, 1993). Interview questions focused not on whether the women actually did abort their fetuses but on the reasons behind the decisions. Inviting commentary about a real dilemma created two differences between her findings and Kohlberg's. One was that the people she interviewed did not separate beliefs and actions as sharply as Kohlberg's respondents did: believing in the good and acting on it often were part of the same story. Another difference was that the focus of moral development changed: her interviewees talked less about rights and fairness and more about relationships with and responsibilities to others. The result was a true ethics of care. After a series of studies of moral development, furthermore, Gilligan and her colleagues heard this caring "voice" a bit more strongly in women than men and more often in girls than boys. But it is important to note that the gender difference was small. Individuals of both sexes, it seems, can show concern for caring relationships, and both can show concern for justice as well (Gilligan, 1996; Gilligan, Ward & Taylor, 1988).

Using her approach for learning about moral development, Gilligan identified three positions or levels of thinking about care and relationships. Table 13.2 summarizes the positions. Development from one position to the next represents changes from more selfishness and to more

TABLE 13.2   Forms of Moral Caring According to Gilligan

Position	Features
Position 1: Survival orientation	Egocentric concern for self, lack of awareness of others' needs; "right" action is what promotes emotional or physical survival
Position 2: Conventional care	Lack of distinction between what others want and what is right; "right" action is whatever pleases others best
Position 3: Integrated care	Coordination or integration of needs of self and of others; "right" action takes account of self as well as others

Source: From Kelvin Seifert and Robert Hoffnung, *Child and Adolescent Development*, Third Edition, Houghton Mifflin, copyright © 1994, p. 419. Reprinted by permission.

responsibility for others. Compared to Kohlberg, however, Gilligan and her associates have not occupied themselves with establishing a hierarchy among the moral positions or with showing that individuals normally move from one position to the next as they get older. Instead they have been more concerned about clarifying subtle differences in the positions among individuals of essentially the same age, usually adolescents or young adults (for examples, see Brown & Gilligan, 1992, or Taylor, Gilligan & Sullivan, 1995).

Position 1: Surviving

In the most basic position, an individual is concerned primarily about self and survival. A girl considering an abortion, for example, might focus her concern only on the pregnancy's effects for her. If having the child is less disruptive to her life than having an abortion, she will choose to have the child. If it is the other way around, she will make the opposite choice. In the *survival position,* she does not think much about the needs and opinions of others. Later, if she develops a caring orientation more fully, she may regard this position as "selfish" or inconsiderate, and therefore undesirable ethically. For now, though, she is oblivious to this possibility. Her ethical world does not yet include others; it includes only herself and her own welfare or survival.

Stacy, Surviving

Stacy remembered when her dad died of cancer; he was only forty-five, and Stacy was twelve. Her mom must have been upset; Stacy remembered her crying a lot at unpredictable moments. She remembered people calling—sometimes at inconvenient times—to offer condolences. She remembered several of them telling her, "Be strong for your mother; she needs you right now." Or something like that.

But she also remembered not thinking about her mother very deeply at the time. What she did remember was feeling immediately angry: angry that they had to move. Her mom had to go back to work; she would not earn as much as dad, everyone had said; they could not afford their house and needed to sell it. Besides, it was too full of memories, said her mom. And then she cried again.

So they were moving. Case closed. Stacy would lose her new friendships in the neighborhood. She would lose the wonderful basement that she had adopted as her own secret place. She would lose her mom's attention once her mother went back to work. And, of course, she had already lost her dad.

In Your Own Voice

What might be wrong with an adult telling twelve-year-old Stacy to "be strong" in this situation?

Can you think of a better response or comment to give a girl of this age?

So the advice "Be strong for your mom" rang hollow. She just couldn't make herself care about her mother, no matter how many people told her it was the right thing to do and no matter how much her mother cried. Instead she thought about how to keep her own dignity: how to make sure that at least she, Stacy, would be concerned about Stacy. She would not betray her love for that old house and her old basement for life as it used to be. But to do that, she could not think about her mother. At least not just then. She could be strong, all right, but strong for herself rather than for others—including even her own mother.

Can a survival position find its way into everyday classroom life? Hopefully not on a widespread scale; life could indeed be difficult if most students cared only about themselves. But it is quite possible to find individual students, such as Stacy, whose lives are disrupted enough to make self-survival their way of "caring." In many schools, for example, there are students whose parents are divorcing or experiencing stress. There are also students who are suffering abuse or have done so in the recent past. And in some schools there are students who chronically get too little to eat, or who lack proper clothes for winter or even a reliable place to sleep each night (Kozol, 1995). Under these conditions, as both Gilligan and other educators have pointed out, thinking about others may have to wait until the student can remedy these difficulties or can arrange for others to do so (Taylor, Gilligan & Sullivan, 1995; Maslow, 1987).

Position 2: Caring Only for Others

In a more developed morality of care, a young person equates what is right or good with caring for others (Larrabee, 1993). Survival is not the issue here so much as pleasing others. In considering an abortion, for example, a woman in the *caring for others position* will consider what others in her life might want—whether *they* would approve or disapprove, and how they might evaluate her choice. What is right becomes whatever her community of people seems collectively to want. This is essentially what also happens in Kohlberg's third stage of moral development, which focuses on interpersonal conformity. This new position therefore is more ethical than the previous ones because it is the first time that a person really tries to balance the competing needs and wishes of several others. But it is not fully satisfactory as an ethic of care because it ignores the person's own needs and beliefs. Everyone counts except yourself. Later you may notice this omission; but for now you do not, simply because what others want still is what you want.

Stacy, Living to Serve

Eventually, of course, Stacy came out of her shell. Everyone liked her much better then, when she began being helpful. She learned to study diligently, but not too diligently; she worked just enough to please her mom and her teacher, but not enough to call attention to herself among friends or teachers. She learned to sit attentively during class, even when she was not really paying full attention. But she also learned to pay just enough attention so that if she did have to speak, she would sound as if she had done the assignment, even if she had not. And she learned to listen to her friends' conversations—and especially to boys' conversations—as if she knew and cared about what they were saying, even when she did not. All in all, it seemed, she developed a pleasing personality—or, more precisely, a personality designed to please.

The following year, her mother and teacher both commented on how much happier Stacy seemed after these changes began. "Maybe she's learning from her difficult loss," said a school counselor. "Maybe she's maturing into a young woman," said her mother. She was so helpful, they all said, so considerate. The fact was, Stacy later believed, that she had become "nice" to a fault. Too nice for her own good.

Vaguely Stacy still sensed discomfort. Hearing everyone's comments, she thought she *should* be happier than when her father first died. But was she really? Why was she often so uneasy? She felt as though everyone was always watching her, always expecting grace and perfection. Vaguely she knew she resented sitting through boring classes, all the while looking as if she were interested. And vaguely she resented pretending to care about conversations that meant little to her. And not at all vaguely, she saw how some kids, especially girls, got in trouble "for their big mouths," as she put it. Speaking up, asserting yourself, stating your views and sticking to them: all of that meant risking conflict and criticism, and ultimately risking relationships.

Stacy wondered what she meant by *relationships*. Those mattered to her a lot. But how could she achieve genuine connection with others, true relationships, without losing her true self in the process?

For a teacher, Position 2 creates students who are kind, considerate citizens of the classroom. Socially, a student can seem very helpful but not overly helpful. Academically, he or she can seem good rather than outstanding or excellent. Emotionally, he or she can try to fit in, but will

In Your Own Voice

Of course, a person might behave in the manner described here for reasons other than Position 2 ethics.

For example, you might be motivated by survival.

Attending to others might keep others from criticizing you or treating you badly—essentially Position 1.

If you were the teacher, is there a way you could distinguish among types of caring—among survival motives, conventional motives of caring for others, and the motives of integrated caring for self and others described in the next section?

hang back from leadership. And so on. By definition, the student who cares only about others will try to balance everyone's expectations against one another. What gets neglected, and consequently remains undeveloped, is the student's identity: his or her own academic goals, his or her own ways of forming relationships. The student in Position 2 is officially caring, but failure to care about the self contradicts this attitude.

Position 3: Integrated Caring

In Gilligan's model, the most developed form of ethics involves *integrated caring*, the coordination of the needs of self and those of others. In this position, what is right is what takes account of everyone, *including* yourself. In considering an abortion from this position, a woman would go beyond pleasing others and think as well about how she herself would feel about the decision and its consequences. Integrated caring therefore is a more truly comprehensive ethics than the previous position, in which care is focused only on others. Being comprehensive does not, however, prevent a person from experiencing dilemmas about right and wrong; in fact, the more people one takes into account in an ethical decision, the more difficult it will be to please them all and the more likely one will confront dilemmas.

Stacy: Caring in Principle, Caring in Practice

At least, thought Stacy, I handled my job hunting better than my junior high experiences. In fact, my father would have been proud of me. Stacy remembered what a crisis that job search had been! Eleventh grade: to work or not to work? Her mom sure had a lot to say about her working; she dragged her heels, start to finish. "It'll hurt your school work," she had said. "We can afford for you not to work, even with Dad gone." Stacy had no doubt that her mom was right in a sense. But she also noticed her mother's assumption that making ends meet was the only reason to work.

Her friends also had a lot to say. Half of them had already found "McJobs," if not literally at McDonald's, then at other places with low pay and little future. But they all sang the praises of working: "It gives you money of your *own*," Regan pointed out. "You can go places, do stuff." As if the only reason for working was to *spend* the money you made!

Then there was Ms. Carter, her favorite English teacher. When Stacy said she was thinking about getting a job, Ms. Carter didn't reply directly. She just said, "Do you want to go to a university out of the state?" A hint, meaning: you should consider seeing a new part of the world. And also meaning: it costs money to move far away, and a job might help with the cost. All things to think about, admittedly.

"But what to do?" she wondered—her usual question these days, it seemed. In the end, Stacy both took all the advice and ignored it. She listened respectfully to her mom, suspecting that she was trying to make up to Stacy for the emotional disaster of her dad's death years earlier. It was kind of her to promise financial support, but Stacy felt there was no sense denying it: she *was* poorer since her father passed away. So she found a job anyway, in spite of her mother's advice.

She listened courteously to her friends, making few comments, but realizing they often did not have the same financial concerns she did, nor the same college plans. But she did like the idea of having spending money. So when she began her job, she did spend part of her wages on recreation.

And she listened to Ms. Carter's indirect hints, but revised them in her mind: yes, she would apply to college out of state, but on the other hand she might not be admitted there. So she made a plan, announced only to her mother, to bank half of her wages every month. "It's my going-away present to myself," she confided to a friend. "Either I will use it to go out of state, or I will spend it next summer to see Europe."

In the end, I might note, no one person determined Stacy's decision totally, nor was anyone totally ignored, including Stacy herself. Or put differently: no one got everything they wanted, but everyone did get something. Combining responsibility to self and to others guided the decision.

Note, too, that in reaching this more universal position, Stacy's ethics of care begins to resemble an ethics of justice like Kohlberg's discussed earlier in this chapter. The difference between Stacy's thinking and Kohlberg's highest, principled stages, however, is explicitness: Stacy does not necessarily think of the decision to find work as being guided by a conscious principle. For all we know, her decision strategies were unconscious or intuitive: she may have simply made a habit of listening to others while still making up her own mind. In Kohlberg's model, on the other hand, a highly principled thinker necessarily knows he or she has principles and can tell you what they are.

Garth looked at Stacy with new respect. "Seems to me that you, not Seifert, have the last word about care and justice," he said. "You've filled your life with moral choices. Seifert has only been talking about them."

Stacy looked up, having finished reading about herself, over and over, in Chapter 13. "Mmm?" was all she said.

"Yeah," he continued. "This chapter needs more about moral action—

In Your Own Voice

Is conscious knowledge of your principles valuable, or might consciousness create emotional detachment and distract you from moral action?

This is an especially important and tricky question for teachers, who are expected every day both to make "good" choices quickly and to be able to justify the choices consciously.

As a teacher, would you emphasize one over the other—action over consciousness?

about how to be more caring in practice, how to be fairer. We don't need just to talk about those things, just to sit in an armchair and talk."

Stacy smiled mysteriously at her friend. He was a good sport, really, but sometimes he could be so dense! Here she had just finished revealing her life to unknown readers, made herself vulnerable to their criticisms. But all Garth could do was make generalities: expound on what an ed psych text should say or on what an author should write. Instead of criticizing Seifert's writing, maybe Garth should reveal some of *his* moral choices; then he would know how she felt.

Of course, Garth did have a point, she realized. As a teacher, she really *did* want ideas about how to encourage students to ethical action and not just to ethical belief. So she smiled her mysterious smile again and felt new respect for Garth.

Fostering Care and Justice

*S*TACY and Garth's point is a good one. As teachers, we are concerned about encouraging students toward worthwhile actions and not just toward worthwhile beliefs. It is one thing to believe in saving the natural environment and another to organize and act to do so. It is one thing to believe in treating classmates with respect, regardless of race or cultural background; it is another actually to do so regardless of biases or pressures from peers, family, or society. The gap between belief and action is widespread, and teachers have a responsibility to reduce it. But how? We can get some clues by looking at research on people with exemplary moral lives and at what those lives suggest for developing similar qualities in students.

Qualities of Exemplary Moral Lives

Anne Colby and William Damon studied the lives of twenty-three adults who showed extraordinary commitments to the welfare of others (Colby & Damon, 1992; Phillips & Benner, 1994). These people were not especially rich or famous, but they were highly committed to a life of human service. Colby and Damon interviewed them at length about their lives, and followed them through their daily routines to understand their motives and circumstances more fully. One of the people was Suzie Valadez, a resident of the border city of El Paso, Texas. Suzie (as she preferred to be called) assisted residents of Cuidad Juarez, the neighboring town on the Mexican side of the border. Every day for thirty years she packed sandwiches and other supplies and drove to the Mexican town, where she distributed the food to poor and homeless people at the town dump. On most days, she also visited a school and medical clinic serving the area that she helped to create. Various friends and family help with these daily activities, but Suzie provides the energy and direction to sustain the whole operation. Residents have nicknamed her the "Queen of the Dump" to honor her efforts.

Suzie had several key qualities that accounted for her commitment and that Colby and Damon found in others leading morally exemplary lives. Some of the qualities contradicted qualities of moral leadership that the researchers expected to find. For example:

- *Willingness to take risk:* Although Suzie was aware that she was visiting an area (a town dump) every day with more than its share of crime, disease, and violence, she was not deeply concerned about the risk. Contrary to Colby and Damon's expectations, she never struggled with fear or needed to work herself up to her task, even when she first began doing it.

- *Clarity about underlying rightness:* With the wisdom of maturity, Suzie was sure that assisting the poor was both the right thing to do and effective for the people she served. She no longer seriously wondered whether her underlying commitments were appropriate. Sometimes she had questions, though, about specifically how to implement her plans effectively.

- *Steadfast optimism:* Even though she witnessed dismal poverty every day, Suzie remained optimistic about the lives of the people she served, as well as about the future of her efforts to serve them.

- *Intimate, trusted supporters:* Throughout her years of service, Suzie had a circle of friends, family, and coworkers who supported her work and with whom she felt able to relax, be herself, and confide. Contrary to one commonly held impression of the "do-gooder" who feels incapable of forming close relationships, Suzie's life was never solitary, nor was it grim or dull.

- *Following as well as leading:* Suzie listened to others' advice and experiences consistently, and at times found herself following others as much as she was leading them. She did not simply "preach at" or boss others with preconceived ideas; in fact, she developed many of her ideas by borrowing projects from others.

- *Continuity with the past:* Over the years, Suzie's service to the poor grew naturally out of earlier activities, including some from her child-

In Your Own Voice

This conclusion seems to be good news for most teachers: if you want to develop your commitment to students, you can draw on past experiences and commitments in doing so!

Can you think of any in your own life that form a basis for your current interest in and concern for students?

hood family, in which she had already practiced being helpful to others. An exemplary life of moral commitment therefore did not require her to make a radical break with the past; on the contrary, it built on it.

Even though Suzie's circumstances differ radically from those of most classrooms and students, the qualities she showed offer clues about how we, as teachers, might encourage moral commitment in students. To see this, it helps to look at successful teaching practices. I have chosen two, reciprocal teaching and philosophy in the schools, each of which supports different combinations of Suzie's moral qualities.

Risk, Support, and Leadership: Reciprocal Teaching

Reciprocal teaching is a widely used, successful strategy for building students' thinking skills (Palincsar, 1986). Although it was not originally devised to promote moral development, its design actually encourages three of the six qualities of moral commitment that Colby and Damon identified. In reciprocal teaching, students take responsibility for teaching one another how to reflect on reading material. First, they watch the teacher as he or she models key techniques of reflection: how to summarize a passage, for example, or how to clarify difficult points, compose a central question, or predict what will come next in the passage. As they become familiar with these techniques, they gradually begin practicing them on one another. In essence, they become one another's teachers and begin "taking care" of one another. That is what happened to Kurt in the following dialogue; he tried to formulate a question about the main point of the paragraph for the benefit of other students, though he still needed a bit of help from the teacher. Kurt is in third grade.

Kurt was reading from a book called *Sara and Her Umbrella:* "One day Sara was walking home from school, when it started to rain. 'Oh I wish I had an umbrella,' said Sara. Presto! It started to rain umbrellas—all sorts of umbrellas. Big ones, little ones, red ones, blue ones. All sorts. . . ."

Kurt paused here, thinking about how to phrase a main question about what he just read. The other students looked on expectantly.

After several seconds of silence, the teacher said, "What's the passage about?"

Kurt's face lit up. "Sara; umbrellas!" He started over, speaking directly to other students: "What happened when . . ." But he hesitated; looked at the teacher; looked at the students.

"What happened when . . ." repeated the teacher, with an encouraging smile.

"What happened when Sara made a wish?" said Kurt triumphantly. Two hands went up, and Kurt called on one of them, who answered correctly—not surprisingly, perhaps, given the dialogue that had preceded the question.

"I have a prediction," continued Kurt. He glanced at the teacher to see if he could continue; she looked interested, so he went ahead. "I predict that every time she makes a wish, something else will fall on her head!" This brought a few chuckles from others.

In this example, Kurt took over much of the teaching about this story, first asking a summarizing question and later making a prediction about what the story would contain. He did not do it perfectly, but his hesitations are not the point. What matters is that the teacher encouraged him in his efforts. Eventually he will gain skill at taking a turn as the teacher.

What matters, too, is that in fostering reciprocal teaching, the teacher encourages some of the moral qualities shown by Suzie Valadez. For one thing, it provides students with trusted supporters; by working cooperatively they learn to help one another, not only in learning the reading passages themselves but also in learning how to phrase questions that stimulate reflection. In the process of providing a circle of support, furthermore, reciprocal teaching allows students to take risks: since everyone must take the risk of composing thought-provoking questions, apprehension about looking foolish decreases, and focus on the task at hand increases. And as with Suzie, everyone sooner or later serves as both a leader (the questioner) and a follower (the responder to questions). By sharing participation in this way, the approach helps to move students beyond merely conforming to one another's wishes and opinions (Gilligan's Position 2) and on to integrating their personal learning needs with those of other students. Note, too, that reciprocal teaching creates diverse participation structures in the classroom—a positive benefit to students, as we discussed in Chapter 8.

But reciprocal teaching cannot do everything. In particular, it does not speak directly to three of Suzie's other qualities noted by Colby and Damon: achieving clarity of underlying values, creating optimism, and ensuring continuity with students' pasts. Reciprocal teaching might realize these goals indirectly as the incidental result of successful experiences with teaching and learning among peers. But they are not its primary purpose. To succeed more fully with developing Suzie's remaining qualities, teachers need an approach focused more directly on students' reasoning.

Clarity, Optimism, and Continuity: Philosophy in the Schools

A number of educators, beginning as long ago as Kohlberg himself (1970), have argued that children and youth are quite capable of systematically reflecting on philosophical questions, and they have in fact created curricula for encouraging students to do so (Mathew, 1994; Pritchard, 1996). One widely used program for "doing philosophy," for example, involves a series of stories and books about a fictional character named Harry Stottlemeier, who has various puzzling experiences that stimulate his own philosophical thinking (Lipman, 1974, 1993). Harry finds himself puzzling about the nature of reality, for example, and about how we can ever know reality if it must always be filtered through our senses. He also reflects on questions of ethics—on how to decide between right and wrong—in much the same way we have been doing in this chapter. Curriculum materials associated with the stories invite students to reflect on what Harry Stottlemeier and other characters in his stories say and do. In the process, students become more aware of their views about a variety of philosophical topics, including ethics in particular.

In Your Own Voice

Educators have debated whether it is better to teach about ethical and moral issues as a separate subject or to weave the issues into all other subjects.

Which approach do you think might be more effective, all things considered?

By directly helping students to become aware of their moral values and beliefs, this approach helps to develop the other qualities Suzie shows in great abundance: clarity, optimism, and continuity. Students' reflections on personal values help to clarify those values and add to students' sense of "rightness" about what they believe morally. The combination of clarity and certainty, in turn, sustains optimism about beliefs: if you are sure of what you care about, you can sustain commitment to it for extended periods of time. And clarity reveals connections among the past, present, and future: to decide now what you will value in the future, you have to know what you used to value, even if only to reject it.

Moral Students, Moral Classrooms

PERHAPS the real challenge in encouraging moral commitment in students is to rethink teaching strategies so as to create entire classrooms—indeed, whole schools—that foster concern for care and justice. Teachers need to examine all activities for ethical overtones, for the messages each activity sends, directly and indirectly, about what is good and valuable. In a kindergarten class, for example, what does the teacher's policy about tidying up the room "tell" the children? That each child bears responsibility for the group? That each child is not helpless but capable of contributing to the group? Or that the teacher values the materials in the room more than the children? Somehow the teacher must make sure that the first two messages, and not the third, get through to the children. These questions are raised, at least implicitly, whenever the teacher decides to manage the class in one way rather than another. They cannot be answered, though, unless the teacher makes himself or herself aware of the possible moral implications of even simple decisions such as these.

As this example suggests, there may be no classroom actions or activities that lack moral implications. Even if I, as a teacher, try hard to be neutral in presenting a controversial theory or idea, for example, my very neutrality is a moral position: I am making an implied statement to students that being neutral is good. In general, even if I say nothing about care or justice verbally, I cannot get away from "saying" something about care and justice through my actions. By the same token, my students cannot escape making moral "statements" of their own. Because I am professionally involved with students and other members of the public, I am part of a moral universe.

But take heart: the "trap" of moral predicaments surrounding teachers is not as intimidating as it may at first seem. In fact, entire books describe ways to live with the moral dimension of teaching and of making constructive use of it (e.g., Noddings, 1992). Entire curriculum guides offer ways to assess and develop the moral character of students (e.g., DeVries & Zan, 1994; Sharp & Reed, 1992). Care and justice are in fact a large part of the tradition of teaching, even if you also are entering the profession because you love a particular subject matter.

So my only parting advice in this chapter is to relish being trapped, enjoy the constant presence of problems of care and justice. Whatever else you do, enjoy the privilege of assisting students to make choices, of caring for and being fair to them, and of watching for signs of their own care and justice toward one another.

It was the last hour of the last day of the school year. The students had left; Mr. Fisher was cleaning up materials and storing them away for next fall. He checked one last time inside students' desks. They were supposed to have cleaned them out completely before leaving, and indeed most of them had done so.

But not Alison. Inside her desk he found one piece of paper, neatly folded and with his name printed carefully on the outside: "Mr. Fisher—do not open until after we have gone."

Well, they've all gone, he thought. So he opened the piece of paper and found the following:

Roses are red, violets are blue,
You try to be fair, but know how to care too.
It's like when we came by, at noon or at 3,
You helped us a lot, in fact more than you see.
Have a good summer!
Matt, Joelle, Diane, Craig (and others who left too quick to sign)

Not exactly Shakespearean quality, he thought, but definitely from the heart. He folded the paper back up, tucked it safely in his pocket, and walked out.

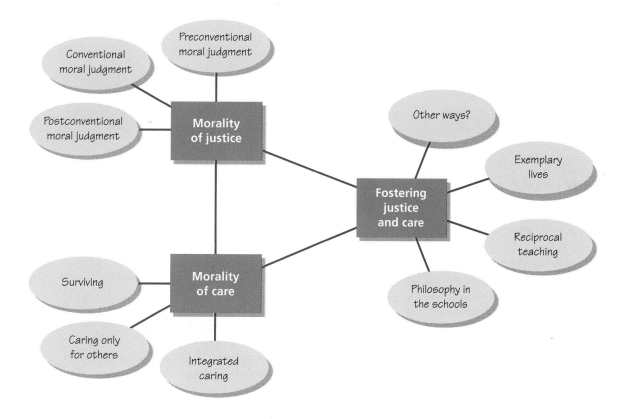

Chapter Re-View: Care and Justice in Teaching and Learning This Chapter Re-View suggests directions in which the chapter might have taken your thinking—though, of course, other directions are also possible. It expands the Chapter View, which suggests a starting point, conceptually, for the chapter. But this Re-View does not suggest an ending point. Like the Chapter View, it represents just one perspective among many.

Key Terms and Concepts _____

morality of justice (450)
preconventional moral
   judgment (454)
conventional moral judgment
   (454)
postconventional moral
   judgment (454)

morality of care (461)
Position 1: surviving (465)
Position 2: caring only for
   others (466)
Position 3: integrated caring
   (468)
reciprocal teaching (472)

philosophy in the schools
   (474)

Annotated Readings _____

Colby, A., & Damon, W. (1992). *Some do care: Contemporary lives of moral commitment*. New York: Free Press. This is the book cited in the chapter that describes case studies of individuals whose lives embody moral commitments. Most of the individuals are not well off or renowned, but a few are relatively well known. The book makes interesting reading for teachers, whose working lives also require moral commitment in important ways.

Molnar, A. (Ed.). (1997). *The construction of children's character: 96th yearbook of the National Society for the Study of Education*. Chicago: University of Chicago Press. This book is written by a number of authorities on moral development and moral education, and reviews important and recent research in the area. The book itself takes no stand on the relative merits of different theories of moral development (e.g., about justice versus care), but some of the individual authors do so.

Noddings, N. (1992). *The challenge to care in schools: An alternative approach to education*. New York: Teachers College Press. One of the foremost advocates for a "care" orientation to ethics, Nel Noddings explains what this orientation implies for teachers, principals, and others concerned about education. Unlike myself, Noddings seems to believe a care orientation is the only approach to ethics that teachers need. I encourage you to read the book and see what you think.

Internet Resources _____

<www.wittenberg.edu/ame>, <www.uni-konstanz.de/SIG-MDE> These are both web sites for professional associations of educators, psychologists, and others concerned about the nature of moral development and moral education. The first address belongs to the Association for Moral Education, and the second belongs to a section of the American Educational Research Association called the Special Interest Group in Moral Development in Education. Both sites contain newsletters about the orga-

nizations' activities, information about becoming a member, and links to other sites related to moral development.

<www.uic.edu/~Inucci/MoralEd> This web site belongs to the Office for Studies in Moral Development and Character Education, a department of the University of Illinois. The site contains information for teachers and other educators concerned about moral development (e.g., parents and religious leaders), including downloadable articles, teaching ideas, and links to other sites related to moral development.

V

Reflections

If you have read the book this far, you have engaged in a complex journey. You began with your existing views about teaching and learning (Chapter 1) and continued with explorations of individual change in students, relationships in the classroom, the social context of education (Parts 1, 2, and 3). Then you looked at how these features of teaching and learning determined the overarching problem of education—to decide on and choose what is good, desirable, and successful (Part 4).

Part 5, which contains only Chapter 14, integrates the issues from all of these earlier parts by returning to your own beliefs and purposes. Chapter 14 suggests the qualities, knowledge, and skill that you will need to become a truly successful, professional teacher. What do you really need to know, it asks, about students' individual change? Or about their relationships? Or about their context and about judging their success? But the chapter goes beyond merely naming these questions; it also examines the resources that you already have for answering them and that you can expect to acquire as a beginning teacher. The picture that it therefore presents of your future as an educator is both hopeful and challenging. It suggests that it is not easy to teach well, but it is also not impossible to do so.

Challenges in becoming
an accomplished teacher

Your resources for becoming
an accomplished teacher

Chapter View: Looking Ahead This Chapter View is a concept map that indicates one among many ways of thinking about the chapter. It suggests a starting point, conceptually, for the chapter but is incomplete by itself. At the end of the chapter is a Chapter Re-View, which expands on the Chapter View, suggesting directions for taking your thinking further—though, of course, other directions are also possible.

14

Looking Ahead

Education is everything. The peach was once a bitter almond, and the cauliflower is nothing but a cabbage with a college education.

Mark Twain (1899)

Bitter almonds to peaches, and cabbages to cauliflowers? Is that what teaching is all about? And suppose it is; suppose teaching is a process of transforming students, of sculpting the elegant and useful from the everyday. Consider what this might mean for your future as a teacher. What will teaching feel like when you begin? Suppose you have found a teaching position (a challenge in itself!) and face the prospect of educating students. You may be expecting to see as few as twenty each day or as many as a hundred. You may be expecting to hear languages from some students that you cannot understand and to discover special educational needs in some that you can only guess at now. As a newcomer to teaching, you are comparatively unfamiliar with the curriculum the school authorities expect you to implement; how, you wonder, can anyone fill an entire semester or school year with the curriculum, let alone motivate and excite students with it?

The worries are daunting, but they are balanced by other thoughts that are less stressful and more hopeful. You may remember experiences from your past with children or youth: times when you got along wonderfully with them, times that started you thinking about teaching as a career. Or you may remember teachers—not only the ones whose methods you want to avoid but also the ones whom you admired. Or you may remember courses or topics that caught your imagination: subjects that seem especially worthwhile, especially worth sharing with others. The positive memories sustain you while you look ahead to the stresses. Teaching, it appears, will be challenging, but it will be worth the challenge. You are inclined to agree with Mark Twain: education is indeed everything, and you may indeed be able to create some peaches and cauliflowers.

This chapter invites you to look ahead at the challenges and to consider how you may want to grow to become a teacher who is not just good but truly excellent. I cannot know exactly what concerns will be uppermost in your particular mind, of course, but I can suggest challenges for you to consider that other new teachers, and veterans as well, have encountered. I can also suggest strengths and resources that you may already have, or can soon acquire, for addressing your concerns and moving yourself closer to the kind of teacher you want to become. The suggestions are related to topics discussed earlier in this book, but they do not correspond precisely to those topics. In naming them as challenges, I have been guided mostly by knowledge about life in classrooms, both my own and other educators'. The importance of the challenges to you, though, will depend on your particular history and circumstances. Not everyone needs to grow in the same way or has access to the same supports. In reading this chapter, then, ask yourself these questions: What are the challenges that I feel I must meet to teach well? What strategies will I need to use to meet the challenges?

These two questions, and the reflections they lead to, are familiar to teachers who strive for excellence in their work. They are also familiar to government agencies and educational researchers and writers who have considered what it means to teach well (Sizer, 1996; Strange, 1997; Task Force on Teaching as a Profession, 1986). The agencies and researchers often frame the problem as one of identifying **professional teaching standards,** the qualities and complex skills needed for the finest possible teaching. In effect, professional teaching standards are long-term challenging goals for teachers. They identify levels of performance that not every teacher can attain easily but nonetheless are attainable given time, experience, and dedication to students' learning. Professional teaching standards, therefore, should not be confused with standards for teacher certification, which refer to minimal legal qualifications (often expressed as a set of university credits) required to begin a career as a teacher. Professional teaching standards refer to performance that is not minimal but maximal.

One prominent statement of professional teaching standards has been published by the National Board for Professional Teaching Standards (1997), a coalition of nonprofit foundations and professional associations related to education. Relying primarily on advice from classroom teachers themselves, the board proposed several ideas that describe highly accomplished teaching, presented as five propositions. The propositions are listed in Table 14.1. They make a useful framework for considering where you need to develop as a teacher in the years ahead and which aspects of teaching you may find especially challenging. They also help in assessing what skills and qualities you already have that can contribute to your own excellence in this profession. In the next part of the chapter, therefore, I explain some of the thinking behind each proposition, rephrasing it as a challenge to develop in your own work with students. You may find that you do not feel as well prepared in some areas as you would like—though, by the same token, you may also believe you have already made a good beginning toward excellence in other areas. As the discussion unfolds, and especially in the final part of the chapter, we look at how you might find ways to grow where you think you need it and why you can expect to succeed at doing so.

In Your Own Voice

Before reading the next section, stop and think about your own strengths as a potential teacher.

What do you consider your best quality or skill?

What, on the other hand, do you think you will need to develop further as you gain experience?

Keep your reflections in mind as you read the next section.

TABLE 14.1   Five Propositions of Accomplished Teaching

Proposition 1:	Teachers are committed to students and their learning.
Proposition 2:	Teachers know the subjects they teach and how to teach those subjects to students.
Proposition 3:	Teachers are responsible for managing and monitoring student learning.
Proposition 4:	Teachers think systematically about their practice and learn from experience.
Proposition 5:	Teachers are members of learning communities.

Source: National Board for Professional Teaching Standards, 1997.

What Will Challenge You About Teaching?

Becoming Committed to Students and Their Learning

In many ways, commitment to students and their learning is the "bottom line" of excellent teaching; without it, there is no point in even having a teaching career. Yet it is not a specific, identifiable skill acquired once and for all so much as an attitude that develops over time, eventually permeates all aspects of excellent teaching, and calls for constant renewal with each group of new students. The intangibility can be troubling, as it is for Brieanne Edgeworth, now in her second year of teaching middle school:

After reading the sentences above, Brieanne wondered if *she* was truly committed to teaching, and when she would know if she was. How can I know for sure? she thought. Will I ever know? I sweated bullets last year, surviving that first year of teaching. Surely that counts as commitment! But sometimes

One challenge in becoming a professional teacher is to know your subject well. Reaching this goal is a never-ending task: there is always more to be learned. But it is still possible to know your subject well enough to get started as a teacher.
© Elizabeth Crews

Another challenge in becoming a professional teacher is to support, and be supported by, the knowledge of other teachers. Becoming part of a learning community of teachers can help in meeting other goals, such as learning more about the subject you teach.
© Elizabeth Crews

then I did question my decision to go into teaching. There were days when the kids frustrated me more than I dared to say. And nights when I couldn't sleep on account of my work: I kept planning and revising the next day in my mind, even though it was 2:00 A.M. and I should have been asleep. Does insomnia show commitment to students, or just show stress?

The fact is that commitment to students and their learning is an ideal, something that teachers develop but never fully reach. What is important, therefore, is not so much being perfectly committed (there will always be times when you are not) as reaffirming commitment and developing it further. Looked at as a process, commitment is accessible no matter how much or how little experience you have. Brieanne has already engaged the process in her first year of teaching, and presumably will continue to do so in her second year and in later years.

As you gain experience, you may keep discovering new evidence that you do indeed care about students. One kind of evidence will be in your growing understanding of how students learn, think, and develop, because this knowledge allows you to teach more effectively and to make new knowledge and skills accessible. In this book, learning, thinking, and development were topics discussed in Chapters 2, 3, and 4, respectively. Those chapters offered an initial tool for developing useful, workable perspectives on students and their learning. But the information was only initial. You must go beyond the ideas in those chapters by learning more about students' learning, thinking, and development, and by choosing to use these ideas helpfully to benefit students.

Commitment to students and their learning can also be seen in the fairness with which you respond to students, regardless of diversity of race, gender, or disability. Information about students' diversity was discussed in several places in this book: in Chapters 9 (race and gender) and 10 (students with special needs) and, to some extent, in Chapters 7 (with regard to differences among families) and 8 (with regard to differences in expectations about classroom talk). As with the earlier chapters on learning, thinking, and development, however, these discussions took you only to the doorway of commitment to students and their learning. From this starting point you must carry on by yourself, finding out more about your own students' diversity and actually enacting your beliefs by responding to students with understanding and tolerance.

Finally, commitment to students and their learning can be seen in concern for students' self-esteem, integrity, and healthy participation in the communities to which they belong. These issues were discussed most directly in Chapter 13, which looked at how attitudes of care and commitments to justice develop and can be encouraged in both teachers and students. But it also was discussed indirectly in Chapter 7 (with regard to the impact of students' social relationships on their classroom learning) and Chapter 8 (with regard to how teachers' classroom talk can either empower or silence individual students). Taken together, these discussions focused attention on a point so fundamental to teaching that it seems commonplace and easy to forget: that all of our students will someday become adult members of society, whether or not they remember the details of what we teach them. As B. F. Skinner (the behavioral psychologist mentioned in Chapter 2) once put it, "Education is what is left over after everything else has been forgotten." An excellent teacher's job is to make sure, at the very least, that what "gets left over" in students includes qualities of constructive citizenship.

In Your Own Voice

Given these ideas, how committed do you already feel to students and their learning?

Think about what you consider the signs of commitment in yourself—where your interest in students' learning has come from and where you now think it needs to head.

Knowing Your Subject and How to Teach It

Excellent teachers "know their stuff": they know their subjects well and know how to communicate them to students. We talked about the first of these goals in Chapter 5, which discussed the roles teachers normally balance when teaching. One role is the *generous expert,* which refers partly to the enthusiastic, competent sharing of knowledge about a subject and partly to sharing how knowledge in the subject is created in the first place. To be a generous expert is to help students think like scientists (if you teach science), or like musicians (if you teach music), or like competent readers (if you teach reading). Michael Collingwood, an experienced high school science teacher, agrees, and also suggests why enthusiasm and generosity with knowledge can be so effective:

MICHAEL: You know how they're always saying that good teachers are enthusiastic? Well, it's true! I think I know why. When I get excited about science, it's like I'm showing my *relationship* to science. It's like science has become an old, respected friend that I'm introducing to new, young friends—to my students. And each time I visit my old friend, I discover something new, as I might with a real friend. The students see that, and like it. It turns science into something more than a lot of concepts and terms; it makes it something you can become connected to. When I'm enthusiastic, students see that science is not just abstractions sitting "out there" in the universe alone, devoid of human contact and relevance. They see that science is something that is known *by* someone, that stands in relationship *to* a human being. I figure that if I am crazy enough to make friends with science, then maybe some of them will be, too!

In Your Own Voice

At first glance, it would seem that a high school teacher has *more* need to know his or her subject in depth and *less* need to understand connections between the subject and other subjects.

But is this necessarily true?

Do you agree with this idea or not?

But another part of knowing your subject and how to teach it involves good instructional management, another of the roles discussed in Chapter 5. Being an instructional manager means knowing *how* to select and coordinate activities and tasks so that students learn as effectively as possible. A challenge for excellent teachers is to combine the roles of generous expert and instructional manager: they must know not only know what they teach but how to teach it. The specifics of how to forge this combination will depend on exactly what you are teaching. In early childhood education, for example, it may be especially important to know how a subject relates to *other* fields of knowledge. What skills at drawing contribute to a child's learning to read? How would the connections between drawing and reading alter how each of those subjects are planned and taught by an excellent early childhood teacher? How could the connections be conveyed to students effectively? Maybe they should draw what they read and read what they draw. But how exactly should this happen? Maybe computers could also help: they often have programs both for drawing and for reading. But how exactly should the teacher use the computers? These are all questions related to knowing the subject and how to teach it. Although answering them is beyond the scope of this book, they are normally addressed somewhere in every teacher education program, often in a curriculum or "methods" course.

While not a resource for knowledge of particular disciplines or how they might specifically be taught in school, this book is indirectly a general resource for learning how to foster the ability of students to analyze ideas critically and actively, no matter what subject they are learning. In Chapter 6, for example, the illustrations of successful management all emphasized inviting students to be actively involved in their own learning, and even in solving their own behavior disruptions when they occur. In Chapter 8, the best classroom talk was discourse in which students participated freely and actively. All chapters, in fact, either implied or stated the importance of students' engagement with new ideas and skills. Exactly how this should happen in your classes, of course, will depend on exactly what you are teaching. But no matter what that subject or topic is, you will want engagement from students.

Monitoring and Managing Students' Learning

As we saw in Chapter 6, management of activities poses special challenges because of the nature of classrooms, and in particular their unpredictability and complexity. Small wonder that many new teachers rate management as their biggest initial concern and a matter of survival (Jones, 1998; Partin, 1995)! Whether you are new to teaching or a veteran, though, inappropriate behavior by students, either accidental or deliberate, can confuse the sense of order and the purposes you are working toward with your students. Especially as a newcomer to teaching, it is tempting to equate management with self-defense: you may worry too much about how to handle *mis*behaviors and prevent specific disruptions rather than how to orchestrate and coordinate positive, constructive learning. In reality, all teachers do need ways to prevent and eliminate the negatives, but excellent teachers focus much more strongly on creating the positives in the first place (Kohn, 1996). The two sides of classroom management, and the priority of a positive emphasis, were reflected in Chapter 6. In the first part of that chapter we saw how one teacher, Barbara Fuller, gradually created successful learning groups in her classroom; she clearly focused on the positive in doing so. In the second part, we talked about how to respond when things do not go well in spite of your best efforts. Ms. Fuller has more to say about her approach to management:

BARBARA FULLER: Sometimes in my room it's like there's an "economy of attention," like students can attend to only so many things at a time—so many instructions, or tasks, or attractive classmates, or whatever. More attention to one means less attention to another. So I have to be careful about how much I ask them to keep track of. If they're doing group work, I have to be careful about how much I "drop in" to their discussions; if I do it needlessly, I could distract them from their thinking. If they're all supposed to be listening to me, on the other hand, I have to make it clear that their groups are (temporarily) disbanded; I must remind them that for the moment they do *not* need to consult with working partners about whatever we're studying. A lot of minor misbehavior happens when I forget the human limitations on attention. There can be problems when I forget how hard it can be to listen to two people at once or to talk to one person (like a partner) and listen to another (like me) at the same time. If I can remember about the economy of attention, it's easier to focus *my* attention on arranging positive learning rather than on curing "bad" behaviors.

Hopefully, when you teach, you will be able to focus more on coordinating positive learning than on repairing disruptions. Until you actually meet your students and classes, though, it will be hard to predict how *much* more you can tip the balance toward coordination and away from repair. To some extent, the balance will be influenced by factors beyond your control. Some classes are more prone to disruptions than others, and the reasons are not always clear, especially when the students in them behave well as individuals. And some classes may be harder (or easier) to manage than others, simply because you know less (or more) about the subject or about activities appropriate to it for engaging students. That said, keep in mind that the balance between coordination and repair nonetheless is under your control to some extent. By planning thoroughly before class, for example, you can make disruptions during class less likely—though, of course, not completely absent. Planning does so in two ways. First, it improves your tolerance for the unexpected during class. For example, a discussion that is more (or less) noisy or longer (or shorter) than expected may seem more acceptable if you know that students have focused on crucial goals of the curriculum. Second and more important, good planning tends to ensure that students have constructive things to do—tasks and activities that are incompatible with disruptive behavior. Planning can even lead to forms of participation that eliminate the preconditions leading to disruptions. For example, when learning activities are arranged to take place on students' own time using the Internet, some of the crowding of classroom life may be alleviated, and with it your need to repair classroom disruptions when they occur. This realization, though, is not a good enough reason to use computers; they are not meant simply to keep students out of mischief. As Janice Friesen pointed out in the Multiple Voices in Chapter 5, good teachers focus on the positive learning benefits even when using technology in the classroom: "What," asks such a teacher, "will students gain from using the Internet?" Not "What management problems can I avoid by using it?"

In Your Own Voice

What kind of balance do you expect will develop when *you* begin teaching?

Think about what is influencing your choice: your students' personalities, the subjects you expect to teach, the working conditions you anticipate, or . . . ?

But keeping the right mix of coordination and repair is not the only sort of balance needed to manage a classroom well. Another kind, just as challenging, is discovering combinations of teaching roles that are most appropriate and helpful to students. We explored this most explicitly in Chapter 5, which suggested three overlapping roles that all teachers adopt and integrate in some way: the roles of instructional manager, caring person, and generous expert. As I emphasized there, these roles are not mutually exclusive, but are expressed in relationship to one another as you teach. The roles develop in the interactions between you and your students. In those contacts and conversations, you must somehow arrange for students to learn (be a manager), you must value and support students' personal qualities and goals (be caring), and you must share enthusiasm and knowledge about what you are teaching (be a generous expert). At any one moment, one of these roles may predominate over another, but in the long term they all play a part in every teaching and learning relationship. Your job as a high-quality teacher is to discover exactly when and where to emphasize each role—as well as additional roles, perhaps, that you will discover as you gain experience.

The more you can focus on orchestrating learning and balancing teaching roles, the more you can attend to monitoring how well students are actually learning. "Monitoring learning" in essence refers to the challenge of assessment, discussed in Chapter 11. Given the diversity of students' backgrounds and the many ways in which learning occurs, it should be no surprise that high-quality assessment requires multiple, complex methods. Conventional paper-and-pencil tests, for example, may be useful as indicators of some forms of learning, but you will probably need additional indicators if you want a full picture of your students' learning. That is why Chapter 11 emphasized assessment using "authentic" tasks (those related to students' real-world lives and expectations) and portfolios, which deliberately collect a variety of work for assessment and invite students' own comments on it.

Thinking Systematically About Your Practice and Learning from Experience

To teach well, you must gain from your experience; and to gain from experience, you must reflect on it. Self-reflection has been an ongoing theme throughout all chapters of this book; for example, the In Your Own Voice discussions have encouraged it, as have my comments made periodically in the body of the text. Only by questioning your practices can you hope to improve on them. The reason is simple: the best ways to teach are not necessarily the first ones you (or any teacher) try; you must continually consider how else you might have carried out a lesson effectively or what other plans you could have made that might have assisted particular students just as well or better than the ones you actually followed. Maybe you should try the alternatives next time; at any rate, you should keep them in mind.

In addition to daily reflection, it is important to take stock, periodically and deliberately, of general classroom practices and general goals that seem important or that pose chronic problems in your work. If, for example, you are a third-grade elementary teacher, you might ask, "Is there a less abstract way to introduce 'number facts' than what I am now doing?" If you are a tenth-grade math teacher, you might ask, "How can I help students see relationships among mathematical topics so they don't forget each one after it's tested?" If you are a special education teacher, you might ask, "Have I arranged for programs for my students that are truly as challenging and inclusive as possible?" A host of general, reflective questions such as these exist; the ones you choose to think about will depend on your particular teaching concerns and circumstances. Here is a question that had been concerning Karen Dworkin, an upper-elementary teacher for several years:

KAREN DWORKIN: I got interested in a few students who classmates had nicknamed the "bad kids." It seemed to me they were not bad as people, but they sometimes behaved in ways that were difficult to handle. Every year there were always a few students who were inclined to make inappropriate remarks, or crack jokes at the wrong time, or annoy me and others at the wrong times. It was awkward when they did these things. So I started watching these students closely, trying to understand their motives. I kept a journal

In Your Own Voice

What general concerns, as opposed to daily ones, deserve your attention now in looking forward to a career in teaching?

Are they distinct from concerns about daily matters, or are they the same?

entirely about "inappropriate remarks," describing incidents and speculating about the reasons behind each of them. It helped! Eventually I had a whole book's worth of descriptions and interpretations about this sort of "bad" behavior. These students' "bad" behaviors, I decided, were really an effort to reassure themselves that they were not powerless and to convince classmates of their power as well. So my job became one of helping the "bad kids" feel competent, socially and academically, without getting drawn into their power games. And I think I'm succeeding, at least with some. I still get kids like that every year, but my journal—or really the thinking and observing behind my journal—helped me not to worry as much as before.

Karen's work verges on being teacher research, a topic discussed in Chapter 12, because it was a systematic inquiry by a teacher into a classroom-based problem. Karen could also have proceeded, however, by consulting published forms of educational research, some of which were also discussed in Chapter 12. As pointed out there, "research" has diverse qualities and purposes: sometimes it provides perspective, sometimes it offers teaching advice, and sometimes it advocates for new practices, among other things. Much educational research is conducted by specialists (usually university professors), but a growing body of it (called "teacher research") is designed and conducted by classroom teachers themselves. Your challenge, as you become an excellent teacher, will not only be to find research on topics that concern you but also to understand the purposes of the studies you find. You must become an intelligent consumer of research. Look for food for thought, but avoid the junk food—the research that does not prove, or is not meant to prove, what it claims.

To the extent that you can indeed think systematically about your teaching, you can serve as a model of an educated person for students as well as colleagues: you will be someone who is curious, intellectually honest, tolerant of differences of opinion, and fair-minded. These qualities are important parts of the "generous expert" role described in Chapter 5. In fact, they may be the most important parts of that role. In addition, as explained in that chapter, the generous expert also knows the content well that he or she is teaching. But as important as knowledge of content is, it may ultimately matter less than your own love of learning and the example that love provides for others. Which would you prefer students to take from their contact with you as a teacher: would you prefer that they forgot the content you taught them and pick up qualities of curiosity, intellectual honesty, and fairness, or the other way around? Whenever you play the role of generous expert, this question will be central if you also wish to be reflective.

Becoming a Member of a Learning Community

Excellent teaching is not a solitary act; it is more like a collaboration with learners and other teachers. In spite of the stereotype of "solitary" teachers working alone in classrooms and unobserved by other adults, the fact is that high-quality teachers consult with others frequently about students' needs and about the best ways to facilitate students' learning. These conversations may be either deliberate or "accidental," but either way they help teachers to improve their teaching. From others you can gain new sources of good information and materials for teaching. You can also find new classroom activities and learn about priorities and values held by others that deserve your consideration.

Participation in a learning community was illustrated in a number of places in this book, but especially in Chapters 10 and 12. In Chapter 12, we saw the published results of teachers working together either with one another or with other educators. In one example, teacher Wendy Schoener and university researcher Polly Ulnichy cooperated on a teacher research project focused on problems that Wendy had experienced in her classroom. The two of them, along with the teachers and educators who read and discussed their research, formed a learning community (at least temporarily) for the purpose of sharing the results. In another example from Chapter 12, two teachers published the results of jointly exploring why their team-taught classroom had succeeded. By working together and by sharing their experiences with others through publication, the two teachers formed part of a "community" of learners, enriching each other's thinking as a result. Still another example, in Chapter 10, described the efforts of a school staff to plan an individual educational plan cooperatively; arranging a convenient meeting time was difficult, it seemed, but this fact did not by itself prevent collaboration. In the same chapter we also read about a seventh-grade teacher, Sharon, and a special education resource teacher, Pat, who tried teaching together as a team for the benefit of students. In doing so they created the beginnings of a community of learners, even if it was not a complete community yet. The teachers encountered challenges in collaborating, but the challenges did not prevent them from making the effort. Sharon and Pat had more to say in support of their teamwork:

SHARON: Sure, working together got to be awkward—a division of labor emerged that we hadn't expected. But I would work with Pat again if I had the chance! Pat was great. It's just that we need to think more carefully ahead of time about who's going to do what, and why. Maybe I shouldn't expect to

In Your Own Voice

When you first thought about teaching as a career, how much did you expect to work *with* others?

Do you foresee problems with doing so, and if so, what do you think you should do about them?

be the equivalent of a full-fledged resource teacher all at once. Maybe I should focus on just one or two students with special needs at first, and make sure the help I give is really something that I can fit into my day. I still think, though, that teaming can be done. I wish more people would try it for the sake of the students.

PAT: Working in Sharon's class helped me more than I expected. I could see the kids with special needs in their "natural habitats" much better than by visiting just occasionally. Sharon reminded me about how precious a classroom teacher's time can be; Sharon had so many students to pay attention to! Most of them were not officially designated as "special-needs" students, but they were needy anyway. You really have to set priorities if you're a classroom teacher and you take the differences among students seriously.

Of course, Pat and Sharon's way of building a community of learners probably will not fit the circumstances and personalities of every high-quality teacher. But there are other ways to define a learning community and to become part of one. In Chapter 7, for example, we saw a teacher, Ms. Hamilton, struggle to develop rapport with a parent from a cultural background different from her own. Eventually she succeeded in doing so, and in the process created conditions for involving the parent more effectively in the work of the school and of her child's education in particular. In Chapter 6 we saw a teacher, Barbara Fuller, work diligently to help students learn how to work in groups. In the process the students and Ms. Fuller became a learning community in its own right, and students benefited as a result.

A learning community does not even have to exist face to face to be a "community." In Chapter 2, for example, we heard from Jerod and Cheryl, a brother and sister who communicated entirely by e-mail. Even though they lived hundreds of miles apart, they learned from each other—in this case, teaching each other important ideas about the nature of learning at a distance. In that respect, at least, they formed the kernel of a learning community. In the same way, some teachers—including yourself—may participate in some communities where many of the individuals never meet in person or do so only rarely. These are the communities of teachers and other educators who share professional interests, for example, but live in different cities and meet only occasionally at conferences or professional development days. They are also the "virtual" communities of teachers and educators who share interests or questions but communicate as Jerod and Cheryl did, strictly by electronic correspondence. In spite of seeing one another rarely, or even never, these groups also meet the test of a professional community: they provide individuals with support, information, and advice on matters of common interest.

Your Resources for Becoming an Accomplished Teacher

ECOMING an accomplished teacher is indeed challenging, but keep in mind the resources you already have to meet the challenge. Put briefly, there are two: your experiences and your interpretations of experiences. Your experiences give you a basis for caring about students and about education in general, as well as knowledge of particular ways teaching and learning might occur. The interpretations you make of your experiences give you a basis for evaluating experiences and for considering alternatives to them that may be appropriate or desirable.

A major resource in becoming more professional are your own past experiences and memories about teaching and learning—provided that you supplement these with new experiences and ideas from other professionals.
© Elizabeth Crews

Your Experiences, Past and Present

No matter what particular experiences you have had with children, classrooms, and teachers, those experiences are a major source of strength in becoming an accomplished teacher, because they are the only place to start developing your own commitments and skills related to teaching. This idea was discussed in Chapter 1, but it is important enough to bear repeating in this final chapter. Your experiences in schools (and elsewhere) do matter to your development as a teacher, whether they were positive or negative, and whether they involved actions and people you admired or ones you would like to escape from. All of your experiences provide building blocks for your development as a teacher, even if they are fragmented and even if you have interpreted them differently now than at the times they occurred. Take these memories and experiences, all from teachers in their first or second year of teaching:

DENIS ENBERG, second grade: You know what I remember most about kindergarten? Watching the tomato plants grow. My parents said the teacher was concerned about that. Even my parents worried. But I just remember enjoying checking them every day, up close, carefully.

SANDRA WATSON, tenth-grade biology: She [my fifth-grade teacher] took us on a field trip to the park. It seemed like the deepest, darkest woods! I loved it; we all did. The teacher seemed more like a human being that day, less like an official "teacher."

TOM SABOURIN, ninth-grade English: The trouble was, he [my seventh-grade social studies teacher] used to single out one or two students and criticize them mercilessly. I still squirm thinking about it! I never want to teach like that, ever.

MARIA TOEWS, sixth grade: We always felt safe there [in my eighth-grade math class]. Mr. Morgan made everyone feel appreciated—even the girls—in spite of obnoxious remarks from a couple of the boys. That mattered to me, even if I never learned eighth-grade math very well.

In Your Own Voice

What do you remember most about your life as a student?

Is there more than one way to interpret your memory?

For all four teachers, past experience provides a starting point for current thinking about their teaching and their students' learning. This is true even for Tom, who criticizes his experience and vows to avoid it in the future; his beliefs and priorities about teaching might be framed differently if he had never witnessed the teacher who he believed "picked on" students. Denis's and Sandra's experiences offer clues about how to teach particular subjects; Maria's and Tom's offer clues about managing and monitoring students. As we will see shortly, none of the four should *end* thinking about teaching and learning with memories of past experiences—nor should you. But everyone begins there, because there is no place else to start.

Memories of personal experiences need not come from the distant past to be relevant. Teachers begin accumulating new ones as soon as they begin teaching, as these three teachers have done:

SHAWNA BUORS, third grade: I'm a lot more comfortable, now that I've tried it, about having a child with special needs in my room. Jill [my student with special needs] was partially sighted, and it didn't really take much adjustment to accommodate her. Some of the kids like to help when she can't read something; in fact, sometimes I have to keep them from helping Jill *too* much.

EMILY MAURO, senior high human ecology: When I found out how the other teacher [of human ecology] prepares for the tests, it sounded great! She has each student write a version of the test; then has a classmate "take" the test by looking for errors in it; then has the two students discuss the results together. I'm going to try it next term.

DAVID VIS, seventh-grade Spanish: I borrowed an idea from a primary teacher at my school, which was to ask students to create their own personal vocabulary lists. Only she [the other teacher] was doing it in English for early readers, and I'm doing it for "early" Spanish speakers, even though they're in seventh grade. Students' responses to having personal lists was so much better [than before], at least for me! Like day and night compared to before.

Note that in these recent or current memories, two of the teachers (Emily and David) have added a new criterion for what makes experience "relevant." Their comments now imply that teaching includes not only classroom events and activities in the presence of students but also planning and collaboration behind the scenes. Otherwise Emily and David would not have commented on an activity that occurs outside class time, the borrowing of ideas from other teachers. In this way, these two teachers show signs of beginning to think systematically about their practice (Proposition 4 in Table 14.1) and beginning to participate in communities of teachers as learners (Proposition 5 in Table 14.1). They also show signs of drawing on the other major resource available to all teachers: their ability to reflect on their work and thereby extend or transform past experiences.

Your Interpretations of Experience

As helpful as personal experiences will be in guiding your teaching and developing your perspectives about education, they will not accomplish these benefits automatically, without your deliberate thought or reflection. By themselves, memories of learning or teaching experiences often do not have clear, agreed-on meanings, although sometimes they may seem to because of assumptions you (or others) make about them. Usually experiences must be interpreted to be useful: reflected on, considered, mulled over, pondered, wondered about, and so on.

From Thoughtful Reflections

One way to interpret experiences is simply to ask questions about them yourself and to make decisions about how the experiences relate to other memories of learning or teaching, or what they imply for your current work with students. Take a closer look at the four teachers' memories of past experiences from the previous section, and consider what each teacher might ask himself or herself about each particular memory:

DENIS ENBERG: Denis might ask himself *why* he chose to tell us that he enjoyed watching the tomato plants grow. Is he saying that he thinks all students should get more chances to garden in elementary school, and perhaps that he is going to provide the chances with his own second-grade class? Or is he saying that children should be allowed to do quiet activities ("just watching") in class without being prodded by the teacher to be more outgoing or active? Or that teachers—perhaps including himself—should be on the lookout for shy children, such as the ones who "just enjoy watching the tomato plants grow," to draw these children out into the social mainstream?

SANDRA WATSON: Sandra might ask herself what she means by saying that on the field trip, the teacher seemed "like a human being." Are teachers not normally human? She might also think about whether "being human" is necessarily good for all kinds of learning, as she implied it was for the field trip. Would it create difficulties in certain situations, such as when a teacher needs emotional distance to help settle a conflict between students or to assess students' work fairly?

MARIA TOEWS: Maria hints that gender bias is an issue for her and that her eighth-grade math teacher was good because somehow he avoided that bias. Maria might need to consider, though, what she admired about *how* the teacher avoided bias. Was it because he responded in a totally "gender-blind" manner to all students, as if he were not even aware of students' gender? Or was it because he deliberately tried to compensate for girls' unfavored status by explicitly inviting them to participate more?

TOM SABOURIN: Tom implies that his seventh-grade social studies teacher was habitually insensitive to students' feelings. Let's assume for the moment that Tom's diagnosis is accurate (although that assumption probably also deserves a closer look). Tom might consider why a teacher might behave in such an inhumane way, or at any rate would give the impression of doing so to students. Are there some clues in the rest of the teacher's behavior that Tom should be aware of to avoid making the same mistake himself, the mistake of accidentally "picking on" students?

From Dialogue with Colleagues

The four teachers—Denis, Sandra, Maria, and Tom—do not have to confine their reflections to themselves. They can, and in fact should, also engage others in the questions they ask. Many ways to do so are accessible to teachers, regardless of level of expertise or experience. The simplest way to engage others is just to *converse* with fellow teachers: What do *you* think of this experience I have had? What do *you* think I should make of it? But more complex ways to involve others are also not difficult to find. *Group study,* for example, occurs frequently in schools as a result of committee work a school needs; teachers gather for the purpose of bringing themselves up to date on a new piece of curriculum, for example, or planning activities related to a schoolwide theme (e.g., "ecology"). The meetings associated with study groups often lead to considerable dialogue about issues of teaching and learning, including the sharing of experiences by other teachers and of their interpretations of them. For a beginning teacher, study groups are a particularly good way to meet experienced, veteran teachers and to learn from them.

Somewhat more formal in organization are professional in-service programs sponsored by a school or school district. Usually these focus on specific areas of current educational concern in the local schools (for example, implementing a new system for managing conflict). They often meet after school or in the evening, and occasionally on half- or whole days when teachers are released from normal teaching duties. They offer a convenient way to converse with colleagues, especially those from neighboring schools, and especially if you are indeed concerned about the topic of the in-service program.

Still more formal in organization are graduate courses at a local university. These typically focus on broad topics, issues, or curriculum areas in education, and often provide leads to pursue new reading or educational research—including teacher-designed research—that is interesting

In Your Own Voice

This discussion leaves out another way to involve colleagues in reflecting on questions of teaching and learning: discussion groups on the Internet.

For suggestions about where to locate some of these, see the Internet Resources section at the end of each chapter.

How would a discussion via e-mail compare, in terms of helpfulness, to the alternatives: (1) no discussion at all or (2) a face-to-face discussion?

and important to teachers. Like in-service programs, graduate courses provide another place to meet and talk with fellow teachers, but courses are more likely to include colleagues not only from your own school district but from others as well, or even from other cities. Many (though not all) of the courses offer opportunities to share and interpret personal experiences related to teaching and learning. Gaining admission to university courses in education generally is not difficult for teachers, although sometimes the courses require a minimum average grade level or minimum amount of classroom experience (one or two years). And, of course, they have tuition costs.

Blurring Distinctions, Enriching Meanings

 F you have read this book carefully, you may have gotten the impression that it blurs many traditional educational categories and distinctions. Here are a few examples:

- *Teaching and learning.* Teachers, it seems, are sometimes learners, and learners sometimes teach one another. Teaching means learning both how students think in general and how they think about specific ideas or skills. Learning means knowing how to teach something to others.

- *The classroom and the "real world."* The classroom is supposed to provide tasks that are as authentic as possible, tasks that resemble "real-world" activities (as discussed in Chapter 11). The "real world," on the other hand, has turned out to be like a classroom in that important learning and problem solving often occur outside school (as discussed in Chapter 2).

- *Students "with" special needs and students "without" special needs.* Students "with" special learning needs, it seems, can and should be as fully participating as possible, and in this sense are like students "without" special needs (see Chapter 10). Yet all students have "special learning needs" in the sense that they all have unique strengths and problems, both socially and academically.

- *Teaching and research.* Certain forms of educational research—in particular, teacher research—actually resemble classroom teaching in that the research grows from questions and issues created by classroom teachers in everyday teaching. Yet since everyday teaching can involve systematic reflection, observation, and sharing of results, "teaching" itself resembles "research."

The blurring of traditional distinctions such as these can cloud our understanding of teaching and learning, but it also reflects the richness of the key ideas in education and psychology (Davis & Sumara, 1997). *Teaching*, *learning*, and the other major ideas discussed in this book are indeed complex, full of multiple meanings, and laced with connections between and among each other. They therefore deserve careful, conscious reflection by anyone who plans to use them. As I and the other voices in this book have tried to show, there are many ways to accomplish such reflection, to ask good questions about teaching and learning. To the extent that you can do so, you and your students will learn more—though perhaps not always in the ways you first expect. The African American writer James Baldwin (1961) said it well, although at the time he was reflecting on how he came to terms with being an African American. When you reflect deeply on your work experiences, he said,

The questions which you ask yourself begin . . . to illuminate the world, and become a key to the experience of others.

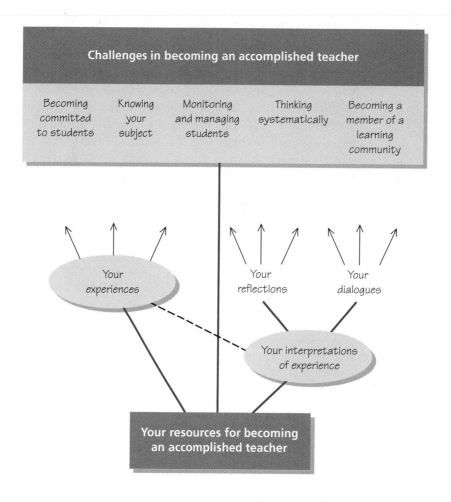

Chapter Re-View: Looking Ahead This Chapter Re-View suggests directions in which the chapter might have taken your thinking—though, of course, other directions are also possible. It expands the Chapter View, which suggests a starting point, conceptually, for the chapter. But this Re-View does not suggest an ending point. Like the Chapter View, it represents just one perspective among many.

Key Terms and Concepts

professional teaching standards (484)

commitment to students (486)

knowing your subject (488)

monitoring and managing students' learning (490)

thinking systematically about practice (493)

learning communities (495)

Annotated Readings

Richardson, Virginia (Ed.). (1997). *Constructivist teaching education: Building a world of new understandings.* London: Falmer Press. Richardson and other educators talk about the challenges of becoming a teacher with a constructivist orientation. Although the authors assume familiarity with constructivism as a point of view about education, they generally write in a very accessible style. In any case, by now you should be becoming familiar with constructivism!

Wasley, P. (1994). *Stirring the chalkdust: Tales of teachers changing classroom practice.* New York: Teachers College Press. The author describes how several teachers undertake new initiatives that make each of them more accomplished educators. Each teacher has unique needs, teaching different subjects, grade levels, and kinds of students; thus each develops in ways that are quite different, yet equally appropriate.

Zemelman, S. (1993). *Best practice: New standards for teaching and learning in America's schools.* Portsmouth, NH: Heinemann. The author describes examples of teachers who explicitly focus on developing skills in the five areas of challenge described in this chapter. On the whole, the teachers succeeded in meeting the challenges—though it was work for them all.

Internet Resources

<www.nbpts.org> This is the web site for the National Board of Professional Teaching Standards. Among other resources, it contains complete explanations of, and justifications for the importance of, the five propositions of accomplished teaching summarized in Table 14.1. It also presents supplementary standards developed by teachers of particular subjects (e.g., mathematics) and grade levels (e.g., early childhood education).

<www.ericsp.org>, <www.yahoo.com/Education/Teaching> Here are two more web sites that emphasize the continuing professional development of teachers. The first is from the ERIC Clearinghouse on Teaching and Teacher Education, a federally funded institute that provides information and support to both new and experienced teachers. Among other things, it includes short, downloadable publications about professional concerns. The second is the site for Yahoo!, a major search engine on the Internet; this particular part of Yahoo! lists various other sites on the Internet that are intended for professional development.

accommodation in Piagetian theory, the modification of knowledge structures as a result of actions (Chapter 2).

age-graded developmental change events or processes that happen to nearly everyone at predictable, chronological ages (Chapter 4).

arts-based research a method of research study that takes advantage of an artistic medium in order to heighten readers' understanding of and response to research findings (Chapter 12).

assessment methods teachers use to identify or diagnose strengths, weaknesses, and unique qualities in students (Chapter 11).

assimilation in Piagetian theory, the interpretation of actions according to preexisting structures of knowledge (Chapter 2).

attention deficit disorder (ADD) a problem with sustaining attention and controlling impulses (Chapter 10).

attention deficit hyperactivity disorder (ADHD) ADD with the addition of hyperactivity or excessive activity (Chapter 10).

attribution theory a cognitive view of motivation that focuses on the reasons a person uses to account for success and failure and the impact those explanations have on the person (Chapter 6).

authentic assessment assessment procedures based on tasks with real, ongoing value to students (Chapter 11).

authenticity integrity or sincerity in expressing one's unique talents and interests (Chapter 5).

behaviorism a set of psychological theories based on the assumption that what a person has learned in life—and particularly what punishments and rewards they have encountered along the way—determines human behavior (Chapter 2).

caring person an aspect of teaching roles whereby the teacher focuses on students as unique individuals and on noting and responding to students in light of that uniqueness (Chapter 5).

case study a method of conducting psychological or educational research that focuses intensively on one or a few participants or situations (Chapter 12).

classical conditioning a behaviorist theory of learning that explains learning by changes in association between stimuli and responses. A response to a previously neutral stimulus is learned through repeatedly pairing that stimulus with another stimulus that already elicits that response. The original, neutral stimulus is called the *UCS (unconditioned stimulus)* and the original response to the UCS is called the *UCR (unconditioned response)*; the stimulus that elicits the new response is the *CS (conditioned stimulus)* and the new response learned is the *CR (conditioned response)* (Chapter 2).

classroom discourse the verbal interactions among members of a class, including the teacher (Chapter 8).

classroom discussion a participation structure in which the teacher sets a topic, issue, or problem and invites comment on it or solutions to it (Chapter 8).

classroom management techniques for maintaining a positive, productive learning environment, consisting of planning, self-assessment, and revision of plans (Chapter 6).

classroom research see *teacher research* (Chapter 6).

classroom test a means of evaluating and assessing student knowledge; classroom tests usually sample knowledge or skill from a larger domain, take place at a designated time and place, and rest on the assumption that learning resides within the individual (Chapter 11).

cohort effects developmental changes that occur in individuals because of historical events and trends in society at large; cohort effects may happen to everyone in a population or only to a portion of it (Chapter 4).

collaborative group work a participation structure in which the teacher sets a general task and students work out the details of implementing it among themselves (Chapter 8).

community a group of people showing civil, respectful concern for each other (Chapter 5).

community of practice a group of individuals who respond to one another and work together to accomplish a common goal (Chapter 2).

concrete operational stage in Piagetian theory, a stage of thinking lasting from about seven years of age to about the age of eleven, during which children can manipulate ideas and memories using logical rules (Chapter 4).

consequential validity the impact of a test on students' motivation and learning (Chapter 11).

conservation in Piagetian theory, demonstrations of reversibility and decentration revealing a belief in an object's constancy or invariance despite visible changes to its outward appearance (Chapter 4).

construct validity how well a test is logically related to the content being tested and thus how well it assesses what it is intended to assess (Chapter 11).

constructivism the belief that knowledge is created or "constructed" by individuals' active efforts to make meaning through interactions with other people and with things (Chapter 1).

content validity see *face validity* (Chapter 11).

control group a group (or condition) that provides a baseline against which to compare a group (or condition) that is the focus of experimental observation or treatment (Chapter 12).

control talk a register of speech marked by implied assertion of authority; often used teachers in classroom talk (Chapter 8).

controls procedures for regulating the conditions of an experiment or observation, so as to identify true causes and influences clearly (Chapter 12).

conventional moral judgment in Kohlberg's theory of moral development, the stage that emphasizes conformity to existing rules, customs, and authorities (Chapter 12).

creative thinking generating ideas that are genuinely new, as well as useful and pleasing (Chapter 3).

criterion-related validity the extent to which a test predicts a particular type of knowledge or skill, regardless of the precise content of the test (Chapter 11).

culture the organized context of behaviors, attitudes, and customs that constitute a distinctive society or way of life (Chapter 9).

decentration in Piagetian theory, a distinct aspect of concrete operational thinking whereby children can focus on more than one aspect or feature of a problem at one time (Chapter 4).

developmental change relatively permanent, long-term alterations in skills, attitudes, or knowledge (Chapter 4).

dialogue the active sharing of views intended to clarify differences and identify common ground; dialogue can be internal, thoughtful considerations of ideas and external conversations about them (Chapter 1).

Down syndrome a genetic disorder that causes some cases of mental retardation; a person with Down syndrome either has an extra chromosome or a particular chromosome that is defective (Chapter 10).

educated guesswork a form of trial-and-error behavior based on experience and knowledge of a problem rather than on completely random responses (Chapter 3).

education research the systematic study of issues or problems of teaching and learning (Chapter 12).

educational psychology the study of educational problems from the viewpoint of individual teachers and students (Chapter 1).

equilibration in Piagetian theory, the interplay of experience and schemata (or *schemas*, in Piagetian terms) that leads to learning (Chapter 2).

equivalent forms reliability an assessment of reliability conducted by finding or writing two parallel forms of a test, which are given to two groups of students; reliable tests will produce similar scores across the two groups (Chapter 11).

evaluation a judgment, often expressed in the form of a numerical score or letter grade, about whether students' learning is worthy, useful, and desirable (Chapter 11).

expertise a teacher's knowledge of content and of how experts usually think about content (Chapter 5).

extinction the unlearning of a conditioned response brought on when the unconditioned stimulus is no longer paired with the conditioned stimulus or when a new, competing stimulus is paired with the response (see *classical conditioning*) (Chapter 2).

face validity the extent to which a test appears to cover what it was designed to test; also called *content validity* (Chapter 11).

formal operational stage in Piagetian theory, a stage of thinking lasting from about eleven years of age into adulthood, characterized by the ability to reason about abstract relationships among ideas (Chapter 4).

friendship a strong, lasting bond between particular individuals marked by shared interests, values, or activities (Chapter 7).

gender patterns of social behavior and attitudes associated with biological sex; note that gender is learned while sex is genetically determined (Chapter 9).

generalization the tendency for a stimulus similar to a conditioned stimulus to produce a conditioned response—usually weaker than the original learned response (see *classical conditioning* and *operant conditioning*) (Chapter 2).

generous expert an aspect of teaching roles whereby the teacher conveys skill and familiarity with a subject and shares that competence freely with students (Chapter 5).

Gilligan's Position 1—surviving according to Gilligan's theory of moral caring, a morality characterized by concern for the self, a lack of awareness of the needs of others, and the promotion of emotional or physical survival (Chapter 13).

Gilligan's Position 2—caring only for others according to Gilligan's theory of moral caring, a morality characterized by a lack of distinction between what others want and what is right and a focus on pleasing others (Chapter 13).

Gilligan's Position 3—integrated caring according to Gilligan's theory of moral caring, a morality that coordinates the needs of the self and of others (Chapter 13).

group focusing the ability to involve all members of a classroom in activities (Chapter 6).

hypothetical reasoning the ability to think about imaginary or counterfactual relationships among concepts—the ability to consider "what if?" questions (Chapter 4).

identity the qualities, attitudes, and behaviors that constitute a person's self (Chapter 9).

inclusion the philosophy and/or policy of educating students with special needs in regular classrooms to the greatest extent possible and beneficial for the students (Chapter 10).

individual education plan (IEP) as required by IDEA, a plan developed annually for each special needs student by teachers, support staff, and parents. The IEP describes the student's current level of achievement, specifies educational goals and objectives for the coming year, and describes how progress toward those goals will be evaluated (Chapter 10).

Individuals with Disabilities Act (IDEA) see *PL 94-142* (Chapter 10).

information processing theory a theory of human learning based on categorization, sequencing, and the application of rules for manipulating information, analogous to the operation of a computer (Chapter 2).

instructional manager an aspect of teaching roles whereby the teacher focuses on orchestrating sets of activities for groups and individuals (Chapter 5).

intelligence the ability to reason, solve problems, and perform skills that adapt an individual to his or her environment effectively (Chapter 3).

interdependent self an identity defined in terms of one's relationship to others and to the community at large (Chapter 9).

interview a method of conducting educational and psychological research by comparing responses to participants to a common set of questions (Chapter 12).

learning a lasting change in behavior or thinking as a result of experience or reflection; learning occurs in all settings, of which classrooms and schools are but two (Chapter 1).

learning as assisted performance a metaphor of learning that sees people's relationships with others as forming a framework for encouraging new skills beyond what they could learn on their own (Chapter 2).

learning as behavior change a metaphor of learning that equates learning with an observable change in action and behavior (Chapter 2).

learning community a group (actual or virtual) of teachers, parents, and students that fosters collaboration and mutual support in the educational endeavor (Chapter 14).

learning disability (LD) a specific impairment of learning related to language that makes a student unable to achieve in some aspect of schoolwork at a level appropriate for his or her age (Chapter 10).

least restrictive environment (LRE) as required by IDEA, a combination of settings that involve special needs students in regular classrooms and programs to the greatest extent possible (Chapter 10).

lecture a participation structure in which the teacher talks and the students listen to the teacher (Chapter 8).

literature review a method of research that discerns trends by examining statistical data and other published studies about a given topic (Chapter 12).

mastery learning a way of organizing learning so that all students learn material at a nearly identical, high level, even if some students require more time to do so than others (Chapter 11).

mental retardation significant limitations in a person's intellectual functioning and daily adaptive behaviors (Chapter 10).

mentor a person who devotes him- or herself to developing the skills of another person, often called the *protégé* (Chapter 7).

metaphors of learning images of learning modeled after particular and familiar objects, situations, and actions (Chapter 2).

morality of care a collection of beliefs and actions based on responsiveness to others and thus tailored to circumstances and individual relationships (Chapter 13).

morality of justice a collection of beliefs and choices that is based on principles of fairness and impartiality and that is therefore intended to apply as universally as possible (Chapter 13).

motivation in the classroom, rousing and guiding students' interests; more generally, an energy that arouses a person to action and gives direction and focus to that action (Chapter 6).

multicultural teaching strategies that support learning by the full diversity of students, regardless of cultural or language background (Chapter 9).

multiple intelligences in some views of cognition, the set of distinct forms of intelligence, talent, or behavior that contribute to a person's adaptation to the world (Chapter 3).

need a biological or psychological requirement for living, such as food, sex, love, or respect from others (Chapter 6).

nonnormative developmental change events or processes that happen to individuals or selected groups but not to everyone; nonnormative changes can be positive or negative and can be present at birth or acquired at any point in one's development (Chapter 4).

object permanence in Piagetian theory, an aspect of infants' thinking whereby concepts begin to take on permanence and exist in the infant's mind even when not being directly experienced (Chapter 4).

operant conditioning a behaviorist theory of learning by which people's behaviors are influenced by the past and immediate consequences. Any action that has immediate consequences for one's behavior is the *operant* (because it "operates" on the environment); any consequence or outcome that causes an action to occur more often in the future is called a *reinforcement* (Chapter 2).

partial reinforcement effect the tendency for an operant behavior to be learned more slowly if reinforcement does not occur on every occasion but also to extinguish more slowly after learning. (see *operant conditioning*) (Chapter 2).

participation structure a set of rights and responsibilities expected from students and teacher during activities (Chapter 8).

peer a person who is your social equal and with whom you have relatively casual or passing contact (Chapter 7).

performance assessment assessment of a meaningful task, usually generated by a student's teacher and by external authorities such as school districts or state education departments, and based on a set of criteria related inherently to the nature of the task (Chapter 11).

Piagetian theory a theory of learning whereby a person gradually fits new information into a preexisting framework of knowledge, while at the same time gradually altering the framework (Chapter 2).

PL 94-142 federal legislation covering special education, which (a) supports the *least restrictive environment* for students, (b) requires *individual education plans* for each special needs student, and (c) funds a variety of services for special needs students. Currently called the *Individuals with Disabilities Act (IDEA)* (Chapter 10).

portfolio assessment assessment of collections (portfolios) of students' work (Chapter 11).

postconventional moral judgment in Kohlberg's theory of moral development, the stage that emphasizes abstract moral principles (Chapter 13).

preconventional moral judgment in Kohlberg's theory of moral development, the stage that emphasizes avoiding punishment and getting rewards (Chapter 13).

preoperational stage in Piagetian theory, a stage of thinking lasting from two years of age to about the age of seven, during which children engage in intuitive, symbolic thinking that does not yet exhibit complete logic or coherence (Chapter 4).

principled knowing the act of stating one's own thoughts in a classroom (Chapter 5).

private talk a register of speech used when only the person addressed can hear and respond to the speech; private talk, by definition, cannot be overheard (Chapter 9).

problem ownership taking responsibility for a behavior as a problem (Chapter 6).

problem solving the analysis and solution of situations that pose difficulties, inconsistencies, or obstacles of some kind (Chapter 3).

professional portfolio a collection of materials a teacher keeps related to the work of teaching; as a management tool, a portfolio can serve both as a record of what went on in a classroom at a given time and as a basis for planning subsequent teaching experiences (Chapter 6).

professional teaching standards the set of qualities and complex skills needed for excellent in teaching; long-term challenging goals for teachers (Chapter 14).

protégé a person to whom a *mentor* devotes time to help him or her develop skills (Chapter 7).

public talk a register of speech that is assumed to heard by persons other than the individual to whom the speech is addressed (Chapter 9).

qualitative research research that relies on verbal descriptions and non-statistical classification or grouping of phenomena or behavior (as opposed to quantitative research, which focuses on statistical frequency of phenomena or behaviors) (Chapter 12).

reciprocal teaching a strategy for building students' thinking skills whereby students take responsibility for teaching one another; although not designed to do so, reciprocal teaching often helps children develop moral commitment (Chapter 13).

recitation a participation structure in which the teacher leads a question-and-answer session, posing questions and calling on students to give answers to them (Chapter 8).

reflection the internal, highly individualized act of interpreting experience to draw conclusions or pose further questions (Chapter 1).

reflective journal a teacher's diary of day-to-day teaching experiences and his or her feelings about them (Chapter 6).

register a pattern of vocabulary, grammar, inflection, manners, and types of comments that people associate with a social role (Chapter 8).

relativity of reinforcers the tendency for some behaviors to be reinforcing only relative to other behaviors; also called *the Premack principle* after the psychologist who identified and studied this phenomenon (see *operant conditioning*) (Chapter 2).

reliability the degree to which a test can be repeated with consistent results (Chapter 11).

response costing removing a privilege, valued activity, or valued resource from a student in an attempt to stop his or her misbehavior or disruption (Chapter 6).

reversibility in Piagetian theory, a distinct characteristic of concrete operational thinking whereby children can mentally go both backward and forward in working through a problem (Chapter 4).

ripple effect the spreading of a classroom disruption or misbehavior from the person initiating it to other students (Chapter 6).

ritual knowledge an unintended effect of some teaching strategies whereby students learn to interpret hints and gestures from the teacher in order to guess correct answers, rather than focusing on the knowledge or problem itself (Chapter 5).

rubric scoring criteria for evaluating complex qualitative knowledge along several dimensions (Chapter 11).

sampling the process of selecting a group of research participants from a larger population such that the smaller group reflects the larger one (Chapter 12).

schemata in information processing theory, a previously acquired set of concepts about life experiences that reside in long-term memory (Chapter 2).

scholastic aptitude tests a standardized test of verbal reasoning, numerical skills, and vocabulary designed to predict school success (Chapter 3).

scholastic aptitude the skills needed to succeed in school, earn high grades, and do well on standardized tests (Chapter 3).

self-esteem feelings of self-worth (Chapter 9).

sensorimotor stage in Piagetian theory, a stage of infants' thinking lasting from birth to about two years of age, during which learning takes place primarily though senses and motor activity (Chapter 4).

shaping behavior initial reinforcement of approximations to parts of behavior, followed by gradual reinforcement of increasingly accurate or complete versions of the behavior (see *operant conditioning*) (Chapter 2).

shyness a predisposition to be extremely concerned about the evaluations of others and especially about the possibility of those evaluations leading to rejection (Chapter 7).

smoothness the ability to make clear and well-timed transitions between classroom activities (Chapter 6).

sociogram a diagram showing patterns of relationships within a social group such as a classroom (Chapter 7).

special education teaching modified to the specific requirements of students with special needs (Chapter 10).

special needs in special education, the unusual physical, cognitive, or emotional qualities or differences in a few students that require adjustment of teaching strategies or curriculum goals (Chapter 10).

speech and language disorders problems with understanding and expressing information, ideas, or meanings (Chapter 10).

split-half reliability an assessment of reliability conducted by creating a test with two halves that address the same knowledge or skill; a reliable test will produce similar scores on each half of the test (Chapter 11).

spontaneous recovery the reappearance of an unconditioned response following its extinction—usually weaker than when originally learned (see *classical conditioning* and *operant conditioning*) (Chapter 2).

stage in the discipline of psychology, age graded changes that appear as patterns of behavior that emerge together, in a predictable order, and in all people as they grow older (Chapter 4).

stimulus substitution in behavioral theories of learning, the replacement of a conditioned stimulus for an unconditioned stimulus (Chapter 2).

student evaluation feedback—oral, written, formal, or informal—from students on the success of a teacher or course (Chapter 6).

student-talk a register of speech used by students in classrooms, marked by indirect efforts to influence classroom dialogue or an individual student's role within the dialogue (Chapter 8).

teacher research the sustained, systematic inquiry into the issues and problems one faces as a teacher; in contrast to formal educational research, the teacher him- or herself defines the problem being researched. Also called *classroom research* (Chapters 6, 12).

teacher-talk the speech registers used by teachers in classrooms, often marked by *control talk* (Chapter 8).

teaching what teachers do to assist students in learning, both outside of class and inside (Chapter 1).

teaching roles patterns of behavior that students repeatedly witness and that thus influence the relationships between teachers and students (Chapter 5).

test-retest reliability an assessment of reliability conducted by comparing the results of the same test given twice; a reliable test will produce similar scores each time (Chapter 11).

thinking the process of forming ideas—a combination of problem solving, creativity, and scholastic aptitude (Chapter 1).

transfer the application of knowledge acquired in one situation to another, related situation (Chapters 3, 11).

validity the degree to which a test measures, reflects, or demonstrates what it is intended to measure, reflect, or demonstrate (Chapter 11).

withitness the ability to be simultaneously aware of everything that is going on in a classroom at any one time (Chapter 6).

zone of proximal development according to Lev Vygotsky, the difference between independent performance (what one can do on one's own) and assisted performance (what one can do with support from others) (Chapter 2).

REFERENCES

Adams, S., & Young, K. (1995). Questions parents ask. In T. Azwell & E. Schmar (Eds.), *Report card on report cards: Alternatives to consider* (pp. 175–182). Portsmouth, NH: Heinemann.

Adelman, H. (1996). Appreciating the classification dilemma. In W. Stainback & S. Stainback (Eds.), *Controversial issues confronting special education: Divergent perspectives* (2nd ed., pp. 96–111). Boston: Allyn and Bacon.

Adler, M. (1984). *The Paideia program: An educational syllabus.* New York: Macmillan.

Agran, M. (1997). *Self-directed learning.* Pacific Grove, CA: Brooks/Cole.

Airasian, P. (1996). *Assessment in the classroom.* New York: McGraw-Hill.

Alberto, P., & Troutman, A. (1994). *Applied behavior analysis for teachers.* New York: Macmillan.

Alexander, S. (1994). *In praise of single parents: Mothers and fathers embracing the challenge.* Boston: Houghton Mifflin.

American Psychiatric Association. (1994). *The Diagnostic and Statistical Manual of Mental Disorders* (4th ed.). Washington, DC: Author.

Amsel, E., Langer, R., & Loutzenhiser, L. (1991). Do lawyers reason differently from psychologists? A comparative design for studying expertise. In R. Sternberg & P. Frensch (Eds.), *Complex problem solving* (pp. 223–252). Hillsdale, NJ: Erlbaum.

Anson, C. (1994). Portfolios for teachers: Writing our way to reflective practice. In L. Black, D. Daiker, J. Sommers & G. Stygall (Eds.), *New directions in portfolio assessment.* Portsmouth, NH: Heinemann.

Apple, M., & Christian-Smith, L. (Eds.). (1991). *The politics of the textbook.* New York: Routledge.

Apter, T. (1994). *Working women do not have wives*. New York: St. Martin's Press.

Arends, R. (1991). *Learning to teach* (2nd ed.). New York: McGraw-Hill.

Arias, M. B., & Casanova, U. (Eds.). (1993). *Ninety-second Handbook of the National Society for the Study of Education: Bilingual education: Politics, practice, and research*. Chicago: University of Chicago Press.

Asher, S., & Coie, J. (1990). *Peer rejection in childhood*. New York: Cambridge University Press.

Azwell, T., & Schmar, E. (Eds.). (1995). *Report card on report cards: Alternatives to consider*. Portsmouth, NH: Heinemann.

Baldwin, J. (1961). *Nobody knows my name: More notes of a native son*. New York: Dial Press.

Bandura, A. (1993). Perceived self-efficacy in cognitive development and functioning. *Educational Psychologist, 28*, 117–148.

Bara, B. (1996). *Cognitive science: A developmental approach to simulation of the mind*. Hillsdale, NJ: Erlbaum.

Barber, P. (1988). *Applied cognitive psychology*. London: Methuen.

Barkley, R. (1985). Developmental changes in mother-child interaction of hyperactive boys: Effects of two doses of Ritalin. *Journal of Child Psychology and Psychiatry, 26*(5), 705–715.

Barone, T., & Eisner, E. (in press). Arts-based educational research. In R. Jaeger (Ed.), *Complementary methods for research in education* (2nd ed.). Washington, DC: American Educational Research Association.

Becker, J. (1995). Women's ways of knowing in mathematics. In P. Rogers & G. Kaiser (Eds.), *Equity in mathematics education: Influences of feminism and culture* (pp. 163–174). Washington, DC: Falmer Press.

Bereiter, C. (1994). Implications of postmodernism for science, or science as progressive discourse. *Educational Psychologist, 29*(1), 3–12.

Berlak, H. (1993). *Toward a new science of educational testing and assessment*. Albany, NY: State University of New York.

Berliner, D. (1990). What's all the fuss about instructional time? In M. Ben-Peretz & R. Bromme (Eds.), *The nature of time in schools* (pp. 3–35). New York: Teachers College Press.

Berliner, D., & Rosenshine, B. (1987). *Talks to teachers*. New York: Random House.

Besag, V. (1989). *Bullies and victims in schools*. Philadelphia: Open University Press.

Binet, A., & Simon, T. (1908). Le développement de l'intelligence chez les enfants. *L'Année psychologique, 14*, 1–94.

Black, L., Daiker, D., Sommers, J., & Stygall, G. (Eds.). (1994). *New directions in portfolio assessment*. Portsmouth, NH: Heinemann.

Bloome, D. (1994). Classroom language. In A. Purves (Ed.), *Encyclopedia of English studies and language arts* (Vol. 1, pp. 189–191). New York: Scholastic.

Bobrick, B. (1995). *Knotted tongues: Stuttering in history and the quest for a cure*. New York: Simon and Schuster.

Boutte, G., Scoy, I, & Hendley, S. (1996). Multicultural and nonsexist prop boxes. *Young Children, 52*(1), 34–42.

Brantlinger, E., Majd-Jabbari, M., & Guskin, S. (1996). Self-interest and liberal educational discourse: How ideology works for middle-class mothers. *American Educational Research Journal, 33*(3), 571–597.

Bredekamp, S., & Copple, C. (Eds.). (1997). *Developmentally appropriate practice in early childhood programs* (Rev. ed.). Washington, DC: National Association for the Education of Young Children.

Britzman, D. (1991). *Practice makes practice: A critical study of learning to teach*. Albany, NY: State University of New York Press.

Brophy, J. (1996, April). *Classroom management as socializing students into clearly articulated roles*. Paper presented at the annual meeting of the American Educational Research Association, New York.

Brown, L., & Gilligan, C. (1992). *Meeting at the crossroads: Women's psychology and girls' development*. Cambridge, MA: Harvard University Press.

Bruner, J. (1900). *Acts of meaning*. Cambridge, MA: Harvard University Press.

Bubeck, D. (1995). *Care, gender, and justice*. Oxford, UK: Clarendon Press.

Bullough, R., & Stokes, D. (1994). Analyzing personal teaching metaphors in preservice teacher education as a means for encouraging professional development. *American Educational Research Journal, 31*(1), 197–224.

Bullough, R., Knowles, G., & Crow, N. (1992). *Emerging as a teacher*. London: Routledge.

Bunce, B. (1997). Children with culturally diverse backgrounds. In L. McCormick, D. Loeb & R. Schiefelbusch (Eds.), *Supporting children with communication disorders in inclusive settings* (pp. 467–506). Boston: Allyn and Bacon.

Calfee, R., & Perfumo, P. (1996). *Writing portfolios in the classroom: Policy and practice, promise and peril*. Mahwah, NJ: Erlbaum.

Canter, L. (1989). Assertive discipline—more than names on the board and marbles in a jar. *Phi Delta Kappan, 71*(1), 57–61.

Carlson, C. (1992). Single-parent families. In M. Procidano & C. Fisher (Eds.), *Contemporary families: A handbook for school professionals* (pp. 36–56). New York: Teachers College Press.

Case, R. (1991). *The mind's staircase: Exploring the conceptual underpinnings of cognitive development.* Hillsdale, NJ: Erlbaum.

Case, R. (1992). Neo-Piagetian theories of intellectual development. In H. Beilin & P. Pufall (Eds.), *Piaget's theory: Prospects and possibilities.* Hillsdale, NJ: Erlbaum.

Cazden, C. (1986). Classroom discourse. In M. Wittrock (Ed.), *Handbook of research on teaching* (3rd ed., pp. 432–463). New York: Macmillan.

Cazden, C. (1988). *Classroom discourse: The language of teaching and learning.* Portsmouth, NH: Heinemann.

Chavkin, N. (1993). (Ed.). *Families and schools in a pluralistic society.* Albany, NY: State University of New York Press.

Cherlin, A. (1992). *Marriage, divorce, and remarriage* (Rev. ed.). Cambridge, MA: Harvard University Press.

Chi, M., Glaser, R., & Farr, M. (1988). *The nature of expertise.* Hillsdale, NJ: Erlbaum.

Chisholm, J. (1996). Learning "respect for everything": Navajo images of development. In C. P. Hwang, M. Lamb & I. Sigel (Eds.), *Images of childhood* (pp. 167–183). Hillsdale, NJ: Erlbaum.

Chomsky, N. (1988). *Language and problems of knowledge.* Cambridge, MA: MIT Press.

Chomsky, N. (1994). *Language and thought.* Wakefield, NJ: Moyer Bell Publishers.

Christensen, N. (1995). The nuts and bolts of running a lecture course. In A. DeNeef & C. Goodwin (Eds.), *The academic's handbook* (pp. 179–186). Durham, NC: Duke University Press.

Clifford, P., & Friesen, S. (1993). A curious plan: Managing on the twelfth. *Harvard Educational Review, 63*(3), 339–358.

Cochran-Smith, M., & Lytle, S. (1993). *Inside/outside: Teacher research and knowledge.* New York: Teachers College Press.

Cohen, E. (1994). *Designing group work: Strategies for the heterogeneous classroom* (2nd ed.). New York: Teachers College Press.

Colby, A., & Damon, W. (1992). *Some do care: Contemporary lives of moral commitment.* New York: Free Press.

Colby, A., & Kohlberg, L. (1984). Invariant sequence and internal consistency in moral judgment stages. In W. Kurtines & J. Gewirts (Eds.), *Morality, moral behavior, and moral development.* New York: Wiley.

Cole, M. (1997, June 21). *Using Piaget and Vygotsky to create new educational activities.* Paper presented at the annual meeting of the Jean Piaget Society, Los Angeles, CA.

Dannefer, D. (1992). On the conceptualization of context in developmental discourse: Four meanings of context and their implications. In D. Featherman, R. Lerner & M. Perlmutter (Eds.), *Lifespan development and behavior* (Vol. 11, pp. 84–111). Hillsdale, NJ: Erlbaum.

Darling-Hammond, L. (1994). Performance-based assessment and educational equity. *Harvard Educational Review, 64*(1), 5–30.

Darling-Hammond, L., Ancess, J., & Falk, B. (1995). *Authentic assessment in action: Studies of schools and students at work.* New York: Teachers College Press.

Davey, G., & Cullen, C. (1988). *Human operant conditioning and behavior modification.* New York: Wiley.

Davis, B., & Sumara, D. (1997). Cognition, complexity, and teacher education. *Harvard Educational Review, 67*(1), 105–125.

DeCharms, R. (1984). Motivational enhancement in educational setting. In R. Ames & C. Ames (Eds.), *Research on motivation in education, Vol. 1: Student motivation* (pp. 275–310). New York: Academic Press.

Delamont, S. (1996). *Women's place in education.* Brookfield, MA: Avebury Publishers.

Denis, D., Griffin, P., & Cole, M. (1990). *The construction zone: Working for cognitive change in school.* New York: Cambridge University Press.

Derry, S. (1992). Beyond symbolic processing: Expanding horizons for educational psychology. *Journal of Educational Psychology, 84*(4), 413–418.

Devlin, L. (1995). The mentor. In D. Glover & G. Mardle (Eds.), *The management of mentoring: Policy issues.* London: Kegan Paul.

DeVries, R., & Zan, B. (1994). *Moral classrooms, moral children: Creating a constructivist atmosphere in early childhood education.* New York: Teachers College Press.

Dixon, R., Lerner, R., & Hultsch, D. (1992). The concept of development in individual and social change. In P. van Geert & L. Mos (Eds.), *Annals of theoretical psychology* (Vol. 7, pp. 279–324). Orlando, FL: Academic Press.

Dorsey-Gaines, C., & Garnett, C. (1996). The role of the Black Church in growing up literate: Implications for literacy research. In D. Hicks (Ed.), *Discourse, learning, and schooling* (pp. 247–265). New York: Cambridge University Press.

Doyle, W. (1986). Classroom organization and management. In W.

Wittrock (Ed.), *Handbook of research on teaching* (3rd ed.). New York: Macmillan.

Drew, C., Hardman, M., & Logan, D. (1996). *Mental retardation: A life-cycle approach* (6th ed.). Englewood Cliffs, NJ: Prentice- Hall.

Eder, D., Evans, C., & Parker, S. (1995). *School talk: Gender and adolescent culture.* New Brunswick, NJ: Rutgers University Press.

Edwards, D., & Mercer, N. (1987). *Common knowledge: The development of understanding in the classroom.* London: Methuen.

Edwards, N. (1989). *Stand and deliver.* New York: Scholastic.

Edwards, V., & Redfern, A. (1992). *World in a classroom: Learning in education in Britain and Canada.* Philadelphia: Multilingual Matters.

Egawa, K., & Azwell, T. (1995). Telling the story: Narrative reports. In T. Azwell & E. Schmar (Eds.), *Report card on report cards: Alternatives to consider* (pp. 98–109). Portsmouth, NH: Heinemann.

Eisner, Elliot. (1991). *The enlightened eye: Qualitative inquiry and the enhancement of educational practice.* New York: Macmillan.

Eisner, E. (1994). *The educational imagination: On the design and evaluation of school programs* (3rd ed.). New York: Macmillan.

Eisner, Elliot. (1996, May). *Qualitative research in music education: Past, present, perils, and promise.* Paper presented at the Music Education Research Conference, University of Illinois, Urbana, IL.

Elbow, P. (1994). Will the virtues of portfolios blind us to their potential dangers? In L. Black, D. Daiker, J. Sommers & G. Stygall (Eds.), *New directions in portfolio assessment* (pp. 40–55). Portsmouth, NH: Heinemann.

Elicker, J., & Fortner-Wood, C. (1995). Adult-child relationships in early childhood programs. *Young Children, 51*(1), 69–78.

Emberley, P. (1995). *Values education and technology: The ideology of possession.* Toronto: University of Toronto Press.

Epstein, J. (1990). School and family connections: Theory, research, and implications for integrating sociologies of education and family. *Marriage and Family Review, 15*(1/2), 99–126.

Erikson, F. (1996). Going for the zone: The social and cognitive ecology of teacher-student interaction in classroom conversations. In D. Hicks (Ed.), *Discourse, learning, and schooling* (pp. 29–62). New York: Cambridge University Press.

Erwin, P. (1993). *Friendship and peer relations in children.* New York: Wiley.

Everett, C. (Ed.). (1994). *Economics of divorce: Effects on parents and children.* New York: Haworth Press.

Evertson, C. (1994). *Classroom management for elementary teachers.* Emigsville, PA: Allyn and Bacon.

Feagans, L., Garvey, C., & Golinkoff, R. (1984). *The origins and growth of communication.* Norwood, NJ: Ablex.

Feldman, D. (1986). *Nature's gambit: Child prodigies and the development of human potential.* New York: Basic Books.

Feldman, D. (1988). Creativity: dreams, insights, and transformations. In R. Sternberg (Ed.), *The nature of creativity* (pp. 271–297). New York: Cambridge University Press.

Fenstermacher, G. (1994). The knower and the known: The nature of knowledge in research on teaching. In L. Darling-Hammond (Ed.), *Review of Research in Education* (Vol. 20, pp. 3–56). Washington, DC: American Educational Research Association.

Finlan, T. (1994). *Learning disability: The imaginary disease.* Westport, CT: Bergin and Garvey.

Floden, R., & Buchmann, M. (1990). Philosophical inquiry in teacher education. In W. R. Huston, M. Haberman & J. Sikula (Eds.), *Handbook of research on teacher education* (pp. 42–58). New York: Macmillan.

Florio-Ruane, S. (1989). Social organization of classes and schools. In M. Reynolds (Ed.), *Knowledge base for the beginning teacher* (pp. 163–172). New York: Permagon Press.

Flowerdew, J. (Ed.). (1994). *Academic listening: Research perspectives.* New York: Cambridge University Press.

Ford, D., & Lerner, R. (1992). *Developmental systems theory: An integrative approach.* Newbury Park, CA: Sage.

Foster-Harrison, E. (1997). *Peer tutoring for K-12 success.* Bloomington, IN: Phi Delta Kappa Educational Foundation.

Francasso, M., & Busch-Rossnagel, N. (1992). Parents and children of Hispanic origin. In M. Procidano & C. Fisher (Eds.), *Contemporary families: A handbook for school professionals* (pp. 83–99). New York: Teachers College Press.

Frederikson, N., Mislevy, R., & Bejar, I. (Eds.). (1993). *Test theory for a new generation of tests.* Hillsdale, NJ: Erlbaum.

Freiberg, J., & Driscoll, A. (1996). *Universal teaching strategies* (2nd ed.). Boston: Allyn and Bacon.

Funder, D., Parke, R., Tomlinson-Keasey, C., & Widaman, K. (Eds.). (1993). *Studying lives through time: Personality and development.* Washington, DC: American Psychological Association.

Gandara, P. (1995). *Over the ivy walls: The educational mobility of low-income Chicanos.* Albany, NY: State University of New York Press.

Garcia, G. *(1994)*. Assessment and diversity. In L. Darling-Hammond (Ed.), *Review of research in education* (Vol. 20, pp. 337–392). Washington, DC: American Educational Research Association.

Gardner, H. (1991). *The unschooled mind: How children think and how schools should teach.* New York: Basic Books.

Gardner, H. (1993). *Multiple intelligences: The theory in practice.* New York: Basic Books.

Gardner, H. (1994). *Creating minds: An anatomy of creativity seen through the lives of Freud, Einstein, Picasso, Stravinsky, Eliot, Graham, and Gandhi.* New York: Basic Books.

Garner, H. (Ed.). (1995). *Teamwork models and experience in education.* Boston: Allyn and Bacon.

Gartner, A., & Lipsky, D. (1987). Beyond separate education: Toward a quality system for all students. *Harvard Educational Review, 57,* 367–395.

Geary, D. (1995). Reflections on evolution and culture in children's cognition: Implications for mathematical development and instruction. *American Psychologist, 50*(1), 24–37.

Gelman, R., & Baillargeon, R. (1983). A review of some Piagetian concepts. In P. Mussen (Ed.), *Handbook of child psychology: Vol. 3. Cognitive development.* New York: Wiley.

Gilligan, C. (1982/1993). *In a different voice: Psychological theory and women's development.* Cambridge, MA: Harvard University Press.

Gilligan, C. (1996). The centrality of relationship in human development. In G. Noam & K. Fischer (Eds.), *Development and vulnerability in close relationships.* New York: Erlbaum.

Gilligan, C., & Wiggins, G. (1988). The origins of morality in early childhood relationships. In J. Kagan & S. Lamb (Eds.), *The emergence of morality in young children* (pp. 277–305). Chicago: University of Chicago Press.

Gilligan, C., Lyons, N., & Hanmer, T. (1990). *Making connections: The relational worlds of adolescent girls at Emma Willard School.* Cambridge, MA: Harvard University Press.

Gilligan, C., Ward, J., & Taylor, J. (Eds.). (1988). *Mapping the moral domain: A contribution of women's thinking to psychological theory and education.* Cambridge, MA: Harvard University Press.

Glasser, W. (1990). *The quality school: Managing students without coercion.* New York: Perennial Library.

Glover, D., & Mardle, G. (Eds.). (1995). *The management of mentoring.* London: Kegan Paul.

Goldberg, S. (1997). *Parent involvement begins at birth*. Boston: Allyn and Bacon.

Goldenberg, C. (1996). Instructional conversations. In A. Purves (Ed.), *Encyclopedia of English studies and language arts* (pp. 630–631). New York: Scholastic.

Golombok, S., & Fivush, R. (1994). *Gender development*. New York: Cambridge University Press.

Good, T., & Brophy, J. (1994). *Looking in classrooms* (6th ed.). New York: HarperCollins.

Goodnow, J., & Collins, A. (1990). *Development according to parents*. Hillsdale, NJ: Erlbaum.

Gordon, E., & Bonilla-Bowman, C. (1996). Can performance-based assessments contribute to the achievement of educational equity? In M. McLaughlin & D. C. Phillips (Eds.), *Evaluation and education at quarter century: Ninety-fifth yearbook of the National Society for the Study of Education* (pp. 32–51). Chicago: University of Chicago Press.

Gordon, T. (1991). *Discipline that works: Promoting self-discipline in children*. New York: Plume Books.

Gormezano, I., Prokasky, W., & Thompson, R. (1987). *Classical conditioning: An assessment*. Hillsdale, NJ: Erlbaum.

Graham, S., & Weiner, B. (1996). Theories and principles of motivation. In D. Berliner & R. Calfee (Eds.), *Handbook of educational psychology* (pp. 63–84). New York: Macmillan.

Greene, M. (1994). Epistemology and educational research: The influence of recent approaches to knowledge. In L. Darling-Hammond (Ed.), *Review of Research in Education* (Vol. 20, pp. 423–464). Washington, DC: American Educational Research Association.

Greenfield, P. (1994). Independence and interdependence as developmental scripts. In P. Greenfield & R. Cocking (Eds.), *Cross-cultural roots of minority child development* (pp. 1–40). Hillsdale, NJ: Erlbaum.

Greenfield, P. (1995, March 30). *Independence and interdependence in school conferences between Anglo teachers and Hispanic parents*. Paper presented at the biennial meeting of the Society for Research on Child Development, Indianapolis, IN.

Greenfield, P., & Cocking. R. (Eds.). (1994). *Cross-cultural roots of minority child development*. Hillsdale, NJ: Erlbaum.

Grize, J. (1987). Operatory logic. In B. Inhelder, D. deCaprona & A. Cornu-Wells (Eds.), *Piaget today*. Hillsdale, NJ: Erlbaum.

Groen, G., & Patel, V. (1988). The relation between comprehension and reasoning in medical diagnosis. In M. Chi, R. Glaser & M. Farr (Eds.), *The nature of expertise* (pp. 287–310). Hillsdale, NJ: Erlbaum.

Grossberg, L. (1994). Introduction: Bringin' it all back home—Pedagogy and cultural studies. In H. Giroux &d P. McLaren (Eds.), *Between borders: Pedagogy and the politics of cultural studies* (pp. 1–28). New York: Routledge.

Guidon, A. (1992). *Moral development, ethics, and faith.* Ottawa, Canada: Novalis Press.

Guskey, T. (1994). Making the grade: What benefits students? *Educational Leadership, 52*(2), 14–21.

Haggerty, B. (1995). *Nurturing intelligences: A guide to multiple intelligences theory and teaching.* Menlo Park, CA: Addison-Wesley.

Hallahan, D., & Kauffman, J. (1995). Toward a culture of disability. In J. Kauffman & D. Hallahan (Eds.), *The illusion of full inclusion* (pp. 59–74). Austin, TX: Pro-Ed Publishers.

Hallowell, E., & Ratey, J. (1994). *Driven to distraction.* New York: Pantheon Books.

Halpern, D. (Ed.). (1994). *Changing college classrooms.* San Francisco: Jossey-Bass.

Haney, W. (1993). *The fractured marketplace for standardized tests.* Boston: Kluwer-Nijhoff.

Hansen, D. (1995). *The call to teach.* New York: Teachers College Press.

Harkness, S., & Super, C. (1992). Parental ethnotheories in action. In I. Sigel & A. McGillicuddy-DeLisi (Eds.), *Parental belief systems: The psychological consequences for children* (2nd ed., pp. 373–392). Hillsdale, NJ: Erlbaum.

Harkness, S., Super, C., & Keefer, C. *(1994).* Learning to be an American parent. In R. D'Andrade & C. Strauss (Eds.), *Human motives and cultural models* (pp. 163–178). Cambridge, UK: Cambridge University Press.

Heath, S. B. (1983). *Ways with words: Language, life, and work in communities and classrooms.* New York: Cambridge University Press.

Heath, S. B., Mangiola, L., Schecter, S., & Hull, G. (Eds.). (1991). *Children of promise: Literate activity in linguistically and culturally diverse classrooms.* Washington, DC: National Education Association.

Herrnstein, R., & Murray, C. (1994). *The bell curve: Intelligence and class structure in American life.* New York: Free Press.

Hickson, L., Blackman, L., & Reis, E. (1995). *Mental retardation: Foundations of educational programming.* Boston: Allyn and Bacon.

Hill, M., & Hill, F. (1994). *Creating safe schools: What principals can do*. Thousand Oaks, CA: Sage.

Hirsch, E. D. (1996). *The schools we need and why we don't have them*. New York: Doubleday.

Hittleman, D., & Simon, A. (1997). *Interpreting educational research* (2nd ed.). Englewood Cliffs, NJ: Prentice-Hall.

Hoffman, D. (1996). Culture and self in multicultural education. *American Educational Research Journal, 33*(3), 545–569.

Hoffman, D. (1996). Culture and self in multicultural education: Reflections on discourse, text, and practice. *American Educational Research Journal, 33*(3), 545–570.

Horn, J. (1989). Models of intelligence. In R. Linn (Ed.), *Intelligence: Measurement, theory, and public policy* (pp. 29–73). Urbana/Champaign, IL: University of Illinois Press.

Hourigan, M. (1994). *Literacy as social exchange: Intersections of class, gender, and culture*. Albany, NY: State University of New York Press.

Howard, R. (1987). *Concepts and schemata: An introduction*. Philadelphia: Taylor and Francis.

Howe, M., & Rabinowitz, F. M. (1992). Development: Sequences, structure, and chaos. In P. van Geert & L. Mos (Eds.), *Annals of theoretical psychology* (Vol. 7, pp. 65–72). Orlando, FL: Academic Press.

Hubbard, R., & Power, B. (1993). *The art of classroom inquiry: A handbook for teacher-researchers*. Portsmouth, NH: Heinemann.

Hudson, P., & Lee, W. (1990). *Women's work and the family economy in historical perspective*. New York: Manchester University Press.

Humphreys, L. (1989). Intelligence: Three kinds of instability and their consequences for policy. In R. Linn (Ed.), *Intelligence: Measurement, theory, and public policy* (pp. 193–216). Urbana: University of Illinois Press.

Hunt, E. (1991). Some comments on the study of complexity. In R. Sternberg & P. Frensch (Eds.), *Complex problem solving* (pp. 383–396). Hillsdale, NJ: Erlbaum.

Imel, S. (1996). *Learning in groups*. San Francisco: Jossey-Bass.

Ingersoll, B. (1993). *Attention deficit disorder and learning disabilities: Myths, realities, and controversial treatments*. New York: Doubleday.

Ishikawa, E., & Swain, D. (1981). *Hiroshima and Nagasaki: Physical, mental and social effects of the atomic bombings*. New York: Basic Books.

Jacobson, J., & Mulick, J. (Eds.). (1996). *Manual of diagnosis and professional practice in mental retardation.* Washington, DC: American Psychological Association.

Jiménez, R., García, G., & Pearson, D. (1995). Three children, two languages and strategic reading: Case studies in bilingual/monolingual reading. *American Educational Research Journal, 32*(1), 67–98.

Johnson, D., & Johnson, R. (1991). *Teaching children to be peacemakers.* Edina, MN: Interaction Book Company.

Johnson, D., & Johnson, R. (1994). *Learning together and alone: Cooperative, competitive, and individualistic learning* (4th ed.). Englewood Cliffs, NJ: Prentice Hall.

Johnson, K. (1995). *Understanding communication in second-language classrooms.* New York: Cambridge University Press.

Johnson, P., & Johnson, D. (1989). *Cooperation and competition: Theory and research.* Edina, MN: Interaction Book Company.

Johnson-Laird, P. (1988). *The computer and the mind: An introduction to cognitive science.* Cambridge, MA: Harvard University Press.

Johnston, R. (1991). *Attention deficits, learning disabilities, and ritalin: A practical guide.* San Diego, CA: Singular Publications.

Jones, V. (1998). *Comprehensive classroom management: Creating communities of support and solving problems.* Boston: Allyn and Bacon.

Kagan, J. (1994). *Galen's prophecy: Temperament in human nature.* New York: Basic Books.

Kaiser, A., & Gray, D. (1993). *Enhancing children's communication.* Baltimore: Paul Brookes.

Kamii, C. (Ed.). (1990). *Achievement testing in the early grades: Games grown-ups play.* Washington, DC: National Association for the Education of Young Children.

Kant, I. (1959). *Foundations of the metaphysics of morals.* New York: Liberal Arts Press. (Originally published 1785).

Katz, L., Evangelou, D., & Hartman, J. (1990). *The case for mixed-age grouping in early education.* Washington, DC: National Association for the Education of Young Children.

Katz, P., & Walsh, V. (1991). Modification of children's gender-stereotyped behavior. *Child Development, 62,* 338–351.

Kellaghan, T., Sloane, K., Alvarez, B., & Bloom, B. (1993). *The home environment and school learning.* San Francisco: Jossey-Bass.

Kennedy, J. (1993). *Drawing and the blind.* New Haven, CT: Yale University Press.

Kentucky Systems Change Project for Students with Severe Disabilities (undated). *The Kentucky Alternative Assessment Portfolio Project.* Frankfort, KY: Kentucky Department of Education.

King, P., & K. Kitchener. (1994). *Developing reflective judgment: Understanding and promoting intellectual growth and critical thinking in adolescents and adults.* San Francisco: Jossey-Bass.

Klein, S., & Mowrer, R. (1989). *Contemporary learning theories—Pavlovian conditioning and the status of traditional learning theory.* New York: Wiley.

Kliewer, C., & Biklen, D. (1996). Labeling: Who wants to be called retarded? In W. Stainback & S. Stainback (Eds.), *Controversial issues confronting special education: Divergent perspectives* (2nd ed., pp. 83–95). Boston: Allyn and Bacon.

Kluger, R. (1976). *Simple justice: The history of* Brown v. Board of Education *and Black Americans' struggle for equality.* New York: Knopf.

Koehler, M. (1990). Classrooms, teachers, and gender differences in mathematics. In E. Fennema & G. Leder (Eds.), *Mathematics and gender* (pp. 128–148). New York: Teachers College Press.

Kohlberg, L. (1970). The moral atmosphere of the school. In H. Overly (Ed.), *The unstudied curriculum.* Washington, DC: Association for Studies in Curriculum Development.

Kohlberg, L., Levine, C., & Hewer, A. (1983). *Moral stages: A current formulation and a response to critics. Basel*: S. Karger.

Kohn, A. (1996). *Beyond discipline: From compliance to community.* Alexandria, VA: Association for Supervision and Curriculum Development.

Kounin, J. (1970). *Discipline and group management in classrooms.* New York: Holt, Rinehart and Winston.

Kozol, J. (1995). *Amazing Grace.* New York: Crown Publishers.

Lane, P. (1995). *Conflict resolution for kids: A group facilitator's guide.* Washington, DC: Accelerated Learning.

Larrabee, M. (1993). *An ethic of care: Feminist and interdisciplinary perspectives.* New York: Routledge.

Lave, J., & Wenger, E. (1991). *Situated learning: Legitimate peripheral participation.* New York: Cambridge University Press.

Leaper, C. (1994). Consequences of gender segregation on social relationships. In C. Leaper (Ed.), *New directions for child development, #65: Childhood gender segregation* (pp. 67–86). San Francisco: Jossey-Bass.

Leder, G. (1990). Teacher/student interactions in the mathematics classroom: A different perspective. In E. Fennema & G. Leder (Eds.), *Mathematics and gender* (pp. 149–168). New York: Teachers College Press.

Lee, V. (1988). *Beyond behaviorism*. Hillsdale, NJ: Erlbaum.

Lemke, J. (1990). *Talking science: Language, learning, and values*. Norwood, NJ: Ablex.

Lerner, J. (1993). *Learning disabilities: Theories, diagnosis, and teaching strategies* (6th ed.). Boston: Houghton Mifflin.

Lerner, J. (1994). *Working women and their families*. Thousand Oaks, CA: Sage.

Lesgold, A. (1988). Problem solving. In R. Sternberg & E. Smith (Eds.), *The psychology of human thought* (pp. 188–213). New York: Cambridge University Press.

Lesgold, A., Rubinson, H., Feltovich, P., Glaser, R., Klopfer, D., & Wang, Y. (1988). Expertise in a complex skill: Diagnosing X-ray pictures. In M. Chi, R. Glaser & M. Farr (Eds.), *The nature of expertise* (pp. 311–342). Hillsdale, NJ: Erlbaum.

Lewin, T. (1997, October 9). In California, wider test of of same-sex schools. *New York Times*, pp. A27, A22.

Lifton, R. J. (1982). *Indefensible weapons: Political and psychological case against nuclearism*. New York: Basic Books.

Lightfoot, C., & Valsiner, J. (1992). Parental belief systems under the influence: Social guidance of the construction of personal cultures. In I. Sigel & A. McGillicuddy-DeLisi (Eds.), *Parental belief systems: The psychological consequences for children* (2nd ed., pp. 393–414). Hillsdale, NJ: Erlbaum.

Linn, R. (Ed.). (1989). *Intelligence: Measurement, theory, and public policy*. Champaign/Urbana, IL: University of Illinois Press.

Linn, R., & Baker, E. (1996). Can performance-based student assessments be psychometrically sound? In J. Baron & D. Wolf (Eds.), *Performance-based student assessment: Challenges and possibilities: 95th yearbook of the National Society for the Study of Education* (pp. 84–103). Chicago: University of Chicago Press.

Lipman, M. (1974). *Harry Stottlemeier's Discovery*. Upper Monclair, NJ: Institute for the Advancement of Philosophy for Children.

Lipman, M. (Ed.). (1993). *Thinking children and education*. Dubuque, IA: Kendall/Hunt.

Lipsky, D., & Gartner, A. (1991). Restructuring for quality. In J. Lloyd, N. Singh & A. Repp (Eds.), *The Regular Education Initiative: Alternative perspectives on concepts, issues, and models* (pp. 43–57). Sycamore, IL: Sycamore.

Lipsky, D., & Gartner, A. (1996). Inclusion, school restructuring, and the remaking of American society. *Harvard Educational Review, 66,* 762–796.

Lloyd, B., & Duveen, G. (1992). *Gender identities and education.* New York: St. Martin's Press.

Lowe, R. (1994). *Phonology: Assessment and intervention applications in speech pathology.* Baltimore: Williams and Williams.

Macbeth, F., & Fine, N. (1995). *Playing with fire: Creative conflict resolution for young adults.* Philadelphia: New Society Publishers.

Maccoby, E. (1990). Gender and relationships: A developmental account. *American Psychologist, 45*(4), 513–520.

Maccoby, E. (1994). Commentary: Gender segregation in childhood. In C. Leaper (Ed.), *Childhood gender segregation: Causes and consequences: New Directions in Child Development,* #65 (pp. 87–98). San Francisco: Jossey-Bass.

Maccoby, E. (1995). The two sexes and their social systems. In P. Moen, G. Elder, & K. Luscher (Eds.), *Examining lives in context: Perspectives on the ecology of human development* (pp. 347–364). Washington, DC: American Psychological Association.

Maccoby, E., & Mnookin, R. (1992). *Dividing the child: Social and legal dilemmas of custody.* Cambridge, MA: Harvard University Press.

Malina, R. (1991). Physical anthropology. In T. Lohman, A. Roche & R. Martorell (Eds.), *Anthropometric standardization reference manual.* Champaign, IL: Human Kinetics Press.

Marrett, C., Mizuno, Y., & Collins, G. (1992). Schools and opportunities for multicultural contact. In C. Grant (Ed.), *Multicultural education: From the margins to the mainstream* (pp. 203–217).

Martin, C. (1994). Cognitive influences on the development and maintenance of gender segregation. In C. Leaper (Ed.), *Childhood gender segregation: Causes and consequences: New Directions in Child Development,* #65 (pp. 35–52). San Francisco: Jossey-Bass.

Martin, J. (1992). *The schoolhome: Rethinking schools for changing families.* Cambridge, MA: Harvard University Press.

Maslow, A. (1987). *Motivation and personality* (3rd ed.). New York: Harper and Row.

Maslow, A. (1970). *Motivation and personality* (2nd ed.). New York: Harper & Row.

Mathew, G. (1994). *The philosophy of childhood.* Cambridge, MA: Harvard University Press.

McAlpine, L., Eriks-Brophy, A., & Crago, M. (1996). Teaching beliefs in Mohawk classrooms: Issues of language and culture. *Anthropology and Education Quarterly, 27*(3), 390–413.

McCaleb, S. (1994). *Building communities of learners: A collabora-*

tion among teachers, students, families, and community. New York: St. Martin's Press.

McClelland, D. (1985). Human motivation. Glenview, IL: Scott, Foresman.

McCormick, L., & Loeb, D. (1997). Characteristics of students with language and communication difficulties. In L. McCormick, D. Loeb & R. Schiefelbusch (Eds.), *Supporting children with communication difficulties in inclusive settings.* Boston: Allyn and Bacon.

McKeachie, W., Pintrich, P., Lin, Y., Smith, D., & Sharma, R. (1990). *Teaching and learning in the college classroom.* Ann Arbor, MI: National Center for Research to Improve Post-Secondary Teaching and Learning.

Measor, L., & Sykes, P. (1992). *Gender and schools.* New York: Cassell.

Mehan, H. (1986). *Handicapping the handicapped.* Stanford, CA: Stanford University Press.

Mekos, D., & Clubb, P. (1997). The value of comparisons in developmental psychology. In J. Tudge, M. Shanahan & J. Valsiner (Eds.), *Comparisons in human development* (pp. 137–161). New York: Cambridge University Press.

Messick, S. (1989). Validity. In R. Linn (Ed.), *Educational measurement* (3rd ed., pp. 13–103). New York: American Council on Education.

Messick, S. (1994). The interplay of evidence and consequences in the validation of performance assessments. *Educational Researcher, 23*(2), 13–23.

Miller, B. (1995). Precepts and practices: Researching identity formation among Indian Hindu adolescents in the United States. In J. Goodnow, P. Miller, & F. Kessel (Eds.), *Cultural practices as contexts for development: New directions in child development* (pp. 71–86). San Francisco: Jossey-Bass.

Miller, N. (1992). *Single parents by choice.* New York: Plenum Press.

Mitchell, C. (Ed.). (1995). *Gender equity through physical education and sport.* Reston, VA: National Association for Girls and Women in Sports.

Moll, L., & Dworin, J. (1996). Biliteracy development in classrooms: Social dynamics and cultural possibilities. In D. Hicks (Ed.), *Discourse, learning, and schooling* (pp. 221–246). New York: Cambridge University Press.

Morris, B. (1994). *Anthropology of the self: The individual in cross-cultural perspective.* London: Pluto.

Morrison, J., & Rodgers, L. (1996). Being responsive to the needs of children from dual heritage backgrounds. *Young Children, 52*(1), 29–33.

Moss, P. (1994). Can there be validity without reliability? *Educational Researcher, 23*(2), 5–12.

National Board for Professional Teaching Standards. (1997). *What teachers should know and be able to do* [online]. Available at <www.nbpts.org/nbpts/standards/intro.html>.

National Council of Teachers of Mathematics. (1996). *NCTM assessment standards.* Reston, VA: Author.

National Organization for Women. (1996, November/December). Public funds for single-sex education. *Newsletter of National Organization for Women* [online]. Available at: <http://www.nyct.net/~now nyc/ssedu.htm>.

National Research Council. (1996). *National Science Education Standards.* Washington, DC: National Academy Press.

Nelson, K. (Ed.). (1989). *Narratives from the crib.* Cambridge, MA: Harvard University Press.

Newmann, F., Marks, H., & Gamoran, A. (1996). Authentic pedagogy and student performance. *American Journal of Education, 104*(4), 280–312.

Noddings, N. (1992). *The challenge to care in schools: An alternative approach to education.* New York: Teachers College Press.

Norris, J., & Hoffman, P. (1993). *Whole-language intervention for school-age children.* San Diego: Singular Publishers.

Norris, S. (1992). *Generalizability of critical thinking: Multiple perspectives on an educational ideal.* New York: Teachers College Press.

Nye, N., Delclose, V., Burns, M., & Bransford, J. (1988). Teaching thinking and problem solving. In R. Sternberg & E. Smith (Eds.), *The psychology of human thought* (pp. 337–365). New York: Cambridge University Press.

O'Connor, M., & Michaels, S. (1996). Shifting participant frameworks: Orchestrating thinking practices in group discussion. In D. Hicks (Ed.), *Discourse, learning, and schooling* (pp. 63–103). New York: Cambridge University Press.

Ogbu, J. (1994). From cultural differences to differences in cultural frame of reference. In P. Greenfield & R. Cocking (Eds.), *Cross-cultural roots of minority child development* (pp. 365–392). Hillsdale, NJ: Erlbaum.

Osborne, A. B. (1985). Practice into theory into practice: Culturally relevant pedagogy for students we have marginalized and normalized. *Anthropology and Education Quarterly, 27*(3), 285–314.

Ostrofsky, M., Kaiser, A., & Odom, S. (1993). Facilitating children's social-communicative interactions through the use of peer-mediated interventions. In A. Kaiser & D. Gray (Eds.), *Enhancing children's communication* (pp. 159–186). Baltimore: Paul Brookes.

Otto, M. (1995). Mentoring: An adult developmental perspective. In M. Wunsch (Ed.), *Mentoring revisited: Making an impact on individuals and institutions.* San Francisco: Jossey-Bass.

Overton, W. (1991). The structure of developmental theory. In H. W. Reese (Ed.), *Advances in child development and behavior* (pp. 1–37). San Diego: Academic Press.

Paley, V. (1986). *Mollie is three.* Chicago: University of Chicago Press.

Paley, V. (1997). *The girl with the brown crayon.* Cambridge, MA: Harvard University Press.

Palincsar, A. (1986). The role of dialogue in providing scaffolded instruction. *Educational Psychologist, 21* (special issue on learning strategies), 73–98.

Partin, R. (1995). *Classroom teachers' survival guide: Strategies, maangement techniques, and reproducibles for new and experienced teachers.* West Nyack, NY: Center for Applied Research in Education.

Pavlov, I. (1927). *Conditioned reflexes.* London: Oxford University Press.

Pellegrini, A., & Perlmutter, J. (1989). Classroom contextual effects on children's play. *Developmental Psychology, 25,* 289–296.

Perkins, D. (1992). *Smart schools: Better thinking and learning for every child.* New York: Free Press.

Perrone, V. (Ed.). (1991). *Expanding student assessment.* Alexandria, VA: Association for Supervision and Curriculum Development.

Philips, S. (1983). *The invisible culture: Communication in classroom and community on the Warm Springs Indian Reservation.* New York: Longman.

Phillips, D. C. (1992). *The social scientist's bestiary: A guide to fabled threats to, and defences of, naturalistic social science.* New York: Permagon Press.

Phillips, D. C. (1994). Telling it straight: Issues in assessing narrative research. *Educational Psychologist, 29*(1), 13–22.

Phillips, S., & Benner, P. (Eds.). (1994). *Crisis of care: Restoring helping behavior in the professions.* Washington, DC: Georgetown University Press.

Piaget, J. (1952). *The origins of intelligence in children.* New York: International Universities Press.

Piaget, J. (1965). *The child's conception of the world*. Totowa, NJ: Littlefield, Adams.

Piaget, J. (1965). *The moral judgment of the child*. New York: Free Press. (Originally published 1932).

Piaget, J. (1977). *The development of thought*. New York: Viking Press.

Piaget, J. (1983). Piaget's theory. In P. Mussen (Ed.), *Handbook of child psychology* (Vol. 1). New York: Wiley.

Piaget, J. (1985). *The equilibration of cognitive structures*. Chicago: University of Chicago Press.

Piaget, J., & Inhelder, B. (1974). *The child's construction of quantities*. London: Routledge and Kegan Paul.

Pinard, A. (1981). *The conservation of conservations: Toward integration of Piagetian studies*. Chicago: University of Chicago Press.

Pintrich, P. (1990). Implications of psychological research on student learning and college teaching for teacher education. In W. R. Houston (Ed.), *Handbook of research on teacher education* (pp. 826–857). New York: Macmillan.

Premack, D. (1965). Reinforcement theory. In D. Levine (Ed.), *Nebraska Symposium on Motivation* (Vol. 13, pp. 123–180). Lincoln: University of Nebraska Press.

Pritchard, M. (1996). *Reasonable children*. Lawrence, KA: University of Kansas Press.

Procidano, M. (1993). Families and schools: Social resources for students. In M. Procidiano & C. Fisher (Eds.), *Contemporary families: A handbook for school professionals (*pp. 292–306). New York: Teachers College Press.

Procidano, M., & Fisher, C. (Eds.). (1992). *Contemporary families: A handbook for school professionals*. New York: Teachers College Press.

Puka, B. (1994). *Moral development: Vol. 4. The great justice debate*. New York: Garland.

Ramsey, P. (1991). *Making friends in school: Promoting peer relations in early childhood*. New York: Teachers College Press.

Resnick, L. (1987). Learning in school and out. *Educational Researcher, 16*(9), 13–20.

Resnick, L., Levine, J., & Teasley, S. (1991). *Perspectives on social shared cognition*. Washington, DC: American Psychological Association.

Rice, M. (1993). "Don't talk to him; he's weird." In A. Kaiser & D. Gray (Eds.), *Enhancing children's communication* (pp. 139–158). Baltimore: Paul Brookes.

Richardson, V. (1994). Conducting research on practice. *Educational Researcher, 23*(5), 5–10.

Riordan, C. (1990). *Girls and boys in school: Together or separate?* New York: Teachers College Press.

Rizzo, T. (1989). *Friendship development among children in school.* Thousand Oaks, CA: Sage.

Roach, V. (1995). *Winning ways: Creating inclusive schools, classrooms, and communities.* Alexandria, VA: National Association of State Boards of Education.

Rubin, K., & Asendorpf, J. (1993). Social withdrawal, inhibition, and shyness in childhood: Conceptual and definitional issues. In K. Rubin & J. Asendorpf (Eds.), *Social withdrawal, inhibition, and shyness in childhood.* Hillsdale, NJ: Erlbaum.

Ruhlman, M. (1996). *Boys themselves: A return to single-sex education.* New York: Holt.

Russell, T., & Munby, H. (1991). Reframing: The role of experience in developing teachers' professional knowledge. In D. A. Schön (Ed.), *The reflective turn* (pp. 164–187). New York: Teachers College Press.

Rutter, M. (1995). *Psychosocial disturbances in young people.* New York: Cambridge University Press.

Saltzstein, H., Millery, M., Eisenberg, Z., Dias, M., & O'Brien, D. (1997). Moral heteronomy in context: Interviewer influence in New York City and Recife, Brazil. In H. Saltzstein (Ed.), *New directions in child development: Culture as a context for moral development: New perspectives on the particular and universal* (pp. 37–50). San Francisco: Jossey-Bass.

Schmar, E. (1995). Student self-assessment. In T. Azwell & E. Schmar (Eds.), *Report card on report cards: Alternatives to consider* (pp. 183–195). Portsmouth, NH: Heinemann.

Schön, D. (Ed.). (1991). *The reflective turn.* New York: Teachers College Press.

Schrader, D. (1990). *The legacy of Lawrence Kohlberg.* San Francisco: Jossey-Bass.

Scott, A. (1995). Why I teach by discussion. In A. L. Deneef & C. Goodwin (Eds.), *The academic's handbook* (pp. 187–191). Durham, NC: Duke University Press.

Scriven, M. (1991). Beyond formative and summative evaluation. In M. McLaughlin & D. C. Phillips (Eds.), *Evaluation and education at quarter century: 90th yearbook of the National Society for the Study of Education* (pp. 19–65). Chicago: University of Chicago Press.

Seifert, K. (1991). What develops in informal theories of development? *Journal of Learning About Learning, 5*(1), 5–14.

Seifert, K. (1992). Cognitive development in early childhood. In B. Spodek (Ed.), *Handbook of research on young children* (3rd ed., pp. 9–23). New York: Macmillan.

Seifert, K. (1992). What develops in informal theories of development? *Journal of Learning about Learning, 5*(1), 4–11.

Seifert, K. (1995, March). *The social construction of the child: A review of five studies.* Paper presented at the biennial meeting of the Society for Research on Child Development, Indianapolis, IN.

Seifert, K. (1998, March). *Consistency: Real and apparent among teachers of young children.* Paper presented at the Nineteenth Annual Forum on Ethnography in Education, March 6–7, Philadelphia, PA.

Seifert, K., & Handziuk, D. (1993, March). *Ontological commitments to the child.* Paper presented at the biennial meeting of the Society for Research on Child Development, New Orleans.

Seixas, P. (1993). The community of inquiry as a basis for knowledge and learning: The case of history. *American Educational Research Journal, 30*(2), 305–324.

Selman, R. (1980). *The growth of interpersonal understanding.* New York: Academic Press.

Selman, R., & Schultz, L. (1990). *Making a friend in youth.* Chicago: University of Chicago Press.

Serbin, L., Moller, L., Gulko, J., Powlishta, K., & Colburne, K. (1994). The emergence of gender segregation in toddler playgroups. In C. Leaper (Ed.), *Childhood gender segregation: Causes and consequences* (pp. 7–18). San Francisco: Jossey-Bass.

Serbin, L., Powlishta, K., & Gulko, J. (1993). The development of sex typing in middle childhood. *Monographs of the Society for Research on Child Development, 58*(2, Serial No. 232).

Serbin, L., Tonick, I., & Sternglanz, S. (1977). Shaping cooperative cross-sex play. *Child Development, 48,* 924–929.

Shanahan, M., & Elder, G. (1997). Nested comparisons in the study of historical change and individual adaptation. In J. Tudge, M. Shanahan & J. Valsiner (Eds.), *Comparisons in human development* (pp. 109–130). New York: Cambridge University Press.

Sharp, A., & Reed, R. (1992). *Studies in philosophy for children.* Philadelphia: Temple University Press.

Shepard, L. (1993). Evaluating test validity. In L. Darling-Hammond (Ed.), *Review of research in education* (Vol. 19, pp. 405–450). Washington, DC: American Educational Research Association.

Shepard, L., & Bliem, C. (1995). Parents' thinking about standardized tests and performance assessments. *Educational Researcher, 24*(8), 25–31.

Shotter, J. (1993). *Cultural politics of everyday life: Social constructivism, rhetoric and knowing of the third kind.* Toronto: University of Toronto Press.

Shuell, T. (1996). Teaching and learning in a classroom context. In D. Berliner & R. Calfee (Eds.), *Handbook of educational psychology* (pp. 726–764). New York: Macmillan.

Shulman, L., & Quinlan, K. (1996). The comparative psychology of school subjects. In D. Berliner & R. Calfee (Eds.), *Handbook of educational psychology* (pp. 399–422). New York: Macmillan.

Siegal, Michael. (1991). *Knowing children: Experiments in conversation and cognition.* Hillsdale, NJ: Erlbaum.

Siegel, B. (1996). Is the emperor wearing clothes? Social policy and the empirical support for full inclusion of children with disabilities in the preschool and early elementary grades. *Social policy report: Society for Research on Child Development, 10*(2 & 3). Ann Arbor, MI: Society for Research on Child Development.

Sizer, Theodore. (1996). *Horace's hope: What works for American high schools.* Boston: Houghton Mifflin.

Skinner, B. F. (1974). *About behaviorism.* New York: Knopf.

Slavin, R. (1995). *Cooperative learning: Theory, research, and practice* (2nd ed.). Boston: Allyn and Bacon.

Smith, C., Wood, F., & Grimes, J. (1987). Issues in the identification and placement of behaviorally disordered students. In M. Wang, M. Reynolds & H. Walberg (Eds.), *Handbook of special education* (Vol. 2, pp. 95–124). New York: Permagon Press.

Smith, M., & Levin, J. (1996). Coherence, assessment, and challenging content. In J. Baron & D. Wolf (Eds.), *Performance-based student assessment: Challenges and possibilities: 95th yearbook of the National Society for Studies in Education* (pp. 104–124). Chicago: University of Chicago Press.

Smith, M., & Shepard, L. (1989). Kindergarten readiness and retention: A qualitative study of teachers' beliefs and practices. *American Educational Research Journal, 26*(3), 307–333.

Sosniak, L. (1990). The tortoise, the hare, and the development of talent. In M. Howe (Ed.), *Encouraging the development of exceptional skills and talents* (pp. 149–164). Leicester, UK: British Psychological Society.

Spain, D. (1992). *Gendered spaces.* Chapel Hill: University of North Carolina Press.

Spindler, G. (1987). Transcultural sensitization. In G. Spindler (Ed.), *Education and cultural processes* (2nd ed., pp. 467–480). Prospect Heights, IL: Waveland Press.

Stenhouse, L. (1985). *Research as a basis for teaching*. London: Heinemann.

Sternberg, R. (1990). *Metaphors of mind: Conceptions of the nature of intelligence*. Cambridge: Cambridge University Press.

Sternberg, R., & Frensch, P. (1991). *Complex problem solving*. Hillsdale, NJ: Erlbaum.

Stipek, D. (1996). *Motivation and instruction*. In D. Berliner & R. Calfee (Eds.), *Handbook of eduction psychology* (pp. 85–113). New York: Macmillan.

Strange, J. (1997). *Evaluating teachers: A guide to current thinking and best practice*. Thousand Oaks, CA: Corwin Press.

Strauss, S. (1993). Teachers' pedagogical content knowledge about children's minds and learning: Implications for teacher education. *Educational Psychologist, 28*(3), 279–290.

Streitmatter, J. (1996). Justice or caring: Pedagogical implications for gender equity. In D. Eaker-Rich & J. van Galen (Eds.), *Caring in an unjust world* (pp. 31–46). Albany, NY: State University of New York Press.

Swearingen, R., & Allen, D. (1995). *Classroom assessment of reading processes*. Boston: Houghton Mifflin.

Tanner, James. (1981). *A history of the study of human growth*. Cambridge, UK: Cambridge University Press.

Task Force on Teaching as a Profession. (1986). *A nation prepared*. Washington, DC: The Forum.

Taylor, J., Gilligan, C., & Sullivan, A. *(1992). Between voice and silence: Women and girls, race and relationship*. Cambridge, MA: Harvard University Press.

Tharp, R. (1994). Intergroup differences among Native Americans in socialization and child cognition. In P. Greenfield & R. Cocking (Eds.), *Cross-cultural roots of minority child development* (pp. 87–106). Hillsdale, NJ: Erlbaum.

Tharp, R., & Gallimore, R. *(1991). Rousing minds to life: Teaching, learning, and schooling in social context*. New York: Cambridge University Press.

Theall, M., & Franklin, J. (1990). *Student ratings of instruction*. San Francisco: Jossey-Bass.

Thorkildsen, T., & Jordan, C. (1994). Is there a right way to collaborate? In J. Nicholls & T. Thorkildsen (Eds.), *Reasons for learning*. New York: Teachers College Press.

Thorndike, R. (1997). *Measurement and evaluation in psychology and education* (6th ed.). Columbus, OH: Merrill.

Thorndike, R., Hagen, E., & Sattler, J. (1986). *Stanford-Binet Intelligence Scale* (4th ed.). Chicago: Riverside Publishing.

Thorne, B. (1993). *Gender play: Girls and boys in school.* New Brunswick, NJ: Rutgers University Press.

Trefil, J. (1997). *Are we unique?* New York: Wiley.

Tucke-Bressler, M. (1992). Giftedness, creativity, and productive thinking: Towards a unification of theoretical concepts and empirical research. In J. Carlson (Ed.), *Cognition and educational practice* (Vol. 2, pp. 131–149). Greenwich, CT: JAI Press.

Tudge, J. (1990). Vygotsky, the zone of proximal development, and peer collaboration. In L. Moll (Ed.), *Vygotsky and education.* New York: Cambridge University Press.

Tudge, J., Shanahan, M., & Valsiner, J. (1997). *Comparisons in human development: Understanding time and context.* New York: Cambridge University Press.

Turiel, E. (1983). *Development of social knowledge: Morality and convention.* Cambridge, UK: Cambridge University Press.

Twain, M. (1899). *Pudd'nhead Wilson.* New York: Harper, 1899.

Ulnichy, P., & Schoener, W. (1996). Teacher-researcher collaboration from two perspectives. *Harvard Educational Review, 66*(3), 496–524.

United States Department of Education. (1993). *Single-sex schooling: A special report from the Office of Educational Research.* Washington, DC: Office of Educational Research, United States Department of Education.

United States Department of Education. (1995). *Seventeenth annual report to Congress on the implementation of the Individuals with Disabilities Education Act.* Washington, DC: Author.

United States Department of Education. (1996). *Eighteenth annual report to Congress on the implementation of the Individuals with Disabilities Education Act.* Washington, DC: Author.

United States Department of Education. (1997). *Nineteenth annual report to Congress on the implementation of the Individuals with Disabilities Education Act.* Washington, DC: Author.

United States Department of Labor. (1994). *Working women count! A report to the nation.* Washington, DC: United States Government Printing Office.

U.S. Department of Labor, Bureau of Labor Statistics. (1992). *Marital and family characteristics of workers.* Washington, DC: U.S. Government Printing Office.

Valencia, S., Hiebert, E., & Afflerbach, P. (Eds.). (1994). *Authentic reading assessment: Practices and possibilities.* Newark, DE: International Reading Association.

Van Houten, R., & Doleys, D. (1983). Are social reprimands effective? In S. Axelrod & J. Apsche (Eds.), *The effects of punishment on human behavior.* San Diego: Academic Press.

Voterra, V., & Erting, C. (1990). *From gesture to language in hearing and deaf children.* New York: Springer-Verlag.

Vygotsky, L. (1978). *Mind in society.* Cambridge, MA: Harvard University Press.

Wagner, R. (1991). Managerial problem solving. In R. Sternberg & P. Frensch (Eds.), *Complex problem solving* (pp. 159–182). Hillsdale, NJ: Erlbaum.

Walker, K., Taylor, E., McElroy, A., Phillip, D., & Wilson, M. (1995). Familial and ecological correlates of self-esteem in African-American children. In M. Wilson (Ed.), *African-American family life: Its structural and ecological aspects: New Directions in Child Development* (pp. 23–34). San Francisco: Jossey-Bass.

Wallace, D., & Gruber, H. (Eds.). (1992). *Creative people at work: Twelve cognitive case studies.* New York: Oxford University Press.

Weiner, B. (1986). *An attributional theory of motivation and emotions.* New York: Springer.

Weiss, G., & Hechtman, L. (1993). *Hyperactive children grown up: ADHD in children, adolescents, and adults* (2nd ed.). New York: Guilford Press.

Welker, R. (1991). Expertise and the teacher as expert: Rethinking a questionable metaphor. *American Educational Research Journal, 28*(1), 19–35.

Wells, G. (1993). Reevaluating the IRF sequence: A proposal for the articulation of theories of activity and discourse for the analysis of teaching and learning in the classroom. *Linguistics and Education, 5,* 1–37.

Welsh, O. (1993). *Research and practice in deafness: Issues in education, psychology, and vocational service provision.* Springfield, IL: Charles Thomas.

Wenger, B., Kaye, H. S., & LaPlante, M. (1996). *Disabilities statistics abstract #15: Disabilities among children.* Washington, DC: United States Department of Education, National Institute on Disability and Rehabilitation Research.

Wertsch, J. (1991). *Voices of the mind.* Cambridge, MA: Harvard University Press.

Wielkiewicz, R. (1995). *Behavior management in schools* (2nd ed.). Boston: Allyn and Bacon.

Wilkinson, L. C. & Marrett, C. (Eds.). (1985). *Gender influences in classroom interaction.* Orlando, FL: Academic Press.

Willen, W., & White, J. (1991). Interaction and discourse in social studies classrooms. In J. Shaver (Ed.), *Handbook of research on social studies teaching and learning.* New York: Macmillan.

Wilson, S. (1995). Not tension but intention: A response to Wong's analysis of the researcher/teacher. *Educational Researcher, 24*(8), 19–22.

Wineburg, S. (1991). On the reading of historical texts: Notes on the breach between school and academy. *American Educational Research Journal, 28*(3), 495–519.

Wishnietsky, D. (1996). *Managing chronic illness in the classroom.* Bloomington, IN: Phi Delta Kappa Foundation.

Wolf, D., & Reardon, S. (1996). Access to excellence through new forms of student assessment. In J. Baron & D. Wolf (Eds.), *Performance-based student assessment: Challenges and possibilities: Ninety-fifth yearbook of the National Society for Studies in Education* (pp. 1–31). Chicago: University of Chicago Press.

Wolff, S. (1995). *Loners: The life path of unusual children.* London: Routledge.

Wong, E. D. (1995). Challenges confronting the researcher/teacher: Conflicts of purpose and conduct. *Educational Researcher, 24*(3), 22–28.

Woodhead, M. (1997). Psychology and the cultural construction of children's needs. In A. James & A. Prout (Eds.), *Constructing and reconstructing childhood* (2nd ed.). London: Falmer Press.

Wunsch, M. (*1995*). New directions for mentoring: An organizational development perspective. In M. Wunsch (Ed.), *Mentoring revisited: Making an impact on individuals and institutions.* San Francisco: Jossey-Bass.

Zabel, R., & Zabel, M. (1996). *Classroom management in context: Orchestrating positive learning environments.* Boston: Houghton Mifflin.

Zimbardo, P. (*1990*). *Shyness: What it is, and what to do about it.* Reading, MA: Addison Wesley.

Zuelke, D., & Willerman, M. (1992). *Conflict and decision-making in elementary schools.* Dubuque, IA: William C. Brown.

Learning (*cont.*)
theories of, *see* Metaphors of learning
unique meanings for, 6–9
value of one's own ideas about, 14
value of publications about, 13–14
voices creating psychology of, 13–15
Learning as assisted performance, 54–60
community of practice and, 54–57, 58–60
teacher and, 58
web site for, 66
zone of proximal development and, 55, 56, 57–58, 59
Learning as behavior change, 32–46
classical conditioning and, 34–41
learning disabilities and, 340–341, 342
motivation and, 180–181
operant conditioning and, 34, 41–46
prevention and, 191
web site for, 65–66
Learning as thinking, 46–54
information-processing theory and, 46–51
Piagetian theory and, 51–54
Learning community, excellent teacher becoming member of, 495–497
Learning disabilities (LDs), 326, 338–344
behaviorism and, 340–341, 342
body of literature on, 360
constructivism and, 343–344
definition of, 338–340
individual education plan for, 328–332
information-processing theory and, 341–342
percentage of students with, 337
prevalence of, 339
reasons for, 340–344
teacher aide for, 328, 331, 357
see also Special needs students
Least restrictive environment (LRE), 323, 324, 325, 326, 333
Lecture
children's play taught with, 252–254
classroom arrangement for, 249–250, 253

evaluation of, 262–263
topics appropriate for, 276
Lesson plans
ethics of boring *versus* helping students in, 448
gender options in, 301
Listening
lectures and, 253
recitation and, 256
Literature, teacher as generous expert teaching, 153
Locus of control, attributions about success or failure based on, 181–182
Logical reasoning, for problem solving, 92
Long-term memory, in information-processing model, 48, 49, 50
LRE, *see* Least restrictive environment (LRE)
Lunch time, no student-teacher interaction in, 249

Management, *see* Classroom management
Manager, teacher as, *see* Teacher as instructional manager
Managers, problem solving by, 84, 85, 91
Marginal students, in community of practice, 57
Market exchange, ethics of, 453, 455
Master planner, teacher as, 158–159
Mastery learning, 381
Mathematics
age-graded developmental changes and, 107
core of, 386
girls minimizing knowledge about, 290–291
learning disability relating to, 340–344
portfolio assessment for, 382–387
report card grades on, 367–377
rubric for, 401, 403
self-assessment in, 386, 388–390
taught in class *versus* at home, 70–72
teacher as caring person teaching, 145–146
teacher as translator teaching, 157–158
teaching roles for teaching, 156

Maturation, 103. *See also* Developmental change
Meaning, importance of, 50–51
Meetings, *see* Class meetings
Mensa, web site for, 99
Mental retardation, 354–359
adaptive and functional skills in curriculum for, 357–358
assistance for teacher in individualizing curriculum for, 357
body of literature on, 360
classmates helping child with, 358–359
definition of, 354–355
inclusion for, 358–359
percentage of students with, 337
prevalence of, 355–356
teaching children with, 356–359
time and practice for, 356–357
transition from school to real world and, 355
see also Special needs students
Mentoring relationships
for child with mental retardation, 358
learning disability due to lack of, 343–344
parents and, 229–231, 232, 238–239
between students, 217–221
Metacognitive awareness, learning disability handled with, 341–342
Metaphors of learning, 32
developing own, 61–62
reconciling, 61–63
use of, 62–63
value of, 61
see also Learning as assisted performance; Learning as behavior change; Learning as thinking
Methylphenidate (Ritalin), for attention deficit disorder, 348
Mexican Americans, interdependent self and, 307–308
Microsoft Corporation, web site sponsored by, 161
Mild mental retardation, *see* Mental retardation
Misbehavior, 185–194
choosing right response to, 194
classroom rules preventing, 186, 191

Paper-and-pencil tests, 74
Parents, 209, 228–231
    assessment and, 371–374
    conflict among students involving, 227–228
    constructivist assessment and, 400
    discourse by, 272
    divorce and, 232, 233, 234
    individual education plan and, 328–332
    involvement of, 227–228
    as mentors, 229–231, 232, 238–239
    mothers working outside home and, 232, 234–235
    portfolio assessment and, 387–388
    report cards viewed by, 371–374
    shyness and, 222
    speech of *versus* teacher-talk, 267
    stages defined by, 113, 114–115
    teachers compensating for unavailability of, 231
    teachers' roles overlapping with, 228–231
    see also Families; Parent-teacher relationship
Parent-Teacher Association, web site for, 242
Parent-teacher conferences
    with bilingual and bicultural families, 227, 235–238, 239–240
    creative scheduling of, 239
    difficulty of arranging, 233, 238–239
    newsletters instead of, 239
    notes following, 239–240
    phone calls instead of, 23, 239
Parent-teacher relationship
    appropriate responses to parents and, 238–240
    school involvement and, 233–234
    see also Parent-teacher conferences
Partial reinforcement effect, in operant conditioning, 43, 44
Participation
    as classroom discourse goal, 275, 490, *see also* Participation structures
    collaborative group work and, 261
    discussion and, 258–259
    lectures and, 253–254
    recitation and, 255

Participation structures, 248–259
    adjustment of to subject or topic, 276–277
    individual dialogue, 249
    learning and, 250–263
    multicultural teaching and, 309–310, 313, 315
    physical arrangements of classroom for, 249–250
    recess breaks and lunch time, 249
    reciprocal teaching and, 473
    rules of, 249
    students' comfort with, 276–278
    success of, 263
    using variety of, 276
    see also Classroom discourse; Collaborative group work; Discussion; Lecture; Recitation
Pavlovian conditioning, *see* Classical conditioning
Peer opinion, ethics of, 453, 456–457
Peer relationships, 210–213. *See also* Students' relationships
Pencil-and-paper tests, *see* Classroom tests
Performance assessment, 378, 380–381
Performances, multicultural teaching and, 315
Permitting, as response to misbehavior, 187, 188, 189, 194
Philosophy, schools teaching, 474
Phone calls, for parent-teacher communication, 23, 239
Physical education teacher, expertise of, 151
Piagetian stages, 51–54, 115–122, 215, 452, 453
    age-graded change and, 121–122
    concrete operational, 119–120, 122
    formal operational, 120–121, 122
    preoperational, 118–119, 122
    sensorimotor, 117–118, 122
    usefulness of, 121–122
    web site for, 65–66, 129
Piaget, Jean, Society, web site for, 65–66, 129
Pictures, for multicultural education, 312
Pitch, in teacher-talk, 265
Planning
    for classroom management, 166–169, 491–492

misbehavior due to teacher flaws in, 185–186
Planning diary, teacher as instructional manager using, 138
Play, *see* Children's play
Playmates, choosing compatible, 289, 295, 297–299. *See also* Friendships among students
Police, conflict among students involving, 227
Portfolio, 197. *See also* Portfolio assessment; Professional portfolio
Portfolio assessment, 378, 380, 382–390, 392, 398, 399
    alternative assessments summarized with, 401–403
    rubrics for, 401–402
    self-assessment of, 386, 388–390
Postconventional stage, of moral development, 453, 454, 458–461, 469
Power
    assessment and, 379
    fair use of, 450, *see also* Care, morality of
Preconventional stage, of moral development, 453, 454–456
Premack principle, *see* Relativity of reinforcers
Preoperational stage, 118–119, 122
Preventing, as response to misbehavior, 187, 188, 191
Primary grades
    teacher as caring person in, 156
    teacher as generous expert in, 151–153
Principal
    conflict among students involving, 227
    individual education plan and, 328–332
Principled knowing, 141
Privacy
    caring teacher and invasion of, 148–149
    role-played conflict and, 226
Private talk *versus* public talk
    gender differences in, 287–288
    while students do independent work, 301
Problem fixer, teacher as, 158
Problem ownership, misbehavior and, 190

Problem solving, 73, 80–91, 96
  as ambiguous, 88, 89
  clarity of problems and solutions
      and, 91
  in classroom, 82, 85–91
  commonalities in, 85–86
  creativity and, 95
  definition of, 81
  by doctors, 83–84, 85–86, 91–92
  educated guesswork for, 85–86, 87,
      89, 91
  imagination for, 89
  by lawyers, 84–85, 86, 90
  logical thinking for, 91–92
  by managers, 84, 85, 91
  in nonschool settings, 82–85, 86,
      90, 91
  personal value on, 73
  problem definition and, 90, 91
  by psychologists, 84–85, 86
  questioning for, 88
  reflection for, 86, 87, 88, 89
  small groups for, 89, 90
  as talent, 95
  transfer and, 88, 90–91
  types of, 82–85
  zone of proximal development for,
      87
Professional development activities, 197
Professional journal, on participative
      structures, 262
Professional portfolio, for classroom
      management and motivation,
      21, 197–198, 201
Professional teaching standards,
      481–485
Prop boxes, for multicultural teaching,
      311
Protégés, students' mentoring relation-
      ships with, 217–221
Psychologists
  individual education plan and,
      328–332
  problem solving by, 84–85, 86
Public Law 94–142, *see* Individuals
      with Disabilities Education Act
      (IDEA)
Public performances, multicultural
      teaching and, 315
Public talk *versus* private talk
  gender differences in, 287–288
  while students do independent
      work, 301

Punishment and obedience, ethics of,
      453, 454–455

Qualitative research, in educational
      research, 426
Questionnaire, multicultural teaching
      evaluated with, 315–316
Questions
  dialogue with text encouraged
      with, 21
  indirect, 141
  open-ended, 200
  for problem solving, 88
  student answering with question,
      269–270
  for student evaluations, 200
  on tests, 265, 267, 271–272
Quizzes, random, unannounced,
      182

Race
  segregation and, 290
  shyness and, 222
  see also Culture; Ethnic culture/
      ethnicity; Multiculturalism
Reading
  age-graded developmental changes
      and, 107
  difficulties or impairments in, *see*
      Learning disabilities (LDs)
  research on impact of bilingualism
      on, 424–428
  teacher as generous expert teach-
      ing, 151–153, 157
  teacher as instructional manager
      teaching, 157
Real world
  as classroom, 502
  problem solving in, 82–85, 86, 90,
      91
  school-based thinking *versus*,
      70–73, 96
  transition to for child with mental
      retardation, 355
Recess breaks, no student-teacher
      interaction in, 249
Recitation, 249
  children's play taught with,
      254–257
  cultural differences and, 309
Recollections, teachers' knowledge
      about developmental change
      based on, 123–125

Reflection, 7, 11, 503
  on classroom management,
      195–202
  on developmental change, 127
  for excellent teaching, 493–494,
      500–502
  on experience, 7
  learning disability handled with,
      341–342
  on multicultural teaching activities,
      315–316
  for problem solving, 86, 87, 88, 89
  self-assessment for, 389
  sharing with friend, 175–176,
      195–197, 198, *see also* Dialogue
  for teacher research, 434, 436, 437,
      438, 439, 440, 442
  unique meanings of teaching and
      learning and, 7–9
  see also Professional portfolio;
      Reflective journal
Reflection-in-action, 11
Reflective journal
  for classroom management and
      motivation, 198–199, 201
  for classroom or teacher research,
      199
Reflexes, inborn, 38
Register, 263. *See also* Student-talk
      register; Teacher-talk register
Reinforcement/reinforcers
  learning disability and, 340–341,
      342
  motivation as, 180–181
  in operant conditioning, 42
  relativity of, 43
Relationships, personal metaphor of
      learning considering, 62. *See
      also* Classroom management;
      Misbehavior; Motivation; Par-
      ents; Parent-teacher relation-
      ship; Students' relationships;
      Teacher-student relationship
Relativity of reinforcers, in operant
      conditioning, 43
Relevance, of educational research,
      415, 422–423, 427, 429–430
Reliability
  of alternative assessments, 397–400
  of classroom tests, 392–393,
      395–397
  of educational research, 421
  equivalent forms, 393

Reliability (*cont.*)
   rubrics and, 401
   split-half, 393
   test-retest, 393
Repair, for classroom management, 490–492
Report cards, 367–377, 378
   parent's perspective on, 371–374
   prevalence of, 378
   student's perspective on, 369–371
   teachers' perspective on, 374–377
   see also Assessment; Grading
Reprimanding, as response to misbehavior, 187, 188, 192–193, 194
Research, *see* Educational research; Teacher research
Resource teacher, 333–335
   individual education plan and, 328–332, 335
   for student with mental retardation, 357
Response
   conditioned, 35, 36
   unconditioned, 35, 36
Response costing, as response to misbehavior, 187, 188, 193, 194
Responsibility
   attributions about success or failure based on, 181, 182
   in morality of care, 461, 462–463, *see also* Care, morality of
Retention of students, 114
Reversibility, in concrete operational period, 119–120
Review of literature, for educational research, 429
Revision, in classroom management, 166–167, 171–179
Revoicing, in teacher-talk, 265–266
Ripple effect, of misbehavior, 186–187
Risk, in morality of care, 471, 472–473
Ritalin, for attention deficit hyperactivity disorder, 348
Ritual knowledge, 141
Role playing
   of significant conflicts, 226
   student with speech or language disorder participating in, 353
Roles, 136. *See also* Teaching roles
Rubrics, alternative assessments summarized with, 401–403

Sampling
   by classroom tests, 391, 398
   in educational research, 421
Schemata
   in information-processing model, 50–51
   in Piagetian theory, 51
Scholastic aptitude, 73, 74–75, 96
   as one talent among many, 77–78
   personal value on, 73
   as single, global ability, 77
   see also Intelligence
Scholastic aptitude tests, 73, 74–80
   ambiguous responses on, 78–81
   errors on, 79–80
   history of, 76
   qualities of, 75
   school success predicted by, 77–78
   strategies for taking, 79, 80
   see also Intelligence tests; *specific tests*
School-based thinking, everyday thinking *versus*, 70–73, 96. *See also* Scholastic aptitude
School counselors, conflict among students involving, 227
School success, standardized tests predicting, 74. *See also* Scholastic aptitude tests
Science
   control talk by teachers of, 264–265
   hypothetical reasoning in, 120–121
   learning as form of doing and, 51–54
   rubric for, 402–403
   social relationships learned along with, 30–31
   teacher as generous expert teaching, 151, 153
   teacher as translator teaching, 157
Segregation
   gender, 289–291, 298–299
   racial, 290
Self
   cultural differences in meaning of, 307–308
   interdependent, 307–311, 313
   self-esteem and, 310–311
Self-actualization need, 183

Self-assessment, 386, 388–390, 392
   in classroom management, 166–167, 169–171
   constructivist assessment and, 400
Self-chosen universal principles, ethics of, 453, 459–460
Self-determination need, 183
Self-esteem, culture and, 310–311
Sensitivity, *see* Care, morality of
Sensorimotor stage, 117–118, 122
Shaping behavior, in operant conditioning, 43, 44
Short-term sensory store, in information-processing model, 48, 49
Shyness among students, 211, 221–224
   web site for, 242
Side talk, in control talk of students, 269, 272, 273
Signing, 350–351
Silence, in student-talk, 270
Single-parent families, 232, 233–234
Single-sex schools, 290
Small groups, *see* Collaborative group work
Smoothness, for classroom management, 169, 170, 171, 173
Social context, of teaching and learning, 53, 244
Social contract, ethics of, 453, 458–459
Social isolation, as response to misbehavior, 187, 188, 193–194
Social relationships, *see* Students' relationships
Social systems orientation, 453, 457
Social workers, conflict among students involving, 227
Society for Research on Child Development, web site for, 129
Sociogram, friendship patterns and, 211–213
Sorting, constructivist assessment and, 400
Speakers
   teachers nominating, 264, 271, 272
   teachers terminating and interrupting, 264
Speaking object, in discussion, 300
Special education, *see* Special needs students

Special Interest Group for Arts-Based Methods of Research in Education, web site for, 99

Specialist classes, collaborative group work and, 179

Special needs students, 321–362
ambiguities regarding categories of, 335, 336, 338, 360
body of literature on, 359–360
government support for range of services for, 323, 332–335
individual education plan for, 323, 325, 326–332, 333, 335, 495
least restrictive environment for, 323, 324, 325, 326, 333
legislation for, *see* Individuals with Disabilities Education Act (IDEA)
percentage of in U.S., 337, 360
resource teacher for, 328–332, 333–335
as students without special needs, 502
teacher of, 158–159
web sites for, 362
see also Attention deficit disorder; Inclusive education; Learning disabilities (LDs); Mental retardation; Speech and language disorders

Special-needs teacher, as broker and master planner, 158–159

Speech and language disorders, 326, 349–354
body of literature on, 360
communication deterioration and, 351–352
definition of, 349–350
modeling good language and speech for, 352–353
patience and acceptance for, 352
percentage of students with, 337
positive strategies of communication minimizing, 352–354
practice at communication for, 353
prevalence of, 349
speech-language pathologist for, 353–354
stuttering, 450–451, 462–463
see also Special needs students

Speech-language pathologist, 353–354

Split-half reliability, 393

Spontaneous recovery, in classical conditioning, 37–38

Sports, gender segregation and, 290

Stability
attributions about success or failure based on, 181, 182
change *versus*, 17, 101–102
of children, 16–17

Stages, 111–115
everyday meanings of, 112–115
of friendship (Selmar), 214–215
parents' meanings of, 113, 114–115
parents' *versus* teachers' meanings of, 114–115
teachers' meanings of, 113–115
see also Developmental change; Piagetian stages

Stand and Deliver (Edwards), 80

Standard English, 231, 307

Standardized tests, school success predicted by, 74–75. *See also* Scholastic aptitude tests

Stanford-Binet Test of Intelligence, 74–75

State of Kentucky Department of Education, web site for, 204

Stepfamilies, 232, 234

Stigma, shyness and, 222

Stimulus
conditioned, 35, 36
unconditioned, 35, 36

Stimulus substitution, in classical conditioning, 40

Stories, 22
for teacher research, 436–437
teachers' knowledge about developmental change based on, 123–125

Student-centered teachers, cooperative learning groups and, 178

Student evaluations, 142
for classroom management and motivation, 198–201
of multicultural teaching, 315–316

Students
assessment and, 369–371
caring teacher rejected by, 145–146
comfort of with participation structures, 276–278
gender roles and, *see under* Gender
knowledge held back by, 141–142

report cards viewed by, 369–370
responsibility of teacher to curriculum *versus* to students and, 144–147, 149, 258, 259
revoicing strengthening contributions of, 265–266
self-assessments by, 386, 388–390
teaching evaluated by, *see* Student evaluations
unintended effects of actions of teacher as manager on, 140–143

Students' relationships, 207–228
diversity of, 208–209
enemies, 224–228
friendships, 213–217, 289, 295, 297–299
interdependent self and, 307–311
mentoring, 217–221
peer relationships, 210–213
shyness and, 211, 221–224, 242
side talk and, 273
teachers and, 209, 210–213
see also Parents; Teacher-student relationship

Student-talk register, 267–270
answering with question in, 269–270
breaking rules of, 273
calling out in, 269
for control or motivating learning, 272
control talk in, 267–269, 272, 273
eye contact in, 270
multiculturalism and, 270
silence in, 270, 272

Stuttering student
morality of care for, 462–463
morality of justice for, 450–451

Subject knowledge, for excellent teaching, 488–490

Success, motivation as attributions about, 181

Support, in morality of care, 471, 472–4673

Survival orientation, in morality of care, 464, 465–466

Symbolic thinking, in preoperational stage, 118, 119

Systematic thinking, for excellent teaching, 493–495

MULTIPLE VOICES layer direct responses of other educators to this text's discourse, helping readers deepen their own interactions with its ideas.

MULTIPLE VOICES
MULTIPLE VOICES
MULTIPLE VOICES
MULTIPLE VOICES

Two important issues arise here. First, Professor Seifert raises a question for Ms. Althouse: "Knowing that most students have no intention of becoming professional mathematicians, should she respect and support their nonmathematical priorities or work to create an intrinsic love of mathematics . . . ?" The two goals are not completely incompatible. I would choose to make the first primary and show my respect for the nonmathematical talents of my students. But I would also teach in such a way that these students might, at least occasionally, enjoy math and understand why some people love it as they love, say, art. Working together, we would "get through" as much math as minimally required by the school's standards; but, more important, we would come to respect one another's interests and talents.

The second issue reflects a widespread misunderstanding of what it means to care. Some students, like Murray, do indeed protest that they don't want to be "cared for." But these students, like many of my professional colleagues (who also make such a protest), *do* want people to detect and respond positively to their preferences with respect to styles of human interaction. So they actually do want care! To respond as carer means exactly this: to receive the other and respond as nearly as one can (consistent with your own moral commitments) to what has been received. Caring cannot be done by recipe. It requires sensitivity, flexibility, and a continuing commitment to increase our competence in human relations.

Nel Noddings, Professor, Stanford University

MULTIPLE VOICES
MULTIPLE VOICES
MULTIPLE VOICES
MULTIPLE VOICES

So how
don't!
ing in
phasis
failure
who w
overwh
find ti
who ha
Now, t
many t
The mo
build o

Tech
instructional manager will naturally lean toward using a classroom computer to keep records, to make plans, schedules, and class lists, and to print labels since these are organizational tasks. But the computer can also help the instructional manager in the other roles talked about in this chapter. Technology can aid in reaching individual students with diverse backgrounds and experiences. For example, sharing the rich resources of the World Wide Web and good searching techniques can enhance the "generous expert" role.

Janice Friesen, Technology coordinator, Columbia, Missouri

MULTIPLE VOICES
MULTIPLE VOICES
MULTIPLE VOICES
MULTIPLE VOICES

In essence, Kevin asks here whether teaching interferes with research. Some might argue that it does, that there is a great divide between teaching and research. This happens, I think, because we tend to think of research in terms of surveys and statistics, and not as something engaging and self-renewing. The verbs used to represent teaching are *act, choose,* and *decide* as opposed to *understand* and *observe* for research. In my opinion, though, the "chasm" is irrelevant and artificial. Empirical inquiry should not be viewed as a separate entity with goals different from teaching. As a teacher, my choices and decisions are based for the most part on my understanding and observations of my students—which are essentially research activities. Observing the subtleties and nuances of students' behavior is the key, and this can often be done best by a teacher who knows the students on a daily basis.

Yvette Daniel, High School English Teacher, Toronto, Ontario, Canada